The Prophet & The Virgin

The Prophet & The Virgin
The Masculine and Feminine Roots of Teaching

Errol Miller

Ian Randle Publishers
Kingston • Miami

First published in Jamaica, 2003 by
Ian Randle Publishers
11 Cunningham Avenue
Box 686, Kingston 6
www.ianrandlepublishers.com

© Errol Miller

National Library of Jamaica Cataloguing-in-Publication Data

Miller, Errol
    The Prophet and the Virgin: Masculine and Feminine Roots of Teaching/ Errol Miller

        p.; cm

        Bibliography : p.

ISBN 976-637-052-4 paperback

1.   Educational sociology   2.   Gender identity in education
3.   Education - History

I.   Title

306.43 dc 21

Cover & Book design by Shelly-Gail Cooper
Set in Adobe Garamond 10pt

Printed in the United States of America

Dedicated to my daughter

Catherine Lauren-Louise Miller

Contents

Acknowledgements

In researching and writing this book, I incurred numerous debts of gratitude to several institutions and many individuals. These debts can only be partially repaid by acknowledgements here. Indeed, only a partial listing is possible. My sincere thanks are extended to the following institutions and individuals:

The Centre for International Exchange of Scholars (CIES) and the government of the United States which granted me: (i) a Fulbright-Hays Fellowship for Senior Academics in 1988 which allowed me to collect data for this book and (ii) a Fulbright Scholarship (September 1995 to March 1996) which allowed me to complete the research and write the bulk of the text. Without these awards, it would have been impossible to have conducted this study. In this regard, I thank the United States Information Service in Kingston for nominating me for these awards and, particularly, Mrs Angela Harvey for guidance and assistance on both occasions. I am also grateful to Miss Janice Byrd (who administered the Fellowship) and Mrs Marylin Saks-MacMillion, and her assistant Miss Alision Gavine, (who administered the Scholarship) for the efficient and professional manner in which they discharged their duties.

The School of Education, Stanford University, that accommodated me during the Fellowship. Apart from the superb facilities that were at my disposable everyone was so helpful. Thanks to Prof. Hans Weiler for coordination of my programme and valuable feedback. Thanks also to Professors Martin Carnoy and David Tyack, and Dr Myra Strober for enlightening discussions and useful pointers on sources of data on US education. Thanks to Prof. John Myer and Dr Francisco Ramerez for allowing me to share in their weekly seminar on schooling and its relationship to the development of world systems. Thanks also to Marc Vantresca for quickly realising the relation of my work to the seminar and for introducing me to it. I am greatly indebted to the Librarians of the Stanford Library System, especially to Mr W.D. Rozkuszka in the Johnson Library of Government Documents and Mrs I. McKinley in the Cubberly Library. How could I ever forget the Caribbean contingent at Stanford and Palo Alto who made sure I remained sane. My particular thanks go to Prof. Ewart Thomas and his wife Odette, Dr Jeff Charles, his wife Susan and family and to Mr Patrick McDonald and his family. My stay in Palo Alto was made more memorable because by my landlady, Mrs Pearl Nicolino, who is simply a great human being.

Dr Phillip Burnham for facilitating my access to the Libraries of London University, particularly to those of the Anthropology Department and the

Institute of Education. Dr Burnham not only helped me solve the logistical problems related to the access to libraries, but pointed to important sources and engaged me in discussions that were particularly helpful in clarifying several ideas.

The staff of the Public Records Office in London for their assistance in sourcing and photocopying crucial documents, and generally for being helpful.

The Harvard Institute for International Development and the Harvard Graduate School of Education for not only providing me with accommodation but access to the marvellous facilities and technical support of the University between September 1995 and January 1996. I am deeply indebted to the Librarians of the Andover-Harvard Theological Library, the Widener Library, the Gutman Library, the Map Library, Hilles Library, the Tillis Peabody Museum and the Lamont Library. I am particularly indebted to Prof. Noel McGinn, and his assistant Miss Susan Rarus, for all the support given to me and particularly to Noel for his unobtrusive but generous spirit and friendship. My stay in Cambridge was made even more enjoyable by Dr George Caruso, his wife Ann and their daughter, Maria, who opened their home to me and shared their fellowship.

Teachers College, Columbia University which provided me with accommodation and access to their vast resources during February and March 1996. I am particularly indebted to my friend and colleague Prof. Lambros Comitas for pointing me to several sources, including books from his personal library and for the lively discussions on several aspects of Caribbean and American Education and on the history of Greece. Mrs Marylin for helping me to settle in and navigate New York. I also benefited greatly from several of the courses put on by the Computer Centre of the College.

The University of the West Indies, for granting me the leave necessary to bring this study to completion. I am grateful to the Librarians of the Mona, Cave Hill and St Augustine Campuses for assistance in accessing information on Caribbean education.

Dr Ruby King for not only reading several of the chapters on the Caribbean and commenting on them, but for suffering through my ramblings in the course of clarifying and developing many ideas. In the wider university, I thank Prof. Roy Augier for reading the chapter on Sumerian society and education, Prof. Rex Nettleford for numerous illuminating discussions on several aspects of culture, particularly Caribbean culture, and Prof. Hilary Beckles for his great insight into so many aspects of Caribbean history.

My sister, Mrs Audrey Dehaney, and her husband John for providing me with accommodation on my several trips to London and for their support and encouragement; my cousin, Mrs Sheila Miller-Weston, and my son Garth and his wife Andree for similar support and encouragement on my visits to New York. I also thank Garth for his assistance in helping me learn some of the basics of Geographical Information Software and its applications to this study.

Rev. Dr Burchell Taylor, my pastor, not only for his inspired sermons and Christian example, but only for his careful reading and helpful comments on the chapters on Judaism and Christianity.

Archdeacon William Thompson of St Agnes Church in Nassau Bahamas who not only took a lively interest in my work and commented on the chapter on Christianity, but organised several discussion groups which were intellectually simulating and illuminating.

Ian Randle Publishers for publishing the manuscript. Particularly, I wish to thank Mr Ian Randle for his support in this project, Miss Lisa Morgan for her management of the entire exercise and Mrs Glory Robertson for her careful editing of the text and constructive suggestions. Certainly their efforts have improved the presentation of the book and its quality.

My wife, Sharon, whose love and support during the years of my researching and writing this book have never wavered or faltered. Although the Fulbright Scholarship took me away from home during the last six months of her pregnancy with our daughter Catherine, she coped with the demands of her job and pregnancy alone without complaint and never ceased to encourage me to stick to the task and complete it. There aren't enough words to express my gratitude to her.

Finally, to all of the above and many whom I have failed to mention by name, I express my heartfelt and sincere thanks.

One

POSING THE QUESTIONS

Schooling was invented somewhere around 2500 BCE. All the available evidence points to the fact that from that time up to about 150 years ago the vast majority of teachers were men. This was true of every level of schooling, from elementary school to university. Although over the last 150 years large numbers of women have become teachers, the vast majority of university teachers are still males. Further, there are several countries in the world in which the majority of primary school teachers are still male.

This long history of male teachers probably accounts for the fact that the masculine origin of teaching is practically taken for granted. The question why was schooling established with male teachers has not been asked or answered. Neither has there been any explanation of why teaching had remained a male occupation for nearly four millennia. Rather, it is the shift to female teachers at the primary and secondary levels of schooling, beginning in the nineteenth century, which has attracted attention and critical analysis. It is the feminisation of teaching, at some levels of schooling, that has generated the probing questions especially from historians. As a result the studies of the gender composition of the teaching professions have invariably concentrated on some period within the last 150 years.

The vast majority of books written on the subject of the gender of teachers begin with the nineteenth century. Very little is researched and written about the gender of teachers prior to that time. This work attempts to make some small contribution in bridging this gap. Accordingly, the account of the gender of teachers reported and discussed in this book ends in the nineteenth century, the point at which most other books on the gender of teachers begin.

This study asks and seeks to answer four main questions. Why did teaching become a masculine occupation in the first place? Why did teaching remain a predominately male occupation for over 4000 years? On what bases did women first make their entrance into the teaching occupation and why? Do the masculine and feminine roots of teaching cast any light on the social nature of the teaching profession? The assumption and assertion here is that the study of the masculine and feminine roots of teaching has the potential not only to place contemporary developments in a better historical context, but also to lead to better understanding of recent changes in the gender composition of teaching as well as greater insights into the social roles and relationships of the teaching occupation itself.

Tackling the first three of the questions should lead to greater insights and better understanding of changes in the gender composition of the teaching occupation since the middle of the nineteenth century. Accordingly, this study seeks to survey and gain insight into the gender composition of the teaching occupation from the inception of schooling around 2500 BCE to about the middle of the nineteenth century.

THE OVERALL APPROACH AND METHODOLOGY

It is necessary from the outset to outline the broad approach and assumptions that informed this work. Admittedly, the aim of this study is outrageously ambitious. It seeks to trace gender in the teaching occupation over the long haul of many centuries and in different cultures. The search is ultimately for more universal explanations that cut across space and time, Old and New World, East and West. The attempt is to find the conceptual keys that unlock the doors to understanding the patterns observed globally, with less attention to contextual nuances in particular localities.

In this regard this study is out of step with contemporary trends within academia. The current tendency is to prize case studies generating rich contextual details of particular situations and settings, emphasising the lived experiences of real people. This study is not about the life histories of men who first became teachers in ancient times. Neither is it about the life histories of women, ancient or modern, who broke the barrier to become the first female professors, or the first female secondary school teachers or the first female primary school principals working in settings where only men were previously employed. It is neither case studies or oral histories of men, ancient or modern, who continue to teach at the primary or infant school level, despite its low status, social derision or even ostracism. Where it is possible, insights will be drawn from such studies but this study attempts to develop a historical sociology of the teaching occupation, with specific emphasis and focus on its gender composition. The primary intention is to formulate a more comprehensive and satisfying macro historical and sociological framework within which to situate, interpret and understand the origin and changes in the gender composition of the teaching occupation.

A major assumption of this study is that the masculine and feminine roots of teaching are better understood in relation to the creation and evolution of schooling as the latter was transformed in response to changes in the organisation of society and the spread of civilisation. By identifying and tracing the masculine and feminine roots of the teaching occupation historically, there should be a better understanding of the gender structure of the contemporary occupation. The general hypothesis being pursued is that as schooling differentiated into different levels, spread to include more age groups and became more inclusive in terms of the groups in society that had access to formal education, changes occurred in the gender of the teachers at some levels of the education system in some settings. The search is for the critical social factors that account for the conservation or change in the gender composition of teaching in some places and at some levels of the school system.

This approach of necessity dictates a comprehensive historical study of the gender composition of teaching since schooling was invented in the ancient world. However, it is impractical even to contemplate a study that would attempt to trace the evolution of schooling in all regions of the world in any depth. At the same time some depth of knowledge about schooling and society in particular settings is critical to the understanding of the gender composition of the teaching occupation. To match these imperatives with what was practical, it was necessary to select the periods, the civilisations and the countries that would be included in this study. It was recognised, however, that in choosing particular periods, civilisations and countries questions could be raised about the criteria used and the selections made. While recognising that it would be impossible to limit the study without raising challenges that are not easily defended, it is hoped that such challenges would lead to other studies, thus adding a new dimension to the study of gender in the teaching occupation.

Writing was invented, and later schools were created, in the ancient civilisations of Egypt, Mesopotamia and the Indus Valley. Given the objective to identify and trace the masculine and feminine roots of teaching, it is necessary to start the study in the ancient world. The particular interest of this study is the purpose for which writing was invented and subsequently the roles and functions that schools were created to perform in the ancient world. Bearing in mind that the script of the Indus Valley civilisation has not yet been deciphered, the choice for inclusion in this study narrowed to Egypt and Mesopotamia.

Mesopotamia Sumer was selected on two grounds. First, there is increasing evidence to suggest that writing was first invented in Sumer. Second, because clay was the material used in Sumer there is more available information of writing and schooling at an earlier time than in the case of Egypt. Because of the perennial controversy concerning primacy between Egypt and Mesopotamia in the evolution of civilisation, making a choice between them is fraught with danger. The selection of Sumer was made because the object of this study is not to settle any controversy related to primacy but rather to gain some understanding of the origin of schooling and teaching, and in particular the gender roots of the teaching occupation, in the ancient world.

After its origin in the ancient world, schooling served the interests of religion. If one were to follow the evolution of schooling in relation to religion globally, from ancient times, then it would be necessary to probe schooling in relation to such religions as Hinduism, Judaism, Zoroastrianism, Islam, Christianity, Buddhism, Confucianism, Shintoism and ancestral worship. Each of these religions enjoyed a classical period in which they informed and underpinned almost all aspects of societal organisation and social intercourse of the civilisations of which they were an integral part. It is imperative to understand the ways in which schooling was transformed in the Age of Religion, from its antecedents in the ancient world. Indeed, the transformation of schooling in the Age of Religion could possibly cast more light on the gender roots of teaching in contemporary society than the origin of schooling in the ancient world.

The decision was made to probe the evolution of schooling, and the gender roots of the teaching occupation, in relation to Judaism, Islam and Christianity. This decision was taken mainly with respect to my own knowledge and familiarity than to any other factor. Hopefully, this work may induce scholars knowledgeable about the other religions to attempt similar studies in relation to those religions. Of equal importance is the fact that these three religions largely underpin religious experience in the western world, in which the subject of gender in teaching has been most studied.

The Age of Religion gave way to the Era of the Nation-States. This brings us to contemporary times. This study does not include contemporary times. That analysis is done in a companion work, The Feminisation of Teaching in the Nation-State. There was, however, a rather protracted period of transition from the Age of Religious Empires to the emergence of nation-states that could be traced roughly from the time of the Reformation to the beginning of the nineteenth century. The decision was therefore taken to include in this work the evolution of schooling and teaching in the United States and the Commonwealth Caribbean up to the end of the nineteenth century. The inclusion of these states helps to bridge the gap between teaching as an occupation in the Age of Religion and in the Era of the Nation-State.

ELEMENTS OF THE APPROACH

1. In pursuing the gender composition of teaching in the ancient world and its evolution in the Religious Age every effort was made to develop a historical sequence, based upon the most reliable sources and data available, in relation to the societal imperatives that shaped the creation and expansion of formal schooling. The assumption is that factors determining the gender of teachers are best understood, in each instance, with benefit of historical sequence as these emerged in the particular settings. By seeing sequential patterns emerging over time it should be possible to identify consistencies and commonalities.

2. The most fundamental assumption of the study is that the evolution of the teaching profession is best understood in the context of the societal factors shaping the creation and spread of schooling in the world. The school, college and university are social inventions in particular societies in specific periods of history that have now become part of the common stock of social institutions in societies, globally, and indeed part of human heritage and civilisation. The key to understanding the gender composition of teaching, and changes over

time is identifying why schooling was invented and why and how it has spread across time and space to become part of the infra-structure of modern society.

3. The assumption is that there is an intimate and close relationship between how the institution of the school was shaped and configured by societal factors and who were recruited to the teaching occupations so created.

4. The corollary is also true. By understanding why teaching was invented, the factors that have driven its spread in the world and who have been the teachers we are peering into the very nature of human civilisations, in all their varieties. Schools, colleges and universities, their teachers and the gender composition of this occupation are not fickle or fashionable institutions or social phenomena with superficial meaning. Rather, they are cornerstone social institutions and substantial phenomena whose evolution represents fundamental and profound changes in civilisation, society and history.

Many previous studies, by attempting to conceptualise schooling in the narrow context of industrialisation or the hegemony of ruling elites in particular countries and specific periods of history, missed the essence of the nature of schooling and teaching by the exclusivity of the conceptual categories generated. The challenge, taken up here, is to look at schooling in its widely different social and cultural settings throughout history and to identify its enduring and inclusive distinctive features. The Eduba of ancient Mesopotamia; the Academies of ancient Greece; the Museums of Alexandria and Antioch; the Kuttab, Mattak and Madrasah of Islam; the palshaohof and temple school of the Hindus, the talmudic institutions of Jewish education; the song, reading and grammar schools and university guilds of medieval Europe; the public school, community and land grant colleges of the United States; and contemporary primary and secondary schools and universities in modern society all share a common core as formal institutions of learning.

Teaching as an occupation is not viewed here as either unique or peculiar, requiring special treatment and consideration. The assumption here is that the same principles applied to understanding the gender composition of the teaching occupation, and its changes over time, are applicable generally to all other occupations once their socio-cultural nature is fully understood and appropriately related to the rest of society.

What teaching provides us with is an occupation with a long history, that is global in scope and numerous in its population. Its size, history and distribution make teaching an excellent candidate for exploring the nature of gender changes in occupations generally and the factors occasioning such changes. This point is well illustrated by the fact that primary schools now exist in areas in which there are no roads, no running water in houses and no electricity. They are to be found in villages with no hospitals, fire stations, churches, mosques, synagogues or temples and no police stations. Teachers sometimes live in areas in which their only neighbours are subsistence farmers and fishermen and their families. At the other end of the continuum, some primary schools exist on university campuses in large metropolitan centres and are fully equipped with the latest information technology. Across these two extremes teachers teach the basics of literacy, numeracy and moral values. No other occupation covers this range of ecological settings. The same kind of claim can be made about institutions of higher learning in history. Only the temple and the palace can reasonably claim prior origin as public institutions. Likewise teaching at all levels probably employs more people than any other single occupation. This is not to speak of its role in preparing entry to those other occupations.

The methodology employed utilised three main tools. First, the bulk of this study is based upon the collation and review of a wide variety of archaeological, historical, anthropological and sociological studies judged by the author to be of relevance to the object of this investigation.

This was done through standard library searches with the benefit of the considerable resources of the library systems of Columbia, Harvard and Stanford Universities. Two Fulbright Fellowships made this possible, one in 1987 at Stanford and the other in 1995–1996 at Harvard and Columbia. The basic strategy employed was that of establishing search parameters consistent with the objectives of the study. The studies obtained were screened through a first reading. Then through a process of crosschecking of their sources the best studies relative to the focus of this study were selected. The final step was to distil and interpret the material in these studies in relation to the gender composition of teaching in the particular setting.

Second, in selecting the studies upon which to rely, the preference of the author was for those studies in which the historians or archaeologists or anthropologists or sociologists separated the reporting of fact from their interpretation. While recognising that fact and theory cannot be totally or easily separated, as both interact in perception and explanation, one was biased towards those researchers who exerted themselves to maintain some distinction between that which was objectively verifiable by other researchers as against their own interpretation and understanding of the particular phenomenon. Particular attention was paid to those studies in which the researchers pointed out where their observations and findings did not exactly fit their preferred theory. Put another way, this author relied on studies that attempted to accurately describe sequence and fact before the argumentation related to the interpretation of their meaning within some theoretical framework employed by their authors.

Third, the writer attempted a reconstruction of the findings from the various sources that would account for the evolution of formal schooling in the particular setting and within that framework account for the gender composition of the teaching occupation in the particular context. Invariably the reconstruction and reinterpretation of the findings from the various sources took account of the power and resource relations, the beliefs that justified account and the routinised relationships that resulted.

PATRIARCHY, ITS DEFINITION AND ORIGINS

The approach adopted in this study is that of tracing schooling and teaching over the long haul of recorded history. In these circumstances it is almost impossible not to refer in any way to the phenomenon of patriarchy. It is therefore imperative, at the outset, to define patriarchy and its origin as it is conceptualised and applied in this study.

The seminal theoretical contribution of feminist scholarship to social theory has been that of the radical feminist in firmly placing patriarchy as an important category in social theorising and analysis. However, the problematic has become the definition of patriarchy. Weber (1947) had defined patriarchy as the women and younger men being ruled by older men, who were heads of households. While a few feminist theorists have followed the Weberian definition, the more common approach has been to discard the generation difference between men and define patriarchy as that system of social structures and practices in which men dominate, oppress and exploit women (Walby 1990). In other words, the most prevalent tendency in feminist scholarship has been to adopt a narrower and more exclusive definition than the Weberian formulation.

To define patriarchy solely in terms of men's domination of women is to treat both men and women as two separate undifferentiated groups that have sustained their coherence over time and between different cultures. This posture has attracted sharp criticism especially from Black feminists and post-structural and post-modernist theorists. Hooks (1984), for example, argued that while White feminists have traditionally conceptualised the family and the home as major sources of women's oppression, this is not the same among Blacks where the family is not a major source of women's subordination. Indeed, as more and more Black women become heads of households the family and the home have become major loci of their liberation from traditional patriarchal roles.

Collins (1990) extending the arguments of Hooks took the position that race, class and gender constitute three interlocking axes of oppression that are part of an overall matrix of domination. She further made the point that while most individuals have no difficulty identifying their own victimisation, however, they routinely fail to see how they contributed to the suppression of others. White feminists typically point to their oppression while they resist seeing how much their white skin constitutes a social privilege. Likewise African-Americans, eloquent in their analysis of racism often persist in their perception of poor White women as symbols of White power. Failure to see gender as part of the matrix of domination leads inevitably to such contradictions in the approach to and perception of oppression.

The post-modernist critique maintains that neither man nor woman is a unitary category. Post-modernists argued that the categories men and women are a number of overlapping and crosscutting discourses of masculinities and femininities, which are historically and culturally variable. In their view the notion of women and men dissolves into shifting and variable social constructs which lack stability and coherence over time. Walby offered some rebuttal by her observation that the post-modern feminists draw heavily, theoretically, upon the deconstructionism of Derrida (1976), the discourse analysis of Foucault (1981) and the post-modernism of Lyotard (1978) who are all guilty of not paying serious attention to gender. Indeed, post-structural and post-modernism theorists have been no different from modern or classical theorists in their benign neglect of gender in social analysis.

Miller (1991) approached the definition of patriarchy from the opposite direction of the radical feminists. He argued that the main limitation of Weber's definition of patriarchy was its omission of the kinship relations, factual or fictive, that usually exist between the older and younger men and women that constitute the household. Patriarchy needs to be defined as that system of reciprocal social obligations in which final authority rest with older men of the kinship collective, who exercise that authority over its individual male and female members in the overall interest of the collective.

The differences between these three sets of definitions of patriarchy are the elements included. Most feminist scholars have confined their definition of patriarchy solely to gender relations. Weber's definition included the elements of gender and generation. Miller explicitly highlighted the genealogy element in addition to gender and generation and insisted that recognition of the genealogy is critical if the complexities of patriarchy and gender are to be better understood.

Miller argued that the gender and generation elements relate mainly to the internal relations of the collective while the genealogy element defines its external boundaries and relations. From one perspective genealogy extends kinship outside of the immediate circumstances of the household or family by establishing links with other collectives through common ancestry. At the same time it defines collectives that are not kin. This is a critical consideration both conceptually and empirically. The essence of Miller's argument was that conceptually and historically patriarchal collectives had major difficulties with other collectives that fell outside the covenant of kinship, and particularly with the men of those collectives. When patriarchal collectives interacted outside boundaries where kinship could be established, whether factual or fictive, then one group had to submit to the hegemony of the other. Failing such compromise, violent confrontation became the means of establishing dominance. Miller traced the practices of genocide, where one collective sought the physical elimination of another, the killing or castration of male captives, and the almost permanent enslavement of men, as historical outcomes of conflict between collectives which did not share the covenant of kinship or where that covenant had been breached. In all of these circumstances Miller showed that patriarchal collectives found it easier to incorporate women of non-kin groups than the men of such groups. He maintained that the external relations with men of hostile collectives are as much an element of patriarchy as the internal relations with women.

Miller took the position that within the patriarchal collective, generation or age, in addition to genealogy, moderates the relations between men in that, because age is mutable, in time the younger males succeed the older men. Genealogy and generation combine to define the younger males as potential heirs of the older men. Succession dictates male solidarity manifested in the older men grooming and apprenticing the younger men who reciprocate by waiting their turn. While generation contributes to male solidarity within the collective through the process of succession, gender excludes women who are left marginalised within the kinship collective by virtue of such exclusion. Within patriarchy, therefore, women are marginalised in the internal relations of the kinship collective. However, the genealogical relations between men and women of the collective, ameliorates women's marginalisation by virtue of the filial bonds and especially in circumstances where the collective is under threat.

Miller further argued that the genealogy element, defining the external relations of patriarchy, defined non-kin men as potential threats and possible enemies. In these circumstances of relations between unrelated collectives the subordination of one collective relative to the other, voluntarily or by violence, becomes the only means of establishing the bases of interaction. By definition, therefore, patriarchy includes the marginalisation of men of the unrelated collectives, in one way or another.

The essence of Miller's contention therefore is that patriarchy does not only involve the marginalisation of women within the kinship collective but also of men of unrelated collectives over which dominance has been established by whatever means.

However patriarchy is defined, a pertinent question is how did it arise? The historical evidence points to the fact that from the dawn of civilisation human groups were patriarchal, (Lerner 1986). The reasons for this have been the subject of much speculation by numerous theorists. Fredrick Engel, Sigmund Freud, Simone de Beauvoir, Nancy Chodorow, Susan Brownmiller, Elizabeth Fisher, Mary O'Brien and Claude Levi-Strauss have all offered different single factor explanations, the limitations of which have been amply demonstrated by Lerner (1986). She also showed the inadequacies of the biologically determinist explanation of Wilson (1975) which employed multiple factors. In their place Lerner offered her own explanation of the creation of patriarchy.

Lerner's explanation is posited on four factors that can be summarised as follows:

1. Women's reproductive capacity was vital to the survival of early human groups. Related to this was the veneration of women's life giving

powers through the symbol of the Mother-Goddess.

2. Man's engagement in warfare and defence led to the creation of institutions to bolster male ego and self-confidence to counter the awe and veneration of the Mother-Goddess imagery of women.

3. Women's reproductive capacity came to be recognised as a tribal resource that had to be protected from other groups. Over time women's reproductive capacity evolved into being regarded as the property of the ruling warrior elite.

4. The development of agriculture led unintentionally to greater leisure for men, resulting in greater opportunity to develop skills, initiate rituals and manage surplus. Women, on the other hand, continued to be confined to the species specific activities in the form of child rearing and the nurturing of the group. Men's greater freedom and routine tasks increased their status in the group, resulting in women's even greater subordination.

Miller (1991), while agreeing with Lerner on several points, constructed his own explanation of the creation of patriarchy along different lines. Miller's explanation can be summarised as follows:

a) Early humans lived in small groups because the adaptive advantage resided in communal living. Individuals attempting to brave the hostile environment, in which they lived, with the then state of knowledge and technology, did not survive. Those who stuck together to form these early groups were most likely to be those sharing common ancestry. These early groups therefore tended to be descent groups sharing genealogical bonds.

b) Given the relatively short life span of early humans, long life constituted a communal resource. It represented the resident memory of the group that was a critical factor in enhancing group survival. Long life was therefore venerated resulting in the aged being revered. In this regard it should be noted that men at that time enjoyed longer life expectancy that women, because of the mortality that attended childbirth and the frequency of pregnancies.

c) Gender in early human groups was differentiated on the sexual division of powers relating to life giving and life taking. These small isolated autonomous descent groups had to deal with the entire range of human and social reality, including the preservation and taking of life. Biology determined that women gave life, and therefore should be socialised from birth to preserve life. By default therefore life taking fell to men. Men and women in early human societies participated in this sexual division of power.

d)   In group dynamics, life taking proved to be more empowering than life giving, resulting in men exercising final authority in the decision-making within the kinship collective and therefore in women's marginalisation in the group.

From this standpoint the genealogical, generational and gender imperatives of early human groups, living as small isolated entities, combined to produce patriarchy, that is, older men, fathers and grandfathers, of the kinship collective exercising final authority in the descent group.

OUTLINE OF THE BOOK

Chapter 2 explores the masculine roots of teaching as schooling was created in the city-states of ancient Mesopotamia after writing was invented and monarchy and ancient empires were inaugurated. It examines the connections between these three momentous developments in the history of civilisation. Some comments are made about the links between the origin of schooling in Sumer and the evolution to its zenith in ancient Greece. An attempt is made to identify the essential social features of schooling and teaching and their distinctive features as social institutions.

Chapter 3 traces the masculine roots of teaching in Judaism as formal education was adopted and adapted by Judaism to serve the cause and interests of a small margin state permanently under the sceptre of annihilation by the contending superpowers of the ancient Mediterranean world.

Chapter 4 looks at the rise of Islam, both as empire and as religion, and discusses the masculine and feminine roots of teaching in the classical period of Islamic history.

Chapter 5 takes an in-depth look at the masculine and feminine roots of teaching in Christianity. In particular it looks at the emergence of England, the Anglican branch of Christianity and the traditions these spawn with respect to the gender composition of the teaching profession.

Chapter 6 examines schooling and teaching as they are transformed from their religious roots to serve the end of nation building. The particular nation-state chosen is the United States.

Chapter 7 examines schooling and teaching as they are transplanted within the British West Indian colonies and forced to adjust to the prerogatives of the abolition of slavery in circumstances in which ex-slaves constituted the overwhelming majority in the population.

Chapter 8 seeks to answer the four main questions posed at the beginning of this Chapter by synthesizing the findings and understanding gained from tracing the origin of schooling and evolution of the teaching occupations.

Two

MASCULINE ROOTS OF TEACHING IN SUMERIAN CIVILIZATION

History begins at Sumer declared Kramer (1981) who cited thirty-nine firsts in recorded history accredited to Sumerian civilisation. Among the impressive list of achievements of this little known but highly creative people are the inventions of the wheel, writing, literary debates, the chariot, bronze and schools. These and others of their achievements remain a part of the cumulative heritage although the Sumerians as a state, people and distinct society disappeared nearly four thousand years ago. It is therefore appropriate that the exploration of the masculine and feminine roots of teaching should begin at Sumer as it is here, with the inventions of writing and schools, that the teaching occupation was first inaugurated. The circumstances of these beginnings could throw light on several opaque issues related to gender in the teaching occupation.

The civilisations of the Nile and the Indus are competitors of Mesopotamia Sumer, as claimants for primacy for the commencement of civilisation. China also has a long history, but Chinese civilisation is clearly later. It cannot rival these three for primacy. Each of the three has its protagonists. The choice of Sumer in this study is made because the weight of the evidence for primacy in the invention of writing and schooling falls in Sumer's favour. North Africa represented by Egypt, Western Asia represented by Sumer and Southern Asia represented by the Indus valley led human kind into the phenomenon called civilisation. The rest of the world was barbarian, from their point of view. It is clear that the table of civilisation turns, and is still turning.

A few cautionary notes are appropriate from the very outset. First, almost all that is known about Sumer and the Sumerians comes from the work of archaeologists whose findings are constrained by the sites of their explorations and the fragmentary nature of some of their artefacts. Second, Sumerology as a field of specialisation within archaeology is relatively new, just over 100 years when evidence of this unique civilisation was first discovered. Third, based on both its recency and the nature of the evidence, new interpretations of existing material and new evidence are repeatedly coming to light qualifying previous conclusions or sometimes refuting them. More than many other branches of knowledge, therefore, a sense of work in progress needs always to be borne in mind. Sweeping generalisations have to be approached with some degree of caution, but at the same time it is necessary to connect fragmentary details within some coherent framework in order to make sense of the hard evidence that is available.

At best therefore the treatment of the invention of schooling at Sumer, and with it the inauguration of the teaching occupation, has to be regarded as a sketch and not a full-blown portrait complete with all the fine details. To begin with, as Van de Mieroop (1989) observed, the exact chronological boundaries of Sumerian history are difficult to determine since there is no certainty about the exact time of their arrival in Mesopotamia and no precise date of their disappearance as a people. Although they were the creators of the cuneiform system of writing, their writing cannot be used to date them since it was developed after they arrived and persisted for well over a millennium after all trace of them disappeared from the historical record. There is definite evidence of their presence by 4000 BCE and up to 2000 BCE there is still some evidence of their existence. In this sketch some events and developments before 4000 and after 2000 BCE will be mentioned that are crtitical if classical Sumerian civilisation is to be properly perceived.

AGRICULTURE AND SEDENTARY LIVING

There is general agreement among archaeologists that the first evidence of human civilisation comes from the great riverine areas of the Tigris and Euphrates, the Nile and the Indus. It is in these areas that there is the first evidence of the growing of crops for food production and the domestication of animals – that is, of agriculture and sedentary living. Prior to that, the evidence is of nomadic clans, of about 25 to 50 persons, shifting locations while sustaining themselves through hunting and gathering. The beginnings of civilisation therefore coincide with the agricultural revolution in river valleys in western Asia, north Africa and south Asia.

Schmandt-Besserat and Alexander (1975) highlighted the fact that agriculture was evident in Mesopotamia, bounded by the Tigris and Euphrates, from shortly after 10,000 BCE. This places this area first among the cradles of civilisation or settled living, currently known by the evidence available. They noted, however, that apart from an abundance of water and silt deposits, this section of Mesopotamia is lacking in the most elemental raw materials such as timber, stone or metal. In addition, the climate is noted for scorching heat in the summer. Apart from water and soil potential, the area is therefore not marked by either plenty or favourable climate. Crawford (1991) queried whether Sumerian civilisation would have emerged as early were it not for the challenges posed by the ecology of that locale. Water and fertile soil are great resources, but they are not sufficient by themselves for the development of productive agriculture yielding large surpluses.

The earliest inhabitants of the area were divided into two types: those living in permanent settlements and those wandering between settlements and other places with their animals. Within the settlements villagers planted crops and raised animals. Nomads not only wandered between settlements but also had permanent camps on the outskirts of the larger villages. Crawford

(1991) was of the view that these two ways of life were complementary. Pastoralists were able to provide goods and services to settled farmers from whom they received grain in return. The pastoralists also provided some means of communication between settlements. Thus the relationship between nomads and farmers was on the whole symbiotic although not without points of conflict and tension. For example, on the whole the people in settled villages often regarded the nomads as uncouth barbarians.

Not only was the relationship symbiotic, but also it was dynamic. Crawford pointed to the fact that the richest and the poorest nomads had the tendency, for opposite economic reasons, to join the settlers. The largest flocks would suffer from diminishing returns, thus prompting the clans concerned to invest their profits in more secure and lasting areas, like property in the settlements. On the other hand, the poorest were often forced, by necessity, into settlements to find work. In these ways the sedentary villages grew in population as former nomads added to their numbers.

By 6500 BCE there is clear evidence of farming communities, villages, with a material culture that strongly suggests long experience of sedentary living. At the Jarmo site, for example, articles recovered include mortars, pestles, blades and stone vases. There were also male, female and animal figurines, pottery from baked clay and geometric tokens of various shapes and sizes. The agricultural activity is clearly of a subsistence nature although the tokens, or calculi, give evidence of the exchange of goods suggesting some surplus.

With respect to the latter Schmandt-Besserat (1977) pointed out that tokens, calculi, along with human and animal figures and beads appear together in Mesopotamia, from the ninth millennium BCE, and represent the first use of clay by man in the Middle East and long occupation of the area by sedentary groups. In other words, trading or exchange of goods appears to have emerged very early in the region, and as Zagarell (1986) noted may have included internal as well as long range operations.

Schmandt-Besserat (1977) provided evidence to show that with the development of agriculture a system of record keeping and calculation was developed using seals, tokens and bullae, which was widespread throughout Mesopotamia. The tokens were of four main shapes: spheres, discs, cones and tetrahedrons. They were globular and never angular. There were no squares, rectangles or triangles. Clay balls, bullae, were used as virtual envelopes. Seals were the means of establishing ownership. Both the tokens and the bullae were the means by which farmers recorded and kept track of their herds and crops as well as their transactions in transporting produce or animals to the temple and other places. Different tokens had different numerical values, using either the base six or ten. By their combination quantity was recorded.

From the point of view of education, Schmandt-Besserat's work could be interpreted to mean that numeracy, and with it systems of counting and accounting, were invented and widely used soon after the emergence of agriculture. The surplus from agricultural production was exchanged or stored. The counting and accounting system allowed farmers, merchants and the temple to establish ownership through seal stamps and to record and keep track of production, storage and exchanges through tokens and bullae.

A further stage in development of settlements is marked by monumental architecture, in the form of temples; built by people of the Eridu culture around 5300 BCE. Later the Ubaid people built more and even larger temples. The temple seems to represent permanent housing for the gods, related to the settled existence of the people. The gods, like the people, were being provided with a permanent abode. The temples were the centres of village life, often at the actual centre of the village locale.

Childe (1952) observed that Ubaid culture was that of peasants with a typical rural lifestyle. The vast majority of people were engaged in subsistence farming. Priests, a few potters and metal workers were the only ones who appeared not directly engaged in agriculture. In fact the temple played a central role in the community's economy in that it was the place where the agricultural surplus was stored, redistributed and traded. The temple represented what could be regarded as the first signs of a nascent public sphere. All the available evidence is that the social organisation of these settlements was on the basis of patriarchal clans and large extended families. They constituted the private sphere, and the temple their only point of substantial interface. It would seem incorrect to regard the temple as the public sector for as yet there was no overarching authority over these several and separate patriarchal clans and families. The clans and families met in the temple on equal footing.

An interesting point that emerges from these early agricultural villages was that the temples were not only the centres of religious life but also the places of commercial exchange of agricultural produce. The basis of the linkage was that the land belonged to the gods who owned it. The farmers occupied and farmed it at the pleasure of the gods. The priests therefore presided over the storage and exchange of the surplus. The temple was therefore not only the centre of religious rituals and observances but also at the heart of the commercial exchange. It would appear that, at this time, the doctrine that claimed that the gods owned the land, farmed by the clans at their pleasure, was more to establish a basis of authority in spiritual and commercial matters, than it was evidence of temple totalitarianism in the political economy of the villages.

The controversy between Oriental scholars such as Falkenstein, Gelb and Diakanoff, concerning the extent of private ownership of land, and therefore the extent of public ownership by the temple, could distract attention from a major consideration. It would appear that debate about public and private ownership at the dawn of civilisation is projecting contemporary conceptions on the ancient past. What does not appear to be in doubt is that the temple was the major player in the nascent economies and early commercial transactions at the dawn of the ancient civilisation of Mesopotamia.

The larger point, therefore, is that when human kind started to settle in agricultural communities, produce more than their subsistence, and trade this surplus, the inaugural commercial transactions were done in temples and presided over by priests. Economics and religion were conducted and practised in the same place by the same people. Ritual observances, commercial exchange and redistribution of surplus were intimately linked. In other words, economics and commerce was inextricably linked with the ethical vision and cosmology of the people. Commercial exchange was transacted and economic redistribution effected in the holy place. These exchanges were presided over by those who represented sacred trust and divine presence. Note has to be made of this ancient association, while resisting contemporary controversy about ownership.

When looked at as a whole, the first five millennia of agriculture and sedentary living in Mesopotamia produced a culture based on three main pillars. First, a subsistence mode of production manifested in its major economic activities in farming, fishing and animal breeding. Second, counting and record keeping, numeracy and accounting, emerged as the primary instruments of establishing ownership, keeping track of production and the basis of exchange. Third, temple centred villages worshiped a pantheon of gods. In addition, this culture was continually challenged to accommodate new arrivals converting from nomadic existence to sedentary living. As such it was also kept rooted to the social organisation typical of patriarchal clans practising the nomadic lifestyle. Within the clan final authority rested with the eldest male, who, through reciprocal rights and obligations, exercised that authority over younger males, women and children to ensure the survival of the clan. The challenge of maintaining settled community among groups that knew nothing else but nomadic existence must have been formidable.

The task of maintaining community in the villages fell to the temple. Religious bonds were the means of binding blood-related autonomous clans together in corporate living. Ritual observances and worship were therefore the first activities transferred from the private sphere of kinship, to the public sphere of corporate existence of non-kins. The blood bonds of kinship were dissolved in the solvent of ritual piety. The common gods worshipped by the clans became the glue of non-kinship solidarity that made village community possible.

It is in this context that the temple's involvement in the village economy and commercial activity must be understood. The redistribution of surplus, and the trade of surplus between the clans and with outsiders, were being conducted in the only common space and shared beliefs of the separate clans of blood related kin. The gods themselves had to preside in transactions being conducted outside the covenant of kinship. The priests, the gods' representatives, were however directly accountable to the faithful and as a consequence had to oversee the transactions and redistribution. The temple itself had to develop the doctrinal basis for its authority, and did so by its assertion that final ownership of the land, the source of subsistence, rested with the gods. Equally important, this doctrine established the basis of the temple's authority and secured its continued existence through gifts and donations from those who exercised earthly stewardship over the various plots of land owned by the gods.

The temple's existence, however, could not be left solely to philanthropy. In the context of self-reliant clans, it had to have the means of generating its own subsistence. Apart from its impressive architecture, compared to the rest of the village, temples also had their own lands, the means of generating their own subsistence. This endowment of the temple, seemed to have been more than just an original gift but appeared to be added to from time to time, as piety inspired philanthropy on the part of the faithful, and as the gods were thanked for the bounty that periodically blessed agricultural production.

TECHNOLOGY, URBANISATION AND WRITING IN SUMER

By the year 4000 BCE the Sumerians were firmly settled in Mesopotamia. When they arrived is uncertain. Where they came from is still a matter of speculation. Crawford (1991) maintained that Sumerians and Semites inhabited Mesopotamia from the earliest settlements. She based that conclusion on the fact that there are no physical differences between the earliest and the more recent population of the area. There are others, however, Kramer (1963), Landsberger (1974) and Schmandt-Besserat (1977) who hold to the view that the Sumerians were late arrivants in Mesopotamia.

Two things are sure. First, the Sumerians were not Semites. They along with the Semites constituted the two major ethno-linguistic groups in southern Mesopotamia at the beginning of the fourth millennium. Second, they were another set of clans exchanging nomadic existence for settled living. There is some speculation that they arrived by sea and not overland, but that is also an issue of debate. By whatever route they arrived, Schmandt-Besserat and Alexander (1975) noted that they settled on the banks of the Euphrates, the less unpredictable of the two rivers.

Whenever they came, and by whatever route, by the beginning of the fourth millennium they had emerged as the dominant group within southern Mesopotamia. They were not the only occupants of the area. Semites were also present and Semitic dialects were also spoken. The Semites steadily increased in numbers and were particularly numerous around Kish in the north. While Sumerians were undoubtedly the dominant founders, the Semites were subordinate co-founders of Sumerian civilisation.

TECHNOLOGICAL REVOLUTION

The starting point of any description of the contribution of the Sumerians to the development of civilisation has to be the technological revolution they engineered in the fourth millennium. Revolution is currently out of style in academic analysis. Social phenomena are now interpreted in evolutionary sequence to show the connectivity with the past. However, notwithstanding the long gestation in each of the areas that Sumerian inventiveness tackled, the volume and interconnection of their contributions justify the revolutionary caption, in that their combined effect catapulted a significant break with the past.

To begin with the innovative Sumerians engineered a more sophisticated system of irrigation that turned much of the swamps and silt-banks into fertile soil on which they planted crops of dates and barley and raised sheep and cattle. Their first settlements were villages, consistent with the patterns that had become traditional for agriculture in Mesopotamia.

For all of human kind's previous history, as revealed by archaeology, hunting, gathering and then agriculture employed stone tools of a wide variety as the major implements. The Sumerians effected a major technological revolution, by their skill in metallurgy, through the development of metal tools made of bronze. It is still a matter of debate whether they invented bronze; however, most authors credit them with its first production and use. What is not in dispute is that they were the first to use bronze in the production of metal tools for agriculture.

Schmandt-Besserat and Alexander (1975) noted that metalworking was one of the outstanding skills of ancient Mesopotamia. By 3000 BCE the technical aspects of the craft had been fully developed. Casting, hammering, repousse, chasting, riveting, engraving, inlaying, gilding, smelting and refining were all not only practised but also fully mastered. Though latecomers to the region, Sumerians soon became its leading metal workers. Childe (1952) underscored a point, more subtlety made by Schmandt-Besserat, that Sumerians did not come into the region with a ready made and superior culture, which they imposed upon the region. Rather, they brought fresh vigour to the traditional strengths in Mesopotamia, hence their achievements built on foundations that had been previously laid. Their smiths first worked in gold, silver, lead and copper.

Exactly when bronze replaced copper is hard to specify. However, bronze by being better for casting, harder and more durable represented a considerable technological advance. The metal plough was one of their outstanding inventions. It was far more effective that similar devices made of stone. However, the metal plough by itself would not have brought about the advance made in field preparation had not the Sumerians found a new source of energy for ploughing.

The Sumerians also developed the harness and were the first to use domesticated animals, the ox and later the horse, as the source of energy and power in ploughing fields. By 3500 BCE there are pictograms of two oxen drawing metal ploughs through fields. Men drawing stone ploughs, were now replaced by oxen drawing metal ploughs. The implications for agricultural production and productivity were revolutionary in terms of time, speed and cost of land preparation and the size of the fields that could be planted.

Sometime after 3500 BCE Sumerian inventiveness created the wheel and applied it to transportation. The first wheels were solid discs made of three planks of wood clamped by a transverse piece and fitted with copper studs or leather tires. The Sumerians were therefore the first people to advance metalworking to the point where wheeled vehicles could be manufactured. As Schmandt-Besserat observed, this implied the use of sophisticated tools including saws. Wheeled vehicles revolutionised transportation and communication and facilitated the faster movement of large amounts of agricultural produce.

The Sumerians in their era of technological breakthroughs also invented the potter's wheel. Both the wheels for carts and the potter's wheel appeared almost at the same time. Which came first is impossible to say. However, the potter's wheel became the first application of wheel technology outside of transportation of one kind or another. While pottery was a cottage activity, the potter's wheel opened the possibility for industrial production, although it would appear that its potential was not immediately seized, and pottery remained a hand made craft for several centuries after the invention of the wheel designed specifically for this craft.

Crawford (1991) noted that the Uruk period in the fourth millennium was one of striking technological innovation and invention over a vast range of fields. Indeed, it was the most inventive period in Mesopotamian history. The other periods including the Dynastic, Agade and Ur III periods are not marked by similar inventiveness, or for that matter later periods of Mesopotamian history. Crawford raised the possibility that not all the inventions were by Sumerians themselves but some may have been brought by immigrants from the Iranian plateau. In other words, Sumerian civilisation not only spawned invention from among its own but also inspired and welcomed inventions and innovations from outside, which it then appropriated as its own.

What is not in doubt is that the technological inventions and innovations increased the amount of land that could be brought into agricultural production, improved agricultural productivity of the land and as a result significantly expanded the surplus generated. This was the foundation upon which the expansion of population, urbanisation and the rise of Sumerians to dominance in Mespotamia rested.

URBANISATION

Simultaneous with the technological inventions and innovations pioneered by the Sumerians, was the growth of cities in Sumer. Schmandt-Besserat and Alexander (1975) pointed out that while the earliest Sumerians settlements were villages, by about 3500 BCE cities began to make their appearance in Sumer. Ur, Nippur and Kish were the first three; Lagash, Uruk, Fara, Eridu and Sharrupak later attained city status. Kramer (1963) noted that around 3000 BCE there were about a dozen or more cities in Sumer.

A necklace of smaller towns, villages and hamlets surrounded each city. Each city was separated from the next by long stretches of unirrigated land, swamps and semi-desert. Apart from providing a buffer between cities, this stretch of land provided grazing for livestock and the thorn bushes and scrub provided fuel. Each city was therefore isolated from the next. The spaces between them also allowed nomadic tribes areas in which to continue to roam. Initially the population of each city was estimated at no more than 5,000 to 10,000 inhabitants.

Kramer (1963) described the typical Sumerian city as being walled and entered by gates. The temple was its most outstanding architectural feature. Situated on a high terrace, the temple was the tallest, largest and most important building. Typically it consisted of a massive staged tower called a ziggurat, a rectangular central shine and surrounding rooms. Usually the large complex included several shrines, courtyards, magazines, storehouses and dwelling places for temple personnel. Crawford (1991) noted that in several of the larger cities the ziggurat was separated from the temple and was itself a most impressive religious monument. Indeed, it was the most imposing architectural feature of the city. The construction of the ziggurat arose from the tradition of raising temples on platforms or terraces above the surrounding buildings. While the exact religious purpose is still a matter of much debate, its form was consistent with the tradition of holy places being high places, raised closer to heaven, the home of the gods. It was the site of many religious festivals and observances and showed that the central importance of religion in Sumerian civilisation was retained, as the transition was made from village to city living.

As Schmandt-Besserat and Alexander (1975) observed the concept of city implies more than just a large congregation of people. Central to the concept of city are the ideas of a community of specialists working full-time in various fields, unity under some form of leadership and, by taxes or indenture, extensive works undertaken for the welfare of all residents. Factors necessary for the formation of cities include:

- A surplus of food, thus allowing a fraction of the population to engage themselves full-time in occupations other than agriculture.
- Some system of redistribution and exchange in which agricultural surplus goes to non-agricultural workers who in turn deliver technological and other services to the food producing sector.
- Public administration and a legal system to both record and account for transactions as well as to plan and co-ordinate actions, resolve problems and conflicts.

Sumerian cities met these criteria. The technological revolutions they engineered allowed for a level of food production that could support large numbers of persons in other occupations than agriculture. While the majority were still farmers, animal breeders and fishermen, for the first time in human history large numbers of people were engaged full-time in occupations other than those concerned with their own subsistence. These included smiths of various types, carpenters, potters, weavers, administrators, priests and merchants.

Interestingly, the layout of the city reflected nascent social stratification. The city centre around the temple had straight and wide unpaved streets. Within the same neighbourhood were public buildings and the dwellings of the elite. Further away were the shops and dwellings of the craftsmen. On the outskirts were the houses of the poorer people reached by narrow alleys.

The farms related to the city were outside the city walls. By the time the Sumerian cities appear, farms were owned both by the temple and individual clans. While the temple was the largest landowner, it had no monopoly on ownership. Many clans owned land of varying size. Temple lands were rented out to sharecroppers. Priests, and the temple, however, continued to be the backbone of public administration, commercial exchange and of redistribution in the economy.

THE INVENTION OF WRITING

Writing is viewed by many as Sumer's most lasting contribution to civilisation. There is some controversy as to whether writing was invented only once and then imitated elsewhere or independently invented in different locations. The dates of different systems of writing vary from 3500 to 3300 BCE in Mesopotamia, 3100 to 3000 BCE in Egypt, 2500 BCE in the Indus Valley and 2000 BCE in China (Robinson 1995). Whether one holds to the mono- or polygenesis explanations of writing, what is not in doubt is that the oldest texts are from Sumer. Cooper (1989) maintained that there are no challengers to Sumerian primacy in either true writing or urbanisation. Katz (1995) maintained that all writing, as we know it, with the exception of Chinese and pre-Columbian script, originated in the ancient Near East between 4000 and 3000 BCE. He went on to cite urbanisation, formal religion and active trade as the collective stimuli for the development of writing since all three required written communication.

The question of why writing emerged in some agricultural settlements and not in others is an issue of much debate and outside the scope of this study. More germane are the factors that contributed to its emergence in Sumer. Schmandt-Besserat (1977) maintained that writing was not brought into Mesopotamia by the Sumerian newcomers, but rather represented another step in the evolution of a sophisticated system of record keeping which was indigenous to Mesopotamia from the ninth millennium BCE.

Schmandt-Besserat (1977) traced the stages in the evolution of writing from the accounting system as follows:

- From the ninth millennium BCE an accounting system was established based on seals and geometric tokens of various shapes to which different values were attached.
- Between the ninth and fourth millennia BCE there was little change in this system.

- At the beginning of the fourth Millennium a marginal invention took place, which employed clay envelopes called bullae, to hold the tokens of a particular transaction and bear the relevant seals.
- Check marks were placed on the surface of the bullae to repeat for convenience the number of tokens inside. Soon these check marks supplanted the old token system, since they represented the tokens symbolically.
- Pictograms next appeared, representing words. Nine hundred different symbols can be recognised.
- Ideograms constituted the stage where abstract ideas are included in the text. For example, a foot assumes walking, or the sun implies heat.
- The final step or stage was phonograms used to represent sounds. For example, 'eye' also meant the sound.

In commenting on this evolutionary sequence, Schmandt-Besserat (1981) raised the question as to the point at which notations could be considered writing. In her view, the answer depends on the definition of writing that is employed. Some definitions stress the emergence of graphic symbols, while others lay emphasis on the assignment of a phonetic value to the sign. Using the latter definition, writing would only have existed at the final step of the sequence described. Pictograms and ideograms would best be classified as proto-writing, emphasising their transitional character. In this regard, the shift from three-dimensional tokens to their graphic representation constituted the most significant event in the evolution of the recording system into writing.

Schmandt-Besserat (1975) noted that writing employed the same clay materials that had been used for tokens and bullae. Writing was done using a stylus to draw the pictograms on damp clay tablets, which were then baked. Originally the pictograms were arranged vertically but around 2800 BCE they began to be written left to right. After writing was invented tokens and seals continued to be used. Schmandt-Besserat was of the view that urbanisation and trade were two critical factors in the invention of writing in Sumer. Katz (1995) noted that clay was a plentiful and cheap material in Mesopotamia, and very suitable not only as a writing surface but also as a record in that once baked tablets could last forever.

Green (1981) challenged Schmandt-Besserat's notion of an evolutionary sequence in the development of writing. She maintained that from its inception cuneiform was not merely a collection of individual symbols but rather a coherent information system for which written characters were the main, but not the only, component. Further, she maintained that cuneiform writing did not evolve by itself, but rather was invented within the framework of a bureaucratic organisation which controlled not only the distribution of goods and services, but also status and information. That institution created the demand for a control technology for which cuneiform writing was the eventual realisation. Indeed, one of the earliest recognisable objectives of the writing system was the exploitation of the maximum data storage capacity of the texts.

Green was of the view that it was the demands of public administration rather than accounting that led to the invention of writing. The existence of a technology, which could reliably preserve information, facilitates the control and management of information, which is the primary task of public administration. The socioeconomic base of such a system is a stratified society, a redistribution system, and voluminous transactions, all of which pre-existed in Sumer. Writing allowed the administration to grow, through written liability, and maintain direct authority over even the lowest level of personnel and clientele.

Cooper (1989) was of the view that while Schmandt-Besserat's argument that cuneiform was invented through a number of precursors is not entirely convincing what it establishes beyond any reasonable doubt is that the invention of writing in Sumer, for the Sumerian language, is not an ex nihilo event but the culmination of a long development of notation in clay. What she had done is to give cuneiform a documented pre-history in Mesopotamia and to construct a sequence that leads directly to the tablets on which cuneiform signs were written.

Powell (1981) agreed with Green that writing was invented as a coherent system and did not evolve by a slow accretion of sign after sign, generation after generation. He pointed to the fact that in the history of writing there is not a single instance of a communal-evolutionary invention of a script. In his view an individual, probably of the city of Uruk, invented writing after which the community of users modified, adapted, elaborated, refined, added and eliminated various aspects to produce the system that continued to be used for centuries. At the same time, like Cooper (1989), Powell credits Schmandt-Besserat's work with establishing the long conceptual development that undergirded the emergence of writing and the stages through which the record keeping system evolved, which was the precursor to writing.

Goody (1986) is of the view that writing is not an essential element in state formation or in the creation of cities. The historical association of these in Sumer and the Near East may be accidental rather than developmentally necessary. He points to the fact that comparable cities and states arose in America, Africa and Polynesia without the development of writing, in the fullest sense, although all had record keeping systems. In his view, the critical element in the creation of writing systems was bureaucracy, of the city or the state.

What is interesting is that writing was invented in the temple, but its early use was for bookkeeping and record keeping rather than for recording myths and rituals. Legal transactions dealing with material considerations in the form of sale, rental and lease agreements, marriage contracts and wills were the main documents produced by the earliest writing system. Material concerns, not ethical vision or ritual observance, were the early objects of writing, notwithstanding the temple location of its invention. The apparent contradiction may be more for the modern mind attuned to a different cosmology from the Sumerian perspective. A more literal interpretation may be warranted. That is, in Sumerian civilisation the material was sacred and not secular, spirit and matter were one. At least, this hypothesis is worthy of being tested.

Goody noted that written treaties between two cities were said to be witnessed by the gods of both cities. Great oaths were taken in the names of the gods pledging commitment to the agreements reached. Further, curses were in store for those who broke the contracts. This highlights the ethical aspects of contracts and treaties that seemed to have been part and parcel of Sumerian practice. While many scholars have noted the connection between accounting and writing, and the appearance that the former led to the latter, not much attention is paid to why the temple was the locus of such matters.

Green and other have stressed the element of control, through written liability, that a system of writing confers upon the institution employing it. From this perspective priests employed writing for hegemonic purposes. However, the notion of a Sumerian temple theocracy has been shown to be a misrepresentation of the contexts and a misunderstanding of the texts on which that notion was advanced. It is likely therefore that the use of writing for bureaucratic and hegemonic purposes may be overstating the importance of these in the invention of writing in the middle of the fourth millennium.

At the same time it must be acknowledged that writing is a means of establishing or maintaining credibility and integrity in circumstances where serious questions are likely to be raised on a variety of levels by numerous parties. With the great increase in wealth that was generated by the technological revolution in agricultural production and productivity, the volume of transactions they had to both oversee and execute must have overwhelmed the temples. Writing, therefore, may have been one means by which the temple sought to maintain its role and image of sacred trust, and by the esoteric nature of this new invention, even the aura of divine presence. In other words, the system of accounting was also the means of accountability by which priests could be trusted. Writing expanded their capacity to continue to be trusted in circumstances that were far in excess of the demands that could be met by the accounting system that was devised to meet the needs of subsistence agriculture of a relatively sparsely populated area.

Cooper (1989) added an important footnote to the saga of the invention of writing by his observation that while cuneiform was invented for the Sumerian language, and was only later adopted for the writing of Semitic and other languages, scribes who wrote the earliest known Sumerian literary texts had Semitic names. In other words, Semites were intimately involved in learning and writing cuneiform from the time it was originally invented. This in his view emphasised the close relationships that existed between these two ethno-linguistic groups in southern Mesopotamia.

Note must also be made taken of the invention of the cylindrical seal, which together with the stamp seal, served in Sumer as a second recording system to writing. In fact, like writing, the cylindrical seal appeared in the technologically inventive and innovative Uruk period. Shaped like a cylindrical bead, and usually pierced length-wise, the seal was usually decorated with scenes which when rolled on damp clay, produced a continuous frieze. Like the stamp seals, cylindrical seals were used to stamp objects as a sign of ownership and also as a signature. As Crawford (1991) pointed out, in a largely illiterate society the seal served an important function in validating documents and transactions. Parties to a contract, before witnesses, would roll their seals on the relevant tablets that recorded the terms of the deal. Having the seal of the appropriate temple official affixed to it would strengthen the entire transaction. Crawford is of the view that the seal functioned is some ways similar to the modern credit card and its loss had to be announced publicly at several points in the city of its owner, to avoid being held accountable for debts and shady deals accumulated by the thief.

The cylindrical seals were used not only for economic transactions but they became the means by which information was conveyed about the owner of the seal, historical events and heroic deeds. Over time these seals varied in style. Crawford noted that scenes varied in different eras from pastoral, banquet, combat, rituals and prayers. In later periods inscriptions were added to the scenes suggesting that more people could read them. In addition, ownership of seals appeared to become more widespread.

It is important to briefly take note of the comparative perspective with respect to the invention of writing in the ancient Near East and particularly in Mesopotamia. Ullman (1980) was of the opinion that while speech was a momentous invention in human history, writing was not as epochal but was much more important than one would suspect. He quoted Thomas Astle as saying that speech was the noblest acquisition of mankind, and writing was the most useful art. The first distinguishes man from the brute creation, while the second, draws the distinction between the civilised and the savage. Katz (1995) observed that when the Sumerians and the Egyptians created writing in the ancient Near East, Europe was a cultural wilderness. The typical European was a nomadic hunter.

Finally, it must be noted that although writing was invented in the middle of the fourth millennium, schools and schooling do not appear in this period although writing must have required long training before scribes could have been produced. Green (1981) pointed out that the occupation of scribe was not differentiated from that of priest for some time. Indeed, the scribal occupation was not listed among occupations until the third millennium. It would appear that scribal training was incorporated in the training of some priests and remained exclusively within the temple. The invention of writing therefore did not immediately lead to the creation of schools.

Kramer (1963) observed that writing was one of the supreme achievements of Sumerian civilisation and that the invention of schools was a direct outgrowth of that invention. He noted, however, that while the oldest known documents, which were found in Erech, were largely bits of economic and administrative memoranda, they contained word lists intended for study and practice suggesting that as early as 3000 BCE some scribes were thinking of teaching and learning. However, progress in the emergence of formal schooling was slow in the centuries that followed and it was not before the middle of the third millennium that formal schools appeared throughout Sumer.

To account for the lag of almost 1000 years between the invention of writing and the first appearance of schools, to teach writing, it is necessary to examine several other aspects of Sumerian civilisation. These include religion, government, war, social organisation and gender relations.

SUMERIAN RELIGION

The people of Sumer were polytheistic. They worshipped a pantheon of anthropomorphic gods. The pantheon was hierarchically organised in a manner similar to the patriarchal family complete with goddesses (Falkenstein 1974). The three basic categories were:

a)   The great gods and goddesses, among whom were the creative and the non-creative gods and goddesses;
b)   The gods and goddesses of functions and parishes; and
c)   The personal gods and goddesses assigned to and protecting each individual, (Gadd 1948).

There were four primary gods, three male and one female. Enlil, the god of the earth, was the father of all gods and the most important god in the pantheon. He together with An the sky god, Enki god of the ocean and Inanna goddess of love and war constituted the top echelons in the pantheon (Landsberger 1974). The primary gods were creative while the lesser were non-creative gods of appropriate ranks. Together they ruled over all the forces in nature, all the functions in society and all areas of the world. The gods played an important part in everyday life although their functions were separate. The gods were all human in form but superhuman and immortal. While they preferred truth, justice and righteousness they were also capable of evil and falsehood, Kramer (1963). However, not even the supreme god, the father god Enlil, ruled without challenge to his authority or without the prospect of revolt. The pantheon therefore was in constant dynamic action, including conflicts between the gods.

According to Sumerian myth, after the creation of the ordered world and its inhabitants, under the leadership of Enlil, the gods parcelled out the domains among themselves. Gods were assigned to different cities and functions, (Gadd 1948). Each god represented one divine person and each possessed a cult city, at which he or she was worshipped. Enlil, the father god, assigned himself to Nippur, which therefore became the religious capital of Sumer. Enlil therefore was not only the supreme god of heaven but also of earth. The cities, like the gods, were therefore organised along the lines of a patriarchal family. Inanna was the goddess of Uruk.

Depending on the god or goddess of each city priests and priestesses of special classes were assigned to temples. Asceticism, transvestism and cult prostitution only represented the extremes of this polymorphic cosmology (Landsberger 1974).

The patron god of each city was expected to defend the interest of their own city in the council of the gods in which all decisions were made. To illustrate the ways in which gods not only defended but also promoted the interest of their city, Sumerian legend had it that at one time the city of Eridu had all the arts and crafts of Sumer as its sole prerogative. Inanna anxious to advance her own city visited Enki, god of Eridu and her father, and requested these gifts from him. After a banquet with much to eat and drink, Enki gave her of his *me* that which constituted these special gifts in art and craft. Inanna departed by boat with her precious cargo, but on awaking Enki repented of his generosity and sought to recover the gifts. Inanna was able to retain her cargo and arrived at Erech with them. According to the legend that was how her city, and all of Sumer, got hold of the special arts and crafts that characterised Sumerian civilisation.

Landsberger (1974) noted that an enduring and unchanging feature of Sumerian civilisation was its belief that the earthly order paralleled cosmic order. All worldly occurrences were therefore merely a reflection of heavenly events. Earthly life therefore participated in cosmic events. The temple at Nippur was not only the centre of Sumer but also the pinnacle of the world. The cultic order was symbolic of world order. Landsberger observed that the wonder and riddle of Sumerian religion was its capacity to adapt the local cults to the cosmic pantheon without resort to artificial speculation. As such Sumerian religion had no theology, no speculative strain. The world order and the cosmic order were one. The challenge was to observe and list the order revealed. By such observation priests created a canonical list with the names of nearly 15,000 gods.

In addition to the pantheon of creative and non-creative gods, each person had a protective god or goddess. It they became impure, or sinned, the guardian deities would abandon them. It must be noted that the wrath of the gods was incurred for ritual incorrectitude and their pleasure gained by ritual correctitude. Lamentations, or prayer combined with magic, or appeal to one of the great gods, had to be invoked to get the personal gods to return to the particular individual.

There were always people on earth, priests and oracles, who knew what was taking place in heaven and through whom the gods communicated. In addition to their direct contact with heaven, the gods communicated through omens, dreams and other means. One rather esoteric means that was very popular was the entrails of sacrificial animals, particularly their livers. The gods were supposed to write their messages in this organ. Identifying the message and interpreting the meaning became an area of specialisation among priests.

Gods and goddesses like people needed housing, food and drink which it was the duty of people to provide. Indeed, human kind was created to provide for the needs of the gods. In addition to providing for their sustenance, human kind needed to observe the monthly and annual celebrations and festivals related to the gods of their city, occupations and other relationships. The most important of these festivals was that of the New Year at which the sacred marriage, and ritual coitus, between the king and a priestess, were re-enacted. Pleasing the gods was much more related to rites, ritual observance and the performance of duty than to personal morality. At the same time, the authority of the gods over the people was never exercised by command or direct relationship through ownership of property, Landsberger (1974).

The influence of the gods over the people was spiritual, effected through the *me* and the *nam*. The *me* was an aura emanating from the gods and the temple in mystic manner magically drew the pious into its spell. The *nam* was the fate, or formula, decreed by the gods, which determined the future. The gods decreed the fate by the divine word. The *me* kept things going or in place once they had been created or decreed (Kramer 1963).

The Sumerian religion included belief in life after death. After death the spirit descended to the nether world that was ruled by a god like all other aspects of society. The nether world, however, was dismal and wretched. It was only a pale imitation of life on earth. In descending to the nether world the spirit was emasculated, hence there was no better life to come in the next world. The present life was superior to the life to come. Further, the nether world was hierarchically structured along the same lines as the present world. Hence notables and kings would receive better treatment, even if the conditions were generally worse. As with the gods, material provision had to be made for life in the nether world (Kramer 1963).

In Sumerian cosmology earthly life was a reflection of the divine. In a nutshell there was only one order, one reality, transposed into three different spheres with a different quality attached to each. The divine world was out of the reach of humans. The nether world was worse than the present life. Hence the present life, from the human perspective, was the best that there was and would be.

Within the context of this cosmology and worldview, manifest in their religion, Kramer attempted to sketch the values and attitudes and general character of the Sumerian people. The main features of this sketch can be summarised as follows:

- Sumerians were achievement and success oriented, with strong tendencies for establishing superiority.
- They were competitive, aggressive and predisposed to rivalry.
- They prized life, since as far as they were concerned this was the best that would be since the nether world was worse than the present. Since there was no better to come, the best was to be made of the present.
- Sumerians were materialistic. Prosperity was seen as a sign of divine approval and blessing and poverty the reverse. They prized wealth,

possessions and prosperity and loathed, despised and were unsympathetic to poverty and the poor for whom they had no consolation. Their attitudes were well documented in their wisdom literature which included sayings like 'when a poor man dies do not try to revive him' or 'when he has bread he has no salt, when he has salt he has no bread, when he has meat he has no condiment and when he has condiment he has no meat.'

· They cherished all of humankind's most desirable virtues and qualities: truth, goodness, justice, freedom, wisdom, learning, courage and loyalty.

· They constantly lamented the treatment of widows, orphans, the poor and refugees from the perspective of justice and fairness. In other words, while they loathed poverty and were generally unsympathetic to the poor, they were concerned and even outraged if these were the result of unjust or unfair use of power. An active social conscience was alive in Sumer premised on justice rather than on sympathy.

· Great importance was attached to law and order. Kramer was of the view that this was because of their contentious and aggressive behaviour pattern and their recognition of this rather than from the fact that they were naturally law-abiding.

Landsberger (1974) made the observation that one of the enduring features of Sumerian civilisation was its ordered form and the ordering function of thought. The principle of order was implicit in all activities of the Sumerian mind. Manifestations of this feature of Sumerian character were the cadastral catalogues or lists of municipal real estate with field plans; lists of city population separated into classes; lists of gods; lists of everyday objects; poems carefully divided into stanzas; and pictorial presentations carefully divided into groups and scenes. The ordered form was expressed in concrete terms. This classificatory way of ordering the world was also manifested in the peculiar cognitive style of the Sumerian language. Nouns are grouped by type and all verbs are transparent. Hence all processes of speech were from the mouth and all nuances of sight from the eye. Indeed the system of writing they developed embedded this determinate way of thinking.

Another important insight into the Sumerian outlook and worldview was given by Gadd (1948) who cited the religious poem that described how the god of the nomadic Amorites took his place in decent society. He observed that all the other gods had a wife and establishments, he alone seemed like an outcast. He therefore besought his mother to find him a wife, which she did from a neighbouring god. Whereupon, he married her, built a home in the city of Ninals and installed himself as the lord of that place. Gadd noted that the nomadic Amorites were regarded as barbarous and uncivilised. To become civilised their god had to have a wife, a temple and a city in his possession. No god of consequence could exist without these.

Glassner (1989) noted that in the Sumerian epic of Gilgamesh, Enhidu the stranger who is one of the two heroes of the epic, became human through his initiation to sexual intercourse, bread, beer and the wearing of clothes. His acceptance into the community, however, revolves around participation in a meal to celebrate his arrival, a challenge to prove his worth centred around the defence of marriage, a fight observing normative rules and finally his acknowledgement of the rights of the Sumerian god-king Gilgamesh. Interestingly, Enhidu is initiated into humanity through sexual intercourse with a prostitute, the outside woman, and is accepted into community after his defence of the wife, the inside woman.

Based on the descriptions of the major elements of the religion and the selected insights noted by some scholars the essence of Sumerian religion appeared to be:

i)   A polytheistic pantheon of anthropomorphic gods hierarchically ranked reflecting inevitable inequality in the cosmic order, mirrored by parallels in the earthly order and in the nether world

ii) Resignation to the prerogatives of the gods, whose ways could not be comprehended, but who were to be served through rites, rituals and adherence to duties and obligations.

iii) Acknowledgement of sex, marriage and the patriarchal family as the basis of civilised society.

iv) An acceptance of the here and now as the best that will be in human existence and therefore the imperative to aggressively seek the most and the best material benefits available in this life.

v)   An ethical framework within which to conduct the aggressive pursuit of material ends. Prosperity was to be earned as the reward of ritual correctness and the fulfilment of obligations to the gods.

Within this framework the location of economic and commercial activity in the temple was totally consistent with Sumerian religion. Indeed it was an integral part. The ideal was to compete aggressively for material rewards in this life but to do so in a rule governed ethical manner. Conducting commercial transactions and effecting economic redistribution through the temple was, at least in theory, subjecting them to the scrutiny of these ideals even if human frailty manifested itself from time to time. The debate among scholars with alternative conceptions of the temple operations as centrally planned or private enterprise imposes the ideological debates of the 1980s on the realities of 3500 BCE. What is missed is the essential nature of Sumerian religion, their worldview and the predisposition of the people consequent upon these.

It is these distinctive features of the Sumerian civilisation that accounted for the invention of writing, as against other civilisations located in other riverine areas of the world with a similar agricultural mode of production and comparable sedentary lifestyles. In this regard the creations of Sumerian civilisation cannot be seen in linear relationship to any other civilisation, except where through their own imperatives those civilisations borrowed directly from Sumer or indirectly through third sources.

FROM TEMPLE CENTRED DEMOCRACY TO AUTOCRATIC CITY-STATE

Previous reference has been made to the fact that at the start of the fourth millennium BCE the temple not only dominated village architecture but was also the centre of the religious, commercial and economic life of the community. The technological inventions applied to production in agriculture made urbanisation a reality for the first time in human history. With increased wealth and urbanisation involving the incorporation of villages into cities, greater disparity and differentiation in the social organisation of the society became manifest as well as greater rivalry within and between Sumerian cities. It is important to examine here the implication of these transformations for the evolution of government in Sumer.

Jacobsen (1943) traced the evolution of the form of government in ancient Mesopotamia and concluded that the general direction of the change was from primitive democracy to autocracy. Jacobsen acknowledged that the definition of democracy he employed was the classical gendered version instead of its modern form. However, working within that limitation, democracy was defined as the form of government in which internal sovereignty resided in all free adult men without distinction of class. As such

- Major decisions required their consent. For example, to conduct war.
- Citizens constituted the supreme judicial authority.
- Rulers and magistrates obtained their positions by consent.

On the other hand autocracy is defined as that form of government in which major political, judicial and executive powers are concentrated in a single person.

Jacobsen observed that initially Sumer accommodated a mosaic of diminutive, self sufficient, autonomous villages, which gradually grew into cities. Political powers rested in the hands of the free citizens and an ensi or city governor who discharged his authority in the name of the god of the city. Where decisions had to be made that were vital to the community as a whole, then a general assembly of all free adult males needed to be consulted to decide on the action to be taken. In other matters a council of elders made the decisions. Kramer (1963) referred to this arrangement as a bicameral assembly of an upper house of elders and a lower house of all free adult males. In the case of war the general assembly appointed, from among them, a leader on a temporary basis for the duration of the engagement. In a similar manner the judiciary rested with the general assembly, which settled conflicts that arose in the community.

While the temple played a central role in the life of the community, it would be improper to regard the arrangement as a theocracy. Sovereign power did not rest with the priest, with respect to politics or justice. Executive authority, such as existed, rested with the governor. The role of the priest was with respect to the ritual defence of the community and the administration of economic and commercial exchanges. In large measure the priests were accountable through the recording system that was in place. What existed is therefore better described as temple administration of the economy rather than theocracy.

Jacobsen observed that in light of the fact that government in these growing villages and emerging cities was still in a primitive condition, in that various functions were not specialised, the power structure was loosely defined and the machinery for social co-ordination was imperfectly developed, it could be said that at the commencement of urbanisation and organised warfare, clan democracy prevailed in Sumer. The governor, with a council of elders of the clans and a general assembly of all free adult males exercised political, judicial and executive power in the context of consent and consultation on various matters. Final authority rested with the general council in matters of war, with the elders in other matters and with the governor in terms of administrative routine.

The process of transformation began with the appointment of temporary military leaders for specific campaigns. Usually these were younger men who, for that campaign, had supreme authority. Several of these temporary generals became heroes. Unwilling to relinquish the office and the power after a specific campaign was over, they sometimes initiated conflicts, or maintained that the danger had not passed or could come from another source. In time these heroes were appointed as kings, mandated to establish regular standing armies. Part of the agricultural surplus now went to serve this military establishment, headquartered in the palace. Through this process kingship became hereditary, with the consequential establishment of dynasties.

Crawford (1991) observed that there were three titles, En, Ensi and Lugal, used, over time to describe the person responsible for the city administration. The first suggested priestly status, the second equates roughly to governor or civilian leader while the third had the closest meaning to king. Lamberg-Karlovsky (1986) interpreted the titles as En, chief priest, Ensi civilian governor, and lugal, military leader. Some kings had additional designations like Kings of Kish, or King of the four quarters of the world. Crawford interpreted the changes in designation as indicative of the process of secularisation of political power in Sumer. In other words, originally the person with executive powers in the village or the early stages of city formation could have been the chief priest, who later became a civilian governor, both exercising their responsibilities in conjunction with the council of elders and general assembly. The shift from governor to king represented the completion of the secularisation and concentration of political power. This process of centralisation can be traced in the following brief outline.

- At first kingship was temporary, or even part-time, specific to particular military operations.
- When kingship became full-time, in the early dynastic period, kings did not enjoy absolute power; they were military leaders, lugal. They were primarily responsible for raising and equipping the army and for maintaining the defences of the city, including its protective wall, Schmandt-Besserat and Alexander (1975).
- From being military commander, the king next acquired the executive powers of the civilian governor, Ensi, who then became redundant.
- Later the king acquired control of the judiciary. The king was then commander in chief, president and chief justice.
- At some point along the way, the king also became high priest, En. Finally, Naram-Sin, grandson of Sargon the Great, completed the centralisation of power by reaching the ultimate level of autocracy by declaring himself god. His example was then followed by all the kings of Sumer until the end of the dynasty of Ur III, that is, to the end of Sumer as a political entity. It is ironic that when kingship peaked in the effulgence of its power, the kingdom was so weak that it expired.

Jacobsen (1943) made the point that the transformation between primitive democracy – the preference here is for the label temple centred democracy – to autocracy was such that in the transition stages, some aspects of power would be centralised while others remained democratic. For example, while the king may have been commander in chief and president, the judiciary was still controlled by the assembly. However, by the last two centuries of Sumerian civilisation political power was fully centralised, in the single figure of the god-king. Council and assembly were non-existent and the king appointed judges. It was the king's justice that was meted out to the people.

It is important to note the redefinition of patriarchal power relationships that is effected in the course of Sumerian civilisation. To begin with political power was almost totally exercised by men. The En, council of elders and the assembly were all males. As Jacobsen rightly pointed out the definition of Sumerian democracy was highly gendered. In time, however, power shifted from the patriarchs, the older males, to the younger males. Warfare was the vehicle through which the generational shift was executed. The epic of Gilgamesh explicitly demonstrated the shift. Gilgamesh wanted to engage in warfare and approached the council of elders who decided against such a course of action. But he took his case to the younger men of the assembly who agreed with him, and therefore whose counsel he took. Over time, power shifted from its generational mooring to military might exercised by the young.

Associated with this transformation of power was the rise of the state symbolised by the palace. The first kings reported to have lived in palaces were those of Ur in the early dynastic period. The palace was located in the centre of the city, beside the temple, (Schmandt-Besserat 1975). The rise of the palace has to be approached and appreciated from several perspectives.

Jones (1975) studied administrative records for the Lagash in which the 12 or more temple establishments were mainly responsible for cultivation of most of the arable land of that city. The main crop was barley and in any one year there was better than 2,000,000 bushels. Priests, who engaged in much forward planning and careful monitoring of the entire production cycle, managed the operation. Jones found about half the crop covered the cost of production in terms of the cost of labour, feed for draught animals, seed etc. A quarter went to the king as a royal tax, while the remaining quarter was kept by the priests for their own consumption, some was kept as seed grain, some was sent as grain for milling and quantities were sent to the temple in Nippur.

The findings of Jones's study indicate the basis upon which the palace could begin to rival the temple in wealth as it began to assume state powers. A tax of twenty five per cent would not be imposed only on the temple, but on all other revenue earning enterprises of the city. Some records indicate that nothing escaped the tax collectors of the palace not even divorce or death. Crawford (1991) made the point that not only did the palace become wealthy but also the king and his family. Schmandt-Besserat and Alexander (1975) noted that kings soon acquired large estates, established courts at their palaces replete with servants and entertainers, and created the demand for luxury goods in the form of jewellery, fine woodwork, rare and delicate materials and other exotic indulgences.

It must also be noted that the palace entered the economic arena, alongside the temple, large landowners and merchants. In addition to estates, the palace acquired workshops and other productive enterprises. For example, whereas previously only the temple was engaged in large scale metal production, the palace workshops soon became their rivals both in the production of metal and in its external trading. In addition to being a consumer of the surplus generated by the rest of the society, the palace joined the productive enterprises, employed large numbers of free and slave workers and generated some of its own wealth.

The palace therefore added to its military and defence portfolios, state functions including executive activities, diplomacy, taxation and the judiciary. This required the establishment of its own bureaucracy parallel to and separate from that of the temple. The temple bureaucracy was related to its religious, production and commercial activities. That of the palace became the civil service of the city-state.

Kings also used their office, the spoils of conquest and the massive wealth they accumulated, to create a persuasive system of patronage which they used to reward supporters and to co-opt potential adversaries (Foster 1981). Probably it is through this means that the elders of the council, influential priests and strategically placed members of clans were co-opted or neutralised in the process of the kings' acquisition of total power (Lamberg-Karlovsky 1986).

The relationship between the temple and the palace seems worthy of special mention. First, the rise of the palace did not fundamentally alter the functions and operations of the temple. In some respects the palace became a parallel and competing institution. The religious, commercial and economic activities of the temple continued as before. This would suggest that the temple was not primarily an institution of state as some have concluded. Second, in cases where cities successfully advanced their cause against that of other cities, the temple often benefited from the booty since the contest was conducted in the name of the god of that city. Ritual rectitude required such thanksgiving from the victors. There is evidence that many of the female captives from conquest were donated to the temple thus providing additional members of its workforce (Zagarell 1986). The palace kept the male captives for itself. Third, the temple, it would appear, gave support and legitimacy to many of the activities of the palace. Indeed in the ascent of kingship many kings became high priests and participated in the rituals of the temple, particularly the annual re-enactment of the sacred marriage in the new-year festival.

The strain and tension in the temple-palace relationship came in the gradual extension of the hegemony of the palace over the temple resources and authority. Prior to the rise of the palace, the temple was the centre of public administration. In time the centre of public administration shifted to the palace, although by virtue of its continued economic and commercial involvement the temple never ceased to be a significant bureaucracy.

Another area of tension was that some kings sought to appropriate and deploy the resources of the temple for their own ends. In some of the reforms effected upon the change of dynasties, reference is made to former abuse in using god's plough and god's animals to work the king's fields. Also there are counter-charges from the palace of impropriety in the conduct of temple affairs. The elevation of Urunimgina to the throne 2351–2342 BCE, and his social reforms, highlighted the discontentment of the state of affairs between palace and temple as well as the extent to which the exploitation of the many by the few had become the subject of widespread resentment. Kramer (1963) noted that in some cities, in particular eras, there was much bitterness between temple and palace.

Sargon's appointment of his daughter as the high priestess of the moon god at Ur could be interpreted as another instance of kings attempting to extend their hegemony over the priests. The later practice of kings elevating themselves to divine status, during their lifetime, could be seen as the ultimate step along that line. The point is that kings and the palace invariably attempted to extend control, appropriate resources and acquire temple functions. This was not without some amount of resistance or resentment from the temple. In large measure both palace and temple became two pillars of the public sphere, many times in competition with each other, the palace being clearly the state and the temple, if not part of the private sector, then more like a statutory corporation.

What is clear is that while symbolically the king-god was the supreme autocrat with powers over the army, state machinery and the temple, in actual fact, this development came sufficiently late in Sumerian civilisation to ensure that the temple was never completely under the control of the palace. At the same time, the relationship between palace and temple was uneasy and ambivalent in several respects. In some matters they were parallel and competing institutions in production and trade. In others matters they were symbiotic and mutually supportive, like in the conduct of war and in some ritual observances. The point of greatest tension was the extension of palace control, not only over temple resources and surplus, but also over its operations and activities.

An appropriate conclusion on the establishment of the monarchy in Sumerian cities and over all Sumer is that kingship became one of the primary symbols of civilisation during the ancient era of world history. Not to have a city and a king, with a standing army at his disposal, was to be ranked with the barbarian savages still in need of civilisation. Democracy and egalitarianism belonged to the backward past. The upper house of the council of elders and the lower house of the general assembly of all free men were ancient traditions that had to be discarded in the name of progress. The king had the momentum and legitimacy of the times on his side. Even the temple had to genuflect to this wisdom.

It was only towards the end of Sumerian civilisation that a single city, and its king, was able to establish hegemony over the entire region and even beyond. It was Sargon the Great who initiated imperial kingship over all Mesopotamia. This, however, was the pattern that would follow and become a hallmark of history: the city-state empire.

WARFARE AND THE SUMERIANS

Bronowski (1973) claimed that war is not a human instinct. Rather it is a highly planned and co-operative form of theft. He traced this form of theft to the dawn of the agricultural age, 10,000 BCE, after which nomads of the deserts perennially robbed farmers, in settled villages, of the accumulated surplus which they themselves could not provide. Gabriel (1990) maintained that war must be differentiated from aggression, violence, murder and raids. He traced the first evidence of organised violence of some scale, to around 6500 BCE, where at Jebel Sahaba in the Sudan, 59 men, women and children were killed at a single site by repeated arrow wounds and spear thrusts. He identified a period just prior to 4000 BCE when the first evidence of fortified towns was found in Jericho, as the conclusive sign of warfare as a feature of human civilisation. The Jericho walls enclosed an area of about ten acres and had a length of about 765 yards. Like Bronowski, Gabriel contended that war was not a feature of the Stone Age, but began to be practised a number of millennia after some groups opted for sedentary living.

Wright (1965) in a large scale study of 633 so-called 'primitive cultures' noted a high correlation between war and agricultural economies. Gabriel

(1990) explained the connection between war and agriculturists not only in terms of defending against theft from nomadic tribes but rather in terms of defence of residence and the potential loss of all possessions. In addition, identification with a single site could be bolstered with religious beliefs as some areas became invested with a sense of the sacred. Agriculture and sedentary living narrowed the territorial sites and heightened the stakes involved, compared to nomadic existence. In addition, he identified two 'parasitic classes' that were spawned by agricultural societies – warriors and priests. Both classes consumed much but produced little and justified their existence on the basis of protecting the society as a whole.

Gabriel made the more general point that warfare on any scale requires at least the following structures:

1. A stable population of a large size, enough to produce a surplus population freed from traditional economic roles.
2. A territorial attachment specific enough to change the psychology of a group so that it thinks of itself as both special and singular.
3. A warrior class with social influence in the decision-making process.
4. A technology of war.
5. A complex, role-differentiated social order.
6. A larger mental vision of human activity that stimulates the generation of artificial reasons for behaviour.

From all the available records, war was practised before Sumerian civilisation came into being. War itself cannot be added to their many firsts in human history. However, they were among the earliest practitioners of modern warfare. The Bronze Age is generally recognised as a period in which warfare was revolutionised in its organisation and weaponry. In this regard, Sumerians, through their inventiveness and organisational genius, contributed to the revolutionising of warfare, just as they did to agriculture. Many of the new weapons and stratagems of war emerged very early in Sumer.

Sumerian civilisation was among the first, along with Pharonic Egypt, to replace stone age weapons with metal weapons such as the composite bow, the sword, the axe, mail armour, helmet, shield and dagger. Applying its technological revolution in transportation to warfare, Sumerians added the chariot to the weaponry and with it new military tactics. The Sumerian chariot was a massive box-like vehicle running on four wheels with a receptacle for spears jutting out in front. It was equipped with a crew of two helmeted soldiers, one the driver and the other raining spears on the infantry of their opponents. The contraption was pulled by four mules harnessed abreast. As important as the weapons were, military formations, the tactics by which they would be used and the army that would use them were all of critical importance. Sumerian armies gave evidence of mobilisation, planning, training and great skill.

Gabriel made the point that advance in weaponry by itself does not increase the scope, scale or horror of war. Rather, clear superiority could be a deterrent.

The critical elements, in his view, are the psychological transition from the extended family or tribe to the state, and new social structures that enable resources to be marshalled to equip a standing army. Bronze weapons were the artefacts of these larger social and psychological transitions that had taken place, or were taking place, in Sumerian society.

Humble (1980) observed that Mesopotamia had no metals or timber on which much of the Sumerian economy rested. The Gilgamesh legend shows the warrior king making an expedition to the Cedar Mountains, destroying its guardians and felling the cedars. Childe (1952), however, maintained that most of the raw materials for Sumerian industry was obtained through trade conducted by merchants and while Sumerian princes boasted of expeditions to obtain raw materials this was never a major source of supply. Gabriel maintained that nomads descending on the city were more of a nuisance than a real threat to Sumerian civilisation.

Gabriel, Childe and Humble all seem to agree that more of the warfare was conducted between Sumerians cities, than with external foes. Indeed, it was not until almost the end of the third millennium, around 2200 BCE, that the Gutians seized control and established hegemony over all of Sumer. Even then their rule was for a relatively short period, 50 to 70 years before they were expelled. Warfare involving external foes occurred when Sumer with superior might annexed or subdued its weaker neighbours rather than when Sumer was attacked from without. For example, Lugalzagesi of Uruk expanded his territorial borders to the Mediterranean, Sargon of Agade in addition to the Mediterranean conducted expeditions in Anatolia and outward to the Gulf. Naram-Sin his grandson expanded his domain to the Zargos mountains.

Humble was of the view that the narrow orbits of the city-states placed them in constant collision for supremacy, mainly for economic reasons. Childe cited the reasons as disputes over water rights between closely juxtaposed communities with expanding populations. Crawford (1991) cited competition between the ambitious princes of the various cities to become ruler over all of Sumer as a major cause. Other reasons included growing disparity in wealth within and between cities leading to discontent, agitation and aggression. These became the sources of well-orchestrated and organised war efforts. For example, the southern cities developed at a much faster rate than those of north. The polarisation created became one of the axes of conflict.

It would appear that all of these reasons contributed to some degree. What is not in doubt is that Sumer at the height of its urbanisation, technological revolution, increasing production and productivity also became a hotbed of military contest with warfare being conducted along lines easily recognisable by modern military strategists. With these wars came a succession of dynasties culminating finally in the Ur III dynasty, the last king of which was carted off ignominiously by the Amorites in the last decade of the third millennium.

The military machine probably reached its height with Sargon the Great of Akkad, who put 54,000 men on the battlefield on a regular basis. As Humble (1980) pointed out Sargon was a commoner, a Semite, who started his career in the service of the King of Kish and reached the position of cupbearer or butler. Through the first recorded coup d'etat, Sargon seized the throne and made himself king and established history's first empire which stretched from the Persian Gulf to the Mediterranean. This territory was acquired by force of arms and ruled by a central government. Sargonic control, from Sargon I to his grandson, as Cooper (1989) observed, was varied in degree and mode. Rebellion was chronic in outlying provinces and Sumer. Schwantes (1965) commented that the Akkadian empire was created by a family of exceptionally able rulers but did not outlast their ability. This could be said of nearly all the dynasties that arose.

The Akkadian empire lasted for a hundred years. Gutians, mountain tribes subdued by Sargon, overran the empire and took control of Mesopotamia only to be repelled by Utuhegal of Uruk, establishing the kingdom of Sumer and Akkad. Ur-Nammu who established the Ur III dynasty, and his successor Shulgi were traditionalists who tried to recover the former glory of Sumer. They rebuilt the sacred places and ziggurat, re-established scribal schools, introduced new weights and measures, reformed the civil service and Shulgi's son even built a great wall to keep out the Amorites of the west.

Shulgi's reign was marked by great prosperity, a fortune not shared by Ibbi-sin the last king who reigned over a period of substantial decline in agricultural production leading to major economic problems. The very Amorites whom his predecessor tried to keep out by the massive wall took Ibbi-Sin away in chains. With that final ignominious act in 2006 BC, Sumer as a political entity passed into history and their identity as distinct people followed not long after.

War is about power. It is the supreme human expression of might, military and otherwise. When warfare in Sumer is looked at as a whole, over the period of Sumerian civilisation five broad generalisations appear warranted:

1. The contest for power was internal. It was between Sumerian cities contesting hegemony over all Sumer or seeking the advance of one city at the expense of another. As such coalitions and alliances were constantly being formed, dissolved and reformed in new combinations.
2. The leaders of war who succeeded invariably converted the power and position gained into family and clan advantages, thus making kingship hereditary and creating dynasties, which succeeded each other consistently as the power was shifted from one line to the next after a few generations. Kinship and blood prevailed even though these wars were fought in the name of the gods and financed by all in the city.
3. The locus of power shifted in Sumer from south to north, as successive cities up the river superseded those lower down (Wakeman 1985).
4. Power shifted between groups from the dominant Sumerians to subordinate Semites, first Sargon of Agade, and the city of Kish and

later Semites outside the original borders of Sumer. Indeed, it was the Amorites, recent arrivals from the western desert, who drove the final nail in the coffin of the Sumerian empire.

5.   The only city that was never attacked and remained apart, if not aloof, from the intercine warfare was Nippur, the city of the father god, Enlil. Nippur, and its temple, was constantly involved as the source that recognised and legitimated the dynasties seizing power in the different cities. Demonstrated here is the power and influence of Sumerian religion, and with it the enormous power of the patriarchal symbolism. While the brother and sister gods and goddess of the pantheon, and their cities, competed for power and imperium, the patriarch, the father-god and his city, remained aloof or was left out of the contest.

SOCIAL ORGANISATION

Most writers on Sumerian civilisation make reference to its tendency for hierarchies and hierarchical organisation. However, Schmandt-Besserat and Alexander (1975) observed that initially Sumerian social structure was fairly straightforward, if not simple. There were few large or rich landowners. Most were free citizens owning small plots. The majority were farmers or animal breeders, while some were boatmen and fishermen. Slavery existed as an institution with the slaves coming from a variety of sources: captives of warfare, civil offenders serving sentences and children sold by their parents largely for reasons of debt.

Diakonoff (1982) established that regardless of occupation or size of land ownership the society was organised on the basis of a patriarchal clan differentiated into smaller kinship groups. Property was collectively owned, and while it could be alienated, sale had to be with the consent of the entire group who were usually witnesses of the transaction, (Kramer 1963). Usually lineages within the clan owned contiguous property; hence the clan holdings were in a particular locality. Stone (1982) made the important observation that even though corporate property could be alienated, it had to be sold within the clan. Usually the direction of the sale was between major and more minor branches. Such transfers led to the polarisation of wealth in the clan thus threatening lineage solidarity, the very bedrock of the social system.

The extended family or lineage, a collection of agnates, was the basic unit of social organisation. Individuals belonged in and to their lineages. Membership of the society was through the lineage. Individual membership of the society was not possible. It was the family or lineage, that had moral authority, personality, legal persona and that owned property, not individuals. The lineages were bonded together through material bonds that were sanctioned by religion and therefore sacred, and strictly enforced by law.

Each clan was a multi-storied collection of extended families or lineages. Each lineage had its own leaders (Gelb 1979). Each lineage was structured on the classic patriarchal criteria of kinship, age and gender (Zagarell 1986). Lineages were to a large extent not only autonomous but also almost totally self-reliant. Because corporate property was not easily disposable or recoverable, lineages faced with serious economic constraints sometimes sold members into slavery, especially for debt, and redeemed them in more favourable times. Debt slavery reached such proportions by the end of the early dynastic period that rulers were declaring periodic debt amnesties, releasing slaves and returning them to their lineages (Zagarell 1986). Donating members to the temple appeared to have become an alternative to debt slavery.

The temple was the only social organisation that to some extent fell outside the corporate kinship structure that characterised the rest of the society. It was the corporate alternative to clans and lineages. Membership was based on institutional rather than kinship ties (Stone 1982). Like the clans, the temple owned land, was autonomous and largely self-reliant. It distinctiveness was that blood relationship, or kinship, was not a requirement for membership. As such it was the only non-kin social institution in Sumerian society. Kramer (1963) maintained that the temple organisation was structured into two hierarchically related groups: temple administrators and the most important craftsmen on the one hand and the mass of temple personnel on the other. Schmandt-Besserat and Alexander (1975) suggested that the categories of the hierarchical structure were priests, secular employees who conducted the business of the temple and slaves, with sub-divisions within each group.

It is extremely important to note that these two types of social institutions, clan and temple, were interrelated and not totally differentiated from each other. As Lamberg-Karlovsky (1986) noted some members of lineages were attached to the temple in one way or another while others of their members were independent of the temple. Therefore, kinship extended into the temple and probably may even have influenced its hierarchical structure. Indeed, in the practice of donating members to the temple clans may have been using the temple's neutral relation to kinship to cope temporarily with either hiatus or fall-out in the patriarchal arrangements.

The most fundamental social change that the palace seemed to have promoted was that of individual ownership of land. Stone (1982) was unsure whether city government imposed individual ownership for reasons of taxation or conscription or some other reason. She noted, however, that the collective ownership of land was the very heart of the lineage system that was the bedrock of the society. The fact that successive city governments, over several generations and regimes, persisted with this policy would seem to suggest, first that they recognised its implication and second that their continued implementation of the policy was deliberate.

Crawford (1991) made the point that allowing individual property ownership permitted the king to acquire and control large masses of land, which not only afforded him personal wealth, but also allowed him to consolidate his own political position through patronage in the form of grants of land to supporters on whom he could rely. By weakening the power base of the clans, while increasing that of the state in the person of the king, the palace was further consolidating the power base and hegemony of the newly created monarchy. It does appear however, that such a fundamental assault on lineage power could hardly have been sustained without some support from the clans. Also not withstanding military might and high priestly status, kings were practising politicians mindful of what was possible among their constituents, even if they were called subjects.

It must be remembered that clans themselves were having problems with ownership as wealth was being polarised among them. For those being dispossessed the king may have been one of the more important means of repossession. At the same time, for wealthy lines individual ownership of land allowed some members the possibility of amassing fortunes independent of clan-owned property. It also allowed them to acquire enough agricultural surplus to become the basis of external trade, without risking the family patrimony. By the end of the Ur III period, independent merchants operated alongside the palace and the temple in long-term trade.

Zagarell (1986) recognised these developments and relationships but conceived them differently. In his view the state took an active role in furthering state production through centralised means and in the process unintentionally created the conditions for independent merchants and for a third economic force to emerge in the society. The essence of Zagarell's thesis is that the palace and the temple, priests and kings, controlling the public/communal mode of production and using mainly female slave labour, generated surpluses that were far above the capacity of the kin mode of production. By systematising production, and the use of the surplus generated, through a centralised bureaucracy utilising scribes, writing and accounting, levels of output were achieved that could be effectively and profitably disposed of in external trade. The process legitimised the formation of the state while at the same time weakening the kin controlled organisation and polity. An unintended result of this strategy was decline in collective rights and the rise of private ownership. Zagarell's tightly argued thesis has generated much debate, which is beyond the scope of this study.

An alternative scenario is that through the opportunities created by inter-city rivalry, usually conducted by means of warfare, some clans seized the opportunity to subordinate others. Skilfully utilising the power placed in their control of the newly created standing army, they adopted a two-pronged assault. First, these clans appropriated as much of the surplus and resources of the temple as was feasible. Second, they weakened other large rival clans through the imposition of private property, which was the means by which these militarily empowered clans could more legitimately acquire property. In other words, the actions of the palace has to be seen not in terms of an assault on kin-structured society itself, but on rival clans. The palace was not attempting to change the fundamental basis of the society, but rather was promoting the interests of clans it represented at the expense of others.

From this perspective, the palace itself has to be seen as a kin based organisation. Kingship was hereditary. It was dynasties that ruled, albeit for varying periods of time. In effect the monarchy and its allies constituted nothing more than the elevation of some clans over others by means of military might. While the military power was directed outward against the enemy from other cities, its inward effect was a fundamental reordering of the relative relationships of lineages and clans within cities. From a position of relative equality, with an En or Ensi and his lineage being *primus inter pares*, there was now the king and his clan who was unmistakably dominant. The division among the clans was now between royalty and commoners. The hereditary state had now been created. The next step to the hereditary imperial city-state was a short one.

That the centre of imperial power shifted progressively from south to north did not obliterate the royal families created, although the range of power they exercised was restricted. Further the geographical shift of the centre of power from the better developed south to the less developed north, would suggest the successive empowerment of new elites. What is suggested is that particular clans formed coalitions and alliances, predicated on popular grievances or aspirations within cities, which they used to advance themselves at the expense of other clans. In this regard, the palace was a fundamentally different institution from the temple. Membership in the palace was not based on institutional ties, but kinship. In essence the palace represented the ruling clan or alliance of clans. As such the palace represented kin controlled organisation of the polity.

By assuming effective control of much of the new wealth of the society, the palace led the way in the creation of a whole new range of occupations including courtiers, as well as to increased opportunities for employment in previously existing occupation in the cities. By controlling the wealth that it had not created, the palace increased its influence by the considerable patronage it offered. Cities and towns had increased numbers of occupations that joined priesthood and the military as non-agricultural vocations. What emerged could be construed as a middle class consisting of scribes, priests, merchants, diviners, craftsmen of various kinds and the more successful farmers, animal breeders and marine personnel. In other words, by the end of Sumerian civilisation the society it spawned was much more socially differentiated than it had been 2000 years before.

An appropriate final note on the social organisation of Sumerian society may be with respect to its funerary practices. Crawford noted with there is no evidence of any changes in the burial of the ordinary people over the 2000-year history of Sumerian civilisation. They continue to be buried in the same types of sites, in the same manner and with the same objects to take with them into the nether world. The differences that emerge are those to do with the nobility or aristocracy that was created with the social differentiation that occurred within the period and in particular with respect to the burial of royalty. Not only are the tombs themselves more elaborate and more ornamental but the provisions made and the materials taken into the nether world are not only more in quantity but vastly improved in quality. The social distinctions that emerged in the society are also manifest in death.

The changes with respect to the burial of royalty are not only more substantial but also more bizarre. Some kings were buried with their chariots and military regalia, but also with wives, courtiers and guards. Kramer (1963) noted that there is no evidence of violent death among those who accompanied their king in death. Hence it would appear that they voluntarily joined him, probably by drinking poison. For a people who so prized life, and saw no good prospect in death, such loyalty can only be regarded as exemplary. It may be indicative of the personal charisma of some of the personalities who ruled in ancient Sumer, or of the inevitable fate for those left behind when regimes changed. Much more remains to be done to more fully explain these practices.

GENDER IN SUMERIAN SOCIETY

Languages record more than their words but also their habitual modes of conception. It is of some importance that Sumerian language did not differentiate, grammatically, between male and female. Even names were not gendered; males and females were often given the same name. Also many of the public records did not record the gender of the parties involved. Bearing in mind that the written language was invented largely for administrative purposes, a working hypothesis could be that in public exchanges in Sumer gender was not an operative consideration. In other words, at that time gender was a matter for the private sphere, but public dealings were 'ungendered'. The locus of operation of gender was in the lineage, the family, but when conducting public affairs the particular member, male or female, was of no particular significance save the authority to undertake such action.

Mention has already been made of the fact that among a father-god headed pantheon of Sumerian gods there were many goddesses. Indeed among the four primary and creative gods there were three gods and one goddess. Hence there were cities where the people worshipped a goddess, most famous of which was Inanna of Uruk. In the Sumerian cosmology therefore the pantheon was gendered, but only within the context of lineage patriarchy. That is, although Inanna was below the rank of Enlil, and therefore subject to his wisdom, she was divine and shared the same statue and status of divinity as her brother gods. The limitations of Inanna's femaleness were only within the pantheon and with respect to the father-god, but not with respect to the exercise of her divinity in the world or ritual obligations due to her by mortals.

Schmandt-Besserat and Alexander (1975) took the position that in Sumerian society women were mainly mothers and housewives. Marriages were arranged at an early age, and involved dowries, but love matches were not unknown.

Usually men had one wife but a second wife, or concubine, was permitted in the case of childless couples; however, the second wife always remained subordinate to the first. Single women were rare. Marriage was the widely accepted norm for males and females in the society.

Van de Mieroop (1989) and Zagarell (1986) differed from Schmandt-Besserat and suggested that most Sumerian women were more than mothers and housewives. These authors maintained that women were a large part of the workforce. A large number were involved as agricultural labourers carrying out tasks such as transporting grain, cutting thorns, cleaning furrows, oil pressing and winnowing. Considerable numbers were also employed in the textile industry as weavers in the temple and also in cottage operations. In these textile operations in the temple and sometimes the palace, women were organised in groups of twenty with either a female or a male supervisor.

There is general agreement that women were not only employed in the workforce but owned or managed many business operations including large agricultural estates and commercial enterprises. Such women were usually royal women, the queen or the governor's wife, or members of wealthy clans. However, ordinary women owned bars, shops and other small-scale enterprises or were the overseers of workshops or supervisors of groups of workers. In other words, women could be found in all kinds of economic activities and at all levels of various businesses. In addition, in the temple there were priestesses. Further, the high priestess was an important position. Usually she was chosen at an early age on the advice of an oracle.

Women could give evidence in court and initiate legal action on their own. They could sell, lease or loan property or serve as guarantor. They were accepted witnesses of transactions. There were no legal restrictions on women's role in business and legal affairs and they actively exercised their franchise. In the records of Lagash no gender distinctions are noted with respect to several religious and administrative functions in terms of advantages, privileges, rations received or resources they had at their disposal.

Glassner (1989) warned, however, not to rush to hasty conclusions that these facts mean that gender equality existed. He pointed out that in reporting their presence scribes invariably described women in relation to their husbands, fathers, brothers or sons with whom they shared rank, but seldom in their own right. This is not to say women lived totally in the shadow of their male relatives or that they had no identity of their own. To illustrate the nuances of the relationships Glassner observed that in paying tribute to the king, husbands and wives gave separate gifts. This indicated the wife's identify separate from that of her husband. However, invariably the husband's gift was larger, probably underscoring his primacy.

This point is further illustrated with respect to the disposal of property. If a husband and wife were simply witnesses to a sale they were of equal rank. If however, the husband was the seller, or one of the sellers, then she would be on the same level as her children not the husband. This demonstrated the differences that existed in Sumerian society, in which the subordination of women was internal to males in the family but not to all males in the society. When she faced outsiders, she was a member of her clan and her internal position within the clan was of no account.

Many of the women in the workforce in Sumerian society were slaves, foreign women captured in conquests. Zagarell (1986) noted that when male captives were taken, which was not always, they were usually hobbled and kept by the palace while the standard practice was to give female captives to the temple. He suggested that this was probably because the temple lacked the coercive restraints to deal with males, and that females could be more easily incorporated since they were less likely to resist. This argument by itself is not entirely convincing since slave women were not the only women being donated to the temple. It would appear that the donation of slave women to the temple has to be interpreted within the wider practice of donating women, of all ranks, to the temple.

WOMEN AND THE TEMPLE

Three general points are worth noting at the outset about women who were part of the temple institution. First, they were located outside the lineage organisation and structure at least temporarily or partially. Second, they were living under the protection of the god of the temple. This suggests that they would be more vulnerable if located elsewhere. Third, they were beneficiaries of the temple's care in one form or another. Harris (1989) made the point that women of the temple were normally not mothers, or nurturers, or wives or daughters-in-law but it was not unknown: generally speaking these were women living outside the traditional definitions of patriarchy. Some elaboration is necessary concerning each of the categories of women who were part of the population of the temple.

1. Priestesses. Elite, and not so elite women, served as priestesses. Some were cloistered others were not. Some could have children others could not. Some were married others were not. The high priestess was usually chosen by an oracle at an early age and usually came from a prominent clan. It is acknowledged that these women had a special status in Sumerian society, but little is known of them or why such various requirements were imposed on them. One can reasonably assume that piety and religious considerations dominated the reasons why women, like men, entered the priesthood.

2. The Arua Institution. Women donated to the temple fell into two categories.
   a) Some wealthy families donated some of their daughters to the temple. It has been suggested that this was done for reasons of piety. However, some earthly considerations appeared to have been operative. One such consideration was the inability to find

a suitable husband for a daughter, but wanting to give her some form of independent life, not possible as a single woman in the society. Such families donated daughters to the temple and provided appropriate support. Living as a single woman was possible in the temple culture and organisation, since the temple was a social organisation whose structure could accommodate a measure of independence that the clan and the general society could not. The temple became social surrogate for the clan and extended family, and within that framework women could be afforded a measure of independent life.

b) Poor families donated not only daughters but widows, waifs and handicapped members (Van de Mieroop 1989) for whom they were unable to provide care. Without a source of sustenance from their clans, these women were obliged to work in the temple organisation. Some worked on the temple estates doing jobs in agriculture. Others were deployed in the textile factories. They received rations from the temple production. In the case of these women from impoverished families, it would appear that the reason for donation was destitution, and that the temple served a welfare function. The temple, as a non-kin organisation was literally 'picking up the pieces' of the fall-out of lineage society.

3. Prostitutes. The Epic of Gilgamesh and Enhudi portrays the prostitute as part of Sumerian society. As a group they were recognised and regulated by Mesopotamian law. Generally they were recruited from the ranks of the poor, from among female captives and foreigners. In several instances, for example at Sippar, it was the temple or a temple official who had jurisdiction over groups of prostitutes. Harris (1989) noted that no in-depth study had been done of prostitutes in the ancient Near East. Their relationship with the temple is not immediately self-evident.

4. Female slaves captured in warfare or raids. These women as slaves were natally alienated from their clans. They were foreigners, and female. As such they were the most vulnerable group in Sumerian society. Zagarell has maintained that the temple and the palace exploited these women in the generation of the wealth that facilitated the formation of the state and the emergence of private ownership. Without wishing, or being able, to challenge Zagarell's thesis on their impact on the political economy of Sumer, it would appear that the rationale for donating female slaves to the temple may have been for reasons other than economic and political exploitation, even if this may have been its consequence. Female slaves could have been viewed as just another category of women who had, for a different reason, fallen out of lineage society. The same ethical reasons that applied to

prostitutes and donated women could have been applied to female slaves.

5.   The Naditu Institution. The naditu institution while not coming to full flower till the old Babylonian period, was an adaptation of the Arua institution and bears mentioning here as illustrative of the ongoing relationship of the temple and women in the dynamics of lineage society. Stone (1982) studied naditu in Nippur, while Harris studied it at Sippar. The term naditu derived from the root nadu, which meant – 'to leave fallow.' Naditu women were devoted to different gods, lived under different regulations, but were all prohibited from having children.

Naditu were daughters of wealthy and powerful families, who were cloistered in a special compound in the temple premises, but lived in their own houses complete with slaves to do household chores. They had all the provisions of a life of ease. They came to the cloister complete with dowry, gifts of land, jewellery, furniture and utensils. The naditu was entitled to a share of inheritance equal to that of a full heir, that is, like her brothers. Her provisions for life in the cloister and her rights of inheritance were the rewards for accepting the status of naditu. Prohibited from participating in lineage patriarchy's most fundamental definition of the role of women, having children, the naditu could be treated as a son. She had the power to conduct the full range of business operations including selling, leasing, granting and obtaining loans and guaranteeing agreements. The naditu could sell property within the clan as well as to another naditu. At death, however, her assets reverted to her brothers or their heirs. Harris noted that some families used the naditu institution while others did not. Moreover, those who used it did so over several generations.

An interesting angle of the naditu institution not explored by either Harris and Stone is the difficulties Sumerian society had with daughters-in-law. The wisdom literature portrayed her as the devil himself. Kramer (1981) cited the following poem to illustrate the point.

The desert canteen is a man's life
The shoe is a man's eye
The wife is a man's future
The son is a man's refuge
The daughter is a man's salvation
The daughter-in-law is a man's devil.

Daughters-in law were placed at the intersection of three generations: as daughters, as wives and as mothers. Daughters-in-law appeared to have complicated several kinship relationships. One cannot but wonder, if the naditu institution was not, if even in a small and indirect way, related to this difficulty.

Some wealthy families decided, probably in conjunction with others to whom they were obligated, to induce some of their daughters to stay clear of this complication.

Both Stone and Harris explained the naditu institution in terms of action clans took to minimise the dispersion of the patrimonial estate as pressure grew on clans to shift from collective to individual ownership. Of equal importance was the fact that at a time when clans were restricted from selling property outside the clan, by being able to sell to other naditu, the restrictions were circumvented. In all their transactions naditus usually acted on the advice of their brothers and always in the interest of their clan. The naditu belonged to the temple based on institutional ties, and to the clan based on kinship ties. By virtue of this duality she was able to serve her clan in ways her brothers could not. The naditu institution was only possible because of the peculiar relationship that existed in Mesopotamian society between women and the temple, and the degrees of freedom this gave to elite families to manoeuvre in the best interest of their clan.

In looking at the temple and its relationship with women, it becomes evident that the temple served women from all levels of Sumerian society. It does not appear to have encompassed men over the same range of social space. Wealthy and powerful families seemed to have related to the temple for different reasons than impoverished families. The latter sought its assistance for welfare support. The former used the temple to preserve and promote their clans or to circumvent fall-out from lineage living. Prostitutes and slave women are not as easily explained. One must only note that they too were living outside the institution of family and kinship. Further research is needed here.

Wakeman (1985) in tracing the women's movement from Sumer opined that Inanna Goddess of Uruk pointed backward and conserved the values of a time when power was female and communal and when the fruitful integration of the powers of heaven and earth were celebrated. She also pointed forward to the acceptance of historical process as real and human initiative as sacred. Eridu and Uruk provided two types of religious sanction of power. Uruk invoked the image of sacred marriage between heaven and earth, while Eridu projected the phallic force of fertility. In the end it was the Eridu model that prevailed.

Without commenting on Wakeman's theological interpretation of Sumerian cosmology, as it applied to gender, it does not appear that there was any substantial change, for better or worse, in the position of women in Sumerian society over the course of its history. Glassner (1989) hinted at some change by juxtaposing Sumerian records against those of Akkad in the time of Sargon and noting the absence of comparable references to women, provocatively implying that with the shift in the ethnicity of power, there may have been some negative shift in gender relations. Without any more substantial evidence it would seem fair to say that Sumerian civilisation, while it lasted, afforded women a great deal of independence although they did not enjoy full equality with men.

Women's lower status was within their clans and families and not with respect to all men. Wives, sisters and daughters interfaced with the public as the equals of their male kin. The anomaly was that Sumerian society saw them in the names of those males, based on its patriarchal ideology and its method of labelling clans and families. However, the same was true of males. The society did not see them as men, but as members of clan, lineage and family and named them accordingly. The strictest interpretation of the evidence seems to be that neither men nor women acted in individual capacities, but rather as representatives of their clans, lineages and extended families. Relations and interaction across the kinship divide were not gendered. Who represented the clan or family, where and how, appeared to have been determined on the basis of strategic and comparative advantage.

Further, Sumerian society seemed to have had some concern for women who, for whatever reasons, fell outside the mainstream of lineage lifestyle or of major patriarchal definitions. The temple was the institution that gave practical manifestation of this concern. While the temple may have reaped significant material benefits for its good works, to see only the realpolitik but ignore the ethical dimension of an institution whose mission it was to act in this way, is to view these ancients through the lens of modern cynicism and nihilism and to disrespect their penchant for ordering their world, and striving to maintain that order.

To borrow, vary and apply Wakeman's imagery, the temple in its social construction and structure went beyond the lineage configuration of society. It was premised upon relationship to god, irrespective of kinship, and therefore based upon institutional ties. In this regard the temple pointed forward to the future of human society. At the same time, in many of its roles and functions, it reached backward and conserved kinship as the basis of social organisation. It was a point of rescue and retrieval of the fall-out and mal-function in patriarchal society and a focal point of resistance to threats to kinship and clan. This feature of the temple was most manifest in its relationships to women. If this duality in the character of the temple is missed, it is possible to misconstrue most of its interactions with the kinship elements of Sumerian society.

THE INSTITUTIONALISATION OF SCHOOLING AND TEACHING IN SUMER

Writing was invented around 3500 BCE. It was quite likely an invention of temple personnel, most probably in Uruk, as Powell suggests. There is evidence of its immediate and far-flung spread by virtue of the distribution of the written tablets (Vanstiphout 1995). This would imply that scribal training began shortly after writing was invented. However, the scribal occupation is not recognised or listed as such until centuries later, neither is there any record of where or how scribes were trained. As Green (1981) remarked any secret, or esoteric wisdom, confers high status on those who possess it if it is viewed positively. The myth of Lord Enmerkar of Uruk inventing writing, sending his messenger to Aratta with a written message and the resulting confusion and despondency invoked on the ruler of the latter, indicates that from its inception writing was viewed as an instrument of power. The priests no doubt realised this and kept it to themselves. The scribal art became an exclusive prerogative of the temple, and probably particular clans among the priests.

The institutionalisation of scribal training does not appear to have taken place until the middle of the third millennium. The earliest records are of 'school textbooks' found in ancient Shuruppak dating back to 2500 BCE (Kramer 1963). They contained lists of gods, animals, artefacts and an assortment of phrases and words. Kramer concluded that from the tens of thousands of tablets found, and the thousands of scribes of which there was evidence, schools seemed to have flourished in the latter half of the third millennium BCE. Kramer noted that the earliest documents about schools do not deal directly with the school system, although they give clear evidence of the operation of schools and formal scribal training. Details of the school system come from the last century of the third millennium and the early decades of the second.

THE SUMERIAN EDUBA

The institution established to train scribes was called the eduba, or tablet house. The literal translation meant school, library and scriptorium. This implies that schooling, librarianship and publishing were given institutional form at the same time and in the same organisational arrangement. Teachers, librarians and publishers are hewed from the same rock. If further reference is made to the eduba only as school, then it must be recognised that it is solely for the sake of convenience, bearing in mind the focus of this study.

Like all areas of Sumerian life, education and the scribal art had its divine patron. It was the goddess Nisaba. Vanstiphout (1978) translated a hymn of praise to King Lipit Istar, which was commonly used as a school text, which included the following verse, devoted to the patron goddess.

> Nisaba, the woman radiant with joy,
> The true woman scribe, the lady of all knowledge,
> Guided your fingers in clay,
> Embellished the writing on the tablets,
> Made the hand resplendent with a golden stylus,
> The measuring rod, the gleaming surveyor's line,
> The cubit rule gives wisdom,
> Nisaba lavishly bestowed upon you.

The eduba was established to provide professional training for scribes. It was a higher education institution rooted in practical knowledge clearly evident in the hymn of praise to the king and the celebration of the goddess Nisaba. Its purpose was to train scribes to satisfy the administrative and bureaucratic requirements of the temple and palace. This purpose never changed throughout its existence (Kramer 1963).

Given this purpose, and the fact that scribal training had been carried out in the temple for nearly a thousand years, it would appear that the establishment of the eduba as an institution grew out of the need of the palace to secure appropriately trained scribes for its own needs. It can only be inferred that the palace was not sanguine about recruiting its scribes from the temple and whatever processes it used to train them. Formal schooling, it would appear, arose to consolidate the formation of the city-state and to provide some distance between the locus of training of state employees from the temple. During the Ur III dynasty, 2100–2000 BCE, for which there is clear evidence of the establishment of schools, it was the king who was the prime mover. Shulgi, in his attempt to restore some of the traditions lost during the period of foreign occupation, re-founded schools in Nippur and Ur, the religious capital of Sumer and the seat of his dynasty.

Kramer (1963) observed that there was little to distinguish an eduba building from a house, except that the former contained a large numbers of tablets. In one site a building was found with several rows of benches, made of brick, which seating capacity for two to four persons. The first schools had no distinctive architecture. The most critical point appears to be that the eduba had its own building.

The question of whether these early schools were autonomous or related to either temple or palace remains unsettled. Kramer (1963) and Vanstiphout (1995) seem to suggest that these schools were independent operations and that junior and senior scribes from the palace and the temple were attached to them. Vogelzang (1995) took the position that edubas were attached either to the palace or the temple, palace or temple schools. All the edubas for which evidence exists, offered exactly the same training irrespective of their attachment.

Smith (1955) was of the view that temple schools were the earliest schools and that scribes not connected with the temple may have trained scribes of minor positions privately. Landsberger (1974) made the point that it would be erroneous to regard tablet houses as temple schools or their scholarly work as being of a religious nature. He was of the view that from its inception the eduba was purely a secular institution. It occupied itself with mastering the art of writing, language and its refinement, belles lettres, and list literature. Gadd (1956) maintained that the schools were not part of the temple or necessarily attached to it. Schools have not been found in temple ruins of ancient Sumerian cities as diverse and widely dispersed as Nippur, Ur, Kish, Ashur, and Sultan-tepe. All the schools found have been the same as private dwellings. He suggested that these dwellings might have belonged to the person in charge of the school. Further he was of the view that fees and contributions from patrons supported the schools.

Vanstiphout (1995) noted that while ritual texts that existed in the eduba seem directly related to the temple, these are kept apart from the eduba catalogues, and their performers were constantly being mocked in the lighter modes of literature. The temple singer, or kalu priest, was presented as a figure of fun, known for his arrogance and stupidity. This is in sharp contrast to the hymns of praise to kings that were frequently part of school texts. This would seem to suggest that not only was the content of the education provided by the eduba secular, but also its ethos was more deferential to the palace than to the temple. What is undisputed is that the eduba trained scribes for both the temple and the palace.

Kramer (1963) quoted a study, done by Nilalous Schnieder, of persons listing themselves as scribes in the year 2000 BCE. This study took account of the social background of these scribes mainly in terms of the occupations of their parents. Schneider found that scribes were descendants of governors, city fathers, ambassadors, temple administrators, military officers, sea captains, tax officials, priests, accountants, supervisors, foremen, scribes and archivists. Scribes were the offspring of persons, who with the exception of priests were pursuing occupations created in the rise of the urbanisation and the city-state. Apart from those who were descendants of foremen and supervisors, scribes came from families of specialists, many of whom would have had scribal training themselves. Interestingly none of these scribes were descendants of farmers, pastoralists or fishermen, the main producers of the wealth upon which Sumerian prosperity rested. The scribes were the children of fathers engaged in the new non-manual occupations created by urbanisation and the city-state.

Sumerian tradition was that children were expected to follow in their father's occupation; hence the rough correspondence of occupation of descendants should be interpreted in this context. Kramer cited a popular school text used in the eduba, which highlighted the frustrations of a scribe whose son refused to follow in his footsteps. Part of his exhortation to his son included the assertion that Enlil, king of all gods, had decreed that a son should follow his father's profession. Also of interest is that the distraught father upbraided his son for preferring materialistic success rather that humanistic endeavour. In pressing his case, the father uses the word humanity to 'mean conduct and behaviour befitting human beings'. Kramer is of the view that this is the first document to use the word not only to mean mankind but in its broader meaning. The content of this school text, and its use as instructional material in the training of scribes, suggests at least four important implications.

First, that many of the students in scribal training may have come from a scribal family background consistent with the traditions of lineage patriarchy. Second, that the economic opportunities in the city-state posed some threat to this tradition as sons could make other choices. Third, that scribes appeared to be developing a code of ethics concerning their role in Sumerian society that included the concept of civilised behaviour, service to their fellow human beings and the public good. Fourth, this nascent code of ethics was embedded in materials used as teaching texts for instruction in the practical skills of writing.

A further example of an emerging ethical code embedded in school texts comes from another stanza of the hymn in praise of Lipit Istar quoted previously.

> Great mind knowing all things,
> Saving people from evil and oppression.
> Sin and destruction you know how to free them.
> The mighty does not perpetrate robbery.
> The strong does not make the weaker ones into hirelings.
> To Nippur you are scribe, provider for all.

Seeing that this hymn was used in edubas long after Lipit Istar's reign, it would appear that the praise was not for the king's benefit, but for the promotion of moral values among the students in scribal training. Evil, oppression, sin, destruction, the mighty engaged in robbery, and the strong exploiting the weak on the one hand, are in sharp contrast on the other hand, to the association of Nippur the religious capital, with scribes and provision for all. This contrast seems to differentiate between the reality of the world in which scribes worked and the moral stance they were exhorted to adopt through their training. This seems to indicate that in the eduba in the training of scribes, a start was made toward ethical behaviour on the part of the profession, beyond ritual rectitude that was normative for the society. Values and virtue became an early component of schooling along with writing and reading.

Instruction in the Eduba

It is difficult to use the term curriculum at this inaugural stage of formal education. Stages of instruction appear more appropriate. Indeed, the most comprehensive accounts of instruction and teaching methodology come from the Ur III and Old Babylonian period when Sumerian was no longer spoken and had been replaced by Akkadian. Nevertheless the scribal art continued in Sumerian, since mastering cuneiform script and the scribal art could not be accomplished without knowledge of Sumerian. Vanstiphout (1995) noted that the successors to the Sumerians had no difficulty with this. They saw the Sumerian invention as a boon to mankind and a legacy to appropriate. To learn to write was to learn Sumerian: script, grammar, vocabulary and literature. The Sumerian language therefore continued in the eduba long after the people who originally spoke it had disappeared.

Vanstiphout (1995) gave a comprehensive account of stages of instruction in the eduba that can be summarised as follows:

1.   Introductory stage.
     · Mastering the three basic strokes of cuneiform writing: vertical, horizontal and oblique.

- Learning Sumerian signs.
- Learning the linguistic values of the signs.
- Learning Sumerian grammar.
- Learning the structural relationships between the Sumerian and Akkadian languages.
2. Intermediate stage.
    - Copying long texts in a purely imitative way
    - Exercises in composition.
    - Use of model documents drawn up in different branches of administration.
    - Instruction in mathematics, particularly measurement and calculation.
    - Learning the rulebooks about running agricultural, pastoral, and industrial activities.
    - Principles of trade and law.
    - Letter writing: personal and official.
    - Singing and music.
3. Advanced stage
    - Drawing up lists of almost every thing.
    - Literature of all types.
    - Disputation and argumentation.

Sjoberg (1975) pointed out that the education given scribes included the technical language used by smiths, jewellers, shepherds, master shippers and priests of several classes. It also required that they mastered the terminology and techniques of surveying fields, and numerous mathematical and accounting operations including balancing accounts. In other words, scribal training involved not only mastery of the techniques of writing but included sound knowledge and understanding of the enterprises that they would administer as well as general principles of public administration.

The general rationale undergirding the sequence of instruction was that the scribes were given general training in the eduba, followed by work, usually for life, in a specific branch of administration where they would become more accomplished in the nuances and 'tricks of the trade' of that branch.

Vanstiphout (1979) through grammatical analysis attempted to reconstruct the methodology of language teaching used in the eduba. His conclusions were that the instruction strategies used could be characterised as follows:

- Practical, using text as the starting point.
- Exemplary, structures taught in the context of usage.
- Concentric, several structures introduced at the same time.
- Contrastive, different structures played near to each other for contrast.
- Sentence bound, corresponding parts of speech were not taught in isolation.

- Progressive, gradual movement from the simpler to the more complex form.

Looked at as a whole it would appear that the language teaching methodology employed in these early schools was quite modern in addition to being pedagogically sound.

Scribal training was standardised in all edubas of the different cities for which there is evidence: Nippur, Kish, Sippar and Ur. The exact mechanism for this common instructional pattern in the different centres is not known. Neither is there any indication of how long this training took, except that the period involved was considerable. However, there is evidence of examination tablets suggesting that graduation was dependent upon achieving set standards.

Teachers and Scholarship in the Eduba

While the substantive mission of the eduba was to provide professional training for scribes preparing them to meet the requirements of public administration, there is abundant evidence that the actual work of the eduba went beyond its practical purpose and encompassed academic pursuits. Scribes teaching in the eduba appeared to have pursued literary and scientific interests. Vanshiphout (1995) noted that they had ideas and wrote about them. While, in the first place they recorded many aspects of the oral tradition, these first teachers went beyond this and wrote about their own interpretation of these matters.

Vanstiphout credited these first teachers with creating literature. He noted that at that time there was no literature outside the eduba. Writing had been used mainly to conduct and transact business and legal affairs. The range of literature they created was impressive. It included the following:

- Narrative literature recording major myths of Sumerian civilisation, the exploits and accomplishment of famous dynasties, epic poems the most famous of which are the Gilgamesh epics, and various important episodes in the first united kingdom of Mesopotamia, Agade.
- Lyrical literature, including hymns; odes to kings, temples and cities; appellation poems appealing to royalty or gods; psalms of praise, prayers and love poetry.
- Lamentation and wisdom literature including historical complaints on the destruction of Sumer; proverbs and riddles.
- Didactic literature, which which were often about agriculture.
- School literature of which the disputation poems recording scholarly debates and examination texts were the main categories.

Hallo (1975) made the point that Sumerian literature leads all the world's written literature in terms of antiquity, longevity and continuity. Its beginning can be traced firmly to the middle of the third millennium BCE, when schools were inaugurated, until 85 CE. In other words, Sumerian literature continued to be produced for more than a thousand years after the langauage ceased to be spoken, and the people who spoke it had disappeared. Between these two dates it was copied and preserved with a remarkable degree of textual fidelity. Sumerian foreshadowed Latin, but with greater longevity.

Vanstiphout also made mention of the fact that through dialogues and disputations within the eduba, based on if-then propositions, teachers in the eduba engaged in exploration of issues related to science, jurisprudence, law, and divination if not theology. As such teachers in the eduba constituted a small but important intellectual class and inaugurated the academic career. The interests of these early scholars were liberal, general and humanistic, indicating that they enjoyed a fair measure of independence within the eduba. In addition, it must be noted that the initiation of dialogues based on if-then propositions, within these first schools, commenced the long journey of reflective thought that runs the gamut of intellectual activity from philosophic speculation to scientific inquiry.

THE FIRST TEACHERS AND THEIR GENDER

The terminology used to designate the teachers in these inaugural schools is highly instructive of both the gender of those who taught in the eduba and the absence of technical terms at the inauguration of schooling. The head of the eduba was the Ummia, the literal translation of which was school father. The teachers were the ses-tab-ba, translated brother fellows. The students were school sons, one of whom was referred to as the big brother, probably the most senior (Vanstiphout 1995). Graduates of the scribal schools were called school sons of past days (Kramer 1963). The terminology was borrowed and transposed directly from the institution of kinship and family. Just as the school building could not be distinguished from the family dwelling, so too was the terminology used to designate the occupants: the teachers, students and their relationship.

Gadd (1956) and Vogelzang (1995) took the position that the eduba was organised on the basis of a crafts guild. Volgelzang suggested that the ummia-father was the master, the student son the apprentice and the big brother probably a supervisor. The fact that smiths and craftsmen were a prominent part of the Sumerian workforce and had to be trained by attachment to a master, and that writing was perceived as a craft, seems to have prompted Gadd and Vogelzang to interpret these designations in the model of the guild and apprenticeship. It has to be noted, however, that neither the guild nor apprenticeship assumed or required kinship. To the contrary, they are premised on no blood relationship between master and apprentice, only substantial differences in skill, knowledge and experience. To interpret the terminology of the eduba in terms of guild and apprenticeship appears to be projecting a European mould upon the Mesopotamian past.

What cannot be overlooked is that the terminology used to designate teachers and students assumed kinship. From all appearances the kinship being invoked was fictive. The ummia was not the father of the students neither were his assistant teachers his brothers. However, schooling was being conceived within the framework of kinship and family relationships in circumstances in which such relationships did not obtain, for at least the vast majority of the persons involved. The incongruence of this situation is patently clear and must have been to the Sumerians themselves.

From the available evidence it is not possible to give any definitive answer as to why the kinship model was adopted. It is only possible to speculate. One obvious possibility is that scribal training, from the time writing was invented, was passed on from father to son, or among brothers, within particular clans. When schooling was formalised, the terminology used in the training within the lineage setting was simply carried over into circumstances in which it was not entirely appropriate. This could also explain why the school buildings were dwelling houses; fathers could have simply expanded their teaching beyond family to include children from other families.

Another possibility is that because formal schooling was being invented and therefore had no precedents, there was no ready-made terminology. In this new and uncertain situation, use was made of well-known terminology, which was likely both to convey some meaning as well as receive wide acceptance. The terminology of kinship was used because it was not controversial and was well understood.

Yet another possibility is that because the society was organised on the basis of kinship ties and the unit of the extended family, hence it had to conceive and label even emerging non-kin types of social institutions within this paradigm. The society was therefore not at the stage where it could conceive and label members of the school in their individual capacities without reference to kinship and the lineage system.

Although the preference here is for the latter explanation, there is no available evidence that would unequivocally validate any of them. In all likelihood more than one factor was operative. Hopefully future research may throw further light on this question.

It must also be noted that the kinship terminology used is highly gendered. The eduba has father, sons and brothers, but no mother, sisters or daughters, at least not in its terminology. This bias in the terminology appears related to the gender bias among scribes. Kramer noted that among the 500 scribes of the year 2000 BC, studied by Schneider, only one was female. He concluded that there were very few female scribes. Gadd (1956) also reached this conclusion. Women in the priesthood, scattered references to female scribes, and the eminence of some of them for example, Enheduanna, Sargon's daughter seem to suggest that while scribes were overwhelmingly male the ratio may not have been as low as 500 to one. It could be assumed, therefore, that in the few instances where there were females among the teachers or students in the eduba the same kinship terminology would be applied to them, that is, they would have become school mother, sister fellow, big sister and school daughter. The gender terminology of the written records may not have indicated any structural gender bias in the nature of the eduba itself, but rather may have been simply reflective of its predominant competition.

The divine patron of the scribal art, and of scribes, was female. This could be interpreted to mean that in the Sumerian mind, scribes ought to be women. At the very minimum it implied no bias against females becoming scribes. The observed difference between the Sumerian cosmology and the earthly reality among scribes is not self-evident and therefore somewhat puzzling. This difference is brought into even sharper relief when it is juxtaposed against the fact that women were a major part of the Sumerian workforce and very present at all levels of business, the priesthood, and sometimes in government. Further, there does not appear to have been any form of discrimination, on a categorical basis, seeing that Semites were evident among the earliest scribes (Cooper 1989).

The substantive question becomes, why was the eduba so heavily male biased? What were the masculine roots of teaching in Sumer? Clues to the possible answers to these questions come from two sources, Zagarell (1986) and Stone (1982).

First, Zagarell noted the high level of corporateness that existed among clans and extended families in Sumerian society. This allowed families to readily sell members into debt slavery. At the same time it would not appear that this was callously done, nor was there unconcern if members could not be redeemed. That the rulers regularly declared debt amnesties which allowed debt slaves to return to their lineages and clans would seem to suggest that the inability to buy back family members was a matter of some obligation and priority which prompted families to seek political means of retrieving their relatives where market forces failed.

Building on this very critical observation of Zagarell, it is important to make explicit at least some of the qualities implicit in corporate kinship. These were reciprocal rights and duties commanding compliance and cooperation among members of the kin-group in prosecuting the best interest of the collective. This was the most inclusive level of the covenant of kinship. Age and gender established internal rank within this covenant. Where the broad interests of the kinship collective were at stake, internal rank was of no account. Women's high profile and authority in Sumerian society has to be interpreted within the context of the prosecution of the corporate interests of their families, lineage and clans and not in their individual capacity as females. Neither male nor female, at that time, acted in their individual capacities. This was to emerge later, probably as a consequence of some of the very social, political and economic changes that Sumerian civilisation was initiating.

Second, Stone noted that the institution of naditu went into decline in Nippur after 1800 BCE, and finally disappeared when temple offices, which were a form of property, could be alienated. Prior to this temple offices were inherited but could not be alienated. They were therefore retained in the families that held them. The naditu institution constituted the only mechanism through which lineages could exchange property between themselves, but it was unwieldy because of the indirect relationships that were involved. When the temple at Nippur entered the private sector, the market, by allowing its offices to be traded, it provided clans with a new vehicle of property exchange that allowed them to join a risk-sharing redistributive institution that offered some of the same advantages of the traditional lineage ownership. Moreover, it allowed direct economic ties between the male members of the lineages, which were preferred over the indirect ties through the naditu.

Stone rightly qualified her findings by noting that because of the special position of Nippur, as the religious capital of Sumer, temple offices there assumed a level of importance and value that was not replicated elsewhere, hence her finding could not be generalised to the naditu institutions in other cities. While this may be true about the specifics of the naditu institution, the general principle of lineage practice implicit in Stone's findings seems to be of wide generality and applicability. This generality goes way beyond the naditu institution, which was just another example of its application. That general principle is, internal lineage rank, based on age and gender, is relaxed where the collective interest is at stake, but re-imposed when the threat is removed or new opportunities arise. Faced with threat to its most fundamental criterion, kinship, clans deployed their young and female members in their defence. In circumstances where there was no threat to the collective, internal rank was imposed in the allocation of advantage.

The essence of the synthesis of these two clues, or insights, is that the new occupational opportunities, offered by the creation of public administration and schooling, presented to clans prospects of advancement or consolidation of their position in society, without any threat to kinship. In these circumstances, families chose their sons rather than their daughters to be trained as scribes. Put another way, the opportunities opened up and afforded to clans by way of scribal training, and the teaching of scribes, were not sufficiently great to require them to go beyond their sons in appropriating the advantages. Interestingly, the clans appropriating these advantages were those that were already highly placed within the prevailing lineage.

It is very important to note that by this process of ordering advantage by internal rank, clans were exporting the internal rank from the private to the public sphere. The gender of teachers and scribes appears to be an early manifestation of this pattern and trend as families, clans and tribes made the transition to more complex forms of association required by larger polities including non-kin.

THE TRANSFORMATION OF THE EDUBA AND TEACHING

The assertion was previously made that it was the rise of the hereditary state, the monarchical city-states, that led to the invention of schooling as the palace, the centre of state power, sought to obtain personnel for its operations. Because of the fragmentary nature of the evidence available, as well as the newness of the institution of the school, the essence of the relationship between the eduba, teachers and the palace has to be highlighted with the aid of developments after the institution was borrowed and transformed by the city states and empires that succeeded Sumer.

Vogelzang (1995) studied the relationship between the eduba, scribes and the last kings of the powerful Assyrian Empire, which then exercised hegemony in ancient Mesopotamia. The study covered the period 721–627 BCE. His findings can be summarised as follows:

1. Scholars were divided into five specialist groups.
   - Scribes, those specialised in observations, interpretation of omens, miscarriages and other such phenomena.
   - Haruspices, soothsayers reading the will of the gods in matters of great importance for example, war and plague. Inspection of the entrails of scarified animals was the major methodology of these specialists.
   - Exorcists, who through magic tried to influence and fight supernatural forces with spells, rituals and curses.
   - Doctors, who prescribed medicines and other treatment.
   - Singers, conciliating the supernatural forces through the singing of complicated chants and the use of drums.

2. The first circle were scholars of high social position who were part of the court, although they did not appear to have much personal contact with the king. The second circle was not a part of the court and was comprised of groups of scholars with leaders.

3. Scholars were grouped into two circles in relation to the king. Scribes of the first circle were all from the same prestigious families with continuous connection with the scribal tradition and the court for at least 250 years. Within this group it was exceptional for the sons not to succeed their fathers and this spelt disaster to the families concerned. However, succession was not automatic, the king made the decision and took various factors including accomplishment into consideration. Where the son did not succeed the father, the position went to another family with long connection to the scribal tradition. Rivalry for positions among these families seemed to have led to the widening of the scribal art to include the five fields of scholarships described.

4. The relationship between the king and the scholars was on the same basis of provincial governors, top military officers and top administrators. It was that of master and servants. Social connections

to knowledge were useful to the king and the state. It provided the king, his family and court with medical assistance, protection against magic, explained strange happenings and prophesied the future. This connection with knowledge and learning also strengthened the legitimacy and authority of the state.

Vanstiphout highlighted the fact that by the Sargonoid period of 721-627 BCE all evidence of liberal, humanistic and works of general value that had characterised the Sumerian and old Babylonian eduba had disappeared. Intellectual and literary pursuits were no longer undertaken. Scribes and scholars were merely public servants. All knowledge was subservient to the needs, plans and policies of the royal person and the state. The purpose of the palace in creating the institution called school had by then been fully realised. Also it is virtually impossible not to notice the quaint, and spurious, specialisation in scholarship which were produced by the combined and prolonged interaction of scholars protecting vested family interests, kings exercising control over scholars and both subservient to the prerogatives of power and policy demands of statehood.

ACCOUNTING FOR GENDER COMPOSITION

The gender of teachers in the first schools has to be explained largely in terms of the factors that accounted for the gender composition of the scribes themselves, since the teachers were selected from among scribes. Teachers were male largely because the vast majority of scribes were males, and therefore, there were extremely limited opportunities to select women as teachers.

Six interacting factors seem to have accounted for scribes being almost all males:

1. Schooling was inaugurated as a single level institution restricted to the training of scribes who began their training during childhood and continued it until they were young adults. Education in these first schools began with basic literacy and culminated in professional training for the scribal occupation.
2. The emerging bureaucracies of the temple and monarchical state were very small in comparison to the size of the population. Therefore, the numbers being admitted into scribal training annually were relatively very small.
3. Clans competed to appropriate particular non-manual occupations in the public sphere and then to perpetuate themselves in these occupations through heredity.
4. Clans appropriated and allocated the opportunities available to them on the basis of the ranked position of their members by age and gender which gave older siblings and males first preference.

5. Thus the competing clans could satisfy the demand for scribes from among their sons, who enjoyed ranked preference over their daughters. All the data indicate that by the end of Sumerian civilisation younger sons began to be disinherited, as division of the patrimony of clans was proving more and more difficult. Clans actively sought opportunities for these sons.

6. Sumerian society perpetuated family advantages in public office through inheritance, thus allowing sons to inherit their fathers' positions.

The exception that confirms this general pattern comes in the form of daughters of royal clans who became scribes. In some instances, the number of opportunities that were available to royal clans exceeded their supply of sons. In such circumstances royal clans had to draw upon their daughters in order to fully appropriate or preserve the opportunities available to them. Usually, this was only a temporary hiatus in male succession, which was corrected in subsequent generations.

Note also that for the minority of clans that became dominant in Sumerian society, business opportunities were sufficiently numerous to allow them to deploy sons and daughters, husbands and wives, sisters and brothers in the appropriation of those opportunities. The greater involvement of women in the field of business in Sumerian civilisation can be explained in terms of ownership of enterprises by clans and their efforts to retain these enterprises within their clans. Where these enterprises demanded more personnel than the clans had male members, then female members were mobilised. In other words, clans with the greatest access to the opportunities in Sumerian society went as far down the patriarchal queue as it was necessary to maximise their advantage. The fact that this entailed giving women of the clan access to opportunities in the public sphere was not as important as preserving or appropriating advantage to the clan.

Opportunities for scribal training, and therefore entry into the teaching occupation, was much more competitive because it was open to a much larger number of clans in the society. The evidence suggests that scribes were drawn largely from among the offspring of members of the new non-manual occupations that were being created in the city-states. Many of these persons would have themselves received scribal training. In this more competitive, and restrictive context, clans met the demand from among their sons, because the opportunities available were much less than the demand. Scribes were therefore mainly male, and as a consequence so were the teachers.

Three critical implications of this framework must be noted. First, by taking rational decisions within this framework, clans began to export to the public sphere the internal ranking that had marked their internal structure. The public sphere, in some occupations like teaching, therefore began to be structured on the same basis as the clans themselves. Second, male preference began to span both the public and private sphere, thus beginning the process of generalising women's marginalisation. In the clans, brothers were preferred to sisters, sons to daughters, and husbands to wives. In the new occupations that were created in the public sphere men began to be preferred to women, without any mediation from kinship. Third, the preference for men in the new occupations, including scribes, had no other ideological underpinning or philosophical justification except that of advancing the interests of the clans who virtually took ownership of these occupations. Teaching became a male occupation largely because of relatively low demand for teachers in the context of an oversupply of sons from those clans claiming virtual ownership of the teaching occupation.

Bearing in mind the focus of this study there are three developments in Sumerian society that need restating and highlighting.

- Among these predominantly male scribes, soothsayers claiming powers of divining became a specialisation of particular interest to kings because of their alleged capacity to forecast, envision or prophesy the future. It could well have been that some scribes moved into specialisation because kings, and their courts, demanded knowledge of this kind.

- The naditu institution was premised on the principle that women who chose to be childless virgins, had a special role to play in the public sphere in preserving the interests of their clans. Daughters, who chose to be childless through the naditu institution, were accorded the same rights and privileges as sons. The disadvantage attributed to women by bearing children and motherhood was absolved by remaining virgin. The virgin women of those clans, participating in the naditu institution, became male for all practical purposes.

- The prevalence of women in business in Sumerian society provides an early example of a type of feminisation that is the result of partnership of men and women of dominant clans. The institution of the naditu amply illustrated this form of feminisation that involves the co-operative and collaborative actions of men and women of a particular group seeking to preserve and promote those groups' interests in circumstances in which those interests are best served through their female members. In such circumstances, group solidarity overrides gender differentiation resulting in the relaxation of patriarchal closure thus allowing women of the group to access opportunities in the public sphere. In this collaborative effort the men of the clan were the senior partners and the naditu the junior partners.

Although the divine patron of the scribal art was the Goddess Nisaba, almost all the scribes were male. All references to those who taught in the eduba are to male teachers. Teaching has no feminine roots in Sumer. The masculine roots of teaching in Sumer are related to public administration constructed in relation to the emergence of monarchies in the ancient city-states. The occupation of teaching is related to the mechanisms by which the newly enthroned kings exercised power over their subjects by non-violent means. Schools and teaching are intimately intertwined with the consolidation of power, gained by violent means, but which must govern by less coercive methods. In this regard knowledge of forecasting the future became an important specialisation.

Writing, schools, scribes and their teachers were all part of the power structure of the newly created monarchies. They were all part of the means by which power was exercised, justified and affirmed.

POSTSCRIPT

Taking into consideration that this study attempts to trace the history of schooling and the teaching occupation from their genesis in the city-states of Sumer to modern times, it is virtually impossible to escape or avoid making some comments about Greece and Africa. While each is a substantive field of study in itself, only some brief comments are appropriate here in this postscript.

FROM SUMER TO GREECE

Western European civilisation has invariably treated Greece as the beginning of civilisation. This has to be understood as myth, in that ancient Greece was part of the ancient civilisation and not part of the western European world, which was still primitive. Further, the legacy of ancient Greece did not pass directly to western Europe from the ancient world. In a nutshell, this myth has to be understood and accepted as that of a latecomer to civilisation reaching back to connect with the ancient past largely on grounds of ethnicity. In the process the myth distorts reality, as myths generally do. The major distortion is that the myth treats Greece as a beginning. In reality, Greece was part of the conclusion of the beginning of civilisation for which Sumer, Egypt and the Indus Valley were part of the genesis. This in no way diminishes the enormous contribution of ancient Greece, it simply puts it in a more appropriate historical perspective. Civilisation began in Sumer, Egypt and the Indus Valley and then passed to Greece.

Within this framework it is necessary to take brief notice of what Sumer, Egypt and the Indus valley started and what Greece brought to fruition. To see this clearly it is necessary to list the features they all shared, at least at the beginning of classical Greek civilisation. These features were:

- A polytheistic pantheon of gods.
- Patriarchal clan and the extended family as the units of social organisation.

- Women occupying an inferior status within the clan or extended family.
- Material bonds and materialism as central values.
- City-states that regularly engaged each other in warfare.
- Competitiveness and rivalry as a prominent feature of social relations.
- Epic literature and heroic art.
- Writing.
- Formal schooling.

The peculiar contribution of Greece was not the origination of these hallmarks of ancient civilisation, the primacy of which belongs to Sumer, and to Egypt its chief competitor. Rather, Greece transformed several of these into the highest forms attained by the ancient world. The genre of ancient civilisation described did not reach Greece directly from Sumer. The passage was through the Babylonian, Assyrian, Phoenician and Persian civilisations which themselves added to their inheritance from Sumer and Egypt. For example, the Sumerians had invented writing but no alphabet. The alphabet was invented in the Levant in the Babylonian period. Writing, complete with alphabet, reached Greece through the Phoenicians. Schooling was passed down in an unbroken succession as scribes were trained for governmental purposes.

The Greek Empire was part of the successive rise and fall of city-states, and the empires they spawned in the first wave of civilisation. It came late in the wave, more than 2500 years after the beginning at Sumer and Egypt. Accordingly, Greece knew primitive beginnings, domination by prevailing powers, ascent to central supremacy and fall from the pinnacle of power. Within its own sphere it had rivalry between its own cities, for example Athens and Sparta with each making its own peculiar contribution when it dominated the confederation. Its own contribution to the ancient world was based on the doses of marginal energies released as cities rose from marginality to centrality, and the confederation as a whole rose on that energy relative to the world of which they were part.

A full explication of the Greek transformation of ancient civilisation is beyond the scope of this study; a mere listing of the general directions will have to suffice.

1. In the process of seeking to reconcile their own polytheistic pantheon with those of the Minoans, Persians, Egyptians, and Phoenicians, which all impacted on Greek civilisation, gradually mythology became discredited in Greece (Davidson 1903). In time the unreflective thought of religion was replaced with the reflective thought of philosophy. Reason replaced revelation as the cornerstone of Greek civilisation.

2. From the notion that the gods decreed all things, man became the measure of all things, even if Socrates substituted the universal man

for individual man as originally claimed by the Sophists. Happiness and pleasure replaced ritual rectitude as the major pursuit of life. Separated from their moorings in religion, things in life were to be pursued for their own sake. Hence, warfare was to be pursued to ennoble the human spirit through acts of valour and courage. Learning was to be undertaken for the sake of understanding and knowing.

3. From the notion that the extended family, or lineage or clan, was the basic unity of society, with moral personality, Greek society moved to the individual as the primary unit of society, possessed of worth and capable of self-determination. Notions of private property that had emerged in Sumer, were now enlarged to encompass the much wider meaning of self-knowledge. Accordingly, ethical bonds between individuals replaced material bonds between kin as the glue of societal cohesion.

4. From the beginning of women's modest presence in the public sphere, noted in Sumer especially in business, women were virtually excluded from the public sphere and almost totally confined to the private sphere in Greek civilisation.

5. From the notion that people were servants of the state, the state was now conceived as the servant of the people, thus giving birth and form to ideas of democracy.

6. From focusing only on the gods, heroes and triumph in war, art and the aesthetic shifted to highlight beauty and enjoyment. From seeking to edify and arouse action, they moved to satisfy the senses and invite contemplation (Davidson 1903).

7. From writing being the exclusive domain of the temple and the palace, its uses and products were made more universally available as books began to be traded and libraries were established. In so doing the Greeks broke the hammerlock which scribes, the temple and the palace had on writing and opened up to written self-expression and the wider dissemination of written works Katz (1995). With respect to the alphabet the Greeks added vowels, dropped some consonants and standardised the direction of writing from left to right thus bringing it very close to its modern form (Ullman 1980).

8. From formal schooling being for the purpose of training scribes for government offices, schools were transformed into institutions for the pursuit of learning and the development of scholarship in all fields. Elementary education was introduced to spread basic literacy in the general population (Harris 1989). From a single level system of education, schooling evolved in Greece into a two tiered structure. Plato even advocated education for all free men. Even through this was only philosophical speculation the idea of universal education was born in Greece.

Interestingly, ancient Greek civilisation added little to warfare except to its psychology. It did little to change the strong rivalry and brutal competition that marked ancient societies. However, in the humanistic values that it added to the civilisation of the ancients, it brought to full flower and fruition what had been first planted at Sumer and repeatedly germinated and mutated in the civilisations that succeeded it. But like Egypt, Sumer, Babylon, Assyria and Persia, and Rome that succeeded it, the plant and the flower died. Greek civilisation did not disappear completely. Unlike Sumer, Akkad, Rome and others of these city-states, the Greek language survived, more or less. Quite likely because of the islands related to her territory and the tendency of islands to conserve social form. In the course of human history, the coincidence of geographical, cultural, political, social and linguistic borders of islands tend to conserve more than contiguous entities within continental land masses.

Ironically, the legacy of Greek civilisation was transmitted to the present through the very aspect of society that Greece did so much to supplant, religion. The only difference was that these religions were not the polytheistic variety of Sumerian/Greek vintage but that which declared one universal god. It is through monotheistic religions that the ancient civilisation of the Near East, started at Sumer and Egypt and of which Greece and Rome were heirs and successors, has been transmitted to the modern world. The path from this past to the present must, of necessity, go through universalistic religions. For it was among them that the seeds of the dead plant of ancient civilisation was to germinate, grow and flower yet again.

THE AFRICAN ORIGIN OF CIVILISATION

There are many who insist that Egyptian civilisation was the first in human history, and therefore pre-dated that of Sumer. By accepting Sumer's primacy in the invention of writing and schooling, this study is by no means advocating Sumer's primacy in the origin of civilisation generally. What is indisputable is that Egypt and Sumer are arch-rivals in the claim for primacy in the origin of civilisation and that they rely on different accomplishments in staking their claims. In the accomplishment of writing and schooling Sumer's claim is supported by the greater weight of evidence, but this cannot be generalised to all other areas.

It is widely accepted that the civilisation of Pharonic Egypt was the mature form of a civilisation that had most likely started in the Great Lakes region of Central Africa and which travelled northward entering the Nile Valley through Nubia (Parsons 1932). In the terminology of the times it had its origins in Ethiopia, where the latter is understood to mean the land of the 'burnt face' or black people. This generic meaning of the term Ethiopian was widely used in ancient writing and references (van Sertima 1995).

While there is uncertainty about the origins of the Sumerian people, claims have been made to the effect that they were of Ethiopian origin. Rawlinson (1878) traced the Sumerians to origins in Ethiopia and Perry (1937) took a similar position. Kramer (1963) noted that Sumerians referred to themselves as the black head people. Jackson (1995) suggested that 'black face' would be the best modern translation of the Sumerian phrase, 'black head'. Bearing in mind that Sumerian language was very literal in its anatomical references; there is much to be said for Jackson's translation and conclusion that the Sumerians were black people.

Several British archaeologists, including Hall (1916) and Crawford (1991), implicitly accept that the Sumerians were 'black face people', by advancing the position that Sumerians were Dravidians migrating from the Indus Valley. In this regard it must be remembered that the civilisation of the Indus Valley is another claimant to the crown of primacy in the origin of civilisation. Unlike the Egyptian or Sumerian civilisations, that of the Indus Valley manifested little evidence of central authority. Their largest public buildings were baths, not temples or palaces. Despite these and other differences, there are many similarities shared between these three early civilisations. The writing of the Indus Valley civilisation is still to be deciphered, and therefore still to reveal its secrets concerning its origins and interrelationships.

The fact that all three early civilisations arrived in their separate locations almost full blown and mature, invites the hypothesis of common origin. Ethiopia becomes the most likely candidate of that common starting point. Sumerian records and literature contain numerous references to Ethiopia, and there are many artefacts that establish connections between these three ancient civilisations. An alternative hypothesis is that these three civilisations arose independently, around roughly the same time, and subsequently established links between themselves.

What is interesting is that the hypotheses attempting to explain the variants of early human civilisation mirror a similar set of hypotheses concerning the origin of Homo Sapiens. Wolpoff, Zhi et al. (1984) put forward the multi-regional hypothesis of the origin of modern humans by claiming that Homo Sapiens evolved during the last million years from Homo Erectus in parallel developments in Africa, Europe and Asia and then spread over the three continents by virtue of a high rate of selection, migration and interbreeding. Cann, Stoneking et al. (1987) put forward the alternative common origin, 'out-of-Africa', hypothesis that has been segmented into four independent parts by Wilson, Stoneking et al. (1991). These are:

- The most recent common ancestor of Homo Sapiens lived about 200,000 years ago.
- Homo Sapiens arose from Homo Erectus in a single region of the world.
- Africa is the most probable region for this transition.
- There was later a spread out from Africa, eventually replacing earlier Homo groups.

Penny, Steel et al. (1995) tested both the multi-regional and 'out-of-Africa' hypotheses over a wide range of genetic data including diversity in mitochondria

DNA sequences, diversity of nuclear alleles frequencies and the evolutionary tree derived from restricted fragment length polymorphism (RFLP). They concluded that the multi-regional hypothesis failed numerous tests in predicting gene dispersal over the whole range of human precursors. On the other hand, a wide range of data including nuclear and mitochondrial sequences, stochastic mechanisms of mutation and allele frequencies, supported the 'out-of-Africa' hypotheses. In addition, the DNA data were consistent with considerable archaeological evidence including times of arrival of Homo sapiens in various regions, appearance of modern artefacts in the archaeological record and similar evolutionary trees derived from genetic information and languages.

Interestingly Penny et al found that the genetic data revealed an exclusively African group, with the greatest genetic diversity, and a 'general' group of Africans, Europeans, Asians and Australopapuans. Further, the Europeans, Asians and Australopapuans, and the Africans belonging to this 'general' group, appeared to be subsets of the diversity within Africa. Also Native Americans and Polynesians are subsets of Asian lineages, and these Asian lineages are subsets of those occurring in Africa.

Penny et al. developed a two-phase model split into two equal periods of 75,000 to 100,000 years, of the emergence of the Homo Sapiens population. In their view in the first period Homo Sapiens evolved into a constant average population size, and then experienced an expansionary phase in the second period. It is during this expansionary phase that Homo Sapiens moved out from Africa into other parts of the world. They were of the view that the discovery of sophisticated tools in Zaire about 90,000 BCE, Yellen, Brooks et al. (1995), which are twice as old as equivalent ones outside of Africa, is consistent with their time frame for expansion from Africa. Further, Noble and Davidson (1991) proposed a cultural explosion model in the expansion of Homo Sapiens population that appears to accord more with the archaeological and genetic data than models based on climatic changes.

Strong support for the common ancestor and out-of-Africa hypotheses in the origin of Homo Sapiens raises the question that if Homo Sapiens arose out of Africa, and not by independent regional mutations, why should civilisation not have followed the same course? In other words, why should the almost full-blown civilisations that emerged in Egypt, Sumer and the Indus Valley not have a common origin in Africa? Indeed, a common African origin is more in keeping with the existing archaeological records, than the hypothesis of independent origin. These data suggest that the hypothesis of a common origin of human civilisation in Africa has greater plausibility when compared to other alternatives and to comparable developments in the human population.

A further point to note is that research evidence from genetics casts serious doubts on the notion of race as a biological fact. Also the hypothesis of a common African origin of civilisation raises questions concerning the relative meaning of the terms civilised and primitive. If civilisation arose in Africa and then spread from there to Mesopotamia and the Indus Valley, then at one stage

Africans were civilised and the rest of the world was primitive. Since then the cycle seems to have come full circle in the usage and application of these terms.

Wakeman (1985) and others have claimed that Sumer was the starting point of western civilisation. However, western Europe has far less claims on Sumer than either Africa or Asia. Sumerians wrote of their interactions with Ethiopia and the Indus Valley, and there is an abundance of evidence of the exchanges between Sumer, Egypt and India. There is no similar record of direct contact with Western Europe and any of these ancient civilisations. The position taken here is that the legacies of Sumer, Egypt and the Indus Valley are part of the common ancient civilisation and therefore the controversy concerning the primacy of Sumer or Egypt is redundant.

Writing, schools and the teaching occupation were the inventions and creations of this ancient civilisation and belong to that common legacy bequeathed to all people by the ancients. No modern variant of civilisation can claim exclusivity. If ancient pedigree and origin are to be claimed those attributes belong to Africa, more than to any other.

Three

THE MASCULINE ROOTS OF TEACHING IN JUDAISM

Judaism marked a fundamental break with the religious orientation and civilisation of an ancient world characterised by polytheism, hedonism, materialism and the belief that the present life was better than the one to come. Its tenets of monotheism, austere adherence to law and dependence upon spirit are almost the antithesis of the cosmology of Sumer and Pharonic Egypt. At the same time Judaism, as the fountainhead of two other great monotheistic religions, has been a major shaper of the world as we know it today. It is therefore appropriate to continue to trace the evolution of schooling and within it the masculine and feminine roots of the occupation of teaching in the period of classical Judaism.

It is impossible to discuss Judaism without reference to the Jews. While much controversy surrounds the Jewish people there are several points that are generally conceded:

1. Jewish history goes back to the second millennium when city-states, and the empires some created, were the hallmarks of the era.

2. Israel and Judah were small marginal political and economic entities that existed between the imperial powers that controlled Mesopotamia on the one hand and Egypt on the other hand. Even at the heights of the united kingdom, under David and Solomon, they were largely confined to Palestine and mainly to the hills. For most of their history, except for two periods of just about 100 years each, Israel or Judah were tributary or vassal states of a major power, whether Assyria, Babylon, Persia, Greece, Egypt or Rome. David and Goliath can be regarded as an accurate metaphor of their experience between the powers of their day. The Bible celebrated the victory of David over Goliath, probably because it was so uncommon. The history of Israel and Judah has many instances where the major powers were triumphant.

3. Notwithstanding these circumstances of political and economic marginality, Jews have survived as living testimonies of their existence as a people and have maintained their identity, language and culture while many of their powerful conquerors have long disappeared and are only known from historical records. Probably, it is from this

perspective that the victory of David over Goliath is to be reconstructed as a religious metaphor, as against the historical reality that was the opposite.

4. Notwithstanding this history of political, economic and social marginality, Jews can rightly claim to have given birth to two major religions directly, Judaism and Christianity, and one indirectly, Islam. The adherents of these three religions, who all trace their beginnings to Abraham, currently number more than half of the world's population. While it is usual to claim that politics, economics and social forces shape society, Israel and Judah present classic cases of the influence of belief in shaping society including its political, economic, social and cultural dynamics. It is from this perspective that the masculine roots of teaching in Judaism will be traced in this chapter.

THE FORMATION OF ISRAEL

Genesis traces the origin of the Jews to the Hebrew Abram who was said to have originated from the territory of the old Sumerian city of Ur. He is recorded as having migrated to Harran in north-western Mesopotamia. Archaeological evidence has established the fact that Ur was completely destroyed and disappeared from history in the early seventeenth century BCE. There is also evidence that Harran flourished in the nineteenth and eighteenth centuries BCE. Abram's migration would need to have taken place within these time boundaries, if the Genesis account is to be regarded as having a historical basis, which some doubt, and not restricted to being a reconstructed myth of Jewish beginnings.

Albright (1966) insisted that the historical basis of the western Mesopotamian origin of the Jews, as given by the Genesis account, must be conceded for the following reasons:

- Between 2000 and 1800 BCE Amorite princes displaced their Akkadian and Sumerian counterparts from the Zagros Mountains to the Mediterranean.
- Freedom of movement obtained and motives for movement, as attributed to Abram, were common in that period.
- Personal Amorite names included Abram, Jacob, Laban, Zebulun and Benjamin among others.
- The divine and tribal names, recorded in Genesis for the period of the Patriarchs, are independently established from Babylonian tablets, and have no correspondence with the cosmology of Canaan.

Egyptian records, independent of the Bible, showed that Israel existed as a recognised people in Palestine from at least 1200 BCE. How they reached there, however, is another matter of some controversy between those who accept the Genesis account as being of general historical value, as against those who insist that it is a mythical reconstruction not corroborated by the archaeological evidence. Main points of controversy are the enslavement and exodus from Egypt and the conquest of Canaan. While the points of view and accounts are myriad, they coalesce either around the basic outline of the Biblical account, or a reconstruction of the available archaeological evidence and sources independent of the written Jewish records. Considering that excavations of sites are ongoing and published research of previous excavations are always coming out, that the positions of the maximalists relying almost totally on the Bible and the minimalists disregarding the latter are constantly being revised, it is probably prudent to outline the essence of these two positions concerning the formation of Israel as a people and state and to integrate them.

THE BIBLICAL ACCOUNT

Because the Biblical account is so well known only its main points will be listed here.

1.   The Hebrew ancestors of the Jews voluntarily went into Egypt during a period of famine and received favourable treatment when Joseph was alive but eventually became enslaved after his death.

2.   Under the leadership of Moses the enslaved Israelites made a dramatic exodus from Egypt and had an epochal experience at Sinai where the covenant with God was renewed and the written commandments were given to Moses.

3.   Following this the Israelites were condemned to wander in the desert and wilderness largely because of their lack of faith in Yahweh's promise and their disobedience, primarily in the form of idolatry.

4.   Finally, led by Joshua, they were allowed to enter the promised land but this had to be accomplished through conquest, as there were people, mainly the Canaanites, living in the land. Several battles were fought in which they destroyed numerous cities in Canaan including Jericho and Ai.

5.   For the period in which they were becoming settled in the land, judges ruled the twelve tribes under the guidance of Yahweh.

6.   Eventually, beginning with Saul and followed by David and Solomon, the monarchy and the kingdom of Israel were established with Jerusalem as the capital city. The temple was built in which the Ark of the Covenant was housed and the royal court was established.

7.   After Solomon's death the united kingdom was divided into the Northern Kingdom, Israel with ten tribes, and the Southern Kingdom, Judah, with the other two tribes, Judah and Benjamin.

8.   As a result of sin, particularly that of idolatry, Israel was destroyed.

9.   Judah entered into captivity in Babylon for much the same reason in later years as the word of the Lord was neglected and the nation sinned.

The essence of this account is that the Israelites who had been slaves in Egypt came to Canaan already worshipping Yahweh. As such they were new arrivants in Canaan and different from the Canaanites. These latter people had originally settled the land and established their own cosmology that was entirely different from Israel's. Further, Israel acquired the land by conquest and destroyed the cities of the Canaanites. Following the conquest of the land the twelve formerly semi-nomadic tribes settled in the land and in time became a kingdom replete with a king, a city and a palace, as was the pattern of those times.

THE ALTERNATIVE EXPLANATION

Many scholars contest the biblical account maintaining that it is not supported by archaeological evidence. Bearing in mind the purpose of this study, only one such position will be outlined here. It is that of Ahlstrom (1986) who by tracing the name of Israel posited an alternative explanation to the biblical account. Ahlstrom based his account mainly on archaeological evidence and other sources independent of the Bible. The essence of Ahlstrom's account is set out briefly as follows:

- The biblical account of the conquest of Canaan and the formation of Israel is a reconstruction and reinterpretation of the history of the Jews at a time when their right to the land was being contested after the Babylonian captivity. The biblical story of conquest is therefore ideological and not historical and must be understood and interpreted as such.
- There is no archaeological evidence of a well-organised military conquest of Canaan, the destruction of cities or the arrival of any new group in Canaan at the time that the Israelites are projected as arriving in Canaan. Further, there is no evidence of any change in the material culture of the hills as would be expected from new arrivants with a different culture.
- Palestine was under the general control of Egypt for the period in question. The prisoner of war list of the second campaign of Amentotep II (1453–1419 BCE) provides a glimpse of the population of Palestine in the fifteenth century BCE but shows no evidence of Israelites in the land. That list included the Canaanites and other ethnic groups and a group labelled, the apiru. In fourteenth century texts the term apiru was generally applied to those opposed to state policy, disruptive elements, robbers, raiders, rebels or social outcasts.
- The hills of Palestine were virtually empty. New settlers were virtually pioneers. They constructed their dwellings and villages on unoccupied lands. These pioneers were city dwellers and lowland peoples fleeing the city-states. They chose virgin but difficult terrain in which to live.

This provided them with refuge from the devastating effects of wars that were prevalent at the time, escape from taxes and the seizure and destruction of property by rulers. They lived in cluster dwellings suggesting extended families. Originally, villages may have been clusters of unrelated families, but in time through inter-marriage kinship ties developed and clans arose.

- As the population of the hills grew improved production and conservation measures were introduced, including terracing, the areas under production were increased and with these the sizes of villages.
- Expanding population in neighbouring villages led in time to conflicts that in turn induced smaller and less aggressive clans to affiliate with larger and more aggressive clans. Aggressive clans with similar expansion interests created feuds and wars, requiring a more organised society with capable leaders steering the communities and organising defences. In time this process created the very city-state structure in the hills, from which the pioneers had originally fled.
- There is evidence of Jacobites moving into the hills and settling around Shechem at a relatively early date. As settled people within the hills, they along with the apiru may have been the first to be called Israelites, people of the hills of Palestine.
- Israel appeared to have been a name used to differentiate the hills from the coastal areas of Palestine. The latter were populated and cultured, while the hills were sparsely populated and the people practised an impoverished version of the city culture. The material culture of the hills was Canaanite. Israel was therefore first used as a territorial name within Canaan. It was the name for the entire hill country. Judah appeared to have been the old name for the southern hills within the range.
- Later after the process of social and political organisation had reached the point where the monarchy had been established under Saul, David and Solomon, Israel became a political name, that of the kingdom.
- After the kingdom was split following the death of Solomon, and the ultimate demise of the Northern Kingdom, which had taken the name Israel, the prophets of Judah began to appropriate the name Israel as an ideological name to represent the cultic congregation of Yahweh. This trend continued and intensified after the destruction of the kingdom of Judah in 586 BCE. This constituted a theological reconstruction of the name Israel, to mean congregation of Yahweh not limited by territory or nationality.
- Yahweh was an Edomite deity. Several Edomite clans were among those that had migrated to the hills of Palestine. El was the name of the head of the Canaanite pantheon. This suggests that the name Israel may have been related to the worship of this Canaanite deity. Yahweh became the God of Israel through certain Judges and the fact that Saul and David, his son in law, were Yahweh worshippers.

In essence, this reconstruction by Ahlstrom (1986) is that there is no evidence of a mass exodus from Egypt but rather voluntary departures from coastal cities of Palestine for the hills by people seeking to escape the vicissitudes and fall-out of the ancient city-states. They along with other disparate groups recreated, in the hill country of Palestine, the same cycle of village settlements expanding into urban conglomerates and, with rivalry between them, the emergence of city-states and monarchies. As such, Israel and Yahweh worship emanated largely from within Canaan and from a process of evolution from Canaanite parent culture and assimilation of some of the other groups that migrated to the area.

AN INTERMEDIATE POSITION

Albright (1966) and others posited an intermediate position between the biblical account as historical fact or as an artificial recreation of a later period totally lacking in any historical basis. He maintained that there is evidence in support of conquest within Canaan at around the time Joshua would have invaded the hills of Palestine. He maintained that his own findings at Tell Beit Mirsim and Beth-el provided evidence of the destruction of Canaanite towns around 1230 BCE, which would have been toward the end of the period of conquest. However, he agreed with Ahlstrom that apiru, who in his opinion were mainly semi-nomadic Semitic raiders of the northwestern region, were among the people who came to populate the hills and to comprise the Israelite community.

In his view, the Israelite movement into Canaan came at a time when Egyptian power was in decline in the region after 1225 BCE. The movement into Canaan was of disparate elements made up of the slaves led out of Egypt by Moses, freebooters in Palestine, and groups migrating from elsewhere. They, along with the Canaanites who originally occupied the land, were eventually moulded into the single polity that eventually emerged. The native Canaanites of old lineage were the aristocrats and patricians of Palestine. Their rich mythology and dramatic rituals were to be contrasted with the austere and simple religion of Yahweh. Their highly developed civilisation of Phoenician cities on the coastal plains was to be contrasted with the unsophisticated newcomers in the hills with rustic ways, little or no art and few craftsmen. This division between the newcomers and the original inhabitants was a fundamental distinction that marked the major polarities in the society which emerged. Another of these markers was religion.

Leadership of the disparate groups came from the Israelites who operated under a federation of the tribes grouped around a central religious symbol, the Ark of the Covenant, which unified them by politics and religion, as well as language and customs to some extent. The country was not suited to central political organisation. Hence, charismatic tribal leaders, judges, provided central leadership where such was required. Wisdom and impartiality in making decisions according to tribal customs, and fame as an arbitrator were features that marked most of the judges, some of whom for good measure were also military leaders. These judges played the important role of preventing blood feuds and restricting lawlessness.

The stimulus to unite and form a single kingdom came from the Philistine threat. They invaded Palestine by sea and land about 1187 BCE, about 50 years after the climax of the Israelite invasion. They along with other seafaring people from the Mediterranean overwhelmed the Canaanites on the coast and came close to invading Egypt itself. The Egyptian king made a virtue of necessity and allowed them to settle on the coast between Gaza and regions further north.

In time, the Philistines turned their attention to the hill country of Palestine. Their attempts to conquer the territory were substantial and sustained. Recognising the symbolic importance of the Ark of the Covenant, the Philistines captured it. The response to the attack on territory and its religious symbol provided the basis for the unification of the tribes and disparate elements that comprised the country. The end result was the creation of the monarchy, begun around 1013 BCE by Saul and consolidated on David's succession in 1000 BCE following Saul's death in a hopeless battle against the Philistine army.

After defeating the Philistine army, and therefore containing the threat, David moved to consolidate his power and that of the monarchy by seizing Jebusite territory and establishing Jerusalem on territory outside that of the twelve tribes, and between the two halves of the kingdom. Actually, Jerusalem was the city of David, totally dependent on the monarch for its original meaning. Further, he distributed the priests and Levites across the kingdom, thus weakening them politically but contributing to the spread of normative Yahwism.

Smith (1955) took a position that was very similar to Albright. He noted that Solomon who succeeded David did not attempt to extend territory. Rather he moved to consolidate monarchy and the state that had been created. He reigned from the death of David in 961 to 922 BCE. Swift (1919) adopting the same line or argument listed the following as hallmarks of Solomon's reign. He:

- Built the temple, the palace in Jerusalem, fortified cities and constructed new roads.
- Established a navy and large-scale commercial trade.
- Established districts and appointed governors in each so as to better administer the territory.
- Created numerous alliances through marriages, leading in the process to a large harem that was a virtual register of the friendly relationships he established.
- Imposed onerous taxes to pay for his various projects.
- Imposed forced labour as a means of carrying out public works and projects in alien lands.

While Solomon in his lifetime was able to effect these projects and policies, these were not without substantial dissension and considerable resentment. Upon his death, the kingdom was divided. The hundred-year period of the monarchy did not provide an internal reason for unity. With the Philistine threat no longer a unifying force, schism set in as it had done in the past, at the point of succession on the death of the ruler. Israel fractured as a united political force after a period involving only three monarchs. Contributing factors were the nature of the territory which promoted local autonomy, the history of a people resistant to urbanisation and the modest wealth of the country, which provided little incentive for imperial compliance. They all conspired to undermine unity.

The unique precedent created by this fracture was the innovation of two sovereign kingdoms serving the same God, Yahweh. This was highly unusual for this period of history. In the ancient world gods were both territorial and national. Each kingdom and its territory had its own god. That two kingdoms should serve only one god constituted unprecedented magnanimity in the realm of the divine and a unique cosmology.

The first half of the eighth century BCE was one of relative ease for the kingdoms in Palestine. Smith noted that the monarchy in Israel emerged in the period when Egyptian power in the region was at a low ebb. At the same time, the Assyrian empire was struggling to recover from a devastating plague that had ravaged the population, (Schwantes 1965). By 745 BCE, this was no longer the case. The larger northern kingdom, Israel, made alliances that appeared hostile to Assyria. Sargon II terminated its existence in 722 BCE, exactly two hundred years after its break from the united kingdom. The immediate cause was Hosea's mistake in choosing to pay tribute to the King of Egypt instead of to Sargon II of Assyria. Hosea misread the relative strength of the two powers and Israel paid the price with its existence. Sargon II destroyed the capital at Samaria, deported 27,290 persons, including many of the most important cadres, scattering them in cities beyond the Euphrates (Schwantes 1965).

One lasting contribution of the kingdom of Israel was that in a backhanded way it nurtured the rise of the prophets. The monarchy in united Israel was never wholeheartedly embraced, and kings and their courts were always regarded with suspicion that was evident from the time of David and Solomon.

These tendencies were manifested in the Northern Kingdom in even larger writ, exaggerated by palace intrigue and assassinations, internal strife and turmoil, disruption and devastation, as different clans championed and promoted their interests (Kretzmann 1916). In addition, Baal had come to be associated with Canaan, its aristocratic ways, stratified society and great disparity in land and wealth. Baal was the god of urban, commercial and aristocratic Canaanites, palace intrigue and strife. On the other hand, Yahweh was the god of clan democracy, mutual responsibility, social justice and suffering commoners. While Yahweh was the state religion, the worship of the Canaanite deities continued in private and without sanction. Israel's drift was perceived by some to have been away from Yahweh and towards Baal. Those hostile to all that Baalism represented became the nucleus of the prophetic group.

Prophets constituted a separate group from priests and Levites. The latter were responsible for shrines, rituals and organised religion. Prophets had no such appointment. They appeared in groups, and exercised their prophetic functions with the aid of music, dancing, inspired speech and interaction with their peers. Yet, at the same time they also operated on an individual basis.

Sachar (1948) described the prophets as being extraordinarily complex by the contradictions that they appeared to embrace within themselves. They were supremely individualistic yet preached restraint and conformity to law. They were intensely patriotic but smote the idea of a territorial god or narrow patriotism and threatened the kingdom with destruction. They were highly religious but despised the form that religion took. They laboured for plain moral requirements to replace elaborate ceremonies and formal creeds. They were fearless in their self-appointed mission to defy kings, priests, and populace while bearing abuse with sublime patience. In Sachar's view, they were the poets of statesmanship and the living Hebrew conscience.

Above all the prophets were champions of social justice. They identified Yahweh and his laws with social justice. On one occasion, Elijah journeyed from Gilead east of the Jordan River to Samaria to protest the King's seizure of Naboth's vineyard. In Smith's view, this was the truly original element in prophetic thought. Ancient religions were founded on ritual rectitude and formal observances without regard to personal ethics. The Hebrew prophets broke though this barrier and linked ethical action with serving Yahweh and viewed ritual observances as virtually meaningless without corresponding ethical action.

Apart from creating the synthesis between religion, Yahweh, and social idealism, the prophets also were major proponents of an exclusive monotheism. The ancient world was characterised by religious tolerance. The underlying assumption was that gods were territorial; hence people worshipped the gods of the territory in which they lived. Further, in the polytheistic world there was no objection to adding gods to the pantheon if people so chose. The prophets introduced an uncompromising hostility to other gods and cults by the notion of Yahweh being jealous. In the evolution of their thought, they came to the position that Yahweh was a universal god. It was Jeremiah and the second Isaiah who probably were the first to declare Yahweh alone as God and all other gods as inconsequential and non-existent. As part of their complexity, the prophets were the authors of both narrow religious intolerance as well as the majestic conception of a universal God and its corollary the unity of all human kind.

Eby and Arrowood (1940) made the point that the Hebrew conception of deity was the result of the integration of the ideas of eternal creative energy with that of the ethical life of the universe. Yahweh was a genuine personality, creative, omnipotent, universal, just and righteous in all his dealings. As the only God, he was the Lord of all nations who embraced all peoples in his providential care at the same time he was exacting in his requirements for the observation of his laws.

Finally it must be said of the prophets that they more than any other groups were the repository of Hebrew resentment of the monarchy. Kings had interposed themselves between Yahweh and the people. Before the kings, God led the people directly. Kingship was therefore not part of the divine plan but only allowed by His providence. In this regard, the prophets of Israel objected to monarchic government even when that form of political organisation was in its heyday. Furthermore, they forecast its demise.

Judah, as a kingdom, lasted about 130 years longer than Israel: long enough perhaps for the experience of Israel to make an indelible impression. Caught between the superpowers of Egypt and Mesopotamia it was only a matter of time before the small kingdom of Judah would make a wrong choice in terms of ally, which by default also defined enemy. Before the fateful day, it would appear that the words of the prophets found more receptive soil in both palace and temple. Hilkiah, the high priest, discovered the book of the Law, Deuteronomy, in the temple. Following this discovery in 622 BCE, Josiah the King embarked upon religious reform which included clearing the temple of all foreign gods, destroying their local sanctuaries, dismissing their priests, instituting wide-ranging social reforms and canonising the extant version of the Book of Deuteronomy as sacred scripture. For the first time in history, a book had been declared sacred scripture and the ultimate divine authority.

An important point in these reforms was the distinction made between priests and Levites. To this point, priests and Levites were synonymous. All priests were Levites (Swift 1919). Josiah's reform appeared to integrate the prophets into the priesthood since some of the distinctions between priests and Levites related to those functions that had been traditionally performed by prophets: divination, soothsaying and teaching.

However, it would appear that Josiah, and some of the prophets as well, had not internalised the full implications of the new religious path on which they had embarked. Hence, acting within the paradigm of kingship, and not that of prophetic insight, Josiah quietly but unmistakably took steps to recover territory that had formerly belonged to Israel, probably hoping to re-unite the kingdom established by Saul and David (Steinsaltz 1984). Josiah died in a military escapade to extend national territory at the same time he was implementing social action based on the notion of a universal god not bound by territory and notions of humanity independent of lineage.

Assyria's powers in Palestine had waned over the years after Sargon's invasion. The new power, notwithstanding Egyptian intentions, was the Chaldeans. Nebuchadnezzar's army invaded Judah and Jerusalem three times between 592 and 586 BCE carrying off captives, destroying the temple, removing its vessels, destroying the fortifications of Jerusalem and establishing alternative government for the area. The kingdom of Judah was at an end.

OBSERVATIONS

These three different approaches to recounting the formation of the Jewish people are illustrative of the range of reconstructed history of the Jews, but are by no means exhaustive. Unlike most people of the world, the Jews have a written history of themselves by themselves. While this constitutes a great advantage, as Frerichs (1989) pointed out, the biblical account has all the disadvantages of a single source. As Neusner (1990) insisted the biblical account is not the autobiography of the experience of a single person, neither is it an account of the entire nation or people. The selective perspective that it transmits is that of those who identified themselves as part of the genealogy of Abraham, the children of promise. While this may be sufficient for matters of faith, it is only one contributor to the understanding of history.

Understandably, therefore, over the last two hundred years scholars have sought corroboration from archaeological sources. However, even here the approaches have varied on a continuum from those who seek to rely almost entirely on archaeological sources with little reference to the biblical record, to those who approach the study of archaeology through the Bible. The result is wide divergence even with respect to circumstances in which there is evidence from different sources. Since this study is directed at understanding the creation of formal schooling and the teaching profession as these were influenced by Judaism; only passing note is taken of the differences in the account of Jewish history. Even then, it is for establishing needed background for this study.

As with all areas of study, there are numerous questions that need to be asked about what happened, when, where, how and why in Jewish history. Fortunately for the period in which formal education was established in the history of the Jews, there is little controversy of what and where, but rather much greater debate on when, how and why.

It is important to observe that none of the accounts of the history of the Jews to the time of their Babylonian captivity includes any description of schools or formal education. The only biblical reference to any school is to that of the school of the prophets. There are also numerous references to scribes but no mention of how they were trained. The book of Jeremiah states that the king tried unsuccessfully to arrest both the prophet and his scribe. Through seals that have been found, archaeological evidence has established the existence of Baruch son of Neriah who was the scribe of Jeremiah. In addition, it would appear from all sources that writing was not uncommon, at least after the establishment of the monarchy, although there is no record of how it was taught.

Swift (1919) was of the view that prophets rose with the monarchy and related to the need for seers at the court to declare the will of Yahweh. From this point of view, prophets would be one type of scholar in the genre that developed in the Babylonian and Assyrian empires for which there are better records. There is therefore the possibility that priest, scribe and prophet could have been part of a royal institution of the palace, which offered training in the different areas they represented. However, there is no record to establish this as fact during the periods of either the united or divided monarchy.

THE BABYLONIAN CAPTIVITY AND PERSIAN RESTORATION

The period of Babylonian captivity commenced in 597 BCE and ended in 536 BCE. The Persian restoration that followed commenced in 536 BCE and was completed by 455 BCE, at the occasion of the Great Assembly. This is another monumental era in the history of Judah and of the Jewish people. This period marks the establishment of Judaism and with it the creation of formal schooling including a new institution, the synagogue, which was the agent of both. It is therefore necessary to discuss, in summary fashion, the major elements of this period.

CONQUEST AND DEPORTATION

The army of Nebuchadnezzar invaded Judah and captured Jerusalem in 597 BCE. Consistent with the ancient code of warfare and conquest, the victors took as captives the heir to the throne, Jehoaichin, his court, many leading subjects as well as the best craftsmen. Zedekiah, the regent, continued resistance by conspiring with the enemies of Babylon contrary to ancient code and therefore had to bear the consequences. The Babylonian army returned, devastated the countryside, laid waste Jerusalem and destroyed the temple, which had been spared in the first invasion. Further deportations of notables followed this second invasion.

Gedaliah, former mayor of the palace, was appointed governor of Judah; consistent with the ancient practice of imperial powers to allow the locals to govern themselves once they accepted overlordship, obeyed the laws and paid taxes. Many Jews, who had fled for reasons of security, returned and accepted the authority of Gedaliah. Even the military chiefs, who had fled into the wilds, entered into negotiations with him. However, Ishmael, an ultrapatriotic member of the Davidic clan assassinated Gedaliah, killed many of his supporters and inflicted casualties on the Babylonian army stationed at Mizpah. This resulted in a third invasion and the deportation of the remaining notables and skilled persons in 582 BCE (Albright 1966).

Following the assassination of Gedaliah, the army chiefs gathered a large number of Jews along with their soldiers and fled to Egypt, where they entered into military service and were stationed as garrison troops on the northern and southern borders. The Jewish community at Elephantine owed its genesis to this voluntary exile of this loyalist resistance of the Babylonian invasion.

While the forced deportation to Babylon, and the voluntary deportation of those fleeing to Egypt, had considerably reduced the population of Judah, it would be a mistake to believe that the entire population had been dispersed. While accurate estimates of the numbers involved are not available, Smith's contention that Judah was not depopulated and that the majority of Jews remained in Palestine, seems a reasonable inference. The period of exile applied only to a minority of the population of Judah. The most profound effect was the removal of the dominant clans of the stratified society that had been created by urbanisation and the monarchy. The majority of these leading families were either deported or fled. The majority of those remaining were those families engaged in subsistence through agriculture and animal breeding.

CAPTIVITY IN BABYLON

From all accounts it does not appear that those taken captive to Babylon were treated harshly (Smith 1955). Jews were mentioned in the rations of the royal court and Jehoiachin was still referred to as the King of Judah (Albright 1966). Moreover, it is clear that many were not only redistributed to well disposed locations but also were allowed to rise to positions in public office as well as to conduct business. The only requirement was adherence to the ancient code of conquest, which is, acceptance of political dominance, obedience to the law of the imperial power and the payment of taxes.

For those taken captive into Babylon the period of exile was traumatic but also exciting. In the first place, they were exposed to a more advanced civilisation in terms of formal schooling, scholarship; architecture and the arts. Secondly, the Chaldean empire of Babylon was much wealthier than Judah. Thirdly, opportunity was not denied them and there was apparent freedom of movement and association. The Book of Daniel recorded that Nebuchadnezzar instructed that young men 'without blemish' and full of all wisdom, from among the captive Jews, should be selected and taught 'the knowledge of the Chaldeans'.

Jews in captivity in Babylon, warned by the oblivion which had befallen Israel, were determined to avert the same fate for Judah (Swift 1919). The answer was clearly not military might. The prophets had warned against this option repeatedly and highlighted the folly of such an approach. Instead, the prophets had preached an ethical religion as the antidote to oblivion. This was the option therefore that was fully explored in the period of captivity.

The essence of the prophetic message as it applied to their situation can be reduced to the following principles:

a)   National calamity was punishment visited upon the people, by Yahweh, for disobedience and sin. As such, the Chaldeans were the instruments of Yahweh performing His will since Yahweh was also God of the Chaldeans.

b)   If Yahweh's law were kept, and His will found, restoration was assured.

c) Judah's mission, as God's chosen people, was to make Yahweh
     known to all peoples.

It is clear that there was much discussion and debate about these matters
in the Exile community. Drazin (1940) maintained that synagogues began to
be constructed in Babylon, as Jews mourning the loss of the Temple devised
alternative arrangements for worship and prayer. Ebner (1956) insisted that
the synagogue was a communal centre not only for worship and prayer but
also for the discussion of local and national matters as well as a meeting place
for scholars and students. In reconstructing the sequence, it would appear that
worship, prayer, study and discussion preceded the construction of a building.
Apparently, the ferment in the Exile community as Jews sought to interpret,
understand and cope with their circumstances led to the creation and
construction of this new institution, the synagogue. It was the focal point and
physical expression of the communal exertion to re-interpret and re-define
themselves.

One view, and line of action, that seemed to have prevailed was that the
Deuteronomic reform begun during the reign of Josiah had to be continued
and brought to completion. The history of Israel and Judah and the messages of
the prophets were redacted, re-interpreted and written. Original works were
also written in this period. These included Ezekiel, and the Second Isaiah,
while new editions of the extant books of Amos, Hosea, Joshua and
Deuteronomy were produced (Swift 1919). The history of people recited orally
for centuries now took written form. The words of inspiration and revelation
spoken by the prophets for the benefit of their hearers were now written for
the edification of succeeding generations. This scholarly effort also produced
the Pentateuch, the five books of Moses.

It seems erroneous to assert, as some do, that there were no written scriptures
prior to the captivity. Mention has already been made of the Book of
Deuteronomy that was declared scripture prior to the period of captivity.
Reference has also been made to the fact that scribes recorded some of the
messages of prophets. More to the point would be the assertion that prior to
the captivity extant works had not yet reached the point of normative consensus
of being scripture. However, the process of acquiring canonical authority had
certainly begun as declaration of scriptural authority of some materials had
already been made in some quarters. It would appear that the enterprise, during
the period of exile, was to pull these disparate sources and materials together,
collate and edit them to the end of producing a comprehensive and complete
document. The evidence of their success, in this regard, was the Pentateuch,
the Torah. In addition to this redaction, original works were also produced,
which later became scripture as well.

The first record of formal education being established by Jews is that of the
school created in Babylon during the period of captivity. It was a school for
scholars and not neophytes. Little is known about the details of its organisation
and operation (Swift 1919). Neither is anything known about its role in the

scholarly work done to produce the Pentateuch. Whether its contribution was direct, or indirect through the preparation of the scholars who undertook the work under auspices is not known. Neither is it known if the school was modelled on Chaldean academies. It, however, can reasonably be assumed that the school was created to assist in the preservation of the Jewish way of life and culture. In addition, Jews were educated by the Babylonians in academies sponsored by the royal court.

RESTORATION UNDER PERSIAN SPONSORSHIP

Just as the fall of Judah and captivity was brought about by a superpower, so was its restoration. In 538 BCE, the Persians defeated the Chaldeans. Darius, the conquering king, died and was replaced by Cyrus in 536 BCE. Among his first official acts was to allow the Jews to return to Palestine with permission to rebuild the Temple. Leading the first group to return were Zerubbabel, Jehoiachin's grandson who was then the head of the house of David, Joshua the high priest and the prophets Haggai and Zechariah. They undertook the rebuilding of the temple, which was completed in 516 BCE. Contrary to the hopes of some, the Persians did not allow the monarchy to be restored. Judah was to have religious liberty but not political sovereignty.

While there is much controversy concerning the sequence of events after the return of this first group, the position adopted here is that the next phase of restoration, and movement back from captivity, was the arrival of Nehemiah. He was cupbearer to the King of Persia, and therefore quite likely was a eunuch. Through these connections, he had gained royal approval to rebuild the fortifications and restore Jerusalem. This he achieved despite opposition from the governor of Samaria. Nehemiah provided military muscle combined with religious zeal, which together restored Jerusalem to city status. This paved the way for the final stage of the restoration, Ezra's ideological and social reconstruction of the society (Steinsaltz 1984).

Ezra arrived in Jerusalem as the Persian commissioner. His mission was to establish the reconstituted state of Judah. In addition to Persian authority, he had the Mosaic Law, the Pentateuch, which was to become the constitution and the law of the new state. Judah would be a theocracy. The high priest would be the head of state. There would be no king. The temple not palace would prevail not only in matters of religion but also in affairs of state. As such, there would be no distinction between sacred and secular; both would be one. In order to obey the law everyone had to know the law. Education was therefore critical for compliance with the requirements of the theocratic state. The launching of this new state, and religion, occurred at the Great Assembly at which all men, women and children were gathered.

THE ESSENCE OF THE RESTORATION

Several critical points must not be overlooked. Each in itself is worthy of in-depth commentary and discussion, but this is outside the scope of this study. Only brief mention of their essence is possible.

1. The restoration was not a single dramatic act accomplished by a large number of Jews returning from Babylon to Palestine. Rather it was accomplished over many years and in stages. Those returning first appeared to be those with hereditary ties to land and office. However, they were followed by those whose principal motivation was religious and nationalistic. Exact dates are difficult to come by as different sources vary, but it would appear that the entire process took upwards of 80 years. During this period, there was dynamic interaction between the Exile community in Babylon and the Jews in Palestine.

2. Only a minority of the Exile community returned. The majority remained in Babylon. However, it seems simplistic to assume that those who remained were either unconcerned or had become assimilated and absorbed in Babylonian society. There is abundant evidence of their existence as a distinct community in Babylon with continued connections with Palestine for the next 1000 years at least (Bickerman 1966). What seems more to the point is that it was their connections and influence in the centre of power that was the motive force sustaining the leadership of the restoration. It was their re-conceptualisation of Judah and Israel that was implemented. The complex reality appears to be that the thrust of and leadership for the restoration of the religious and national centre in Palestine came from the Jews located in the centre of geopolitical power in Babylon. It was Persian sponsorship, engineered by Jews in Exile, which made the restoration in Palestine possible. Judaism was launched in Jerusalem with Persian blessing and Exile leadership. The Laws of Moses were established with the sceptre of Persian power.

3. It does not appear that those who were left in Palestine were any more absorbed and assimilated into the society, which evolved in the interregnum, than those who were exiled. However, the restoration efforts did not appear to have found a comparable movement from within the homeland. This appears to be explained more by social than religious factors. It seems very likely that those who remained, along with newcomers, had benefited from the lands from which the elite and notables had been evicted. They may have been fearful of the return of the exiles. It would appear that the abolition of the Jubilee year, in which all property fell back to the original owners, might have been a concession to those who had remained and now occupied the property. This reform gave them tenure in perpetuity. Accordingly, those returning could not reclaim their old property. It had passed permanently to the new occupants. The nobility created by the monarchy was at an end.

4.   In making this forward movement Jews were also taking two backward
     steps. One was religious to the Mosaic Law, the other was in political
     organisation. Prior to the invention of the hereditary monarchy clan
     democracy, under the umbrella of the Ark of the Covenant, had
     prevailed. The judges governed along with the heads of the clan, the
     elders. The monarchy had sidelined this model of governance. Judah
     was to be re-established within this old model of political organisation
     in which the high priest, and priests generally, would govern in
     conjunction with the Council of Elders. As Bickerman (1966) pointed
     out, in governing their empire the Persians preferred priests to a
     military aristocracy, which the monarchy represented. While they
     were willing to allow Judah's autonomy they were unwilling to install
     potential military competitors.

5.   The patterns emerging from the creation of Judaism out of the
     experience of exile and restoration bore the elements that marked the
     paradigm within which the religion had redefined itself in the context
     of major calamities experienced by the Jewish people. Importantly, it
     reached back into the past history of Israel and linked other episodes
     with the exile experience and from that extracted their essential core,
     which was codified in the edited version of scripture they produced.
     But the paradigm went beyond conscious and deliberate redaction to
     include the very actors themselves. For Ezra and Nehemiah were types
     of Joseph, Jews in the courts of the prevailing imperial power, who by
     their connections were able to ameliorate the circumstances of their
     people.

THE BASIC TENETS OF JUDAISM

Neusner (1990) insisted that there has never been a single Judaism, but
several Judaisms. There is a definitive human experience that each Judaism
reworks in its own circumstances and context, all at once, including all the
misery and magnificence of life. Further, no Judaism stands in linear or
incremental relationship with any other, but all repeat the paradigmatic
experience of the Torah of Moses authored by the Jews in exile in Babylon.
That experience, in theological terms, rehearses the conditional moral existence
of sin and punishment, suffering and atonement, and reconciliation. He further
stated that the lessons learned from the exile were that the life of the group is
uncertain and subject to conditions and stipulations; that nothing is set or
given, all things are gifts, land and life itself; exile and restoration marked the
group as special, different, select. Certainly, this was the case compared to the
fate of the Israelites of the northern kingdom.

Neusner also maintained that any religious system, and any Judaic system,
is not a theory or a book distinct from social reality. Accordingly, it can be
identified by three elements:

a) An ethos: a world-view that by reference to the supernatural and natural worlds accounts cogently and harmoniously for how things are.

b) An ethic: a way of life, which expresses in concrete action the world-view, and which is explained by the world-view.

c) An ethnos: a group of people who give expression, in everyday life, to the world-view and are defined by the way of life, that is, its ethics.

It is against this background that it is necessary to take note of the tenets of Judaism which emerged from the experience of the Jews between 586 and 445 BC. The ethos could be summarised from Hertzberg (1962) as follows:

1. God is.
2. God is one.
3. God is moral.
4. Life is law.
5. Israel, Jews, are chosen by God to be his corporate priesthood and therefore to live in covenant relationship with him. Accordingly, God demands of Israel a higher standard than all other people. This covenant is unbreakable, but God will punish Israel for sin.
6. The Torah is God's revealed word setting out His laws concerning life and how it should be lived.

The ethic is simple: live the law of God. Strictly observe the Torah in daily living. The ethnos is the cultic congregation called Israel.

The contradiction and irony of this formulation of Judaism were that the Samaritans, who were descendants of the Northern Kingdom, Israel, were excluded from the new congregation of the faithful. This is despite that fact that they worshipped Yahweh, and accepted the Torah as God's revealed word. They were part of the ethos and the ethic but were excluded from the ethnos. They had worshipped at the ruins of the temple after 586 BCE. They had demanded a share in its reconstruction. Their objection was to the fortification of Jerusalem, since its re-establishment as a city would rival their northern city.

The magnitude, magnificence and majesty of the conception of God expressed by the restorers are to be contrasted with the exclusiveness of those who were admitted to the congregation of Israel. Sounds of ethnic prejudice ring clear in the exclusion of the Samaritans. Politics can be unmistakably heard in the whispers that accompany the public proclamations. These are the undertones of realpolitik of the ancient world, and echoes of ancient local quarrels. All are distinctly audible in the cacophony of praise. These echoes and undertones are typical of strains of frailty embedded even in the most earnest human efforts to connect with divine presence. Hence, in the inauguration of Judaism there are the profound contradictions of the Torah needing pagan props and believers from Ephraim and Shechem being excluded from the congregation of Israel.

FROM RESTORATION TO DISPERSION

The boundaries of this study of the masculine roots of teaching in Judaism are the period between the restoration under Persia, after 536 BC, and the period immediately after dispersion which occurred under Roman auspices in 70 CE. Formal schooling was inaugurated in this period. While the factors inherent in the restoration outlined above can account for the inauguration of formal schooling, the factors that shape its evolution, and that of gender, are embedded in the wider societal factors that shifted and changed between the restoration and the time of the dispersion.

The period between 536 BCE and 70 CE can be conveniently divided into the following four subsections:

1.   Judah under Persian rule between 536 and 332 BCE.
2.   Judah under Hellenic rule between 332 and 165 BCE. After the death of Alexander the Great his generals subdivided the empire into three power centres: Seleucids in Syria, Ptolemies in Egypt and Macedonians in Europe. This period is treated as one since the underlying cultural framework remained unchanged.
3.   Autonomy under the Hasmonean princes between 165 and 63 BCE.
4.   Judah under Roman rule between 63 BCE and 70 CE.

THE PERIOD UNDER PERSIAN RULE

The Persian Empire ruled from the Indus valley to Ethiopia. Jews in Palestine during this period were therefore not caught between the two traditional centres of political power that hitherto had historically resided in Egypt and Mesopotamia. Further, Persia offered imperial protection from Philistine power from the sea or Arab invasion from the desert, either of which could have easily overwhelmed the reconstituted but diminutive Judah. Again, by influence at the royal court, the Diaspora, acting on behalf of Jews everywhere, could impose a uniform standard of faith and behaviour.

A papyrus unearthed at Elephantine, of a communication sent in 419 BCE, contained instructions to the Jewish settlement there concerning rules that should be observed with respect to the feast of unleavened bread. These instructions were forwarded to the Satrap of Egypt from the King of Persia (Bickerman 1966). Persian sponsorship was not simply the act of a particularly sympathetic ruler but a policy in managing its empire which was evident over several generations of rulers, amplified by bribes and diminished by arbitrary interference here and there, but which was consistently supportive. Persian support for the high priests and their associates went beyond providing political backing and included exemption from taxes, the benchmark of sincerity in alliance in the ancient world. The high priests, other priests, Levites, the Council of Elders and servants and slaves of the temple were all exempt from tolls, taxes and customs. The temple, however, did not possess any property outside its site and their emoluments came from the offerings of the believers.

The high priest was not only head of the temple operations but head of state. He was President of the Great Assembly, later the Council of Elders, comprised of the leaders of the clans. The temple in Jerusalem was not only the headquarters of Judaism, but also the location of the central government and its administration. The office of priest, including that of high priest, became hereditary. Religious and state offices were converted into lineage advantage. The theocratic state spawned a priestly aristocracy not only in terms of status and power but also wealth. Nobility derived from the administration of piety and not military might, as was the case of the monarchy.

Other major changes in the society when compared to pre-exile days could be listed as follows:

a) Much of the Hebrew Bible was canonised as the authoritative scripture. Written scriptures replaced inspired speech as the major vehicle guiding the faithful.

b) Synagogues were widespread, especially in provincial towns, and were a fundamental part of devotional life. This institution invented in captivity was now implemented in the new society as a major instrument of establishing congregational life, particularly for those living outside of Jerusalem.

c) Prophets and scribes became the main teachers of the people. (This subject will be developed fully later).

d) Aramaic, the language of the Persians, gradually became the vernacular language.

e) Yahweh's name was decreasingly used publicly and became increasingly restricted to use in the Temple services and in administering oaths. God of Heaven was the commonly used reference. Incidentally, this was the same phrase used in reference to the supreme god of Persia.

f) Jews in the Diaspora lived on equal terms with the natives, transacted business with people of all nationalities, intermarried, served Yahweh, accepted the authority of Jerusalem but also acknowledged local gods and ritual related to the places in which they lived. In this respect they began to diverge from those in Palestine.

THE PERIOD UNDER HELLENIC RULE

The Persian empire fell to Alexander the Great in 333 BCE. Jerusalem readily submitted to Macedonian rule. On the other hand, the city of Samaria revolted against Macedonian rule in 332 BCE. After the revolt was crushed a Greek colony was established there. Probably to placate the people a temple was established at Shechem, the most ancient capital of Israel. Samaritans now worshipped Yahweh and observed the laws of Moses from a religious centre in their own territory, creating a new item in the ancient quarrel between the northerners and the southerners of the hills of Palestine.

Notwithstanding this provocation, sponsored or allowed by the new imperial masters, Jews generally, and Jerusalem in particular, warmly embraced the new imperial power, which treated them with equanimity within the ancient code for vassals. Bickerman (1966) noted that the Greeks were generally curious about Jewish culture with which they first came in contact through Jews in the Diaspora. Jerusalem was not on the coastal trade routes and therefore not well known to the Greeks initially.

The features of Jewish culture that caught the attention of Greeks, to the point that they wrote about them, were as follows:

a)   The operation of a theocratic state, which gave the High Priest such importance and power.

b)   The obstinacy of Jews in defending the Law.

c)   The intolerance of Jews to other religions and the religious practices of other people.

With respect to the latter, it was traditional in the ancient world to regard all beliefs as different rays of refraction of divine light. The normative code was to respect the religious beliefs of others and to observe the religion of the land in which you were resident. However, outsiders were excluded from the major rituals of the local religion. The Jews did not follow the religion of the people in whose land they lived, regarded all people as pagan but at the same time allowed everyone on their soil to participate in many of their ritual observances, to the end of converting them. To the Greeks the Jews had turned religion on its head.

At the same time there were several elements of Jewish religious thought that were very similar in form to Greek philosophical speculation. The theocratic state resembled in many respects Plato's Republic in which philosopher-kings were the rulers. Further, Plato had also argued in favour of immortality. Monotheism was consistent with Pythagarous and his concept of a single supreme intelligence who had ordered the world, the harmony of which could be expressed mathematically. Also, the absence of images in worship and the abstract conception of God were in tune with the working of the Greek mind.

Despite these common aspects to both cultures, what divided them radically was orientation (Smith 1955). The Hebrew mind tended to mysticism, as such, the Jews accepted moral law and would not go beyond it. The Greeks bowed to no law but self-expression. The Jewish mind continually confronted the question, what must I do? Greeks were preoccupied with the question, why should I do it, or better yet, why should I not do it. On the one hand the Jewish ethos was that of living by revealed law, the Greek ethos was that of self-expression as determined by reason.

For these reasons the Greeks found Jews fascinating, a feeling that Jews reciprocated towards the Greeks. However, the challenge posed by Greek civilisation was not merely to the fundamental difference with respect to orientation to reason and revelation. The major challenge was the physical presence of Greek culture and its threat to literally overwhelm Jewish culture by the sheer weight of that presence. While previous empires had engaged in the practice of maintaining imperial control by defeating, deporting and dispersing those who challenged or threatened their rule, the Greeks engaged in preventative action. Hellenic cities and enclaves were set up all over the empire they controlled. Palestine had numerous Hellenic cities. In addition, Jerusalem and Judah were crowded with Greek officers, civil agents, traders and residents. Greek culture, commercial activities and presence had penetrated village life in Palestine. Greeks were literally to be found on Jewish doorsteps in Palestine and in the Diaspora.

Judah, Jews and Judaism had reconstructed themselves to deal with the uncertainties of existing as a small relatively unimportant polity between two great powers, but the challenge posed by the Greeks was that of a unipolar world in which the imperial power had culturally penetrated their vassal states: all the axes of power of that time had been Hellenised. Egypt and the Seleucid empires were thoroughly Hellenic in cultural orientation. Greek culture had to be confronted from the heights of political power to the doorsteps of village life. Greek civilisation could not be ignored.

The forces of imitation and assimilation were strong. Power was combined with presence and therefore many Jews wanted to be seen as Helene. Greek influences began to undermine spiritual life and promote licentious tendencies. Greek reasoning promoted scepticism and indifference. The Book of Ecclesiastes, written during this period, reflected this new mood in its repeated refrain, 'all is vanity'. Equally disturbing was the notion of extending God's bounty to the heathen, who without the yoke of the Law, were to be treated on the same basis as those who practised its observances on a daily basis. The Book of Jonah documented this resentment by many Jews.

The debate on how to address this challenge posed by the penetration of Hellenistic culture divided Jewish society and Judaism. Those who took the general position that the future direction was that of adjusting Judaism to the realities of the Hellenic world and thought were the Letzim, Hellenists, while those who held to traditional Jewish values were the Hasidim, Puritans. The former maintained, for example, that many of the dietary and other laws served only to isolate Jews from the rest of the world and needed to be reformed. The latter interpreted such proposals as heresy.

The depth of the fissure created was not just political, but also religious and socio-economic. Bickerman (1966) noted that while in Egypt, Babylon and Syria it was the priestly class that resisted the Hellenic penetration, in Palestine it was the priests of the temple who promoted Greek culture and advocated its adoption. Neglecting the sacrifices in the temple, they hurried off to Greek athletic games. It was the scribes of the synagogue who held to the traditional position. Temple and synagogue, priests and scribal sages, prophets, were now opposed to each other. From a socioeconomic perspective, the patricians favoured the Hellenic position and the plebeians favoured the traditional Judaism. No aspect of Judaism was left unchallenged. The Hebrew Scriptures were translated into Greek, the Septuagint.

JUDAH UNDER HASMONAEAN RULE

Judah came under the control of the Ptolemies from Egypt, 301 BCE, in the aftermath of the break up of Alexander's empire. In the year 200 BCE a Jewish militia helped the Seleucids dislodge the Ptolemaic regiment from Jerusalem. The Seleucids immediately confirmed the rights and privileges of self-government and religious liberty that Jerusalem had previously enjoyed. Later they reversed that decision by royal edicts that imposed the adoption of several Hellenic forms. Bickerman (1966) pointed to the fact that such a course of action was rare in the ancient world, and also unprecedented in Greek civilisation. He insisted that the new High Priest, Menelaus, who saw force as the only means of imposing what needed to be done, engineered this imposition from the imperial power. In seeking imperial backing the High Priest was simply following the pattern set by Ezra and Nehemiah who on the basis of Persian sponsorship had imposed the Torah.

The enforcement of the Hellenist position required Seleucid military power and included persecution of the opposition, imprisonment and murder of some of their leaders, and all the attendant atrocities and obscenities of coercion. The folly and miscalculation of this course of action was soon evident in the Maccabean revolt, led by an old priest and his sons supported by those who took the traditionalist position. The Maccabean brothers and their supporters succeeded in their resistance and the Seleucids rescinded the edicts and restored religious liberty. This famous victory brought in its aftermath several outcomes that many who fought and resisted had not bargained for.

In the first instance Jonathan Maccabeus manoeuvred himself into the office of high priest. Simon Maccabeus, the third brother, successfully managed to make the office hereditary to the family based on the claim of descent from Zadoc, the first High Priest of Solomon's time. His son changed the government to that of a kingdom, and declared himself king. The long-standing ancient practice of amalgamating the offices of High Priest and King was now enacted in Jewish history, something not done even by David. The resurrection of the monarchy brought an end to the theocratic state. Judah was brought again within the prevailing political paradigm of the ancient world, that of the city-state ruled by a royal clan. To cap it all, the Hasmonaean monarchy succeeded in gaining political independence. Many Jews applauded, and were even ecstatic about this renewal of sovereignty after so long an experience of being a subject people.

The success of military operations that expanded territory equal to that of the original kingdom of Saul and David, briefly distracted attention and divided and muted opposition to this gross departure from the path and premise of the restoration. However, it could not be ignored that the prophets, the Torah, and the sacred literature that had been written since the restoration, had almost unanimously counselled against statehood founded on military might. However, kingship, kinship and ethnocentrism now combined to defeat the wisdom of the restorers, the traditions canonised in scripture and the voice of prophetic counsel.

The Hasmonaean princes, notwithstanding their multifarious departures from the very traditions from which they were liberating Israel, had to deal with the Greek question. The Hellenic position was now represented by the Sadducees and that of the Hasidim by their successors, the Pharisees. In the fight against the Seleucids the Hasidim had supported the Maccabees, who soon embraced the Hellenic faction and turned against their former allies, the Pharisees. They then carried out against the Pharisees persecution and atrocities similar to those that had fomented the revolt in the first place. However, the Pharisees enjoyed popular support and an assault against them could not be sustained without serious damage to the newly created monarchy. Hence in the reign of Queen Alexandria the persecution against the Pharisees was halted.

Following the death of Queen Alexandria in 65 BCE, conflicts engulfed the Hasmonaean clan itself. Two brothers engaged in a bitter struggle for the right to the throne, resulting in civil war. By then Rome was the new superpower in the ancient world. Unable to resolve the differences internally, the Hasmonaeans committed the very folly that had brought honour and prominence to their clan, but a practice that had numerous Hebrew precedents. They sought the solution from the superpower. Both pretenders turned to Pompeii, the Roman general in the region, in support of their cause. In the midst of his deliberation on the matter, a third party arrived requesting the abolition of the monarchy itself. In 63 BCE Pompeii imposed the solution that suited Rome. He invaded Judah, ended the period of independence, reduced Judah to the status of a vassal state again but retained the monarchy, installing the king of his choosing.

Greek cultural penetration was now compounded with Roman political rule. Judah now faced Goliath in a form never faced before: Greek reason and hedonism administered with Roman efficiency and law. However, the greater problems for Judaism were from within and not from without. The prophetically discredited institution of the monarchy had been reinstated. It suffered from the same social and spiritual distance from the people, as was the case in the past. The congregation was hopelessly divided into sects. Further, the Hasmonaean experiment with independence had reactivated long dormant nationalist resentments against the vassal status. External cultural penetration and political strength were now matched against internal spiritual weaknesses through sectarianism and intolerance.

Sovereignty and independence had removed the external force that had long maintained internal unity. The intolerance, noted by the Greeks, that characterised the Jewish outlook to other peoples and religions, was now refocused inside Judaism itself. Congregations became hardened into sects each firmly persuaded of its monopoly on universal truth. Each sect was resolute in its intolerance of the views of others. Minutiae of the Law were given exaggerated importance and often became the cause of fatal battles. Sects included the ascetic and monastic Essenes, the anti-ecclesiastic New Covenantors, the Morning Bathers, the Water Drinkers, the Worshipers at Sunrise and no less than a score of other tiny but determined groups (Finkelstein 1938). Judaism and the kingdom were splintered into factions holding to their own views without an overriding unifying vision.

While there were numerous factions, many emphasising minute differences, probably four basic tendencies can be identified. First, the withdrawal from active engagement to perfect the faith in isolation, as exemplified by the Essenes. Second, conforming and accommodating to the dictates and exigencies of imperial rule as typified by the Sadducees. Third, detachment from the social and political realities except in circumstances where they impinged on the practice of the faith, as exemplified by the Hasidim. Fourth, engagement with the social and political concerns of the people to the point of challenging the imperial power, as typified by the Zealots.

Neusner's assertion that there is not a single Judaism, but several Judaisms, that none stands in linear or incremental to any other, but that each repeats the paradigmatic experience documented by Ezra and Nehemiah with respect to the Babylonian captivity seems applicable here. To this should be added the observation that each Judaism is an authentic lived experience, which enacts its own interpretation of its predecessors and leaves its own legacy for posterity. The Judaism of the Maccabees appeared to have committed its own transgression. What was to follow immediately was the punishment administered by Rome, which Judaisms of that time would of necessity experience. Suffering, atonement and reconciliation would be even further in the future, for even other Judaisms to deal with.

THE PERIOD UNDER ROMAN RULE

Faced with the complexity of this situation it is little wonder that during the period of Roman rule the people looked to Messiah for answers, for only He could resolve the magnitude of challenges that had to be met. Much of the Apocalyptic literature written in this period manifests the preoccupation with the coming of Messiah. The question of whether Messiah did come and did provide the answers to these profound questions is a matter of fundamental disagreement between Judaism and Christianity. Ebner (1956) noted that two currents of thought were noticeable. One spoke to the universal human experience and associated the Messiah with a period of spiritual reawakening.

The other concerned itself with the immediate restitution of the Davidic dynasty and the vindication of Israel's chosenhood. Christianity arose from the first. However, since it did not satisfy the nationalistic element in Israel's Messianic belief, it was incapable of becoming popular among the Jews. The second became the line that most Jews followed and ended in the dispersion as Rome decimated Judah.

The relationship between Judah and Rome could be appropriately summed up in one word, war! First, in 63 BCE Judah fought the Roman army that invaded the country and ended its flirtation with independence. Judging from both the history of Israel and the difference in military might one would have expected that that first war would be the end of the matter until a new imperial power arose. However, this was not the case. It is incredible to think that this small city-state located in the hills of Palestine had the audacity to challenge the might of the Roman empire at its peak. But it did so on two other occasions. On the first occasion Rome responded by destroying Jerusalem and the Temple in 70 CE. On the second occasion many Jews believing that Messiah had come in the form of Bar Kokhba challenged Rome yet again in 132 CE. At the end of that war in 135 CE Rome not only completed the destruction of Jerusalem but devastated most of Judea and forbade Jews to even enter Jerusalem. This was not only exile but also dispersion.

A BRIEF ELEGY

The elegy here is not for Judaism or Judah, for Judaism still lives and Israel was reborn. Jews are back in Jerusalem. The elegy is for Rome that died, and with it the civilisation of the ancient world based on the political paradigm of the city-state, the cosmology of polytheism, the philosophies of hedonism and materialism and the social institution of slavery. The only aspect of Rome that lives comes from its dying embrace of Christianity, its deathbed confession so to speak. The mismatch in political power between Rome and Judah gave all the appearances of another occasion when Goliath won. Jerusalem, the city, including the palace and the temple were destroyed. Jews were dispersed as a people without a city and a state. But from the perspective of the pious, David won. Not David the king, but the David of prophetic vision whose house had embraced a universalistic religion, from which two others were to rise.

Symbolically, the confrontation between Judaism and Rome was one between the old and the new. Rome represented the old order of ancient civilisation, started at Sumer, which Greece and itself, in different ways, had brought to its highest expressions. The new order, in the form of Judaism, expressed a new view of God and humanity, a new framework for societal organisation and a new world-view. The old order was finishing its course in Rome. The new order was beginning in Judaism. The new was arising within the old. Only the most discerning could have seen it. Also the confrontation between Rome and Judaism symbolically represented the confrontation between reality and mysticism, reason and revelation, a perennial conflict in human experience.

However, the new world-views of humanity did not arise in circumstances that can be romanticised. They emerged in circumstances of war, defeat, captivity, exile, fear, schisms, intrigue, distrust, intolerance and hate. In situations manifesting the worst in human nature, the loftiest conceptions of that nature and God emerged. The contrast invokes mystery, the very core of religious experience. Defeat, captivity, exile and fear of oblivion as a people, were the midwives of Judaism. Sectarian strife, civil war, national defeat, imperial oppression, palace intrigue, religious intolerance, injustice, atrocities and hate were the attendants at the birth of Christianity. War not peace, poverty not prosperity, marginality not centrality, colonial dependence not imperial power, adversity not sufficiency, pain not pleasure, suffering not well being were the correlates of divine revelation. This is not to suggest that there is any sadistic element in revelation. Rather, it is to observe that circumstances of manifest mortality, weakness and tragedy appear to be related to times when humans tend to see beyond self and listen to other than reason.

THE SOCIAL STRUCTURE OF JEWISH SOCIETY

Whether one accepts the conquest or the voluntary migration approach to the formation of ancient Israel, or some intermediate position, early settlements were established in under-developed, rugged, rocky and under-watered hill country. Group survival depended upon large families living and staying together to supply the labour and defence requirements. Clusters of dwellings catered to extended families. Household units were relatively autonomous and self-reliant. Each had its own storage, commodity processing capabilities and was relatively isolated from its neighbours through the absence of public works (Meyers 1989).

The units of social organisation were the extended family, clan and tribe. The locus of power was the extended family, at the bottom of the lineage organisation, manifesting a fair measure of equality from the relatively flat and loose structure of the organisation. Bird (1989) reconstructed the evolution of the society of ancient Israel as follows:

1. Village agrarian society engaged in diversified subsistence cultivation supplemented by livestock husbandry was originally largely self-reliant, self-sufficient and autonomous.

2. With the expansion of population these autonomous villages were increasingly drawn into a market economy dominated by urban political centres influenced by external military and trade relations.

3. From extended families the movement was into the formation of larger kinship units of clans and tribes, then into a confederation of tribes and finally into the monarchic state through the transitional chiefdom of Saul's kingship.

4. The fracture into two separate and often hostile states, Israel and Judah, did not alter the underlying social organisation of either state, but simply marked the division in tribal associations. The defining features of the monarchic state were urbanisation, centralisation and stratification.

5. The final period was marked by colonial dependence, with local autonomy in religious and cultural life, in which Jerusalem retained priority.

There are three features of Jewish society that remained unchanged for the period covered by this study. While at different times there may have been shifts in degrees of their effect, or the numbers affected, these three factors combined to give the society is shape and texture. These three features were kinship, geography and land. Drazin (1940) noted that after the restoration the Jews who returned found that large tracts of land had come under the ownership of foreigners who laid claim to them. Further, that there was not enough land for all the Jews, hence many had to seek other forms of livelihood through becoming artisans, craftsmen, traders or hired labourers. Thus the Babylonian captivity and the Persian restoration fundamentally altered the composition of the society particularly in relation to the proportion of the population that owned and lived by the land, and those that were landless.

Finkelstein (1938) gave a full description of the social structure of the society, which will be summarised here in relation to geographical areas.

JERUSALEM

Jerusalem had only about ten per cent of the population of the country, 75,000 approximately in the first century BCE, but enjoyed an importance greatly in excess of this proportion. Jerusalem had no second city that was its rival. In the state of Judah, it was set as a huge head with fascinating deformity upon a meagre body. The temple was the heart of the city. Among its records were carefully maintained genealogies of the families and clans of the two tribes that constituted the state, Benjamin and Judah. The characteristics of the social groups that comprised the city could be summarised as follows:

a) Large landowners constituted a lay nobility. Their estates worked by slaves, hired men and tenants from whom they collected rent. These patricians married within their own clans. So prevalent were such marriages that plebeian sects, in their resentment, declared marriages between uncles and nieces incestuous. These families were more willing to manumit their slaves and marry their grown daughters to them than to marry outsiders. Most of the patricians were unlearned. Making a sign, instead of writing one's name, was so common among them, that the use of the seal became a symbol of nobility. In style and views, they adopted the ways of the external power whether Persia, Greece, Egypt or Rome. Their intimates were the officials of these powers stationed in the city. Prestige was measured in acres, and their lifestyle marked by opulence. To the rest of the city, they were viewed as ignorant and boorish but wealthy. However, many men and women from among them were engaged in numerous charities and humanitarian works. They also invited the poor when they had feasts and assisted poor boys to be raised in accordance with Levitical purity.

b)   Priests constituted a nobility separate and distinct from the patricians, of whom they were not tools. Priestly office was inherited including that of the High Priest. When the Hasmoneans ousted the High Priest of that time they, or their clients, invented a genealogy to legitimise this action and perpetuate the acquisition. The vast majority of the priestly families were independently wealthy. While the Torah prohibited priests from owning land, ingenious interpretation of the scriptures rendered this inapplicable by stating that the biblical injunction applied when priests were from a single tribe and was with reference to that situation but not to individual ownership. They were as unlearned as the patricians. In the last days of the Temple there were High Priests who could not read the Bible. They also practised marriage within the priestly families and hedged this around with law. They were the only Jews who did not marry proselyte women. Their daughters could not marry members of the laity. Priestly views and cultural orientation were similar to those of the patricians. However, solidarity within the group was not total. Those clans with the greatest advantages did everything to maintain and enhance these advantages, resulting over time in a few priestly families becoming impoverished.

c)   The Levites were the plebeians of the Temple. They were landless. They received their sustenance through wages paid from the tithes given by the faithful and decreed by the *Torah*. Like the priests their positions were inherited from one generation to the next. Indeed, Levites were the first priests in Israel. However, the Zadocites displaced them during the period of the unified kingdom. Notwithstanding this displacement they had remained faithful to their heritage of dedication to Yahweh and His worship. Over time Levites were divided into singers and gatekeepers in the Temple. They maintained these distinctions among themselves. They led the opposition to the nobility inside and outside the Temple. Levites were an effective force in spreading the ideals of equality and liberty of thought among the people. In this regard they found common cause with the plebeian elements in the city.

d) Artisans, merchants/traders, scribes, poets, prophets and scholars were the plebeians of the city. Their houses were located in the narrow streets, less auspicious areas and even in the slums. They differed from the nobility not only in wealth and occupation but also in material culture. This was not only marked in differences in marriage customs, funerary rites and festival observances but also with respect to the embrace of learning. They regarded themselves and were the intellectual superiors of both the priestly and lay nobility. In actual fact they represented solidarity of opposition to the spiritual authority and economic dominance of the nobility. In addition, they did not accept the manners or the culture of the patricians as respectable standards. As the mass of the population they imposed their own forms and norms as standards. While as a group they struggled to maintain their cultural forms against economic adversity, the market place of Jerusalem was engaged not only in the exchanges of goods but also religious and intellectual ideals and ideas. The market was the intellectual, cultural and religious dynamo of the city. If Jerusalem became the Holy City it was the result of the masses of the slums, supported by the Levites of the Temple.

e) Slaves occupied the lowest status and rank in the city. As a group they were culturally ineffective.

The various groups in Jerusalem appeared to have been united around what could be called a Jerusalem ideology. At least three elements formed this ideology. First, this Jebusite city, appropriated by David, acquired a royal theology centred on the concept of the House of David. Probably it had notions of royal roots from its Jebusite origins, before David. Second, associated with this royal theology was the notion of its inviolability. Come what may Jerusalem would remain, it would stand forever. Third, as the site in which the Temple was located, Jerusalem was the geographical centre not only of Judaism but the world.

THE PROVINCES

The division between Jerusalem and the rest of the country, the provinces, was not only geographical. From as early as 835 BCE this difference is recorded when after the revolt against Queen Athaliah the historian of the period reported that all the people of the land rejoiced, but the city was quiet. While this difference in views and interpretation of events remained, the relative relationships between city and province changed over time, revealing the social structures, attitudes and antagonism embedded in them.

Jerusalem, the Jebusite city, was outside the traditional territory of Israel. It was captured and converted into the capital city by David. Its status and position therefore depended on the monarchy and its supporters, since Jerusalem had no indigenous integrity within Israel. The main and most loyal supporters of the monarchy, and therefore of Jerusalem, were the clans of the provinces of Judea and the Transjordan, Galilee. The large landowners, the gentry, of the provinces were both powerful and highly respected. They paid the bulk of the taxes, provided most of the militia and were major players in plotting the course of Judah's history. While the princes and nobles usually led them, it was with their consent and agreement on the objectives. From as early as the ninth century BCE they formed a corporate body with recognised rights, privileges and power and accordingly were labelled the *am ha-arez*, then a term of respect and honour. They assured the internal legitimacy of Jerusalem within Israel. They remained faithful to Jerusalem when the other tribes withdrew and established their city elsewhere. They led repeated revolts against Assyria and Babylonia, ending with the destruction of the temple and Jerusalem.

With the restoration under Persia, the relationship between Jerusalem and the provinces changed radically. Jerusalem's existence was now assured by external dependence on the imperial power. The nationalism of the *am ha-arez* was out of step with the times, their military support was superfluous and their taxes brought no prestige. In addition, the wealth of the *am ha-arez* declined relative to the patrician landowners, and there was no compensating increase in their learning. The term *am ha-arez* was no longer a title of honour and prestige and progressively changed from to its literal meaning, people of the land, to more negative combinations of meanings including brutish, villager, dunce, unconverted, ignorant and illiterate. The term was no longer used simply for the gentry and leaders but applied to all provincials.

From the height of esteem as loyalists and patriots *am ha-arez* descended to being despised as the lowly unlettered country folk, the proverbial division between sophisticated city folk and so-called country people. In this regard all levels of Jerusalem society considered themselves superior to the people of the provinces, who returned the compliment in their own manner and with their own opprobrium.

But like everything else in Israel, the contempt expressed by Jerusalem city folk towards the provincials, did not remain only social, but became codified in ritual and law. The laws established by the Levitical code was for the entire country, but could most easily be observed in Jerusalem. While some acts of ritual contamination could be rectified by ritual bathing, others required visits to Jerusalem, ceremonial sacrifices and even sprinkling of the ashes of the 'red heifer'. Even the pious among provincials by virtue of distance, geography and transportation could not comply with these requirements. They were therefore declared ritually impure. Social contempt for the *am ha-arez* now mingled with ritual sanction.

The distance between Jerusalem and the provinces widened further with respect to taxes. The Torah required two taxes of ten per cent; the first to be paid for the support of the Levites, the second to remain with the giver but to be spent in Jerusalem. The *am ha-arez* were suspected of refusing to give the first or to take the second to Jerusalem. The Jerusalem folks considered such flagrant disregard for scripture as nothing short of heresy.

To cap it all the *am ha-arez* neglected to participate in all ceremonies in which writing was involved. These included ceremonies involving the wearing of the phylacteries and placing scrolls on the doorposts. The reluctance to participate was related to the inability to read and to lack of knowledge of the ceremonial responses. In addition to social contempt, ritual impurity, suspicion of heresy, the *am ha-arez* became recognised, as those who did not wear the phylacteries or fringes and could not read the Shema.

The *am ha-arez* was not a uniform group by any means. Wide differences of wealth and culture separated the rugged peasant farmers occupying the relatively unproductive rocky plots of the Judean hills from the large landowners of the plains. They were divided between the tribes of Judah and Benjamin. Neither were the *am ha-arez* uniform in their views. The wealthy farmers looked to the patrician priests for guidance. The peasant farmers were influenced by the Levites of the Temple and artisans and traders in the Jerusalem market. It was among them that Christianity first took root. Several sects found room among them. On the whole, however, they were the zealots of Jewish nationalism.

The differences in views between the citizens of Jerusalem and the provincials were not confined only to differences in perception and practices. One authority of the law maintained that the *am ha-arez* should be restricted in the following ways:

     i)   Not to be asked to be a witness.
     ii)   Not to be permitted to testify.
     iii) Not to be entrusted with secrets.
     iv) Not to be appointed trustees of the estates of orphans.
     v)   Not to be permitted trustees of charities or funds.
     vi) Not to accompany one on one's way.

Rabbi Meir a leading scholar maintained that to marry one's daughter to an *am ha-arez* was like unto binding her before a lion. He maintained that the *am ha-arez* would beat his wife and then embrace her. Yet another authority insisted that on no account should a man marry his daughter to an *am ha-arez* because they were despicable and their wives were like vermin. To say that the weight of social prejudice was against the *am ha-arez* is to state the obvious.

Notwithstanding the views of their more sophisticated countrymen, the *am ha-arez* defended Jerusalem and fought the Romans against all odds. They suffered most under Herodian and Roman oppression. It was mostly their land that was confiscated and their families that were impoverished. It was their leaders who were tortured, crucified and thrown to the lions. It was mostly their children who were sold into slavery and driven into exile. The Romans hated them for their nationalism. The Jewish scholars despised them for their 'ignorance' and in their suffering they did not receive solace from the respect of their countrymen.

The relation between the former city, especially the scholars, and the *am ha-arez* was not advanced when in the midst of the war with the Romans between 68 and 70 CE, the scholars, through Johanan Ben Zakkai, convinced the Romans of their pacifism and won concessions to relocate the Sanhredin and the college to a site in Jabneh. While this move appeared wise, far-sighted and highly skilful, to the *am ha-arez* it was nothing short of betrayal.

The destruction of Jerusalem, not only levelled the temple and the city, it shortened the social distance between *am ha-arez* and the city folk. They all now lived together in close proximity in provincial territory. The ritual distinction was eliminated, since they were all ritually impure. Centuries of animosity could not be expected to vanish overnight. Hence hostility and animosity marked the forced association on provincial soil.

The polarities of these intense feelings were most marked between the scholars and *am ha-arez*. One of the foremost scholars of the time Rabbi Eliezer remarked that if the *am ha-arez* did not need scholars for purposes of trade, they would slaughter them. Another remarked that the hate, which the *am ha-arez* bore towards the scholar, was greater than that which the pagan bore toward Jews. But this hatred was not one sided. In a period of famine R. Judah, prince among scholars of the Tannaim, opened his granary but excluded the *am ha-arez* from the distribution. As these two hostile groups of Jews faced each other on provincial soil, among the few social bridges between them were the institution of the elementary school and the occupation of elementary school teaching.

GENDER IN JUDAISM AND ANCIENT JEWISH SOCIETY

Frerichs (1989) insisted that gender in ancient Jewish society has to be seen and understood in the context of a small marginal vassal state struggling to maintain itself and to ensure the survival of its people against the pressures of power and oppression. As an agrarian society with little industrial expression it did not have the incentive of great wealth to ameliorate social challenges. Meyers (1989) highlighted several of the methodological problems in reconstructing gender relations in ancient Israel in that men wrote most of the Bible records. Also, the Bible was mainly concerned with public and national life which was almost entirely male dominated. Further, ethnographic research shows disparity between societal ideology and social behaviour, as well as between normal customs and normative roles.

In this light Meyers maintained that contemporary assumptions of male prerogatives and privileges being more valued than those of females should not be superimposed on ancient society. Likewise the notion of patriarchy, with the implicit connotation of a hierarchical arrangement that devalues females cannot be easily applied to ancient Israel. Accordingly, patriarchy and its assumption of male superiority should be avoided in any analysis of ancient Israel. Meyers' reconstruction of gender relations in ancient Israel can be summarised as follows:

1. Large families were an advantage because of the labour requirement in the rugged hill country. Fertility was therefore emphasised and the maternal instinct was strong.
2. High labour demands required that women be involved in agrarian work, especially in circumstances where men were engaged in sporadic military encounters. However, productive and reproductive roles of women were not incompatible, since child bearing did not disrupt the agrarian routines of life.
3. The relative absence of imported ware or any other signs of a market economy highlight the importance of household production in the villages and their relative self-sufficiency.
4. The fact that dwelling units were approximately the same size points to an egalitarian social structure within the villages.
5. The housing units were clusters, indicating that they were not nuclear but extended family units. In other words residential compounds with several dwellings sharing the same production, processing and storage facilities.
6. In this setting where women were involved in all aspects of economic life, and lived in large extended family units, senior females would have some measure of authority over younger males and females.
7. In these circumstances women had near parity with men and gender complementarity probably existed. The Book of Judges, with its several stories of women's involvement in all aspects of the life of the Israelites appears to give some biblical support to the archaeological evidence and this anthropological reconstruction.

Bird (1989) took a very different position from Meyers. She insisted that ancient Israel belonged to the group of ancient societies that typically manifested relatively sharp sexual division of labour and role differentiation marked by significant asymmetry of power and prestige. At the same time women were restricted not only in the public sphere, but they also lacked authority in the domestic sphere where formal authority rested with either father or husband. Women had little or no role in decision-making. As a consequence of this asymmetry men determined culture and values that saw their views and position as universal and women's as special or aberrant. In Bird's view failure to recognise the asymmetry in power and authority, such as in ancient Israel, leads to misreading of data by interpreting complementarity of roles, especially when accompanied by expressions of honour, as evidence of equality. At the same time, overemphasis on the structures and symbols of power would blind interpreters to the informal exercise of power by women and to authority exercised by wisdom and affection.

From her survey of religious practices in ancient Israel Bird concluded that:

·   Male participation was predominant and leadership was almost exclusively male in public worship and kin-based communal observances.

- Women were not excluded but were not obliged to participate while men were obligated.
- Family worship replicated public worship and communal observances in terms of male leadership and obligation.
- There was evidence of female cultic specialists, for example, Miriam the sister of Moses and the sacred prostitutes, but these were exceptional cases.

Biale (1984) observed that while biblical laws reflected a clear social order, they do not appear to have flowed from systematic legislative thinking. There was no explicit formulation in the Bible that excluded or exempted men or women in any set of obligations. Mishnah, however, did contain an explicit statement about the differences in legal obligations between men and women and attempted to systematise them. These can be set out as follows:

a)   All positive commandments that are time-bound, men are obligated and women are exempted.
b)   All positive commandments, which are not time-bound, are binding on both men and women.
c)   All negative commandments, whether they are time-bound or not, are binding on men and women.

Time bound exemptions of women from the positive commandments have been explained on two bases. First, on grounds of practical considerations of the duties of housewives and mothers and the difficulties that these present in fulfilling these requirements of the law. Second, on theological grounds by reference to the fact that in these matters women are obligated to both God and their husbands and therefore required to serve two masters. To resolve the conflict on the basis that no one can serve two masters, the requirements to God are relaxed. God not being as jealous as husbands bows out of the competition.

Biale took the position that the difference between the halakhic and religious positions of women demonstrate the strain between two visions of women evident in scripture and most aspects of Jewish life. On the one hand there is the fundamental ethical and theological position, held by God, which recognises no stratification or hierarchy among human beings and therefore no difference between men and women. On the other hand, husbands hold to a view rooted in daily life and social reality in which women are inferior to men in economic standing, social status, legal rights and importance. This tension appears in the two creation stories in Genesis. One account shows men and women created in equality, the other account related woman's creation in relation to man's need. From Biale's perspective these two versions haunt all attempts to interpret gender in Jewish and Israelite society.

Niditch (1991) summarised the interpretation of the portrayal of women in law and society in the Hebrew Bible as follows:

- Women were legally governed by their fathers before marriage, and their husbands afterwards.
- Before marriage she should be a virgin and after it a faithful wife. Sexual activity before marriage and adultery during marriage brought the same punishment, death by stoning.
- Adultery by the man was only with another man's wife and not with an unmarried woman. In adultery the man's crime was that of theft. Seduction or rape of a virgin required the payment of bride price to the woman's father. In both instances it was property rights that were abused which was remedied by appropriate payments.
- Barren wives or women who displeased their husbands could be divorced.
- Wives were entirely subject to the will of their husbands in divorce. However, the courts could direct, on the request of the wives, that husbands divorce them.
- Married women who did not have children became particularly marginalised. It was children that formed the bond with her husband's clan. Young childless widows constituted a particular problem, which was regularised by marriage to his brother and the raising up of children in the name of the dead husband. However, the widow was subject to the will of the brother who had the alternative to release her or marry her by the ceremony of halitza; without the former a widow could not remarry in the lifetime of her husband's brothers.
- The birth of a child to a woman late in life who had been regarded as barren was a favourite motif, marking the birth of heroes, as was the case in several other cultures. Childlessness is presented as a special cultural worry.
- Women did not normally inherit property except in families in which there were no sons, and in special cases where wives inherited their husband's property.
- Laws of purity declared menstruating women unclean and forbade women having sexual intercourse for seven days. During the period of menstruating sitting in the same seat, lying in the same bed constituted contamination. Men having sex with women during this period were regarded as impure for seven days.
- After the birth of a son mothers were unclean for seven days and needed a further 33 days for blood to become pure again. The period for the birth of a daughter was double, 14 and 66 days respectively.
- Men were obligated to perform conjugal duties pointing to power of women in the private sphere.
- Prostitution was outlawed.

To this list Drazin (1940) added the following restrictions:

a)   Women were not permitted as witnesses or judges.
b)   They, like slaves and minors, were exempted from observing several biblical precepts.
c)   Women were exempted from studying the Torah.
d)   They could not be counted in the quorum of ten adults necessary for divine services in the synagogue.
e)   Women had a separate gallery in the temple, and were segregated from men.
f)   Women could not wear the phylacteries or the fringes.
g)   Polygamy was permitted only to the Jewish man.

Drazin argued that while these constituted restrictions and handicaps on women it would be erroneous to assume, on the basis of these, that women were considered inferior to men in ancient Israel. From his perspective these handicaps and restrictions before the law should not be used to infer social status. For example, women were placed on the same level as minors and slaves in terms of being judges and witnesses, but so too was the king of Israel. He could not serve as a judge or be a witness. If the king's social status cannot be inferred from his position in the law neither could women's. Again, while the law permitted polygamy not a single case was ever reported. It was permitted legally but not practised socially. In addition, every negative statement with respect to women's position could be matched by a positive statement. In Drazin's view both the Bible and Mishnah had to be understood in their overall context before gender inferences could be made.

Drazin explained the observed preference among parents for sons rather than daughters on two grounds. First, for reasons of religious piety parents preferred sons because they could worship God to the fullest extent. Second, because of the care and anxieties related to bringing up daughters. With respect to the latter he quoted Ben Sira as follows:

The father waketh for the daughter when no man knoweth, and care for her taketh away sleep: when she is young lest she pass away the flower of her age; and being married lest she should be hated; in her virginity, lest she be defiled and gotten with child in her father's house; and having a husband, lest she should misbehave herself; and when she is married, less she should be barren.

A morally lax daughter was the greatest calamity that could befall parents.

Zolty (1993) took a similar position to Drazin on several points. For example, she reviewed several sources and authorities to show that exemptions of women from the positive commandments did not represent exclusion since women could perform them if they so chose. The exemption she maintained did not represent discrimination, which is negative, but made a positive distinction, based upon practical considerations, which in no way either diminished women or accorded them a lower status. Similarly Morris (1937) argued that while women in their roles as daughters and wives were marginalised, in their role as mothers they were given equality with fathers in many aspects of the law and also given great social recognition. Women's position in Israelite society had to be assessed in relation to all the roles they performed, and their status could not be derived from any single role or relationship.

Wegner (1991) developed this line of argument even further with the distinction she drew between dependent and autonomous women and their treatment by the law. She defined minor daughters, wives and levirate widows as dependent women whose biological functions were owned by father, husband and brother-in-law respectively. In this respect they were treated as chattels. If a minor daughter were raped damages were paid to the father because this lowered her market value and diminished his returns with respect to bride-price. Likewise, the husband had exclusive rights to the sexuality of his wife. However, outside of the area of sexuality in which they were chattels, the law recognised them as persons. For example, the property that a wife brought to the marriage was hers and could not be sold by her husband without her consent. Further she could appoint agents to act on her behalf and could act as her husband's agent.

In the case of autonomous women – adult daughters, widows and divorcees – they owned their own sexuality. They negotiated their own marriages. In the case of rape, damages were paid to them. They also enjoyed the rights as persons as other women. In this regard, they were fully recognised as persons before the law, in that there was no duality with respect to ownership since their sexuality belonged to themselves. From this perspective it would be dangerous to generalise women's status in the society without reference to whether they were autonomous or dependent. Among dependent women mothers had the highest status and were revered.

Castle (1961) noted that the family was central in Jewish society and there were several aspects related to family and gender that marked Jewish society as different from other ancient societies, including Greece and Rome, and their contemporaries in Palestine. For example, infanticide was almost unknown among the Israelites although it was quite common in Palestine among non-Jewish communities. Where child sacrifices are mentioned in the Bible, it is to condemn the practice. Hebrew law recognised the child's right to his own life centuries before similar legal enactment in Roman law, which only came about in the sixth century CE as a result of sustained Christian pressure. Very early Hebrew law removed the right of fathers to kill their children. Parents could take a rebellious son before the Elders, and if they accepted the report, the erring son would be stoned to death. It was the elders not the father who decided and administered capital punishment. This represented a diminution of patriarchal power among Jewish men, similar curtailment of which had limited precedent in the ancient world.

Kraemer (1991) in a study of Jewish women in the Diaspora in late antiquity noted that such women appeared to have lived outside several of the restraints and constraints of their peers in Palestine. He cited the case of Rufina, a Jewish woman of some means, with a Latin name, who lived in Asia Minor in the city of Smyrna. She was head of the synagogue, head of her family, prominent in the public sphere and took action without reference to any man, whether father, brother, husband or son. Reviewing the data on the seclusion of Jewish women, Kraemer concluded that the evidence was contradictory and suggested the following:

- Some women did live their lives in relative seclusion, rarely leaving their homes except in carefully defined circumstances.
- Social class, geography and religious perspective were critical factors determining seclusion.
- Seclusion may have been limited to middle and upper class women.
- In some communities only unmarried women were secluded, to guarantee their chastity. After marriage they participated in public activities.

Cantor (1995) attempted to reconcile these two contrasting interpretations of gender in ancient Israel and Jewish society in general. She took the position that Jewish society was always organised as a patriarchy and belonged to that genre in which men were dominant and women were more or less powerless. However, she contended that patriarchy exists on a continuum with considerable variation in eras and territories. As such it is necessary to analyse the specific character of patriarchy in a particular context.

In Cantor's view the experience of Jewish history, as a society, parallels women's experience under patriarchy. For almost all of their history they were a small beleaguered nation, or lived in small communities in the Diaspora, in the midst of hostile populations. As a vassal state or minority community, Jews often lacked the capacity to defend themselves from attack. In these circumstances Jewish society reformed patriarchy in several important respects. These reforms were imposed by the necessity to ensure communal cohesion as the foundation for survival in these hostile circumstances.

Cantor's reconstruction of gender role definitions of reformed patriarchy in Jewish society during its history as a country in Palestine, and in the period of dispersion following 70 CE, can be summarised as follows:

1. The emergency of exile required that the home and community be a safe haven, hence male violence had to be eliminated. Male dominance was therefore maintained but male power was stripped of the use of force and redefined as the power of the mind and intellect. Masculinity was redefined as spiritual resistance: the intellectual labour of studying the Torah, performing public and communal rituals, ceremonies and other observances.

2. Women's roles and femininity were redefined as enabler, with two distinct components. First, to facilitate what men decided was their

work and enable this by maintaining the complex home support systems. Second, to accept and endure exclusion from the public sphere of men's work turf so that in the absence of women from it, manhood could be defined.

3. Third, breadwinning, which defines masculinity under classical patriarchy, was gender neutral in many periods of Jewish history. Women in these periods were responsible for the entire support of the family, as part of their enabling role, thus allowing men to devote themselves to spiritual resistance.

4. Women were encouraged to be strong, assertive and resourceful in their enabling role instead of being passive, helpless and dependent. This has led to an erroneous view of matriarchy in Jewish society. Jewish women never exercised power but rather enabled men as they perceived and defined community interest. In this regard women's roles were always altruistic, that is, in the interest of the community.

While Cantor's reconstruction of gender relations within the overall context of patriarchy goes a far way in reconciling the conflicting positions recited previously, and advances understanding of the processes involved, it probably overemphasises the spiritual elements in the reforms identified and underestimates the material considerations. Wealth, office and occupations were inherited throughout the history of Jewish society. Through inheritance advantage was passed from one generation to the next, in circumstances where these were not in abundance. It would appear that it was in the interest of every one in the clans, men and women, to co-operate to preserve their advantage. The preservation of patriarchal structures seemed to have served both the internal position of clans, as well as assisted the external defence of the community as a whole. Both of these processes, spiritual defence and the continued inheritance of material advantage, maintained patriarchy, if even in a reformed structure of gender relations.

THE EVOLUTION OF SCHOOLING

The only schools mentioned in the Bible were those of the prophets. The exact form of those schools is not known. Greenberg (1966) presumed that priests and Levites had a school seeing that they started their occupation at age 30 and 25 years respectively. He was also of the opinion that scribes must have received formal training during the monarchical period probably at an academy that was part of the royal court. However, there is no historical record of any of these institutions, apart from the reference to the school of the prophets. The possibility also exists that because these occupations were inherited, and because the Israelite tradition was for fathers to instruct their sons, the home and not formal institutions could have been the source of education and training. The biblical record could indeed be accurate in reporting that the only schools that existed during the monarchical period were those of the prophets.

The formal school system, associated with the state, was created in Judah after the restoration in 536 BCE. It was the principal means used to achieve the objective of preserving Israel through religion (Swift 1919). Prior development to organising and institutionalising education included the following:

1. The development of the complete code of the law, the priestly code.
2. The adoption of the Pentateuch as the constitution of the state, which made its observance binding on all and therefore knowledge of it a prime necessity.
3. The growth of a sacred literature, oral and written, which became along with the law the educational content to be transmitted.

The creation of formal schooling was part of the overall reforms, introduced by Ezra, which inaugurated Judaism, made the Torah the constitution of the state and the foundation of congregational and spiritual life, and required all citizens to comply through the legal requirements of the theocratic state that had been created (Greenberg 1966). Formal schooling started with academies and not elementary schools. Following the ancient precedent, the creation of formal schooling in Judah was top down. However, by the time of the destruction of the Temple by the Romans in 70 CE a comprehensive educational system had evolved.

Drazin (1940) observed that the nationalistic ideal of the Second Commonwealth, as established by Ezra and Nehemiah, was to make religious education the goal of Jewish nationalism. Religious piety was founded on two pillars: a full knowledge of the law and strict observance of its tenets. Knowledge, character and conduct were inextricably linked. The evolution of the formal system of schooling to give effect to this ideal can be traced through three distinct periods: the reforms of the Great Assembly of 445 BCE, the reforms of Simon Ben Shetah in 75 BCE and the reforms of Joshua Ben Gamala 64 CE. Each of these periods will be discussed in relation to the different levels of the education system developed.

THE REFORMS OF THE GREAT ASSEMBLY

The Great Assembly of 445 BCE decreed that every spiritual leader of Israel should endeavour to secure large numbers of students to whom they should give advanced instruction in the law. This decree provided the basis for the founding of colleges. Prior to this it was customary for the great masters of the law in every generation to concentrate their efforts on teaching their sons, and if they were not capable of receiving such instruction, to find some unusually gifted student upon whom they would concentrate their efforts to hand down the Torah in its entirety. The reform was intended to widen access to Torah knowledge (Drazin 1940).

Drazin explained that because agriculture was a seasonal activity, Jews had sufficient time to advance their own education and instruct their children. However, with the rise of crafts and industry after the restoration, many people had to work year round to secure their livelihood and so had little time either to advance their own education or to instruct their young. Education suffered as a result. The decree of the Great Assembly was intended to provide education through schooling to many adults, through the great masters of the law, who previously devoted their efforts to a few individuals, mainly their sons. By instructing adults, youths and children would learn since it was the responsibility of fathers to teach their children.

Another explanation for the decree of the Great Assembly was that the selective process for higher learning was successful as long as prophecy flourished in Israel. With the decline in prophecy the Great Assembly feared that the masters might make erroneous choices, or that the chosen scholar might die young, before he had a chance to hand down the traditions, which would then be lost. Making education in the Torah more widely available was seen to be essential to its survival.

The Establishment of Academies

The academies that were expected to be established in Jerusalem by the great masters were expected to attract students from all over the country. However, the response to the reforms was not as overwhelming as expected. Academies located in Jerusalem were not easily accessible to residents from outside, the entry requirements were high and the costs involved were outside the means of most people. While several academies were established, they were all small institutions. Toward the end of the period of the Great Assembly these small academies were amalgamated into a single institution. This single college continued to operate in Jerusalem for over two hundred years (Drazin 1940).

This academy was built on the Temple mount and consisted mainly of one auditorium large enough to accommodate all the students. There were no separate classrooms. Its location allowed not only the members of the Sanhedrin, the highest Jewish judiciary tribunal, but also priests and Levites to participate in the discussions and polemics of the college. Sabbaths and holidays were the most convenient times for such interaction since the courts were not in session and the sacrificial services at the temple were minimal. The location of the academy also allowed students to be influenced by both the ceremonials of the temple and the operations of the court.

The entire academy operated as one class and all students were expected to attend all sessions and to participate in general discussions. Initially the academy had no seats. Teachers stood to deliver their lectures and students stood to receive them. The standing posture was regarded as a sign of reverence to the Torah and other scripture that was being studied. It was symbolic of the posture in which the law was received from God on Mount Sinai. After this custom proved a hardship on the students and seats were introduced, many older scholars felt that the 'glory of the Law ceased'

Greenberg (1966) pointed out that the Kenesset Ha-Geholah, the Great Assembly, exercised three-fold functions: as legislature, court and academy. The education of the prospective new masters of the law was obviously done within the context of the operation of the old masters who were enacting new legislation and rendering judgements on the basis of existing statutes. While a separate institution executed each of these functions they were integrated under the umbrella of the Great Assembly.

In 200 BCE, when the Seleucids became the dominant power, the Great Assembly was dissolved and replaced by the duumvirate, the Zugot. This came about from a new charter of the city of Jerusalem. One member of the Zugot was the president of the academy, while the other was the Father of the Court. This new arrangement separated the court and academy but also allowed each to relate to the other. The principle of learning the law in the context of the administration of the law was preserved. It would appear that the students of the academy in addition to formal instruction would observe the operations of the court, benefit from the knowledge of its personnel and even play minor roles in the research and deliberation leading to judgement on various issues.

Following reforms after 75 BCE there was a significant increase in the number of students available. The Zugot arrangement was terminated in 10 CE with the Sanhedrin taking the place of the court. The result was that the academy was divided in two and the last pair of Zugots, Hillel and Shammai, each presided over one academy. These two academies operated in Jerusalem until its destruction in 70 CE. In the heat of the battle with the Romans Johanan B Zakkai, through clever manoeuvrings, gained the permission of the general, Vespasian, to re-establish the academy at Jabneh. Both the academies of Hillel and Shammai were reunited into one academy under Zakkai's leadership. After the death of Zakkai, a number of his best students settled in other communities, gathered students and established academies. Accordingly, after the dispersion, academies of almost equal rank were established in Palestine, Babylonia and Rome. The academy system established during and immediately after the captivity not only continued during the period of the Second Commonwealth but continued into the exile after the destruction of Jerusalem and the second Temple.

It must be noted that, under Roman sponsorship, the academy established at Jabneh, and its successor in Palestine, exercised the function of court and legislative body for Jews remaining in Palestine. Instead of having 71 members in the Sanhedrin, the number of Sages was reduced to 23, however, their numbers could be augmented by advanced students of the academy as situations demanded. The Sages sat in a semi-circular row of 23 seats, and the advanced students in three similar rows of 23 seats each. The junior students sat in back rows or on the floor (Drazin 1940). In this respect the operation of the academy in Palestine after the destruction of Jerusalem resembled that of the Great Assembly after the restoration, except in its exact composition. Involvement in the judicial and legislative functions kept the academy, its staff and students, in contact with the daily life of the members of the communities, so that its purely intellectual pursuits were grounded in and guided by the demands of practical living (Greenberg 1966).

The Synagogue

The synagogue has been described as the greatest practical achievement of the Jewish people, (Morris 1937). Established as a meeting place, house of prayer and centre of instruction during the period of captivity, it became the focal point of community life in Judah after the restoration. Synagogues were established all over the country and were easily accessible. It was not only a fundamental part of devotional life but the centre for instruction of adults in the Torah. The synagogue was the first centre for popular or adult education ever created. Greenberg (1966) described the synagogue as the most democratic and universal Jewish educational institution outside the home.

Morris pointed out that once per week, on the Sabbath, most people would come to the synagogue where one would read and another explain some passage from the scriptures. The Great Assembly had decreed that the scriptures be read in synagogues every Monday and Thursday, market days, when many people were in the towns. By systematic reading, the entire scriptures could be covered in about two years. Itinerant teachers were also sent out from Jerusalem to offer instruction to the people, using the synagogue as the meeting place.

As knowledge and traditions increased, various schools of thought and methods of investigation arose around similarly minded scholars. The synagogue became the meeting place for such like-minded scholars and students interested in their views. The room of the synagogue in which these local lovers of the law met for their deliberations became known as a Bet Midrash, a house for studying and interpreting the Torah. This distinguished it from other rooms used for other purposes, for example, the Bet Tefilah, the room for prayer or the Bet Sefer, the room for instructing the young. In time a small collection of books, a library, became associated with the Bet Midrash (Greenberg 1966).

The Two Pronged Strategy

The twin elements of spreading knowledge of the Torah established by the Great Assembly were to democratise access to full knowledge through the creation of academies in Jerusalem, thus ensuring that there would always be several sages versed in the Torah in every generation, and to spread as much knowledge as possible to all families through the local synagogue in towns and large villages. These two prongs of the strategy broke radically from the previous educational premise of Israel, and that of all tribal systems. That premise was that education of the younger members of the tribe, clan or family, was the responsibility of the elders of that particular kinship collective.

One weakness of this approach was that to become a master of the law, one had to go to Jerusalem. In addition, because Jerusalem had the masters the informal dissemination of the Torah through the synagogues could be most effectively done there. Another weakness was the assumption that families and clans could be as effective in transmitting Torah knowledge of the Torah as they had been in transmitting the peculiar knowledge of their clan or tribe.

THE REFORMS OF SIMON BEN SHETAH

In 75 BCE Simon Ben Shetah introduced reforms that provided free education for males 16 to 17 years old. Scholars differ on the educational and institutional interpretation of these reforms. Swift (1919) came to the conclusion that they were to establish higher schools for orphan boys over 16 years old in Jerusalem and provincial towns. Morris (1937) was of the view that these reforms were to regularise and spread popular education particularly as this related to the Oral Law. Drazin (1940) was of the view that the Ben Shetah reforms established free and compulsory secondary schools for all male adolescents to prepare them for higher education. Ebner (1956) disagreed with these interpretations and insisted that these reforms, while directed to all adolescent males, were to provide elementary education.

Morris, Drazin and Ebner are agreed that the background to this reform was the factional strife of the Maccabean period. They are also agreed that Simon Ben Shetah, brother of Queen Alexandria, was the leader of the Pharisees, after the latter had been reinstated following their persecution by Hellenist priests and Hasmonean princes. Ebner's reconstruction of the factors leading to the reforms was as follows:

a)   While Jewish tradition dictated that parents were responsible for the education of their children, and should carry out this instruction themselves, many wealthy Jews employed private tutors to teach their children.

b)   Schools for children existed in Palestine, mainly Greek schools in Hellenist cities or in places with mixed populations. The advantages of public versus private instruction were obvious in terms of both economy and the time of fathers. Jews therefore adopted the Hellenistic practice but created their own type of school to avoid the dangers of Greek cultural penetration.

c)   The growing complexity of teaching the Torah, in light of the oral interpretation of the law, increasingly became an assignment that surpassed the ability of the average father. Teaching the Torah involved not only a literal translation from the Hebrew to the Aramaic vernacular, but also explanation in harmony with the oral interpretation of the law. It was therefore logical to replace the teaching of the father with a more competent professional teacher.

   d)   In the struggle between Sadducees and Pharisees for leadership in Jewish life, the founding of public schools constituted an important means to spread Pharisaic teaching among the people. During the revolt against Syrian rule the Pharisees, who enjoyed broad popular support, had fought with the Hasmonean princes. Subsequently, the Hasmonean rulers had turned to the Sadducees for support, and with that shift the Pharisees had been ejected from positions in public administration, the courts and temple organisation. In addition, many were slain or exiled. In the reign of Queen Salome Alexandria, 75–67 BCE, the situation was reversed. Pharisees were recalled and reinstated under the leadership of Simon Ben Shetah. They sought to entrench their position by securing lasting and widespread acceptance of their doctrines among the people.

   e)   The establishment of schools in all provincial towns was to ensure accessibility, the admission age was set at 16 or 17 years to allow older boys, who had not received any education, to be so instructed. These adolescents were beginners not advanced students. The level of education being delivered was elementary not secondary.

From Ebner's perspective the reforms sponsored by Ben Shetah were the commencement of the establishment of the elementary school system. They established a two-tier education system: elementary schools and academy. From Drazin's perspective they established a two-tier system, but the tiers were academy and secondary. In Morris's view a two-tier system was established: academic education for specialists and popular education for youths and adults.

THE JOSHUA BEN GAMALA REFORMS

Joshua Ben Gamala was high priest between 63 to 65 CE during a period of great turmoil and upheaval just before the cataclysmic events of 70 CE. He enacted legislation that decreed that every community should provide teachers for all boys over the ages of six or seven years old. One teacher should be provided for every twenty-five pupils. If the numbers exceeded twenty-five but were less than fifty then one teacher and an assistant should be provided. While the ordinance took immediate effect, it is doubtful than much in the way of implementation could have been done before 70 CE.

Drazin maintained that these reforms introduced the third level of the educational system, the elementary level. In his view the institutional evolution of education in Judah had proceeded from college, to secondary and finally to elementary over the period 536 BC to 70 CE. Ebner took the position that the Ben Gamala reforms completed what Ben Shatah had started by reducing the age of entry to six or seven years and specifying both community responsibility and the basis on which teachers should be provided since this constituted the greatest cost. All scholars are agreed that elementary schooling as a norm for

Jewish communities did not exist before 70 CE and was accomplishmed during the period that followed.

The available evidence seems to support Ebner in that at the time of the destruction of Jerusalem it was reported that there were 396 elementary schools. It is hardly likely that such a great number of schools, with teachers, could have been established in only six years. In Ebner's interpretation these schools would have been established over a period of just over a century, which appears more likely. In addition, elementary school teaching was a recognised occupation with a distinct social status prior to the destruction. This could not have emerged over a short time.

Eby and Arrowood (1940) interpreted the evidence very differently from Swift, Kretzmann, Drazen, Morris and Ebner. In their view the initial plan to set up colleges in Jerusalem was judged to have failed. This led to experimentation with a system of district academies for youths 16 to 17 years old as prescribed by Ben Shetah. This too failed. Ben Gamala therefore required elementary schools to be established throughout Palestine, and made attendance compulsory, in an attempt to establish a sound and comprehensive educational system.

THE INSTITUTIONAL LEGACY OF THE SECOND COMMONWEALTH

The elements of the education system that emerged in the Second Commonwealth were elementary schools, popular education provided through the synagogue, which included neophytes and scholars, and higher education in the form of an academy educating scholars and accommodating the judges of the law. These constituted the structures that Jews took with them into the period of statelessness. These three educational institutions were now to operate without a state, but in communities where Jews lived. The elementary school and the synagogue became the universal institutions, established in almost every Jewish community in the Diaspora. Academies, on the other hand, were established in particular centres to which Jews from all parts of the Diaspora sent those students who were selected or were desirous to receive higher education.

The captivity in Babylon raised the fear of oblivion. Restoration set in train developments that anticipated that these circumstances could recur. When it happened again, with the dispersion following Israel's conflicts with Rome, Jews were better prepared not just by memory of the previous occurrence but with respect to the educational institutions developed during the Second Commonwealth. Further, education now emerged as the highest priority in Jewish communities. The urge to ensure identity, to secure solidarity and build common bonds between all the factions could all be pursued through the educational infrastructure that had been put in place. Neither the school nor the academy was an original Jewish institution. The former was borrowed from the Greeks; the latter was a legacy from the Sumerians. The synagogue and popular education represented Jewish genius inspired by captivity and nurtured by the geography and social realities of the society of the Second Commonwealth.

THE CURRICULUM

The entire focus of Jewish education was knowledge of the Torah and behaviour consistent with such knowledge. Knowledge, character and conduct were integrated into a coherent whole. Everything else was studied as a means to achieve these ends. This applied to all levels of the educational system. This meant that history, geography, mathematics and the sciences were studied only as they related and were integrated with some aspect of understanding the Torah or sacred scriptures. Accordingly, they were not studied as subjects but as aspects of the law.

The Torah as far as Jews were concerned was not only knowledge but it had supernatural powers. The Torah had curative and protective powers because of its divine character end knowing it was critical in partaking in the divine character and experiencing the curative and protective power. The responsibility of education was to faithfully and accurately transmit Torah from one generation to the next. From this perspective the curriculum for education was knowledge of the Torah. Because the latter was permanent and unchanging, so too was the curriculum (Ebner 1956).

With this in mind, some brief mention will be made of the curriculum at the different levels of the educational system.

The Elementary School Curriculum

The content and curriculum of the elementary school was directed at transmitting knowledge of the written law, Torah, and developing conduct consistent with this knowledge. Elementary education was provided between the ages of six or seven and twelve years. Normally the course of study could be covered in four to five years. The curriculum could be set out as follows:

a) Learning the aleph-bet, the Hebrew alphabet.
b) The study of the Pentateuch. It is interesting to note that after the defeat of Bar Kokhba by Rome in 135 CE elementary schools started the study of the Pentateuch with the book of Leviticus and not Genesis, as was previously the case. This was because the leaders were anxious to minimise despair and promote hope by holding out the promise of the rebuilding of the temple and the re-instatement of priestly service.
c) The study of the other books of the Hebrew Bible.
d) The liturgy including the eighteen benedictions, grace after meals, the Shema and the hallel.

e) The basics of writing, but not writing as an art form. That is, writing was taught for functional purposes including signatures, letters and business transactions but not for creative expression.

f) General knowledge that included historical, geographical, scientific and mathematical knowledge, as these were important for understanding the scriptures.

Ebner took the position that by the end of the Tannaitic period, 220 CE, elementary schools had become almost universal in Jewish communities in Palestine and the Diaspora. While all boys received an education until age 12 or 13, some were given more advanced education. These advanced students studied the Oral Law. According to Drazin the Oral Law constituted the curriculum of secondary education and was provided mainly to boys between the ages of 13 and 17 years.

The Popular Education Curriculum

Popular education was originally centred around public readings of the Bible on the Sabbath and on market days, Mondays and Thursdays, once a quorum of ten adult males was present. It also included study groups where ten or more adult males could organise themselves into classes and secure an instructor to lead them on any subject they wished to study in the oral or written law.

As knowledge of the written law became more general and oral law became more complex, the focus of the synagogue-based popular education shifted to the Oral Law, which was redacted as Mishnah during the Tanniatic period, 10 to 220 CE.

The Higher Education Curriculum

The curriculum of the academy could be summarised in three brief statements:

1. Detailed and in-depth study of the Written Law, and the scriptures generally.
2. Study of the Oral Law as this had been developed to address the general principles enunciated in the Written Law and as applied to the changing and practical existence of the congregation.
3. Study of Talmud, the commentaries on the Written and Oral Law as these were developed over time by the Sages and in opinions given in judgements handed down.

As was pointed out previously the colleges or academies throughout the Second Commonwealth were located organisationally and administratively in relation to the legislature enacting law and the courts interpreting the law.

Students were therefore educated not only by formal lectures in the three areas outlined above, but also in the context of the application of the law to the lives of the people. Advanced students sometimes participated in the deliberations leading up to resolution of matters before the courts and legislature.

Immediately after the destruction in of the Temple and Jerusalem, and with the relocation of the academy to Jabneh, all Jews looked to the sages in Palestine for authoritative guidance in matters of faith. Later with the establishment of academies in Babylonia and the rise of those institutions, after the sixth century it was the Babylonian academy that assumed intellectual leadership among institutions of higher education, and in the guidance of Jews of the Diaspora.

SCHOOL ORGANISATION AND FINANCE

Elementary schools were located either in the private house of the teacher, or in the synagogue in the room for teaching the young, bet sefer. Most elementary schools were located in synagogues. The teacher was usually seated on a chair, while the students sat on mats on the floor with scrolls on their knees. The textbook was the Hebrew Bible. Because of the expense of books at that time, separate scrolls for each of the five books of Moses, the Pentateuch, were produced for school children.

Parents or the community paid the teachers. The tradition of communal responsibility for education was established with the reforms of Ben Shatah in 75 BCE. The Ben Gamala reforms made it mandatory for communities to ensure that the teachers were paid. If tuition fees, paid by parents, were insufficient or non-existent as in the case of orphans, then the community had to make up the deficit. A community could impose a tax for this purpose.

The academies had their own building and organisation as previously described. During the period of the Great Assembly and the time of the Zugot tuition fees were charged. The Shammai academy continued this practice in keeping with their belief of exclusiveness with respect to who should be allowed to study the Law, while the Hillel academy consistent with its open and more liberal beliefs abolished fees. After the academies were merged into the single institution at Jabneh, the Hillel tradition prevailed.

Only boys were students in Jewish schools. Starting from the premise that education was a family responsibility, and that this was traditional Hebrew practice, when public education was created only the education of boys was transferred to the public sphere. The education of girls remained a family matter. As Swift (1919) noted the education of girls was entirely domestic and given to them mainly by their mothers.

PRINCIPLES OF JEWISH EDUCATION

Jewish education was premised within the father's responsibilities towards his son. These were to circumcise him, redeem him, teach him the Torah, teach him a trade and to marry him off. To fail in any of these constituted grave moral failure as a parent. The elementary school emerged to assist fathers with the obligation to teach sons the Torah.

Maller (1966) summarised what in his view were the fundamental concepts of Jewish education as it was developed in the Second Commonwealth. He identified the following ten principles as fundamental:

1. Human character is modifiable and can be improved.
2. Learning and doing, knowledge of ethics and conduct must be integrated.
3. Education is a lifelong and continuous process.
4. Environment is a critical and important factor in instruction.
5. Individual difference must be recognised.
6. To be effective education must start early.
7. Responsibility for education is shared between parents and the community.
8. Learning must proceed from the known to the unknown, the simple to the complex and the immediate to the remote.
9. Training for work is essential and honourable
10. Teaching of history is critical to a sense of continuity and meaning of Jewish experiences.

TEACHERS IN JEWISH SCHOOLS

By the end of the monarchical period in Israel and Judah, 586 BCE, there were two sharply different spiritual tendencies struggling for supremacy. On the one hand, there was the priestly tradition with its realist view of life, its ceremonials and sacrificial rituals hedged around with mystery, its religious outlook centred in tribe and locality, and its arena of operation fixed to shrine and temple. On the other hand, there was the prophet tradition with its stubborn refusal to submit to facts, its vigorous insistence on an ideal social order and its lofty and noble universalism denying importance to territory or ethnicity. In Morris's view the one represented the static and the other the dynamic elements in Jewish society. In a single stroke the destruction of the first temple and Jerusalem, wiped away the world of the priest. In captivity the elite of Judah, in circumstances of extreme necessity, had to confront the world-view of the prophet. The conclusion in captivity was that the survival of Israel rested firmly with the prophets' world-view.

Ironically, the restoration started with the rebuilding of the Temple. The world of the priest was reinstated. This seems more related to political necessity rather than religious strategy. The monarchy was abolished. The Persian sponsor placed government in the hands of the priests. They filled the political vacuum created by the abolition of the monarchy. Temple and government demanded the full-time attention of the priests. Political necessity therefore created the room for the prophets to become the teachers of the people. This was convenient because the conclusion of captivity had been that it was their message that had to form the core of Judaism. Who better to teach Judaism than prophets?

THE TEACHERS OF HIGHER EDUCATION

Prophecy did not decline in the Second Commonwealth, prophets became the teachers of the people in the new ethos of Judaism. They became the Soferim: the sages, scholars or scribes. Inspired speech gave way to insightful oral interpretation of the Written Law as applied to the changed circumstances of the lived experience of the people. As Bickerman (1966) observed, formerly the priestly families had kept to themselves knowledge concerning rituals and morals. Now prophets were charged with the responsibility to democratise access to this highest form of knowledge in the country and to make it widely known. Knowledge of the Torah, which was previously retained for family advantage, was now to become a national resource. Further, authoritative decrees from the High Priest had to take account of learned argument from the sages. The old polarities and tension between prophet and priest were not abolished, only transferred to new arenas. While the priest now acted in the place of the king, it was the prophet who held spiritual sway as depicted in Psalm One: it is not the priest but the sage who is honoured as he meditates on the law day and night.

The scribes, scholar/teachers, took over the prophets' mantle in the Second Commonwealth. The teachers in higher education, and the judges who interpreted the law to guide daily living, the living authorities of the law, were the very core of both the ethos and the ethnos: Judaism and the community that gave practical expression to this world-view. They were key citizens of the Second Commonwealth who were recognised, and recognised themselves as such. But they became important in another respect. Judah was a vassal state ruled by various imperial powers at different times. As Bickerman pointed out foreign rulers needed expert advice on the laws and customs of their subjects. This was particularly so about a group that must have appeared quaint in an ancient world from which they diverged in so many ways. These scholar/ teachers therefore became important to the imperial rulers in ways different from the priests controlling the government. Johanan Ben Zakkai must have understood this fully when he successfully negotiated with the Romans for the survival of the academy when the temple and city were slated for destruction.

What is interesting is that while patronage and influence from the imperial powers did crack the solidarity of the scholar/teachers as a fraternity, as evidenced by the opposing tendencies within the group: Hellenist against Hasidim, Sadducees against Pharisees, assimilationists against traditionalists, and Shammaites against Hillelites, the lines of fracture were such that the core tenets of Judaism remained intact even if at times it appeared compromised. Greco-Roman culture broke on the rock of Judaism largely because of the work of these men. Ebner (1956) quoted Seneca, the Roman philosopher of the first century CE, as saying 'They, (the Jews) at least know the reasons for their ceremonies, but the mass of the rest of mankind do not know what and why they do'. By the time of the Roman termination of the Second Commonwealth, these scholar/teachers had so effectively discharged their task as the nation's teachers, that the consciousness of the ordinary Jews was sufficiently raised that not even the might of the greatest political power of the ancient world could destroy their identity or shake them loose from their religion.

These scribe scholars were drawn from all social strata, but most came from the ranks of the plebeian traders, artisans or farmers. While the priests enriched themselves by virtue of their control of the state machinery, and over time became part of the nobility of the Second Commonwealth, the scholar/ teachers did not advance economically by virtue of their social and political importance in the society. They regarded and believed the Law, Written and Oral, to be holy and their task sacred. They taught without pay. Those whose background provided no source of support, provided their sustenance through some trade or craft. The distance they maintained between themselves and the acquisition of material wealth enhanced their credibility as the keepers of the spiritual heritage of the nation. Their sacrifice of material gain enhanced their social standing in addition to preserving the perception of their spiritual integrity, by the wider community.

While it would appear that the scholar/teachers continued to maintain a healthy distance between themselves and affluence, Sperber (1990) examined codes of rabbinical conduct during the Talmudic period and concluded that in time they took on to themselves some of the etiquette of the nobility of Jerusalem, which their plebeian predecessors had so stoutly resisted. For example, they had to know in advance with whom they would dine, before accepting a dinner invitation, or with whom they would sign before witnessing documents. In other words, having assumed power in the community, scholar/ teachers underscored their position by social distinctions rather than by material gain.

They also created their own myths concerning the sacrifices that had to be made with respect to the sacred task that was their charge. Simon Ben Shetah, President of the Sanhedrin, it is said was stern and strict in his interpretation and administration of the law. His enemies sought revenge by inciting two false witnesses to accuse his son of a capital offence for which he was tried and convicted. On his way to execution Simon's son so vehemently protested his innocence that the two witnesses recanted and confessed their falsehood. When the judges were about to set him free he pointed out to them that to accept the recantation of a witness proven to be false was itself a violation of the law. To his father he remarked that if he wished Israel to be saved by his effort, then he should consider him the threshold over which he must cross without compunction. Both father and son, it is said, proved themselves worthy of the supreme task of guarding the integrity of the law: the latter by sacrificing his life and the former by ignoring parental love (Swift 1919).

This anecdote is typical of several others cited by historians to illustrate the devotion of the scholar/teachers to the law. However, it would appear that in their effort to maintain the integrity of the law, justice was relegated to second place. The law was no longer the servant of justice but its master. The law of God, who is moral, was to be preserved even with injustice. The zeal of the scholars in performing their sacred trust to achieve holiness through the law began to warp the alignment between God, justice and the law. Ironically the scholar/teachers appeared to have become guilty of an error similar to that of the priests, whom the prophets had previously accused of allowing their ceremonies and rituals to cloud their vision and understanding of Yahweh.

The destruction of the second temple, and Jerusalem, by the Romans changed the Jewish world radically. The world of the priests was again reduced to rubble because their office was tied to locality and ritual at a particular site, the Temple in Jerusalem. Priests and Levites virtually disappeared. The Jews of the Diaspora were led by the scholar/teachers. Their universal vision did not depend on place or rite. It proved portable. It could be carried anywhere. Accompanying the faithful were the institutions they had created after the restoration: the synagogue, the academy and the elementary school all rooted in the study of the sacred scriptures and the law.

Swift made the point that rabbi originally meant master or leader and was applied to any group. For example, the leaders of the hangmen and weavers, were rabbis of hangmen and weavers respectively. Increasingly the term was used for teachers although this did not entitle them to teach or preach. Eventually the term rabbi became used almost exclusively in reference to the scholar/teacher.

In the period after the Roman dispersion the religion became identified as Rabbinical Judaism since they were now its leaders. The prophets did not vanquish or destroy the priests, the latter disappeared because their static and narrow conceptions gave them no future outside the locality or times to which these were relevant and appropriate. The terminology used to label prophets changed to scribes, sages, scholars, teachers and finally into rabbis, but their universal conception of God and humanity proved timeless and independent of territory.

Maller (1966) noted that after 220 CE it became rare to find a Jewish community without a synagogue and an elementary school. The most respected person in the community was the scholar/teacher, the rabbi. Drazin noted that after the destruction of the temple, Jews of the Diaspora, to support the academy then redirected the contribution that previously had gone to the upkeep of the Temple. The teachers were then paid a salary, the remainder going to the upkeep of the building and other expenses.

TEACHERS OF THE ELEMENTARY SCHOOL

The task of the elementary school teacher was to teach the children the Bible, starting with the Pentateuch or Torah, by expanding the literal interpretation with explanations from the oral law. The requirements for being an elementary school teacher were:

a)   Reasonably knowledgeable of the Bible and possessing a working knowledge of the Oral Law.
b)   Good character, as judged by the community.
c)   Male, the law debarred women from being elementary school teachers.
d)   Married, and living with his wife, according to some authorities.
e)   Exercising patience with children.

The elementary school teachers were called scribes, sofer. However, by then the term scribe had changed from its original meaning of scholar/sage to mean one who copied scrolls of the Bible and official documents in legal transactions. The other derivation of the term was from bet sefer, house of learning for the young. In many small communities the same person held the offices of scribe, copyist, and elementary school teacher. Elementary school teaching was also combined with other offices, for example, that of synagogue attendant, hazzan. The latter performed several minor duties related to the Torah and its reading on the Sabbath and festival days. The fact that many elementary schools were housed in synagogues meant that several hazzans were utilised as elementary school teachers (Ebner 1956).

Payment of elementary school teachers posed some problems for the reformers who established the system. It was generally accepted that 'without bread there could be no Torah'. The elementary school teachers' existence depended on material provision. At the same time, the Torah should not be the source of material gain. The compromise that was eventually struck by the Talmud was that accepting remuneration was permissible for elementary but not secondary education. The ruling was based on two lines of argument. First, payment to the elementary school teachers was for "watching the children and preventing them from mischief", baby-sitting. Second, the restriction on payment only applied to the oral and not the written law, the latter being the emphasis in elementary education. The basis for calculating the pay of the teachers was actual time lost, and therefore earning foregone were they doing trades or comparable jobs. Payment to elementary school teachers was therefore always modest and needed supplementation from other sources, which was achieved by its combination with other offices.

All sources make the point that elementary school teachers were lavishly praised. Ebner agreed but added that despite this high praise, they were often spoken of in less than complimentary terms. High praise had to be compared with social reality. For example, God Himself was compared to the teacher of children, but the latter was at the bottom of the social register. On the scale of desirable marriages the teacher's daughter found herself at the lower end of the list, just above the *am ha-arez*. Similarly when enumerating the ten essential institutions and persons a city should have, the elementary school teacher was mentioned last after the scribe and barber.

Ebner explained the relatively low status of the elementary school teacher on the following grounds:

1. He was not considered a scholar, not being sufficiently advanced in mastery of knowledge of the law. Low status was silent reproach for not ascending the higher rungs of the ladder of Torah knowledge.
2. There were laymen in the community who were as learned and pious as he was.
3. He was paid for his work. He had to accept a fee for teaching God's word. Purity of the ideal was contaminated by materialistic considerations.

The relatively low status of the elementary school teacher has to be contrasted with the high status of the scholar/teacher of the academy. Kretzmann (1916) quoted Talmudic references, which stated that a city that did not have at least ten unemployed men who devoted all their time to the study of the law must be considered a village. While city status depended on having at least ten scholars, the elementary school teacher was tenth of the list of persons the city should have. The scholar was a high official of the state, served without pay and was the repository of and authority on the highest values of Jewish culture, Torah. The elementary school teacher was usually a functionary of the synagogue, received pay and had only a limited mastery of the high culture. Moreover, the former taught adults while the latter taught children. While the law defined teaching as man's work, the role of fathers, baby-sitting was female responsibility. Part of the elementary school teachers' role was defined in such terms, at least for pay purposes. These differences were sufficient to regard teaching in ancient Israel as two distinct occupations: teaching at the academy and teaching at the elementary school.

THE GENDER OF TEACHERS

The gender composition of ancient Jewish schools and academies was straightforward and simple. All the students were boys, and all the teachers were men. Women and girls were excluded from both. The short explanation for this structure was straightforward, the ordinances that prescribed public education so decreed. This was the law. The foundation for the law appears to have been derived from a particular line or reasoning. Torah made teaching the responsibility of fathers. The Oral Law exempted women and girls from learning Torah but made it mandatory for men and boys. The father's obligation was therefore to teach his sons, but he was allowed discretion with respect to teaching his daughters. When teaching became a communal and not simply a parental responsibility the legislation required boys to be educated and men to teach them. The ordinance decreeing public education was mirroring Torah, in its prescriptions for education in the home.

The flaw in this line of logic is, why was the discretionary power given to fathers in the education of their daughters, not also transferred to the public sphere? Torah did not exclude girls from being taught, it did not make it mandatory. Public education excluded girls. Also the Torah did not exclude mothers from teaching their children, it made it mandatory for fathers so to do. Public education excluded women from teaching. In addition, this exclusion could only be meaningful as an ordinance because there were women who could meet the other criteria established. Zolty (1993) made the point that from the spiritual plane, the obligatory basis of the participation of the men and boys in Torah learning, as against the voluntary basis of women and girls, could be interpreted in favour of the latter. In the divine providence females could be relied on to learn Torah, but males could not, hence the coercive nature of their participation. Evidently the men of the Great Assembly and later Simon Ben Shatah and Joshua Ben Gamala did not share this interpretation. Girls were not allowed voluntary participation in the school system they were excluded from it.

Drazin and Ebner explained the reasons for not creating a coeducational school system on the basis of the concern of families in ancient society to protect the chastity of their daughters who were usually married at an early age. Legally girls could be married from age three years and one day old, and had the legal status of wives, although they remained in their father's house until age 12 years. While these circumstances could have weighed heavily against co-education the same arguments would not obtain for schools for girls taught by women.

Wegner (1991) insisted that the sages and rabbis systematically excluded women from the 'life of the mind'. Women were excluded from leadership positions in the synagogue, the school and the courts. They were prohibited from forming women's fellowship groups to study the Torah. Women therefore could not study Torah together, only independently or with family members. In Wegner's view women were deliberately excluded from the most intellectually and spiritually rewarding practices of traditional Judaism, and also from the most prestigious enterprises of rabbinical culture. The expectation was that women would spend most of their lives in the realm of domestic affairs.

Swift (1919) was of the view that women's position in Israelite society deteriorated progressively from the period of the Judges through to the Tannaitic period. He noted that while there was no time at which women enjoyed equality with men, their position in society was more equal in earlier times. For example, there were no early restrictions on women in religious observances and they participated in all the essentials of the cult, both as worshippers and officials.

Some deterioration in women's position can be noted in the First Commonwealth, with the establishment of the monarchy, but women were numbered among the prophets, through not among the priests. Their position deteriorated in the Second Commonwealth, after 536 BC, in that women were not among the Scribe/Sages who succeeded the prophets.

Ebner (1956) agreed with Swift and noted that women's position deteriorated in the Tannaitic period compared to the Second Commonwealth. For example, during the Second Commonwealth women used to mingle freely with men in the synagogue but were later segregated and confined to a women's gallery mainly as spectators and not participants. Likewise, during the Second Commonwealth women could be among the seven readers of Torah on the Sabbath, but the Rabbis of the Tannaim discontinued this practice. In other words, women's exclusion from the public sphere was progressive as the scholar/teachers gave their interpretations and developed the Oral Law. By the time the school system was established the public exclusion of women was far advanced and the discretionary power of fathers to educate their daughters was not extended to the public sphere. This deepened the restriction of women to the private sphere of the home.

Comparatively speaking as far as education was concerned Judaism, and Jewish society, did not differ from the rest of the ancient world in its proscription of the education of women and girls. Those women and girls who were taught learned in their homes from family members. Educated women belonged to families that had a tradition of scholarship or belonged to the elite who employed private tutors to teach them. The Greek declaration of universal education, and the Jewish implementation of it, excluded girls. It also excluded women as teachers.

There is a strange silence, from almost all of the sources, on explaining women's exclusion as teachers in Jewish society. Their exclusion is reported but not explained. Because women learned in the home, the arguments for their exclusion as pupils in the public system cannot be automatically applied to their exclusion from the occupation of teachers, without the imposition of some other consideration. Mothers in the home were responsible for the education of daughters. This activity was not transfered to the public sphere in the creation of schools for girls. However, mothers must have executed some educational tasks with respect to their sons, especially mothers who were literate and learned in the Torah. Why could such women, married mothers, not be employed as teachers? Chastity or fidelity could not be material considerations. The possibility of ritual impurity, cultic pollution, is also suggested (Wegner 1991). Surely this must be a justification for the exclusion not its cause.

One explanation that seems likely is that women as elementary school teachers would have created dangerous legal precedents with respect to male authority in Jewish society. The interpretation of the Genesis injunction that men should rule could have been applied in constructing the school system. Another explanation could be that as gainful occupation was at a premium in ancient Jewish society, women competing with men for the few jobs that were available could advance some families with two incomes, while leaving many with none. Competition for family/clan advantage was therefore restricted to their men. Leaving as much room as possible for male employment was one measure adopted to maintain social cohesion and community peace. It was one of the counter measures to some others that were tearing the society apart. It is not possible to rule out both factors as contributing to women's exclusion as elementary school teachers.

There was only one woman recorded as a master of the law through private study or the guidance of scholar relatives. This was Beruriah (Zotly1993) who according to Babylonian Talmudic sources, was the wife of Rabbi Meir, himself a noted scholar, and the daughter of Rabbi Hanihah Ben Teradyon, who was martyred in the Ben Kokhba rebellion in 135 CE, and sister of another noted scholar. By family and marriage Beruriah was surrounded by scholarship. She became a noted commentator on halakhic tradition. She was more brilliant than her brother and the peer of her famous husband. She was credited as the source of at least two guiding principles eventually accepted and incorporated in the Talmud.

The end of Beruriah was shrouded in mystery. Talmud reported that Rabbi Meir ran away to Babylonia where he eventually died. It gives alternative reasons for his departure one of which was 'the incident with Beruriah'. One historian reported that the incident referred to was that one day Beruriah ridiculed the rabbinical dictum that women were temperamentally light headed and tended to succumb under intense pressure. Rabbi Meir, her husband, soon after ordered one of his students to test her virtue. After repeated urging on the part of the student, Beruriah yielded to his advances. She committed suicide out of remorse for what had happened. Overcome with guilt Rabbi Meir fled into Babylonia. As Zolty (1993) pointed out there has been much controversy over the accuracy of this account. Wegner (1993) took the position that whether the report is accurate or not, the legend of Beruriah was intended to justify the exclusion of women from the academy and was also used as an example of what happens to women who step outside the norms prescribed by the culture.

CONCLUSION:
THE MASCULINE ROOTS OF TEACHING IN JUDAISM

Ancient Israel and Judah were marginal states in the ancient world. From the perspectives of power and resources they would be mere anecdotes in discussions of the ancient world were it not for the religion they created. From marginality among the city-states of that era, and obliteration as political entities, they rose to be a global force in religious expression. This underscores the importance of belief in human society and its capacity to shape the nature and form of the other dimensions of community. There was no aspect of Israelite society that was outside the influence of religion. Belief shaped political, cultural, economic and social expressions of Jewish life.

The vulnerability of Judah was evident from the time Israel went its own way. The destruction and disappearance of this larger entity forewarned of Judah's future fate. The scholars whose speciality it was to predict the future, the prophets, anticipated the events of that future, developed a paradigm for survival of these marginal people and fearlessly proclaimed it. The essence of that paradigm was that Judah's future resided in marshalling spiritual qualities. Judah as a marginal state could not survive on the basis of military might, economic resources or political power. The continuity of Israelites as a people depended upon spiritual energy and exertion: 'not by might nor by power but' by spirit. The power, resources and materialism of the ancient imperial city-states could only be successfully resisted by spiritual integrity.

When the Babylonian captivity came Judah was not entirely unprepared. What was predicted, as a distinct possibility, by the prophets had become reality. This gave legitimacy and credibility to the prophetic vision and world-view. Strategies were developed in the period of captivity to fully implement the elements of that paradigm. Persian termination of the Babylonian empire gave Judah the reprieve it had hoped for.

During the Second Commonwealth the prophets' spiritual paradigm was given institutional form in the Pentateuch as the written constitution of the state; in the Oral Law and courts addressing changing circumstances; in the synagogue as the centre of congregational life and adult education; in the academy as the institution in which knowledge of the Torah was developed and scholars prepared; and in public elementary schools which disseminated Torah knowledge to male children. The destruction of Jerusalem and the Second Temple and the obliteration of Judah by the Romans did not therefore end the existence of the Jewish people. Judaism had been established for over seven hundred years and had prepared Jews, as much as any people could have been prepared, for this calamity.

The imperial city-states of the ancient world offered marginal city states only two options: either submission marked by ceremonial tributes and paying taxes in return for a fair measure of internal autonomy or oblivion. City-states that chose oblivion experienced the destruction of their city and its shrines, the public display and humiliation of their elite if they had not been killed, and the deportation and dispersion of the majority of their political and technical cadres among other city-states. In these circumstances they were absorbed as they assimilated into the cultures into which they had been dispersed. Through Judaism, Jews defied and survived oblivion. They created their own option, that of being a distinct community even when dispersed. Large numbers never assimilated despite enormous pressure, physical and psychological, directed against them. They maintained their identity and culture while exiled in different places, over thousands of years, starting from the Babylonian captivity in 586 BC.

Exile represented an even more marginal condition than being part of a vassal state dominated by an imperial power. Being stateless and city-less in a world organised on the basis of city-states constituted a considerable disability by virtue of loss of rights and privileges. In addition, being exiled meant living as aliens. When both were combined, stateless exiles, the marginalisation was even more extreme. Being exiled by a regime has far greater prospects that being exiled by virtue of having no state. Regimes change in time. Restoration of exiles whose states continue to exist is usually only a change of government away. Restoration of a state and city are far more difficult to contemplate much more effect. Jews in exile lived in the most extreme form of political marginality.

Cantor (1995) made the point that in exile Jews were never an integral part of the societies in which they took refuge. In her analysis of their social position she maintained that Jews did not own the means of production neither did they belong to the working classes that produced the goods that society regarded as essential. In feudal times they did not belong to either the landowning nobility or to the peasants working the land. As such Jews were continually located in the interstices of the economic structures of the societies in which they lived. In these positions they were constantly caught in the crossfire of ethnic and class battles in these societies. On the one hand they often were found in the role of oppressor surrogates as ruling classes utilised their skills and services in exercising their hegemony over the rest of the society. On the other hand, the same ruling classes often used Jews as lightning rods to deflect the rage of the oppressed, when this had reached boiling point. As marginal minorities without a firm stake in any society, Jews of the Diaspora were always expendable.

Cantor maintained that Jews in exile developed a number of strategies to mitigate the effects of their powerlessness. These can be listed as follows:

- Cultivating protectors among elements of the ruling classes, just as women often seek powerful male protectors to prevent attacks by other men.
- Being useful to those factions of the ruling classes that needed their services most, in the hope of receiving some protection in return.
- Relying on trusted Jews in high places: 'Court Jews', those of their number who managed to secure high position in the society.
- Bribery, paying protection money to reside in particular places or engage in particular economic activities.

Cantor insisted that while all these strategies were tried, and often succeeded, there were numerous instances in which they failed with disastrous consequences. In Cantor's view the only real defence that proved effective against physical and psychological oppression were those enunciated by the prophets: spiritual resistance and communal cohesion. Spiritual resistance was essential in shoring up psychological defences against anxiety, hopelessness and depression. Communal cohesion was critical to the preservation of Jewish identity. Exile required collective responsibility for survival, and did not have room for individual solutions. It was treated as a national emergency that drew upon the traditional Jewish world-view of one history and destiny and corporate survival.

Cantor was of the view that the exile experience forced the incorporation of several feminine traits into Jewish society through the reform of patriarchy. Her reconstruction of the reform of patriarchy can be summarised as follows:

1. Rabbinical scholars, who assumed leadership of the Jewish people in the first centuries of exile, were convinced that the use of violence against the Romans was the principal cause of the terrible consequences that resulted. If physical resistance to the powerful was not effective as a nation then it had even less chance in the circumstances of exile, when communities were scattered over many jurisdictions. They therefore systematically attempted to eliminate violence as a means of resistance to subordination and oppression.

2. Another consideration was that oppressed people were very likely to use violence against each other leading to the breakdown of community. The retention of Jewish identity and solidarity required communal cohesion. Communities therefore had to become violence free zones, at least from members of the community itself.

3. Violence against women had to be specifically outlawed since this could become the source of multigenerational blood feuds.

4. If spiritual resistance were to become the principal means of defence, then men had to be free to express their opinions and ideas in debates and discussions without fear of physical reprisal. Masculinity was therefore reconstituted and redefined. It was stripped of glorification of violence, rugged individualism, rapacious exploitation, machismo, rampart cruelty, military conquest, physical heroism and abuse of women. Masculinity was redefined in terms of knowledge, learning and study of Torah. Man as scholar replaced man as macho-fighter.

5. Because the study of Torah was the major component of this new definition of masculinity its pursuit had to be democratised to include all men. It became a means of upward mobility for some, since it was open to all.

6. By depriving Jewish men of power through physical resistance, relative to other men of the general society, they were reduced to the same level of powerlessness as women. To compensate for this loss men were allowed to dominate all other aspects of communal life: legal, social, intellectual and religious. By excluding women, particularly from the study of Torah and intellectual work, its definition as man's work was assured. It made this turf exclusively masculine.

7. The role of the Jewish woman was that of altruistic, assertive enabler of men's public performance of spiritual resistance. Her task was to take care of the complex support systems of the household. The home was the major support system upon which Jewish life rested. This was particularly so because so many ritual observances and ceremonies took place in the home.

8. Women accepted their role and endured exclusion from the life of the mind, because what was at stake was the survival not only of the family, but the community as a whole. At times women became sole breadwinners, to ensure that men could continue in the task of spiritual resistance to ensure long-term survival. While they entered the public sphere, with their husbands' permission and undertook several occupations, men retained scholarship and teaching as their preserve.

While issue can be taken with Cantor's reconstruction from the perspective of its historical correctness, in that many of the patterns and tendencies she attributed to Rabbinical Judaism were certainly evident within the Second and even the First Commonwealth, the essential core appears sound. Three elements seem undeniable. First, patriarchy was consistently retained in Judaism, and Jewish society, its content was continually revised to mitigate and ameliorate the status of women and children as well as the relations between men of different kin groups within the community. Second, men and women perceived and performed their separate and different roles voluntarily and knowingly within the context of the common cause of Jewish survival as a distinct society. Third, the common enemy was men of the dominant society who exercised power mainly through violence and other coercive means against which Jews had little protection.

The masculine roots of teaching in Judaism and Jewish society stemmed from its highest value and its principal means of ensuring survival, spiritual resistance of imperial power. Unlike Sumer and imperial city-states like Babylon, Rome and Macedonia in which scholarship and teaching were part of the means by which power was legitimised, consolidated and maintained by non-coercive means, in the marginal state of Judah and during the exile of the Jewish people, scholarship, education and teaching were the principal means of resisting the powerful, of maintaining communal identity and of retaining personal integrity in the face of overwhelming odds. From being a weapon of the powerful, teaching and scholarship in Judah were transformed into shields of resistance by the powerless. Teaching and scholarship were no longer the exclusive tools of monarchs and their courts, but also the instruments of the people to be used by the weak and marginalised in their confrontation with superior might.

It must be noted that teaching and scholarship in Judah constituted an affirmative form of resistance and not a resisting form of opposition. Inspired by Judaism, teaching and scholarship positively asserted values of an alternative ethos and ethic to that which guided and inspired the imperial forces that continually held Judah as a vassal state. As such teaching and scholarship were not negative but positive in resisting superior force. In a nutshell Jewish history provides a classic example of the institution of schooling and the occupation of teaching being transformed into mechanisms by which the powerless prevail against overwhelming odds of political and military might, great disparities in economic resources and enormous differences in social prestige.

It is in this context that it must be noted that teaching had no feminine roots in classical Judaism. However, women's exclusion from schooling and teaching was not simply a consequence of a general exclusion from the public sphere. These were not mere examples of the types of restrictions to which women were subjected. Women's exclusion was specific to scholarship and teaching. Wegner's phrase 'women's systematic exclusion from the life of the mind and spirit' seems very appropriate because it highlighted the specific areas of the public sphere which men maintained as their exclusive zone, notwithstanding the humanising concessions to the personhood of women and their legal persona and rights enshrined in law. It is in this context that women accepted their exclusion since its was predicated on the very survival of the group itself. The only females who broke through these barriers were a few from some families of exceptional scholars, especially where there were no sons.

The scholar/teachers became the powerful in Jewish society during the exile. Certainly by the end of the Talmudic period, they were the 'centrals' in Jewish society. What arose could best be described as pedagogic or rabbinical patriarchy. While fathers still made the final decision in their families they did so within the framework established by the rabbis. Rabbis were the decision makers and the leaders of the wider communities. Faced with the subordination to a dominant society, the adversity of living as aliens as well as all the uncertainties of exile existence, the scholar/teachers reformed patriarchy and exercised power more humanely, democratically and transparently than was the norm of their time. They relied less on coercion and more on participation; engaged more in mutual assistance especially of those in need; and maintained community solidarity. In many respects the fractious, acrimonious and hostile relations noted between different groups in Judah were transformed into working and functional communities that retained solidarity and unity despite diversity in views.

In this regard the seminal contribution of elementary school teachers to Jewish society should not be overlooked. Given the animosity and deep hostility that existed between scholars and *am ha-arez* at the commencement of the Tannaitic period, that Jewish society in exile overcame this hurdle, was testimony to the work of elementary school teachers. They bridged the gulf between scholar and *am ha-arez*, which led in time to almost total disappearance of this group, or at least to the stigma. It was the elementary school teachers and not the scholars who disseminated Torah knowledge beyond what most homes were capable of teaching.

Four

THE MASCULINE AND FEMININE ROOTS OF TEACHING IN ISLAM

Islam and Christianity and their civilisations were the successors of the civilisation of the ancient world. While conserving many aspects of ancient civilisation they ushered in the second civilising wave in human history. Embedded in both civilisations was Judaism, their precursor and fountainhead. Judaism had signalled the future, but did not itself lead the charge to that future. Judaism, Christianity and Islam are all Semitic monotheisms that trace their roots back to Abraham (Stoddart 1985). The new age and civilisation which succeeded the ancient city-state empires was that of the Semitic monotheistic religions promulgated by theocratic empires.

Like most major transformations in human history, dates are hard to fix. Hence any fixed dates for the end of the civilisation of the ancient world based upon polytheism, materialism, the city-state and slavery and the beginning of the theocratic age of the monotheistic religions are bound to be arbitrary. However, a convenient marker of the end of the first civilising wave, was the sacking of Rome in August 410 CE by Alaric leading the Gothic campaigners of the invading Germanic tribes. It signalled the beginning of the end of the Roman Republic, the Empire it had captured and the ancient civilisation it had embodied. Ancient civilisation had been built up over 4000 years. It therefore did not die quickly. From its prolonged death in Rome new directions can be traced along three paths, which represented the course of the new age. These paths can be labelled by the terms Eastern Orthodox Christian, Western Roman Christian and Islamic empires. The Islamic Empire, as a full-blown theocracy, was the first to arise and flower.

The conventional label for this period of human history is the Middle Ages or Dark Ages or Mediaeval times. This designation is rejected here because of its Eurocentric bias, which accepts the ancient genesis but conceives of Western Industrial civilisation as a terminus of human history. The in-between era then becomes the Middle Ages, the Dark Ages or Mediaeval Times. The position taken here is that the era following the demise of ancient civilisation must be designated in terms of its essence, which was monotheistic religious empires.

THE RISE OF ISLAM: RELIGION AND EMPIRE

Prior to the founding of Islam, Arabs were still mostly discordant nomadic tribes roaming the Arabian Peninsula. They were Semites who had tormented the ancient cities, but had been kept out, or stayed in the margins, of the ancient world of city-states. Their history, traditions and mores were transmitted through a rich oral tradition, which gloried in poetry and honoured poets. By the sixth century Judaism and Christianity had penetrated the Arabian Peninsula. Arabs heard their teachings but inspired by Mohammad they did not convert to either. Rather, they assaulted the decaying city-state civilisation with their own version of monotheism, Islam.

Mohammad was born in Mecca in 571 and died there in 632, but in his lifetime, as the Messenger of God, he and his colleagues of the Quraysh tribe unified the Arabian tribes and established Islam. The confessional basis of this new religion was a declaration of faith and five simple tenets or pillars. The shahada, or statement of faith, is 'There is no god but God: Mohammad is the Messenger of God'. The five pillars of Islam are:

1. Faith: assent to the shahada, There is only one true God, and Mohammad was his Prophet.
2. Prayer: in recognition of the sovereignty of God, worship and prayer are required, five times daily at dawn, noon, afternoon, sunset and night.
3. Almsgiving: one's goods must be given to assist the poor and to sustain the faithful.
4. Fasting: the abstention from food and drink from dawn to dusk during the month of Ramadan is obligatory.
5. Pilgrimage: to Mecca, at least once in a lifetime, is desirable.

Islam ordained no clergy, but commissioned all the faithful to convert unbelievers, not by sword but by persuasion and, if need be, force of circumstances. An important tenet of Islam was that the state and religion existed in unity with God hence there was no difference between the laws of God and those of man. The result of this fusion was the imperial religion, the theocratic state, which the new believers set out to establish universally.

Armed with their new faith, the Arabs proceeded, within a hundred years of the death of the Prophet, to establish an Islamic empire with borders that encompassed territory greater than the Roman Empire at its height (Stanton 1990). The Muslim army overran the Sassanian Persian Empire, reduced the territories and powers of the Byzantine Empire, pushed westward from Egypt through North Africa and subdued the Berbers all the way to the Atlantic coast, pushed into South Asia as far as the Punjab, Sind and Cujart overtaking Hindu territory, and invaded Latin Europe capturing Spain and Sicily (Nakosteen 1964). In this vast area there was one state, one law, one official religion and one official language.

In this vast area, the Arabs established their hegemony over widely different peoples. Encompassed within this new empire were Jewish, Greek, Hindu, Persian and Christian cultures. Nakosteen made the point that by touching three continents and embracing so many peoples and cultures Islam became the avenue of cultural traffic in this era of world history. Within the limits imposed by geography, East met West through Islam.

Stanton makes the very important point that unlike many previous conquerors the Arabs did not plunder and lay waste the cities and peoples they subdued. They followed the ancient precedent and principle of conquest. They allowed internal autonomy to those vanquished peoples who accepted their fate as vassal states of the new empire. Neither did they enforce conversion by the sword. Persecution of Jews and Christians, or the burning of libraries as happened in Egypt and Iran, was the exception rather than the rule. The general practice was to leave in place the institutions – temples, churches, synagogues, schools and hospitals – that they found. Christians remained the majority population in several provinces formerly in Egypt, Byzantium and Persia. Tibawi (1972) underscored this point by his observation that the Muslim military commanders were so unconcerned with details, initially, that they allowed official records, including those for taxes, to remain in the hands of the native people and in their own languages, and not in Arabic the official language.

Cragg (1991) while agreeing in principle with this position, posited several important qualifications. Cragg maintained that Islamic tolerance for the Jews and Christians, and by extension other religions, was largely a contractual arrangement. The essence of the contract was protection, or refuge, in exchange for political submission. The protection could be withdrawn at any time Muslim power determined that the terms of the contract had been breached. Jihad, waging holy war, was exchanged for the subordinate dhimmi political status of being a non-citizen in the empire. Cragg noted that under the terms of these arrangements religious minorities enjoyed reasonable security in Islam.

The details of the dhimmi contract spelled out a number of obligations for both the Islamic power and the religious minorities. Scriptured people could maintain their own worship and worship places, teach their own children, and administer their own laws of personal status through their own community authorities. In return for these privileges they had to accept political submission and pay jihad, poll tax. As non-Muslims they were exempt from giving alms. Over time several other restrictions were legally imposed. These included the following:

- Prohibition from building new or repairing old places of worship.
- The obligation of Jews and Christians to wear distinctive dress.
- Avoidance of the use of cherished Arabic words.
- Protocols in exchanging greetings with Muslims.
- Building their houses lower than Muslims.
- Dismounting from donkeys if in the presence of Muslims.
- Refraining from ringing bells and the public use of crosses.

· Prohibition against bearing arms.
· Not being able to give evidence against Muslims in the courts.

It is important to note, however, that because of the religious basis of the political and social division, the dhimmi status could not be regarded as religious apartheid for it could be changed by religious conversion. The political, legal and social restrictions were, therefore, strong incentives for conversion and could be justified and legitimised as part of the evangelistic mission. Apparently, over time, many came to see the truth of Islam through the contrasts between hardships imposed by the dhimmi restrictions and the benefits obtained by conversion. Also, the Muslim authorities were not at all averse to this outcome. Cragg reported the rebuke that came from Caliph 'Umar, in the eighth century, when one of his officials became concerned about the cost of conversion to the treasury became of the reduced numbers of dhimmis paying taxes. 'Umar was said to have reminded the revenue conscious bureaucrat that Mohammed was the Prophet and not a tax gatherer. For those who held to their faith, the price was unrelieved political and social dominance of Muslims, second-class membership in the empire and the payment of heavy taxes.

Cragg went on to highlight the fact that while the occasions for venality were legion, Muslims displayed decency and humanity in not abusing their powerful position relative to these subordinated minorities. In addition, non-Muslims were not debarred from holding public positions including custodians, accountants and tax collectors. These, however, did not alter their inferior political or social status. Herrin (1987) observed that in several countries in which Jews and Christian sects had been persecuted, the conquering Islamic army was welcomed as liberators. Goldin (1966) was of the view that Jews, in the classical period of Muslim history, fared better than previously. This was especially with respect to the new opportunities that opened up to them in trade and financial services. The Jewish connections in the Diaspora worked to their advantage in an empire that allowed them freedom of movement and permitted them free access to the world of commerce.

Goldin (1966) also noted that Jewish and Christian settlements were given the opportunity of abundant self-government, which allowed the Exilarch to become quite a powerful figure. He attended the court of the Caliph and had his general blessing in exercising authority within the Jewish community. Further Islam's treatment of the Jews differed sharply from that of the Roman Empire, including the period after Rome had adopted Christianity. For the Jews, Islam brought welcome relief from persecution and offered genuine prospects for a good deal of prosperity. The extent of the change can be measured by the fact that during Islam's classical period, Babylon became the de facto capital of Judaism, replacing Palestine.

Greek scholars persecuted by zealous Roman Christians, who closed their schools in Athens, found refuge in Islam. Some were commissioned by the Caliphs to translate the Greek classics from Syriac and Greek into Arabic. Nestorian and Monophysite Christians, excommunicated and persecuted for heresy by the Eastern Church, certainly welcomed the Arabs initially as liberators. They were embraced by the Ummayyad Caliphs and given important posts as court physicians and translators. Many Jews also found refuge in Islam.

The division between Muslim and Non-Muslim was not merely political and social. More fundamentally it reflected religious superiority (Naff 1981). In Islam polytheism was idolatry and paganism the work of the devil. In the case of Judaism and Christianity, Islam regarded itself as superior by virtue of recency of revelation. Judaism and Christianity were recognised as related religions that Islam had superseded and replaced.

A passing note should be entered on Zoroastrianism, the state religion of the conquered Persians. Like Judaism, Christianity and Islam, Zoroastrianism is monotheistic. From one perspective, it could be said to have almost crumbled under the weight of dhimmi pressure, unlike Judaism and Christianity in its several varieties. From another perspective it could be claimed that Zoroastrianism was assimilated into Islam and emerged as one of its main denominations, Shi'ism, as Persians pursuing social and political objectives converted to Islam. Evidence in support of the latter comes from the fact that the concept of the infallible Imam is consistent with the Zoroastrian creed while inconsistent with the Quran. Also the majority of its adherents were initially Persians.

The extremely rapid spread of the Arab empire is not only remarkable and impressive, but demands some comment. After all it subdued the Persian Empire, which had existed for nearly one thousand years. It made significant inroads into India, and overran part of the Byzantine and Roman territories. An immediate contrast between the conquerors and the conquered was a newly united and empowered people, galvanised and inspired by a new religion, and decaying empires that had settled into fixed classifications of their people, oppression of minority groups and fractional conflicts among their leaders. Another equally important contrast is the egalitarian and democratic message of Islam, of equality before God, and the highly stratified relationships of the hosts of oppressed people in the decaying cities of the ancient world. In this context, the Arab conquerors appeared as liberators to many, and Islam a hope of a new life here on earth for the dispossessed.

The historic defeat of the Muslim army near Tours in France in 732, and its retreat southward across the Pyreness, signalled the end of this phase of conquest, and the dawn of the classical period of Islamic civilisation. The initial vision of these Arab leaders of Islam was to establish both a world religion and a global state. Retreat at Tours dampened, if not permanently stalled, the universalistic dream and gave rise to consolidation of the empire in the regions conquered. It is important to note that these newly empowered Semites were not stopped by the forces of Rome, but rather by the newly empowered Goths, who themselves were carving out their own empire from the ruins of the ancient world. Two newly empowered peoples confronted each other at Tours.

The core of the empire, which these Semites now controlled, was the ancient empires of Egypt and Mesopotamia. The periphery was the Western Mediterranean borders of Europe, and the excursions into Central and South Asia. Europeans of the Mediterranean borders had captured the ancient civilisations of Western Asia and North Africa from the Semites and Africans, who through the Arabs and Islam were now retaking that world from the Europeans. The civilisation begun at Sumer and in Egypt was not European. As latecomers on the geographical periphery, Greece and Rome had been the beneficiaries of Western Asian and North African inspiration, energy and enlightenment. If the light went out in Europe, it was the reflected light of the glory of ancient civilisation reflected and refracted by Greece and Rome. Europe was now being forced to create its own light from its indigenous energies and inspiration.

The end of the period of conquest was soon marked by the first of many changes in the dynastic rule of the Islamic empire. By 750 the Ummayyad Dynasty, that had so brilliantly led the conquest, were almost annihilated and replaced by the Abbasid Dynasty, Persians who had married into Arab families. They prevailed for over 400 years, in what Stanton (1990) labelled a Pax Islamica during which the empire for the most part enjoyed freedom from external invasion and minimal internal strife. This period is often described as the classical period of Islamic history in that it was during these times that scholarship reached its heights not only in the great historical personages that emerged but also with respect to the collective contribution of that era to civilisation generally. It is against this general background that both the rise of schooling, establishment of the occupation of teaching and the masculine and feminine roots of teaching in the Islamic world and religion need to be understood and interpreted.

SCHOOLING IN ISLAM

Islam proclaimed the unity of religion and state. A caliph, who was warrior, 'priest' and king, therefore ruled the new empire. The caliph led the faithful in battle, prayer and the affairs of state. The caliph was recognised as the successor to Mohammad, but at the same time he was not a prophet. While the state was highly centralised and clearly defined on paper and in practice, the religion was only centralised on paper. Also there were no specific instructions for the establishment of any centralised bureaucracy to administer the faith. From the beginning the caliph's claim to infallibility in matters of faith, morals and behaviour was regarded not only as a violation of the Quran and the teaching of Mohammad, but also challenged especially by respected religious leaders. These religious leaders opposed the caliphate on the grounds that not even the Prophet had that status that was accorded to the caliph.

Challenge to the caliph's position within the religion emerged during the period of conquest. This challenge centred on the issue of whether it was only members of the prophet's family who were eligible for the office of caliph. It was a major point of contention with the Ummayyad caliphs. It represented the first major rift in Islam. Immediately after the period of conquest ceased, the state and the religion began to proceed on different paths. The state and empire remained centralised. The religion began to devise decentralised structures and forms to match its revelations. The peace that prevailed facilitated the evolution of these forms and the teaching needed to support them.

The evolution of schooling and teaching are best understood in relation to the separate needs and requirements of the Islamic empire and Islam the religion. While by doctrine there was unity between state and religion in actuality different trends developed in relation to the exercise of imperial and state power and the principles and practices of the believers. The synergy and tensions related to the assumptions of unity and the reality of diversity provided the broad contours and the dynamic that shaped and energised the evolution of schooling and teaching in Islam and the Islamic empire.

This evolution can be traced through three distinct phases. There was a preparatory or incubation period during the first century of Islam. This was followed by a period of spontaneous developments stretching from the eighth to the tenth century. Finally there was a period of increasing standardisation as the state increased its influence in schooling between the eleventh century and the thirteenth century. By that time the institutional structure, curriculum and legal framework of schooling in Islam were firmly established and ready to be exported elsewhere. For the purpose of this study, attention will only be paid to the evolution of the system to the point at which it was firmly established in shape and form, that is, by the thirteenth century, the end of its classical period. Brief comments will be made on the preparatory and incubation period highlighting its generic features; the other two periods will be treated in an integrated manner and by the levels of the education system created.

SCHOOLING IN THE PERIOD OF INCUBATION.

During the century of frantic conquest following the death of Mohammed, several other significant developments took place that impacted on the development of schooling and the teaching occupation. These could be regarded as preparatory steps to the creation of schooling in Islam. The four most important developments can be listed as follows:

1. An authorised version of the Quran was finally settled in 651. Muslims now had their 'book' comparable to the books of the Jews and Christians, whom Mohammad referred to as the people of the 'book'. The importance of the Quran was not only in terms of putting the new religion on a comparable literary status with the religions it claimed to supersede, but more importantly its educational significance as the most important text of learning in Islamic education. While the oral tradition of the Arabian Peninsula carried over into Islam, and

memorising the Quran became a challenge that many accepted and accomplished, mastery of the written word had far wider educational implications.

2. An Arabic grammar was codified. Arabic is the sacred language of Islam. Indeed, it is the only liturgical language of Islam. To Muslims it is the language in which God spoke to Mohammad. However, up to the middle of the seventh century Arabic had no standard written grammar. Through the work of al Duala in producing the first written grammar, by about 688, this important breakthrough occurred which facilitated the use of Arabic in instruction. Arabic, like any language whose diverse oral uses had to be converted into standard written form, went through a slow evolutionary process in the standardisation of its grammar. This required inspiration, patient application, accepted standards and applied genius. As Shalaby (1979) noted people from the desert served as the standard for both speech and grammar. Scholars like al Duala exercised the patience, had the inspiration and undertook the brilliant work required for the Arabic grammar to be codified. Without a standard grammar the teaching of the fundamentals, of any language, is challenging to say the least.

3. Hadith, exemplary behaviour of the Prophet and his colleagues, became a guide to determining right behaviour and an amplification of the principles enunciated in the Quran.

4. Consensus among the ulama, respected religious leaders in the community, became the modus of resolving issues where neither the Quran nor hadith were sufficient to decide practical matters or determine behaviour.

These internal developments established the decentralised instruments of defining the faith and the means by which the religious community could manage the faithful. Almost at the same time that these instruments had been established, the warriors had reached the limits of territorial expansion. The timing of these two sets of factors facilitated the creation of the school system almost immediately after the exertion of conquest had ceased.

It is necessary to take account not only of the internal developments that laid the foundation of schooling in Islam, but also an important technological development that proved to be a great boon to the educational efforts that were to follow. This was the invention of paper in China and the transfer of the process of its manufacture to the Islamic empire. The implication for both the spread of the new religion and the development of education were enormous. Books became more readily available and more affordable. Knowledge from books became more easily accessible than ever before.

At almost the same moment four separate sources of energy were released in the Islamic Empire. First, political will, in terms of the enthronement of a new dynasty, was ready to promote new directions. Second, the religious zeal of the new religion was no longer fettered by warfare; hence it could give full expression to missionary zeal. Third, technical matters related to the dissemination of the Quran and Arabic grammar had been decided. Fourth, technology in the form of the invention and production of paper provided a more affordable and convenient medium of disseminating both knowledge and belief. These concatenated to forge educational developments in Islam. Periods of convergence of such different sources of energy are not common in history. They are in fact very special. To the credit of Islam the potential was recognised, the prospects clearly seen and the opportunities fully grasped. For these reasons Islam and the Muslim empire shone brightly while Christianity and Europe had yet to come to terms with their own fundamentals. As Nakosteen (1964) observed while Charlemagne and his nobles were learning the alphabet in the courts of Europe, Islamic savants were debating the finer points of Plato, Aristotle and Socrates.

As Totah (1926), Tritton (1957) and others have pointed out Islam placed great value on learning and education. Totah cited the following injunctions, all attributed to Mohammed:

·   To seek learning is the duty of every Muslim man and woman.
·   Seek ye learning from the cradle to the grave.
·   Pursue knowledge though it be in China.
·   The learned are the heirs of the prophets.
·   The ink of the learned is as precious as the blood of the martyrs.
·   Honouring the learned man is worth honouring seventy prophets
·   The learned hold the third rank, preceded only by God himself and his angels.

It is against the background of these injunctions, and the preparatory steps that laid the foundations for constructing schooling that the Assidis caliphs moved to promote and support the efforts of the ulama in developing learning as the principal mechanism for deciding matters of the faith as well as defending it against the challenges posed by the peoples and cultures that had been subdued by military means. On the other hand, schooling and teaching in Islam can be viewed as being fashioned to meet the needs of a new religion that, with breath-taking speed, had converted large numbers of people who were now faced with the challenges of post-conversion living by the new faith.

Of equal importance were the demands of managing the empire. As Tibawi (1972) observed there was urgent need for literate and numerate clerks and accountants to transact the affairs of state. The educational demands of the faith were religious and sacred, while that of the state was essentially secular, although Islamic dogma envisioned no separation between religion and state. The reality that emerged was that schooling required was not the same with respect to the needs of the empire and the demands of the religion. Two separate but interrelated systems of education emerged. Each system had it own institutions and teachers. Each will be discussed in turn.

THE ELEMENTARY SCHOOL SYSTEM

Legend has it that at the Battle of Badr in 624 CE Mohammad took some of his Quraysh tribesmen captive. Those who could, redeemed themselves through the payment of a ransom. On learning that some of those who could not muster the required sum could read and write, Mohammad accepted payment in kind by allowing each literate captive to purchase his freedom by teaching ten Muslims to write. The point of this legend was the value Mohammad placed on education, and teachers, and his willingness to accept non-Muslims as teachers (Totah 1926).

It is generally accepted that at the time of the establishment of Islam, there were very few literate Arabs. Totah cited the records of al Buladhi that stated that there were only 17 men and four or five women in Mecca who were literate in 622. While schools existed before the arrival of Islam such schools were run by Christians and Jews, who were also the vast majority of the teachers. Shalaby (1979) maintained that very few Arabs were engaged in teaching in pre-Islamic times. Also that such schools as existed aimed at teaching the fundamentals of reading and writing. Until many more Muslims were made literate, Islam relied on non-Muslims to teach literacy and numeracy.

Tibawi (1972) made the point that early Islamic religious communities established no institutions for teaching the fundamentals of education and the Islamic state assigned no funds for direct expenditure for teaching literacy and numeracy to children. Basic education was regarded as the private concern of parents. Indeed, this remained the policy throughout the classical period of Islam.

While making no provisions for basic education, both the exigencies of the state and the and the imperatives of the new religion, made demands for literate and numerate people. Shalaby (1979) noted that many administrative departments and posts emerged within the mushrooming state bureaucracy that required writing, accounting and record keeping. In addition, only learned persons were expected to teach the faith. While literacy and numeracy were not critical to learning the faith, they were the basic skills essential to teaching the Quran. Empire and religion demanded basic education, for different reasons, but allowed the latter to be supplied by private enterprise.

The Kuttab

Sensing the need and noting the lack of provision by the state or the religion, private teachers offered children instruction first in their homes and later in specially designated places. Tibawi maintained that both the demand for basic instruction and the needs of the teachers to secure their livelihood promoted the formalisation of this service. Thus the kuttab, or maktab, was established. Tibawi states that both terms derive from the Arabic root 'to write' and are used interchangeably. The former was the more popular term during the classical period while the latter has been the more often used term in more modern times. Makdisi is of the view that, in at least some places, they were different institutions, the kuttab being the more advanced institution. Given the decentralised nature of the system, it is not impossible that is some places both institutions could have existed with some differences between them. What seems indisputable is that the kuttab/maktab constituted the institution offering formal elementary education.

Shalaby (1979) was of the view that in the first century of Islam the kuttab only offered basic education: reading, writing and arithmetic. Religious education was taught through oral instruction in the home and mosque. However, after the Quran had been written and copies were readily available, and Arabic grammar had been formulised, religious instruction became a dominant element of elementary education and the Quran its main and sometimes only textbook. In fact, this latter development resulted in the proliferation of kuttabs with different curricula.

Three main curricula varieties of the kuttab can be identified:

a)   Kuttabs that continued to offer only basic education without religious instruction. These would be patronised mainly by non-Muslims.

b)   Kuttabs that offered only religious instruction. These were mostly associated with mosques.

c)   Kuttabs that offered both basic and religious instruction. This was by far the most popular type and could be found throughout the empire.

All three types continued to exist for several centuries. In addition, Shalaby pointed out that through endowments, kuttabs were established for poor boys and orphans whose parents could not afford to pay for basic education. Such philanthropy sought to ensure that gifted boys of poor parentage had a chance to be educated. Kuttabs founded on this basis existed throughout Syria and Mesopotamia.

Note must be taken of the fact that teachers could only receive pay for teaching the secular subjects but could not accept pay for teaching the Quran or for offering religious instruction. While kuttab education was a private matter between teachers and parents, the Quran became so pervasive in basic education that the jurisconsults felt constrained to regulate its operation. Based on the revelation that the believers had the responsibility to evangelise the world, that the Quran was the word of God and thus a principal element of evangelism, no charge could be affixed to the proclamation of its message. Therefore instruction in the Quran was free.

The Sufis, the mystics in Islam, extended this concept to include all instruction. Hence schools run by them, zawiyah, were free. These schools offered an enriched basic education but were cognates of the kuttab. The legendary al Ghazali, who later in life embraced the mystic way of life, was of the view that students should make no payment for instruction. Further, students' gratitude to teachers was out of place. Rather, teachers should be grateful to students. The basis of the teachers' gratitude should be that students entrusted the nurturing of their hearts to teachers and in performing this service teachers gained merit in the eyes of God and reward in the next life (Chaudhri 1982).

The kuttab, or maktab, was the school of the common people. Nakosteen (1964) maintained that this institution could be found in almost every village and town in the empire during the classical period of Islam and that literacy was almost universal. While Totah, Tibawi and Shallaby agree that kuttabs made elementary education widely available, and that it was democratic in that it was open to all, there is disagreement that either participation or literacy was almost universal. Chaudhri quoted Ibn Khaldun, writing at the end of the classical period, as saying that the common people did not see education as indispensable, regarded the investment as considerable and the returns delayed, and therefore did not attach the same value to it as investments that led to more immediate returns. It would appear that Nakosteen's claim may be highly optimistic.

The Adab, The Palace School

In addition to the kuttab, initiated by the common people, there were adabs, palace schools, to serve princes and children of wealthy families. Included in this genre were private tutors employed by princes and notables to teach their children in their homes. They offered an enhanced elementary education. In addition to religious instruction and the three Rs offered in the ordinary kuttab, these institutions offered instruction in oratory, good manners, conversation, ethics, history and traditions.

The difference in the curricula reflected the difference in the clientele. As Nakosteen (1964) observed both the princes and the sons of the wealthy were being prepared for positions in the government of the caliphs, and for social intercourse in the court and elite society of the times. This was elementary education with all the pretensions of court and class. In a context in which education was open to all, rich or poor, this was education that was more equal than that offered in the kuttab patronised by the common folk.

Childhood in Islam in the Classical Period

The basic educational institutions and practices developed in Islam during the classical pereiod represented a considerable advance in the conceptualisation of human development. Gil'adi (1992) studying childhood during the classical period of Islam, made the point that childhood in Islam during this period was longer than in Europe at the same time and cited as one of the reasons the widespread existence of the kuttab and its de facto definition of childhood and the absence in Europe at that time of any similar institutional definition of childhood. Children entered the kuttab at about seven and remained until about 10 or 11 years. Gil'adi also cites Ibn Sida's dictionary which showed that the Arabic language had over 40 terms to describe infants and children and various phenomena related to their development. In other words, apart from the institutional definition given by the kuttab, popular Arab culture at that time recognised the uniqueness of childhood and stages of its development This is to be contrasted with Europe at that time, where the conventional view was that as soon as children could live without constant attention from their mothers or nannies they belonged to the adult world, which was conceived to start at about seven years or earlier.

It must also be noted that the various schools of law of Islam defined childhood and several eminent jurisconsults wrote treatises on childhood themes and the obligations of parents and teachers to children. Gil'adi cited as examples Ali Mohammed's 'The Treatise Detailing the Condition of Students and the Laws Governing Teachers and Students' and Ibn Qayyim's. 'A Present for the Beloved on the Rules Concerning the Treatment of Infants'. However, the most celebrated treatises on childhood were those written by the legendary al Ghazali between 1095 and 1106. Only a mere listing of some of the more salient views of al Ghazali can be mentioned here:

·   A child is by way of being 'on loan' in care of his parents.
·   If he is made accustomed to good and he is taught, then he will grow up in goodness and his parents and teachers will share in the reward.
·   Childhood education is critical because the child is pristine and pure and therefore open and susceptible to influence.
·   The main purpose of education is to ensure the future of the believer in the next world.
·   The age of discernment, at which the child become able to make distinctions between good and evil is the point at which instruction must begin, this is by about age 7.

What is evident here is that as the Islamic empire and religion tackled the problems of settlement they not only addressed issues related to the management of the state and concerns of the faithful relative to matters of doctrine, behaviour and faith, but they also addressed issues related to human development and devised humane approaches that were well in advance of contemporary thinking in the Christian empires of those times. Stanton observed that there is no evidence of teachers abusing their students either physically or verbally. Indeed the injunction, from the ulama and jurisconsults, to both teachers and parents was to be moderate and gentle in their child rearing and disciplining practices. The kuttab, an institution created largely by private initiative, without direct intervention from state or religious community, the adab for notables and the schools run by the Sufi mystics were examples of such a response.

General Observations on Elementary schooling

The establishment of elementary education in Islam received a significant boost from the invention of paper in China, and which became widely available in the empire during the eighth century. It facilitated the copying and distribution of the Quran which became the main text book of all types of elementary schools. It also facilitated the teaching and learning of writing. Stanton noted that in the first century of Islam children in schools wrote their lessons in the sand. Clay tablets became popular but were soon replaced by paper, which allowed children to write in manuscript form. It was not the availability of paper that caused elementary schools to spread across the empire, but the technological breakthrough represented by paper facilitated and supported the social innovation represented by the elementary schools.

Stanton (1990) noted that in the subjugated lands, outside the Arabian peninsula, the kuttab and elementary school generally, became coveted institutions because they provided the means by which non-believers as well as converts to Islam could learn Arabic in order to accommodate to the new empire and the opportunities for advancement and prosperity that it offered. Social mobility prospects, through this new educational institution facilitated by the technological advancement paper presented to education and learning all came together to offer new experiences and opportunities to a large number of previously marginalised people.

COLLEGE EDUCATION AND ITS DEVELOPMENT

Initially both state and religion were led by the Ummayyad dynasty and caliphate. They sought to determine both the form of the empire and what it meant to be Muslim. In many instances this was done by force rather than by dialogue. Slowly the knowledgeable religious leaders, the ulama, began to challenge the caliphate with respect to the authority to determine normative behaviour within the faith. At issue was whether orthodoxy was to be determined by central authority. This question arose particularly in sections of the empire where the local population accepted Islam but rejected the authority of the caliphs, (Hawting 1986). The resolution of this issue brought about the first major rift in Islam but, in time, gave rise to one tradition that accepted the caliph as the successor to the Prophet, but rejected his authority as infallible in matter of faith and morals.

The vast territory made it impossible for the caliph to teach the faithful and adjudicate issues in the same direct manner as the Prophet had done. The Quran provided the scriptural basis for community resolution of matters. Learning and knowledge was the means by which the true meaning of revelation should be unravelled. Learned men from among the faithful, the ulama, therefore slowly appropriated the authority to lead the faith, with the caliph serving largely ceremonially functions as Primus Inter Pares. This devolution to the ulama was facilitated by the change of dynasty from Ummayyad to Abbasid. While the former deferred on decentralising decision-making in matters of faith the latter accepted it, in a manner not uncommon to changes in political regimes and the practice of granting concessions to groups that were allies in opposition to the previous government. Shalaby (1979) noted that by this transfer of religious authority to the ulama, the caliphs essentially became political chiefs only, conceding religious leadership to the learned among the faithful.

It is necessary to keep in mind that neither the Quran nor hadith, the exemplary behaviour of the Prophet and his companions, were sufficient to deal with the practical issues of every day living by the faithful or the requirements of administering an empire encompassing so many different peoples and cultures over such a vast area. The revelation to the Prophet envisioned this challenge and had left this task to the community stating in the Quran verse, 'My Community will never agree on an error'. This formed the basis of the decentralised nature of authority that developed in Islam and the premium placed on the consensus of the community. Consensus became the third leg on which the religion rested, in addition to the Quran and hadith, tradition. The Quran was revelation, tradition represented exemplary behaviour, consensus of the community constituted the mechanism of addressing the dynamics of faithful living.

Accepting the responsibility of leadership in the new faith, but without the benefit of ordination, the ulama initiated formal education as a means of preparing themselves and their successors for adjudicating matters of faith and morals in Islam. This determined the character and parameters of the education that was established for this purpose. It was religious in content, legalistic in nature, geared to adults, located in mosques and pitched at the higher levels of educational attainment.

The community was not specified by Quran but came to be accepted, by tradition, as those persons who were learned in the sacred scriptures. It was to these learned persons, the ulama, that the faithful turned for guidance in dealing with the dynamics of the faith as they confronted the challenges of daily living. Members of the ulama, muftis, were approached for opinions, fatwa. The Quran exhorted muftis to engage in 'ijtihad', the utmost scholarly exertion, free from any external influence in arriving at their fatwa. The mufti was rewarded in heaven, even if he was wrong, provided he had engaged in ijtihad. He was doubly rewarded if he were right.

Makdisi (1995) outlined the process that evolved by which consensus was achieved in determining the orthodoxy of the faith. These stages can be briefly summarised as follows:

- The mufti approached on a matter gave his fatwa based on his personal research and free from any external influence.
- The layman was free to consult as many muftis as he wished, or could afford, and was free to accept any fatwa he chose from among those he

had received.

- His choice invested the opinion with the first level of consensus.
- The second level of consensus was unanimous acceptance by the ulama, representing the Islamic community.
- Usually, however, there were several opinions on a single matter that had been invested with the first level of consensus resulting in conflicting opinions.
- The ulama therefore engaged in disputation as the method of determining the opinion that was the strongest and worthy of unanimous consensus.
- Where no single opinion prevailed, but where two opposing views proved equally strong both were considered orthodox. This became the sic et non, yes and no, questions which generated the most prolific legal literature of Islam and so doing became the means of recording both the orthodoxy and its history.
- In the absence of any central authority in Islam – pope or bishop, synod or council – consensus was established negatively and retroactively by the absence of any known authoritative dissent.
- Consensus was always provisional since authoritative dissent could arise with new data and interpretation.

Ahmed (1992) offered a different perspective to Makdisi's observation that consensus was always provisional. While agreeing with Makdisi that the process of reaching consensus was long and arduous, and that the points on which the ulama reached consensus were binding, she maintained that these points of law, having been vested with such authority, were deemed infallible and extremely difficult to change. To repeal a past consensus, while theoretically possible, because of the authority vested in it, was highly unlikely. In fact to contradict such an agreement was viewed as heresy. From Ahmed's perspective Makdisi's outline represents the process and its rationale. His observation on the provisional nature of consensus represents the theory rather than the reality.

The position taken here is that the merit of both perspectives is best appreciated against some time-frame. Ahmed's perspective is substantiated by empirical observations about several points of Islamic law on which consensus was reached several centuries ago that are still operative today. There is also the consideration that the continual provisional status of consensus could lead to perpetual flux by repeatedly revisiting the same issues in rapid succession. Makdisi's outline of the rationale of the process highlights the fact that there is no final or fixed point even with respect to those aspects of the law that appear intractable even at the present time. An authoritative and sustained challenge could result in change in the future. The caveat is that it will need to conform to the stages he outlined. In other words, one cannot deny that even at the present time some aspect of previous consensus is in the process of change. Current challenge, conflict and tension over points of previous consensus could lead to the repeal of the old and replacement with a new consensus at some future time provided the challenge was sustained and persuaded some future set of the ulama of its merit.

The critical point to recognise is that in a religion with no central authority but rather a decentralised process of addressing issues arising from the dynamics of the faith, consensus is achieved often across generations and not necessarily in the generation raising the issue. Also consensus having been achieved is difficult to change. The conservative nature by which it is achieved is probably exaggerated in its repeal. Given the sustained effort required to establish consensus on any point, and the longevity of those arrived at, points of consensus may have the appearance of infallibility and finality. The factors most likely to alter the appearance of infallibility and the rates of both reaching and repealing consensus may be those related to external threat to the entire community.

The purpose of the system of higher education created by Islam was to train muftis to issue fatwa, responsa to the faithful who sought guidance in applying the faith to the circumstances of life. In the first instance the training had to cover the Quran, hadith, Arabic grammar and the methods of both analogy and disputation. The scholar had to know the scriptures, be conversant with the tradition, and possess the ability to interpret written texts correctly through his knowledge of Arabic grammar. He had to master analogy, the means of comparing the situation he was presented with, or its opposite, to some known situation for which the answer was established. He had to be able to choose the appropriate analogy. Further, he had to master the scholastic method, the very essence of jurisprudence.

But the training of the mufti did not end there. The matters on which he could be consulted could come from any area of daily living or of the affairs of the state. Theology and law had to be buttressed with knowledge in other areas. Because the pursuit of education was very much up to the scholar, rather than prescribed by the institution, members of the ulama versed themselves in practically all areas of knowledge.

The Institutional Structure of the College System

Makdisi (1981) made the point that the first institution of higher learning in Islam was the mosque. He points to the distinction between the jami, the congregational mosque in which the Friday sermon was delivered, and the masjid, the non-congregational mosque that was a place of teaching and prayer. He identifies the masjid as the first educational institution of Islam. The masjid was the community mosque, with a professor who usually doubled as the imam, who after the ritual prayers, taught the students enrolled or visiting his lectures.

The congregational mosque, jami, had to be authorised by the caliph, and was located in large centres of population. It was also an educational institution through the halqas, study circles, which met there. The study circles were common to all jamis and were the places of teaching where the shaikh, professor, leaning on pillar or wall, taught the students seated in circles around him. Sometimes the circles were so large that a repeater assisted him. In the jami the preacher, delivered the Friday sermon, and several shaikhs taught different study circles at other times. The format of teaching the halqa was quite standard. The professor would announce the topic and outline the sub-headings. Having delivered the exposition on the topic he would invite responses from the students who were sometimes provoked into discussion. The shaikh, sometimes assisted by the repeater would examine the notebooks of the students, make corrections and offer comments. The student largely determined the length of time he remained in a particular study circle. At the time of leaving he could request a certificate by the shaikh, a license, specifying his achievements in studying with him. The number of licences received by a student, and the shaikhs with whom he had studied, would bear testimony to his learning and credibility as a scholar.

Makdisi (1981) highlighted the fact that the mosque was the central point in the life of Islam. From its pulpits the faithful were edified through preaching. From those very pulpits policies of the state were proclaimed. From its floor professors taught those striving after knowledge and wisdom, and within its walls justice was dispensed. The point to note here is that scholars, preachers, college teachers and judges were interchangeable vocations for which virtually the same preparation was given.

Makdisi traced the evolution of colleges from their beginning in early Islam as masjids, mosque-colleges. By the eighth century khans, wayside inns or hostels, started to be located adjacent to some masjids or in close proximity. While serving others, they also provided accommodation for out-of-town students. By the tenth century the masjid-khans, mosque colleges with residential accommodation, became flourishing educational complexes. By the eleventh century the final stage in the evolution of colleges took place, with the establishment of the madrasah, the residential college separated from the mosque.

The evolution of new forms did not result in the elimination of the previous forms, hence masjids continued to operate after masjidkhans became popular and both after madrasahs became the mainline institution. While masjidkhans emerged out of the fact that masjids were located in towns but offered opportunities to students coming from other places, the emergence of the madrasah was more profound. The madrasah was a college not physically connected or related to a mosque. It marked the point of separation of the college from the mosque. It represented a fundamental departure from tradition. Shallaby (1979) noted that while the other types of colleges continued to exist, the madrasah became the main institution of college education as most of the students and teachers shifted to this institution. Further comment, at a later stage, will be made concerning the factors related to this shift in institutional organisation.

Apart from the mosque and the madrasah, there were several other institutions through which higher education was offered. While some were colleges, like the madrasah, others were places where classes were given by individual scholars, in a manner similar to the halqa in the jami. Nakosteen (1964), Makdisi (1981) and Stanton (1990) between them listed the following types of institutions.

a) Ribats, colleges located in monasteries, staffed and run by the Sufis. While the curriculum was similar to that of the masjids and madrasah, other aspects of life specifically related to the mystic traditions of monastic living were also included in the course of study.

b) Bookshops not only sold books but were also centres of learning in that they were the location of several study circles, halqas. The invention of paper gave rise to this new kind of commercial enterprise – places where books were both copied and sold. Bookshops could be found in urban centres throughout the empire. Stanton noted that Baghdad alone had over 100 bookshops and all major cities had multiple bookshops. They became clearing houses for the dissemination of ideas and places where scholars gathered for discussion. Scholars became attached to particular shops and often formed and taught study circles there. Sometimes the owner himself would form and teach a halqa at his shop in a subject in which he was competent.

c) Public libraries were another centre of learning. Not only did they house books but also had rooms in which study circles could be held. All major cities had public libraries. Stanton reported that Baghdad had thirty-six public libraries. He also noted that the book stocks of the public libraries ranged from 100,000 to 1,000,000 books covering all major disciplines of knowledge at that time. He also noted that in both Cairo and Baghdad, some public libraries had as many as 40 to 50 rooms, several of which were used for halqas.

d) Private libraries. Many princes and wealthy notables had private libraries of some magnitude. Several private libraries had more than 100,000 volumes. Some acquired important and rare manuscripts that they would make available to scholars. Several of these libraries also housed study circles. Because of the status of their owners, and the fact that they were private and not under the control of state or ulama, many private libraries had collections that were not necessarily approved by the orthodoxy of the particular time, but allowed scholars to continued to study those subjects.

e) Hospitals were the seat of medical education. They received support from public funds and were routinely inspected by the state to ensure that they continued to meet the standards that would maintain their grants from the public purse. In return for their public support, hospitals provided free treatment to their patients. In addition to the public grant, hospitals were invariably the beneficiaries of endowments, through the law of waqf, which also paid staff, constructed and maintained buildings. Stanton reported that in 1160 Baghdad had 860 licensed physicians and over 60 medical facilities, clinics or hospitals. There were also famous hospitals in Cairo, Damascus, Cordova and Seville. Hospitals usually had waiting halls, treatment rooms, patient accommodations, pharmacies, study halls and libraries. Medical education, especially clinical training, followed much the same pattern as is common today. Physicians made rounds with the students, theory was integrated with practice and noted physicians were employed to carry out the training. Unlike the other areas of higher education, physicians were licensed by the state after taking the Hippocratic oath. In addition to medical education, hospitals were also sites for study circles particularly in science-based subjects and the speculative subjects. Consistent with the concepts of education of the times, physicians also studied philosophy, religion, theology, astrology and astronomy. Hospitals also provided facilities for study circles for such scholars and their students.

f) The literary salon was an innovation by the caliph which later spread to governors and lesser rulers and merchants with an interest in learning. While participation was by invitation and therefore highly selective, it provided an important forum in which scholarly exchanges took place and where topical issues regarding affairs of state received the benefit of intellectual analysis. The proceedings of the salon followed strict protocol. The sponsor would choose the topic and select the invitees, the latter including scholars, officials of state, political appointees, religious leaders and theologians. All invitees would be expected to read the appropriate manuscripts or books and come prepared for discussion. Over time the particular salon discussed a wide range of topics in various fields. The reputation of the salon depended upon the level of the ruler issuing the invitation and the quality of the scholars invited. Young scholars and aspirants to various positions eagerly sought invitations.

g) There were a few observatories in the empire and each of these was also a centre of learning. Equipped with scientific equipment and libraries they were centres for studying astronomy and astrology.

h) Shallaby (1979) noted that before mosque colleges were established in the first century, the homes of scholars were the main centres of higher learning. Afterwards, while the colleges became the major loci, the homes of scholars continued to be a site of higher learning. Ahmed (1968) observed that the biographies of many of the 8831 scholars who lived or worked in Baghdad in the four hundred years between 762 and 1185, showed that the homes of scholars were centres of learning especially in the early years of the evolution of the system. The home of one scholar was used for classes for over 50 years. Ibn Hanbal taught female students at his house in the evenings. al Ghazali after he retired established a study circle at his home and taught there for several years.

i)   Shops were also a place of learning. Several scholars were also merchants. For convenience they held classes at their businesses (Ahmed 1968).

From the above it can be seen that the institutional base of higher education in the classical period of Islam showed great variation and a high degree of sophistication in several areas. Students basically studied with a particular shaikh, professor, who taught a particular subject and then moved to other shaikhs as they deemed fit. The institutional arrangements tolerated a remarkable degree of individualism because the basic arrangement was between the shaikh and the student and only secondarily with the institution. Probably only medicine was the exception to this general pattern.

The quintessential nature of the system is manifest in the halqa of the jami. The students were in the study circle of a particular professor teaching a particular subject. Having studied with that scholar for some time, if the student came to master the book or subject the professor was teaching, then the professor was obliged to give the student a license, certificate, specifying the level of competence achieved by the student in that particular area. The student then moved to study another subject with another professor. Essentially this meant that the period of studentship was protracted; perennial students were not unknown, studying up to fifteen to twenty years in some instances. Students studied with a large number of professors in a wide variety of subjects, located in many different places. The students themselves largely determined their course of study. The investment in scholarly pursuits, therefore, was considerable.

This picture, while essentially typical of the system, must be qualified in terms of time. The image or stereotype of peripatetic students sitting at the feet of learned professors in several distant lands is more true of the early than the later centuries of the classical period. As masjid-khan, ribats and madrassah made their appearance studentship became more settled in these institutions as professors of different disciplines taught in a single location. Further, the system of licensing became more formalised, particularly with respect to jurisprudence. Hence, while the system never lost its decentralised and individualistic tendencies, at the end of its evolution it offered formal professional education and training in institutions as well as knowledge a la carte.

The Challenge of Greek Thought

As noted previously the ruling dynasties of the empire adopted the policy of assimilating and not destroying the cultures of the peoples they had conquered. Included in the amalgam of people were several religions. The tenets of faith of the Nestorian, Coptic and Monophysite Christians, the Jews, Zoroastrians and Neoplatonist Gnostics were not far removed from Islam. They all believed that God was One, in a spirit world between God and man, in communication between the spirit world and mankind, in justice, service and good deeds. Hinduism was somewhat different, but it had a scripture and was also far removed from the centre of the empire and faith. While it could be shown that Islam through the process of assimilation was influenced by all of these, the major challenge came from Greek non-theistic thought. The religions encompassed in the Islamic empire were accorded an inferior status and confined to their own people, with the weight of conversion and attrition resting against them. On the other hand, Greek thought challenged the Islamic mind.

In the quest for knowledge the intellectual achievement of the Greeks could not be ignored. Both Ummayyad and Abbasidic caliphs in the first two centuries of their 400-year rule commissioned translations of the Greek classics into Arabic. This included the entire range of disciplines from philosophy to medicine. It was philosophy that particularly engaged and intrigued some Islamic scholars. It gave rise, in time, to the rationalist movement in Islam, which attempted to Islamise Greek thought. This resulted in the development of philosophical theology, which placed reason higher than revelation. Reason was already being employed by the ulama to address the challenges of daily living by the faithful for which there was no apparent revelation. It may have been this paradox in the practice of Islam that made Greek thought attractive to some segments of the ulama and prompted them to give reason priority in the contest with revelation.

Both Makdisi (1995) and Stanton (1990) referred to the tension which developed between the rationalist movement and the traditionalist reaction which called the faithful back to the teaching of the Prophet that revelation was the primary basis of religious life. The traditionalist movement had developed a juridical theology based on the revealed law of the sacred scriptures, and while admitting that reason was important could not accept its primacy over revelation.

The struggle between these two movements, for supremacy in determining orthodoxy, led in the ninth century to the Inquisition carried out by the caliph, with the rationalists as the persecutors. The focus of the controversy centred on whether the Quran was the created or uncreated Word of God. The traditionalists endured fifteen years of persecution, which included humiliation, imprisonment, torture, and even death of some who refused to accept that the Quran was created, but maintained that it was the very Words of God Himself. Eventually the traditionalists prevailed when the new caliph ended the Inquisition. The traditionalist victims emerged triumphant. Revelation had prevailed against reason through long-suffering. The persecuting rationalists had failed to advance the cause of reason by the instruments of coercion.

Cragg (1991) made the very interesting point that Muslim scholars in the Inquisition were being split on the nature of the Quran, in a manner similar to the divisions among Christian scholars concerning the nature of Jesus. They were also facing similar problems to those that split Jewish society in the time of Hellenic influence, and brought about the divisions between Pharisees and Sadducees. Greek philosophy espousing reason, rationality and reality posed problems for monotheistic religions embracing revelation, and faith as their defining values. At different points in their histories, monotheistic religions embracing the ethical utopian society confronted the inherent contradictions of human society and sought to reconcile Greek rationalist thought with their ethical vision based on revelation.

Following their victory the traditionalists took a number of important steps to defend the faith, and themselves. These steps were designed to achieve the twin objectives of greater independence from the caliph, on whom they would prefer not to depend, and excluding the rationalists who had sought their demise. First, they closed ranks. In the preceding two centuries of Islam over 500 schools of laws had been created across the empire, each reflecting various nuances in interpretation. These began to contract after the Inquisition as they coalesced around four leading jurists. Second, they marshalled resources to establish masjids and masjid-khans with professorships that were exclusively devoted to the study of law and excluded the foreign sciences including philosophy. Third, they reformed the issuing of licenses so that only those who were issued with the 'license to teach and to issue legal opinions' could give fatwa to the faithful.

In one respect the cause of education benefited because of these developments. With the expansion in the number of colleges, students found it easier to pursue their studies in that there were more institutions and in many cases they did not have to go to so many different locations to find teachers. Also they had more convenient lodgings in the locations in which they studied. In another sense education lost in that colleges now restricted their curriculum to the study of law, where previously they covered the entire range of disciplines studied in higher education. The study of the 'foreign sciences' was now consigned to the more informal institutions in which the ecclesiastics exercised little control. These were the study circles, halqas, literary salons located in bookstores, hospitals, observatories and libraries. Interestingly, medicine became the main refuge of philosophy after the Inquisition (Makdisi 1981).

Factors Related to the Evolution of the Madrasah

The physical separation of the madrasah from the mosque marked a turning point in higher education in Islam more fundamental than the reaction of traditionalists after the Inquisition. If the traditionalists tried to gain greater independence from the state through the masjid-khan, the state reacted to establish its own hegemony over the college system. The formation of the madrasah was a deliberate move to shift control of higher education away from the ulama and place it more conveniently under political and state control. Two factors lay at the root of this development.

Schism in Islam resulted in sectarian strife and competition. Iraq, Syria and Egypt had come under Shi'ite rule. The conquest of Baghdad in 1069 had led to the replacement of a Shi'ite by a Sunni dynasty. The orthodox Sunni maintained that the caliphs were not infallible, while the Shi'ite faction insisted on the infallibility of the Imam. The Sunni's regarded the Shi'ite position as heresy. One function of the madrasahs created in the eleventh century was to teach Sunni orthodoxy thereby supplanting the Shi'ite heresy (Shallaby 1979).

Totah (1926), Nakosteen (1964), Stanton (1990) and others, maintained that the more powerful reason was to gain popular acceptance of the Turkish rulers who had assumed political leadership in Islam as the sultans. At the point of Arab conquest the Turks were slaves. In four centuries of Abbasid rule they had risen as both a military and political force in the empire. Also, they had converted to Islam. However, while being Muslim, they had no direct line of connection with the Prophet. They therefore lacked pedigree in terms of tracing their origins to the fountainhead of the faith. By founding madrasahs in the eleventh century the sultans hoped to advance their popularity and acceptance with the people, while at the same time winning some support from the religious community and professors by the benefits accruing through these new institutions, which were the closest approximations in Islam to state colleges. The madrasahs enrolled large numbers of students, and offered them free accommodation and scholarships. They also provided for staff of all levels, including professors, better pay and pensions for the first time. While a few masjids and masjid-khans had libraries this was by no means a standard provision. The new madrasahs all included substantial libraries.

While the political motives of the Turkish sultans in directing the resources of the state to establish madrasahs can be easily demonstrated, it must also be admitted that this innovation addressed many of the weaknesses in the system that had emerged with mosque colleges. These related to the terms and conditions of service of the staff, limited access of students to formal institutions, the hardships placed on students in finding accommodation and the Spartan nature of the learning facilities. By addressing these structural weaknesses within the masjid system, the sultans and the Sunnis hoped to jointly advance their interests through one comprehensive reform.

Shalaby observed that in addition to the political and sectarian motives there were practical reasons for separating the colleges from the mosques.

Mosques had literally been overtaken by their educational functions. Apart from Friday prayers they were in constant use as colleges. In a way this detracted from the mosque as a place of worship and reverence. Further, mosques were not ideal for instruction because they had to serve religious purposes. The separation, therefore, was to be expected at some point in history.

The madrasah marked a new era in Islamic education. Political patronage and sectarian strife now made their entrance into higher education in an open and undisguised form. While the Sunnis created it to promote their brand of Islam, the Shiites responded with the establishment of madrasahs of their own. Islam was now fractured on denominational lines. In addition, the caliphate was now marginalised, and the new rulers sought acceptance through patronage by supporting the education and training of the future ulama.

By this innovation the system of higher education in Islam had evolved to its final form in the classical period. After the Inquisition mosque colleges narrowed their range of studies to include only the law. With the establishment of the madrasah the study of law was contracted to four orthodox positions, each presided over by its own guild.

In early Islam, both learning and matters of faith dictated that the ulama needed to adjudicate all-embracing issues requiring a wide breath of knowledge and an appreciation of its unity. The tradition of the scholar, and the colleges, followed more or less the same pattern as the Greek polymath or the Renaissance scholar. The Islamic haqim at first not only sought mastery in the law, but also mastery of some combination of the following fields: grammar, philosophy, mathematics, lexicology, astronomy, alchemy, poetry, literature, history, geography, medicine or logic. By the eleventh century, however, that concept had essentially been abandoned. The jurisconsult would largely be only a doctor of the law and not a shaikh as before, although he continued to bear the title.

One result of the separation of the college from the mosque, achieved by founding the madrasah, was the rapid expansion of higher education. To fully understand this expansion, which cannot be accounted for entirely by sectarian rivalry or political patronage, some scrutiny is necessary of the law of waqf, the charitable foundation, upon which formal higher education institutions were founded.

The Law of Waqf and the Charitable Trust

One of the five basic tenets of Islam is charity. This was one way by which affluent Muslims could find favour with God. This religious tenet found legal expression in the law of waqf that provided the institutional framework for charity, the trust. Makdisi (1981) gives a full account of the law of waqf, of which only a few salient points can be stated here.

The founders of the trust had to be of age, in their right minds and outright owners of the asset.

- Founders had great latitude in determining the objects of their charity provided these were consistent with the tenets of Islam.
- Founders could impose their will with respect to the administration of the trust, the appointment of trustees, the designation of beneficiaries and the distribution of income.
- Once the trust was established even the founders could not change it. In other words, the founders themselves were bound by the trusts they had established. The trust was sacrosanct; it had the authority of the lawgiver himself, God.
- The trust was in perpetuity. The asset donated could not be alienated by sale, mortgage or gift. It could, however, be swapped for comparable property to continue the trust if for some reason the property donated could no longer fulfil the purpose of the trust.
- The asset donated had to be tangible and immobile, with the exception of books.

If the object of the charity was a mosque, the gift was to God and the founder had no further control of it. If the trust was for any other purpose, while the purpose could not be changed or the asset recovered, the founders, or their successors in law, could maintain control of the management of the trust. Every trust had to have a trustee, since Islamic law recognised only a person as a legal entity, unlike Roman law that recognised a corporation as a legal persona.

Mosques were major beneficiaries of the law of waqf particularly in the early centuries of Islam. Inspired by piety thousands of masjids, mosque-colleges, were established all over the Islamic empire with at least one professor who also doubled as the imam. Higher education therefore was founded upon the philanthropy of the wealthy faithful. However, the donors had no control over their endowment since it was a gift to God. Such control fell to the ulama in the particular location. By this measure neither the content nor the processes of higher education was determined by the philanthropists who donated the resources. It does not appear that this mattered very much because these institutions were responding to the urgent needs of a new religion in its formative stages as it euphorically strove to meet all the challenges presented. The faithful needed guidance, the ulama needed training, while the wealthy owed much of their bounty to the exertions of both empire and religion.

Other favourite objects of charitable trusts were monasteries, hospitals, bridges, the release of prisoners from the prisons of unbelievers and alms for the poor. After the eleventh century madrasahs were added to this list. The law of waqf provided the legal framework for the practical fulfilment of one of the five basic tenets of Islam – giving alms and supporting the faithful. In this context the major motive for charitable trusts was obedience to the faith. The patrons hoped for spiritual advancement through leaving a tangible legacy of good works.

However, as Makdisi and Stanton point out, there were very earthly and practical reasons that made the madrasah a favourite object of charity. Because of their connection to such a basic article of the faith, charitable trusts were exempt from taxation and therefore became a means of escaping taxation. Also because the trust was sacrosanct, it became a way of guarding against confiscation of property and assets by powerful personages of the state, which was not an uncommon practice of the times. Further, it provided the wealthy, including the princes, with a means of patronage for which their beneficiaries and their descendants would quite likely be eternally grateful. Makdisi suggested that the charitable trust was also a mechanism used by families to thwart or restrict the excessive prodigality of some sons.

The significance of both the heavenly and earthly motives of charitable trusts to the founding of madrasahs was that the separation of mosque from college gave the founders greater freedom with respect to certain aspects of their endowment. Stanton pointed out that because the masjids and the masjid-khans were mosques, even though their primary functions were as colleges, the local religious authorities exercised the rights to appoint the imam although he was also the shaikh, the professor of the college. In other words, the local ulama shared authority with the trustees in administering certain aspects of the trust. By separating the college from the mosque, the direct control of the local ulama was removed and the trustees gained sole responsibility for the administration of the endowment.

In addition, the priority of the distribution of the income changed in favour of the professor and his helpers, whereas with the masjid the support of the imam took precedence to the shaikh. Even more importantly, the excess of the trust income over the expenses of its charitable purpose could be distributed to descendants. Through the general protection offered by the law of waqf, and the separation of the college from the mosques, endowing madrasahs became a secure way of ensuring that the descendants of the generous benefactors would share in the inheritance.

It was through these subtle but significant shifts that the invention of the madrasah permitted state control and sectarian direction. When the state with Sunni support established madrasahs, through the law of waqf like every other endowment, they could secure control of its administration including the appointment and pay of professors. This control would be in perpetuity. In the madrasahs that the state founded, it could impose its will without reference to the ulama. Interestingly, at the same time that the Sunni ulama were empowering themselves generally through their alliance with the state, the local ulama were being disenfranchised. Complicity in the scheme brought little or no resistance at the local level, as Shiites, who were being excluded by this manoeuvre, simply established their own madrasahs.

The same circumvention by which the sultans and the Sunni could advance their interests through patronage, and Shiites could defend themselves, allowed individual donors to retain greater control over their endowments to education since the restrictions related to religion and the direct control of the ulama had been sidelined. Founders and their heirs could now administer the trust without ulama intervention, they could specify the appointment of professors and their assistants. In brief, the invention of the madrasah gave wealthy families a more perfect instrument of retaining their wealth within their lineage. The madrasah served their earthly motives of genealogical preservation even better than the several other objects of waqf that were still tied to religious ends.

Stanton drove home the significance of this practice by drawing attention to the fact that madrasahs were not established in Spain and Sicily. Both these places followed the more conservative Maliki school of law, which interpreted the law of waqf in ways that did not allow the founders, or their heirs, to appoint the professors and his assistants, or for the founders to appoint themselves or their heirs as trustees. The school of law followed in Spain and Sicily continued to interpret the law of waqf in the same manner that had obtained for the masjid. Benefactors in Spain and Sicily would therefore gain no greater control over their endowments by establishing madrasahs as against masjids or masjid-khans. Endowments in education in these two provinces continued in the traditional relationship with the mosque, as no earthly advantage would be gained by establishing the more secular madrassah.

Education and students profited from this wider range of benefactors. More places were available for higher education. Scholars could now complete their studies in a single place instead of being peripatetic. Libraries were now part of the facilities of the madrasahs. The size sophistication, standards and facilities of higher education in the eleventh and twelfth centuries were the most advanced in the world at that time. What was less apparent was that the factors that had brought this system to this level of maturity, had fomented, nay virtually ensured, its future decay.

By the beginning of the thirteenth century the two-tiered educational system had developed to full maturity with all its constituent components in place. The large madrasahs in the major cities constituted its crowning glory. Not only did they have magnificent buildings but they included boarding accommodation, library and administrative support staff. Students enjoyed free tuition and boarding and professors were paid better than before and had pensions. In terms of pedagogy and scholarship, the system had developed the scholastic method that still formed an essential part of legal education. The madrasah itself became the precursor for the universities that were to be fashioned in Europe.

The Mongolian invasion of 1250 and the holocaust which followed, in a backhanded way, served to expand and spread Islamic education even further. The sources of this new thrust were three fold. Religious piety was invoked by many who interpreted the events as punishment from the almighty. The new rulers anxious to gain acceptance turned to patronage though education. Khan (1967) and Ali (1983) both noted that the faithful fleeing to the Indian sub-continent and elsewhere in Asia took with them the institutional forms and other educational paraphernalia and implanted them in the places in which they sought refuge.

GENDER IN ISLAM

Since this study is focused on the gender of teachers it is essential to examine the conceptions of gender and the evolution of gender relations in Islamic society in the classical period. A usual and convenient starting point for such deliberation has been reference to the cultural practices and norms that obtained in the Arabian peninsula prior to Islam. Engineer (1992) and others make reference to the fact that pre-Islamic nomadic Arabian tribes manifested traditional patriarchal cultural forms in which males were clearly dominant and females distinctly subordinated in almost all relationships. Several oppressive measures were commonly practised against women. A few of these can be enumerated as follows:

- The killing of female infants, some of whom were buried alive.
- Polygamy in which men had eight to ten, or even more, wives
- Contractual marriages in which dowry was paid but confiscated by the male members of the bride's family.
- Husbands were able to take a vow not to have sexual relations for as long as two years with a wife who had fallen into disfavour for whatever reason.
- Men were able to divorce women but could reserve the right of consent to any future marriage.
- Men divorcing their wives, but retaining control over them, by declaring them to be a female relative: mother, sister or aunt.
- Women having no rights of inheritance.

Islam, through the Quran and the Prophet, mitigated many of these oppressive measures. It totally forbade the killing of infants and exhorted the faithful to treasure female offspring. It enunciated a preference for one wife, but set a maximum limit of four. It made the dowry the sole possession of the bride, limited the vow of abstinence by the husband to four months and 10 days and gave women rights of inheritance. It outlawed the husbands' right to consent to the future marriages of their divorced wives or to divorce them by declaring them to be female relatives.

Further, in terms of religious obligations before God, the Quran made no distinction between men and woman. Indeed, several passages recited the equal obligations of men and women to seek after right living and right relationships. In its explanation of creation it made no distinction between men and women. The Quran had no comparable story to that of Eve. Men and women were created at the same time, from the same substance emanating from God, thereby implying their equality.

Mortley (1981) was of the view that Islam advanced the situation of women, over what previously obtained in Arabia and what was common in tribal society. However, this advance was evolutionary and not revolutionary. In other words, Islam, represented by its dicta and practices, made advances over contemporary times in the treatment of women but it did not fundamentally change their status in relation to men. To substantiate his view Mortley points out that while there was an entire chapter devoted to the regulation of womens' behaviour there was no comparable chapter setting out that for men. Also, the literal interpretation of several verses implied male superiority over women particularly as their managers and protectors. While women were given the right of inheritance their share was less than male claimants. Where wives committed adultery the Quran sanctioned corporal punishment by the husband, while in the case of adultery by the husband the wife was counselled to seek reconciliation.

Taking a different position to that of Mortley, Ahmed (1992) made the point that looking at gender relations in Islam solely in terms of what existed prior to Islam in the Arabian peninsula may lead to inaccuracy or be even simplistic. While she agreed with some of the descriptions given concerning practices prior to Islam she cited the fact that there were other practices that would suggest that women had a more egalitarian position in pre-Islamic Arabia. She maintained that women participated fully in war as nurses, motivators of the troops and even soldiers. Some women in Mecca protested the teachings of the Prophet, and rejoiced at his death with the hope that the demise of the religion would soon follow. The source of their concern was anticipated curtailment of their freedom, if the religion took hold. From Ahmed's perspective, while account must be taken of the pre-Islamic situation there are other factors that are of more profound import.

It was noted in Chapter 2 that the subordination of women in ancient civilisation became institutionalised in the public sphere with the rise of urban societies and city-states in the region, first in Sumer and then elsewhere. As tribal groupings made the transition from lineage society to non-kinship forms of association, as represented by the city-state, women who were marginalised by patriarchy with respect to their fathers, husbands, uncles, brothers and sons began to be marginalised with respect to all men. Further, it was noted that as successive city-states gained ascendancy in Mesopotamia, patriarchal forms in the public sphere became more entrenched and women became even more marginalised as family patterns were consequently adjusted.

Arabian tribes, mobilised by Islam, had little or no experience with city living. Mecca and Medina were not large urban centres. While women were subordinated in the tribe and lineage, their marginalisation may not have been as generalised to all men as was the case with their peers with a longer history of city-state civilisation. Ahmed demonstrated this point dramatically with her contrast of the circumstances of Mohammad's first wife Khadija and his youngest wife Aisha

Khadija was a wealthy widow who employed the young Mohammad to oversee her caravan. She made marriage entreaties to Mohammad who was twenty-five when they were married, she being forty. Not only was she much older than Mohammad, but no male intermediary negotiated on her behalf. She remained his only wife until her death at sixty-two. Her financial means and general encouragement were an important factor in facilitating Mohammad's pursuit of his mission. The entire circumstances of this marriage to a woman of pre-Islamic Arabia suggest mutuality and a great deal of equality.

Aisha was born to Moslem parents and was married to Mohammad when she was nine. She along with co-wives began to be secluded and practised veiling. While recognising the special circumstances that occasioned these events and acknowledging that Mohammad himself did treat his wives in a manner to provide the basis for the patterns that developed, Ahmed made the point that this contrast between Khadija and Aisha symbolically anticipated what was to develop in time in Islam. The process at the root of this evolution was adjustment to the cultures of the peoples that Islam had conquered.

Ahmed noted that in early Islam women attended mosques, took part in religious services, listened to Mohammad's discourses and participated in feast days. By the end of the Abbasid caliphate, women were absent from all the cultural arenas of central community affairs. They could no longer be found in mosques, on the battlefield or in cultural life. Women were restricted to the household and to the private sphere. In Ahmed's view the weight of Abbasid society gave rise to androcentric teaching within Islam. It represented more the ideology of gender of a Persian society than of Islam.

Within a hundred years the Islamic empire had conquered peoples whose cultures based on city-state living had evolved over several millennia. The Persian Empire and Sassanian civilisation, which had existed for over a thousand years, was virtually next-door. Because of both proximity and numbers of captives taken, Sassanian civilisation posed the greatest social and cultural challenge to both the new empire and nascent faith. If Greek thought challenged the Muslim mind, then Persian culture challenged its social organisation and mores.

First, that Zoroastrianism, the state religion of the Persians, was monotheistic made the challenge even greater because of the similarities it immediately established between conquerors and conquered. The theological distance of conversion was shortened for the conquered Persians, and the moral heights of declaring them infidels were lowered for the Islamic conquerors. From another perspective the common monotheism of Islam and Zoroastrianism facilitated confession of Islam while still holding to the tenets of Zoroastrianism.

Second, large numbers of captives were taken and transported to Arabia including royalty, soldiers, women, children and slaves. Among these captives were women liberated from enormous harems of wives and concubines that the princes and wealthy notables of Persia were renowned for keeping. Status and wealth in the Persian empire were judged, if not displayed, by the sizes of these harems appropriately guarded by eunuchs. The Persians also had large slave holdings, the majority of whom were female. Part of the bounty of conquest therefore was large numbers of women of different status, who became available to their conquerors. Large numbers of these captured women were redeployed in household service.

Third, the rewards of conquest were so great and the proximity of Persia so close, that large numbers of Arabs participated in the bounty. Stanton was of the view that one of the reasons that the conquest was so prolonged was that having formed such a large army, it was difficult to disband it hence it just kept going. Ahmed saw it differently. For her the huge wealth and booty that accrued to the generals and soldiers provided ample reinforcement to both increase the size of the army and to keep it going.

Ahmed implied that the temptations of this largesse proved too much even for those whose mission it was to establish Islam universally. She gave as an example al Zubair, Aisha's brother-in-law, who had one thousand slaves and one thousand concubines when he died. Caliph Ali, married to Mohammad's daughter Fatima, and who lived monogamously until she died, thereafter acquired nine wives and several concubines. Hasan, his son, married and divorced 100 women in his lifetime.

Fourth, given the policy of assimilation that was practised generally by the Arab victors and the process of adjustment that was inevitable, fusion with Persian culture set both the context and the text of Islamic gender relations. But it was not only the excess of the soldiers and the ruling elite that set the parameters of cultural assimilation rather it was the daily interaction between the conquering Arabs and conquered Persians that led to Persian conversion to Islam and Arab adoption of many aspects of Sassanian culture. It is not uncharitable to say that notwithstanding several points of congruence between Zoroastrianism and Islam, the Persian elite had much to gain from conversion to Islam. At the same time, many of the recently enriched Arabs were unaccustomed to the ways of the palace and had much to learn from the more sophisticated Persians. The assimilation between Arabian and Persian culture was much more rapid among the wealthy and the rulers than in the empire as a whole. The evidence of this is that almost a hundred years after the death of the Prophet, Arabs who had married into Persian families or vice versa, seized the government and became the ruling Abbasid dynasty that lasted over 400 years.

Ahmed underscored her argument that it was Persian influence that was mainly responsible for gender ideology in Islam by observing that men creating the text of the Abbasid age – literary and legal – grew up in households experiencing and internalising structures of power governing the relationships between men and women of cultures imported into Arabia. Further, they observed women in the new ethos in which the woman's only means of securing the survival of herself and children was manipulation, falsehood and poison, instruments of the powerless. Later most of the women they related to were those that they owned. In these circumstances, increasingly, Abbasid nobles adopted the practices of Sassanian nobility. These included large harems, emphasis on virginity and disgust at remarriage.

As Ahmed so eloquently observed, there are two voices in the Quran and the traditions of the Prophet, the ethical vision and the pragmatic accommodation to the times. The former speaks to the equality of men and women in their spiritual duties and obligation before God and is 'stubbornly egalitarian' in its postures. The other addresses the issue of what seems practical in the circumstances. The rulers of the empire and the wealthy in Persia and Arabia quickly heard the voice of pragmatism and made their adjustments calculating their immediate gains or losses. The shape of Islam, however, depended to some extent on which voice the ulama heard.

In Ahmed's view the ulama hardly heard the voice proclaiming the ethical vision but invariably responded to the imperatives of pragmatic regulation. She maintained that the general ethical injunctions of the Quran were rarely transformed into enforceable law but only recognised as binding as a matter of conscience. She pointed to the entrenchment of patrilineal family patterns which put women at a considerable disadvantage in marriage, the continuation of polygamy, the development of the convention of the seclusion of women, the institution of veiling and elaborate rules relating to menstruation and ritual purity. By these means women's position in Islam became more unequal under the Abbasid dynasty than it had been during Mohammed's time.

This assessment of the ulama seems harsh in that it ignored many aspects of Persian laws, customs and mores concerning women and the family which Islam successfully resisted including those related to incestuous marriages and women's rights in inheritance. Also it would appear that the ulama did not engage in the excesses frequently referred to and were at odds with the caliphs, certainly the Umayyads, on several points. Again, while the vast majority married and shunned celibacy, it would appear that most lived monogamously. Ahmed's general point, however, cannot be denied. Instead of moving forward inspired by the ethical vision, Islam under the guidance of the ulama stagnated by making pragmatic accommodation to the historic circumstances.

Yet this accommodation was not without dissent. The sustained dissent came from the Sufi, the mystic tradition of Islam. Clearly the Sufis heard the ethical voice and responded accordingly. Their position was that the only real basis for action was the vision of the Quran. That even Mohammad's exemplary behaviour was the ephemeral aspects of the religion relating only to the particular society at that point in history. This was the antithesis of the ulama's position, that orthodoxy was independent of history and circumstances. The Sufis passive dissent survived cloistered in monasteries, ribats, and clothed in piety, asceticism and mysticism.

The position taken by the Sufis fundamentally challenged the postures of both the political and religious establishment. Their challenge was in deeds more than words, in example more than entreaties. They renounced materialism. They would not accept money they did not earn by their own hands or work for more that their daily needs. While celibacy was not mandatory it was the preferred lifestyle. By emphasising the spiritual over the material, by refusing to exploit the labour of others where slavery abounded, and by despising sexuality in the face of unbridled sexual expression by men, they put in sharp relief the disparity between the ethical vision of Islam and the pragmatic expediencies of the times.

It is against this background of the development of the educational system, and the evolution of gender relations in Islam, from its inception to the end of its classical period that we must describe and assess teaching and the teaching occupation of that period.

Theoretically the injunction to seek knowledge was incumbent on all Muslims, male and female. In addition it was important for all the faithful to know their obligations required by God. Ethically there should be no difference in Islam between male and female access to education and schooling. The fact that there were obstacles highlights the predominance of the pragmatic over the ethical in implementing doctrine.

Berkey (1992) made the point that Islamic tradition was not hostile to the education of women. He asserted that analysis of the al Sakhawi's bibliographic dictionary of medieval times listed 1075 women, and showed that 471 had received some form of education, ranging form memorising the Quran to receiving some type of certificate. To explain the well-known disparities that existed between the education of girls and boys Berkey cited social conventions and family practices in addition to exclusion from the formal system. While we shall return to the latter, it is necessary to discuss the former here.

Berkey underscored the fact that in Islam education was the responsibility of the family. The decision to educate children was decided in the home. The early marriage of girls and their seclusion in the home dictated the practice of many families either to educate girls in the home or not to educate them at all. Where families were not able to provide the education themselves they could decide to purchase education for them at some kuttab. Some families did. The majority did not. With respect to higher education entry to the masjid or madrasah occurred at precisely the time when seclusion of girls was enforced most rigidly.

In this regard it is important to note that the ulama took special care to educate their female offspring. Shalaby (1979), Ahmed (1992) and Berkey (1992) all concurred that the vast majority of girls and women who were educated were the children of the scholarly elite, the ulama. These historians highlighted the fact that these daughters of scholars received their education mainly from their male relatives – fathers, grandfathers and uncles. In a few instances even husbands were mentioned in this regard. In these circumstances some could even claim that the ulama, by their practice, advocated the education of women in accordance with the ethical vision.

The point being made here is that in a highly decentralised and individualistic system in which family responsibility, private enterprise and philanthropy were the dominant structural determinants, it is not possible to explain the great under-representation of girls and women in education simply in terms of the dictates of the ruling elite or the dogma of the religious authority. This line of argument is even more difficult where the ulama were the very elements in the society that gave girls and women, albeit their daughters, any form of education. The obstacles to the participation of girls in education especially with respect to the daughters and women of the folk, must reside in structural factors outside of education and voluntary action within these structures.

The contradictions of the situation are compounded even further. One of the issues on which the ethical vision was indeed implemented was the right of women to inherit, own and dispose of property on the same basis as men. Like men women donated property through the law of waqf to the purpose of education. Both Ahmed (1992) and Berkey (1992) recorded numerous instances in which women endowed mosques, madrasahs, ribats and hospitals. Also because founders of these colleges, monasteries and hospitals could, through trust deeds, require that their descendants be the trustees it was common practice for women to be the trustees and administrators of these endowments.

The irony of this situation is that while women donated and endowed, and often were the administrators of endowed colleges, they were not among the students. The only endowed institutions which offered education to women were the ribats for females run by the Sufis. These ribats provided refuge for women who were abandoned by their husbands, widows and divorcees. Until they married again, or returned to their husbands, they lived in the ribats and included in their program were classes run by the Sufi shaikhas.

The education of women therefore took place largely outside the formal institutions, and largely in the non-formal arrangements that were so pervasive in Islamic education. Many scholars ran halqas for women in the homes and at other venues. These matters will be examined further when the topic of the gender of teachers is discussed.

TEACHERS AND THE TEACHING OCCUPATION

From the foregoing description of the education system it is clear that teaching consisted of two distinctly different occupations. Elementary education was quite widespread, but was related to the pragmatic demands of the state and the basic educational demands of religion. Higher education on the other hand, and its teachers, were profoundly related to the core of Islamic society, religious education and the professional preparation of its jurists. While the former extended to Muslim and Non-Muslims, probably to different degrees, the latter was restricted to Muslims almost entirely. Bearing this fundamental distinction in mind it is necessary to look in greater detail at who were the elementary and college teachers in Islam.

KUTTAB AND ADAB TEACHERS

The system of elementary schooling that emerged in Islam was totally private. Parents paid teachers for instructional services given to their children. By Islamic laws payment was restricted to services related to the teaching of the fundamentals – reading, writing and arithmetic – and other secular subjects.

Elementary school teachers selected themselves; they were not recruited by the state or mosque. Neither the state nor the religious community placed any restrictions on who could offer themselves as teachers. Certainly there were no restrictions by virtue of religion or nationality. The religious minorities – Jews, Christians, Hindus or any others – organised schools for their children taught by teachers of their choosing. Only Muslims could teach the Quran or offer religious instruction in Islam. However, kuttabs were not required to offer religious instruction in Islam. Further, non-Muslim teachers taught Muslim children and non-Muslim parents purchased education in kuttabs teaching the Quran and Arabic.

All the available evidence points to the fact that the vast majority of kuttab teachers were men, although children were being taught. Totah (1926) claimed that both girls and boys attended kuttabs. Shalaby (1979) disagreed with Totah and claimed that the former misinterpreted the sources he cited as evidence. Shalaby insisted that he could find no instance of girls being educated with boys or outside the home. In support of his contention he cited cases where notables employed teachers to provide their daughters as well as sons with basic education. However, separate instruction was provided for boys and girls.

Stanton (1990) described the economic circumstances of the majority of kuttab teachers as genteel poverty, notwithstanding the fact that Islamic law exempted teachers from some taxes. Shalaby (1979) described similar circumstances to Stanton pointing out that the financial position of these teachers was poor, although payment varied in different locations. In Sicily total fees for kuttab teachers did not amount to as much as 10 dinars per year. In several locations cash was supplemented by gifts of milk, bread or corn. This practice was more prevalent in villages than in urban centres. There is also some evidence that payment was sometimes associated with achievements of the students. Parents would give teachers gifts after their children had successfully recited chapters of the Quran or mastered some aspects of reading or writing. Many could not survive on the income received from teaching and therefore supplemented their pay by doing other jobs including that of labourers, craftsmen and performing functionary duties in the local mosques.

Ahmed (1968) analysed the Ta'rikh Baghdad, one of the best known dictionaries of the Middles Ages. Among the 8831 scholars who lived or taught in the city from its founding in 762 to 1070, when its author died, he could hardly find any that had been elementary school teachers. Also the few references he found had very little information about the persons concerned. Ahmed concluded that either elementary school teachers were not considered prominent enough to be classed as scholars or there were not many notable scholars among them. To illustrate the level of education of these teachers he cited the case of al Sikkit who taught in his father's school while learning grammar and preparing himself to get a job as a private tutor.

Teachers in the adabs, palace schools, were both better educated and more highly paid. Ahmed (1968) noted that of these teachers listed as scholars in this dictionary. Some gave classes and lectures in various study circles. Their wealthy employers provided them with horses, furniture, concubines, travel and, of course, access and association with elite society. Shalaby underscored this point by observing that in many instances the private tutors adopted the name of the family that employed them, for reasons of social prestige.

In Spain teachers entered into partnerships and ran schools jointly. They also developed formal agreements with parents that included clauses with respect to student absence, holidays, method of instruction, amount and period of payment and the educational objectives to be achieved. Apparently these agreements proved more lucrative than the customary relationships that prevailed in the rest of the empire (Chaudhri 1982).

There is general agreement among the various sources that kuttab teachers did not enjoy high status or prestige. Tiwabi and Totah quoted al Jahiz who wrote about education in the tenth century and who cited some popular but unfavourable proverbial sayings about teachers of the kuttab. One saying was 'more foolish than a kuttab teacher' and another was 'how could intelligence and wisdom be found in one who rotates between an infant and a woman'. Al Jahiz while quoting these proverbs stoutly defended kuttab teachers pointing out that these unfavourable statements were certainly not applicable to all teachers or even all kuttab teachers in the villages. Al Jahiz insisted that 'for they, like any other class or men, include the superior and the inferior'. Ahmed reported similar findings from his research that speak of the low status of kuttab teachers.

Nakosteen (1964) added two other proverbs to those quoted by Tibawi and Totah. 'Do not take advice from teachers, shepherds and from those who sit much among women', and 'Stupidity is found among tailors, teachers and weavers'. In his view, the status of teachers was dependent on place and level of the system. In some parts of Islam there was a long tradition of respect for teachers; in those places they enjoyed high status but not everywhere. With respect to level, Nakosteen opined that kuttab teachers being the least learned, and sometimes being of mediocre minds, enjoyed the least status.

Shalaby highlighted the following:

- Kuttab teachers generally lacked real education, although a great number of learned men emanated from its ranks including theologians, philologists, calligraphers, judges, politicians, judges and poets.
- Some tried to exploit the fact that they taught the Quran, and were therefore bearers of truth, by appearing frequently in court as witnesses, but sometimes proved to be less than reliable.
- Many kuttab teachers were Christians, or converts to Islam. This seemed to have affected the status accorded to this category of teachers.

What does not seem to be in doubt was that kuttab teachers were generally perceived to be small minded, of modest social status and despised by some. At the same time they were expected to be humble and unpretentious in lifestyle, not young, of good character and not gossips (Stanton 1990).

It would appear that the kuttab teacher in Islam, in the classical period, suffered from many limitations not of their own making. By occupation they were confined to the lowest level of the educational system. Most of them came from the lower social ranks of society. They could not derive status from their students, since they taught the children of the common folk. The teachers of princes and the children of notables overcame the same stigma by virtue of their association with power and influence and the privileges they enjoyed by way of patronage. At the same time the Sufis, cloistered in monasteries, had captured the moral high ground by offering their services free, thus emulating the Prophet.

Kuttab teachers could not afford to give their services free for they had to finance themselves and their families. They had to teach for material reward, contrary to the exhortation of the religious tradition. They taught prospective functionaries of the state and provided the foundation for those who in time could become scholars. However, their relationship to both power and scholarship was indirect. Trapped in the lowlands of materialism, confined to the first level of education, surrounded by the ordinary status of their students, and hobbled by the low status of their own origins, kuttab teachers became the butt of social derision which remains the lot of their modern successors and largely for the same reasons.

Comments on the Gender Composition of Kuttab and Adab Teachers

All the available evidence points to the fact that the kuttab and adab teachers were all males, from the inception of Islam to the end of its classical period. The circumstances surrounding the all male status of these elementary teachers are most interesting, as can be seen from the nature of the kuttab system that had developed.

First, the kuttab system was established solely on the basis of private enterprise and a limited amount of philanthropy in some places. These teachers were responding to market driven demand for basic education as empire and religion spread. Neither state nor religious authority imposed any legal or religious restrictions on who could become a teacher. Hence the market was not regulated in this regard. The only regulations were with respect to prohibition for charges for Quranic or religious instruction. Any person within the empire could establish a school and teach provided parents were prepared to purchase the services offered.

Second, men were the teachers notwithstanding the low salaries associated with teaching, its low social status in the society and the expressed negative association with women's work. This negative association with women was expressed in numerous sayings. Yet these considerations were not sufficient to deter men from voluntarily taking up teaching as their enterprise.

Third, not even women's virtual exclusion from the public sphere, by itself can explain the absence of women from the ranks of kuttab teachers, seeing that some women taught at the college level.

Fourth, none of the historians or researchers, of this period of Islamic history, offered any explanation of the gender composition of elementary school teachers. They appeared to have taken for granted the fact that all elementary school teachers were men hence there was no need for an explanation.

TEACHERS OF HIGHER EDUCATION

Constant reference has been made to the ulama, without an exact description of who they were. The ulama were the learned faithful whose mission was to teach the faithful and keep the faith. Ahmed (1968) observed that there was no difference between Muslim scholars and Muslim teachers. Every Muslim scholar was a teacher and every Muslim teacher, at the higher level, was a scholar. This inter-changeability between teachers and scholars reflected the link between who they were and what was their mission. Learned scholar was who they were. Teaching was what they did. Every Muslim scholar at the end of his studentship received the license to teach, from his teachers. This was the process of pedagogic succession, analogous in a real sense to apostolic succession. The ulama were the unofficial priesthood of Islam, ordained by learning received from a succession of teachers starting with the Prophet.

Islam never accepted that learning was independent of faith. The Greek notion of learning for its own sake, which separated learning from faith, was not adopted by Islam. The issues that led to and weighed heavily upon the Inquisition revolved around this separation. The outcome of the Inquisition was that reason was essentially a method that should always be the servant of revelation. Learning was for the sake of teaching the faith, giving guidance to the faithful, making wise judgements in problematic situations and for resolving disputes.

The teachers of higher education in Islam were therefore the leaders of the religion and the keepers of its ideological apparatus. While they became the community, identified by the Quran, the modus operandi was individual opinion. There were no fora or councils in which the community voted or collectively decided matters. Learning and guiding the faithful was to be achieved by the utmost scholarly exertion done individually and independently. Each scholar was to perform his teaching mission through individual understanding of God's revelation. The common agreements from among those independent understandings became the orthodoxy of the faith.

While at the beginning there were no restrictions on which members of the ulama could contribute to the pool of common understandings, after the Inquisition it was only the jurisconsults from among the ulama who could so do. Faith became a matter of law. While all the ulama remained teachers, only some, the jurisconsults, could give fatwa, opinion, to the faithful.

While the system that emerged had its formal institutions and its non-formal structures, it never lost its core, the intimate nexus between teacher and student. The students studied with a particular teacher whether it was in a madrasah or a study circle in a shop. The teacher student relationship was primary, the institutional arrangement secondary. Wherever the site, the subjects, methods, instruction and award of certification was basically the same. In other words, it was the same pool of teachers who spanned the space between formal institution and non-formal study circle.

The disciplines represented within the pool of scholar/teachers were law, hadith, grammar and Quranic sciences. They constituted classical Islamic studies. Medicine, mathematics, sciences, logic and philosophy constituted the so-called foreign sciences. In the aftermath of the Inquisition only the Islamic subjects were taught in the formal institutions while the foreign sciences were taught in hospitals and the non-formal structures. The difference that this made to teachers was that it perpetuated and concentrated the location of non-Muslim scholars in hospitals and the non-formal arrangements. Non-Islamic scholars were never integrated into the formal institutions, and were therefore concentrated in the foreign sciences where, as Chaudhri (1982) noted, they were sometimes the leading authorities. They were mainly physicians, mathematicians, logicians, alchemists, astronomers and tax collectors. This included Jewish, Christian and Hindu scholars who were accommodated in the higher education system in Islam but as outsiders, dhimmi, never integrated into to masjid, masjid-khans or madrasahs.

The point to note is that while the foreign sciences were never the sole preserve of non-Islamic scholars, they were disproportionately represented in these areas. In other words, while there were Islamic scholars in all of the fields, Jews, Christians and Hindu scholars were mainly physicians, mathematicians, logicians, alchemists and astronomers. Higher education in Islam reserved space for non-Muslim scholars in fields that provided services or were not central to its primary defining tenets as a religious society. It excluded them from the institutions that defined its core values, its holy educational places.

The place in society occupied by teachers in higher education and their mission, dictated by the Quran and tradition remained unchanged from the inauguration of Islam until the end of its classical period.

1. They were the ultimate earthly authority in matters of religion and faith in an empire where the state and religion were, by doctrine, one. Their decisions, arrived at by consensus were binding on the state. They determined what was orthodox and authoritative in belief for state and people.

2. They shared with the state the authority to determine normative social behaviour, not only through their pronouncements on faith, but also

by their roles in the formulation of the law and the judiciary.

3. They exercised considerable political influence by virtue of the intermediary role between the people and the state bureaucracy. In many respects they were the de facto representatives of the people in the lower house of opinion even if the caliph and his ministers were fully in charge of the upper house of decision making.

Another factor that impacted on the influence and importance of teachers, scholars, in the society was that caliphs, sultans, princes, governors and lesser rulers were subject to sudden changes and short tenure. The teacher/scholars of the ulama were far less subject to change and held office usually for life. Also they were usually resident in a particular town or city which acquired status based on the scholar's reputation. Their stature, stability and longevity provided an anchor that steadied and balanced community life, which was not matched by any other source.

It is clear from the above that the authority and influence wielded by the teachers in higher education was considerable by any standards, in any place or any age. Their authority and influence were only mitigated and constrained by the individualistic manner by which these were exercised and the lengthy process of consensus building. Major differences between these teachers of higher education and the state seldom involved the entire community, and were also never resolved by the generations in which they occurred. This diffusion of differences, and protraction in their resolution, contributed substantially to longevity of these arrangements.

While these powers, social and cultural relationships of teaching prevailed in Islam, it must also be borne in mind that it was the belief dimension that was dominant. Teaching was conceptualised as ministry, sacred service, or even worship. It was one of the highest means of serving God. Al Ghazali maintained that teaching should only be undertaken for heavenly and not material reward. The implications for teachers were that even if they accepted material reward, a minimum condition would be that it should be modest.

Another implication of this intimate relation between teachers and the belief system of Islam was the requirement that teachers should live by the highest moral standards. Teachers were expected to be exemplars of piety and paragons of virtue. Character and scholarship were inextricably combined. The teachers' private life was properly a matter for public scrutiny.

Teaching and Related Occupations.

Ahmed (1968) concluded from his study of scholars of Baghdad, between 763 and 1070, that teaching was not a professional occupation but rather was done by learned people who had other occupations; it was a part-time and not a full time occupation. However, Berkey (1992) who studied higher education in Cairo between 1250 and 1500, reported that scholars were invariably full time teachers in the various madrasahs and masjids. This difference seems reflective, not so much of place but of time and the transformation the occupation of teaching underwent between its emergence in early Islam to its maturity and full development by the end of the classical period.

The transformation of the occupation of teaching from part-time to full-time has to be understood in terms of the evolution of the institutional structure of higher education with its early reliance on non-formal arrangements and its later dependence on formal institutions. The transformation from part-time to full-time is also indicative of other trends in the transformation of the occupation itself.

It would appear that initially most of the scholar/teachers were persons of independent means. Ahmed noted that the Bibliographic Dictionary of the scholars of Baghdad revealed that the majority were merchants and craftsmen. His estimation was that 75 per cent of the teachers fell into these two categories. Totah (1926) observed that in Islam teaching was not a business. Khan (1967) was of the view that it was Muslim merchants who were principally responsible for spreading Islam in the Indian sub-continent. From the record of Islam's early teachers of higher education it would appear that businessmen were missionaries and taught for reasons of piety. An interesting correlation in this regard was the age at which most of these early teachers entered teaching. Most were in their forties, suggesting that in the case of merchants they may already have either acquired some wealth or had their businesses fully established.

Chaudhri (1982) made the same point about the part-time nature of teaching from the opposite direction by stating that many teachers could not maintain themselves from the income they received from teaching and therefore supplemented it by taking other jobs. He lists crafts, cabinet making, gold beating, copying, part-time work in offices of correspondence and chanceries. Notwithstanding the difference in direction both establish the links between teaching and private means of income generation. Chaudhri went on to observe that teachers were restricted from supplementing their income from hairdressing, tannery, dyeing and money-exchange. These restrictions seemed to have been focused on women's work and filthy lucre.

The main difference between these two portrayals is that of primary commitment. Were the early practitioners of teaching business people who taught, or teachers who dabbled in other types of work to ensure their economic survival? Probably this distinction is irrelevant. It is difficult to differentiate them except from the perspective of the individuals themselves. To different degrees, the balance shifted between part-time and full-time teaching at different times, different institutional arrangements and in different circumstances.

Makdisi (1981) reported that throughout the classical period teachers were imams in mosques, particularly masjids in which they taught, led ritual prayers and gave counsel, advice and comfort to the faithful. The professors of law were also muftis, who issued fatwas, legal opinions on religious and civil matters.

From among the muftis the caliph appointed judges. However, such appointments were often avoided or resisted by many scholars. Appointment by the caliph represented being paid by the state and therefore being an agent of the state; it also meant passing judgement on the fatwa of colleagues, by selecting from among them. Professors of law also served as notaries public witnessing documents. This lists highlights the teachers intimate links to both the religious and legal life of the community

Posts, Ranks and Appointments.

Makdisi (1981) described the ranks of teachers in colleges as professors, deputy or assistant professors, and repeaters. These ranks existed in the various disciplines of jurisprudence, tradition, grammar and Quranic science. The deputy's job was to act for the professor in periods of absence. That of the repeater, who in the early period could be a senior student, was to assist the students with the lessons. Makdisi pointed to the fact that in masjids and masjid-khans, there was usually only one professor. Colleges also tended to be focused around a single discipline.

As the system became more complex with the invention of the madrasah there were several professors in the colleges, however, only one in each discipline. However, the posts of deputy and repeaters were retained since they continued to assist the professor who was the one granting certification, and with whom students studied. In the early periods many deputies and assistants succeeded their professors when they retired or died.

Makdisi (1981) and Chaudhri (1982) both reported that their studies indicated that initially appointment to posts was based on superior qualifications, the agreement of the local ulama after consultation with the retiring holder of the post and sometimes with the students. In numerous instances scholars were approached and offered professorships in colleges in recognition of their eminence. In some instances it was the most able student, or the deputy after these posts were established, who was promoted to professor. In either case the occasion of appointment was a matter of great ceremony, through the inaugural lecture, in which the scholar would display his erudition to an audience including other scholars and persons of high standing in the community.

After the addition of the madrasah, however, it was possible for the founders not only to name the professors who should be appointed initially to the endowed colleges, but also to prescribe that the descendants of the professor should hold the professorship in perpetuity. This fundamentally changed the process of appointments. Makdisi, Berkey and Chaudhri commented on the practice of professors simultaneously holding appointments in several colleges. Instances were identified where a single person held as many as 17 such appointments. Berkey cited several instances in which the infant sons of professors were appointed to posts, which were then taught by deputies until the sons were able to replace them many years later. In time, the inheritance of posts became the norm rather than the exception. This practice led to many abuses including the sale of posts. While initially the scholar class was an intellectual elite, through the practice of inheritance of posts its recruitment of talent was constricted, its social base narrowed and its competence diminished.

Sources of Income and Prestige

Several researchers insisted that most teachers of higher education in Islam were not wealthy, in fact, some were destitute at different times in their lives. However, they all enjoyed high social prestige. Chaudhri cited the amusing anecdote of a scholar's wife, frustrated by hardships of eking out a living and his unconcern, who served him his lecture notes for supper. On the other hand, Shallaby was of the view that scholars made a good living and were quite well off. Careful reading of the available evidence seems to suggest that the two moved in inverse relation over the period under review. Initially when the teachers' remuneration was more precarious, and teachers supplemented their income from elsewhere, they enjoyed higher prestige than in the later circumstances where income was more assured, and higher. In a nutshell, prestige was lost with patronage, while pay increased. That was the trade off over the period. Scholars resisted this trade off for centuries but it was made, eventually.

Initially teachers of higher education received income from student fees, endowment funds or college budgets and where these were inadequate from other work they undertook in areas previously outlined. In some cases it was the other way around. They earned income from their businesses, which allowed them to carry on their scholarly activity without much concern for low pay from such activities. Chaudhri, Makdisi, Ahmed and others all cited cases of destitute teachers, many of whom proudly refused assistance from the state.

The attitude of many teachers seemed to be captured in Chaudhri's quotation of Ibn Khaldun's views, of the factors that explained the scholar's socioeconomic position and their acceptance of it. A paraphrase of his explanation is as follows:

- Education required great investment and delayed returns, which diminished its attractiveness to those seeking more immediate returns.
- Scholars were unwilling to engage in the self-abasement and adulation that was the secret of success, but of which as men of learning and religion they could not approve.
- Preoccupation with intellectual pursuits did not give scholars time to wait on princes and nobles.
- The honour and consideration received by the learned class from the people was compensation enough.

Ibn Khaldun, regarded by Gellner (1981) as the greatest sociologist of Islam, appears to have had a crystal clear understanding of the scholar's position in the society. In paraphrase he seemed to be saying that learning, and its possibilities, was really not open to all. Those who pursued it had a price to pay both to acquire it and to disseminate it. In this regard independence and dignity were to be defended at all cost. The pay off was the trust, regard and esteem of the people who appreciated the eloquence, the sound judgements, carefully crafted opinions, wise counsel and learned advocacy of positions they held but were unable either to articulate or to argue.

An issue of perennial contention among teachers was their independence and the means of safeguarding it. This was not a matter of consensus among the ulama. There were those who were of the view that patronage from the state, especially form the ruling elite, was to be avoided like the plague. Others saw advantages in patronage through links made with the political class. Ahmed noted that some scholars boycotted and ostracised other colleagues who appeared to too cosy in their relationships with persons in high authority or of great wealth, particularly the caliph and his lieutenants. Others readily accepted and even sought such patronage. In the early period the balance seem to have been struck in favour of distance from state power and wealth. In the later period the fulcrum shifted in favour of close relationship. The ordinary people's trust, regard and esteem shifted in the opposition direction to patronage. The founding and spread of the madrasah seem to have marked the turning point.

Gender of Teachers of Higher Learning

From all the studies and records of the period under review, it is clear that the vast majority of teachers were men. Ahmed (1968) reported that from his analysis of the 8831 scholars listed in the bibliographic dictionary of Baghdad, between the years 762 and 1070, there were 7799 men and 32 women. In other words, 99.6 per cent was male and 0.4 per cent was female, that is less than one half of one per cent. One has to be careful in generalising these statistics for Baghdad for the whole of Islam since it is only one site and it was for the period before higher education was more widely available.

Totah (1926) maintained that there were several women scholars in the classical period of Islam, including women professors in the madrasah. He supported his contention by citing the fact that Ibn Khallikan, Abu Hayyan and Al Maqqari listed several women scholars with whom they had studied. He also cites several other women, including Shahdah daughter of Abu Nasr, as both belonging to the learned class as well as teaching several men. He made reference to the fact that Al Shaffi once listened to a lecture on hadith given in Cairo by Nafisah, daughter of Abu Muhammad. Katibah, daughter of Ubari, was the author of a famous book on hadith, and Miriam of Seville granted several licenses to men who had studied with her. Totah's contention was that while women were under-represented among teachers in higher education they were not excluded, as many claim.

Ahmed (1992) offered some support for Totah's position but qualified it by noting that this small minority of women were mainly of the ulama class. She agreed that many became renowned scholars and taught men and were particularly known for the teaching of hadith. She also pointed to the fact the Sufi did not discriminate against women and included females among their leaders. Several women Sufi became well-known and respected teachers and scholars, shaikhas. Al Ghazali, born in Spain was taught by two women Sufi teachers. Shallaby corroborated Ahmed's observation of the relationship between women scholars to the ulama class and cited several instances in which they were daughters of booksellers.

Shalaby (1979) maintained that women had far less opportunities that men in Islam, but insisted that this was no different from other parts of the world at that time. He claimed that journey away from home was one factor that militated against higher education among women. Nevertheless, he insisted that there were many women scholars in jurisprudence and tradition. He cited the various bibliographic dictionaries produced up to the end of the classical period listed 1543 women teachers of tradition. However, by not quoting the number of male scholars listed in these dictionaries it is not possible to establish what proportion of scholars were female. It must be noted that Shalaby's listing of dictionaries included the Tarikh Baghdad quoted by Ahmed (1968), and al Daw al Lawi quoted by Berkey. If the total number of women scholars listed by Shalaby is calculated as a per cent of those listed only in the Tarihk Baghdad, even then women scholars only amounted to 17.5 per cent. Shalaby also listed calligraphy, poetry and medicine as fields in which women scholars were found.

Berkey (1992) researched the later period, between the middle of the thirteenth century to the end of the sixteenth century in Cairo, and reported that he did not find a single instance of a woman holding an appointment of professor, or any teaching post in a madrasah or masjid, nor any female students in a institution providing an endowed student fellowship. On the other hand, there were numerous women administrators or trustees of such institutions. Berkey concluded that women were systematically excluded from the formal institutions of learning and received their education as 'outsiders', that is, through the non-formal structures.

Berkey corroborated Ahmed (1992) in her identification of hadith and Sufism as two areas in which women scholars were concentrated. He found very few women who were teachers of jurisprudence. With respect to hadith he made the observation that reciters of hadith invariably listed the authorities on which they recited. He cited a list of 172 authorities of which 19 were women and another of 130 authorities of which 33 were women. Al Sakawi, the author of the bibliographic dictionary on important women, listed 68 women teachers with whom he had studied hadith, 46 of whom issued licenses to him. Berkey offered three reasons that, in his opinion, explained women's competition on an almost equal basis as men in one of the most prized areas of Islamic scholarship, the reciting of tradition.

First, it was possible to receive a license from a scholar without actually studying or reciting a work in his or her presence. Women could therefore participate in the transmission of hadith without always or actually encountering male students or teachers. Also families of scholars of hadith, subject to certain conditions, had the right to issue licenses. Family connections were therefore crucial and very beneficial.

Second, in the transmission of hadith it was highly advantageous to have studied with a shaikh of wide knowledge and blameless reputation. Reducing the number of transmitters in a chain was another critical consideration. This gave the reciter greater authority, the higher up in the chain they were. It was therefore preferable for young scholars to study with old teachers who fit the first two criteria. For male or female, the privilege of being the sole survivor, in a city or region, to transmit hadith on direct authority from a prominent shaikh was to be highly prized. On this level women could compete directly with men. Ulama families placed their daughters in advantageous position in this regard either through family members or close friends and associates. Girls who heard traditions, at an early age from authoritative transmitters, themselves became authoritative transmitters in their advanced years.

Third, the transmission of hadith did not involve analysis or judgement. The skills involved were accuracy and memory. While disputes could arise these could be resolved with reference to records or other sources. As such the transmission of hadith by women did not threaten men, because the transmitter was not required to exercise judgement.

THE MASCULINE ROOTS OF TEACHING IN ISLAM

The two main masculine roots to the teaching occupation in Islam in the classical period were related to the exigencies of empire and religion. These were also the two fountainheads from which schooling evolved in Islam: the masculine roots of teaching were directly related to the same two sources that made schooling a necessity. Each requires some discussion.

THE MASCULINE ROOTS OF ELEMENTARY SCHOOL TEACHING

The empire acquired by force had to be administered by more than coercive means. The state bureaucracy that had to be hastily established needed clerks, bookkeepers, tax gatherers and record keepers who could write. The fact that the vast majority of the Arab warriors who had won the empire were illiterate made the creation of schooling almost inevitable and mandatory. The institution of schooling became one of the means by which newly gained power was consolidated and perpetuated. In this regard the Islamic empire was no different from the Sumerian city-states of Mesopotamia. Schooling was established to serve the needs of public administration.

The particular institutions that were created to meet this need were the kuttab and the adab, elementary schools. The kuttab provided schooling for the common folk, while the adab did the same for notables and nobles of the court. Schools required teachers.

At least four interrelated factors seem to have been associated with the fact that almost all the kuttab and adab teachers were men.

- Although schooling in Islam, between 700 to 1300 CE, was more widespread than in any other part of the world at that time, it was by no means universal. The relatively modest size of the school system appears to be related to the relatively modest size of the state bureaucracy and the life long tenure of persons employed.

- One of the great challenges of the vast empire so hastily won, was that of providing opportunities for advancement for all who desired it. Initially this problem was faced in relation to demobilising much of the army that had acquired the empire. Thereafter, a perennial problem for succeeding generations was providing opportunities for all Muslims and citizens who desired the same. Teaching was one of the occupations that provided some modest relief to this dilemma.

- Because there was a strong secular component in elementary education, the elementary teaching occupation was among a limited number of occupational spaces open to non-Muslims and new converts to the faith. The rulers of the Islamic empire adopted and practised the ancient code of conquest in which vanquished people, who accepted their defeat, were allowed a measure of autonomy in governing their communities and permitted some measure of assimilation into Islamic society. Non-Muslims, accepting the hegemony of the dominant Muslim group, and confined to their legally defined dhimmi status in the society, could safely be recruited to perform certain types of functions within the empire. These areas related to matters in which the dominant faction might have been reluctant to engage, either for religious reasons or because they lacked competence. It was therefore expedient to patronise the conquered groups. Other examples of such areas were tax collecting, medicine and foreign sciences. In these areas Jewish, Christian, Greek and Hindu scholars were patronised by the Muslim holders of power and wealth. For much of the period under review elementary school teaching was populated by large numbers of Non-Muslims and new converts to the faith.

- Patriarchal tradition within families and clans dictated that in circumstances of scarcity of opportunities preference went to the male members of the kinship collective.

Elementary education was a private business arrangement between teachers and parents. The education received was largely utilitarian, either for employment in the state bureaucracy or to gain access to higher education. The teachers were either Non-Muslims, of dhimmi status, or lower class Muslims unable to find better employment. The students were mainly those of the folk. These factors combined to give the elementary teaching occupation low status, low remuneration and social derision. Despite these disadvantages, elementary school teaching remained a male occupation. This was because there was no shortage of men to teach; the supply of available men outstripped demand for teaching services at the elementary school level.

The masculine root of elementary school teaching in Islam was grounded largely in governance and public administration. The process followed a similar logic, if even in different circumstances, to that described in Chapter 2 in relation to Sumer. The limited demand for teachers in relation to the abundant supply of persons that could offer the teaching service, and the logic of patriarchal tradition of all the groups that comprised the society, concatenated to produce the outcome whereby the vast majority of elementary school teachers in Islam in the classical period were male. In the case of Sumer, the masculine roots of teaching were directly related to the emergence of the monarchy in the ancient city-states. With respect to Islam, one of the masculine roots of teaching was part of the means by which the empire was consolidated and ruled.

THE MASCULINE ROOTS OF TEACHERS IN HIGHER EDUCATION

The issue of why teachers at the higher education level were mainly men is directly related to why the ulama was predominantly male. The masculine roots of the ulama, and therefore of teachers in higher education in Islam, were the same. It appears to have rested on the interaction between three factors:

- The relationship of the ulama, and therefore of teachers of higher education, to the pinnacle of the belief system of Islam.
- The imperatives of a vast theocratic empire.
- Lineage patriarchy, which continued as the basis on which clans gained or defended advantage in society.

Each of these requires some elaboration.

Teachers of Higher Education, the Ulama and Islam

Islam as a religion has no synod or sanhedrin, no pope or zugot, no bishop or high priest and no ordained clergy. The decentralised structure of the religion consigns its leadership largely to self-appointed adherents. A principal criterion for self-appointment to leadership in Islam, and recognition by others, is to be learned. This community of learned faithful has come to be labelled the ulama. As scholars, the ulama are the leading exemplars of the faith, the most convincing exponents of its ethic and the accepted experts of its theology. They regard themselves, and are regarded, as the guides, the guardians and the gurus of the faith. High on the list of functions of the ulama is the acquisition and dissemination of knowledge of the faith. They are the teachers of the faithful and more importantly of those who would elect to be the ulama in succeeding generations.

Muslim college teachers, scholars and the ulama, therefore, were one and the same. College teachers and scholars were the clergy of Islam without ordination. They not only constituted the teaching occupation but also were the principal leaders in religious matters. College teachers, therefore, resided at the centre of the Islamic belief system. Factors determining the gender of college teachers went to the core of the ideological, social and political imperatives of Islam.

The control by the ulama of the religious apparatus of Islam, through their role in the formulation of doctrine, their responsibility in handing down judgements, the binding authority of consensus among them on the state and the people, their location in communities, and their distribution across the empire without control from central authority made them a potent countervailing force to that of emperors, governors and other political power brokers. Alignments, coalitions and alliances inevitably arose among the ulama and men holding state power, in time these alliances fractured the religion and diminished but did not eliminate their political influence. Notwithstanding these shifts in their relationship with state power over the years of the classical period, the ulama remained the glue of the religion.

Higher education was a defining criterion of the ulama. It was virtually impossible to be a member of the ulama without being learned. Such learning had to be certified by professors with whom one had studied, privately or in a college. Entry to higher education was therefore a critical factor for inclusion in the ulama. Any factors that totally or partially excluded women from admission to higher education would limit their access to the ulama and also to college teaching. Women were highly restricted in their entry to higher education institutions in Islam.

Berkey explained the exclusion of women from formal institutions of higher learning on the bases of legal restriction, social convention and religious concerns of ritual purity.

1. Women were excluded by law from participation in the institutions that offered training in jurisprudence. One matter on which the ulama had reached consensus was that a woman could not serve as qadi, as judge. This consensus was reached on the authority of the Quranic verse, which declared that men were the guardians of women, because God had set the one above the other. To act as a judge would be to exercise authority over men.

2. Women were excluded by virtue of social convention in that their presence in an institution housing young men was deemed to pose an intrinsic threat to sexual boundaries and taboos. The corollary to this was the social convention that developed that men should be educated in a sexually isolated environment to avoid distraction as well as temptation. Some colleges required that students be unmarried.

3. Women were excluded by virtue of concerns about ritual purity of those engaged in the transmission of knowledge which was regarded as sacred. Menstruating women would threaten ritual purity. One college's trust deed went as far as permitting only the professor to be married.

The masculine root of teaching in Islam in the ulama bares strong relationship to the masculine root of teaching among the prophets in Judaism. Common to both were the stubborn hold on the ethical vision, as they perceived its revelation, the vision of the future they inspired themselves and others to bring to pass and their undying faith in teaching as the means of spreading their beliefs and passing them on to succeeding generations. Also common to both were self-appointment based on revelation, being exemplars of the core values and the strong condemnation of those who deviated or were perceived to deviate from the canons of the faith, and a stubborn disregard for facts when these confronted faith. The ulama were the prophets of Islam, although none would claim that title in deference to Mohammed.

Empire, Empowerment of Men and Male Solidarity

Men's power in the public sphere was dramatically increased by the authority of empire. Their dominance was not simply within the clan or over a few neighbouring tribes but over vast numbers of different clans, tribes, religions and cultures. It was the empire that marginalised women even further and not the religion. Faced with the imperatives of this imperium, Islam compromised its ethical vision. Ahmed's (1992) description of the connection between Islam's assimilation of Persian culture and the increased marginalisation of women is accurate. However, her conclusion that this marginalisation was due solely to assimilation of Persian culture identified the process but missed the source, which was the heightened and far-reaching power that Muslim men wielded during the rule of the Abbasid dynasty.

Allied to the vastly expanded power that accrued to Arab men, and to their successors as the power elite in the Islamic empire, was the challenge of assimilating the large numbers of vanquished peoples. The Islamic empire had adopted and honoured the ancient code of conquest which rewarded conquered groups that accepted their vassal status. They allowed the vanquished city or tribe or clan autonomy in managing their own affairs, maintaining their culture and practising their religion on condition that they accepted the hegemony of their conquerors. The reward also allowed limited opportunities for upward social mobility to the most able and competent among the vanquished. The egalitarian posture of Islam and its evangelistic mission to convert the vanquished further mitigated the approach to those that had been conquered.

While the Islamic empire arose and spread with spectacular success in a very short period of time, the rise of Islam was not accompanied by any new breakthrough in technology associated with substantial improvement in the creation of wealth or economic opportunity. The dramatic military achievement of the empire was not matched by substantially increased material means and opportunities for meeting the desires and demands of the peoples concerned. The seclusion of women appeared to have been one of the means by which obligations to vanquished groups who accepted their vassal status were met. The exclusion of women from the public sphere created more space for opportunities to be allocated to the conquered groups.

The effect was to expand and to strengthen patriarchy. By accepting their vassal status, the vanquished groups did not challenge the hegemony of their conquerors. By allowing the vanquished groups some autonomy in managing their affairs and retaining their culture and beliefs, the internal structure of these groups were left intact. The patriarchal traditions of both dominant and subordinate groups were preserved. The seclusion of women from the public sphere generalised their marginality beyond their kinship collective to include men of all clans. Women's inferior social status was not now only with respect to their fathers, brothers, sons, and husbands but to all men. In the process male solidarity was deepened across clans.

College Teaching, Patriarchal Tradition and Clan Competition

The policy and practice of common citizenship within the empire underscored the egalitarian posture of the religion. However, religion itself became the major axis of inequality. College teaching became an occupation mainly for Muslim men, the ulama, and only to a limited extent for non-Muslim men. Initially teachers for higher education were recruited from all clans within the empire. College teachers included persons experiencing both upward and downward mobility. However, it represented a respectable occupation for all. The dynamism of the teaching, and the level of scholarship, was most evident when it was most open to all men, at the commencement of empire and religion, and most inclusive in the areas of scholarship pursued. Interestingly, some of the most brilliant college teachers were non-Arab men of low social status.

College teaching was associated with high status and prestige because of preeminent relationship to the dominant criterion upon which the society was structured, religion. Likewise the social relations of college teaching were always within the orbit of power and wealth, even if some scholars tried to maintain some distance. Equally important the location of these teachers in local communities, and their involvement in the everyday life of the people as jurists, preachers and counsellors made them a formidable force and revered group. Further, college education was founded on philanthropy generated from one of the five basic tenets of Islam, and legally enabled through the law of charitable trust, hence while the occupation did not guarantee opulent living if offered most college teachers a reasonable subsistence.

Decline in scholarship and stagnation in college teaching became clearly marked in the later centuries of the classical period, when scholars attempted to pass on their positions as a matter of inheritance to their children or associates, and also when the areas of scholarly activity were substantially narrowed as a result of sectarian divisions.

At the heart of the rot that set in during the latter centuries of the classical period, was the deliberate steps taken by clans that had gained socioeconomic advantages in the empire, to consolidate and perpetuate those advantages within their clans. While Islam decreed generosity as one of its five defining tenets, and institutionalised it in the law of waqf, wealthy clans so gerrymandered the trusts creating madrasahs that professorships became inherited instead positions of being merited. Genealogy had devised means of compromising divinely decreed generosity. In this regard women of many wealthy clans often administered the trusts through which their male relatives inherited the patrimony of the clan, which ostensibly had been benevolently bequeathed for educational purposes.

Men and women of clans enjoying socioeconomic advantages in the Empire co-operated to retain these advantages within the clan and in the process excluded men of other clans from teaching positions in higher education. Formulations that seek to explain the disproportionate access of men to teaching at the college teaching in classical Islam solely in terms of women's oppression, are fatally flawed by ignoring the genealogical element in the collective and corporate action of both men and women of the clans seeking or defending social advantage.

THE FEMININE ROOTS OF TEACHING IN ISLAM

The areas of teaching and scholarship, at the college level, in which patriarchal closure was relaxed, arose from the highest and most cherished values in Muslim and Arab society. These highest values were its ethical vision and cherished traditions. In Arab society the highest cultural values were in poetry, the ultimate expression of its oral tradition. Medicine represented a high level service, and in a society where high jealousies were associated with the seclusion of women, areas of medicine relating to sexuality and childbirth presented problems if men outside of the family performed them. It was very important to keep these areas within the particular groups concerned.

It is in these areas that patriarchal closure was relaxed to allow some women access to opportunities in the public sphere. In other words, some women were co-opted to act as men on behalf of the religion, or clan or culture.

Women scholars of hadith, Sufi shaikha, women poets and women physicians in obstetrics and gynaecology can all be explained with reference to these considerations. In these circumstances the women of these groups co-operated with their men folk to preserve the interest of their group and to maintain the exclusion of men of the subordinate groups from advancement in these areas during breaks in male succession in the particular groups.

Women scholars in tradition, women poets and female physicians were invariably the beneficiaries of relationships to men of some consequence. They were in most instances the daughters, sisters, wives or mothers of important male personages. In most instances they were standing in some breach in male succession or in the case of female physicians practising in fields of medicine where male practitioners were considered inappropriate.

The Sufi shaikha was different. She held her position in her own right without reference to any man. She stood outside the patriarchal structure and thereby challenged it. She was protected only by her embrace of the ethical vision of the highest values in the society and her backward integration into the social fabric of the society by her good deeds relative to the fall-out from the patriarchal structure, namely widows, orphans, divorced and abandoned women. Paradoxically, while the Sufi shaikha challenged the patriarchal structure of the society, especially the exclusion of women from the public sphere, she preserved at least some notion of gender equality as expressed in the Quran. Many Sufi Shaikha were unmarried women, presumably virgins. At least they were celibate while they practised and performed their interpretation of Islamic religion. It was the celibate woman cloistered in her embrace of Sufi mysticism on the high ethical ground of the religion who was the college teacher in her own right without relational props from any man.

The feminine roots of teaching in classical Islam were tiny compared to their masculine counterparts. Like the masculine roots these feminine roots also arose from their relationship with the pinnacle of the belief system and the high culture of the theocratic empire on the one hand, and lineage patriarchy on the other hand. In instances where male succession was breached, threatening the loss of advantage by clans or families, women of talent in those collectives became teachers of hadith and poetry. By virtue of their becoming teachers in these areas they retained advantage in their extended family, lineage or clan.

It is important to note that the cracks which occurred in patriarchy, were in the area of teaching and with respect to the highest values of belief and culture. In the previous chapters there were examples of political and economic naditu – women allowed to act as men in order to retain power or wealth within the clan. In other words the relaxation of patriarchal closure in circumstances where the higher criteria of social organisation would be breached. In Islamic society, the examples are of the intellectual naditu in the teaching of tradition, in the exercise of piety and the expression of poetry. The point is that while gender is compromised patriarchy is preserved since the expectation is that in time male members will come along to remedy this temporary breach. Until then, a female member of the line would fill the gap. In other words, women teachers were the result of partnership between men and women of the lineages and clans which constituted the ulama, in preserving the position of the clan in circumstances where there was a hiatus in male succession.

The feminine root with the highest degree of integrity was that which was grounded in Sufism, which through its ethical vision and queitism, made the most fundamental departure from deepening and expanding patriarchy (Cook 1981). In that regard there is no more majestic symbolic imagery than that of the Sufi woman scholar residing outside the borders of patriarchy but making trips within its territory to stoop and clean up some of its mess.

It was from the cloister of the Sufi monastery that secluded women in Islam launched their public careers, one of which was teaching. It was from the retreat into the privacy of the cloister that the seclusion of women from the public was breached.

CONCLUDING COMMENT

To Ahmed's charge that the ulama ignored the voice of the ethical vision of gender equality clearly expressed in the Quran, the ulama could enter in their defence that their efforts were directed as preserving the vision itself and not just a part. In seeking to rescue the whole, there is no doubt that they sacrificed a part, women's equality, even if they tried to redeem their own daughters. The point is the empire died but the religion is still alive. Condemnation of the compromise of the principle of gender equality by the ulama must be matched by commendation for their separation of the religion from the fatal intoxication of the imperium.

The uluma, the prophets and teachers of Islam, preserved the religion from the fate of the empire. The Sufi virgins breached the seclusion of women in Islam and opened up a small space in the public sphere, as they became teachers on the same basis as men.

Five
⇌

THE MASCULINE AND FEMININE ROOTS OF TEACHING IN CHRISTIANITY

Christianity arose among the Jews but was not a Jewish religion, although during the early decades of its history it was regarded as a Jewish sect. Unlike Judaism and Islam, Christianity had no ethnic group that claimed to be its natural adherents. The ethnos embedded in its doctrine was 'whosoever will'. While it claimed fulfilment of the Hebrew Scriptures, and acknowledged the covenant with Moses, the new covenant was open to all of humankind. The chosen were those who accepted Jesus as the Christ, God incarnate revealed in human existence.

JESUS AND CHRISTIANITY

Any description of Christianity must of necessity begin with the historical Jesus. Herein lies a great dilemma because of the great diversity of opinions among historians and theologians concerning the Jesus of history and the Jesus of faith. Powell (1998) made the point that prior to the Enlightenment Christian scholars regarded the Bible account as a straightforward history of the life of Jesus. Since the Enlightenment and until the present time, however, a great volume has been written on the subject, including works that have seriously questioned the biblical account as an accurate historical record. A review of the debate about the historical Jesus is outside the scope of this study. However, a rough sketch of the sources of historical evidence and range of views about Jesus by scholars studying these sources are essential.

Powell listed the historical sources from which reliable data can be gathered about Jesus as follows:

- Roman literature. Tacitus, Suetonius and Josephus, the three most important Roman historians of the first century CE, all mentioned Jesus. Tacitus records that Jesus was executed in the reign of Tiberius by Pontius Pilate, governor of Judea. Josephus recorded, that he was a teacher of the people but was crucified by Pontius Pilate following charges brought against him by leading men and that his followers called Christians had not died out.

· Jewish literature. The Babylonian Talmud made reference to Jesus, who was hanged on the eve of the Passover.

· The New Testament Epistles, among the earliest Christian sources, tell little more details on the life and ministry of the historical Jesus than the non-Christian sources, however, they do make several references to His teachings.

· The Synoptic Gospels, Mark, Mathew and Luke, contain much more information about the life and ministry of Jesus. However, a large number of modern scholars reject the notion that they were Gospels written by disciples of Jesus. Given the great overlap of materials between these three Gospels, scholars have come to the conclusion that Mark is the earliest and that Mathew and Luke copied from an earlier Christian document, Q. Accounts that are found in all three Synoptic Gospels are generally regarded as having the greatest authenticity.

· The Gospel of John is regarded as later, probably written in the second century, and less reliable from a historical perspective than either Mark or Q.

· The Apocryphal Gospel was written in the first few centuries of Christianity but ultimately did not become part of the New Testament. Of these gospels only the Gospel of Thomas and the Gospel of Peter are regarded as containing credible historical information about Jesus.

Scholars studying these sources have come to wide ranging conclusions concerning the historical Jesus.

Ellegard (1999) is of the view that all Christian sources that can be dated to the first century CE, including Paul, regarded Jesus as a great Jewish prophet and teacher but one who had lived in the distant past. He was not a contemporary of theirs who was crucified before their eyes. These early Christians present Jesus as a heavenly figure, with scant details about his earthly life. The Gospel picture of Jesus as a Palestinian preacher and wonderworker living and crucified in the first three decades of the first century is a myth created by second century Christians faced with challenges from within and from outside the Church. Ignatius, the highly respected Bishop of Antioch, is cited as the possible initiator of the shift in focus from the heavenly figure to the earthly Jesus portrayed in the Gospels. Ellegard put forward the view that the historical Jesus was most likely to have been the revered founder of the Essenes, regarded as their great prophet and Teacher of Righteousness who was martyred by the Jewish priestly hierarchy toward the end of the second century BCE. Ellegard's view is a new departure. Most other scholars accept that the historical Jesus lived and died in the first three decades of the first century CE.

The most common depiction of the historical Jesus is that of prophet. Schweitzer (1968) concluded that the historical Jesus was a misguided eschatological prophet who was twice wrong. First that God was to send the Son of Man and second that the Kingdom of God was at hand. Sanders (1985 and 1993) has revived Schweitzer's view of Jesus as a prophet of the end time who was wrong. Wright (1996) agrees that Jesus was an eschatological prophet of the oracular mould bearing an urgent apocalyptic message for Israel. Wright insists that the historical Jesus was indeed right because he foretold a coming political, military and social disaster that would bring about the total destruction of Jerusalem and the Temple.

In Wright's opinion Jesus ran afoul of the priestly hierarchy because of a clash of key symbols of Israel's distinctiveness. Feasting was to replace fasting, open table fellowship was to replace segregating purity codes, healing of the sick replaced segregating them, forgiveness replaced retribution, love replaced hate, blessing replaced cursing and most offensive of all allegiance to Jesus himself replaced Temple and Torah.

Horsley and Hanson (1985) and Horsley (1989) maintained that Jesus stood in the classic tradition of the Hebrew prophet in that he was fundamentally concerned about the social and political circumstances of his day. Indeed, Jesus sought to foment social revolution from the bottom up. As such he was a non-eschatological prophet.

Witherington III (1994) maintained that sage is a more appropriate depiction of the historical Jesus than prophet. Witherington pointed to the fact that Jesus never used the classic formulation of the Hebrew prophet: 'thus saith the Lord'. Rather he spoke and taught on his own authority in a manner similar to the Teacher of Ecclesiastes and the author of Proverbs. Further, he pointed to the fact that Jesus in his teaching used parables, riddles, beatitudes, and personifications, which are forms of speech of the wisdom tradition that made equal claim to divine inspiration.

Downing (1988) and Crossan (1991) have both depicted the historical Jesus as a cynic philosopher with some resemblance to those of ancient Greece but with marked differences. Cynics defied social conventions and worldly entanglements and in so doing invariably practised eccentric lifestyles. Downing is of the view that cynics were outspoken and courageous protesters who stood up for individual liberty and freedom in an oppressive society. Crossan put forward the view that the historical Jesus acted in ways that involved shattering convention with respect to several aspects of everyday life including dress, meals and family obligations. Jesus tried to inaugurate the brokerless kingdom of God in which there was no room for social hierarchies, domination and subordination, patron-client relationships and patriarchal family structures.

Borg (1984 and 1988) depict the historical Jesus as a religious mystic. His portrait of Jesus includes images as healer, sage, social prophet and movement initiator. He relates these four images to two primary foci: the social and the spirit world. Borg concludes that the historical Jesus was primarily a spirit person, a religious mystic, who sought union and communion with a reality beyond the visible world of ordinary experience. It is this spiritual quality and core that integrates the four images and holds them together.

Smith (1978) maintained that most early opponents of Christianity presented the historical Jesus as a magician. In Smith's view a balanced account of the historical Jesus must not only include what the adherents of Christianity said of him but also ancient opponents of Christianity. In the view of the latter, Jesus was involved in private dealings with supernatural powers. Casting Jesus as a magician has put him in the category of spirit person with the negative connotation of being involved with demons and evil spirits.

Although it is very important to take note what historians can confirm from the available sources about the historical Jesus, the New Testament account cannot be ignored even if it is admitted that several aspects of it have no historical verification. The importance of the Gospel account of the life of Jesus resides in the fact that it has been the source of inspiration and motivation of the adherents of Christianity since the first century. The Jesus of the Gospel account is as important as the Jesus of the historians but for different reasons.

Accepting what most historians now affirm that Jesus lived at the beginning of the first millennium AD, he quite likely received an elementary education in one of the synagogue schools created by Simon Ben Shetah. He could well have attended the weekly services at the synagogue. He quite likely listened to the peripatetic rabbis who visited Nazareth and other such towns to instruct people in the Law. He seemed to have become versed in the Law and drew his sources from the Hebrew Bible. Accepting the Gospel account, in keeping with the Jewish tradition he learned a trade, carpentry was his choice. He spent most of his thirty-three years in Galilee. All agree that by birth and culture, Jesus was a Jew.

Like all the founders of great religions he was apparently a transcendent personality. His peers soon elevated him to the status of rabbi, teacher, although there is no evidence that he ever attended either the Hillel or Shammai academies or received higher education. He was accorded the title rabbi because he was a very effective teacher whose forte was the use of parables based on ordinary experiences and common objects. While his approach was direct, his language simple, his illustration ordinary, and thereby easily understood by his audience, the content of his teaching was profound.

Unlike other rabbis whose students applied to study with them, Jesus selected his disciples and invited them to follow him. He and his twelve disciples formed a learning community that did not fit easily into the Jewish education system that had developed over the centuries. The operations of the historical Jesus and his disciples resembled the school of the prophets more than either academies of Hillel and Shammai.

Eby and Arrowood (1940) noted that like Socrates, Jesus was informal and conversational in his approach but unlike Socrates he was not argumentative or dialectical, seeking to provoke the intellect to thought. Jesus was affirmative, directing his attention to the conscience and will. His teaching was authoritative without being arrogant, fearless while retaining serenity, and demanding commitment while respecting the sanctity of an individual's will. The impact on some who heard and followed him was transforming.

Many of the teachings of Jesus reiterated concepts of God and humanity previously proclaimed by the Jewish prophets of the Old Testament. Several of his tenets were not dissimilar from some of the conclusions of the Greek philosophers. However, Jesus in addressing the contemporary issues of His day added several new dimensions to all of these. In the ancient world kinship ties in defence of the honour of family and clan, and patriotic citizenship were the bases of moral action. As Eby and Arrowood observed the growth of individualism was seen as both the result and the cause of moral decay that was increasingly evident as the civilisation of the city-states disappointed increasing numbers of people.

Jesus through his life and teaching established new ideals for human personality and individual life. Inner peace, satisfaction and personal fulfilment were to be found in bearing the cross of self-denial and sacrifice in the service of God and others. The subordination of sensual appetites to the dominion of goodness was the way to holiness and wholeness. Following Him as the Way, the Truth and the Life was the path to divine acceptance and approval. Maintaining goodwill to all, even to those who were enemies, was the sure way to transform relationships and society.

Jesus offered a new community in which each individual could find acceptance and fulfilment. That community was the Kingdom of God in which there was no stratification, no discrimination and no injustice. Each individual shared equality with all others and treasure, that could not be appropriated. Individuality and personality had to be related to community in order to realise the full potential of humanity. Human communities had gone astray as the few appropriated the benefits of community to the exclusion of the many. In the Kingdom of God, which is eternal, justice prevailed and each individual could find fulfilment, security and actualisation.

Jewish teaching had proclaimed the spiritual essence of God, His creative nature, holiness and justice that were beyond manipulation by magic. However, while God was personal He was a jealous judge, particularly about obedience to His Laws. While Jesus underscored the ethical and universal nature of God, he emphasised His providential care, His benevolence, His fatherly concern and approachability. God was not remote and inaccessible except through rituals and law, but He could be approached directly by each individual on the basis of His being a loving Father. In fact, sincerity of heart took precedent over rituals, ceremonies or legality.

Plato, Pythagorus and other Greek philosophers had emphasised the importance of the humanistic values of wisdom, justice, courage, temperance and endurance as virtues in communal living and moral behaviour. Jesus went beyond these reasonable virtues and added faith, hope and love. Indeed, he went even further and contracted all the other virtues under the rubric of love by his injunction: love is God and keep his commandments and love your neighbour as yourself. In so doing platonic love was transformed from an abstract philosophic ideal to a concrete operational principle applicable in daily living.

If the Gospel sources are believed Jesus lived the paradigmatic Christian life. The essence of that life can be summarised as follows:

- Personal and close communion with God the Father.
- Consistent devotion to the good of others, even those who harmed him.
- Bearing the cross of self-denial and self-sacrifice even to death.
- Abandoning material gain in pursuit of spiritual perfection.
- Fearless resistance of the powerful in defence of right and righteousness.
- Upliftment of the outcasts, the derelicts, the destitute and the downtrodden in society as brothers and sisters of inestimable worth.

He was crucified at the height of his ministry. He died leaving no writings. He left a few followers who were scattered and frightened by the sudden and unexpected end of their leader. He left them with few instructions. The essence of his strategic plan as understood by his earliest adherents was to wait on the 'Spirit, which shall teach you all things'. The survival of Christianity in the context of this most woolly and unclear strategic approach itself evokes mystery.

Another view of the rise of Christianity is that its earliest followers came from among those who were not only marginal but also disenchanted and disaffected with what the ancient world had to offer. Most were from among the slaves, the dispossessed and the destitute. This is not to say that there were not some people of means and importance among the early Christians. Rather, it is to highlight that early Christianity was a proletarian mass movement and mass conversion was the engine of its growth. From this perspective the path of its acceptance by the powerful was complex.

Stark (1996) offered an alternative and more plausible explanation of the rise of Christianity that can be summarised as follows:

- Christianity started as a sect of Judaism. Early converts to Christianity were largely Jews of relative privilege with friends and relatives in high places. Generally they were of a higher level of education than the rest of the population.
- Christianity had its greatest appeal and success among discontented and inactive Hellenised Jews of the Diaspora because of its cultural continuity with Judaism while at the same time addressing many of the social and intellectual problems they had with practicing the law outside of Palestine. Early Christian missionaries concentrated on the Hellenistic Jews of the Diaspora and were allowed to teach in their synagogues. Much of the New Testament assumed an audience that was familiar with the Septuagint. As Christianity emerged as a new religion many of the early churches were located in the Jewish sections of the cities of the Diaspora. In the first two centuries of the

rise of Christianity it is not inappropriate to speak of Jewish Christianity.

- Christianity did not grow as a result of mass conversions but drew its converts mainly from among those who had strong attachments to members of the new cult. A growth rate of approximately 40 per cent per decade by and large accounts for the growth of Christianity over its first several centuries.

- Two epidemics, which swept the Roman Empire first in 160 and again in 251, played a significant part in the rise of Christianity. These epidemics destroyed a substantial proportion of the population and left behind large numbers of people without the interpersonal attachments that bound them to their conventional moral orders. Unlike many pagans, Christians did not run from the epidemics but nursed their own and others in need of assistance. This resulted in higher survival rates among Christians than the rest of the population as well as many survivors who owned their survival to Christian assistance. These epidemics not only altered the proportion of Christians to pagans in the empire but also gained for Christianity many new converts. Cyprian, Bishop of Carthage, and Dionysius, Bishop of Alexandria, both noted these outcomes.

- Most of the primary converts to Christianity were women of all social strata. They in turn were influential in gaining many secondary converts from among their households. Christianity appealed to women in the Roman world for numerous reasons. Christian wives enjoyed greater marital security and equality. Christian widows were not under pressure to remarry and those in need were better provided for than their pagan peers. Christian girls married at a later age, usually well beyond puberty. Christianity banned all forms of abortion and infanticide. Abortion was highly dangerous and often fatal. Infanticide of girl babies and boy babies with defects was legal and widely practiced in the Greco-Roman world. Christianity's ban on infanticide allowed many more girls born to Christian families to survive. The early Church offered women greater status than in pagan society. Many women occupied posts of responsibility within the church.

- The Polytheistic religion of the ancient world was in decline. It required elaborate temples, professional priests and extravagant festivals the funds for which came from the state or a few wealthy donors. Evidence of this decline comes from a fall off in state and donor support, a lack of public reverence and the sudden rise of new cults from the Orient. These seem to indicate a decline in the plausibility of paganism.

- Central doctrines of Christianity prompted and sustained attractive, liberating and effective social relations and organisations. Christianity offered a coherent culture entirely stripped of ethnicity. All were welcome without need of severing ethnic ties.

Apart from the earliest days of the Jesus movement there probably has never been a single Christianity. Diversity not unity has marked the religion. The deep desire for unity, manifested by the numerous councils and synods in the history of Christianity, testifies to this diversity that has perennially searched for commonality. Yet the very ethos of the religion marked by spirit, spontaneity and personal conviction, has literally dictated different churches, and not one church. The Christian landscape is therefore littered by differences as reflected in the labels Orthodox, Catholic, Ethiopian, Eastern, Western, Greek, Roman, Protestant, Puritan, Monophysite, Arian, Armenian, Nestorian, Coptic, Evangelical, Charismatic, Pentecostal and so many others.

These characteristics of Christianity pose a serious problem in attempting to trace the masculine and feminine roots of teaching in this religion. First, it is outside the scope of this study to attempt to follow the different lines of Christianity in different countries and regions as these evolved from their beginnings within the ancient world. Second, any choice of a particular country or people is in the end arbitrary. Notwithstanding the dangers of this second course, it is the only feasible option that can fit the scope of this study.

The choice made is to trace the masculine and feminine roots of teaching in Christianity as these developed in England. The choice of England relates to five considerations.

1. First, Britain was a marginal entity of the ancient Roman empire, which Rome abandoned, in the later stages of its empire. Little remained of the early Roman settlement in the England that later emerged.

2. Second, England was heathen and then converted to Christianity in the second half of the first millennium. The English, therefore, were never a part of the pagan ancient world of the city-states. They were truly a people formed in the new Age of Religion.

3. Third, from heathen and marginal beginnings England became a centre of both Christianity and imperial power in the modern world. England's rise is simultaneous with and an integral part of the rise of Western Europe and with it emergence of Western Christianity and civilisation.

4. Fourth, England, and Western civilisation, was Christian before it was scientific and industrial. Christianity was one of its first and foremost defining features.

5. Fifth, in terms of missionary enterprise in spreading Christianity worldwide, England ranks among the most effective of the countries of Western Europe, probably surpassed only by Spain.

THE ANCIENT WORLD'S LEGACY TO WESTERN CHRISTIANITY

The First Millennium CE witnessed fundamental changes in the world. At the beginning of this millennium the so-called civilised world was still organised on the basis of polytheistic city-states ruled by the Roman and Sassanian empires. At the end of the First Millennium the ancient world had disappeared and with it both of those empires. In their places, and firmly implanted, were Eastern and Western Christian civilisations and Islamic civilisation each with its own constellation of competing political entities and Judaism nested precariously in all three. Indeed, this situation lasted well into the Second Millennium and did not begin to change until about the eighteenth century. The period from about the sixth to sixteenth centuries is best described as the Age of Monotheistic Religious Civilisation. The usual labels Medieval or Middle Age are misnomers, and are only sometimes used in this study for reasons of convenience.

The decline and fall of the Roman empire has therefore to be interpreted in the wider context of the death and decay of ancient civilisation and the rise of the new Monotheistic Religious Age. While this transformation is clearly seen when the First Millennium is seen in its entirety, exact transitional dates are difficult to pinpoint. Different interpreters have attached varying degrees of importance and significance to different events and dates according to their particular perspective. However, the reason for the difficulties is not simply the lack of records or data or the interpretation of those available, but more fundamentally the fact that there was continuous interaction between the new and the old, as the ancient world declined and the monotheistic religious world rose to replace it.

Five separate but interrelated strands to this transitional interactive process can be identified. These are:

1. The decline of the ancient world under the weight of its own economic, political, social, cultural and ideological contradictions. Only modest and incremental advances had been made to the technological revolution in agricultural and industrial production that had been pioneered by Sumer in the Fourth Millennium BC. This in itself placed limits on the wealth that the ancient world could generate. Given its materialistic orientation and the vagaries of plagues, drought and other factors there were always uncontrollable changes in fortunes. The city-states were by and large political, social and cultural entities economically dependent upon the surrounding countryside from which they extracted most of their wealth. Internally they were highly stratified societies in which wealth and status were polarised. The imperial city-states were those strong enough to coerce some others into tributary relationships, largely on the basis of providing security services. Through these military and policing

services the imperial states permitted, guaranteed and facilitated trade and the free movement of people between cities within its sphere. As Herrin (1987) pointed out, in the latter part of the Roman era cities began to decay and with it the movement of the more wealthy citizens, who owned estates, into the countryside, while the impoverished from the countryside began moving into the cities.

2.   The invasion of tribes from Eastern, Western and Northern Europe in search of a better life. Materially Eastern, Western and Northern Europe were part of the 'Third World' of the ancient world. The term used then was 'barbarian' as against the 'civilised' of the cities. Ancient city-states, city plus surrounding countryside, were always magnets that attracted tribes whom they could not incorporate. Part of the role of the imperial city-state was to protect, or at least offer assistance to, client-cities under siege or whose territory had been encroached upon by barbarians. By the later stages of the Roman empire barbarian tribes were not only encroaching on imperial territory but had sacked Rome itself. Indeed, the ferocity of the destruction of Rome in 476 by the Vandals left the word vandalism firmly entrenched in Western languages (Herrin 1987). While the external threat from barbarian tribes was a perennial feature of the ancient world, repeatedly repelled, in the end the barbarians prevailed.

3.   Christianity, arising from within the Roman empire had implicitly and explicitly condemned the ancient lifestyle and culture. The Christian stance against the ancient ways was uncompromising as evidenced by the many who were martyred, firmly holding to the Christian assessment. In addition, the social injustice that characterised many aspects of ancient life was offensive to the early churches. Very early the churches developed ministries addressing the needs of the outcasts and destitute within the empire. Grant (1977) quoted a Roman official who observed that no Jew had to beg and that Christians not only looked after their own poor but 'ours' as well.

4.   The competition between the invading tribes, and marginal groups within the empire, for supremacy as successors to the Roman rulers. There is no sense in which the so-called barbarians of Western, Eastern and Northern Europe could be described as either homogenous or united. While they had a common enemy in Rome, each tribe or group of tribes entertained their own aspirations for ascendancy. For a time Rome exploited these divisions to its advantage, but this only postponed what proved to be the inevitable.

5.   The confrontations and conflicts between the Eastern and Western Christian empires and both separately with the Islamic empire. Perrin's dictum that without Mohammad, Charlemagne would be inconceivable highlighted the fact that had Mohammed not weakened and halted Eastern Christian empire, the latter would quite likely have dominated the West as well. The point to note is that Rome's

importance in shaping the Western world rested largely in being the only city of the ancient world that formed part of Western Christianity as this version developed.

From the five strands listed above one would expect, at first glance, that a natural alliance would have developed between the barbarian tribes posing the external threat to the Roman empire and Christians condemning the ancient lifestyle from within. But human affairs are never that simple or straightforward. For the purposes of this study it is only possible to give some brief description of the interaction of these five factors as they contributed to the development of Christianity in the West and provide a necessary background to understand the evolution of schooling and the teaching occupation as these were transformed in Western civilisation. The account of the development of Christianity, which follows, relies heavily on the analyses done by Hillgarth (1986) and Herrin (1987), unless otherwise stated.

THE EARLY CHURCH AND THE CITIES

The Jesus movement existed and operated mainly in the countryside of Palestine and only briefly in Jerusalem. It was his followers, mainly Paul and to a lesser extent Peter, who took the Christian message to the cities of the Mediterranean: Antioch, Alexandria and Rome being the most important. In each city the believers chose their own leaders. Bearing in mind that they were operating in hostile circumstances, they invariably elected among their leaders spokesmen who could deal with the authorities. In these circumstances of persecution, the office of bishop assumed special rank. Usually the bishop presided over matters, administered property and was empowered to act on behalf of the Christians in his city and those in the surrounding countryside. Many bishops were martyred with their congregations. The episcopal structure of early church organisation emerged in this context.

Faced with decline, the Roman empire experimented with many forms. One of these, in the early fourth century, was the Tetrachy in which eastern and western emperors were appointed each with a co-emperor who eventually succeeded to the post of emperor. This experiment served only to deepen the divide in the empire and Constantine, the eastern emperor, re-united the empire in 324. However, he established his capital at Constantinople, thus leaving Rome without the office of emperor. Through Constantine's conversion Christianity entered the empire from the east, while Rome itself remained resolutely pagan.

As the military situation deteriorated, the state became both more reliant on the church and in return offered them greater protection under the law and more civic privileges. Between 429 and 439 approximately 150 laws were passed defending or defining the Christian faith. Apart from Christianity, only Judaism was recognised as a legal religion. Church property was exempted from taxes. Bishops and the entire Christian clergy were given immunity to trial in the secular courts and many were assigned functions as local magistrates and judges. The clergy increasingly became the arbiters between the central government and the local authorities. Further, they became the intermediaries between rich and poor, while offering sanctuary to all.

As the situation in the cities deteriorated even further and the traditional city administrators abandoned their duties, the role of the church organisation, particularly the bishops, expanded even further by default. Some of the functions undertaken by bishops were:

- Organising the military defence of the city.
- Negotiating with the enemy and ransoming prisoners.
- Repairing damaged utilities particularly aqueducts, cisterns and other sources of drinking water.
- Taking charge of relief measures in times of drought, crop failure and other natural disasters.

The point must be made that while the bishops and the church were engaged in these good works they were rewarded handsomely, materially. A substantial amount of the wealth of the cities found its way into the church. Central and city governments, and wealthy individuals benefiting from sanctuary, all showed their gratitude to the church in cash or kind. Also, some preferred to hand over at least some of their fortunes to the church rather than to allow them to fall entirely into the hands of the invading armies of the barbarians. Probably these gifts were intended to buy favour in heaven. However, their immediate effect was to substantially improve the material fortunes of the church which received immediate material rewards for its social relief, arbitration and sanctuary services.

This process took particular importance at Rome, although the senatorial aristocracy retained control longer than in other cities and remained resolutely pagan. But even here the tide of events was of such that slowly the bishops assumed even greater influence. While the Senate was unable to maintain public buildings, bishops in addition to ministering to the poor, were also building churches. This contrast by itself symbolised the difference in trajectory of church and Senate. Eventually the bishops in Rome turned to assist the Senate as they rebuilt the banks of the Tiber, and restored other public works. In 452 when Attila the Hun threatened the city, Leo I led the diplomatic mission that negotiated on behalf of the city. These negotiations proved successful and the city was spared. Christians and the poor celebrated the achievement of their 'papa', pope (Herrin 1987). By the very importance of Rome, the leading Bishop of Rome assumed preeminent importance as bishops in all cities filled the breach in the twin circumstances of urban decay and barbarian invasion.

The Changed Circumstances of Ancient Learning and Institutions

Classical learning and its institutions had always depended upon imperial or civic sponsorship. As imperial power waned and became Christian, and as cities decayed, centres of classical learning declined along with them. Increasingly, bishops in Western cities became intolerant of classical knowledge, either denounced it as pagan and evil or regarded it as unnecessary. The language barrier facilitated this position in that classical learning was mainly recorded in Greek, which was little known and spoken in the West. While the barrier was by no means insurmountable, it required investment and effort that Western Christians with some notable exceptions, for example Augustine of Hippo, were unwilling to make.

Justian's closure of the long established and famous Academy at Athens reflected the growing tempo of the times. Interestingly, the equally famous Academy of Alexandra, which had come to some accommodation with Christianity through a synthesis between classical and Christian ideology, was allowed to continue to operate. It was not that the Christian church was against learning, but rather that they firmly opposed the ancient world, which they labelled pagan. This included ancient knowledge and institutions of learning. Accordingly, the church in the West deliberately disconnected from ancient learning.

THE EARLY CHURCH AND THE COUNTRYSIDE

While bishops and their flock were rescuing the perishing in the dying cities, and the urban churches were being enriched by the gratitude of the people an equally important movement developed in the countryside. The move to the countryside was driven by the motivation to shun the world, particularly the cities, and serve God alone. The ascetic life pre-dated Christianity. However, Christians enlarged and elevated the ascetic life to an extent not known before. Egyptian Christians were the first to practise and spread this lifestyle in the third century, based on the example of extreme asceticism and self-denial set by Anthony whose model of asceticism was highly individualistic. On the other hand, Pachom, in about 320, moved to a deserted village near the Nile, established a self-supporting community and placed it under the authority of a neighbouring bishop. This became the model for Christian monasticism that eventually spread to and became popular in the West.

Monasticism focused primarily on the highest expression of Christianity: spiritual devotion, holiness and total dedication to God on an individual basis. In time asceticism became associated with celibacy and with this began the association between holiness and virginity. Monastic Christianity challenged the ancient world fundamentally as it turned its back on kinship and family in terms of both their maintenance and their reproduction. Accordingly, young men fleeing arranged marriages and older men avoiding divorce joined the ranks of the monks. Many saw monasticism as a scandal to which they responded with great hostility. In the 380s a crowd in Rome rioted against a monk. In Carthage monks were jeered at and in Spain they were persecuted. However, within the church monks were seen as heroes, and holy. Many cities recruited their bishops from among the ranks of the monks. Many ascetics resisted such recruitment while others reluctantly abandoned their withdrawal from the world to take up leadership duties in city churches.

Monasticism spread from the East to the West. St. Martin, who later became Bishop of Tours 372 to 397, is credited with having established the first monastery in the West. He had been in North Africa and accepted the ascetic way of life. Through the monastery he established, Tours became an important centre of Christianity in the late fourth century. In time the rules of St Benedict became the most widely practised form of Western monasticism.

In the Christianisation of non-Roman Europe, Hillgarth (1986) maintained that it was the monastery and the abbot that were most instrumental and critical. He cited the case of Ireland which had never been politically or culturally subject to Rome and observed that the early course of Christianity there mirrored the path that was later followed in England and Northern Europe. The main elements of Hillgarth's reconstruction of the development of Irish Christianity can be summarised as follows:

1.   In a pastoral and non-urban society, the church's main centres were rural monasteries and not city churches.
2.   Abbots not bishops were the spiritual leaders.
3.   The overriding social importance of the monasteries was their relation to kinship and clan. The founders of monasteries were invariably relatives of royal families. While the abbot was celibate, a member of the family of the founder usually succeeded him.
4.   Abbots played a role in the recognition of kings and over-kings. This political role was helpful in their establishment of monasteries over which they were over-lords.
5.   While the church triumphed over paganism it did so largely by its fusion or accommodation with older traditions. For example, polygamy was legal in Christian Ireland.
6.   The Irish Church divided into two parties, the Roman and Irish. The Roman party in the south adhered more closely to the continent and to Rome, while the Irish party in the North held more firmly to indigenous ways and independence from Rome.
7.   The Irish had their own culture expressed in a vernacular literature that had not been obliterated by Roman overlay. The church in Ireland developed literature in two different languages centuries before parallel development took place in Latin Europe. There were many pagan heroes in early Irish literature, the celebration of whose virtues were later transferred to Christian saints.

NEW VIEWS ON GENDER AND WOMEN

While at the highest expression of its ethical vision Christianity makes no gender distinctions, in applying Christian teaching to ancient society organised on patriarchal lines, early Christian leaders had to address distinctions made between men and women. Acceptance also of the Old Testament, especially the Genesis accounts of creation, made the issue inescapable and so did Paul's letters to the various churches, recorded in the canon of the New Testament.

While Paul had given his interpretation of gender relations within the context of orthodox Jewish teaching, other Judea/Christian thinkers went outside this well known framework. One point of departure from orthodox Jewish teaching was with the views of Philo, the first century BCE Jewish scholar of Alexandria who had been greatly influenced by Hellenic Stoic philosophy. Philo in his commentaries on Genesis had put forward the view that while maleness was the closest human form to the ideal and higher being, and therefore superior to femaleness, virginity on the part of females was the first step to becoming male. Further, Philo argued that the curse on Eve of pain in child bearing and her loss of freedom to men was punishment for having been deceived by the serpent. Virginity on the part of the female absolved her from the curse. On the other hand, Philo saw no particular virtue in male virginity (Mortley 1981).

The Christian school that emerged out of the Academy of Alexandria, in the second and third centuries, followed the curriculum that had been devised by Philo (Broek 1996). Christian scholars of the school of Alexandria embraced and extended Philo's views. Cyprian in his commentary on Genesis 3:16, in 'Dress of the Virgin', argued that virginity compensated for all that otherwise resulted from the curse. The female virgin was free from the sentence of service to the husband and her desire for him. By embracing Christ as her master, she jumped over the intermediate stage of subjection to any ordinary male. In addition to avoiding the pain of child bearing, the virgin achieved equality not only with men but also with angels (Mortley 1981). The essence of Cyprian's position was that female virginity had triple implications: escape from the punishment of Eve, gender mobility by achieving equality with men, and spiritual elevation to the status of angel.

As Elkins (1988) noted, from about the fourth century, the notion of virginity freeing women from Eve's punishment became a familiar theme in female monastic literature. However, while elevating virginity as a desirable state, this view did not exactly portray marriage and child bearing in the most positive light. Wogan-Browne (1995) observed that the notion of female virginity, combined with the piety of monasticism, reflected a peculiar radicalism in relation to lineage patriarchy in that it simultaneously disrupted biological genealogies and created spiritual genealogies. The point of interest for this study is that through the concept of lifelong virginity, a body of Christian thought developed in the early centuries of Christianity which laid the foundation for altering important patriarchal traditions as these related to women.

Gilchrist (1994) commented on virginity in Christianity and its implications for priests and nuns. She maintained that through chastity priests became accessible to others through the public space created by the removal of sexuality. On the other hand, the chastity of nuns created private space since her sexuality was now not available to others. While Gilfchrist's application of the notion of public and private to chastity is neat, in that it highlighted the difference in its implications for men and women, the public analogy is more appropriately applied to priests than the private analogy can be applied to nuns.

Apart from prostitutes, whose sexuality was available to the public, women's sexuality in patriarchy was always part of the private sphere, where private is defined as kinship collective, family, household and domestic. The critical factor was that the daughter's or the wife's sexuality was the property of either her father or her husband. It did not belong to women, personally, although it was private to the kin group and the family. Virginity dedicated to Christ allowed women to claim their sexuality as theirs, personally. It transferred the daughter's sexuality from being the property of fathers, to being the property of Christ who in turn made the daughter the custodian of His property. Virginity dedicated to Christ interrupted the sale of the sexuality of daughters by their fathers to husbands, and transferred it to the personal control of the daughters themselves. This represented a fundamental alteration of patriarchal traditions for those women who chose this option offered by Christian theology.

Of equal importance was the fact that female virginity, consecrated through the vow of chastity, constituted redeeming and liberated purity that opened the path to female public careers within the church. Theoretically, there should have been no restrictions on women. Theologically they were debarred from administering the sacraments, hence denied the status of priests. Here the church made concessions to patriarchal society that were inconsistent with both the ethical vision of the religion and its emerging theology. Christianity was stumbling on the same rocks of patriarchal society as Judaism and Islam. However, within the constraints of these concessions to clan patriarchy there were several public careers created in the emerging religion in which women could be employed in Christianity's advance in the world.

It is very important to note that the women who were permitted to access these public careers were those who opted out of the traditional patriarchal definitions of female roles and functions as wives and mothers. The majority of women choosing these traditional roles were excluded, theologically, from the public sphere. They remained in the private sphere of domestic responsibility. However, women dedicating their virginity to Christ, were not only freed from the penalty of Eve, but by their elevation to equality with men and angels, permitted access to some public careers in the church alongside men.

The prostitute was always engaged in a public career. Christianity did not condone prostitution or incorporate it into any of its rituals. It did, however, develop the theology of the redeemed sinful woman. Unlike the virgin, whose purity permitted her to engage in devotion and missions, the redeemed sinful woman's role was penance-related repentance. Her role model was Mary Magdalene, perennially engaged in useful service especially to suffering humanity. This path was generally open to married women retiring from marriage, widows and fallen maidens. While chastity was an underlying principle, the purity of virginity was not applicable. The operative principle was not purity but repentance and penance.

THE ALTERNATIVE PATHS

From a social perspective it must be noted that Christianity began to offer alternative paths of social mobility to those which had become standard in the ancient world and which did not exist in the barbarian tribal organisation. The loci of these alternative paths were the episcopal organisation of the churches in the decaying cities, with their increasing link to both the imperial government and civic authorities, and the rural monasteries with their ties to the rising barbarian monarchies. For different reasons Christianity, which was part of the ancient world but not of its classical traditions, proved invaluable for both the protagonists and antagonists of the old and new orders. On the one hand the church provided occupational space for people whom the state could no longer absorb, while on the other hand it supplied the needs of emerging and expanding monarchies, which were without bureaucratic support.

By entering the clergy and its episcopal order, or the monasteries, it became possible to rise to public office through paths that were entirely new. Charismatic leaders could bypass the long and gradual rise to public office through various levels of the imperial and civic bureaucracies through union with Christ, ascetic living and celibacy. It is therefore not surprising that the churches and monasteries began to attract not only some of the most creative minds but also some of the most competent leaders of the time. Marginal energy now resided in the churches and the monasteries. Matched with and motivated by piety, the combination was overpowering.

Through virginity the church provided opportunities for both men and women to renounce patriarchal obligations to their clans and lineage in favour of service to God. Christianity was missionary, whether through its bishops in the city churches or its abbots and abbesses in monasteries in the countryside. Many women became part of the ascetic movement. As was the case with abbots, many abbesses were members of royal or aristocratic families. However, the members of the monasteries, particularly in the case of men, came from all strata of society.

It is against this general background that the rise of Christianity in England must be understood and with it the creation of schools and the teaching occupation.

THE CONVERSION OF ENGLAND

For the purpose of this study it is necessary to provide a brief sketch of England from the first decade of the fifth century to the period just prior to the Reformation in the second decade of the sixteenth century. This period breaks naturally into two somewhat unequal parts; from about 410 after the Romans withdrew their garrison and up to the Norman conquest in 1066, and the second period from 1066 to just before the Reformation, about 1520. The first is marked by repeated invasions as tribes from Northern Europe invaded and settled in Britain and began the process of their incorporation into the society. In the second period there were no further invasions and the settled peoples melted completely into the English identity that had started to emerge after the commencement of the Roman withdrawal.

THE MAKING OF THE ENGLISH

Britain was part of the Roman Empire, but on its outer reaches. During Alaric's campaign in Italy between 397 and 410, Roman government began to withdraw its troops from what were considered its less important territories in order to bolster the defences of Rome. The withdrawal of troops from Britain began in 401 and was completed by 410 (Briggs 1994). Britain was left to organise its own defences and work out its own salvation.

Early in the fourth century the Roman administration had settled Saxons in Britain as part of its military forces. The Roman practice of employing mercenary forces from among the barbarians had been a long established pattern in its military organisation. Indeed, by the fifth century many of the leading military commanders were either Germanic or of Germanic ancestry, the scions of marriages between barbarian military fathers and daughters of the Roman aristocracy. In between military duties these Saxon confederate troops in Britain had carried out farming, which was their background.

By the middle of the fifth century all contact between Rome and Britain had ceased. The confederate troops strengthened by new arrivals from the continent, probably through Frisian land at the mouth of the Rhine, proceeded to settle Britain on their own account. It is important to note that the new arrivants were from the same stock as the confederate troops – the Germanic tribes of North West Germany. They did not come as a large invading army but rather as migrating bands whose routes of entry were along the Thames valley, along the river system of the Wash and through the Humber in the north (Mayr-Harting 1991). This migration was not uncontested. It took place against the military resistance of the native British, Celtic, people who were sometimes successful in halting the advance, as at the battle of Mount Badon in 520. But these successes were only temporary.

A century after the Roman withdrawal the towns and villas that had been the cornerstone of Roman civilisation almost completely disappeared from

British life. Mayr-Harting (1991) made the point that the Roman towns had been in decline even before the withdrawal and that the Anglo-Saxon farmers had simply delivered the coup-de-grace. Lyon (1991) noted that the Anglo-Saxons had abandoned the higher contours on which the Roman towns and villas had been built and established their farming communities on lands in the valleys and on the gentle sloping lowlands.

In other words, the Germanic tribes invading Britain were land hungry farmers and not adventurers in search of loot or conquerors seeking tribute or over-lordship of an already established people. They established their settlements and farms on lands that were not previously cultivated, but appeared more appropriate for permanent agricultural settlements. In this regard they were pioneers clearing forests and draining swamps in between fighting to both acquire access to the land and then to keep it.

The critical point to note is the discontinuity between the previous Roman settlement of England and the emerging Anglo-Saxon society. The new settlers were not building on what the Romans had left but creating their own. Britain was a marginal and relatively underdeveloped part of the Roman empire. It had no major cities, no highly entrenched senatorial aristocracy and no episcopate to mediate with the invaders. The circumstances that preserved Roman culture and structures on the continent were non-existent in Britain. As a result there was as clean a break in human settlement as is possible. This is marked symbolically by the fact that the Romans built in stone while the Anglo-Saxons built in wood and that the Roman roads were abandoned probably because of their lack of relationship to the new settlements.

Unlike the Romans, the British natives had remained. However, there is little sign of their presence within Anglo-Saxon society. At the same time there is no evidence of any massive extermination of the native population by the Anglo-Saxon conquerors. Neither is there any reason to believe that the entire native British had withdrawn into the British kingdoms of the west and north of the island. Mayr-Harting put forward the view that the Anglo-Saxons came in small warrior bands and through inter-marriage and slavery assimilated the native population. Hence the native British were simply absorbed with the resulting loss of identity and their invisibility to the archaeologists, anthropologists and historians searching for evidence of their presence. Lyon (1991), on the other hand, was of the view that the Anglo-Saxons came in relatively large numbers and did not inter-marry with the native population to any significant degree. Rather, the subjugation of the native population was sufficiently effective that they assimilated to Anglo-Saxon ways, particularly in language.

There is very little tangible evidence of British survival in the culture of Anglo-Saxon England apart from some place names and probably less than a dozen words in the English language. Of the little that exists most are artefacts that belong to females. This is to be expected in that given the military confrontation that took place it would be expected that men would be killed and women enslaved. Also men enslaved were more likely sold while the women were kept, especially if the invading men came with relatively few women as seems to have been the case (Leyser 1995). The absence of British influence underscored the lack of community between the Roman British society that had previously existed and the new Anglo-Saxon society and civilisation that was in the making based on tribes voluntarily transplanting themselves from elsewhere. Interestingly the term Anglo-Saxon was coined eventually to distinguish between the Saxons who had migrated to the island from those that remained in Northern Germany.

Leadership among the Anglo-Saxons centred on two criteria: nobility of birth and prowess. The first related to tracing ancestry to the god Woden, that is, claiming the mystery of descent from the gods and with it appropriate status. The second related to military success on the battlefield. Theoretically, prowess by itself only made a man a warrior while nobility by itself only established aristocratic breeding. Both produced kingship, or at least royalty. However, in reality exceptional prowess as manifested by great success in warfare would invariably open the way for the genealogical records to be produced establishing the little known or forgotten connections with divine descent.

As these groups fought to acquire and keep land, they coalesced to form larger tribal groups and eventually kingdoms, reaching into to the very heart of the British countryside. Their common enemy were the British who opposed them. At the same time there was rivalry between the Anglo-Saxon invaders for territory, notwithstanding their common origins and similar mission. These two forces produced at least nine Anglo-Saxon kingdoms by the end of the sixth century. These were the southern kingdoms of Kent, South Saxons, East Saxons and West Saxons; the midland kingdoms of East Angles, Middle Angles and West Angles; and the Northumbrian kingdoms of Bernicia and Diera (Mayr-Harting 1991). In the process of creating these nine kingdoms the Anglo-Saxons had managed to push the British into the west and north of the country in which they had their own kingdoms. Quoting Bede's *Ecclesiastical History of the English People,* Lyon (1991) stated that the Jutes were found mainly in Kent, the Saxons in the three southern Saxon kingdoms, while the Angles formed the midland and northern kingdoms in Mercia and Northumbria.

After these Anglo-Saxon kingdoms had been established, the next round of political activity centred on some kingdoms beginning to exercise imperium over others thereby creating over-kings and lesser kings. The northern, midland and southern kingdoms became the first areas of competition. In time the lesser kingdoms became sub-kingdoms within three large three kingdoms: Northumbria in the north, Mercia in the midlands and Wessex in the south. The great achievement of the Anglo-Saxons invaders was their pioneering foundation of England on a substantial agricultural and rural base.

Viking and Danish Invasions

Viking raids began in 793 with the sack of the island of Lindsfarne and the desecration of the cathedral at York. This signalled a new era in the making of the English. This new wave continued with the Danish sack of London in 842 and culminated in a large-scale invasion in 865. The Danes came in large numbers and settled in the north and east of England. They were prevented from conquering the whole country by the Wessex kings, Ethelred I and Alfred his brother who succeeded him. Through a combination of military success and treaty, Alfred not only halted the Danish advance but established peaceful coexistence. The Wessex dynasties then became the Kings of All England. At the same time the Wessex kings had to pay tribute to the Danish court suggesting that the balance of power had shifted fundamentally from what had previously existed.

The Danish invasion of England, like that of the Germanic tribes before them, was part of a larger movement in Europe also spurred by land hunger. Alfred the Great had noted, after hosting an important Dane, that although he was one of the foremost men of his country he land very little land, only about 20 horned cattle, 20 sheep and 20 swine (Briggs 1994). Lyon (1991) was of the view that political consolidation in Scandinavia, itself a sign of prosperity, had produced polarisation in wealth and the distribution of land and with it unrest. The earlier peaceful settlement of Iceland was but the first wave of this movement in search of new land for settlement. The invasion of England was part of a second wave with similar objectives.

Lyon further noted that maturity in boat building techniques had given the Vikings a new mobility that they used to terrorise the rest of Europe through their pirating activities. However, many Vikings were traders and were known as far as the Mediterranean. These new settlers to England brought new skills in the form of ship building and trading. Their first contributions to England appear to be have been law as Danelaw was established in the territory they controlled. Indeed the word law itself is Danish. The reputed ferocity and mayhem of their military conduct, does not match their documented settlement behaviour based on the rule of law, and the acknowledgement of that law as being among the most advanced in Western Europe at that time. Probably future historians will resolve this apparent contradiction from accounts that highlight the Danish perspective.

The Norman Conquest

In less than a hundred years, a second Danish invasion in 978 again altered the political status quo in England. By 1016 a Danish king, Cnut, had become King of England, which was now united under a single monarchy. While in the space of two generations the kingship again came back into Anglo-Saxon hands, this was short lived with the Norman Conquest in 1066. While the

Normans conquered England from Normandy in France, they had originally migrated to France from Northern Europe and were themselves Germanic, notwithstanding the fact that they spoke French.

The Normans were different from the previous invading groups in several important respects. They were not farmers in search of land. They did not invade England to farm it but to rule it. They were not pagans on arrival but Christians, William the Conqueror was a devout churchman. They were not barbarians compared to the settled people. From the evidence available they would appear to have been better educated. Lyon put the matter delicately by stating that the Normans did not feel themselves inferior to the English. Judging by the records of the attitudes they adopted, it would appear that they interpreted the conquest in terms of civilising the English. Arrogance notwithstanding, the Norman addition to the English pool of natural resources was administrative and organisational leadership. Evidence of this is the cadastral inventory which William immediately commissioned, recorded in the Domesday Book, which is certainly unique and unparalleled in content and methodology until modern times.

The Norman period, lasting until the end of the fourteenth century, marked the end of repeated foreign invasions. English society to that point had not known such sustained relief from external threat. In 1348–49 the country was devastated by the Black Death plague, which recurred several times. The population declined by about 33 to 40 per cent as a result of this plague. It did not recover its peak at the beginning of the thirteenth century until during the sixteenth century.

The Normans represented the last ingredient in the English melting pot at the beginning of the second millennium. In essence therefore the English are a composite, and largely transplanted, people drawn from Angle, Saxon, Jute, Norwegian, Danish and Norman stock with an invisible but definite Celtic underlay. It would take some time yet before the vigour of this hybrid blend would achieve the potential claimed to be inherent in such admixture. More that any other peoples the metaphor of the melting pot applies to the English; they were melted in the solvent of a unified church employing the active agent of education. The resultant crystallisation was the new solute called the English.

THE EARLY ENGLISH ECONOMY

Britain had been part of the imperial economy of Rome. Its subsequent development involved a fundamental break with that system. Any discussion of educational development that did not take some note of the economic implications of this break could be deemed to be incomplete. Unless otherwise stated, the observations rely on the economic history of medieval England as outlined by Lyon (1991) and Miller and Hatcher 1978 and 1995.

With the withdrawal of the Roman garrison from Britain in 410, England did not have any meaningful contact with Europe, or the outside world, until the end of the sixth century. Settlers were preoccupied with the prerogatives of internal settlement and the intense strife related to that process and therefore had no time for the world that had effectively left them to their own devices. Further, the circumstances of almost continuous warfare did not allow for much more than subsistence existence. By the middle of the seventh century when some normalcy and routine had been established, the external world itself had taken a new economic shape. Islam had taken control of the Mediterranean, the very heart of external trade in the then known world. That by itself was a critical factor reshaping macro-economic relationships.

Henri Pirenne's reconstruction of the economic history of Western Europe highlighted the following:

1. There was no substantial break in economic development as a result of the Germanic invasion of the Roman empire in the fifth and sixth centuries.
2. The break in economic development occurred in the seventh century as a direct result of Islam and its success in capturing and dominating the Mediterranean.
3. In consequence of the latter, there was economic decline in Western Europe.

Lyon noted that Pirenne's first two points have withstood the most rigorous analysis and vigorous criticisms. His third observation has not been as sturdy because he interpreted as economic decline the fact that gold disappeared from Western Europe and was replaced by silver as the means of economic exchange. Pirenne had also noted that it was not until the twelfth century that gold again re-entered Western Europe as the means of exchange although both the Byzantine and Islamic empires continued to trade using gold. However, the disappearance of gold as the unit of exchange is not by itself evidence of economic decline or of poverty.

Lyon interpreted the change to silver in the West as a deflationary measure. It was an adaptation of monetary symbols to a fall in prices and to a corresponding increase in the value of the precious metal used for coins. The West had no major supply of gold and had no commodity powerful enough to attract gold back from the East. Such commodities were not available until the twelfth century when the West began to export cloth, timber, arms and wheat to the East. At the same time the change to silver appears to indicate a revival of the local economy within Western Europe.

The matter of relevance to this study is that when England emerged from the internal processes that shaped its settlement after the Roman withdrawal, and reconnected with Western Europe, the latter was not an economic force in the world and overseas trade did not play any significant part in the English economy until the second millennium. In the early centuries up to the end of the first millennium England's greatest export commodity was slaves. The chief source of supply was those captured in internal warfare. There is good reason to believe that the native British were not uncommon commodities in this cargo. Indeed, St Patrick of Ireland was a Briton who had been sold into slavery. Another source of slaves was the legal and penal system, which prescribed slavery as the punishment for various crimes. For example, a thief and his family, if the crime was committed with their knowledge, could be sold into slavery. Yet another source was those who by virtue of economic pressure sold themselves or were sold into slavery. The chief imports up to the time of the Norman Conquest were a few luxury goods, wine and pottery.

Miller and Hatcher (1978) accounted for the forces of change in the English economy between the Norman Conquest and the Black Death of 1348, solely in terms of expansion. Vast areas of marshland, woodland and other unused lands were brought into production at the same time that existing land was being more extensively cultivated. New industries and towns were established and existing towns and industries grew and expanded. Trade expanded in scope and scale.

At first expansion of production kept pace with population growth. The amount of land per capita and output per head remained the same. Economic growth therefore was not associated with increasing prosperity; however, standards of living were maintained. Later, expanded production fell behind population growth resulting in declining standards of living. The Black Death relieved the problems temporarily, however, by the time of the Reformation the population had recovered, and the basic deficiencies of the economy were again manifest. The principal deficiency was backward technology as applied to agriculture.

Miller and Hatcher (1978) showed that between the eleventh and the fourteenth centuries, inflation was not excessive. Prices increased, subject to fluctuations some of which were violent. The chief factor related to fluctuations was the size of the harvests as determined by the weather. Expanded production, however, while not improving the standard of living, resulted in substantial increases in internal and external trade. Products exported included wool, grain, hides, dairy products and iron. The chief imports were luxury and semi-luxury goods, especially textiles, arms and armoury, wines, fish, dyes, timber and raw materials. The basic pattern of trade was that the chief imported goods represented quality consumer goods reflecting the tastes and purchasing power of the manorial elite who were the principal beneficiaries of the economic expansion. The exports reflected the main products of the labour of the peasants.

While Norman England rested on the agricultural foundations laid down in Anglo-Saxon England, the economic expansion it sponsored and managed brought with it the growth of towns and medieval industries. Towns became the sites for a range of industrial activities, even though most industries were still in their early developmental stages.

Miller and Hatcher (1995) noted that most English medieval industries producing durable goods were small-scale units, domestic in character, possessing little in the way of capital. It was sometimes difficult to differentiate agricultural from industrial enterprises. Also industrial producers often marketed their own products. In many instances markets were local and restricted. The main raw materials were wood, leather and clay.

Industries related to consumer goods were mainly brewing, production of salt, milling flour, meal and malt, baking and butcheries. Brewing initially involved a noticeable number of women as alewives. In Norwich in 1327 there were 84 alewives among the 252 persons paying tallage. Seeing that many businesses were registered in the names of husbands, although wives did the brewing, the number of women involved would have been much more than those registered in their own names. Miller and Hatcher (1995) noted that most mills were mechanised and used horse, wind or waterpower. For one reason or another manorial authorities were highly suspicious and wary of millers.

Representatives of the building trades were to be found in cities, and large and small towns. The stonemasons and master carpenters were mostly responsible for large projects. However, in each specialisation there were numerous levels of skill. Because most of the buildings were of wood, carpenters were most numerous, however, an increasing number of public building including churches were being built in stone. The construction sector employed a large number of skilled workers in tiling, thatching, carpentry, stone masonry and plumbing and was an important sector in the economy.

Goldsmiths and tanners represented craftsmen whose markets were not either everyday durable or consumable goods. They directed their trades to the tastes and styles of the more affluent members of society. Increasingly, in medieval England large towns had a few craftsmen who became capable of meeting the needs of this affluent group.

Mining and smelting started about the middle of the thirteenth century. Because mines were located in thinly populated areas, the king and lords found that to increase production and profit it was wise to make modest demands on labour. This gave rise to a few highly independent communities, which did not fit into the manorial pattern. In addition, mining involved high risks because it utilised new technologies that were still not proven. Landlords seldom exploited mines directly but took profits from leases, levies on output or the right to pre-empt the output at an agreed price.

The expansion of agricultural production leading to greater internal and external trade also brought with it the growth of ports and cities, London in particular. Trade required currency exchange, credit arrangements, access to markets, transportation and wholesale and retail distribution. Foreign trade required these in relation to overseas operations. In medieval England more alien merchants than Englishmen were involved in importation and exports. The agents of these foreign merchants from Flanders, Italy, Germany, and elsewhere became resident aliens. They came to trade not to migrate.

At that time traditional rules in London required aliens to be lodged with citizens who would supervise what they did. Visitors were not allowed to remain in the city longer than forty days. They could not own houses or form associations of their own. Over time the status of denizen was devised to allow their agents to be treated differently from visitors. A similar situation existed with respect to the financial arrangements necessary to sustain trade. The canon law forbade usury, yet credit and a return on financial investment were indispensable to trade. In a nutshell the emergence of England in the twelfth century into international trade required major adjustments to patterns of living that had been fashioned for a domestic economy centred on subsistence agriculture.

FEATURES OF SOCIAL STRUCTURE

Anglo-Saxon society evolved continuously from its inception. This dynamic quality poses difficulties for brief descriptions. The key to bear in mind is that the social evolution was from pioneering free peasant householders living in a violent Anglo-Saxon society, to more peaceful and ordered English communities in which the residents had lost much of their earlier freedoms. The factors affecting this transformation related to three institutions: kinship or kindred as it was called; territorial lordship; and the state as symbolised in the monarchy. The general trend was for territorial lords and the monarchy to superimpose themselves on kindred, and to emerge predominant although kinship was not eliminated but rather subordinated. The interactions were complex but an attempt will be made to comment on each of these.

Kindred

As in the case of the ancient world, membership in Anglo-Saxon society was predicated upon the kinship collective not on the individual. The word individual in English did not come to have its modern meaning until the seventeenth century (Briggs 1994). Originally individual meant indivisible. People belonged in Anglo-Saxon society on the basis of kindred. Over time kindred came to be composed of a two thirds of one's paternal and one third of one's maternal relatives. Kindred implied blood relationships which carried very strict and sacred obligations. It could be best defined in terms of some of those obligations.

One's kindred were those who:

- Had the right to take vengeance if one was maimed or slain;
- Were paid the blood price, wergeld, if one was slain;
- Paid the ransom if one was enslaved;
- Vouched for one's good name or guaranteed one's conduct;
- Provided food if one was imprisoned;
- Were informed in case of death or if given sanctuary.

Insight into the transformation of the system of kindred is probably best illustrated with respect to taking vengeance if a member of the kindred was killed. The right of vengeance by kin was the primary means of protection in a relatively lawless and unsophisticated society. This was a sacred and unqualified obligation of the clan as part of the system of mutual protection of its members. Sigbert, King of East Angles, was killed by his kindred because they claimed that was he was too apt to spare his enemies and to forgive those that had done him wrong (Mayr-Harting 1991). Forgiveness of enemies was a fatal virtue, especially among one's kindred, since it suggested unreliability with respect to a sacred obligation.

In time as laws were established, if a man was killed his kindred still had the right by law to wage a blood feud against the slayer and his kindred, but the feud could be bought off by paying the blood price of the slain man. Every man had a blood price, including the king. This was nominated in shillings. The over-king had the highest blood price which was between six to 15 times the price of a nobleman, whose price in turn was about six times that of the ordinary free man. Slaves had the lowest blood price. The primary responsibility to pay the blood price rested with kindred and not the slayer. Paternal and matrenal members paid two-thirds to one-third of the established blood price of the slain man. In King Alfred's time the law was modified to allow associates, or the slayer, to participate in the payment of blood price if kindred were unable to pay (Lyon 1991).

In this very brief sketch of this single aspect of kindred several points can be noted.
- First, the original and sacred obligation of revenge by taking life for the life of one of its kindred.
- Second, the moderation of that obligation by compensating the kindred who was aggrieved and payment by the kindred perpetrating the offence.
- Third, the injection of status considerations in the amount of compensation, which accorded varying values to men.
- Lastly, the possibility of non-kin to substitute for kindred if the latter defaulted.

The trajectory of these shifts was to diminish the strength of kindred.

Territorial Lordship

One of the great themes of epic poetry in Anglo-Saxon England was the triumph of loyalty to lord over kindred. Early settlements invariably involved more than a single kindred. Their defence required many clans fighting together. Land would not be equally distributed in the settlements. Larger landowners, with military prowess and success in battle, would in time command loyalty from those fighting with them. This loyalty in time strained kindred ties. Territorial lord and fighting men emerged as a social unit in Anglo-Saxon society that developed its own codes of honour, as a warrior aristocracy emerged in some places. For example, it became a matter of great disgrace if men survived their lord in battle.

Within the several kingdoms that existed, the king would quite likely reward landless men of military prowess, hence lords could emerge from men with or without land. These links would invariably be made and maintained with the king, who emerged as the leader of the warrior aristocracy. Alfred's modification of blood price law gave territorial lords even greater influence over men. In time men sought out lords who assumed many of the functions of kindred, by standing surety, paying blood price, vouching for behaviour, etc. While the notion of a warrior aristocracy was noble, and the relationship between lords and men commanded in battle came to be regarded as special, or even of a spiritual quality, the dependent relationship that developed between land baron and serf descended into the obscene. Yet both of these fused, especially after the Norman Conquest, and gave rise to feudalism.

In Norman England men without lords were outlaws. All land belonged to the king who parcelled it out to a few tenants in chief, barons. They in turn rented it out to over 4000 knights. Each redistribution carried with it social obligations in addition to economic costs. Knights in turned rented out the land to tenants, villeins. As Briggs pointed out, narrowly defined feudalism was knightly service on condition of land tenure. Broadly speaking it was vassalage. The first was based on violence and warfare, the second on the use and tenure of land.

The point is that Norman England fused and consolidated the relationship between territorial lord and fighting men that had emerged in a diffused and undefined way in the Anglo-Saxon period. The general trend over the period was that territorial lordship was gradually elevated above kindred in the organisation of society. Kindred, however, did not disappear; it was only considerably weakened and subordinated to lordship.

The State as Represented by the Monarchy

The notion of being English, and of England, was intimately related to the monarchy. This bond between the English person and monarch was related to the sense of country and people, of wider obligations beyond kindred or territory or lords. The widely held concept of doing one's duty to king and country reflected that wider obligation. The evolution of this association can be traced through the evolution of the monarchy from its earliest stages and the institutions it created in the name of all its subjects.

Lyon made the point that corporate endeavours were required by the early pioneering efforts to establish farming communities. These included clearing forests, draining swamps and ploughing fields; ownership of ploughs, the plough-teams, the allotment of arable lands and the partition of meadows. These were all premised on co-operative principles and practices. While initially this may have contributed to the creation of wider tribal linkages, beyond kindred, it eventually led to wider collaboration beyond tribe. The monarchy was established beyond tribal arrangements as groups prosecuted their interest in acquiring and keeping land.

The first differentiation was the royal kindred from the rest of the society and with it the royal court. Apart from its military mission, the obligations of royalty began to be defined in terms of the common good of the kingdom. Through intermarriages linkages were established both with other courts and important kindred groups within the kingdom. In time both a wider aristocracy was created as well as the amalgamation of kingdoms until finally a single monarchy prevailed uniting the entire country of the English.

The monarchy's primary mission was the defence of the kingdom externally. Closely allied to this was the responsibility to guarantee safety within the kingdom. The Venerable Bede made a point of the fact that it was possible for women to walk safely at night in the kingdom of Northumbria. The king's guarantee of safety spread to markets, as burghs were created around them. Those that continued to thrive became boroughs and finally fortified towns. The king and his nobles guaranteed the security of the burghs. They became the places where money was minted, and courts were established dispensing the king's justice. Defence, internal security, communications, economic exchange and justice all became part of the monarch's role beyond kindred and lord. The monarch connected kindred and lords to form the kingdom, the precursor to country.

To go even further with this gross simplification of what was a gradual and complex process, it must be noted that urban centres emerged based on royal guarantee. From the starting point of numerous fortified burghs, some developed into towns. In this regard the Danish invasion was an indirect but important stimulus, and the actions of Alfred in expanding the burghs proved to be one of his exceptionally far-sighted policies. However, urban growth was slow. By the time of the Norman Conquest there were only 10 towns that had populations of more than 2000 inhabitants. The Domesday survey showed that only four per cent of the people in England lived in towns, and half of these lived in London. Anglo-Saxon England was a rural society and such urban centres as existed resulted mainly from royal action.

Changes in the Society After the Conquest

In Norman England, there was not the violence of war between kingdoms or invasion from Vikings or any external other sources. This is not to say that peace prevailed in England. Violence continued to be a feature of medieval English society. Civil disturbances were quite common. Men were swift to defend their rights by force and to use weapons. Individual violence was augmented by banditry, as gangs were prevalent in the society. The courts were not effective. Many suspects escaped arrest. Many accused of murder were able to flee instead of stand trial (Miller and Hatcher 1978).

Violence was only one of the means by which life could be shortened. Other causes, less visible but as lethal, were legion. The lack of clean water, inadequate sanitation and poor personal hygiene were the breeding ground for disease. While starvation was rare malnutrition was widespread. Together these factors contributed to frequent epidemics involving great loss of life. Infant mortality was high and life expectancy was low. Even the aristocracy could not expect to live much more than 50 years.

The society that evolved in Norman England was one in which political, social, economic and even legal relations rested on personal dependence. Apart from the king, every man was another man's man. The mightiest barons were the king's men. The lesser barons were the men of the mighty barons. Every knight was the man of a baron. Each knight had his men, who in turn had theirs until the chain reached the lowliest peasant. Each tier of the hierarchy consisted of the men of those above them. In this pyramid of personal dependence, knights on oath exchanged military service for the tenancy of land. Peasants exchanged labour for their tenancy of small portions of land of the knight on whom they depended. The glue holding personal dependence in place was land tenure (Miller and Hatcher 1978).

The massive loss of life in the Black Death of 1348–49 and its recurrences in the latter decades of the fourteenth century weakened the manorial lordship system. Obligations of military service and labour became unenforceable. Also, the economic developments related to the growth of towns, mining, manufacturing and external trade further undermined this system. Merchants, managers, lawyers, miners, brewers, millers, hucksters and the like did not fit easily into the traditional categories determined by personal dependence cemented by land tenure.

The church in the form of the clergy had always had an ambiguous relationship with the lordship system. Bishops, abbots and abbesses were lords. But they held the land ex-officio on behalf of the churches and monasteries. At the same time the relationship between priests and bishops, monks and abbots, nuns and abbesses was not on the basis of land tenure. Bishops, abbots and abbesses related to kings and lords, and were often subject to their direction; however, this was more out of expediency than manorial obligation. Then again kings and lords were subject to the church, at least in theory, as the church and its clergy represented Divine prerogatives in the realm. Moreover, the church was a missionary organisation that did not owe loyalty to king and manorial lord.

The new strata of merchants, bankers, millers, brewers, miners and hucksters resembled the clergy more than barons, knights and peasants. Foreigners living in English society were yet another new group. By the time of the Reformation there were numerous social anomalies involving the church and this new class, as well as the anachronisms of the manorial system that had to be reconciled, rationalised and resolved.

THE CHURCH AND ITS MISSION

All the available evidence points to the fact that there was no continuity between Christianity in Roman Britain and the Anglo-Saxon society that replaced it. Christianity departed with the Roman garrison. While the church continued in the British kingdoms in the West and North, no Christian witness appeared to have survived in England. There was no missionary activity across the warring factions of invading Germanic tribes and Celts defending Britain. The British church played no part in the conversion of the Anglo-Saxons within their island. Its evangelistic mandate was trapped by the antagonisms of territorial warfare.

The Anglo-Saxons were polytheistic. The main deities were Woden the god of war and strife against evil forces, Thor the god of thunder who protected their households and Frigg, the consort of Woden who was the goddess of marriage and childbearing. The goddess of spring was called Easter and the Anglo-Saxon new year, which was marked by a great festival, began December 25 (Bonner 1994). Priests promoted beliefs and performed rituals. They were forbidden to ride stallions or carry weapons. Bonner (1994) was of the view that the Anglo-Saxons did not have a single religion but a collection of religions. This along with concentration upon particular gods, utilitarian emphasis, and their lack of creed and theological foundation facilitated their Christian conversion.

The first attempt to convert the Anglo-Saxons came from Pope Gregory the Great who sent a mission headed by Augustine in 597. Mayr-Harting's reconstruction of Gregory's reasons for sending the mission included the following:

a) Britain had been a province of Rome, and the idea of empire figured prominently in Gregory's conception of geography.

b) Anglo-Saxons were the only totally heathen people within the Western empire.

c) Anglo-Saxons were heathens not heretics. Sending a mission constituted an act of original missionary enterprise.

d) Ethelbert, king of Kent had created circumstances that made missionary activity feasible. He had married a Christian Frankish princess, Bertha, and allowed her to retain her religion suitably assisted by her clergy. Ethelbert was probably disposed to conversion.

The mission was received and established at Canterbury. From the evidence available it is not clear whether it was on monastic or parish lines. The usual distinctions between these two forms of Christian organisation were blurred in this original missionary thrust

The Irish church also played a significant role in the efforts to convert the Anglo-Saxons. Osward of Bernicia converted to Christianity while in exile in

Ireland. On returning from exile as King in 635 he invited the Bishop of Iona to promote the Christian faith in his kingdom. In response Aidan established a monastery on the island of Lindisfarne off the coast of Northumbria not far from the royal castle. Lindisfarne superseded Canterbury as the effective missionary centre in England for the next 30 years.

At the Synod of Whitby in 665 the competition between Irish and Roman influence was resolved in favour of Rome. The issue at hand was the date of Easter, which the two churches calculated differently. The wider significance of this decision was aptly captured in Bede's statement that from that time onward England celebrated Easter, not on the calculation of a remote territory but with the whole world. England was joining the emerging Western European community through the auspices of the church.

The conversion process was gradual and not without reversals and relapses, but the early evangelising mission triumphed through its successes in converting kings and their courts. In fact, several members of courts forsook the world and became monks or nuns. While there were no instances of monks becoming kings, the link between Christianity and power was established very early in English history and remained an unchanging feature. King, bishop and abbot stood together for order and authority and mutually supported each other's cause. In addition, the kings' connections with the church in England meant links to the papacy in Rome and along with marriage with other royal houses became an important link in the Western European world that was slowly emerging. Also, being recognised by Rome was important to the legitimacy of kingship.

This is not to say that the relationship between kings and the church was without trials and tribulations. Probably the most diabolical illustration of the depths to which the relationship sank on occasions was the murder in 1170 of Thomas Becket, Archbishop of Canterbury, at the altar of the cathedral at Canterbury by four knights after a long dispute with the king.

By the end of the period under review the church was all pervasive in English life. It was the only religion in the country and as such had no rival with which to contend. Jews had been expelled in 1290 following a century or more of persecution, which included the massacre of some of their numbers at York in 1190. The church christened babies, married almost all couples choosing this estate, was the community-meeting place, and buried the dead. It provided sanctuary, administered oath and ordeal, contributed to the royal treasury and helped supply the army. As Hill (1994) observed it was meaningless to draw any line between church and state. By this time there could be no question that the conversion of England was complete.

Several patterns evolved that had implications for schooling and teaching:

1. Educational standards became part of the requirements prior to ordination into the priesthood. By 1014 those seeking ordination not only had to bring testimonials from their teachers, but had to undergo examination in learning and doctrine in order to qualify. If by

necessy candidates had to be ordained before completing this process then they had to swear that they would complete it. The imposition of these requirements made education mandatory and not optional for service in the church. The effect of this was to increase the demand for schooling.

2.   Among the clergy a distinction was maintained between monks and priests. Monks were bound by the rule of celibacy while priests were not. Priests maintained their relationship with kindred. While the monks on the other hand were regarded by law as having no kindred. They were officially outside the kinship system.

3.   The celibacy of monks placed them outside of kinship and patriarchal system, and therefore enabled them to act as unifying agents within the society. Within the monasteries no social ranks were maintained (Mayr-Harting 1991). Aidan bought slaves and trained them as monks. Many of the stalwarts of the early English Church were men without social distinction. Royalty and slave, rich and poor, peasant and lord, shared common vows, fellowship and mission through virginity and Christ. By so concretely upholding the high ethical vision of Christianity monks were effective in the conversion of the Anglo-Saxons.

4.   As the clergy grew and the church became established, bishops repeatedly tried to maintain standards among priests. At one stage the guidelines for the good priest included the following:

a)   Teaching his people the Creed and Lord's Prayer.
b)   Keeping and using at least a Missal, Gospel book, Psalter and Penitential.
c)   Exhorting the people.
d)   Preaching if possible.
e)   Baptising babies.
f)   Setting an example of public decency and avoiding secular dress.
g)   Eschewing taverns.
h)   Keeping the altar free from mice and the graveyard free from dogs, horses and other animals, especially pigs.

5.   From the seventh century onwards there were hermits and anchorites who lived solitary lives devoted principally to prayer. Usually they lived in cells attached either to a parish church or a religious house. Both men and women were included among this group and their numbers as a whole increased over the years. Most were lay people, but their ranks sometimes included monks, priests and nuns. Essentially they attempted to live a Christian life outside the formal structures of the church and society.

6.   After the Norman Conquest William the Conqueror reorganised the church and in the process created a structure that lasted until the

nineteenth century. The fundamental shift was to elevate the cathedral organisation to dominance over the monastic system. In other respects, patterns that had been emerging were consolidated. Two provinces were created, York and Canterbury, with the Archbishop of the latter being the head of the church in England. Seventeen sees were created, based on territorial and strategic considerations, each with a bishop and cathedral. In areas with prominent monasteries, monastic cathedrals were established. Each cathedral had a corporate structure with four major offices: dean, precentor, chancellor and treasurer. The chancellor was responsible for the training of the clergy and education within the see. In addition to their individual responsibilities these officers served as an advisory council to the bishop (Hill 1994).

7. After the Norman Conquest several new orders began to operate in England. These included Dominican and Franciscan friars who vowed to reform the secular world, particularly the urban poor. They were well educated, were usually located in towns and were trained preachers. Another notable order were the Cistercians known for their austere holiness and refusal to accept any property that had been developed by or required feudal dues. They established great northern foundations on uncultivated lands or territory that had been devastated by war, including that of the Norman army. Augustinian Canons were another new order that worked mainly in education and health, particularly in the establishment of schools and hospitals (Hill 1994). These new orders were facilitated by the fact that William had accepted that he and his lords would do penance for the loss of life in the Conquest by creating foundations in support of the work of the church.

8. The Fourth Lateran Council of 1215, one of the great reforming councils of the Roman Church, had made confession and communion at least once per year binding on all adult Catholics and made marriage before a priest mandatory. The Council also required that church buildings be properly maintained and required regular diocesan synods. Of particular significance for education was the requirement that all vacant benefices and offices had to be filled within three months by men whose fitness had been tested through examination of their learning and doctrine. This further strengthened the practice that the English Church had long been following, but its insistence on filling all vacancies not only prompted action but promoted measures to ensure a continuous supply of qualified persons.

9. The institution of the chantry was established to chant or say prayers on behalf of persons who had left endowments for that purpose. A chantry could be an entire college of priests, such as All Souls College at Oxford, or a single priest saying daily mass in perpetuity for the founder and members of his or her family, or a dozen masses for

which a tradesman had left provision in his will. Chantries became very widespread. By the beginning of the sixteenth century St Paul's Cathedral had 44 perpetual chantries with a further 186 in the parish churches in its see (Tanner 1994).

10. By 1520 it is estimated that there were about 10,000 monks, 18,000 priests and about 2,000 nuns. In addition to these must be added those serving in chantries, as private chaplains, trade guilds, pious confraternities, in universities, as school masters and those waiting to be ordained. All told, Tanner (1994) estimated that there were more than 40,000 people in religious orders in a population of under five million persons. If the assumption is made that about half the population were adults then the church as an employer would have accounted for approximately three per cent of the labour force, a not insignificant occupation from any perspective.

Despite all these signs of growth, organisation, monopoly and widespread acceptance all was not well with the church by the sixteenth century. Miller and Hatcher (1978) made reference to a poem written in the thirteenth century in which the author claimed that whatever could be said of the lay-folk, 'the clergy was lost'. This anticlerical sentiment was not restricted to poetic expression. Priests were killed in popular riots in 1381 and 1480. Tanner (1994) was of the view that the protest was directed more to reform of the clergy and religious order than to their abolition. The point to note is that the clergy had lost a great deal of credibility at the very time that Christianity had become fully and firmly established in England.

Criticism of the clergy and the church came also from the ranks of the church itself. John Wyclif, ordained priest and Oxford don, had attacked the church for its abuses, excessive wealth and orthodoxy of questionable Christian validity. Wyclif had emphasised the centrality of the Bible in Christian life and witness and encouraged its translation into English. Fellow Oxford dons, who formed the nucleus of his supporters called the Lollards, had produced such a translation, which was banned by the Church largely because of its association with Wyclif who was eventually declared a heretic. William Sawtry became the first Lollard to be martyred in 1401 and more than a hundred Lollards were burnt during the fifteenth and early sixteenth century.

Sheils (1994) noted that widening educational opportunities had created a more literate laity, who were increasingly aware of humanistic and evangelical criticisms of much of conventional piety, which was emerging from the great continental centres of learning. Moreover endowments left by the laity for pious purposes did much to sustain the pastoral provision in the parishes and as a consequence the laity was demanding greater say in parochial affairs. The clergy on the other hand was holding fast to its institutional privileges. In his view it was privilege not piety that provided the motor for the reform when Henry VIII, not able to get a divorce, decided to break with the Papacy on matters of jurisdiction.

The factors leading to and causing the Reformation of the Church in Western Europe, and particularly the English reform, have been the subject of exhaustive debate, which is far beyond the scope of this study. But even if one were to accept Sheils' distillation of the matter it would be necessary to add patronage to privilege because it was royal and aristocratic patronage, which had created many of the institutional privileges, against which the laity was in revolt. Ironically the monarchy, the source of that patronage and therefore those privileges, was also in revolt, against the papacy. The convoluted reflexes of this situation made the king a leader of the reform. King and pious laity were on the same side, for very different reasons. Kings were not required to be pious hence Henry's marital problems were overlooked. However, patronage and privilege were fatal flaws in priestly character for which no explanations were accepted. It is an understatement to say the clergy found itself in the utmost confusion.

Power, patronage, privilege and piety had interacted for nearly a thousand years prior to the Reformation. Power through patronage and privilege had co-opted piety to gain legitimacy in a kingdom won by violent means but which had to be governed by less coercive methods. Piety in its own interest had co-opted power to spread itself in the kingdom. In return power rewarded piety with patronage and numerous privileges. The result was that the piety of priests was compromised. Power, however, was now closer to the parishioners who demanded priestly power for themselves as well as the responsibility to restore piety.

The greatest change emerging from the English Reformation was that England had shifted to being a theocracy: the monarch was both head of the state and head of the church. 'The High Gregorian' principles of the supreme authority of the pope over all earthly rulers, the independence of church from secular rule and the repudiation of lay investiture were now threatened fundamentally. However, the very monarchy that had violated these Gregorian principles was holding fast to what had become conventional and orthodox. At the same time, and underneath the violation of high principles and countervailing retention of orthodoxy, was a stubborn and indissoluble resolve on the part of some laity, to read the Bible for themselves and worship God in their own language. As these intractable issues of faith got more intertwined into more mundane political issues related to various sections of the society pursuing vested interests, England was firmly set on a path to civil war.

GENDER IN ENGLISH SOCIETY

All the groups who made up the English were patriarchal in their tribal traditions. With the exception of the Normans who had been civilised before their entry to England, the varieties of the patriarchy of the Angles, Saxons, Jutes, Norwegians and Danes were of the same genre as the Sumerians and Akkadians of Mesopotamia, the Hebrew tribes of Israel and the Arabs of the

Arabian peninsula. The main difference was in their time of entry into the civilisation process.

It cannot be over-stressed that at this stage of English history men and women belonged to the kinship collective, upon which their mutual survival depended, and that gender as it has come to be conceptualised in the twentieth century cannot be meaningfully applied to the way they constructed either their society or lives. Given the violent nature of the confrontation between the Anglo-Saxons and the British initially, the intense conflicts among the Anglo-Saxons themselves for dominance, the equally violent invasions of Scandinavians and the Norman Conquest it is to be expected that patriarchal form would be maintained. Warfare is the ultimate expression of patriarchy. Warriors returning victorious from battle are unlikely to entertain notions of equality with those who were not actively engaged in combat.

Briggs (1994) noted that in Anglo-Saxon England most women cleaned, cooked, made clothes, milked goats and ewes, sheered sheep and made butter and cheese. Even if women of the royal court were exempt from some of these duties, their activities were confined to managing domestic matters. However, women could own and inherit property and could not be compelled to marry someone they did not like. Divorce was easy and could be initiated by wives who could make wills and disinherit sons. After the Norman Conquest, Briggs maintained, many of these protections and freedoms disappeared and women were less free. Leyser (1995) made the point that the change in the situation of women had to be seen in the wider context that the entire society was less free. Women's condition did not deteriorate relative to men, since Anglo-Saxon men themselves were less free. As such it may be inaccurate to see the Anglo-Saxon period as a golden age for women.

If the interpretation of the impact of the Norman Conquest on gender is contentious, then that of Christianity could become vexed. The earliest Anglo-Saxon legal codes showed little Christian content except for the protection of church property. The orientation of the early laws related to gender is illustrated by the fact that there was only one word used for sex and this was used irrespective of context. The words rape, adultery and fornication were still to evolve. As was the case with blood feud, prices were attached to abduction, sex with another man's wife, sex with a maiden or a slave and for the purchase of a wife. Remedy consisted of payment of the price to the party whose property rights had been infringed was usually to men and not the women aggrieved. As with blood price, the price to be paid varied with status (Leyser 1995).

At the same time the law was not totally one-sided. A husband had to pay his wife her 'shame price' for his having had sex with another woman. She was only expected to accept such payment twice. On the third occasion she was expected to leave him. Women could initiate divorce, which was not difficult to obtain.

The first attempts to inject Christian content into the royal law codes began at about the turn of the eighth century when King Wihtred of Kent imposed Christian marriage laws. The influence of Christianity on royal laws became pronounced after the Viking invasions when it was felt that only Christian piety could save England from the heathen invaders. The law codes of Alfred the Great, and succeeding Wessex Kings, manifested this trend. In the evolution of the law that followed from this point, women's position could be said to have deteriorated, and Christianity could be prosecuted as the culprit.

The evolution of women's position in English society, however, is far more complex than attribution to any single source as either champion or oppressor. Three over-riding and interacting processes appear operative in the first 1000 years of English society. These are: increasing regulation and standardisation, increasing centralisation of power and increasing Christianisation. In this regard Christianity is the agent of both the regulation of society and the centralisation of power, which in turn are both agents of Christianity. The interactions are gradual, subject to reversal and recovery especially as cataclysmic events inspire piety or lead to the seizure of greater power and in some cases, both. Within this framework of interaction neither women nor men are unitary groups. Gender is qualified by the caveats of other societal dimensions. In addressing this issue the critical questions are which women, and to whom were they related?

The situation of widows in Anglo-Norman England as described by Leyser (1995) amply illustrates the latter assertion. At that time widows accounted for ten per cent of the population, which did not allow their situation to be ignored. Generally death of a husband was a catastrophe that plunged families into a crisis from which few households emerged unimpaired (Brundage 1995). Remarriage became almost an urgent necessity but this option was constrained by wealth, social rank, age, physical attractiveness and religious disposition. Many did not remarry and played several masculine roles.

The possibility of the husband's death was anticipated at marriage and at that time the husband had to nominate the wife's dower. The law was straightforward. Widows were entitled to one third of the husband's goods and chattels. One third went to the children, if there were any, and one third was reserved for the benefit of the dead husband's soul. Widows could will the inherited property as they chose. However, the same common law presented numerous difficulties against which women had to struggle to appropriate the benefits prescribed. Despite the difficulties, the majority of women were able to secure their rights.

Wealthy widows of the aristocracy had the greatest difficulties and in a sense faced the more hazardous situation. Wealthy widows, like minor heirs and heiresses, became wards of the King. He could give them in marriage as he chose, and for that privilege the estate paid a heavy royal fine. This situation arose because wealth was based on land, which all belonged to the king. On the death of the lord it was the king's pleasure that prevailed in the reallocation of the land. The grievances of aristocratic widows against royal prerogatives were well-known.

Widows in London did reasonably well. City law prescribed that they should have a share of the matrimonial home until death or remarriage. The common law gave her one third rights, combined with the city law London widows received a reasonable package and without any further complicating factors.

Widows of the peasantry fared best. They took over the tenements or if in jointure could take up the holding without further ado. They could also receive other benefits through deathbed transfers. The situation of the peasant widow was mediated by the fact that despite her dependence and servility, the villein could transfer the property by will, without the intervention of the lord. In this context wives were able to benefit from whatever little their husbands left, which interestingly was mainly left to them and not to the children.

The situation of widows in Norman England has to be interpreted in the broader context of the power relations in the society. Lords could not transfer their wealth on their own volition without the assent of the king. Peasants, however, could transfer their dependence and poverty without the intervention of the lord. The structure and operation of the law maintained the power relations. Widows of wealth, had more materially, and enjoyed a life of luxury, but were much more vulnerable to violation as persons than their sisters who had much less, but who inherited the little available in a more dignified manner. While both shared vulnerability and dependence, these were constructed in very different ways. The key factors in the difference were distance from the centre of power and source of wealth. While husbands were alive dignity and distance were positively related but with their death the direction was reversed in the case of inheritance by widows.

The Female Life Devoted to God

The vast majority of English women between the seventh and the mid sixteenth centuries were wives and mothers. Christianity and the church, however, provided opportunities, and inspired or justified lives and careers for some women outside of traditional patriarchal norms. Wogan-Browne (1995) noted that women saints, as they were celebrated in vernacular literature of England, fell into either the category of the virgin martyrs inspired by Mary the mother of Jesus, or the category of the repentant harlot modelled on Mary Magdalene. The virgin martyr's piety rested in purity, while that of the sinful woman was based on repentance and penance. While the real lives of people never fitted neatly into descriptive and analytic categories employed in studies, this categorisation reflected tendencies that emerged from the backgrounds and careers of the minority of women who operated, in Christian England, outside of patriarchal traditions.

Nuns presented occupations predicated on purity through virginity. While married women often joined convents, having renounced their sexuality and having embraced the life of chastity, the ideal nun was always the virgin. Monasteries with abbesses ruling over double houses had their ascendancy in the two hundred years between the seventh and the ninth centuries. Formal re-organisation of churches and monasteries following the completion of the initial conversion phase and Viking invasion signalled a period of decline. In the monastic revival in the tenth century, female monasteries did not fare well as several double houses and even a few female monasteries were re-founded for men only. By the time of the Norman Conquest female monasteries were outnumbered six to one by male monasteries.

In the revival of female monasteries in the twelfth century, few houses had royal foundations. The female monasteries with connections to royalty remained those founded mainly in the Anglo-Saxon period. The smaller less well-endowed monasteries and priories of the twelfth century were founded by wealthy widows and by members of the local gentry and aristocracy generally, just below the king and great barons (Thompson 1991). They were lesser Norman aristocrats on the rise, demonstrating piety, seeking recognition and taking out insurance.

Whether in the period of initial conversion, or after the revival following the Norman Conquest, nunneries were never independent of male support whether for material sustenance through founders or benefactors or spiritual services through priests administering the sacraments. While virginity allowed nuns to retrieve their sexuality from the kinship collective, the pursuit of religious careers depended upon male support. Nunneries therefore maintained strong connections with the social strata that founded them, and from which the majority of the nuns came.

The uniquely English order, the Gilbertine House, which developed in the North of England, drew nuns from all strata of society. However, to survive the Order integrated male and females, usually two third female to one-third male, in order to achieve some level of self-sufficiency.

The solitary life devoted to God had a long history going back to the second century as previously described. Hermits and anchorites were known in England from the seventh century. By the Reformation there were more women than men pursuing the solitary life (Leyser 1995). A distinction is made here between the hermit, male or female, who lived the solitary life on their own without seeking or receiving church support and control and the anchorite who lived the solitary life with the blessing and support of the church. The solitary life as hermit is sufficiently well known not to warrant further description. The point to note here is that several English women chose and lived this lifestyle in the period under review.

The concept of anchorite related to spiritual work done in anchoring the church and the community. Supreme self-denial on the part of a few kept the many buoyant. The church and the community were sustained by the prayers and intercession of anchorites confined to cells. That this highest state of piety should have become female, at the very time that male control was becoming more firmly fixed under Christian auspices, indicated the ambivalence of the inter-relationships between Christianity and gender in English society up to the Reformation. If one was counteracting the other, then the essence of the inter-relationship was female piety interceding for masculine evil.

Bishops subjected those offering themselves for this special task to a rigorous selection process prior to approval. Selection was followed by an awe filled ceremony that shared several features with the burial ceremony including Psalms for the Office of the Dead and the sprinkling of dust, before the closure of the door of the cell to which the anchorite was committed. Cells were annexed to churches or monasteries or convents. Some remained in their cells for up twenty to thirty years and a few for nearly fifty years. Most of the anchorites were lay people. The welfare of these recluses became the concern of kings, bishops and the entire community. They did not lack for patronage. They were sought after counsellors and advisors.

While both the hermitic and anchorite lifestyle embraced chastity, they also embodied penance. This is illustrated by the fact that several nuns and priests became anchorites or hermits. Thompson (1991) outlined the life of the nun Eve who dissatisfied with monastic life became a hermit. By combining purity and penance, some of these recluses became charismatic figures generating a following, which later required formalisation into religious communities. Several nunneries developed around hermits (Thompson 1991). This underscores the observation that sharp lines cannot be drawn between these various styles and occupations that religious men and women adopted in Christianity, and sometimes with the support of the churches.

Note must also be taken of beguines and hospital sisters. They were religious women, who during twelfth to the sixteenth centuries voluntarily adopted the life of poverty, lived in communities generally outside of the control of the church, and engaged in charitable service to the urban poor amongst whom they lived. Women who lived in beguinages voluntarily chose the life of poverty, situated themselves among the urban poor, which were increasing in numbers and without many services, and expressed their Christian concern through charitable works among them. Hospital sisters not only administered to the poor and the sick by attending to the physical and medical needs, but also provided spiritual comfort in times in which illness was linked with sins, and healing with prayer and penance. Gilchrist (1994) maintained that the lifestyles and work of beguines, hospital sisters, hermits and anchorites were all drawn together and linked by their penitential character.

PROMISE AND BETRAYAL

As was observed for both Judaism and Islam, Christianity's high ethical vision contained no gender bias. However, a masculine bias emerged as each sought to apply this vision in societies rooted in lineage patriarchy. This identical pattern is evident in English society in several sequences that can be regarded as promise and betrayal. Three sequences will be cited as mere sketches. These examples relate to royal abbesses, women brewers and domestic servants.

Royal Abbesses

Royal women played a substantial role in the conversion of the Anglo-Saxons not only as wives discreetly influencing their husbands or through arranged marriages linking kingdoms, but also as abbesses. Coupled with conversion was their contribution to the pacification and consolidation of the kingdoms acquired by means of great violence. Many monasteries were double houses with an abbot and an abbess. Invariably the founders were members of royal families. While direct royal connection declined among the abbots it remained strong among the abbesses. These royal abbesses exercised control over men. Hilda, abbess of Whitby led it to become a formidable educational institution renowned for its good works. Many bishops of the church including Wifrid and Bosa were numbered among her charges. When the missionary effort to Germany was mounted in the eighth century Loebo of Wessex, who had been dedicated to the church by her parents, was appointed Abbess of Bischofsheim in Mainz and became the linch pin of the mission led by St Boniface.

Leyser (1995) observed that several kingdoms acquired through bloodshed and treachery were redeemed through the prayers and good works of royal virgins. For fathers and brothers a daughter or a sister in the convent was not a woman disposed of, but a woman put to work to add sanctity and legitimacy to often nefariously acquired lordship. For royal women the cloister was not an imposition but a privilege and a duty since through their consecration to God they were demonstrating their alliance and support for their kindred, by participating in the intense struggle to establish their kindred as dominant, and to pacify and consolidate the kingdoms acquired. In such action they were partners with their male kin in enterprises that benefited their clan. The church and virginity allowed these women to operate outside the normal definitions prescribed by clan patriarchy. With this not only went glory but its attendant risks. The rape of women of the defeated territory became transformed into the victorious lord demanding the sexual submission of the abbess or one of her nuns, a kind of ritual rape. The last documented case was that of Earl Swein who raided Wales in 1046 and raped the abbess of Leominster in celebration of his victory. That many abbesses became saints, no doubt recognised not only their spirituality and good works but also their sacrifices as well.

The promise of this early partnership between royal men and women in Christian conversion and consolidation of kingdoms was betrayed once the mission was perceived to have been accomplished. Leyser was of the view that it was the shortage of men, which led to this active role of royal women. However, further qualification is necessary if this observation is to be sustained. The critical shortage was not of men generally, but of men whose unquestioned allegiance could be absolutely assured. In the intense competition that existed between kindred for dominance in early Anglo-Saxon society, prudence dictated that royal women should be enlisted rather than men of dubious allegiance.

The arrival of Bishop Theodore and Abbot Hadrian in 669 signalled the point at which conversion and pacification was virtually over. In the re-organisation of the church, which was far-sighted and thorough, the double monasteries were not only dismantled but many of their functions were taken over by the bishop himself and or assigned to monks. Menstruating women were excluded from communion, or if they did so, they could not enter a church for three weeks. These new rules of ritual impurity applied to abbesses, nuns and laywomen alike. Earlier, through a ruling by Pope Gregory no barriers to female participation had been constructed. Rules of ritual impurity and the usurping of functions slowly sidelined royal abbesses and nuns, as men whose allegiance was unquestioned now became the chief advisors and allies of their fathers and brothers.

Alewives

Alewife has become part of the English language because many English wives brewed ale. The association has remained even though the practice has ceased. Water was unsafe so people drank ale. While the brewing of ale required some capital, and was an occupation of more mature women and not those seeking their first jobs, the capital required could be accumulated with some thrift. Ale from barley was most common, but from whatever source, it could be produced within the domestic economy of the household. Because the brew did not last for more than a few days it was not feasible to produce it in large quantities, so fresh supplies were a constant necessity. Many families, through their wives, were part of this cottage industry. By the thirteenth century there were laws regulating standards. The vast majority of brewers were women, while the tasters monitoring the standards were men. While the businesses were registered in the names of the husbands, the wives produced the ale and ran the operation (Leyser 1995).

The promise of ale was that women could use it as a launching pad of economic independence from which they could expand into other areas. This promise was betrayed by the technological inventions that made the brewing of beer feasible. Beer could keep for a long time. Hence it could be stored and therefore produced in large quantities. This required capital beyond the reaches of alewives. Warniche (1983) showed that 39 women were listed with the Brewer's Company in 1419 but by the sixteenth century women's names had disappeared from guild records.

Female Domestic Servants

After the bubonic plague of 1348 and 1349, and the attendant drastic reduction in population, a labour shortage resulted. Young women found that market conditions in domestic service offered reasonable returns as well as other advantages. As Kettle (1995) observed, many young women started to enter this field with the hope of acquiring skills, accumulating a dowry, conducting their own courtship free from family supervision, and entering into marriages with companions of their choice.

A century later, as the population slowly recovered from the devastation and economic recession set in, the promise of domestic service evaporated and many girls immigrating from the country-side into the towns and entering domestic service did not achieve their dream of marriage with a dowry, but rather ended up in prostitution. As Kettle (1995) showed in her study of the records of the cathedral town of Lichfield between 1461 and 1466, the path to ruin of many young women included seduction by masters of households to which they were employed, exploitation by landlords, illegitimate pregnancy and destitution. For a small number prostitution became the viable alternative to the promise.

Unlike the Arabs of Islam who within a century of emergence from tribal traditions had conquered an empire, the English did not come to imperial status for over 1300 years. Like the Hebrews, the English suffered invasion but they were never dispersed nor was their aristocracy sent wholesale into captivity. The picture of this period of English history is that of a monotheistic religion with a high ethical vision of gender equality operating against a background of clan patriarchy experiencing mixed military, economic and catastrophic fortunes.

Within these parameters there are numerous instances of the promises of gender equality being betrayed by later circumstances. The sequence is usually that either men or women of some section of the society, or women alone in some instances, prosecute some apparent advantage which later finds women holding the short end of the stick so to speak. The three examples cited above are illustrative and not exhaustive of the pattern. For instance, as early as the fourteenth century most of the hucksters were female. Married women could run business as femme sole from as early as the thirteenth century. However, the promise of hucksters and femme sole becoming wealthy women merchants was betrayed. The merchant class that emerged was distinctly male.

THE CREATION OF SCHOOLING IN ENGLAND

The Anglo-Saxons were not literate people in 597. Kings, warriors, freemen farmers and their households were unlettered and unlearned. Schooling became part of the conversion enterprise because two tasks had to be undertaken with the utmost urgency. First, instruction of the new converts and second, the education and training of a native clergy. Italian missionaries could initiate the conversion, but permanent Christian witness depended on Anglo-Saxon leadership of the churches created. A native clergy was critical to the long-term success of the evangelistic goal. After six centuries of operation the church had devised institutions to effect these tasks, which now had to be transferred to English soil. The two institutions for training clergy were the episcopal church and the monastery.

From these beginnings it is possible to trace the evolution of English education in four stages up to the point just before the Reformation.

- Inauguration between 598 and 793 when Viking invaders destroyed the monastery at Lindisfarne.
- Survival between 793 and 1100.
- Rebirth and re-organisation between 1100 and the Black Death of 1348.
- Recovery and expansion from the Black Death to the early sixteenth century.

The Inauguration of Schooling: 598 to 793

Schooling was inaugurated in England to serve the educational needs of Christianity within the specific requirements of local circumstances. These needs were for the instruction of converts, the preparation of native clergy and support for the liturgy of the church. Formal instruction, given through schools, was related to each of these needs. The churches and monasteries therefore did not set out to create an educational system but rather to employ education in the service of the religious mission of Christianity.

The school of Catechumen delivered instruction to adult converts being prepared for baptism prior to formal admission into the church. Leach (1915) observed that the instruction given was no more than a limited number of formal lectures delivered over a relatively short period of time. Parry (1920) noted, however, instruction of converts was an ongoing activity. Classes were usually held in the porches of churches. Priests given this task were referred to as the masters of the schools of the catechumen. While the instruction given to any one set of converts was limited, the school of the catechumen was always in session as new converts were instructed in the faith. The purpose was not basic education in literacy and numeracy skills. Rather, it was indoctrination in Christian belief.

Singing was a very important part of the liturgy of the church and of the monastery, used not only for singing hymns, but more important for chanting the various offices and psalms. Chants and hymns were important parts of daily mass, baptism, funeral and other services. In the monasteries seven services were sung daily. Song schools were therefore established to offer instruction in musical portions of the liturgy. Choirmasters usually taught song schools.

Leach (1915) regarded the song school as a type of professional school to train singers. Brown (1987) cited the fact that during 685 to 686 an epidemic at Jarrow killed all the choir monks except Ceolfrith and the boy under his instruction. The rule of Benedict, prescribed that in such circumstances the two should dispense with chanting the antiphons to the psalms of the Little Hours of Office, which they did for one week. However, they found the omission intolerable, hence they resumed chanting with the help of untrained brothers until a sufficient number of singers could be trained. It is uncertain whether these early song schools operated continuously or as the need arose or were integrated with the regular operations of the choir.

Monastic and episcopal schools were created for training those preparing for the clergy. The basic difference between monastic and episcopal schools was in their admission procedure. In the former one was admitted to the order as a novice and then educated as a monk. In the latter a candidate offered himself for training and was then admitted, after a period of schooling, to the priesthood through ordination. Education preceded commitment in the priesthood while it followed the vow of commitment in the monastery. While this was a slight difference in religious policy, it was to become a big difference in educational development.

Parry (1920) was of the view that the monastic schools in England were originally modelled on those of Gaul that taught speaking, reading and writing Latin; copying manuscripts, painting, architecture, elements of astronomy and mathematics. Brown (1987) concluded, from analysis of the writings of Bede, that monastic schools taught Latin grammar for reading the Bible, liturgy and history; biblical exegesis and theology related to Christian doctrines; the computus for reckoning the Christian calendar; music for chanting the texts of office and mass; some natural history and geography which was complementary to the Bible; and husbandry, agriculture and domestic management. The main emphasis was on teaching Latin grammar and biblical exegesis.

Leach (1915) reviewed correspondence by Alcuin and concluded that cathedral schools taught the trivium (grammar, rhetoric and logic) and the quadrivium (arithmetic, geometry, music, astronomy) law and above all divinity. The point made by Leach was that these schools followed a liberal curriculum that closely resembled the curricula of the academies of the city-states of ancient Greece and Rome. As Moran (1985) has shown in portraying the episcopal schools in this way Leach was furthering his argument, against the commonly held position of his day, that medieval education was mainly monastic and that modern grammar schools originated from them. Leach maintained that English education developed from the cathedral and not from monastic roots.

Without wishing to become embroiled in this debate by historians of English education, critical or in support of Leach's claims and interpretation, two observations are of vital importance to this study. First, without regard to future historical outcome, an early difference seemed to have emerged in English education between episcopal schools maintaining Greco-Roman aristocratic educational traditions, and monasteries seeking to adjust to rural England and the prerogatives of converting the English. While close examination of the outlines of what both institutions taught shows that they shared much in common, and therefore, this difference should not be exaggerated, it should not go unnoticed. In this lightly shaded difference, monasteries were making adjustments in schooling that would increase its relevance in its setting and effectiveness in its evangelistic mission.

Second, and of even greater importance, the church in Anglo-Saxon England was presented with the golden opportunity of freeing itself from the baggage of pagan knowledge that had cluttered its evolution from within the ancient world. The Anglo-Saxons had never been part of the ancient world and therefore had no knowledge of its high culture. Their illiteracy and lack of learning represented pristine purity with respect to ancient learning. As Mayr-Harting pointed out Gregory was particularly drawn to the fact that the English were primitive barbarians not aristocratic philosophers. The view appeared to have been that in converting the Anglo-Saxons, Christianity did not need to be defended against ancient learning, hence Christianity should not become the vehicle of teaching them pagan knowledge.

Ancient knowledge had been a burden to the church from the first century. It had dogged the Western version of Christianity as it diverged from the East. The four great fathers of the Western church, Ambrose, Jerome, Augustine and Gregory had all received a Roman aristocratic education and then turned irrevocably against pagan knowledge and ancient culture. Gregory expressed this rejection eloquently in his statement that 'the same mouth cannot praise Jupiter and Christ' (Brown 1987). At the same time, the use of Latin prevented a total departure from the ancient world. Gregory recognised this dilemma in his concession that 'in knowing the liberal arts we understand divine words better'.

The challenge of Christianising England was to teach Latin and the liberal arts while reducing their pagan content to the minimum, if not eliminating it altogether, and to use Christian knowledge as the vehicle of education. Bede and his colleague monks shared these views of the great fathers. They regarded philosophers as the 'patriarchs of heresy' and strongly discouraged the reading of pagan literature. They saw the dialectic art as trickery and much of rhetoric as involving cunning deception.

Bede was an Anglo-Saxon boy given by his parent to Abbot Benedict Biscop of Jarrow at age seven. This was consistent with the Germanic tradition of fostering a boy of this age in the house of a prince or noble. The new faith re-directed this tradition to God and the monasteries. Bede spent all his life as a monk at Jarrow. By the time of his death in 735, at age 62, he had written numerous books, provided the computus on which the Christian dating of time was divided into BC and AD, and was an internationally recognised authority on biblical exegesis. The Council of Aachen in 836 enthroned Bede beside the four great fathers of the Western church, and decreed him to have the same authority. Bede never became an abbot or a bishop. Throughout his life he was a teacher, one who wrote prolifically and at a high standard.

Of particular interest to this study are the books Bede wrote for students, his pedagogical texts. Bede obviously found the Donatus satisfactory because he used it to teach grammar and never produced any text for that purpose. The deficiencies he perceived, from his teaching experience, and sought to fill by what he wrote, were as follows:

1. A book on meter, 'De Arte Metrica', which was a systematic exposition on Latin versification. He paid particular attention to verse form in hymns, chants and poetry.

2. A book on figures of speech in Latin, in which he cited seventeen figures of speech and thirteen transferred meanings and provided at least one example of each. What was remarkable about this book is that it did not contain a single example from ancient or pagan literature. Each example was drawn from scripture. Linguistic and Christian symbols were linked in a grammatical teaching text. This was the first example of a school text that totally excluded classical, pagan learning and asserted the pre-eminence of Christian learning. St Augustine of Hippo had enunciated the principle that the scripture should be the basic text of the education of the Christian. Bede was the first to implement it.

3. A book on orthography, dealing with Latin words and their correct usage, arranged alphabetically. It was intended as a reference book for advanced students and for copyists of the scriptorium. In this work, Bede found that pagan examples were unavoidable, but he kept these to a minimum.

4. A book on time and its calculation, a subject on which Bede became the acknowledged master. The entire essence of this work was the dating of events in relation to the birth of Christ, and setting the Christian calendar. The book referred to here is the shorter version for students and not the full treatise for which he became famous.

5. A book on the nature of things, an introduction to cosmology.

6. Books on the history of the saints.

7. Literary interpretations on most books of the Bible. This book was written for a much wider audience than his students and only the most advanced at that. But it has to be included with his pedagogical works for the very reason that biblical exegesis was an area of primary emphasis in the training of the clergy.

Bede's books written for his students at Jarrow became widely used throughout schools in Western Europe. What is clearly revealed is the deliberate and careful steps taken by Bede to eliminate all aspects of pagan learning deemed inconsistent with the Christian faith on the one hand, and on the other hand to promote scripture and Christian literature. There can be no question that Bede, the Anglo-Saxon monk, was pioneering a radical break with the ancient past as far as Christian learning was concerned. Because that learning was being conducted in Latin everywhere in the West its influence was not confined to the monastery at Jarrow or to England. As Brown (1987) pointed out Bede's school texts were in great demand, which sometimes the scriptorium at Jarrow found difficult to satisfy.

A fascinating feature of Bede was that he was second generation in two respects. He was a great admirer of the four great Fathers of the Church, and drew much inspiration from them. However, they were first generation Christians who had been well schooled in Roman and ancient ways before conversion to Christianity. Likewise, both his teachers at Jarrow, Benedict Biscop and Ceolfrith had been steeped in Anglo-Saxon aristocratic ways before conversion to Christianity. They were first generation Christian, but from Anglo-Saxon roots. Bede greatly admired them also. But Bede himself knew nothing personally of either Roman schooling or Anglo-Saxon secular culture. Brought up in the monastery with monks fired with the piety of a new faith, much of what he learned of Anglo-Saxon ways was related to him and not the result of personal experience.

In a real sense Bede became symbolic of the English Christian, and a portent of the faith in that country. It is from this vantage point that he joined in making a sharper break between ancient and Christian learning and in disconnecting schooling in the Christian Religious Age from schooling in the city-states of antiquity. In this regard note should be taken of the fact that at his death Bede was working on an English translation of the Book of John, which he had almost completed. His *Ecclesiastic History of the English People*, made him England's first historian, underscored his sense of English identity, undergirding his deep Christian faith.

The period from Augustine's establishment of the school at Canterbury to the arrival of Theodore and Hadrian, a native of Africa, in 669 can be seen as the initial formative years when schools were under the control of foreign missionaries. Native clergy, in the form of relatives of the royal families and the warrior aristocracy, rapidly took over the educational enterprise. However, the local educational enterprise was in need of international reputation and recognition. Theodore and Hadrian gave the school at Canterbury international prestige and brought to it a higher standard of learning than previously. Aldhem, was the first Anglo-Saxon to be recognised as a Latin scholar of wide reading. He was a student of the monastery at Malmesbury and later studied in both Ireland and Canterbury. He was of the opinion that he received the highest quality of instruction from the latter (Mayr-Harting 1991).

Aldhem born in 639, was a member of the royal family of the West Saxons. After completing his studies he returned at age 30 as abbot of Malmesbury. In striving to meet the demands of his students he wrote a treatise on poetic meter. In the preface he wrote that he was the 'first of the Germanic race to have sweated in this kind of business', (Mayr-Harting 1991). In that work Aldhem attempted to provide both English content and Christian examples for his students. This first generation of English Christian teacher was therefore starting out on a path that second generation Bede was to so brilliantly follow.

In his time Bede was renowned as a biblical exegete and not either as a historian or pioneering schoolmaster. Acclaim as the latter belonged to Alcuin, schoolmaster of York, of whom he was a former student. Alcuin became schoolmaster of the palace school of Charlemagne's court in 782, as well as the leading intellectual of the court attempting to define and lead Western Christianity. Alcuin had written commentaries on various books of the Bible as well as produced his own book on grammar for students grappling with the intricacies of Latin.

Charlemagne also was very impressed by the work of Bede. It was Charlemagne's court that first adopted and used Bede's system of dating according to Anno Domini, the year of our Lord. Bede did not originate this system, which had been developed by Dionysius Exiguus, a monk in Rome. It was Dionysius who had established which year in the old Roman system of dating was to be regarded as the year of Christ's birth and hence to become AD. But it was not widely adopted until Bede used it and Charlemagne's court followed.

It does not seem far-fetched to say that by inviting Alcuin to be part of his court, with special responsibility for his palace school, Charlemagne was not only recognising Alcuin as a brilliant scholar in his own right but also English education as it was undertaking the same challenges as his Frankish court and moving in the same general direction of redefining Christian schooling in Western European and not ancient terms. Alcuin represented English participation in the Frankish led redefinition of ancient Roman civilisation in Western European Catholic civilisation.

Alcuin also helped to draft the 'Libri Carolini', Charlemagne's independent Frankish theology. He was also instrumental in shaping the concept of imperium on which Charlemagne's coronation as emperor of the Holy Roman Empire was predicated. In 796 Alcuin wrote to the Bishop of York suggesting the appointment of separate school masters for reading, song and writing with the implication that this would separate the elementary from the more advanced levels (Leach 1915). This was very similar to the policies Charlemagne had promoted among monasteries and bishoprics, at about the same time. Charlemagne advocated a school for boys separate from more advanced instruction for those being prepared for ordination.

If the fine points of dispute of English educational history are ignored, the broader conclusion becomes clear. Between its founding at the end of the sixth century and the end of the eighth century, English schooling had emerged as a leader in defining Western Christian education apropos ancient pagan education. In this regard episcopal and monastic schools, and their masters, had made substantial contributions, which were recognised and adopted on the continent. The progress made in defining the content of schooling was far in advance of the differentiation of the educational institutions themselves.

The Period of Survival: 793 to 1066

At the same time the period was not without its pedagogic contribution. Aelfric, student of Dunstan and monk, wrote three books for his students: a grammar, a glossary and a Colloquy. What was particularly noteworthy of both the grammar and the glossary was that they were written with English translations. In his preface to both books Aelfric stated that he had written the translation out of concern for his students and conscious of the possible criticism that he had wasted his time in attempting to provide such assistance.

The Colloquy gave a rare glimpse into the working of the Anglo-Saxon school. The Colloquy was a conversation between some boys who approached a schoolmaster begging him to teach them to speak Latin correctly. The master's reply was that they should understand that they would be flogged while learning. Their retort was confidence that he would not resort to the whip unless this was really called for. The conversation continued with boys representing various occupations whose daily routines were described. They included ploughman, fisherman, salter, baker, shepherd, hawker and merchant. The Colloquy ended with exhortations to keep the commandments of God, attend church, bow to the altar, sing in unison, ask pardon for sins and go out again without playing in the cloister or the school. The Colloquy was intended by Aelfric to be a first Latin exercise. It introduced a wide vocabulary, focused attention on well-known people in the community and emphasised Christian behaviour appropriate for young boys, taking into account some of their known tendencies.

At a much more modest level than Bede or Aldhem, Aelfric, amidst the turmoil and uncertainties of his times, pursued the schoolmaster's task of providing appropriate materials for his students' learning. Notwithstanding its modesty two marks stamped the task. First, Aelfric's adherence to the Augustine principles of Christian education and second the nationalism, symbolised by providing an English translation. This first year text was written in Latin, which was the official language of the church, commerce and diplomacy in Western Europe. However it employed an English translation, which tied it to the community of the students. Also the text was punctuated with Christian exhortations related to the mission of the church. Aelfric was undoubtedly carrying on the work started by the schoolmasters Aldhem, Bede and Alcuin even in the most dangerous and precarious circumstances.

Rebirth and Redirection: 1066 to 1348

Schooling was reborn in England in the twelfth century as a measure of stability returned to the country. Redirection came through the reform of the church executed by the Conqueror in placing leadership of the church firmly in the hands of the episcopate and then appointing Norman bishops. This concentrated power in Norman hands since the decentralised powers of the monasteries were taken away and given to bishops appointed to the seventeen episcopal sees into which the country had been divided. At the same time episcopal education, which was premised on an open admission policy, expanded access to schooling since it anticipated but did not require a career in the clergy.

Education under episcopal control had by definition always been secular and public. Organising and standardising episcopal control made the former open and public while at the same time making monastic education religious and private. The imperatives of conversion and the constant emergencies of warfare had obscured this important distinction. The two systems had coexisted and co-operated to their mutual advantage. Monasteries had children not given to the life of rule and not cloistered. Cathedral and collegiate churches provided education mainly for their own clerical needs. In effect the definitional difference may have appeared more semantic than real.

Norman redirection changed the situation fundamentally. However, it took a century or more before the full implications of this redirection would become apparent. It is always much easier to see fundamental change historically, than it is to perceive it in contemporary times. It is against this background that educational development between 1066 and 1348 must be interpreted and understood. Unless otherwise stated, the description of schools and the school system during this period relies on Orme (1973 and 1976).

Schools at the beginning of the twelfth century can be classified as public, private and cloistered. Public schools were those in which the teachers were not necessarily clergy, admission was open to all who chose to attend and instruction did not imply commitment to any particular career. Private schools were those with restricted public access. For example, schools in the household of nobles for the noble's children, wards and protégés, or schools operated by monasteries or convents for children living within but not under monastic vows. Cloister schools were those organised for members of the religious orders who took vows as novices and were then educated. Entry to these schools could only come after the vows to enter the monastic orders had been taken.

Irrespective of the type of school, instruction followed three stages:

a) Mastering the alphabet, reading and pronouncing Latin words.
b) Studying grammar, that is, words and their meaning, syntax, prose composition and speech.
c) The higher studies in the form of the liberal arts, theology, law and medicine.

Schools were one-teacher operations, in which the single teacher taught all levels and all branches of learning. In some schools an usher assisted the teacher. The public schools charged fees and were located in cities and large towns. However, schools appeared and disappeared from the records indicating some lack of continuity. At the same time, because these historical sources were not systematic this seeming instability needs to be treated cautiously.

The trends that began to emerge during the twelfth century can be enumerated as follows:

- Increase in the numbers of schools in cathedral cities and county towns.
- The establishment of minimum ages at which youth could take vows as monks and friars, and the raising of that age to somewhere between eighteen and twenty years. With this new recruitment standard, novices were expected to have had some previous schooling and their education in the monastery was premised on that assumption. In other words monasteries reorganised their education in a similar manner to the secular clergy.
- The increase of monastery and convent schools as the number of monasteries and convents increased, particularly through local endowment from gentry sources. They continued the practice of offering schooling to children of the aristocracy, not under vows.
- The differentiation of the upper stage of instruction from the other levels began as chancellors in the cathedrals assumed the responsibility for this level of instruction, leaving the schoolmaster with the other levels and thus university education emerged.
- The common practice of private tutoring as parents arranged for their children to be taught by priests.
- The use of French as the vernacular especially by the aristocracy, and the submerging of English as the language of the unlettered, rustic folk. In schools translations were from Latin to French, not English. Thus schools were aligned with the power shift in English society.
- Song schools were created.

These trends were clearly evident from the beginning of the thirteenth century and continued to the Black Death of 1348. The university level became clearly differentiated from the other levels and the term school was increasingly applied to the lower levels of learning. Liberal arts, including advanced grammar, law, medicine, theology were taught in the two universities, Oxford and Cambridge. Also while initially the chancellors in the cathedrals had jurisdiction over the universities, universities won the right to elect their own chancellors. Further, notwithstanding the greater integration of the university with the secular clergy, monks and friars began to attend the university, establishing a measure of integration of the universities with monasteries and friaries. In this respect friars were more fully integrated than monks.

The process of differentiating the early and the middle stages of becoming Latinate had begun. This is indicated by references in the records to reading and grammar schools. Moran (1987) showed that in the diocese of York there were references to seven reading schools before 1300, and eighteen reading schools between 1301 and 1350. Also that before 1300 there were references to thirteen grammar schools and to fifteen between 1301 and 1350. Orme (1976) in his study of the West of England noted that after 1300 the term grammar school appeared in records but it was not in common usage.

Schools came under the control of religious authorities and benefited from their patronage. The Third Lateran Council of 1179 had decreed that permitted authorities should license schoolmasters, or appoint them, but not charge them for doing so. By the beginning of the thirteenth century various religious authorities in England began to license, patronise and appoint schoolmasters who had set up schools on their own. Most authorities established control over schools in a single town or area. With control came patronage in the form of rental of buildings at nominal amounts or free of charge; relief of poor scholars studying away from home; and by the early fourteenth century, a few endowments which paid the master's salary, in whole or part, allowing him to reduce fees or not charge any.

Schools began to be founded in smaller towns. These secular schools increasingly became the sources of education; private tutoring began to decline as the numbers of schools increased and patronage assisted some students with access to schooling.

The creation of song schools came about as wealthy laity and clergy began the practice of founding colleges of chantry priests to sing the divine office or celebrate mass, often with elaborate polyphonic arrangements. Small numbers of boys, along with men with mature voices, were engaged to sings parts in the choirs created for such productions. The singers were full time members of the establishments receiving board and lodging at the chantry colleges. Small song schools became part of the chantry colleges

In the rebirth of schooling between 1066 and 1348 it is important to note that schooling was directly related to the needs of the Church. Song schools provided personnel and training for the choral arrangements in the main churches. The higher level of education, whether in monastery, friary or university was for clergy. In the secular clergy an association was established between university education and the major orders, which by default meant that education below this level was associated with the minor orders. While in the initial period of re-birth some amount of unsponsored private enterprise was permitted, this soon came under the firm control of church authority, which in return provided patronage to those schools it did not establish directly.

Recovery and Expansion: 1348 to 1520

Schooling in this period was shaped by four major factors and their consequential interactive effects. These were the devastating effects of the reduction of the population occasioned by the plague in 1348 to 1349 and its subsequent recurrences; the Hundred Years War which deepened animosities between France and England and fostered English nationalism; response to economic developments which favoured urbanisation and non-agricultural occupations; and reconnection with ancient learning.

Orme (1976) and Moran (1985) described five different types of schools that operated in England from 1348 to the Reformation in the sixteenth century. They were:

a) Song schools which were primarily schools to teach choristers the chants, the Psalter and hymns, parts of which they were required to memorise. Songs schools existed at all types of religious institutions: cathedrals, collegiate churches, parish churches, chantry chapels, hospitals and monasteries. The financial incentives were such that they encouraged both men and boys to become choristers. 'Singing men' was an occupation, as was boy choristers.

b) Reading schools, intended primarily as the first stage in becoming Latinate. Boys expecting to pursue careers in the clergy, in commerce and the courts attended such schools since Latin was the language of church, commerce and court. Vernacular languages, French and toward the later part of the period English, were also taught.

c) Grammar schools primarily to train priests, but also for those whose career in commerce and the courts required greater proficiency than reading schools provided. The grammar school education was linked directly to these occupations, but was also the usual prerequisite for university study. Two grammar schools, Winchester founded by William of Wykeham, Bishop of Winchester, and Eton under royal patronage became so well known that they recruited students from all over the country.

d) Writing schools were not very prevalent but were schools to teach the particular skill for the occupation of scrivener. Writing schools were not at the level of grammar schools, but equated more to the level of the reading school.

Between 1300 and 1548 Moran identified 84 song schools, 161 reading schools and 68 grammar schools that operated in the diocese of York. To appreciate the substantive nature of the expansion in education prior to the Reformation it must be borne in mind that the Black Death had reduced the population by about 40 per cent, and that by 1520, the recovery had not yet attained the peak reached at about 1300. The expansion in educational provision had taken place within the context of an overall decrease in population.

Factors that drove the expansion of schooling could be listed as follows:

- The growth of chantries whose priests increasingly took on teaching duties, usually but not exclusively, as masters of song or reading schools, which charged no fees. While most of the chantries did not sponsor schools, those which did were sufficient to constitute a substantial contribution to education.
- Increasing endowment of schools by the laity. Orme (1976) reported that during the first half of the sixteenth century 31 grammar schools were founded in the West of England; of that number 13 were founded by the clergy and eighteen by the laity. Moran (1985) noted a similar

trend in the diocese of York. Between 1500 and 1548 she reported that 43 grammar schools were founded and of the 38 for which documentation about their founders existed, 21 were founded by laity compared to 17 by the clergy.

- The increasing involvement of non-noble benefactors in the founding of schools. Moran noted that less wealthy merchants, artisans, yeomen and well-to-do husbandmen founded many reading schools. The founders of the schools were of the same social background as the children attending the schools. This trend was not restricted to the basic level. At the grammar school level Moran noted that between 1472 and 1548 non-noble benefactors in York founded twice the number of schools than aristocratic and gentry founders.
- The expanding interest of trade guilds in education not only through the founding of schools but also the stipulation of educational criteria for their members (Alexander 1990).
- The belated interest of the aristocracy in public education. While they had always provided basic education for their children this had been mainly through classes in households. Their increasing interest in public education was not only reflected in their children beginning to attend Eton and go on to Oxford and Cambridge in modest numbers but they began founding schools not for patronage but for their children. This was by no means a full embrace of education but more like nodding recognition of fundamental change in the making. The mainstream attitude of that section of English society was reflected in the irate gentleman's rebuttal of praise of education in his presence by the remark that 'I would rather see my son hanged than become a bookworm. It's a gentleman's calling to be able to blow the horn, to hunt and to hawk' (Alexander 1990).

While the above highlights the new actors who began to appear in the provision of schooling it must not be overlooked that the church continued to found schools, and continued to be by far the major owner of schools and source of schooling. While the laity was outstripping the clergy, the margin of difference could not compensate for the monopoly that the clergy had previously enjoyed.

It must also be noted that many founders of schools were women. Alexander (1990), Moran (1985) and Orme (1976) all reported women founding schools in different parts of England. Several women founded grammar schools. However, all the grammar schools were for boys, irrespective of whether the founder was male or female. Girls were provided with education in chantry, monastic, convent and cathedral schools. They were also educated in household schools of the wealthy barons and members of the nobility. However, girls were only given basic education. They were not admitted to grammar schools. Up to 1548, there no were grammar schools founded for girls but this was not because of legal prohibitions on the establishment of schools for girls. In this context, legislation was passed in 1406 that stated that every man or woman was free to send their sons or daughters to take learning at any school they chose within the realm. The decision to send children to schools, whether boys or girls, and the choice of the schools whether to which they were sent were by law entirely matters of parental choice.

Another area that must be noted was the church's efforts to recover from the effects of the Black Death. Alexander (1990) noted that while 35 to 40 per cent of the population of approximately 5,000,000 to 6,000,000 died between 1348 and 1349, the effect on the clergy was even more devastating. Forty five per cent of all parish priests died. A further 15 to 20 per cent fled to avoid contracting the disease. While the recurrences were regional and not nearly as devastating, yet the clergy lost six per cent of its members in 1362 and 13 per cent again in 1391. The bishops remained relatively intact in the original outbreak. They were of the view that the sacraments of the churches had to remain available to the parishioners, especially in such a crisis. Consequently they took immediate steps to replace those who had died or fled. By 1350, all had been replaced, mainly through mass ordinations involving little screening of the applicants.

Cognisant of this deterioration in the level of preparation of the clergy, as soon as the crisis seemed to have passed the bishops implemented measures to raise the educational standards. The main thrust of this effort was concentrated at the university level. Between 1350 and 1450 ten new colleges were added to Oxford and Cambridge. Numerous schemes were implemented to support clergy undertaking study or students preparing for the priesthood. Alexander (1990) concluded that by 1450 the clergy was better educated and intellectually distinguished as a group that ever before. Of the 131 men who became bishops or archbishops between 1399 and 1499, 119, or 91 per cent were graduates of Oxford and Cambridge, and most of the remainder had degrees from foreign universities.

The educational standards of the lower clergy improved at a much slower and less uniform rate. Surrey, where 35 per cent of the vicars and curates were graduates, represented the high water mark, while in some areas little progress appeared to have been made. This probably explained the observation in a few sources to the effect that a few clergy had difficulty distinguishing between Jesus and Judas. The latter no doubt represented the rock bottom reached in the aftermath of the plague.

It must be noted that this effort to improve the standards of education of the clergy was not centred on in-service training but on a long-term upgrading of new entrants, and such incumbents that were so minded and able. Because the clergy was the main occupation for which both grammar and university education was fashioned, such deliberate and sustained efforts by the church to improve educational standards had an overall effect on both education and society as a whole. In addressing the educational needs of its clergy, the church was providing strong educational leadership for the society as a whole, by example and the climate for learning thus created.

The laity in the latter part of the fifteenth century and early sixteenth centuries was actually building and sustaining the momentum that had been created by the bishops, in the century following the plague. Like the bishops the motivation was largely self-interest, but the interests differed. The laity was focused on the socio-economic opportunities available not only through the church, but also through the commercial and industrial opportunities that were being created in the cities and towns. These interests were being grafted onto the educational system created to serve the needs and interests of the church, with little rationalisation of its structure.

The coincidence between the interests of the bishops and the laity was their common location in the cities and county towns. Although England was still nearly 90 per cent rural the momentum was unmistakably in favour of the urban. The monasteries that had been the centre of missionary enterprise in the conversion were now, nearly a thousand years later, on the margin in relation to momentum and location. This was also true with respect to other aspects of the times. For example, while the religious orders had established foundations and colleges at Oxford and Cambridge, and friars and monks had been prominent members of those communities, by the fifteenth century they were less numerous and not as prominent.

The educational improvements noted in the secular clergy were not as marked among the monks. The number of monastic schools had declined. The enrolment of those that remained was small. Monasteries were still involved in schooling, but they were no longer leading institutions of learning, although their schools still enjoyed high regard in some circles. Small size was their main attractive feature (Alexander 1990). Monasteries in England had ignored the potentials of printing, introduced in England by Caxton in 1476, and remained faithful to copying by hand in their scriptoria. Being out of step with the times may be too harsh a categorisation; being out of tune may be more to the point.

French, in the later fifteenth century, was among the most discordant notes in English society. Norman imposition of French was never revoked in England, it evaporated in the heat of the passion of patriotism generated by the Hundred Years War. As Alexander (1990) noted even the nobles of Norman ancestry had to use English during this period. The war started in 1337. The first salvo fired on French was in the form of petitions appearing in English in 1344. This was followed by an English version of the Psalter translated by Richard Role, a Yorkshireman. Oxford dons, led by John Cornwall and Richard Penrich, began insisting that students translate from Latin to English and not French. By 1376 it began to be observed that French had virtually disappeared and English was the standard vernacular language once again.

Monasteries had benefited significantly from Norman endowment, and friars had made their entry following the Conquest. Monks and friars had a prominent role in promoting French. Memory of this past association struck a discordant note in the context of the times. When Henry VIII closed the monasteries and friaries in 1550 and distributed the monks and friars about the episcopal sees and parish churches, he was not only relocating them in areas more consistent with the momentum of the times, but also using them as scapegoats in the prevailing climate and in prosecuting his jurisdictional problems with the Papacy.

It is interesting that the protests from the populace in different areas were with respect to the closure of nunneries, and not the monasteries or friaries. Over the years the nunneries had maintained schools for boys and girls, mainly of the gentry. The records at the Dissolution showed, for example, that at several nunneries the children at the convent schools were all daughters, or young sons, of lords or gentlemen. The prevailing view was that 'daughters were brought up in virtue' by the nuns. In many regions therefore the nunneries were highly regarded by the local population. The Dissolution drew protest and petition about the closure of many nunneries (Alexander 1990).

THE TRANSFORMATION OF THE CHURCH AND SCHOOLING IN ENGLAND: 697 TO 1548

The Church in England, from 697 to 1548, was a parallel society to English secular society although both were interrelated. The Church had its own peculiar mission and its separate organisation with its own laws and courts. It functioned in four distinct capacities. First, up to the Norman Conquest, the Church was the referee and legitimating agency in the contest between kingdoms. More than might was needed to establish the legitimacy of royal clans and their kingdoms. The Church exchanged its recognition of kings and their kingdoms for proselytising access and advantage. Like the Temple and city of Nippur in Sumer, the English Church remained faithful to its refereeing and recognition role and never sought to enter the contest for kingship or territory. By resisting this temptation the Church maintained maximum missionary advantage in addition to gaining material rewards principally in the form of land.

Second, the Church served as a major link between England and the rest of Western Europe. This facilitated international recognition of the kings, diplomacy and trade. International recognition was important to the newly enthroned monarchies arising from virtual obscurity. Through the Church English kingdoms were facilitated in joining the community of monarchies emerging in Western Europe. The papacy functioned almost like a united monarchs' forum. This was not only important for purposes of recognition and legitimacy but also for purposes of alliances. To belong to the nascent community of Western Europe was also important for trade.

Third, the Church was a major agency in the pacification and unification of England. In this regard the Church and over-kings were major allies supportive of each other for different ends. The Church desired to further advance the Kingdom of Heaven, and the monarchs were dedicated to further advance their kingdoms on earth. The Church in England was unified long before kingdoms merged, or collapsed or were conquered, into one kingdom. This unification of Christian efforts was achieved from the Council at Whitby in 664. From this perspective over-kings were as much in need of the Church's endorsement and support as the Church was in need of the king's protection. The power of belief and believing military power were allied in establishing non-coercive forms of government after kingdoms were won or extended by might. The principal foci of unification were Christian belief and the English language. That is, fashioning and fostering the culture of the Christian English from heathen Angles, Saxons, Jutes, and Vikings.

Fourth, the Church was the developer and repository of the high culture of England. Not only was it the keeper and promoter of its newly accepted Christian ethical vision, but also the developer of its learning and language. The statement by the Gothic noble on learning summed up the general feeling of the military aristocracy to learning in Western Europe including England when he stated that a man who is to show daring and be great in renown ought to be free from the timidity which teachers inspire and take his training in arms (Leyser 1995). Nobility was predicated on military prowess not learning. At best royalty and the nobility sought to be literate but not learned. Kings like Alfred the Great and Charlemagne were exceptional. Learning was limited to the Church and the groups that evolved from out of its being. The high culture of England was centred in Latin, shared with the rest of Western Europe. This not only facilitated trade and diplomacy but along with Christian belief fostered a Western European identity of which the English were a part.

As a parallel society the Church stood above the contests and competition between kings and kingdoms. It located itself outside of the kinship system, as it embraced celibacy, and thus became accessible to all kindred. Its link to Rome gave it an international character and continental connections important to small kingdoms on the British island. As repository of the high culture it gave barbarian societies connection with civilisation and with the Latinate high culture of Western Europe. It fashioned its own organisational structure that included learning as a mandatory activity and achievement and merit as bases of promotion. The Church's inter-relationship to secular English society was rooted in its links to all ethnic groups, its presence in all territories, and in its composition, which included men and women, free and slave, royalty and peasant.

The essence of the capacities in which the Church acted in its relation to secular English society can be summed up as follows:

- Power and belief were the major dimensions shaping early English society. They set the broad parameters that fashioned the economy, defined status and determined the cultural content of relationships.
- Initially, the power of the state in the form of the monarchy, and belief in the form of the Christian Church, acted in tandem, mutual support and with reciprocal advantage. The monarchy was legitimised

- and recognised by belief, and belief was spread by the power of the monarchy.
- The monarchy and church, power and belief, cooperated to unify and transform the barbarian Germanic tribes, through coercion and persuasion, into the Christian English.
- The church by its Latin liturgy and its schools provided for the training of its clergy and religious orders became the repository of the high culture of the English.
- Because of its missionary mission, referee and recognition roles, unification functions and papal sponsorship, the church had a status apart and outside of that which stratified secular society. The institutions of celibacy, cloister, canon law and communion – the Eucharist – all facilitated the separate status. The fact that initially the church was almost synonymous with the clergy, in that the laity was small and only nominally Christian, was also a facilitating factor.
- Fierce competition between kingdoms and invasions from land hungry Northern European tribes combined to keep economic activity just a little above subsistence. The church therefore had little or no impact directly or indirectly on economic activity and economic development was shaped by, rather than shaped the circumstances.

The key to understanding and explaining the development of schooling and the emergence of teaching as an occupation, as well as that of the entire English society, rests in tracing the transformation that took place relative to power and belief and to a lesser extent the economy. The transformations can best be seen by contrasting the circumstances at the end of the sixth century when the Christian missionaries first arrived, and those of the mid sixteenth century when the English Reformation had just begun.

By the mid-sixteenth century the foundation of English society in military aristocracy and territorial lordship was already in decay. The Black Death and its recurrences had further weakened territorial lordship and the Hundred Years War heightened the sense of a common English identity especially among the Norman barons.

Of equal importance was the fact that several tasks that the Church had undertaken in its initial missionary activities were coming to full fruition. These included the legitimating of the monarchy, the establishment of non-coercive means of governing of the kingdom, the pacification of the society, the unification of the society and the conversion of the populace to Christianity. The gains made in these areas facilitated economic development, trade and with these increasing urbanisation. All of these had their impact on undermining the society organised on the basis of military lordship related to land and territory.

The Transformation of Power

Power has two main idioms, personal and material. Both are interrelated and always present. Power in the personalistic idiom is transparent, directly linked to the individual exercising it. It is often brutal but transparently honest in its dependence on might and arrogantly frank in its declaration of responsibility. Material rewards, or bribes in the form of tributes, are openly exchanged symbols of personal power. Power in the materialistic idiom is covert, disguised, manipulative and exercised remotely by those holding power. The distribution of materials rests upon rules that claim fairness but often conceal bias. Distance is maintained between those holding and exercising power on the one hand and those over whom power is exercised. Diffusion of the loci of power is also a feature of materialistic idiom. Distance and diffusion allow the powerful to disclaim responsibility, blame intermediaries, confuse protesters and transfer responsibility to the victims (Miller 1991).

Power in Anglo-Saxon England began and remained mainly in the personalistic idiom. The king and his court of nobles were power personified. Norman England accelerated the transformation from the personalistic to materialistic idiom by standardising and expanding administrative kingship. The early stages of the expression of power in the materialistic idiom were crude, in that material reward, in the form of land, was directly and openly exchanged for military service and labour in a hierarchy of dependency of lords and peasants ultimately obligated to the king. So too were the early organisation of the major institutions of the materialistic idiom namely the courts, the parliament and the bureaucracy. For example, power could not be said to be disguised or covert in the manorial courts where lords sat as judges in disputes involving their men. As land was supplemented by additional forms of material rewards such as money, the materialistic idiom became more sophisticated and consistent with its form.

Of particular interest to this study is the initial bureaucracy created in support of administrative kingship. Top holders of civil service positions were required to be unmarried, if not celibate. They were also required to be educated. The only source of education and educated personnel was the church and the school system the latter had created for its clergy. Both the king and the manorial lords had to recruit their administrative staff either from the clergy itself or persons made literate in Latin and educated in the schools designed for educating clergy. Initially the staff came from the clergy, or clerks of the church, either in full or part-time employment.

The legitimacy once given by the Church to kings through recognition, was transferred into the administrative structures through both co-opting clergy into the bureaucracy as well as predicating education of civil servants and personnel of the manorial system with the type and level of schooling given to the clergy. The effect was to give that schooling material value outside of the church. Access to schooling was added to land as a form of material reward. At the same time, the state bureaucracy brought the educated civil servant directly into similar dependent relations to that which previously obtained with respect to land. Jobs for clergy outside of the church could only be had in the dependent relations of the materialistic exercise of state power. The services of the educated were exchanged for patronage, as was military service by the knight or labour by the peasant. Schooling was therefore incorporated into the exercise of power not only in terms of justification and legitimacy but also into the material exchange and reward system as well.

Transformation in the Economy

Over the period under review the English economy was transformed from being largely self reliant and heavily biased toward subsistence, with little external trade, to one in which external trade was buoyant and the contribution of agro-industries and mining was marked if not substantial. Export trade was sufficient to allow the country to return to the gold standard in currency. In the emerging exchange economy guilds and merchants began to establish educational criteria for their members and apprentices. They also began to purchase schooling for their children and to establish schools. Again the schooling that was specified or purchased or endowed was that provided by the church either for its clergy or for some aspect of its functions or liturgy. Schooling, that once only had meaning in terms of church functions and personnel, broadened to have market value in the emerging exchange economy.

Transformation of Belief and Culture

Initially the church consisted of the missionaries arriving from Rome. Apart from a few others, like the Queen of Kent and her entourage, the rest of England was heathen. By the time of the Reformation almost the entire population of England was nominally Christian, and many of the laity challenged the clergy with respect to piety. Likewise, initially the people were Angles, Saxons, Jutes, Norwegians, Danes and Normans; by the time of the Reformation they were then unmistakably English. In regard to both Christian belief and unifying the country, the church could justifiably claim some credit. Cardinal Newman's statement that there was not a man who criticised the church that did not owe it to the church that he could speak at all, implied some ingratitude on the part of the critics. However, also implicit in that statement is the commendation of the church for not only producing examples of missionary zeal but persons capable of critical comment.

At the same time that the church could claim with justification that it had contributed significantly to the making of the English, it would also need to confess that the clergy had been compromised in the process. The close links between the clergy and the pinnacle of power, had benefited the monarchy and nobility in exercising their hegemony over the rest of the society, and also facilitated the spread of Christianity. However, the high ethical vision and the ethics of Christianity had been brought into question by the lifestyle, privileges and relationships of the clergy. In addition, loyalty to Rome which had facilitated the recognition of the monarchy and the acceptance of England as part of the Western European community of kingdoms, now represented dual loyalty in the well recognised and established England.

As a parallel society with its separate mission to spread Christianity, the Church had brought about some unintended outcomes. First, it had created a coalition of pious laity drawn from all sections of English society, from nobility to peasantry. Second, the church had spread literacy and high culture to the peasantry as well as to the nobility. In addition, from the occupational groups that drew their preparation from the education provided for the clergy, the church had created a stratum of society that did not easily fit into either the peasantry or the nobility, but were not clergy. Further some clergy now sought vocations outside the church in new occupations that had been created, and without the supervision of the church. The dons of Oxford University were among the first to effect this partial separation. These groups and coalitions formed alliances within the church, and challenged the clergy for representational rights in the governance of the church as well as the right to be bearers of the high culture and ethical vision of the religion itself.

When Henry VIII seized upon the circumstances of the times, declared himself head of the Church and started what was called the English Reformation he was continuing a process that had already been set in motion. The church was being integrated into English secular society and would no longer be parallel to secular society. Secular English society was being restructured along the lines upon which the church had long been organised as a learning community.

TEACHERS AND THEIR GENDER

In understanding the evolution of schooling in England and within it the construction of the teaching occupation, the role of the clergy is of pre-eminent importance. From an educational perspective, the clergy was a set of communities centred on formal learning.

FORMAL LEARNING COMMUNITIES AMONG THE CLERGY

Monasteries up to the time of the Norman Conquest were under the Benedictine Rule. Reading and study were a set part of the daily routine of the Rule. Oblates and adults were taught the skills of literacy in formal classes, while the Rule itself promoted the habit of reading. Reading one book per year was specified in the calendar of activities, and the period of Lent was set aside for that purpose. Libraries were part of the infrastructure of monasteries, which also produced books through their scriptoria. Educational achievement was measured and marked by set stages. Promotion was based on merit as kinship was suppressed, though never eliminated. Functions such as teaching, writing, copying, choral direction and arrangement and librarianship were assigned to monks on the basis of intellectual aptitude and academic achievement. Monasteries were autonomous and self-regulating, taking the responsibility for the discipline of their members. All of these were predicated on the basis of self-sufficiency as monasteries attempted to be independent by organising their own sustenance.

Some monks reached great heights of learning in particular fields, equal to that of any age. Monasteries manifested all the requirements of formal peer institutions of learning: autonomy and self regulation, formal teaching of literacy and literary skills; requirements to study as part of daily and annual routines, scholarly activities utilising the library as the chief source; formal assessment of learning achievement, promotion based on merit judged by learning achievement; allocation of vocational functions based on aptitude and formal learning, and the opportunity to achieve the highest level of learning possible.

While there has been great debate about the quality of learning in some monasteries in relation to others in a particular era, or of the same monastery in different ages or any combination of these, what remains unshakeable is that monasteries in their essence were communities of formal learning. This defining educational feature existed when monasteries were mainly composed of children donated by parents, growing up in the monastic tradition and then becoming missionaries converting heathen: that is, insiders reaching out. This feature also remained when monasteries changed after the Norman Conquest and admitted adults turning to the contemplative life: that is, outsiders reaching in. Whatever were the changes in the self/other relationship, in their being, monasteries were institutions of formal learning.

In passing it must also be noted that monasteries recreated and resembled the eduba of ancient Sumer. The monastery was a school, it maintained a library, and had a scriptorium in which it copied books. There is no evidence that the monasteries of Western Europe of the second half of the first millennium CE were consciously copying and imitating the Sumerians or Babylonians who pre-dated them by over 3000 years; they were responding to their own imperatives and in the process reinvented a tablet house using paper instead of clay.

The parish priests were a learning community of a different type. The cathedral church was charged, by being the seat of the bishop, with training the clergy for that see. The mission of the priesthood was pastoral care and ministry. The priesthood remained tied to kindred and, its cultural connections. Nevertheless, as dictated by its ethical vision, it was open to all kindred and permitted upward social mobility in the hierarchy of the church irrespective of kindred. Caught in the tensions between culture and ethical vision it devised graded and measured levels of learning which, at the higher levels, eventually led to ranks of learning labelled bachelor, master and doctor when cathedral schools evolved into universities. These ranks of learning became criteria for all kindred to satisfy in order to advance in the clergy.

This reconstruction of the learning community covered at least seven centuries of operations. Transplanted from its urban roots in the ancient cities to rural England, cathedrals played second fiddle to the monasteries in the conversion mission. The Norman reforms gave them a parish structure more suited to a rural setting. Increasing urbanisation brought a momentum different from the conversion phase. Put another way the head church of the diocese, the cathedral, charged with the responsibility of educating clergy for all the churches of the diocese, slowly created a graded programme of learning achievement marked by appropriately labelled academic rank as an incontestable means of resolving the tensions between its ties to kindred and its obligations to equality as demanded by Christian ethics. The learning community was therefore narrow as its mission was to educate for the specific occupation of priest, but it was driven to heights of excellence as it sought to rise above kinship ties. This is to be contrasted with the more broadly configured learning community of monasteries. While the latter had its being in a way of life, the former had its being in singularity of purpose in educating for an occupation.

The debate that has centred on the relative merits of monasteries and cathedral schools, which Leach fomented and which was revived in more recent times, has failed to take account of three facts of enormous proportions. First, monasteries and cathedral churches were in constant interaction. Secular clergy taught in monasteries and abbots became bishops. This maintained constant cross-fertilisation between these two important institutions of the English Church. Second, these two institutions complemented each other and in their totality have left indelible imprints on English schooling and teaching that far outweigh the hair-splitting differences in seeking to isolate sole legacies of either. Third, in their totality the formal learning communities of the clergy became, as it were, the genetic template shaping secular English learning institutions as these, through a long series mutations, evolved into the educational systems of Western Europe.

The Christian clergy and their institutions have left at least four imprints that have indelibly marked English education generally, and teaching in particular. These can be listed as follows:

1. That teachers should be paragons of virtue.
2. That personal worth is measured in units of formal learning achievement.
3. That the higher ranks of learning achievement offset low social rank.
4. Merit, as measured in units of formal learning achievement, is a fair basis of recognition and reward.

THE TEACHING OCCUPATION: DOWN AND OUT FROM THE CLERGY

The teaching occupation was inaugurated at the very top of the hierarchy of the clergy in England. From that beginning the evolution of teaching as an occupation in Christian England followed two basic directions. The first movement was down the hierarchy of the ecclesiastical order, and the second was out of the clergy itself. However, neither of these movements was completed by 1520. Most schoolmasters and schoolmistresses were still members of the Christian ecclesiastical fraternity, and members of the major orders were still teachers. It is with these caveats that the masculine and feminine roots of teaching in Christianity in England must be traced.

The first teachers were the leaders of the Christian church in England. They were the bishops, the abbots and the abbesses. They did not rise to these positions from being teachers. Rather, they were teachers because they held these positions. This was not a peculiarity of English Christianity, but common practice of the Christian church from the inception of its training for its clergy. At the highest level of its ethical vision, Jesus was the teacher of the apostles. Apostolic succession involved not only authority but instruction as well. At the practical level it related to the selection of bishops and clergy. The starting point of the teaching occupation in English Christianity, at the top of the ecclesiastical order, had strong and abundant precedents in the faith.

The first downward movement was that the role of schoolmaster was separated from the functions of the bishop or abbot and made a specialist responsibility of a monk or priest. This separation could be said to have established teaching as a distinct occupation within the clergy, instead of being one of the several duties of the religious leader. In English Christianity this separation took place toward the end of the first century of missionary activity and was marked by Bede the monk and Alcuin the priest. The schoolmaster priest or monk remained the sole specialist teachers in England for the next four hundred years. The only point to note is that schoolmasters now rose to the position of bishop or abbot. Promotion meant exit from teaching as the major responsibility and function.

The location of the teaching occupation within the clergy was not peculiar. As contemporary writers were constantly pointing out English society in pre-Conquest times was divided into three groups: those who laboured to provide sustenance, those who defended the society militarily and those who prayed for both, that is, those who protected the society spiritually. The teaching occupation was one of the means by which spiritual protection was effected. Schooling and teaching prepared the spiritual protectors for their tasks as priests, monks, choristers and converts.

People were born into either the peasant/labourer or warrior groups while both contributed to the clergy. For the peasantry movement into the clergy constituted the only social mobility possible in the society. To the nobility the clergy was a honourable occupation in which to find fulfilment or take refuge.

Teaching nested within the clergy enjoyed these social attributes of mobility and respectability.

Of equal importance was the fact that the clergy provided the bureaucracy of the state. This became particularly so when the administrative monarchy was introduced by the Normans. The clergy occupied the highest positions within the emerging state machinery. By that development equations and associations were also being built with teaching. The secularisation of teaching and the civil service, from the clergy, proceeded simultaneously from the twelfth to the sixteenth century. But the sources of both their ethos and their education was the same, the church and the education and ethics prescribed for clergy.

Another feature of the clergy of consequence to teaching as an occupation was that the Christian clergy was constantly seeking to maintain educational standards. These standards were constantly being applied and raised as applicants outstripped vacancies. As Alexander (1990) showed while the authorities constantly had to deal with pressures from wealthy and influential lords to accommodate their relatives with comfortable benefices, they also countered with the ingenious strategy of insisting that the endowment was sufficient to provide for a competent priest who acted in the capacity of an assistant to the less able or poorly qualified appointee of the benefactors. Teaching, especially tutoring, became almost a natural sideline to the pastoral ministry. The clergy constituted the only reservoir of learning in Anglo-Saxon England. It was from this reservoir that all outlets into other occupations flowed. In time these occupations evolved in their own right beginning in the period after the Conquest.

Of equal importance was the fact that the clergy was large. It accounted for approximately two per cent of the entire population, inclusive of women, children and adults. If the clergy were compared to the adult male population alone, then it would be approximately eight to nine per cent of all adult males. Approximately one in twelve adult males in England in the late Middle Ages was a member of the clergy. As an occupation in itself, without regard for its religious influence, its effect on the society was enormous and pervasive. The schoolmaster occupation embedded in a large learned clergy with a mission to teach enjoyed all the associations related to these attributes.

As was the case with both Judaism and Islam, teaching in Christianity evolved from the highest ethical expression of English society. To be English was to be Christian. Teaching was devoted to forming English Christians. Unlike Judaism and Islam there was no level of education excluded from this mission as it developed. There was not an elementary school that was separate from a college level, the latter being the essence of the religion and the society. Education and teaching as it emerged and evolved, and for most of the entire 1000-year period, had no distinctive levels. The differentiation of levels only began to emerge slowly after 1200. Even then there were only a few elementary schools as such by 1520.

The differentiation that emerged was dictated mainly by the imperatives of the church, and only to a small degree by the dictates of educational organisation. This is reflected in the equation which emerged between types and grades of clergy and the types of schools of which they were schoolmasters. Chantry priests and vicars chorale taught song schools. Chantry priests and clergy of the minor orders taught reading schools. Priests of the major orders taught grammar schools and at the university. This was by no means a strict equation. Some chantry priests and clergy of the minor orders taught grammar. Some grammarians taught song and reading. Level of education, church functions and the teaching for these were mixed. Embedded, however, was a cleavage that was to loom large among teachers as teaching became differentiated from the clergy. That difference was between the elementary schools that evolved from the reading and song schools on the one hand and the grammar and university teachers on the other hand. That sharp cleavage, however, came mainly after the period that is the focus of this study, and is therefore beyond its scope.

The downward movement of teaching in the ecclesiastic order was not reflective of any devaluation of its role and function over time, but rather of the exigencies of the clergy. The minor orders were allowed to marry, however, promotion to the major order required celibacy. Several members of the minor orders, because of marriage were unable to be promoted. Many married men of ability and learning among the minor orders found teaching an occupation, within the clergy, in which their marital entanglements could be accommodated. Bishops must also have taken this into consideration in assigning functions.

Teaching duties were not part of the chantry endowments as stipulated by the wills of the many benefactors. The assignment of teaching duties to chantry priests came in response to criticism of the institution of the chantry itself, first by Wyclif and the Lollards in the latter part of the fourteenth century, and later to an increasing extent by influential critics of the church in the fifteenth century (Orme 1976). Teaching duties added to the responsibilities of chantry priests, not only responded to the growing demands for education in towns and cities, but also provided social justification to a religious institution under threat. Interestingly, when chantries were abolished, their reading schools that they evolved into elementary schools, and chantry priests into the bulk of the first elementary school teachers.

Orme (1976) provided some quantitative indication of the extent to which teaching had moved down the ecclesiastic order and out of the clergy altogether prior to the Reformation. For the period 1200 to 1548 Orme found evidence of 150 schoolmasters who taught in the West of England. Of that number 56 were chantry priests, 27 priests were either self employed or in schools that did not make their employment a requirement of holy orders, 15 clerks of the minor orders of the clergy and 52 whose status were unknown. Orme observed that the majority of the latter were likely to have been laymen. Even if all were laymen, it would still mean that at least two-thirds of the teachers in the West of England in the later centuries of the period under review, were members of the clergy. While Moran (1987) did not give precise figures for the number of clergy and laity among teachers, she was of the view that the composition of teachers in the York diocese was not unlike that reported by Orme for the West of England.

The trend noted by Orme was for chantry priests to be schoolmasters, and for some other clergy to found schools in response to the growing needs of the towns without initial church sponsorship, which sometimes came afterwards. Further, laity founding schools would often employ clergy as the teachers. This is not surprising seeing that the clergy presented a vast supply of learned people, at a time when learning was still limited within the entire population. However, trends in these later centuries underscored the fact that teaching had slowly moved down the ecclesiastic order, as the lowest paid priests, chantry priests became the bulk of the teachers. In addition to this downward movement, some clergy became schoolmasters of their own volition and some laity, having not made it into the clergy sometimes because of marital entanglements, had become teachers. The outward movement from the church and clergy had unmistakably begun but up to the time of the Reformation teaching had only partially become an occupation of the laity.

Among teachers it was university dons that had established some measure of autonomy from the church, in terms of control by the bishops, by winning the right to select their own chancellors to manage their own administrative affairs. Autonomy did not extend to either teaching or learning. This was clearly under the jurisdiction of the church and its rules of heresy and determined by the Pope. Even though the universities had some autonomy most of the teacher/scholars were clergy: priests or friars.

THE GENDER OF TEACHERS

All the available evidence points to the fact that teaching as it emerged in Christian England, whether in the clergy or as it began to be differentiated from the clergy, was mainly a masculine occupation. The evidence is also unmistakably clear that although teaching was overwhelmingly male, women teachers were part of the teaching occupation from its inception in Christian England. Their place in teaching was from the same source, premises and principles as men. Put another way, when teaching was first inaugurated in England in the seventh century, it was only greater numbers that initially gave men a greater presence in teaching than women. Unlike Judaism no law was ever enacted to exclude or ban women as teachers. Unlike Islam, women were never excluded from formal learning. From the beginning women participated in education and were deployed in teaching, premised on the same basis as men.

Christianity in its highest ethical vision did not exclude female teachers. In founding schools and the occupation of teaching in England women were included in the institutions established. Abbesses, like abbots and bishops, were among the first teachers. Female monasteries, nunneries, like their male counterparts operated under the same Benedictine rules of collective identity, celibacy, daily study, annual study of at least one book, formal teaching of literacy, the operation of schools and all the other features of a formal learning community. Nunneries continued to operate schools throughout the period under review. No laws were ever passed restricting women's education or formally banning women from teaching.

Women were excluded, however, from the priesthood and by virtue of that exclusion were not admitted to training in schools attached to cathedrals. Women's access to the teaching occupation therefore was through the convent. This was one important constraint of the numbers of women deployed in teaching compared to men, since the latter had access to schooling and teaching through both learning communities that constituted the Christian clergy.

By the mid sixteenth century, the inequality noted between men and women teachers within the religious fraternity was even more exaggerated. Men as teachers had outstripped females not only in numbers but also by level and quality of learning. While Christianity through the value it placed on virginity, and the exigencies of the initial missionary effort to convert the Anglo-Saxons, had combined to create occupational space for women in religious orders, that space remained small while the demands of the clergy and the male religious houses grew. In other words, it is not that either the female religious orders, and teaching within them, declined over the period under review, but that they never grew much beyond their beginnings. Substantial growth and development of clergy and teaching among religious men, is to be contrasted with little growth or development among the female religious orders and teaching among women.

One can find no comparable downward and outward movement of teaching among nuns, that can be compared with that observed among priests and monks. Teaching remained an occupation among abbesses and nuns. Orme (1976), Moran (1987) and Alexander (1990) found less than ten references to female teachers outside of religious orders between the Norman Conquest and the Reformation. Alexander (1990) reported references to Matilda Marescflete of a school at Boston in Lincolnshire in 1404 in a school at Taunton run by Alice Harper and a few unnamed female teachers of schools in London. There were no such references in Anglo-Saxon England. The vast majority of female teachers in Christian England from the eighth century to the dissolution of the convents in 1550 were nuns in schools in the convent. A few anchoresses were known to teach. However, this was both discouraged as well as inconsistent with the life of solitude.

Teaching remained an occupation of those religious women whose piety was predicated on purity. The later groups of religious women, in the twelfth to sixteenth centuries, whose piety was grounded in repentance and penance, gravitated more towards charitable works among the poor and care for the sick. That is, these religious women tended to occupations in social work and medicine, mainly nursing. The plague and less fatal diseases had resulted in the founding of many hospitals. The new religious orders, including religious women of the penitential orientation, were the pioneers in filling this need. In other words, the numbers of female teachers were not boosted by these later revivals in female piety. While religious men of the vast pool of the clergy were meeting the increasing demand for schooling, religious women of a penitential character, along with some religious men, moved to fill demands related to the social and health needs of the growing urban poor. The virgin, the pure woman, remained the teacher.

The teaching occupation among women, from the eighth to the mid sixteenth centuries remained centred around teaching novices in the nunneries and later teaching children of the nobility and aristocracy in convent schools. In other words, the teaching occupation for women remained in the environment of the cloister. This was not due to lack of enterprise on the part of the nuns. Indeed, they maintained convent schools sometimes against the opposition of the authorities who often restricted the size of the schools by their regulations as to the numbers a convent could accommodate who had not taken the vow. Had the nuns been totally obedient to the authority of popes and bishops, then the only schools and women teachers would have been those related to teaching novices.

Elkins (1988) made the point that there were two competing views of spirituality that guided monastic life. One view rested firmly in piety related to virginity and lifelong observance of the rule of the particular monastic order. The other accepted virginity as its foundation but emphasised learning as the major means of advancing spirituality. In the case of the male monasteries the latter prevailed in most cases and for most of the time. In the case of convents the former was usually the norm although there were periods when efforts were made to shift to the latter. For example, Archbishop Anselm, between 1090 and 1110 took steps to improve educational standards in the nunneries and refocus their life from the first to the second notion of spirituality.

Leyser (1995) observed that in the twelfth century revival, as was true in the initial conversion period; female piety was placed on a pedestal. Holy women were regarded as being on the hot line to heaven. Learning was not critical to achieving the heights of female piety. The first view of spirituality prevailed. Wogan-Browne (1995) noted that the epitome of female piety portrayed in both the tenth and twelfth century revivals of monasticism, was Etheldreda, renamed Saint Audree, one of the four daughters of seventh century King Anna of the East Angles. Saint Audree was of noble birth, beautiful and sought after by many men, twice married out of family obligation, once widowed but remained a virgin through both marriages. She used her dower of the first marriage to establish the monastery of Ely, then voluntarily chose the life of poverty by persuading her second husband to release her to service to God as Abbess of Ely. Physical beauty, royalty and family loyalty on the one hand, matched with faithfulness to virginity and the voluntary choice of poverty on the other hand elevated Audree to the pinnacle of female piety. Audree's sister, who became abbess after her death, and who did much to establish Ely as a centre of learning, while also elevated to sainthood did not become a role model for nuns or English women in this later period, between the twelfth and sixteenth century.

That learning remained circumscribed in nunneries, and teaching within them, was related to the education and status of women in the wider society. Christianity had created limited occupational space for women, and within that space even a smaller place for women teachers, but this could not override the general status of women in English society. The majority of women became wives and mothers and were viewed as bearing the punishment of Eve. They lived lives that were consistent with traditional clan patriarchal norms. This is amply illustrated by the educational history of a family traced by Alexander (1990).

Clement Parson, a Norfolk husbandman, used his savings and borrowed money in the 1390s to send his son and heir William to study law at one of the Inns of Court. To that time the Parsons had been husbandmen of modest means and humble status. After successfully completing his studies, William found employment and eventually rose to become a Justice of the Court of Common Pleas. By the 1490s not only were there several Parsons who were lawyers and prominent citizens, but a few had gone to Oxford and in 1478 Walter, the great grandson of Clement, had entered Eton. The same records revealed only one female descendant of Clement Parson who was literate.

THE MASCULINE AND FEMININE ROOTS OF TEACHING IN CHRISTIANITY

In Christianity, teaching had taproots that were both masculine and feminine because teaching began in the celibate clergy and religious orders. Based on the high value placed on virginity in early Christian theology, women were admitted into religious orders. Although they were denied access to the clergy, they were admitted into the ranks of teachers.

The masculine and feminine roots of teaching in Christianity were firmly set in the personnel, liturgical and indoctrination needs of the church. Teaching was therefore an occupation within the church and the religious orders established to sustain its mission. The patriarchal structure of the priesthood precluded women from that branch of Christian ministry. Hence, teaching the clergy, performing the liturgy and instructing the converts were entirely male dominated. The Episcopal Church was thoroughly patriarchal in its orientation, organisation and recruitment of personnel.

The masculine roots of teaching in Christianity could be traced to Jesus the Rabbi. However, it could be argued that the learning community of his twelve disciples was not a formal school. It is indisputable, however, that the masculine roots of teaching in Christianity are to be found both in the episcopal and monastic traditions within the religion and in particular to the offices of bishop and abbot which were charged not only with leading the faithful but also with instructing the clergy on the one hand and the novices on the other hand. In this regard, the masculine roots of teaching within Christianity are closely related to the prophetic vision and tradition within the religion, as was the case with both Judaism and Islam.

The feminine root of teaching was from monastic and ascetic Christianity, which imposed celibacy as an admission criterion to the religious communities and the doctrine of the church that made no distinction between male and female virgins. Like Islam, women's access to the teaching occupation in English Christianity was at the very height of the ethical vision of the religion. Like Islam it was the cloister that provided women with access to the public sphere through the teaching occupation.

Of equal importance is the fact that the women with the greatest access to this limited occupational space were royal and aristocratic women, assisting their kindred in their consolidation of newly acquired status and position in English society. In other words, women's access to teaching was not only from the height of the ethical vision of Christianity but also from the heights of the social structure of emerging English society. It was restricted to those royal and aristocratic women who chose, or were chosen, to advance the cause of their kindred through spiritual protection rather than follow the traditional patriarchal roles as wives and mothers. They were acting in partnership with the men of their group in protecting, preserving and promoting the interest of their group within English society.

The closure of the monasteries, but the continuation of the teaching functions through the creation of teaching orders among monks and nuns, opened the door to wider social recruitment of religious women. On the other hand, the retention of celibacy as an entry criterion preserved the tradition of the female teacher as the pure woman redeeming the society through her purity and devotion to God.

POSTSCRIPT

The glory that was England's and Western Europe's in the nineteenth and twentieth centuries was neither envisaged nor imagined in the sixteenth century. The self-confidence and arrogance associated with the West, and the British empire, came with modern times and was not inherited from the past. Tanner (1994) noted that the art of the fourteenth and fifteenth centuries was characterised by the portrayal of death. The mood of the times was characterised by pessimism. In addition, Western Christendom lived with a general sense of cultural inferiority. Islam, though the younger religion, was expanding and growing at a faster rate. Christianity seemed to be in decline. Whatever gains had been made in the conversion of Western Europe had been offset by losses to Islam in the Mediterranean and Africa.

In comparisons of the four cultures – Eastern Christianity, Judaism, ancient civilisation and Western Christianity – the latter fared the worse. Judaism was the older and richer culture whose people were renowned in business and the professions. In comparison to Islam the West at that time had no scholars with the reputation of Avicenna, Averroes and Al Ghazali and their centres of learning and architecture were not yet the rivals of Islam. Eastern Christianity was the heir of the wealthier sections of the ancient empire and bore with pride their role as preservers of the ancient civilisation. Further, the ancient world still stood as a colossus compared to the achievements of the West.

Disease, famine and malnutrition and wars and destruction were all prevalent in the pre-Reformation period. These did nothing to instil confidence but much to undermine it. The church itself was under siege as the clergy was charged with corruption and complicity with the powerful in oppressing the poor. This was a far cry from the posture of the early church as the defender of the dispossessed. Further, charges and counter-charges of heresy circulated with monotonous regularity, followed by persecution in vicious cycles of recrimination.

Yet, it was from these circumstances of apparent gloom, inferiority and destitution that Western Europe was to rise to dominance of the world in the short space of 250 years. With this rise Christianity spread to become the most widespread religion in the world. From this marginal position of the Middle Ages, England, the West and Christianity rose to the central position in the modern world. The latecomer to civilisation became its leader.

The key to understanding and interpreting this spectacular turn around is the marginal energy released by the following:

- The laity's challenge to the clergy for full participation in the mission of the church, the consequent emergence of the Protestant churches and the renewal which this inspired in the Catholic church.
- The commoners' challenge to the monarchy's absolute control of the mechanisms of power, and their demand for greater participation, involvement and control of the body politc through more democratic processes beginning with representation through parliament.
- The synthesis of the high culture with the culture of the folk leading to the greatest period of technological advancement since that at Sumer between 4000 and 3500 BC.
- The expansion of Western Europe into the Americas, the New World.

It is probably an overstatement to say that without the New World, there would be no Western Europe as it is currently known. The release of marginal energy emerging from the broad mass of laity in the churches and commoners in the state may have spurred the West forward in any case. However, without the New World Western Europe would not have achieved the same rate or quantum of progress that it did. The colonies of the Americas made possible the magnitude of Western European imperialism and its rise to become the dominant region of the modern world.

Six

THE TRANSFORMATION OF SCHOOLING AND TEACHING IN THE NATION-STATE

At varying times after the sixteenth century religious empires gave way to nation-states from China to Austria, Turkey and the Vatican. In the emerging nation-states religion retreated in the face of the crusading advance of science as revelation yielded the high ground to reason as the prime basis for interpreting, understanding and explaining human origin, experience and actions. At the same time the geopolitical centre shifted from the East to the West, from the Mediterranean to Europe, as the Iberians connected the several different worlds that for the most part had operated to varying degrees in isolation from each other. These transformations changed civilisation fundamentally.

European scholarship has almost invariably classified this new age as modern while labelling what went before as traditional. The transformation is accounted for and explained in terms of the Renaissance, Reformation, counter-Reformation and the Age of Enlightenment. Yet the transformation from religious empires to independent and sovereign nation-states occurred world-wide as the Islamic, Eastern Christian, Western Christian and Far Eastern empires fractured into nations.

Indeed, the nature of the transformation from the Age of Religion to the Age of the Nation State is best seen not in Western Europe but in the United States. The location of the latter in the New World exaggerates the dichotomy of traditional and modern to such an extent as to call into question its validity. Hence, for precisely this reason the United States provides the clearest picture of the rise of the nation-state, from its genesis in the era of the Religious Age.

America's relationship to the rise of the nation-state is very analogous to that of the relationship of England to the rise of Christianity. As England rose from the periphery of the Roman empire to the creation of its own empire and as the English moved from being heathens to the highest prominence in the spread of Christianity, so has the United States risen from its colonial status on the margins of Western European civilisation to being a superpower among nation-states and the leader of the Western world.

The relations of the United States to Western Europe and the rest of the Americas also share several analogies to Rome, the ancient world and Western Europe. Rome was located in Europe but its culture and civilisation was that of the city-states of the ancient Mediterranean. Italy's culture today is not Roman but Western European. In like manner the United States is physically located in the Americas but its mainstream culture is that of Western Europe. A truly American civilisation is yet to be fully constructed and realised. The product of the American melting pot, almost 400 years after its founding, cannot be called American in the same manner as the English when they arrived in the Americas at the beginning of the seventeenth century.

The English melting pot had so melted its diverse strains in 1200 years that it would have made no sense to seek to differentiate the Anglo-English, the Saxon-English, the Jute-English, the Danish-English, etc. Such relics of the original strains were considered but stylistic variations upon the English theme as represented by the idiosyncrasies of the Yorkshireman, the Cornish, the Lancasterman and of course those of the learned Oxbridge tradition. These were variants in the expression of 'Englishness', not bases for seeking or furthering rights. At the same time English culture was very much a version and a part of Western European civilisation.

In contrast, the term American cannot be meaningfully used without some qualifying prefix like Polish-American or Chinese-American, or African-American or Mexican-American. The exceptions to this general rule are circumstances where externally some political advantage is being advocated with respect to other nationalities, or internally when some right is being claimed, or where some group would seek to usurp this ascription based upon some manufactured claims of primacy. The qualifying prefix speaks to the distinctive origin, ancestry and history of groups and their sub-cultures, while the term American asserts common identity, intended oneness and unity still to be attained: the culture in progress, still being constructed from the rich ingredients of the mix. The continued meaning of the various prefixes testifies to the incomplete state of the blend and the continued importance of the past in present social intercourse and relations. In addition, it is only in a vague sense that one can speak of a civilisation of the Americas emerging from its own imperatives and relationships, and America as being a version of that civilisation.

Probably because of its location at a major crossroads in the history of civilisation, American society has many beguiling and infuriating paradoxes reflecting the best and worst in human society. Greatness and banality, nobility and obscenity, foresight and myopia mingle in schizophrenic abandon. One of the most infuriating paradoxes is that of embracing and practising the tenets of equality, liberty and democracy while perpetrating the most blatant forms of discrimination and disenfranchisement of minorities, particularly Blacks and Native Americans.

One of the most beguiling paradoxes, capable of the most complete deception especially of its most ardent proponents, is the claim to the creation and existence of a unique American culture which at the very same time, in most of its elements, is nothing but the complete embrace and elevation of the quintessential elements and content of Western European culture. This is not to say that there is not an emerging American culture, distinct from Western

European culture, but it is to say that the former is nascent and very much a work in progress, while the latter has been mainstream and dominant from the earliest times of American history.

Highlighting this paradox is not by any means an attempt to enter into any polemical debate on the issues raised. Rather it is a statement, of a few hard and cold realities, which is critical from two perspectives. First, it is a guide in connecting the American past to the present. Second, as a reminder that the present is not to be treated as an end point but a stage along a way: not a fixed, final or uniform product but a dynamic and somewhat distorted confrontation with the past in the effort to create the future.

In seeking to better understand the process of transformation in the gender composition of the teaching occupation in the era of the nation-states it is imperative to trace the transformation in schooling. For the reasons outlined above, this transformation will be traced in relation to the United States. It is important to do the following:

1. Highlight particular aspects of American colonial history that are germane to the establishment of schooling and the occupation of teaching, especially those that relate to their English and Christian beginnings.
2. Identify and briefly describe important factors that impacted on the transformation of schooling and teaching in the first 150 years of the United States as an independent country.
3. Briefly sketch the development of education as this relates to Protestants, Catholics, Jews, African-Americans, and Native Americans.

THE COLONIAL FOUNDATIONS OF AMERICAN EDUCATION

The mariner's compass was invented in the twelfth century. It was one of the few inventions of any consequence of that time. The Iberians emerging from Muslim dominance in the thirteenth century looked for power and glory outside of Europe. Exploring the potentials of this new invention, the Iberians in search of trading opportunities sought to connect the then known world, including the Far East, China and the Atlantic coast of Africa. In the pursuit of such ventures an expedition led by Christopher Colombus happened upon the New World, toward the end of the fifteenth century, and made it known to Europe.

The Americas had no aboriginal people. There was no Pithecantropus Erectus Americanensis. The Americas were two continents without people. All its peoples have come from the Old World at different times. The first to come were Asians in pre-historic times. Entering from the north some migrated to inhabit the central and southern regions. The Maya of Central America developed the most sophisticated civilisation of all the groups. Maya civilisation included a complex polytheistic religion, priesthood, writing, mathematics including the abstract concept of zero, advanced astronomy, magnificent architecture and a wide variety of agricultural crops including maize, sweet potato, tobacco and cassava (Morley 1956).

The Incas to the south in the Peruvian highlands, and the Aztecs in Mexico also developed settled civilisations although not as advanced as the Maya. Only the tribes to the north, in the Great Plains, lived a nomadic life in the classical primitive form (Morison and Commager 1942). The three great civilisations of the Americas did not incorporate most of the tribes, which were relatively small. Most tribes lived in selected areas with generally unfriendly relationships with most of their neighbours. The abundance of land, and the abundance of much of the land, provided room for all without the necessity of large scale warfare characteristic of the Old World.

Columbus, in a quandary over his exact location, had mistakenly labelled the first Americans, Indians. Though the Indians received the expedition in a friendly manner and extended hospitality while reflecting leisurely with the aid of cigars, the European visitors labelled them savages. Ironically Columbus was not only wrong about the place he had happened upon, but also the whole of Europe was mistaken about the exact date of that event because of the inaccuracies of the calendar that was being used. However, the Mayan mathematicians, astronomers and priests had exact calculations of the solar and lunar years and a sophisticated method of synchronising them over a fifty-two year period (Morley 1956). They had the date of Columbus's arrival correct. Yet, there was no objective assessment of the civilisation of the First Americans by the Europeans. Rather, as Morison and Commager (1942) pointed out, there was a deliberate attempt to both deny the existence and authenticity of that civilisation and to destroy it.

Europeans, at the time of their arrival in the New World, were anxious to cast off the mantle of savage barbarians that they had so long borne and also the feeling of inferiority that was theirs as the least of the empires of the Religious Age. Indeed, they had only just cast off the mantle of heathen that the early Christians had placed on them, but were depressed by their failure to capture the Holy Sepulchre in Jerusalem and humbled by the advance of Islam (Morison and Commager 1942). With all the insecurities of newcomers to an elevated status, Western Europeans, including the English, imposed a sense of their own superiority on the New World. In a nutshell the New World gave Europeans scope to construct a pedigree. But the Amerindians were not alone in the receipt of the mantle of inferiority. Sharing it with them were the Africans imported as slaves.

The English came to the New World a little over a century after it became known to Europe. They therefore entered this world with more knowledge than the Spanish and the Portuguese who had come a century earlier. The English came to the marginal and primitive continental north because the Iberians had already taken the civilised centre and south, along with the most strategic and prosperous Caribbean islands. The English knew that they were to encounter tribes of North America still living the nomadic life, roaming the expansive plains and hunting the buffalo. They could have expected that this European intrusion in the North would play out yet another variation of the age old saga of agricultural settlements being raided by roaming nomadic tribes as the former encroached upon the territory of the latter in carving out and expanding their settlements. The difference in this variation of the well-known ancient saga was that it was not possible to trace common ancestry between the contestants either in terms of historical or geographical proximity. Their origins were worlds apart. The English knew this before they arrived. It did not take them by surprise.

Some of the reasons for the late arrival of the English in the New World included:

- Spanish naval power at the time.
- The unsettled nature of England's internal prerogatives related to the Reformation.
- The competition for power within the British Isles and the limited resources of England at that time.

However, by the end of the sixteenth century the union of the Scottish and English Crowns, the completion of the conquest of Ireland, the waning of Spanish power and the formation of joint stock companies with public and private subscription, all eased the way for English appearance in the New World. Before the official appearance English adventurers and scholars were engaged in developing plans for "Western Planting", that is, for establishing colonies in the New World. The most comprehensive proposal was developed by a clergyman, the Rev. Richard Hakluyt, at the request of Sir Walter Raleigh, and presented to Queen Elizabeth I in 1584. While the proposal did not have the desired result at that time, the rationale it postulated became the cornerstone of official English intervention in the hemisphere, and Hakluyt its chief proponent (Cremin 1970).

Hakluyt's rationale for English colonies in the New World was:

1. Spreading the gospel to the natives.
2. Enhancing the power and prestige of England in the world.
3. Restoring vitality to English trade as part of the strategy in making the nation economically self-sufficient.
4. Enriching the particular sponsors of the ventures through the profits that would accrue.
5. Alleviating social and political problems by drawing off idlers and vagrants into the colonising venture.

As an aside, it is important to note that the elements of the rationale speak eloquently of the socioeconomic state of England at the time of her entry into the New World. It also indicates the substantial contribution the New World colonies made to the late rise of the British empire.

By 1607, the false starts of Roanoke, inspired by Sir Walter Raleigh in 1585, had been almost been forgotten (Oberg 1994). Circumstances had changed and with them public support in the form of a London joint stock company, the Virginia Company, which financed the venture to establish an English colony in Virginia. Within a few short years English colonies were established on the east coast of the Americas from Newfoundland to Barbados (Cremin 1970). While the gospel was officially the first priority, the venture's organisational form and financing as a stock company clearly implied that profit rather than piety was the pre-eminent concern. Hakluyt was a director of the company, and possibly because of his insistence on the religious aspect of the mission, and the insistence of James I that the gospel be preached, he was appointed rector of the parish of Virginia, although he never set foot in the New World.

Beginning with Virginia, and Jamestown in 1607, the Southern colonies were established with a multiplicity of religious, political, economic, and social goals. The only objective that targeted any aspect of the colonies themselves was the mission to spread the gospel to the natives. All other objectives sought the interest and advancement of England. The missionary objective was entrusted to the English national church, the Anglican Church. This was the thin veneer of piety that overlaid the political and profit motives that prompted private and public sponsorship of the venture. The plantation was the major instrument of profit and power. A motley combination of English aristocratic families and men of uncertain character constituted its personnel.

The North Eastern colonies of New England were founded on a somewhat different basis. Starting with the Plymouth colony, but led by the Massachusetts Bay colony, the Puritans were retreating to the wilderness of the New World to perfect their version and vision of the Christian faith. While they genuflected appropriately to the profit motive, piety was their mission. The venture was planned and executed mainly by the laity covenanting among themselves and with God, to be exemplars of the Protestant faith. Christian zeal was tempered with learning. Among these dissenters against the English national church were many young intellectuals, particularly graduates of Cambridge (Cremin 1970). Their dissenting views as Puritans were not born so much of emotion, as it was informed by learning and rooted in conviction. Sullivan (1946) put the matter diplomatically in her observation that for all their sterling qualities, truth is best served by noting their intolerance.

The Puritans were those members of the English National Church who advocated carrying the Reformation to its logical conclusion. They were against the majority sentiment of compromise, between Rome and the Reformation, which in their opinion left the church 'half popish'. They wished to abolish the ecclesiastical order, except for the parish priest, abolish the Book of Common Prayer and all set prayers, and reorganise the church either on the basis of a hierarchy of councils, or free federations of congregations (Morison and Commager 1942). They abhorred idleness, eschewed mysticism and frowned on monasticism.

Using the mechanism of the joint stock company, the Puritans of the Massachusetts Bay colony bought all the stocks, obtained a charter from Charles I, and voted to transfer charter, government and members, to New England. In other words, the Puritans redirected the instrument of material gain to serve their interest for self-determination. Unlike the Virginia Company, whose charter and directors remained in England, the Puritans of Massachusetts transferred governance to their colonial location. Decision-making was internal and not external to them. Along with the Pilgrims of the Plymouth colony they inspired a migration of Englishmen often without official sponsorship or blessing.

The Puritans were English but they did not come to the New World to advance the imperial power of England, although they were careful to maintain colonial ties. They did not come to Christianise the Indians, although they did more than most to convert them. They came to perfect the Christian faith among themselves. They had no interest in ecumenical co-operation with any other set of believers. They were sure about the truth they possessed and the God they embraced. Their objective was to develop and demonstrate a new England as congregations of confessing Christians living the new covenant in Christ. Piety not plunder, profit or power was their driving force. Profit was honourable only if it was honestly made.

Between the Puritan Northeast and the Anglican South were the Middle Colonies of New York, New Jersey, Maryland and Pennsylvania. English Catholics founded Maryland under a land grant and charter from Charles I in 1632. The other colonies were composed of Protestants, but of various denominations and nationalities, including Dutch and Walloon Calvinists in New Amsterdam, Scottish and Irish Presbyterians in New Jersey; English Quakers in Philadelphia; English Baptists, English Methodists and Swedish Lutherans along the Delaware; and German Lutherans, Mennonites, Dunkers and Reform Church in the mountains of Pennsylvania (Cubberly 1947).

The Middle Colonies were not only located geographically between the Puritan Northeast and the Anglican South, but they occupied the middle ground of piety. The Puritan colonies were characterised by the singularity of passionate, pious purpose that usually marks dissenting sects. The Anglican colonists genuflected appropriately to piety but were busily seeking to satisfy the colonising intentions of the Crown, the profit expectations of the stockholders financing the plantations and personal gain. The Middle colonies were not beholden to such external motives, but neither were they sects perfecting their version of the Christian faith. Rather, they were communities of believers retreating from religious persecution in England and Europe, determined to preserve the integrity of their beliefs in their newly chosen locations in the New World.

The Puritans of the New England and the Anglicans of Virginia and the South shared one important common feature. Their populations were by and large homogenous in terms of ethnicity and religious persuasion. They were English. In this respect they were different from the Middle Colonies who were heterogeneous with respect to ethnicity and pluralistic with respect to denominational persuasion. This factor, combined with the religious and motivational differences between New England and the South, shaped the educational systems that developed in colonial America and the teaching occupation that developed within them.

THE EDUCATION SYSTEM OF NEW ENGLAND

With the exception of Rhode Island, the New England colonies were organised as theocratic governments. The colonial government and the church were one. There were no differences between civil and canon law. Clergymen and politicians were usually the same people. As Cremin (1970) observed because the New England colonies were founded on the premise of permanent self-sustaining communities from the beginning they embraced the institutions of family, church, school, university and print shop. With clarity of vision and purpose they set about establishing English customs, ideas, language, literature and law, recast in and justified by Calvinist theology.

Within the life-span of the first generation of settlers they had not only begun implementation of a school system based on the concept of communal responsibility, but enacted legislation to ensure its continuation. Legislation of 1642 and 1647 established the model in the Massachusetts Bay colony, that was followed by Connecticut in 1650, and became the pattern for the entire region. The Massachusetts Bay Colony legislation of 1642 and 1647 resembled laws enacted by the Scottish Parliament in 1616, 1633 and 1646 that were of similar intent (Anderson 1995). These laws prescribed the following:

- That all children would be taught to read and understand the principles of religion and laws of the colony.
- That all colonists would arrange to settle in towns.
- That all towns of fifty households would appoint teachers to instruct children in reading and writing.
- That all towns with one hundred or more households would establish grammar schools for instruction in Latin.
- That the colony would support a college of advanced learning and perpetuate it to posterity.
- That each church would have a pastor and a teacher whose duty it was to systematically expound Christian doctrine through biblical exegesis.

The extent to which public purpose and private commitment coincided in the early period of the Puritan colonies is demonstrated by the fact that while the legislature had decreed the development of a college and embarked upon the enterprise, the Rev. John Harvard left half of his estate to assist with its construction. In appreciation of this gift, the decision was taken to name the public college in honour of this private benefactor.

It must be noted that the efforts to establish Harvard College, opened in 1636, predated the efforts to establish public primary and secondary education. While the time span between the two was short, a mere matter of a decade, notwithstanding the Protestant tenet that every one should read the scriptures for themselves, educational development in New England followed the top-down sequence previously noted in the evolution of education historically. The purpose of Havard, and all early colleges in the United States, was to train learned men for the Christian ministry. The curriculum covered Latin, Greek, Hebrew, Bible, Logic, Rhetoric, Dialectic, Mathematics and History of a chronological type. New England colleges were modelled on Cambridge, particularly Magdalene College.

From this beginning the New England colonies founded a total of four colleges during the colonial period. The three others were Yale in Connecticut in 1701, Brown in Rhode Island in 1765 and Dartmouth in New Hampshire in 1769. The Congregational Church founded Yale and Dartmouth, while the Baptists founded Brown.

The collectivist pattern of education established in New England was that of teaching reading and religion to all children. This was to be followed by Latin grammar schools for boys who began their preparation for public occupations and higher learning. At the apex of the system were the English type colleges, modelled largely on Cambridge University. Higher education was vocational training for clergymen provided in the long established tradition of classical and liberal education. This was a communal system of schooling paid for by taxpayers. However, Puritan intention proved more ambitious than their capacity to sustain the system they had so clearly and comprehensively conceived.

Four factors undermined full implementation and maintenance of the collectivist school system established in New England.

- King Philip's war of 1675–78, while punishing the Indians and easing the pressure, itself extracted a heavy price both in the destruction of many towns and in the cost of the troops to the colonies, of over 500,000 pounds.
- They were poor. These agricultural colonies were centred largely on subsistence farming.
- Inland settlements moved away from the coastal towns in which the schools were located and the scattered nature of these settlements posed enormous problems for schooling.
- The rise of younger generations that knew neither religious persecution nor the zeal engendered by vigorous challenge to their faith. These later generations became more preoccupied with facing up to the economic and commercial challenges of life in the New World, rather than demonstrating piety to the Old World.

While these factors constrained the full realisation of the potential of the school system conceived and implemented by the Puritan fathers, they left the foundations firmly in place. More than the school system established was the belief and commitment to education that was engendered in the people of New England. They became in time the apostles of education in America, even if the religious zeal of the younger generation did not match that of their forebears.

THE EDUCATION SYSTEM OF THE MIDDLE COLONIES

The Middle Colonies adopted the policy of leaving education for the churches to organise relative to the ethnic communities that were their adherents. Consistent with Protestant beliefs, the various denominations held to the view that all Christians should be able to read the Bible for themselves. On paper the educational policy was therefore to provide schooling for all children. Each denomination was free to organise schooling, as it deemed appropriate.

The pattern of schooling within the Middle Colonies was for denominations to organise parochial schools under the auspices of local churches within their particular communities. This parochial system of schools combined both fee paying and charity schools. The former were schools that catered to children of parents who could afford to pay for the instruction of their children. The latter catered mainly to those members of the particular denomination unable either to teach their children themselves or to pay fees for these services. Denominations differed on the financial arrangements for the funding of their charity schools. Boys and girls were offered basic education in reading and religion in both types of schools.

While several denominations in the Middle Colonies attempted to establish Latin grammar schools, it was the Quakers and Lutherans who were most successful and made the most substantial efforts to sustain them, (Cubberly 1947). The oldest school was the William Penn Charter School of Philadelphia founded possibly as early as 1683, (Good 1956). There were several other Latin schools, including the Log College operated by the Presbyterians and the schools operated by the Lutherans. Some schools like the Anglican school of Philadelphia did not survive until the end of the colonial period. New York City had difficulty in sustaining grammar schools. The last grammar school that operated there during the colonial period ceased operation in 1737. To receive grammar school education boys of New York had to go elsewhere.

The denominations of the Middle Colonies founded a total of four colleges during the colonial period. Princeton in New Jersey was founded by the Presbyterians in 1746, followed by Kings College in New York in 1754 and Pennsylvania in Philadelphia in 1755, both founded by the Anglicans, and Rutgers in New Jersey founded by the Dutch Reformed Church in 1766 (Tewksbury 1965).

While the Middle Colonies were never as systematic or organised in their educational policies, planning or provisions as the New England colonies, they developed schools and colleges which, despite the vicissitudes of the times, survived in some recognisable form.

EDUCATION IN THE SOUTHERN COLONIES

Virginia and the Southern colonies while adhering to the Protestant principle of universal literacy for the purpose of reading the Bible followed the Anglican position, which was that this responsibility rested solely with the family. Public education was only provided through philanthropy, where families were unable to fulfil their primary responsibility.

The English had long developed ideas about the deserving and undeserving poor. The former were those who had some standing in society but had fallen upon hard times, while the latter were those who were deemed to have brought poverty upon themselves through vice or idleness. Generally women and children were more likely to be classified as the deserving poor. Within Southern plantation society the objects of educational charity were White boys of the deserving poor. The instruments of charity were usually the Anglican Church or endowments from individuals expressing posthumous educational concern.

The general pattern of education in the South was for wealthy families to provide private tutoring for their children for the early stages of education. Many then sent their children to England to complete their education. The modestly affluent families patronised private schools. Generally the poor received little or no education, except for a few poor white boys who were allowed entry to the free charity school provided by the Anglican Church or some endowment.

Latin grammar schools were also established in the South in a few large towns. They served the same purpose and followed the same form and curriculum as their counterparts in the other colonies, and in England from which the institution was transplanted.

The only college founded in the South was William and Mary in Virginia, founded by the Anglicans in 1693. In keeping with the differences that marked New England from the South, William and Mary was modelled on Oxford and not Cambridge. While the difference would be regarded as slight to any external observer, to the English and their American descendants of the colonial era, that difference was highly meaningful.

The general axiom in the South was that slavery and formal education were incompatible. Indeed, even, reading and writing were considered subversive activities among slaves. Laws not only prohibited teaching reading and writing to the slaves, but also banned them from acquiring such competence by teaching themselves. Slaves did not lack formal education by default or neglect; they were deliberately and intentionally denied it. This grim educational reality of American slavery cannot be sugar coated. Whatever may have been its African origin, the oral tradition was an institutionalised aspect of Southern slavery. While selective aspects of Christianity were permitted to be taught by carefully chosen Black and White preachers, all instruction had to be given orally.

AMERICAN COLONIAL EDUCATION: A BRIEF PROFILE

By the end of the colonial period both American society and education had acquired definite forms that mirrored each other.

- Formal education was restricted mainly to people of European ancestry. Indians received very limited educational opportunities. Most of the people of African ancestry were excluded mainly because of slavery.
- The purpose, focus and content of education was Christian, and decidedly Protestant. The Catholic version of Christian education was officially banned.
- The institutions providing education were transplanted almost entirely from England.
- The institutional forms were uniform at the college and secondary levels. Latin grammar schools provided the latter, while nine English type colleges provided the former.
- Three distinct regional patterns existed in delivering basic education. These were the collective and communal responsibility approach of New England, the parochial and denominational approach of the Middle Colonies and the philanthropic/charity approach of the South.

The sequence of colonial education was that of zealous and Herculean efforts to establish schools and colleges in the initial period of the founding of the colonies. This was particularly the case with the New England Congregationalists. This initial idealistic period was then followed by decline as the realities of settler life took their toll on the utopian and idealistic formulations. In the end the War of Independence ravaged much of the infrastructure that had been laid down. The involvement of teachers and students in the war interrupted the normal sequence of educational continuity, at least for a time. Notwithstanding these vicissitudes, the colonial era laid the conceptual foundation for education by allowing ideas and ideals largely borrowed from England to be tested in the crucible of New World reality. The experience and confidence gained from this exposure proved invaluable in the post-independence period of construction of the nation.

It is necessary to make some further observations on four aspects of the profile outlined above.

- The English dominance of the founding of American society,
- The transplanting of institutions from England to the colonies.
- Those legally excluded from the education process.

- The pattern of educational efforts directed at the Indians. Each will be commented on briefly in turn.

The English were dominant in the colonial period not only because of authority of imperial sponsorship by Britain, or primacy in arrival but also by virtue of numerical majority. At the time of the first census of the American population in 1790 people of English ancestry constituted 83.5 per cent of the White population, Scots 6.7 per cent, Germans 5.6 per cent, Dutch 2.0 per cent, Irish 1.6 per cent, French 0.5 per cent and miscellaneous others the remaining 0.1 per cent. The New England states varied between 93 and 96 per cent of their population being of English ancestry and 98.5 to 99.8 being British (Cubberly 1947). English hegemony in the colonies was based on three cornerstones: primacy as founders, numerical dominance and their kinship relationship to the imperial power.

The educational institutions transplanted by the colonists revealed mixture and variety and did not constitute strictly one to one correspondence in either place or time. Most of the institutions transplanted were created in England prior to the Reformation. These included the reading or primer school, endowed or charity school, apprenticeship, writing school, Latin grammar school and college. The reading or primer school taught reading and religion. Instruction was tied to progression from horn-book to primer to Psalter to Testament and culminated with instruction in reading the Bible (Monaghan 1988). The writing school admitted students who had learned to read and taught them writing and arithmetic usually in anticipation of a career in commerce. The Latin grammar school, the English college and apprenticeship all took the forms and taught the content established for such institutions in England, and Western Europe generally.

The only post-Reformation institution transplanted to colonial America was the dame school, transposed as school dames. Two factors seem related to the adoption of this institution particularly in New England in the early eighteenth century. First, town authorities became concerned that some children were arriving at the town schools unable to read. Second, as settlements spread outside of towns, and as towns got larger the distances young children had to travel became much greater. To rectify these problems some housewives, school dames, were contracted by town authorities to provide reading instruction, in their homes, to young children unable to travel long distances (Monaghan 1988).

Not all the ideas informing colonial education were drawn from England. The collective and communal idea of education was neither Catholic nor Anglican. That is, it did not originate in either pre or post-Reformation England. It was a Calvinist idea first implemented on the continent, and then in Scotland. This is illustrative of a more general observation. While colonial education had a strong overlay of ethnic derivations, it also had audible undertones of faith. The transplanting not only involved imitation of the past, but mixture with contemporary developments in Western Europe particularly Britain. Further, it involved adaptations of these to New World conditions.

Slavery and its laws excluded people of African ancestry from education. Catholics were not excluded from education per se. However, the Catholic faith was precluded from being taught, and persons holding to the Catholic faith were excluded by law from teaching. Catholics could only be educated on Protestant terms. In a nutshell, education in colonial America was not designed to be inclusive. Though inspired and informed by Christianity, the Christian ethnos of 'whosoever will' was not translated into the ethic upon which American colonial education was premised. The lofty Protestant ideals enunciated by Luther, Erasmus, Calvin and Knox, which inspired heroic actions on the part of some, including martyrdom, were shown to have feet of clay by some of its most zealous exponents on American soil. Race and Protestant confession were prior conditions to the receipt of educational grace.

The position of the Indians requires special comment. Indians were the adversaries from without. They were the peoples whose land and territories were being expropriated by the colonists, often involving brutal and bloody battles. In large measure they were not part of the colonial society. At the same time they were official objects of missionary attention. Both the New England colonies and Virginia raised money in England for the purpose of their education. Wright (1988) has made the serious charge that colonists eager to maintain their fledgling institutions and settlements, capitalised on the religious fervour of the English at home by raising funds for projects to convert and educate the heathen Indians while neglecting to fulfil the terms of the pious mission. He cited four instances in which this pattern played out itself in colonial America.

First, the charter of the Virginia Company included the objective of converting the Indians. Early in its operations plans were drawn up for erecting a college. In 1617, with royal sponsorship it was arranged for Pocahantas, the only Jamestown Indian convert, to visit England in promotion of the cause. By 1620, the public subscription for the college had reached £2043. In 1620 the treasurer of the Company, Sir Edwin Sandys, postponed plans to establish the college, diverted three quarters of the funds collected to other purposes, some of which benefited plantations and commercial enterprises in which he had interest. When the 1622 Indian uprising put an end to the project, most of the funds had already been misappropriated.

Second, later when the College of William and Mary was established in 1693, the mission of Indian conversion and education was included in its charter. The trustees of the Boyle legacy granted an annuity for this purpose. During the 50-year presidency of the founder, who had secured the bequest, no serious effort was made to either convert or enrol Indians in the college although the funds were used to construct a library, buy books and support the education of English students. Following his death in 1743, the new president, in that very year admitted five Indians to the college. The college historian concluded that the bequest had served as an item in the ledgers through which charitable funds could be funnelled to extraneous activities.

Third, prior to the founding of Dartmouth the Rev E. Wheelock had operated the Moor's Charitable School for Indians. Through the visit between 1765 and 1768 of Samson Occum, his Indian protégé, to England and Scotland £12,000 were raised for the purpose of establishing an Indian academy to train missionaries and schoolmasters. Having received a charter and land grant Wheelock relocated to New Hampshire. However, the residents of the latter expected a college to train English clergymen for the Congregational church. To gain access to the funds raised in Britain Wheelock ensured that the charter of Dartmouth stated that the college would exist for the education and instruction of the Indian tribes and also English youth and any other. However, the enrolment of English students outnumbered Indians three to one, and by 1774, the entire subscription had been exhausted in violation of the original intention of creating an endowment. To that time £12,000 was the largest subscription ever raised for a college. Occum insisted that he had been used as a tool to raise the funds, that he had been warned in England that the money would not be used for the purpose for which it had been raised, and that the terms of the subscription had been violated.

Fourth, in 1653 with funds for the Society for the Propagation of the Gospel in New England, an Indian college was constructed at Harvard, which was completed in 1656. The original plan called for facilities for six students costing £100. Facilities constructed cost £400 and could accommodate more than 12 students. The first Indian students entered the college in 1660 and at no time were there more than two students at the college. The facilities were not left idle, but served the purpose of educating English youths.

The relationship between the colonists and the Indians during the colonial period set the pattern that was to be repeated over and over again. It was that of public promise of assimilation and inclusion on the basis of equality, against private self-serving violation of the commitments made. Unlike the Africans, the Indians were accepted as equals, that is, on paper and in promise, in actual fact that equality remained principle and never became performance. The Indians were, for the most part, willing recipients of missionary benevolence.

TEACHERS IN THE COLONIAL PERIOD

It has been shown that types of schools and the content of education in the American colonies did not differ substantially among the colonies or from their English prototypes. Moreover, schooling remained an activity in its aims and content that was almost totally related to the objectives of the church. The main differences were with respect to the organisational framework employed by the church in the different colonies. These organisational differences had important implications for the composition of the teaching force.

The greatest uniformity within the colonies was at the college level. Colleges existed to train clergymen of the respective denominations that founded them. As was the case in England, the occupation of teaching remained within the clergy at the college level. College teaching was one of the assignments within the clergy, like the pastorate. The clergy, and the college students were all male.

At the level of the Latin or English grammar school, the teachers were clergymen or persons who had received training for the clergy but did not take holy orders. At this point there was some separation between teaching and the clergy. But even here that separation was not complete. However, there were several men who pursued careers as teachers who were not clergymen. Cubberly (1947) recorded that in several small towns grammar school teachers also doubled as town clerks, as well as performed several ministerial duties. Given the fact that in several colonies the church and government were not separated, it is not unreasonable to conclude that the teaching at the grammar school was only partially separated from the clergy. It should be noted that the English pattern of excluding girls from grammar schools was continued in the colonies. Grammar schools students were boys and the teachers were men.

The greatest separation of the teaching occupation from the clergy was at the lowest level of the school system. At this level also there was the greatest diversity with respect to the teachers. New England town schools provided for teaching as a career outside of the clergy. The pattern was for men to be employed as the teachers of these schools. They were selected on the basis of religious faith, character and teaching competence. Writing schools taught by scriveners also provided teaching careers for some men, who sometimes conducted schools on an itinerant basis.

The point was already made that as settlement spread inland in the eighteenth century, and as towns became larger school dames were employed to teach young children, up to about age seven. Children taught by school dames at the early ages then moved to be taught by masters in town schools which mainly enrolled boys (Monaghan 1988). This was the first opportunity available for women as teachers in the colonies. School dames, teaching a small number of their students at homes, were usually married women or widows.

Teaching in the Middle Colonies varied somewhat from New England. The denominational parochial system kept teaching at all levels of education closely integrated with the work and personnel of the churches. Many of the teachers in the parochial schools combined school teaching with such church functions as choristers, sextons and bell-ringers. The parochial system served to preserve teaching in a state very akin to pre-reformation England and Europe. The differentiation of the teachers at the basic level noted in New England, from being directly employed by the churches to being employed by town authorities controlled by the church, did not take place in the Middle Colonies largely because of their denominational parochial system.

In the Southern colonies servitude and profit combined to produce some aberrant forms of school organisations as well as unusual sources of teachers. The teachers of the Anglican vestry schools, run for the deserving poor white boys of the parish, bore strong resemblance to their counterparts of the parochial schools of the Middle Colonies. Teachers of the few endowed schools, established for the same clientele as the vestry schools bore closer similarities to the town school teacher of New England. They were employed by the trusts and not the church and therefore not part of the religious establishment.

Servitude and profit were not confined to the Southern plantation, nor exploitation confined to people of African ancestry. Unknowingly drawing on the precedent of ancient Greece where many teachers were slaves, Southern enterprise produced an American version of that genre by using indentured servants as teachers. Many poor Englishmen who in search of a better life in America sold four of five years of service in return for their passage. The purchasers of indentured men of some learning, either leased them out or set them up as private teachers, and took all of the proceeds from the teaching service given (Sedlak 1989). Newspapers carried many advertisements of teachers for let and, not unexpectedly, notice of runaway teachers. Teaching was not an unprofitable business. Some indentured youths were apprenticed by their owners to learn the trade of schoolmaster (Cubberly 1947). In a bizarre way, this represented the most complete separation of teaching and teachers from the clergy and the church in colonial America.

AMERICAN INDEPENDENCE AND NATIONAL CONSTRUCTION

The Republic of the United States of America marked a paradigm shift in political organisation. It represented three simultaneous experiments: independence from colonial subjugation, republicanism, and federalism. None of these ideas were new, but their combination was unique. The fulcrum of the shift was republicanism. It was not simply that the monarchy had been dispensed with, and aristocracy abolished. The shift was not negative it was positive. Neither was it an imitation of the Roman Republic, it was creating a new future in political organisation. The positive, creative and futuristic essence of the shift was the enthronement of the sovereignty of the people in constitutional law, the conception of the state as their servant and the establishment of individual human rights, at least on paper. The American Republic is a convenient marker of the end of the Religious Age, and in its place the rise of the era of Nation State civilisation. The religious civilisations of Western Christian Europe, Eastern Christian Europe and Islam were on their deathbeds, but in 1776 it was the United States that was not expected to survive. The new nation's demise was widely anticipated.

The new era dawned with the rapid rise of the nation states of Western Europe, with the British nation becoming one of the great imperial powers of history. They rose from the obscurity and gloom of the Religious Age to become the ruling powers of the era of the Nation State and in the process dominated the worlds that the Iberians had connected. The American nation while part of this constellation was marginal. The central powers were located in Western Europe. Burdened with debt it thought it could never repay, racked with secessionist threats based on state rights and buffeted by nations still holding to monarchy and aristocracy, the fledging Republic meandered in its first fifty years as it addressed the challenges of nationhood. Indeed, for the next hundred years, the nation building process was no triumphant march, but painful starts then stops, a few reversals and always punctuated with violence either through full scale war, or by semi-serious riots, or by common brawls or gunfights, the latter becoming the trademark of the Western frontier.

The nation-state is defined largely in terms of its political, social and cultural imperatives. Politically it is marked by sovereign government premised upon the consent of nationals by ballot, or bullet, or some combination of both. In other words, upon varying degrees of the mixture of freedom and coercion deemed necessary to make communal living operationally feasible. Socially it is marked by allegiance, identity and solidarity of the nationals, which takes precedence over all other loyalties. Embedded in these cohesive bonds are notions of social equality, equal rights and justice since all share the same relative equality in relation to the nation and the bonds that bind them as nationals. Culturally the nation is marked by unifying symbols of flag, anthem, mores and national myth clothed in spiritual qualities difficult to specify, but firmly held.

The point has already been made that while the Republic of the United States may appear uniquely American it was quintessentially Western European. The entire colonial history of the United States, from Plymouth Pilgrims to Revolutionary war, represented the transformation of Western Christendom from the Reformation to the French Revolution. The first marked the challenge of the laity for supremacy in the church, and the latter the claims of commoners to sovereignty in the state. Both were but different sides of the same coin: the demand of ordinary people to share rulership of church with the clergy and of the state with lords and kings.

However, the issues involved went far beyond sharing governance. It included equity in the distribution of wealth created by society. Further, its scope included profound ideological questions about the church as the repository of truth, the monarchy as the embodiment of the state and ethics as the nexus between church and state. All of these issues that tore Western Europe apart, including civil and national wars were played out on the American stage. The absence of an entrenched landed aristocracy, colonial status and transatlantic location combined to facilitate more clear-cut resolutions of these thorny issues on American soil.

The European character of American nationhood is clearly marked by the nature of the War of Independence and the negotiations of the Peace of Paris. First, it was a European war fought on American soil. The British and Dutch fought on one side, while the French and Spanish fought on the other and Americans fought on both. The English at home were as divided as the Americans in the colonies. The British government found a disinclination of Englishmen to fight their kin, and hired German mercenaries in appreciable numbers. Second, as Morison and Commager maintained, the War of

Independence was actually the first American Civil War. Americans loyal to the Crown fought rebel patriots. This fractured the colonial society in all regions, of all strata, of all ethnic groups and of all religious persuasions. Without American loyalists the British would have had to capitulate to American Independence almost immediately. Without French assistance the patriots could not have succeeded. Even General Washington despaired of public support for the cause (Morision and Commager 1942). The Peace Treaty of Paris did not represent a capitulation of imperial power as a consequence of overwhelming and resounding victories by American forces. Rather, it was a carefully crafted negotiated settlement that incorporated geopolitical interests of the contending powers of Western Europe with all the trade-offs and compromises that accompany such exercises in international diplomacy.

Ironically, while being quintessentially Western European, the United States was the pariah among the new nations of Europe by the turn of the nineteenth century. This was largely because of her Republican status and democratic rhetoric which was offensive to the monarchs and aristocrats, royalty and lords. America was not only a nation of commoners, but held to the view of its manifest destiny to bury all monarchies. Given the ideological polarities of the times, the United States was the militant leftist of the emerging Western European constellation of nations.

Early American nationalism was buffeted with external claims of its inferiority, compared to the monarchies of Europe with their sophisticatedly manicured aristocracies. The obvious disparities of wealth and the recent colonial history did nothing to engender American self-esteem. It could even be argued that wealth and a longer history of independence have not entirely changed the situation and that some undertones of European superiority and American inferiority still mark transatlantic intercourse, even on the part of some Americans. The point to note is that at the turn of the nineteenth century American nationalism had no countervailing compensation or consolation in either military might or material success.

Whatever were the faults of the colonial churches in America, and the education they provided, they bequeathed to the new nation leaders who were aristocrats of learning. The Declaration of Independence, the Constitution of the United States and the process and manner of the construction of the latter are adequate testimony of this fact. Whatever were their faults, and the contradictions of their personal lives, the framers of the Declaration and the Constitution had both the courage and perspicacity to lift themselves sufficiently high above these limitations to enshrine in law the very means by which those contradictions could be eventually resolved. For that the Founding Fathers of the American nation are worthy of the highest commendation and are deserving the encomiums that have been showered upon them.

The principles they enunciated and enshrined in constitutional law were idealistic and noble. Liberty, equality and justice for all are among the loftiest goals of human society. To entrench and enshrine them in constitutional law speaks to idealism of the highest order. However, the omissions were glaring and pragmatic. Slavery was not mentioned, women were not included and the First Americans were not protected. To their credit the Founding Fathers did not justify these omissions as right. Their learning, morality and idealism precluded such perversity. At the same time they failed miserably and morally by not mentioning them as wrong. In the political compromises reached to secure unity between North and South, expediency dictated omission as the only course by which resolution of these issues could be finessed. The effect, however, was that the idealistic principles placed power firmly in the hands of the strong in American society and left the disadvantaged groups to the mercies of pragmatism and expediency. Probably, the Founding Fathers assumed that succeeding generations of Americans would be like them, an assumption that proved to be unfounded in several generations. The history of American nationhood, therefore, can be written from the intersection of principle, pragmatism and power and their implications for promise and performance, assumption and reality, advance and reversal.

It is against this background that the nineteenth century transformation of the American nation from its origin as loosely related colonies to integrated and united states must be examined. It is within this context that schooling was transformed and with it the teaching occupation. These are the circumstances in which teaching became a predominantly feminine occupation at the elementary school level and to a lesser degree at the secondary level. It is critical therefore to outline the major aspects of the transformation although only brief sketches are possible. Note has to be taken of the broad changes that took place in the United States during the nineteenth century with respect to religion, politics, the population, technology and the economy, culture and education. It will also be necessary to note the impact of wars in influencing various aspects of American society.

RELIGION AND THE REPUBLIC

At the time of the War of Independence nine states had established churches, and four did not: Delaware, New Jersey, Pennsylvania and Rhode Island. The Anglican Church was established in the southern states and part of New York, while the Congregationalists were established in Connecticut, Massachusetts and New Hampshire. The Constitution enshrined religious liberty, separating church from state, making religious observance a private and not a public matter. The nation as a whole followed the principles that had been long practised by Rhode Island and the Middle Colonies. States with established churches went through the process of disestablishment starting with New York, Maryland and North Carolina in 1776 and ending with Connecticut 1817, New Hampshire 1818 and Massachusetts in 1833 (Morision and Commager 1942). At Independence the Roman Catholic Church was almost illegal in several states, Methodists were still within the Anglican Church, while the Baptists and Presbyterians were the main dissenting churches campaigning for disestablishment.

Voluntary church membership probably is the most bland and understated representation of the meaning of disestablishment of state churches. Even in circumstances of coercion belief is voluntary, although nominal membership may be a statutory requirement. More to the point is that disestablishment of the churches, established the primacy of allegiance to the nation above all loyalties including religious commitment and the church. The nation was supreme and national allegiance pre-eminent. From the nationalist perspective, God served the nation. The axiom of the Religious Age that the state served God was disavowed. Constitutionally the Republic was agnostic. Within this framework all nationals were free to believe as they wished, although a close reading of the assumptions would suggest that the range of belief envisaged would be variations within the Judeo-Christian tradition.

Disestablishment also removed the churches, their clergy and laity, from the pinnacle of political power, by virtue of religion, and consigned churches to the status of one among many interest groups in society. Severed from state power the churches, particularly those that had been disestablished, not only had to compete with other interest groups in matters of state but also had to compete with other churches in matters of membership. The laity was strengthened and the clergy weakened, in that the latter were now dependent on the tastes, appetites and tolerances of the former. The pulpit had to be mindful of the people in the pew. Inspiration had to take account of interests and tenure unless the preacher was prepared to take the consequences. In this new configuration clergy had to be more sensitive to the needs and views of the laity.

While the Anglican Church had been established in the South, it was a dissenting church in New England; as such it had learned something about competing from the perspective of the challenger. The Congregational church was confined to New England as the established church and knew competition only from the perspective of the challenged. The Presbyterians, Methodists and Baptist were dissenting in all regions, and therefore best placed as the challengers of the status quo, at least at that time.

Douglas (1977) pointed out that in 1800 only one in 15 persons in the United States was a church member, while by 1850 one in seven persons reported church membership, notwithstanding the rapid increase in population over the period. Competition, resulting from disestablishment, appears to have energised the churches and increased their proselytising effectiveness. The denominations that had become dominant over this period were the Methodists, Baptists and Presbyterians: the dissenting evangelical churches. By the end of the nineteenth century, they along with the Catholics had become the major denominations in America. The Catholics had become the largest denomination mainly through migration; the others had arrived at their dominant position by evangelising zeal and effectiveness through revivals beginning with the Second Awakening early in the century. The Anglican and

Congregational churches that had dominated and defined American Christianity during the colonial period had become, within the nineteenth century, marginal denominations in the American nation.

The rise of the marginal dissenting denominations of the colonial period to dominance in the nation, and the descent of the dominant denominations of the colonial era to the margin, did not change the Protestant Catholic polarities even if the Constitution enshrined the rights of the latter to practise their version of Christianity. Other Protestant denominations were rivals, Catholics constituted the enemy. What emerged was a broad coalition between Protestants, particularly the evangelicals, which manifested itself in common societies promoting Sunday Schools, local and foreign missions and the production of literature, among other areas of collective endeavour. The broad contest between Protestants and Catholics centred on the question of which version of Christianity was more consistent with the Republic. The Protestant claim was that principal allegiance to and direction from the Pope and Vatican, authorities outside the nation, were inconsistent with the spirit and destiny of a Republic. Protestant Christianity, rooted in governance on American soil, was the true heir and spiritual guide of the Republic. Catholicism insisted that there was no inherent contradiction between itself and republicanism, and most specifically with the American Republic. Proof of that in time had to come from establishing some distance between American Catholicism and the Papacy.

This was no mere academic, theological or doctrinal debate. Passions ran high. In several instances they turned violent as was the case with the burning of the Ursuline convent and school in Charlestown in 1830, riots in New York in 1853 over replacement of the School Board of the Public School Society, the Philadelphia riots of 1850s associated with the visit of the Papal Legate, the Louisville riots and bloodshed just prior to the Civil War and the tarring and feathering of the Jesuit priest John Bapst (McClusky 1964). At the root of the animosity were compounding nationalistic, religious and social factors related to the rapid growth of the Catholic church through the large number of Catholic immigrants from Europe. The newly dominant dissenting denominations, fired with the fervour of winning the Republic for Christ through revivals, faced their new challenger, the Catholic Church, growing through the agency of immigration. The Protestant alliance closed ranks, and with evangelical zeal damned their new rivals as threats to the Republic by virtue of foreign allegiance, and incorporated in their mission saving the Republic from the popish Satan.

At the same time that the various Protestant denominations were both forming new alliances and fracturing along new fault lines of competition, science posed an ecumenical challenge to Christianity. While tensions between the church hierarchy and scientists can be traced to the time of Galileo, the fact is that most scientists were churchmen, at least nominally. The separation of science from the church was gradual, and followed the same general course related to the decline of the Religious Age and the rise of the Age of the Nation state.

The challenge of science to the church was broad based and pervasive. Reason and logic on the one hand and empirical reality on the other were combined to question all things that could not be reduced to sense experience, inductive probability or nomological deduction. This included both God and faith. In the crucible of scientific experimentation religious belief became little more than superstition. The debate was largely academic when the physical sciences dominated popular discussion, however, when the sphere of influence shifted to biology, through Darwin's Theory of Evolution, the rivalry between the church and the growing scientific community became more intense.

Science became the new popular religion: a rival claimant to truth, a new basis of accounting for societies including differences between them and a new framework for explaining human behaviour. Nowhere was the challenge more intensely debated than between the Genesis account of the origin of humankind and that of the Darwinian evolution. However, the more profound displacement of religion was with the explanation of phenomena in all facets of social and economic life. Objective, rational and empirically based explanations supplanted religious explanations and justifications in a multiplicity of areas even if the new science was only justifying prevailing prejudices. For example, several leading anthropologists, sociologists and biologists concluded from their empirical observations that the children of two mulattos were physically inferior, sickly, mentally feeble, effeminate and shorter lived compared to the offspring of pure races (Smits 1991). These empirical observations were explained theoretically by logical deductions from the theory of the superiority of pure strains and the resultant inferiority of hybrids.

Scientists began to replace the clergy as the chief advisors and confidants of power. The scientific establishment in the Age of the Nation State replaced the established church of the Religious Age. At best the scientific establishment cast itself as agnostic but in the main was atheistic. Religious scientists were by definition almost schizophrenic: atheistic in their scientific work but religious otherwise. Caught in the crossfire of religious dogma that often denied empirical reality and the scientific community that was fashionably atheistic, some scientists professing faith sought to resolve the seeming contradictions between reason and revelation. Likewise, churchmen recognising the virtues of scientific process also sought similar resolution. Similarly, some philosophers probing the interface between Christianity and science also attempted to synthesise faith and sense experience.

The genesis of these controversies was in Western Europe in the eighteenth century. There was nothing neat and tidy about the nature of the confrontation between scientists and churchmen. Churchmen denying science; scientists denying the existence of God; and philosophers, scientists and churchmen seeking reconciliation between the opposing positions all evolved together. Examples of the latter were John Locke the English philosopher, Sir Isaac Newton the English inventor of modern physics, and the Unitarians, a new

Christian denomination. They came to the same general conclusion. They affirmed the existence of God, conceived as a benevolent force, that had brought into being an ordered universe inhabited by reasonable humans who were capable of discovering and knowing God's laws and living by their dictates.

Cremin (1980) traced the translation of these ideas, emphasising the benevolence of God and the perfectibility of man, to the American Republic, first through the writing of Thomas Paine, particularly in his book *The Age of Reason* and then latterly through the works of William Ellery Channing and culminating in the Transcendentalist movement associated with Ralph Waldo Emerson. Whether Cremin's contention that the oft-repeated quip that Unitarian preaching was limited to the fatherhood of God, the brotherhood of man, and the neighbourhood of Boston was more clever than true may be the subject of great debate. What is almost beyond debate in that though small in size and restricted in its location, Unitarian ideology had an enormous effect upon the formation and ethos of American education.

Disestablishment had placed the Congregational church on the margin of the new nation The Unitarian offshoot of the Congregational church, like their Puritan forebears, moved to the frontiers of the emerging society. Those frontiers were the interface with science, the birth of popular culture founded on reading and writing, and the development of education appropriate to nation states. Like their forebears the Unitarians were not evangelical, but their theology was almost the opposite of that of their ancestors. Gone was the dogmatic Calvinism that preached exclusive election, eternal hell fire and the mission to defeat the great deluder Satan. In its place was an inclusiveness that accepted the perfectibility of all persons and held to the prospect of utopia here on earth. Gone also was the stern, authoritarian patriarch and in its place the innocence of children and the power of maternal love. Armed with this new liberal theology, in which love and freedom were conceived to have triumphed over fear and repression, Unitarians moved to face the challenges posed to Christianity in the nation state particularly as they pertained to science, popular culture and education.

Niebuhr (1935) scathingly criticised liberal theology as God without wrath, bringing man without sin into a kingdom without judgement through the ministration of Christ without a cross. Douglas (1977) took the position that liberal theologians had emasculated traditional theological thought. Stepping aside from value-laden judgements, what must be noted is that in nineteenth century America liberal theologians, led by the Unitarians of Boston, had systematically and in a scholarly manner cast Christian imagery and theology in feminine and not masculine terms. As such liberal theology made a fundamental break with Christian imagery as it had been fashioned in warring Europe and sought to refocus it upon the historical Jesus, who had made no claims of being a warrior.

In summary the transformation of Christianity in independent America could be traced as follows:

- The dislodgement of the Anglican and Congregational churches from the pinnacle of state power. All denominations became no more than interest groups within the nation.
- Religious freedom and with it, competition between the churches for membership.
- The rise of the dissenting Protestant denominations to the centre of religious life, replacing the Anglicans and Congregationalists.
- Increasing co-operation and coalition formation, among evangelical denominations in particular, as manifested by non-sectarian co-operation in establishing Sunday Schools, publishing Christian literature, creating home missions and providing education.
- Escalating antagonism between Protestants and Catholics, particularly as the latter grew in numbers and influence largely through immigration.
- The rise of science as an ecumenical challenge to Christianity, and indeed all religions.
- Liberal theology as a response, particularly by the non-evangelical Congregationalists, to both marginalisation as well as to the new challenges facing nation states and Christianity from science, popular culture and education.

POLITICS IN THE REPUBLIC

The church was much more easily detached from political power than the men of class and learning who had held it in every colony. The Federal Constitution established equality in law, but the law is subject to interpretation and the latter is often hostage to entrenched power. The writing of State Constitutions invariably involved confrontations between those who advocated a broader franchise and the conservatives who wished to preserve the more limited franchise based on of property and payment of taxes. As Morison and Commager pointed out the latter held considerable advantages in determining the content of State Constitutions. The most radical outcome was in Pennsylvania where a coalition of Irish, Scot and German frontiersmen along with workingmen in Philadelphia, led by Benjamin Franklin, successfully dispossessed the Quaker elite, and virtually enshrined White manhood suffrage as the franchise in that state. The contest in Pennsylvania not only had overtones of ethnicity and religion but also highlighted the East/West polarity that was to become a defining feature of American politics. At the time of the adoption of the Federal constitution only about 20 per cent of all adult White males were entitled to vote.

The issue of political franchise was ameliorated in the immediate post independence period by the fact that when the properties of the loyalists went on the market they depressed land prices to such an extent that significant land redistribution was effected as small farmers and others were able to acquire acreage at bargain basement prices. Many poor men were enfranchised through this route. However, up to 1815 only four states of the Union granted voting rights to all White males. The admission of Western states into the Union prompted change. These states, without old estates or large fortunes, invariably wrote White male suffrage into their constitutions. White male suffrage therefore became an issue in Eastern states. By 1825, only Rhode Island was without such a law among Northeastern states, although in both Massachusetts and New York there had been strong resistance to this empowerment of this landless, non-taxpaying and largely unlearned mass of White males.

The election of General Andrew Jackson as president in 1828 marked a turning point in American politics, as a sufficient number of states had enacted White male suffrage to allow the election of a 'man of the people'. All presidents before Jackson had been members of families that constituted the colonial elite and all except Washington had been college graduates. They all came from Massachusetts, New York and Virginia. Jackson had little more than basic education, and was from the West. He was elected by men who shared his social background and probably had less education. Jackson won handsomely again in 1832 and by that victory underscored the fact that the change represented a permanent shift in the nature of power and politics in the Republic. White male citizenship in the Republic was now enfranchised.

The social heirs of the Founding Fathers were the first to feel the full political force of the equality so eloquently articulated in the Declaration of Independence and Federal Constitution. Ironically, those who had created the framework of democracy, government of the people, for the people and by the people, did not trust the people. It took over fifty years before the people, through Andrew Jackson's election, gave warning that they would eventually 'seize the sovereignty that was theirs'.

Manhood suffrage was broadened to include Black men in 1869 following the Civil War, emancipation from slavery and consequential Constitutional amendments. However, subsequent challenges by states, and rulings by the Courts, led to limits of the franchise to Black men in several states, a course of action without parallel among whites and in Western democracies.

Women's suffrage did not materialise until 1919. This followed a long campaign for such rights that can be traced to Seneca Falls in 1848. In this matter the American Republic was following and not leading Western nations. England approved women's suffrage in 1918.

Worthy of note is the franchise, which is the most basic right in a Republic predicated on the principles of liberty and equality, took over 50 years to reach poor White men, just under 100 years for all Black men to be added then subtracted, and 143 years to be extended to all women. What is highlighted is not only the time lag between policy and implementation, but also the discrepancies between statements of principle and practice based upon those principles, when implementation is dependent on those who will be dispossessed by compliance with the intent of noble ideals.

Education was not mentioned in the Federal Constitution. Education was a matter for the states. The earliest Federal involvement with and sanction of education was in the tax negotiation with new states joining the Union. Beginning with Ohio in 1802, the Federal Government reached a compromise, which was extended to all new states, of land grants amounting to one sixteenth of the land of each township for the purpose of maintaining schools (Cubberly 1947). The only exception to this pattern was Texas, which joined the Union owning its lands. Essentially these land grants constituted an endowment for public schools. While they may have facilitated the establishment of some schools, they were not the basis upon which public education arose in the nation.

Cubberly (1947) made the point that White manhood suffrage, culminating in the Jackson Presidency, placed the issue of education appropriate for the Republic firmly on the national agenda. The newly enfranchised White males demanded public schooling from elected representatives at the State and municipal levels. He cited the case of the workingmen of Philadelphia in 1829 who asked each candidate for the state legislature to furnish them with a formal declaration of their intention to establish an equal and general education system in the state. He also cited similar action of the Association of Mechanics and Manufacturers in Providence, Rhode Island, seeking improved schools, smaller classes and improved pay for teachers.

Cubberly summarised the arguments for and against a public state school system that were advanced in the national debate on education following White manhood suffrage. The positive arguments in favour of a public state system of education were that it was:

- The civic responsibility of the state and a natural right of a citizens of a Republic.
- A modality by which the state could teach what was necessary for its welfare.
- A means of preventing crime and poverty.
- A way of promoting productivity and wealth.
- A method of preserving the values of the Republic.
- A mechanism of assimilating the immigrants and a necessity in promoting equality.

The negative arguments in favour of public schooling were that private and church schools could not by themselves cope with the demand for schooling. Charity schools stigmatised the poor. Religious schooling was impractical as the means of providing education in a nation marked by religious pluralism.

Arguments against a public system of education were that:

- Education was the sacred responsibility of parents to their children and as such brooked no intervention from the state.

- Defence of the Republic was the only area that warranted public taxation for its support.
- Education was a luxury of the leisured classes and the poor had no time for such luxury.
- It was the hidden hand of the clergy to recreate the state church arrangement.
- Taxing the industrious for the benefit of the indolent constituted an injustice.

Other arguments against state sponsored education were that it was impractical and unworkable, would promote people out of their place in society, would injure private and church schools, break down desired social barriers and require persons without children to pay for the education of their neighbours' children.

Cubberly's thesis that educational reform, creating universal public schooling, was the response to demands for appropriate education by newly enfranchised citizens and provided largely by a coalition of enlightened politicians and humanitarian interests has been substantially revisited and revised by historians beginning with Katz (1968). What cannot be disputed is that the political fall-out of enfranchisement was one of the factors that catapulted education as an item on the national agenda in the third and fourth decades of the nineteenth century. Schooling that had served the purposes of the church and for training its personnel proved inadequate to the requirements of the nation-state premised on equality. Political enfranchisement was one of the factors that brought church schooling into question.

DEMOGRAPHIC CHANGES AND THE REPUBLIC

The young Republic experienced four major demographic shifts. These were the steady reduction of the birth rate and family size of the native-born White population, the increasing influx of immigrants reaching a peak in the first two decades of the twentieth century, migration from rural to urban areas, and migration from East to West. Any one of these presented formidable challenges to the organisation of society; together they constituted challenges of monumental proportions.

Declining Natural Increase in the American Population

In 1800 the rate of live births in the United States was 7.04 per thousand. By 1900 it had been cut almost in half to 3.65 per thousand. At the end of the eighteenth century the average family had eight children, by 1850 family size had been reduced to five children. In 1780 childbearing among American women lasted on average 17.4 years, and mothers survived their last child by four years, on average. A hundred years later child bearing lasted on average 11.3 years, and mothers survived their last children by twenty years on average (Clifford 1989). These indicators all testify to the decline in the natural increase of the American population, and the corresponding improvement in the life expectancy of mothers.

Clifford observed that the decline in family size had profound effects on the nature and organisation of American households. Women's domestic workload was considerably lightened with less mouths to feed, clothes to make and persons to care for. The related phenomena of postponing marriage, having fewer children and increased longevity also had equally profound effects on society, in that women were available for roles that they had not previously played.

Apart from its domestic implications, declining rates of population increase among Americans implied constraints on the supply of native-born Americans to meet the demands of exploiting the vast natural and economic resources that remained untapped during the colonial period. The most immediate means of supplying the shortfall was immigration.

Foreign Immigration

In 1820, immigration to the United States was just a trickle, 8,385 persons. This was reflective of the pattern that prevailed up to that time. By 1825 the number of immigrants reached 50,000 per year. The numbers expanded to exceed the 100,000 mark by 1842. By 1847, immigration reached above 200,000 per year, and did not fall below this level for the next ten years, peaking at 427,833 in 1854. Indeed, except for two years during the Civil War in the 1860s immigration between 1842 and 1930 did not fall below 100,000 persons annually. The peak of the immigrant influx was between 1903 and 1914 when the annual numbers ranged from a low of approximately 750,000 to a high of 1,250,000. In the period 1820 to 1927 immigrants to the United States totalled 36,386,381 as recorded by the official records (Cubberly 1947). This ranks among the largest movements of people in history.

Given the discussion of Jewish education in previous chapters it is necessary to make some brief reference to the migration of Jews to America. The first Jewish immigrants to the United States in the 1650s were actually relocating from Brazil. Following a century of bloody persecution culminating in edicts of expulsion in Spain in 1492 and Portugal in 1497 many Jews in the Iberian peninsula fled to North Africa, Turkey and Italy. Some remained professing conversion to Christianity while privately continuing to practice Judaism. In the wake of concerted efforts by the church to root out crypto-Jews, through the Inquisition, many Jews fled to the New World. Some settled in Recife in Brazil. When Recife was taken by the Dutch in 1630 many Jews who had professed conversion to Christianity reverted to the open profession and practice of Judaism. When the Portuguese retook Recife they were obliged to flee, yet again. Most relocated in New Amsterdam in 1654 (Froner 1969)

In 1790 the total number of Jews in the United States was 1,500. This number increased slowly to 2,750 in 1820. From the 1830s the pace of Jewish immigration quickened considerably and by 1880 the Jewish population. totalled approximately 250,000, which was about 3.8 per cent of Jews worldwide. Most had come from Western Europe, particularly Germany. Between 1881 and 1930 more than 3,000,000 Jews entered the United States. By 1933 the Jewish population stood at about 4,500,000 representing 30 per cent of all Jews worldwide. The largest number were located in New York, which then could have been properly regarded as the Jewish capital of the world. In the migration after 1881 most of the immigrants had come from Eastern Europe particularly Poland and Russia (Ben-Horin 1969).

Yet again Jews had relocated in large numbers to the emerging centre of power in the world. However, in this instance the immigration of Jews was part of a larger movement of Europeans fleeing Europe for economic rather than political reasons. As such the Jewish relocation was nested in this more general surge.

The brunt of the immigrant influx, of all nationalities and ethnic groups, was to the cities of the Northeast. Between 1800 and 1850 the population of the city of New York increased ten fold (Kaestle 1973). In 1800 the United States was still a rural population, over 90 per cent of the people still lived in rural areas. The decades of the nineteenth century witnessed massive internal migration from rural to urban areas. Rural migrants met foreign immigrants mainly in the growing slums of Northeastern cities.

Rural Urban Migration and the Move Westward

The movement from rural to urban areas occurred at the same time that Americans began moving westward. Missionaries seeking to convert the Indians were among the first pioneers on the Western frontier. That pious mission did not stimulate mass movement. Yet with the movement of the Church of Latter Day Saints from Massachusetts to New York and from there through several stops to what proved to be their final destination in the Great Salt Lakes, the pious motive did make a Western statement that resulted in the creation of the state of Utah. In their withdrawal from established society, to perfect their version of the Christian faith, the Mormons were taking a similar path over land, to that of the Puritans over water two centuries before. Interestingly, the first mission field for the Mormons was England, from which came both financial contributions and people to create the New Jerusalem in the West.

Overpopulation in the Northeast had reduced farming to uneconomic levels, creating land hunger in that region. New England farmers began moving West to settle that relatively empty region. Southerners also moved West for similar reasons. While many communities, complete with families, church and school, moved West to establish farming settlements, this mass emigration from the East and South was characterised by the fact that it was overwhelming male. Thus, the internal migration within the United States created a situation in which the West had a high proportion of males, and the East in particular a correspondingly high proportion of females, although the American population as a whole showed no great gender imbalance.

The gold rush of the late 1840s stimulated the Westward mass movement by adding yet another powerful motive, instant wealth. The lure of gold, prompted the most frantic scenes as people from within and outside of America rushed to strike it rich. Persons from all levels of society abandoned their jobs and families, and even the pulpit, to join the frenzy. San Francisco went from village to city status almost overnight and California immediately became the final frontier.

Piety, land and gold not only fuelled internal migration, but also attracted immigrants. Immigration and internal migration were therefore compounded. While most of the immigrants first came to Northeastern cities, many soon moved westward to the new frontier. Piety attracted a minuscule number, mainly to the Mormon state. Land and gold proved much greater magnets. The overall effect was to change both the rhythm and the balance of American society as well as increase the tensions between the long established North East and the South East as each tried to perpetuate its way in the states being created in the West. It took civil war to resolve many of the contested issues embedded in these tensions.

CULTURAL DIVERSITY AND THE REPUBLIC

The combined effects of declining natural increase of the native born population, the major shift in population from rural areas to urban centres and from East to West, and the massive foreign immigration created not only cultural diversity not previously known in American society, but also the perceived threat of dilution of American culture and the fear of loss of control by those who, by descent, claimed authorship of American society. Added to this was the increasing polarisation of North and South as rival claimants of the American heritage. Each of these factors had multiple dimensions.

At independence the American population and society were agriculturally based, overwhelmingly British, English speaking and Protestant. Indians and Blacks were virtual outcasts of mainstream society. Fifty years later as immigration began to cascade, the bulk of the foreign immigrants were Europeans, speaking other languages than English, with a large proportion of Catholics and Jews. Catholics constituted approximately half the foreign immigrants. In 1800 Catholics numbered about 50,000 and were one of the smaller Christian denominations. By 1850 Catholic immigrants numbered approximately 2,000,000, by 1880 that number had tripled and by 1900 it had doubled again. In all there were approximately 18,000,000 Catholics among the approximately 36,000,000 immigrants who came to the United States up to the time massive immigration was stopped in 1930 (Leahy 1991). By 1850 immigration had made the Catholic church the single largest denomination in America.

The city of Boston best illustrates the impact of the cultural diversity imposed by immigration. With some justification Boston could claim to have been the Puritan capital of New England with respect to both its Congregational heritage and its predominance of English ancestry. In 1820 there were about 2,100 Catholic in Boston. By 1840 that number had increased to 32,000, then to over 200,000 in 1866, expanding to over 600,000 in 1896 and reaching 990,000 in 1929. Until 1880 the Catholics of Boston were mainly Irish, but thereafter they included French Canadians, Italians, Poles, Lithuanians, Portuguese and Syrians. At almost the same time that there was a hundred fold increase in the Catholic population of Boston, between 1820 and 1866, native-born people from rural areas of Massachusetts were migrating to Boston, and native-born people from Massachusetts, including Boston, were moving to the West. It is not hard to imagine that in these circumstances, Puritans of English ancestry remaining in Boston could have experienced some amount of distress, if not disquiet or even desperation, over the changed demographic and cultural circumstances. This was true not only of Boston but all major cities of the Northeast.

Another dimension to the diversity was that while the Puritan and Anglican variants of English culture were confined to the Northeast and Southeast, and therefore spatially separated, internal migration now brought them in touch with each other on common ground in the West. This was not merely a question of religious affiliation but the broader issue of competing Protestant heritages. The chosen symbol of the difference was the question of slavery. The free North was pitted against the slave South; Abolitionists of the North holding slavery to be a moral evil were matching wits and words with slave apologists of the South expounding the view that slavery was the greatest missionary enterprise in history for the prospects it offered for converting the Africans (Morris 1981).

With each new state added to the Union the contest was whether it would be allowed to have either a free or a slave constitution. In Missouri the Southerners won the day and that state was admitted into the union as a slave state. In Ohio the New Englanders had their way and it was admitted as a free state. The opening up of Missouri as a slave state diverted the southern migration there. Hence before long New Englanders spread their influence over the entire Northwest. While the practical differences to the lived experience of Blacks in the South or the North were modest, the symbolic difference was enormous. Above all, the principle at stake generated great heat and burning animosity. State by state a battle was fought concerning the principles upon which the new Southwestern states would be admitted to the Union. When the balance shifted in favour of the North when California was declared a free state, the South seceded from the Union, leaving civil war to bring resolution to the contested issue.

Added to the mix in many areas of the West was the overlay of immigrant cultures on top of the North-South polarity. The permutations and combinations of these mixtures depended upon how much of each ingredient was poured into the mix. Each Western state and each of its cities has some different variants, the English American culture was altered and enriched through interactions with the new elements in the American melting pot. However, the mix was not always perceived as enrichment by those of English- American heritage.

The Civil War of the 1860s settled the slavery question three decades after in had been resolved in the British empire. It also settled the question of which variant of English-American culture would dominate the American nation. However, the Civil War raised the question of the basis upon which Blacks would be integrated as full citizens within American society. White supremacy had been openly affirmed in the South, and tacitly accepted in the North. However, it was openly at variance with the premise of equality on which the society was founded, constitutionally. During slavery the issue was submerged, since slaves were property, however, with abolition the question of citizenship of Blacks could not be avoided.

It is against this background that White Americans of English ancestry and Protestant heritage came to regard Catholics, immigrants, Jews and Blacks as threats to the American way of life they claimed as their own. Response to this perception of threat was wide ranging. The least imaginative was that of nativism from groups like the Know Nothing Party, and later the Ku Klux Klan, who saw resolution of the issues in terms of intimidation violence and terror tactics laced with violence. Among the more creative were those who proposed reforms in education as the means of maintaining solidarity, identity and bonds of national unity across the diverse groups.

THE ECONOMY AND INDUSTRIALISATION

Depending upon perspective, one could say that underlying or overlaying the political, demographic, religious and cultural changes in the new American nation in the nineteenth century was its transformation from an agricultural to an industrial economy. In 1800 the United States was a poor, rural, unmechanised country with vast areas of virgin woodlands. The first sign of industrial transformation was in the application of the newly invented cotton gin to the production of cotton in a factory in Beverly, Massachusetts in 1787. However, up to 1804 there were only four cotton factories in New England. By 1831, however, there were 801 factories and cotton manufacturing was the biggest and fastest growing industry in the region (Cubberly 1947). Cotton, therefore, provided threads linking the factories in New England with the plantations in the South, creating increasing wealth for both regions in the early nineteenth century.

At the root of this transformation in mode of economic production were a series of different measures and developments.

- Beginning in 1807 embargoes placed on the importation of consumer goods and various protective tariffs imposed by Congress allowed several infant industries to supply the needs of the American market. The Napoleonic War in Europe that imposed its own de facto embargo on European exports helped this policy initially.
- The importation of European technology first in the form of the steamboat in 1809, the steam railroad in 1826, in the digging of the Erie Canal which opened in 1825 and the completion of a national turnpike to Vandalia, Indiana 1838, which revolutionised transport in the country. In 1826 there were only three miles of railroad. By 1840, three thousand miles of tracks had been laid, increasing to 9,021 miles in 1850 and 30,000 miles by 1860.
- Yankee ingenuity made its own contribution to industrial and domestic technology in the form of the threshing machine, mower, reaper, lock-stitch sewing machine, kerosene lamp, power loom, improved cooking stoves and the power hammer for working iron and steel.
- Attention turned to exploiting the vast natural resources of the country in timber, iron, oil and various minerals.

Almost all of the industrial wealth that was created was concentrated in the Northeast. The South remained firmly wedded to its plantations. The Western frontier became the national breadbasket, as New England farmers found greater acreage and virgin soil on which to grow their crops. As technology boosted economic growth and productivity, the demand for workers and capital grew. The local population could not supply and sustain the manpower demands of the expanding economy. While there were periodic downturns, the general trajectory of economic expansion and growth was positive. Migration was therefore an economic necessity, and in fact sustained industrialisation in America.

Numerous and voluminous tomes have been written about industrial revolution. Five brief comments seem warranted here.

- First, to find a parallel to the technological revolution which made the industrial revolution possible, in terms of its numerous inventions and widespread application to all aspects of life and endeavour, one has to go back in history to Sumer in the fourth millennium BCE. In a sense the term industrial revolution is a misnomer because all aspects of society were affected by the inventions and innovations including homes, entertainment, agriculture, transportation, warfare and of course manufacturing.
- Second, it is this revolution that has catapulted Western European civilisation, and particularly its English variant, to pre-eminence in the Age of the Nation-States and to claims of superiority over all

previous civilisations. The attempt to extrapolate this present position to all of recorded history, and to claim ancient pedigree is myth making, especially where this is intermingled with notions of race as currently defined in America.

- Third, the section of European society that can justifiably claim credit for this technological revolution was neither the warrior group or the farmers, but rather that section of European society nurtured by the church first as clergy and then as pious laity. It is this group that produced the vast majority of Episcopalians, evangelicals, liberal theologians, rationalists, atheists, scientists and artists. It a misnomer to refer to them as the middle class or a status group. What unites them is a piety, even where God is disavowed, which acknowledged a higher power, ethic or principle beyond political authority and personal need and a passion to find fulfilment in faithful service and adherence to that higher other.

- Fourth, the outcome of the technological revolution was the generation of collective wealth at a level that far exceeded what previously obtained. This increased wealth was by no means limited to the state. Indeed wealth rapidly accumulated in the hands of entrepreneurs, who were not always the inventors of the technologies generating the wealth. Massive private fortunes were made but at the same time the overall wealth of the nations increased and was sufficiently widely distributed to allow for the application of this bounty to various projects deemed vital to the future security and advancement of these new nations.

- Fifth, the United States was not among the industrial leaders of the Western world in 1800. In terms of industrial development the new Republic was still agricultural and dependent on European technology, which it imported generously. In the course of the next 150 years America moved from the margin of industrial development to become its central power. In addition to marginal energy released on American soil, two massive and debilitating World Wars were fought on European soil. Together they account for this transformation.

Industrialisation wherever it occurred brought with it rapid urbanisation with attendant social problems as cities were unable to cope with the massive relocation of rural or immigrant populations. Poverty, dislocation of family life, crime and prostitution were invariably correlates of overcrowded slums, dilapidated housing and poor sanitary facilities in those sections of cities in which the new arrivants were located. Coming against the background of the transition from the Age of Religion to the Age of the Nation State, it is not surprising to find that both the people and the circumstances were interpreted in strong religious and moral terms. The people affected by these conditions were often seen to be depraved. Urgent solutions were not only required but also demanded.

THE REFORM OF SCHOOLING IN THE NEW NATION

Against this background the circumstances in which schooling was reformed in nineteenth century America could be summarised briefly as two sets of interrelated but countervailing developments. First:

1. The replacement of the traditional White propertied and learned political leaders of the colonial period by landless White males of modest means and limited learning both as voters and leaders.
2. The relegation of Christian denominations to interest groups in the society, along with the displacement of the traditional denominations of the colonial period by the dissenting evangelical churches as the major Protestant tendencies in the country. Also the meteoric rise of the Catholic Church to become the largest denomination, stimulated broad-based Protestant coalitions opposed to the Catholic Church.
3. The rise of cultural diversity resulting from rural urban migration and East West migration internally, foreign immigration and the emancipation of the Blacks from slavery, at the same time that the rate of natural increase among native-born English Americans was declining.
4. The rapid rate of industrialisation and urbanisation that disrupted traditional family life, overburdened the physical infrastructure of cities and brought with it associated poverty, destitution, crime and prostitution.

The second set of developments was almost a mirror image of the first. If the former were conceived as negative, then these latter were decidedly positive. They were:

a) Enfranchised ordinary White males intent on more egalitarian policies in national affairs and the chastened former elite seeking to recover their lost position.
b) Energised evangelicals intent on redeeming the nation, the displaced traditional denominations committed to renewing themselves largely through a new liberal theology positioning itself on the frontiers of changes in the secular society; and the liberated Catholic church free to promote its teaching within the religious freedom guaranteed by the constitution.
c) Eager immigrants and emancipated freedmen intent on socioeconomic advancement and the full embrace of American citizenship.
d) Enriched citizens, cities and states able to afford social reforms from the earnings and wealth generated from industrialisation.

The combination of these two sets of interrelated and countervailing factors ensured not only the provision of educational opportunities but also the participation of the mass of the population. The critical issues were control of the formulation of educational policies, the content of schooling and the implementation of the consequential reform of schooling. It is in this context that the creation of the national system of education in the United States needs to be understood.

It must be immediately pointed out that the transition from church to national system of schooling did not begin with the leading and most powerful nations of Europe, England and France. Indeed, the first efforts to establish national systems of schooling came from the absolutist monarchies of Central Europe. Prussia introduced a compulsory national system of schooling in 1763, followed by Austria and Bohemia in 1774, although it took many years for these policies to achieve the intended objectives. The implementation of national systems in this instance was top down and not bottom up, as the centralised bureaucracies assumed responsibility for both policy and implementation.

Anderson (1995) listed the following motives as the inspiration for these European reforms:

i) The need for the state to establish more direct contact with citizens as serfdom became obsolete.

ii) To make religious piety and political loyalty dependent upon positive indoctrination rather than outward conformity.

iii) To foster the emerging sense of a national community.

iv) The need for a disciplined work force to support the industrialisation process.

v) Reinforcing the social barriers between elite and popular education.

From this listing it is clear that the motivation in Central Europe and America shared common features and displayed marked differences. In the United States education was not a federal but a state responsibility, where the state accepted such constitutional responsibility. The Southern states did not originally embrace such responsibility. State and church were being firmly held together, in Prussia and Austria, and not being separated as in the United States. Serfdom not slavery was the social Achilles heel. At the same time nationalism and disciplined workers were common themes.

In setting about educational reform in the first part of the nineteenth century, America was following some of the more marginal states of Europe. The denominational system of education still prevailed in England and France, the most industrially advanced nations of Europe. In a nutshell, fundamental reforms in schooling began in the marginal nations of the West in the nineteenth century.

The decentralised federal structure of the United States precludes any centralised description of educational reform in the nineteenth century. A national system of education arose on a state-by-state basis. The remarkable feature of this decentralised context is the uniformity of the system that was created. Two principal factors accounted for this outcome. First was the countrywide scope of the imperatives and challenges that demanded the reform of education. Second was the imitation of the responses of the pioneering states by those coming after. A state-by-state discussion of educational reform is beyond the scope of this study. Description will therefore be limited to sketches of the pioneering efforts and paradigm setting reforms of Massachusetts and New York City, which were widely copied elsewhere.

THE CASE OF MASSACHUSETTS

Much has been written about the common school reforms in Massachusetts including standard accounts by Cubberly (1947) and Cremin (1951), stressing the humanitarian elements in these reforms. A revisionist study by Katz (1968) highlighted the conflicts and class differences related to the reforms. Rebuttals of the revisions have been offered by Vinovskis (1985) substituting functional explanations of the available data. Gordon (1978) offered a reassessment of the reforms by examining the background of the reformers and tracing the institutions through which they exercised their influence in formulating, shaping and influencing the social and education reform movement. Gordon's reconstruction is adopted here in summary form.

From about the middle of the 1820s a small group of college professors and academy schoolmasters began to voice sentiments concerning the need to reform education in Massachusetts and the country. To promote their ideas they founded a journal, published tracts and used the newly formed lyceum movement as a forum for debate. Conservative Federalists harboured great doubts about White manhood suffrage and the enlightenment of most of the newly empowered citizens as well as the implications of these for the welfare of the Republic.

In 1830, two years after the election of President Andrew Jackson, the American Institute of Education was formed in Boston. Of the 250 founding members 70 were from outside of Massachusetts, coming from other states in New England, New York, Philadelphia and Ohio. Of the 180 from Massachusetts, 65 were from Boston and 115 from the rest of the state. The membership included college presidents and professors, academy schoolmasters, clergymen from the main Protestant tendencies, founders of charity schools, lawyers, physicians, booksellers, publishers, newspaper editors and merchants. Educators were in the majority but the non-educators constituted an influential minority. All of the latter were leading laymen of their respective Protestant denominations. Women and district schoolteachers were excluded from membership.

Most of the members were engaged in other reform type activities including the temperance movement, the Sunday School Movement, the Tract Society, missionary societies, the lyceum movement, moral reform and educational reform in Boston and at Harvard College. Some members were actively engaged in national politics and were fervent opponents of Andrew Jackson. While they did not hold office in the Institute, their involvement gave it national stature.

Gordon noted that in all their discourse on popular education, the members of the Institute betrayed deep-seated anxiety about the stability of the Republic. Unitarians and evangelicals alike were convinced that republican society could not survive without a Christian people. Their aim was to mount a purposeful crusade to forge a Christian nation, albeit in the Protestant mould.

They voiced frank distaste for the lower orders of society in the seaports and mill-towns of New England, the mobs who flouted authority and rioted in Boston, the Irish Catholic immigrants who seemed to them unappreciative of republican institutions, the Negroes whose urban enclaves were described as 'sinks of sin', working mothers who were held to have neglected their children, and the offspring of the 'degraded classes' who worked in the mills or swarmed the streets in 'squalid filth and ignorance'. Gordon listed their other concerns as:

·   Emigration of native sons to the West, removing a stable element from rural society.
·   Ignorant, easily swayed men now exercising the vote and who elected demagogues like Andrew Jackson to office.
·   The declining influence of New England in the expanding Union.
·   Waning respect for the country's institutions and for men of talent and education who had founded both the Puritan Commonwealth and the new nation.
·   Fears of the corruption of wealth, and that a future of plenty would invite greed, moral laxity and class conflict, as the rich became insolent and the poor became fractious.
·   Fears for the decline of the church and family, particularly the influence of the latter in matters of discipline.

The reformers of the Institute were well aware of the Prussian state system of schooling. Victor Cousin's celebrated report on the Prussian system was widely read and much quoted. In fact, he was made an honorary member of the Institute. The reformers came to the conclusion that while the influence of the family and the church was waning, the school had to be reformed and elevated as the institution to remedy and redeem the situation. The intention was simple: to create patriot republicans and Protestant Christians through the agency of the school. The republican child would love God and America, obey divine and national authority, read the Bible and respect the nation's laws.

The means of achieving these goals was the common school, to be attended by children of the rich and the poor, the native-born and the immigrant, black and white. These schools would be housed in properly constructed buildings, adequately ventilated and well equipped. They would conform to uniform standards, follow a graded curriculum, mandated by compulsory attendance and staffed with properly trained teachers.

The reformers were convinced that Bible reading, prayers in schools, and textbooks infused with moral values were not enough. Success depended upon the teachers becoming a surrogate priestly caste. Teachers, therefore, needed to be awakened to the holiness of their calling. Normal schools would become the means of their training and Teacher Institutes would be employed as 'revivalist agencies' with the chief task of providing in-service indoctrination of already existing teachers with respect to their sacred occupation.

In a real sense the American Institute of Education was reviving the essence of the original ideas of the Puritan fathers in the transformed setting of the Republic. While the district school system had fallen into disrepair if not disrepute, it had had the germ of the common school from its inception. These early reformers were not entirely original. They were drawing inspiration from the Prussian innovation, not withstanding the fact that royalty and aristocrats operating a highly centralised government intent on maintaining their dominance over commoners had devised that system of schooling. As republicans, in the wider meaning of the term, they could be charged with a measure of inconsistency in their embrace of monarchical measures. However, it must be acknowledged that reformers have never been the best historians, neither have they been held to the strict standards of originality demanded of inventors nor accepted the burden of consistency. In this regard the members of the Institute were no different from their predecessors or successors.

The new Whig Party swept the polls in Massachusetts in the elections of 1834. The party won the Governor's office, all seats in the Senate and over 80 per cent of the seats in the House of Representatives. The vast majority of the school reformers of the Institute were Whigs. James Carter, a schoolmaster, graduate of Harvard and moving figure among the founding members of the Institute, was among the elected members of the House. He drafted the bill to establish the Common School Fund to provide state aid to district schools. In 1836 he also drafted the bill to establish the Board of Education, which was eventually passed in 1837. It was widely expected that he would have been appointed the first Secretary of the Board. However, the Governor selected Horace Mann for that appointment. Mann was not an educator, but was a seasoned politician having been a member of both House and Senate and President of the latter. Mann, a lawyer, a Whig, and an accomplished public speaker, was also a crusader for temperance and institutional care for the insane. Among his first acts as Secretary was to join the Institute, whose members became his firm supporters and constant advisors.

Mann expanded the powers of the Board and Secretary, popularised and politicised the common school movement, mobilised widespread support and inspired the establishment of the state-wide common school system in Massachusetts. His mission was that of the reformers of the American Institute of Education: to establish universal education for children as a means of setting the Republic on the firm foundations of nationalism and Protestantism.

The common school movement of Massachusetts became the prototype for the public school system of education that was implemented nation-wide by the end of the nineteenth century as state after state adopted the Massachusetts model. The American Institute of Education was founded in Boston, consisted mainly of people of Massachusetts, but from the outset conceived of their mission as national by their very choice of name. The linkages and combination between politics, Protestant denominations and educators along with influential members of the public, particularly the press, proved effective not only in developing the common school idea, but in its implementation. Religion, nationalism, politics, class and technical expertise in education were all critical factors in the outcome.

The relationships involved were not straightforward. It was not the newly empowered landless men, of limited income and little learning who were the movers and shakers of educational reform designed to construct a system of schooling appropriate for the new nation. While they may have passed resolutions to this effect, they, or their agents, were neither the planners nor the conceptualisers. Rather they were one of the objects of the system designed. The designers of the national system were learned men, with some amount of property or substantial income, who had been recently dispossessed of political power. The reformers were those who had felt the force of White manhood suffrage empowering landless men of limited learning. Chastened by a degree of marginality, they responded with creative measures to transform their conquerors into themselves, at least in learning. The Massachusetts led New England reforms became the major tributary that eventually became the overflowing national river of public school education.

In reconstructing the role and relationships of the early school reformers of the American Institute of Education it is almost impossible to escape their likeness to the tradition of the ancient Jewish prophets or the bishops and abbots in early Christianity. While the circumstances were different in their contextual configuration, the essence of their actions was the same. Operating in the intersection between the transition from the Age of Religion to the Era of the Nation-State, these prophets of education constructed the paradigmatic school of nationhood, the common school. Its highly defensible ideological justification and rationale is that if all nationals are to share the same identity, be bonded by the same solidarity, embrace the same symbols of national unity and enjoy the rights of nationality predicated on the basis of equality, then the most appropriate educational institution to promote these values and to socialise nationals into this ethos, is the common school attended by all children irrespective of class, or gender, or race or religion or any other.

While they acknowledged inspiration from the efforts to construct schooling in Europe, particularly the Central European monarchies, they rejected the notion that schooling for the nation should retain distinctions of class, wealth, gender or sectarian differences. Building on the spirit of the Declaration and the Constitution, these early reformers were insistent that schooling appropriate for the Republic, and by implications all nations, should be inclusive and not exclusive. The Protestant principle of universal schooling for the purpose of individual salvation and personal communication with God, especially through the reading of the Bible, was recast and re-formulated as the foundation principle of education for the formation and preservation of the nation-state. The institution of the common school was designed to serve the needs of the nation.

In moving forward to construct schooling appropriate for a nation, these early reformers were also reaching backward to preserve their heritage. That heritage was defined as Christian and Protestant. Therefore, in seeking to create and promote the national ethos, these reformers also sought to preserve the Protestant ethic. They were in no way seeking to create secular institutions, but rather non-sectarian Protestant common schools. Herein lay the contradiction or tension in the common schools founded in New England. One interpretation of the Constitution is that schooling appropriate to the nation-state, which guarantees freedom of religion, must of necessity be secular. The guiding principle of these early reformers was that it would be Christian but non-sectarian. By so doing they reasoned the Christian heritage would be preserved in the Republic.

THE CASE OF NEW YORK CITY

The population of New York City stood at 60,489 in 1800. By 1850 it had risen to 515,547 principally through immigration (Gilman 1984). Kaestle (1973) traced the evolution of the school system in the City of New York from 1750 to 1850, that is from the late colonial period until the emergence of the public school system in the period of independence. While the rest of the state of New York had more or less followed the New England system of district schooling, based on the fact that many New Englanders had migrated and settled upstate, New York City itself had followed the system of denominational, parochial schooling characteristic of the Middle Colonies. The parochial system had a mixture of fee-paying and free schools run by the various denominations for their adherents. A summary of Kaestle's description of the evolution of the New York City school system is essential to the illustration of the second tributary that flowed to form the public school movement.

Growing socioeconomic disparity was evident from the beginning of the nineteenth century, and remained the trend for the entire first half of that century. This increasing socioeconomic disparity was marked by income and residential segregation as the more affluent moved uptown leaving downtown to the poor. While the City population grew ten fold over the 50 year period, poverty outstripped population growth. Accordingly, as stately and manicured residential areas appeared uptown, slums mushroomed downtown. The entire Fourth Ward became a slum with numerous tenements, sometimes with more than fifty people in a single house and many people living in cellars. As the socio-economic disparity got larger, class lines hardened and crime lent a sense of insecurity to the already depressing circumstances.

Gilman (1984) observed that at the beginning of the nineteenth century charity in New York City was operated by women of the patrician elite. The poor were regarded as victims who were by and large friendless, pitiable and destitute. By the middle of the century, the operation of charity had been taken over by men who administered it as professional managers. Charity had been moved from the orbit of the social elite into the sphere of the political economy of the City. Moreover the perception of the poor had changed dramatically. The poor were perceived as wicked, vile, alien, dangerous and responsible for their fate.

Periodic economic depression swelled the ranks of the poor, and immigration turned a labour shortage into a surplus, depressing wages which did not keep pace with prices. Many city workers lived barely about subsistence level, although they were employed. In 1847 a survey estimated that a quarter of the population of the City was receiving some time of charity and that 31 per cent of the population was destitute. Kaestle described the 'brute economic circumstances' of the first half of the nineteenth century in New York City; the deteriorating conditions of poor people increasing at a rate faster than the rapidly expanding population; periodic economic depression; increasing distance between the social classes and rampant health and crime problems.

Kaestle further noted that family life and church attendance wilted in those polarised socio-economic circumstances. In many sections of the growing slums, the streets were the only escape for children crammed in the overcrowded living quarters. Indeed many children, especially boys, lived on the streets. Church attendance plummeted. In 1817 a missionary, Ward Stafford, conducted a survey from which he estimated that while about 31,000 New Yorkers attended church, approximately 89,000 did not. More than half the families in the poorer areas had no Bibles in their homes. He also noted that there appeared to have been a shortage of churches and a surplus of taverns in the City. The alienation referred to was not academic. A pious citizen distributing Bibles in a poor neighbourhood was soundly beaten. Street boys were highly suspicious of Sunday Schools and religious exhortation, for they feared that these were nothing more than clever devices to trap them into places of detention.

Contemporaries placed the blame for the problems squarely on immigration. The Society for the Prevention of Pauperism made such a declaration in 1819. Most of the immigrants in New York City in the first half of the nineteenth century were Irish and German Catholics, bringing ways that were regarded as foreign and alien to New Yorkers. These newcomers enjoyed a measure of levity expressed in a spirit that was not always sober, and reserved Sundays for such expressions. Protestants viewed such intemperance and desecration of the Sabbath as gross immortality.

The conditions of the first half of the nineteenth century in the City promoted a spate of missionary and philanthropic organisations and projects. Popular objects of charity were orphans, widows, debtors, the sick and other especially depressed groups. Wide ranging projects were mooted including the expansion of prisons and separation of juvenile from adult offenders, provision of work for those who were able, temperance campaigns, distribution of Bibles and tracts and expansion of educational opportunity for the poor. Institutions adopted to implement these projects were almshouses, orphan asylums, houses of refuge, Sunday Schools and charity schools. The institutions were uniform and united in the mission of moral reformation of their clientele based on religious instruction.

The earliest efforts at educational reform in the City can be traced to the Quakers, led by Thomas Eddy, who inspired the creation of the Free School Society in 1805. The intention of the Society was to supplement the denominational system by providing nondenominational charity schools for the church-less poor. The aim of schooling was moral reformation and Christian foundation. Schooling was proposed as a means of reducing crime and promoting work thus reducing expenses on jails and welfare. The first nondenominational free school was established in 1806 in rented premises in the Fourth Ward. Under Eddy's leadership the school adopted the Lancaster monitorial system developed by Joseph Lancaster in 1798 for London's growing number of poor children. The Lancaster system had won aristocratic approval and royal endorsement from George III. By the 1820s the Society operated eleven schools and claimed to have provided education for over 20,000 children from the most indigent classes in the City.

Up to 1825, New York State had provided financial assistance to denominational charity schools along with assistance to the nondenominational schools of the Society. Consistent with that policy, the Bethel Baptist Church had established three free schools for poor children, and had planned to increase this number to six schools. The Baptist schools were in direct competition with the charity schools of the Society. The Free School Society therefore lobbied vigorously in Albany for the discontinuation of all state aid to denominational schools. In 1824, the state legislature not wishing to alienate either side decided to grant all state aid for education to the Common Council of New York City, mandating that body to distribute the funds as they saw fit. The Free School Society was able to convince the Council that only themselves, and specialised agencies like orphanages, were deserving of public assistance to provide education. From 1825, state aid to denominational charity schools was discontinued. In a sense the Baptists of New York were given a dose of their own medicine, having so vigorously and successfully advocated the separation of church and state.

The Free School Society took the opportunity of the campaign against denominational charity schools to recast their educational approach and to remake and rename the Society. The Society's new approach to schooling was that the rich and the poor, native-born and immigrant should attend public institutions, with the ultimate goal being the formation of American citizens. Nationalism now joined moral reformation and nondenominational Protestantism as major goals of education. The Lancaster system was abandoned. The common school replaced the charity school. The Society received approval of the Council to be renamed the Public School Society and to introduce nominal tuition fees, although those unable to pay would not be debarred. The change of name, introduction of fees and the call for social integration in school were all designed to remove the stigma of the free schools as schools for the poor, and to promote greater social cohesion in a city that was becoming increasingly polarised.

The Public School Society enjoyed a fair measure of success with their new policies. By the 1850s about half of the population of children of elementary school age were in school. Children from a wider range of social backgrounds attended the public schools although children of the wealthy and much of the middle classes continued to attend private schools. The success of the public schools was in taking over the clientele of most of the more modest fee paying denominational schools whose numbers declined significantly. It is accurate to say therefore that the public schools of New York grew out of the charity schools and the denominational schools charging modest fees.

The Controversy about State Support for Catholic Schools

No description or discussion of the evolution of the New York City school system could be complete without reference to the dispute that developed between the Public School Society and the Catholic Church led by Bishop John Hughes. In 1800 Catholics in New York City numbered 1,300. By 1850 their numbers exceeded 100,000. The first Catholic school was established in the City in 1801. Following its own traditions and that of the Middle Colonies, the Catholics established their own parochial system of fee paying and free schools. By 1840 there were eight Catholic free schools, which together with the fee-paying schools, enrolled about 5,000 children. Most Catholic children attending schools went to public schools.

The Catholic clergy had three main objections to public schools. The first was textual: the schools used the King James Version of the Bible while Catholics preferred the Douay Version. The second was catechetical: Protestants insisted that individuals were capable of interpreting the Bible without the mediation of priests, hence Bible reading played an important part in religious instruction while Catholics insisted that specific explication was needed to accompany Bible reading. The third was cultural: Catholics insisted that their history and culture was either totally neglected or portrayed in the most negative light causing distress to the children and negative self-assessment and self-esteem. In addition, slurs against the Irish in particular, and immigrants in general, were degrading as they were invariably projected as drunken and depraved.

Kaestle reconstructed the sequence of events in the conflict between the Catholics and the Public School Society as follows:

- In his message to the Legislature in 1840 Governor William Seward invited the establishment of schools taught by teachers who shared the language and religion of the immigrants.
- In response to the Governor's appeal the Trustees of the Catholic schools submitted to the Common Council a petition for funds to assist schools run by them.
- The Public School Society immediately submitted counter proposals.
- The Common Council decided not to grant funds to Catholic schools.
- Catholics requested a public hearing, which was granted in October. There were further meetings including a famous confrontation between Bishop Hughes, Hiram Ketchum a leading nativist, a representative of the Public School Society and several Protestant ministers in which Catholic grievances were aired and rebutted.
- The Common Council attempted to broker a compromise based primarily on removing offensive passages from textbooks used in the public schools, but this failed to satisfy the Catholics, who organised a petition to the Legislature.
- When the matter reached the Legislature Governor Seward, cautioned by a narrow re-election victory, gave little direction and the matter remained unresolved.
- In the summer of 1841 there was more debate on the issue along with some violence.
- Catholics entered politics directly by nominating a slate of candidates that excluded all Democrats who would not support their claim for educational reform. Democrats won a landslide victory at the polls in November 1841.
- The new Legislature passed the Maclay Bill in April 1842, which removed authority for public schools from the Public School Society and placed it under the general authority of elected officials. A central Board of Education was created which appointed ward commissioners to establish and supervise all new public schools. Sectarian teaching was prohibited in public schools.
- On the night that Governor Seward signed the bill nativists fought Catholics in the streets and Bishop Hughes' house was stoned.

The result was a partial victory for all parties to the dispute, thus leaving all dissatisfied but not without some measure of consolation. The influence of the Public School Society, symbol of Protestant alliance, had been broken. The governance of schools now rested with elected representatives and their appointed officials. At the same time public funds were not granted for the support of Catholic schools, which was the major objective of the Catholic petition, which started the entire controversy. The Public School Society could feel some measure of satisfaction with this outcome since their position on state support for Catholic schools had been sustained. Also the first Superintendent of New York City schools, William Stone, was not less nativist than Ketchum or the Society's leaders. He sanctioned the King James Version and enforced Bible reading 'without note or comment' in all city schools. The Protestant ethos prevailed. Smith (1967) observed that by 1850 Protestantism and American nationality were synonymous in New York City.

Many Catholics agreed with the idea of public schooling to Americanise the immigrant children. They desired to join the dominant culture and mainstream of American society. Orestes Brownson in the 1850s argued that the common school was the order of the day and opposition to it would only perpetuate the perception of immigrants as a foreign colony in America. The Catholic newspaper the *Truth Teller* also supported public schools and the use of English as the language of instruction. Most Catholics opposed public schools, but preferred it to no schooling at all. Their real preference was for Catholic public schools, a prospect that the Protestant majority was unwilling to concede.

The New York controversy attracted national attention. It also foreshadowed conflicts that would assume national dimensions, as public schools became the norm across the country. This became the context in which the Catholic parochial system of schooling became the rival of the public school system, as the Catholic hierarchy and those Catholic immigrants holding fast to their cultural heritage resisted being dissolved in the Protestant solvent clearly visible in public schooling. The essence of the Catholic position was that there was no inconsistency between being American and being Catholic. In this regard the nationalist intention became the cement holding together the public schools, heavily biased to Protestantism, and the Catholic parochial schools.

Kaestle concluded from his study of the evolution of the New York City school system that as the population of the city increased rapidly between 1800 and 1850 the following took place in the purpose and organisation of schooling:

1. Increased reliance on institutional solutions of social problems. Reformers moved to rationalise charity, incarcerate vagrants and standardise schools.
2. Increased reliance on schooling to implement desired social changes as both the family and the churches were perceived to be declining in both influence and effectiveness.
3. Uniformity became the core value in the face of increasing diversity.
4. Schools became the agent of the dominant culture. They became the major instruments of acculturation and institutions of assimilation. As such schools became conformist.
5. The movement to common schooling and a uniform process of acculturation fractured along Protestant and Catholic lines, as neither was willing to compromise.

The New York City route to public schooling certainly had different contextual elements to that of Massachusetts but the similarities were overriding. The differences were nothing more than variations on general themes arising largely from the uniquely different locations. Initially, the big city of New York did not look to the smaller city of Boston for educational ideas but rather to London, one of the leading cities, internationally. Likewise the reformers of the American Institute did not draw inspiration from the Public School Society of New York, that predated their own efforts, but from the absolutist monarchies of Central Europe. The tendencies of colonies to look outside for solutions to their internal problems still survived in the Republic decades after its official disconnection from colonial rule. Whatever were the routes taken, or external sources of inspiration publicly acknowledged, eventually Quakers and Anglicans in New York City and reformed Puritans of Massachusetts came to the same public school destination at about the same time prompted by the same internal stimuli.

Men of the dominant social elite were obvious in their imposition of their conceptions of schooling on the intended beneficiaries. Katz was absolutely correct in pointing to the fact that conflict not consensus surrounded the emergence of public schooling. At the same time explanations of their actions based on narrow class interests do not do justice to, or capture, the breadth of their motivation. While the party alliances and allegiances were different in Massachusetts and New York City, Whigs in Massachusetts and Democrats in New York City implemented public school systems premised on the same common school assumptions and directed to the same national goals. Nationalism proved to be the common solvent in which both Protestantism and Catholicism dissolved, although both did not mix when poured into the common school. Each maintained its distinctive school systems differing in theology but united in producing American nationals.

THE AMERICAN PUBLIC SCHOOL SYSTEM

Beginning with Katz's (1968) seminal but controversial study revising the origin of public schooling in America, there has been much debate among historians, educators and sociologists on the interpretation of the factors related to these reforms. One of the useful outcomes of the heated debate has been the distillation by Vinovskis (1985) of some uncontroversial elements. Restudying the data available to Katz, but using different techniques and with the benefit of additional data unearthed by the controversy, Vinovskis identified the following as being generally agreed:

1. Between the 1820s and the 1860s, Massachusetts was a microcosm of the United States and remained so until at least 1920.
2. The common school reforms pioneered in Massachusetts became the model for the national public school system as the factors that

occasioned these reforms repeated themselves with minor variations across the country. In many instances the Massachusetts reforms were simply copied.

3. Four factors that drove these reforms were:
    a) Immigration, which led to rapid increases in the population and introduced diversity previous unknown in American society.
    b) Industrialisation as the economy was transformed from its previous agrarian base by technological innovations, particularly related to the application of steam power.
    c) Urbanisation as cities grew at rates outstripping population growth and rates of immigration.
    d) Modernisation as reflected in transport by steamship and railroad.

Katz observed that the educational reforms spurred on by these factors transformed every aspect of schooling from administration to pedagogy and financing to the gender of teachers. It is necessary to note that there has been no consensus among American scholars on the importance of either nationalism or religion as factors shaping the reform movement. In many instances these factors are either assumed as axioms of the reforms or disregarded as unimportant. This is not to say that these factors have not been recognised by any scholars. The works of Cubberly (1947), Cremin (1951 and 1980), Smith (1967), Gordon (1978) Tyack and Hansot (1982) all attest to such recognition. The point is that there is no consensus on these factors as there is about immigration, industrialisation, urbanisation and modernisation.

What is at stake in this lack of consensus on nationalism and religion is not so much their importance as additional variables in the educational reform equation, but recognition of the fundamental nature of the transformation of schooling from its form in the Religious Age where it served the liturgy and personnel needs of the church to the era of the Nation State where it became the handmaiden of the state. This transformation was by no means confined to the United States. However, public schooling in American education has a special position in this transition. Limiting of the explanation of the transformation of education in the United States to immigration, industrialisation, modernisation and urbanisation restricts interpretation to the contextual circumstances and ignores its wider historical and global meaning. A mirror image of this approach is the situation in American baseball or basketball when the American Leagues plays the National League, or the Eastern Conference plays the Western Conference in the finals, the championships are referred to as World Series. While this amusing conception of the world may be employed without damage in these sports, extension outside of this arena to interpretation of social phenomena results in distortions in understanding.

The American common school movement with its antecedents in the Public School Society of New York City and the American Institute of Education of Massachusetts must be understood in the wider global context of the construction of schooling appropriate for and consistent with nation building and nationalism at the dawn of the Era of the Nation-State. On the margins of geopolitical power at that time, on the periphery of the industrial revolution, and benefiting from the disconnection from ancestral cultures and its consequential weakening of patriarchal structures, the United States devised and defined schooling more consistent with the tenets of this era than Western Europe in which this new era had its genesis. This fundamental change in schooling was therefore more clearly defined in the United States, than it was in the central imperial nations of Europe, France and England.

Historically, the common school movement represents the re-formulation of schooling from its former mission to serve the needs of the churches, to its new meaning in serving the prerogatives of the nation. Reading schools, writing schools, choir schools, charity schools, grammar schools and colleges training priests gave way to elementary schools, high schools, colleges and universities serving national needs of citizenship and comparative economic advantage in a world system of competing nations. It is against this background that the transformation of teaching as a full time occupation outside of the clergy and the implications of these school reforms for the feminisation of teaching in America have to be understood.

PUBLIC SCHOOLING AND SELECTED GROUPS

It is necessary to discuss briefly the relationships that developed between public schooling and Jews, Catholics, Indians and Blacks. Each of these will be discussed in turn.

Jewish Education and Public Schooling.

Froner (1969) maintained that from colonial times the Jewish approach to schooling in America developed particular patterns and characteristics that have remained basically the same until the present time. These characteristics have been:

1. The separation of secular and religious education.
2. The acceptance and support of non-sectarian schools.
3. The supplementary nature of Jewish education.
4. The uncertain responsibility of the congregation.
5. The low status of the teacher providing Jewish education.
6. Adjustments to Jewish schooling in relation to major developments in general education.

Gartner (1969) was in general agreement with Froner and pointed to the fact that from the beginning Jews were overwhelmingly in support of state sponsored, tax-supported, religiously neutral public schools as means of training all children for American citizenship. As such Jewish children needed to be educated alongside all others in the common embrace of American nationality. Public schools were perceived by Jews to be a symbol and guarantee of Jewish equality and full opportunity in America. He pointed out that the rise of public schools in the United States coincided with the ascendancy of Reform Judaism as the dominant mode of Judaism in America. Reform Judaism, developed in Germany, held as its fundamental premise the conception that Jews should be fully integrated as citizens of the modern secular nation-state.

Jewish education, in light of public schools, became solely religious in content and supplementary to secular public schooling. Through public schooling Jews became Americans. Through supplementary Jewish education delivered in addition to public schooling they perpetuated the Jewish heritage and identify. This was the general pattern although the establishment of private schools providing integrated Jewish and secular education can be traced to the middle of the nineteenth century when some German Jews created and supported such institutions (Grinstein 1969).

The institutions that emerged in the nineteenth century and early twentieth century to provide Jewish education can be listed as follows:

a)   Private tutors, some of whom were poor men operating in their homes in city slums.

b)   Sabbath schools operated by synagogues and in some instances socialist groups teaching secular Judaism.

c)   Talmud Torah classes operating mainly in lower and middle class neighbourhoods providing seven to ten hours of instruction per week, held after public schools, and covering an ambitious curriculum including Hebrew, taught over a five year period. These classes charged fees and were supported with teacher training, textbooks and appropriate teaching materials.

d)   Yiddish schools, catering mainly to Jews of Eastern European ancestry, using Yiddish rather than Hebrew as the lingua franca. In many Yiddish schools secular Judaism was taught sometimes with either a Zionist or anti-Zionist bias.

There were two major development in Jewish education in the post World War II period. First, has been the emergence of the Hebrew school, which has largely replaced both the Yiddish school and the Talmud Torah classes. These schools are synagogue supported, more financially stable, have better paid teachers, teach a more modest curriculum that can be covered in a shorter time, thus relieving students of some of the onerous burden of full public school attendance each day followed by very demanding evening studies for four to five years. A survey in the 1950s showed that 88 per cent of Jewish children attended Hebrew schools.

Second, was the rapid spread of the Yeshiva day schools, which are private schools, integrating general and Jewish education. Gartner maintained that the Yeshiva schools have stirred great controversy in the Jewish community for several reasons. To begin with they raise the question of the support of public schools by American Jews. Within the Jewish community itself divisions are created because the fees are high and therefore cannot be afforded by all. As such, attendance at these schools became a symbol of status.

Pilch (1969) accounted for the rise of the private day schools on the following grounds:

i)   The influx of large numbers of Orthodox Jews from Eastern Europe.
ii)   The aftermath of the Jewish tragedy in World War II which heightened Jewish solidarity and weakened their trust in the nation-state.
iii) The change of parental attitudes from the melting pot idea to the concept of cultural pluralism.
iv)   The impact of American-born Orthodox rabbis who had become influential in the synagogues.
v)   The realisation that Jewish education as an add-on to day-schooling adversely affected its effectiveness.
vi)   The rapid growth of parochial schools among Protestant denominations.

Looked at in its entirety it can be said that Jews in America have been generally supportive of public schooling and have, in the main, tailored and adjusted their traditional forms of education to reduce or eliminate conflict with public schooling for nationals. By so doing they attempted to participate in national schooling without compromising their maintenance of their Jewish identity. In that regard the establishment of Jewish private schools in the second half of the twentieth century is no different from Protestants, the major religious supporters of public schooling, several denominations of which have resorted to schools promoting their beliefs.

Indians and Public Schooling

One of the tenets of colonisation was the conversion of the Indians. Education was accepted as a principal instrument in the achievement of that goal. Wright (1988) maintained that the Indians were tenacious in their adherence to their culture, rigidly resistant to attempts at Christian conversion and did not acquiesce in attempts to integrate them into American society until war and disease had disintegrated tribal integrity and left their communities vulnerable to English-American domination. After many false starts a comprehensive system of education was established for Indians in the latter decades of the nineteenth century. This occurred in the same period that public schools were being established nation-wide.

The promise was that through education Indians would be assimilated into the mainstream of American society as citizens. Thomas Morgan, Commissioner of Indian Affairs, 1889–1893, stated that through American citizenship and education Indians would enjoy refined homes, the emoluments of trade and commerce, advantages of travel, the pleasures of literature, science and philosophy and the stimulus afforded by true religion. The education that was offered to Indians focused on proficiency in English language, Christian beliefs of Protestant orientation and agricultural work habits. Certainly education based on this premise would not readily lead to the realisation of the promise. On the contrary this was the type of education that could be expected to result in most Indians being marginal members of the society.

The general course of the integration of Indians into public schooling can be traced through the case of the Kiowa-Apache-Comache Reservation. Ellis (1994) observed that the negotiations between ten Indian tribes, speaking nine different languages and totalling about six thousand persons and the Federal Government, that created the Kiowa-Apache-Comache Reservation in 1867, had as a major objective the opening up of the Southern plains to permanent settlement. To induce the Indians to agree to this, the Federal government offered a reservation with fixed boundaries encompassing an area about the size of Connecticut, annuities for twenty years, an agency with staff to attend to the needs of the tribes and thirty two schools staffed with teachers on a ratio of one teacher to thirty students.

Following the signing of the treaty the government enlisted Quakers to administer the reservation in 1869. To encourage the tribes to support education the agent created a school board composed of two chiefs from each of the tribes. The first fruits of this policy were increased enrolment of Indian students and their regular attendance. The Federal government on the other hand was not forthcoming in honouring its treaty obligations. By 1884, only three of the promised thirty-two schools had been built. Although the Quakers and other denominations had established mission schools, the total education provision was far below the need; hence schools were overcrowded as Indian participation outstripped the provision.

Ellis noted that the Federal government completely neglected its treaty obligations not only with respect to the Kiowa-Apache-Comache Reservation but also with respect to all Indian reservations across the country. In fact the total provision for education for all reservations in 1884 of $1,100,000 was not sufficient to meet its treaty obligation to the Kiowa-Apache-Comache Reservation. At the same time the latter was more fortunate than several other reservations whose treaty had no clause that obligated the Federal government to support education. Moreover, the Federal government was always in arrears with respect to the payment of the annuities, which the reservation sometimes applied to educational purposes.

In addition to the difficulties caused by the Federal government reneging on several of its treaty obligations, what was actually provided was poorly administered. Factors associated with poor administration included high turn over of agency staff, rampant nepotism in employment, the incompetence of many of the persons employed and the lack of timeliness by the Federal bureaucracy in addressing critical issues outside of the remit of the agency staff of the reservation. For example, within a year of the establishment of the reservation the health problems posed by lack of water and inadequate sanitation were reported along with proposed solutions. No action was taken for more than a decade and it was only after the health problems had reached alarming proportions that any action was taken at all.

The limitations of the administration of the reservation as a whole, was typical of the schools as well. Between 1895 and 1902 the Rainy Mountain School only had one teacher who remained at the school for as long as two years. The rest drifted in and out on an average of six months. Most times the school operated without qualified teachers as agency staff substituted. The schools were not only poorly staffed but also inadequately financed and deficient in their facilities, equipment and materials.

Ellis concluded that the purpose of the treaty was to concentrate the Indians in an area that would open the way for the settlement and exploitation of the rest of the region. The treaty gave the appearance of Indian approval and acceptance and provided legitimacy to the exercise. Once the treaty had been negotiated and signed, the Federal government, and those who benefited from the treaty, had little further interest in the welfare of the Indians. The future fate of Indians were entrusted mainly to Quaker administrators, through the reservation agencies, whose primary goals were conversion and citizenship.

The civilising mission which was entrusted to Quakers, supported by other denominations including the Baptists, Methodists, Presbyterians and Anglicans, was to make the Indian a 'civilised' Anglo-American Protestant. The promise was assimilation into the mainstream. The system of education actually implemented on the reservation was designed to make the Indian an Anglo-American Protestant on the one hand and on the other hand a disciplined worker in a marginal group in the society. In other words, the margin not the mainstream was the intended destination of the 'civilised' Indian.

Ellis was of the view that the civilising mission and the schooling designed to accomplish it were aimed at destroying Indian culture. The Indians, on the other hand, unwilling to surrender their culture completely but aware of the consequences of rejecting the school and education, sought an accommodation that combined both the imposed Protestant-American culture and their own. In his view the civilising mission failed to destroy Indian values, culture and identity but it succeeded in transmitting fluency in English, providing skills that offered Indians careers outside the reservation and in converting many to Christianity.

In the nineteenth century there were no elements of the American society that were not confronted with American nationalism and incorporation into the nation-state. The Indians were no exceptions. The essential content of American nationality was the same, English and Protestant.

Blacks and Public Schooling

Because further reference will be made to Blacks and Freedman Education in the South, to avoid repetition, only a few salient and general points about the relationship between Blacks and public schooling will be addressed here.

- During slavery every Southern state, with the exception of Tennessee, had enacted legislation with barred slaves from learning to read or write or from being taught to read and write.

- One of the first acts of the slaves who were freed was to seek to appropriate openly and legally the education that was only theirs previously by covert and illegitimate means. The freedmen acted on their own behalf in establishing schools before Northern assistance was forthcoming or Federal policy provided a framework for educational development through the Freedmen's Bureau.

- Through the initiatives of the freedmen, assistance from the North and Federal intervention a start was made in the 1860s to establish an educational system which consisted of elementary, secondary, normal and technical schools and liberal arts colleges (Nieman 1994).

- The common school idea was exported to the South through freedmen creating schooling in the aftermath of the abolition of slavery.

- Blacks, in the South and North, were firm supporters of public schools from their inception, or from the time that they could legally participate in schooling.

- Faced with national imperatives embedded in public schooling Blacks, from the commencement of their participation, desired to be Americans. They therefore embraced its English and Protestant assumptions as means of achieving the higher goals of nationality and citizenship.

Catholics and Public Schooling

Catholics offered the strongest and most profound opposition to public schools. Their objection went to the core of the issue. In their view the state was usurping the responsibility of parents, since it had no mandate to teach children but was taking the same upon itself. The Catholic Church insisted that the education of children was the primary responsibility of parents and not the state. In its view, state-provided compulsory education was a pagan and not Christian concept. In any case, the state was an incompetent agent to fulfil parental duties. Compulsory schooling provided by the state was seen as part of a wider encroachment of the latter upon family life. For centuries marriage, for example, was held to be both a contract and a sacrament. Nation-states in Europe in the nineteenth century had reduced marriage to only a contract. Public schooling provided by the state was just another example of secularising interventions into society that had to be resisted.

This was not just the view of American Catholics responding to the emerging public school system. It was the view of the Papacy in response to the rise of the nation-state and its institutions in Western Europe. This was the protestation of the centre of the receding Religious Age as it attempted to counter the cherished axioms of the new era of the nation-state. Leahy (1991) observed that American Catholicism in the mid to late nineteenth century imitated the uncompromising, isolationist stance of Pope Pius IX who sought to defend the church against the secularising trend in society. Instead of wrestling with the new challenges posed by the emergence of the nation-state, the Catholic Church responded by reciting old formulations, thus isolating itself from the profound changes taking place.

In addition to resisting the assertion that nations had the responsibility, and that nationals had the right, to be educated by public means and institutions, American Catholics objected to public schools because of the Protestant slant in their non-sectarian version of Christianity. Reference has already been made to this point hence there is no need to repeat it here except to say that it was an added reason for resistance.

It has to be noted that even before the common school movement took root, the official policy of the Catholic Church in America was to establish schools to teach the faith and morality. This was one of the declarations of the First Provincial Council of Baltimore in 1829 (Sullivan 1946). The Second Plenary Council of Baltimore urged all pastors to establish more schools and challenged religious communities to devote themselves to teaching. Following the Civil War the common school movement began to take hold everywhere. The Third Plenary Council of Baltimore of 1884 took the decision that every Catholic child should receive a Catholic education, through schools established by the church. It made the establishment of a Catholic alternative school system a matter of the highest priority and urgency (McClusky 1964).

What is interesting is that at the very time that the Catholic school system began to be constructed in earnest, public schooling had shifted from being non-sectarian to being secular as religious education came to be reassessed. The position that prevailed was that the very nature of public schooling precluded religious instruction. The latter was a private matter that had no place in the public domain of the school. As a result the common core of Christian teaching that had been promoted by the early school reformers was watered down to belief in God, the golden rule and the Bible. At the same time scientific humanism began to replace religion in public schooling as research and science replaced theology and religious authority as the final arbiters of truth. The Catholic response to secular public schooling was to label it 'Godless' (McClusky 1968). In other words, secular public schools were no more acceptable to Catholics than non-sectarian Protestant public schools.

Tyack and Hansot (1982) took the position that the differences between Protestant and Catholics in America, which led to the Catholic alternative to public schools was, in the end, a misunderstanding. It would have been truly remarkable if several generations of politically astute Catholic bishops, shrewd

Jesuit priests, Ivy League educated Protestant clergy, and learned Unitarian school reformers did not fully understand the issues involved. Some of the most profound differences arise where the participants are very clear about the issues involved, and then disagree. In those circumstances the issue was not one of understanding but rather that of power, whose will should prevail. While acknowledging Protestant bigotry, and the fact that it perpetrated several injustices against Catholics, it seems clear that the only grounds upon which public schooling would have been acceptable to Catholics would have been if it were Catholic. In the absence of that possibility, American Catholics constructed alternative common schools.

Catholic parochial schools were common schools because they addressed the central challenge of public schooling, that of making American nationals of all their students. A defining disagreement in the debate between Catholics and Protestants, in the new American nation, was the Protestant claim that being Catholic was inconsistent with being American as a result of prior loyalty to the Papacy, a foreign authority. On the other hand Catholics insisted that it was possible to be loyal to family and religion and at the same time to be a loyal American national. Denounced as a menace to the solidarity of the American people and accused of attempting to destroy the public school system, Catholic parochial schools were scrupulous in adhering to the canons of American nationalism and in seeking to produce Catholic Americans who only differed from their Protestant countrymen and countrywomen in matters of religious doctrine.

The circumstance that produced this outcome was not only the conflict with Protestants, but divisions among American Catholics themselves. Leahy (1991) noted that by the 1880s two distinct camps were evident among Catholics. The smaller group championed the idea of Americanisation, encouraging immigrants to enter the mainstream of American life. This group advocated mastery of the English language, learning and adopting American customs. Apart from being ardent nationalists, they minimised the fear about the possible loss of Catholic identity in a predominantly Protestant country. The larger group encouraged the maintenance of ethnic identity, the preservation of native languages and manifested great anxiety about the loss of Catholic faith, identity and culture. Members of this group viewed the non-Catholic world with great suspicion and cautioned against quick assimilation into the American mainstream.

The Catholic community not only differed the pace and extent of assimilation into American culture, but manifested cracks along ethnic lines. At first the main fault line was between Irish and German Catholics. In 1886 only fifteen of the fifty bishops were Germans the other thirty-five were Irish. Indeed, Leahy showed that between 1790 and 1960 almost 75 per cent of all the bishops were Irish. Later, what appeared to have been an Irish-German difference widened to include Eastern Europeans, most of whom harboured a similar resentment of Irish dominance. The Irish favoured rapid assimilation.

The Germans and Eastern Europeans favoured slow and cautious assimilation and the retention of ethnic identities and languages.

Opposition from the Protestant community, particularly the nativist elements, fostered some measure of solidarity in the Catholic community thus preventing major eruptions along the major fault lines and fissures that were evident within it. The interplay between conflict with the Protestant majority and divisions within the Catholic minority combined to shape the Catholic system of parochial schools as alternative common schools. Those Catholics favouring rapid assimilation proposed schemes for compromising with the public school system. As would be expected they drew their precedents from Western Europe. In the 1890s they cited the cases of England and Prussia in which schools were conducted according to the dominant religion, with denominational schools being reimbursed for the secular instruction given. Catholics in Poughkeepsie went further and worked out a compromise with the school district where the school board rented the denominational facilities, directed and funded the schools and their operations, and allowed religious instruction outside of regular school hours.

Although most Catholic clergy, and probably laity, opposed the proposed compromises, experiments along these lines were usually defeated, or frustrated, by Protestant opposition often led by nativist groups. For example, intense public opposition premised on the notion that the compromises represented subsidies to the Catholic Church defeated attempts at compromises with the public school system in Minnesota and the Poughkeepsie Plan. Public-parochial schooling in Minnesota ended in 1893 and the Poughkeepsie experiment was terminated in 1897.

The smaller nationalist group within the Catholic community were confronted with the fact that Protestant opposition frustrated their attempts to secure compromises with public schooling. Hence, the majority view for Catholic parochial schools separate from and alternative to public schools prevailed. At the same time, parochial schools had to contend with and accommodate nationalist sentiment while maintaining their Catholic identity and doctrine. The fact that many Catholics sent their children to public schools to become Americans could not be ignored within Catholic parochial schooling. The latter had to promote American citizenship in addition to Catholic doctrine not only to address the views of the nationalist group but also to compete with the public schools.

The Catholic school system did not create any new educational institutions. It modelled its schools either on the contemporary institutions emerging in the public system or reached back into history to long standing types. For example, in Boston in 1870 the Bishop established the Sanctuary Choir of the Cathedral. Two lay teachers gave the boys of this choir regular elementary schooling. The Cathedral Choir School because of its special nature never exceeded 65 students. However, in 1910 students leaving it formed the nucleus of the Cathedral grammar school which was established, the choir school itself evolving into a full-fledged parochial elementary school (Sullivan 1946).

The principal feature of the parochial school system was not its innovative character but rather its faithfulness to Catholic doctrine and loyalty to American nationalism. Its products were Catholic Americans no less patriotic that the Protestant Americans of the public schools. World War I gave the first eloquent testimony of this fact.

Interestingly in the twentieth century as Catholics have been assimilated into the mainstream of American society, the mainstream has shifted to embrace, at least partially, the denominational parochial system of schooling. Evidence of Catholic assimilation into the mainstream can be most easily demonstrated in politics. In the 1880s and 1890s Catholic political influence grew to the extent that they were able to elect mayors in such major cities as Boston, St Louis, New Orleans, Buffalo, Milwaukee and Pittsburgh and to dominate municipal governments in Philadelphia, Chicago, Kansas City, St Paul and San Francisco. However, up to 1932 Catholics had very limited impact on national politics. In 1880 there was only one Catholic Senator and ten Catholics in the House of Representatives. While their number had increased to six in the Senate and thirty-five in the House by 1930, this was far below their proportion of the population. In 1925 Catholics were approximately 16 per cent of the US population but held four per cent of the Federal judgeships, were five per cent of the Federal employees and did not have a single state governor (Leahy 1991).

Beginning with the Roosevelt administration of the 1930s, Catholics have moved into the mainstream of national politics. Apart from winning the Presidency, since 1960 every Congress has had no less than 100 Catholics in the House and Senate. In the 101st Congress in 1988 there were 120 Catholics in the House and 19 in the Senate, this proportion being above their representation in the population.

As Catholics have mobilised politically and moved into the mainstream of national life, the balance has shifted within the Catholic community between the factions favouring assimilation and integration and those supporting the maintenance of a more isolationist and separatist position. At the same time the Catholic school system grew to accommodate a significant proportion of the school age population. In 1963, Catholic parochial schools numbered 10,633 elementary and 2,502 secondary schools with an enrolment of over 5.5 million students representing fourteen per cent of the school age population (McClusky 1964). Interestingly, enrolment in Catholic schools includes non-Catholics. Also large numbers of Catholics continue to patronise the public schools. While at the beginning of the century Catholic schools were viewed as being of poor quality compared to public schools, at the end of the century the situation has been reversed. Educational quality, not religion, is commonly regarded as the defining difference at the present time as Catholic schools are perceived to offer a higher quality than the beleaguered public schools.

THE TRANSFORMATION OF TEACHING IN THE NATION-STATE

It has been shown previously that up to the end of the eighteenth century, teaching was still an occupation that was integrated with religion and still largely an occupation within the clergy. Grammar school and college teaching remained firmly within this sphere although the course of study they offered, increasingly came to be regarded as general and liberal education without specific vocational focus rather than as training for the clergy. Where specific aspects of schooling, such as writing and the elementary level, had been differentiated from the clergy they were often combined with other occupational pursuits. Writing was combined with occupational training for commerce or with the work of professional copyists, scriveners. Reading schools were combined with farming, or studentship, or housework in the case of very young children. In these circumstances some types of teaching had become partially secular, as some teachers were able to earn a living from the services they provided.

While the churches were able to sustain the institutions for training church personnel, particularly the clergy, the Protestant doctrine of universal literacy for all believers for the purpose of reading and interpreting the Bible for themselves proved beyond the resources of the churches. Numerous ad hoc arrangements had to be implemented but even then these proved inadequate even among the Puritans, who were passionately committed to schooling as a communal responsibility.

The most fundamental transformation of the occupation of teaching has occurred in the Age of the Nation State. Under the aegis of the state, and impelled by nationalism, teaching has become a full-time secular occupation at all levels of the educational system. Ramirez and Boli (1987) explained the expansion of schooling during this era as the mobilisation of the national society to compete in the interstate system. They place emphasis on sovereignty as the sign of the transition to this type of political organisation. However, the history of the United States itself would suggest that sovereignty by itself is not a sufficient condition for the provision of a state system of education. Indeed, in the nineteenth century the British West Indian colonies had rates of enrolment that were only surpassed by nine Western European countries, Australia, New Zealand, Canada and the United States (Miller 1992).

It would appear that it is internal political and social imperatives and not the external status relative to other nations that are the critical factors in the spread of schooling. Notions of social equality combined with political ideology premised on democracy appear to prompt states to so act that greater opportunities for schooling are offered than at any other period in history. However this is educed, it is the mobilised resources of the state that have provided schools that then employ teachers on bases different from those which served the liturgical and manpower needs of churches or the missionary or charity purposes of their doctrines.

In the instance of the United States, in which education is not a federal responsibility, the mobilisation of states to provide education was not the result of centralised policies but rather action promoted and organised from within each state. Accordingly, the provision of state-provided education which began in Massachusetts and New York City in the 1820s did not reach its consummation in Mississippi till 1918, almost a century later. A major consequence of this transformation of schooling was the corresponding transformation of teaching.

Teaching as a secular occupation replaced or incorporated the writing schoolteachers, the dame school teachers, the grammar and academy schoolteachers, the town schoolteachers, charity schoolteachers and independent or private schoolteachers. The process involved was neither neat or tidy and varied from place to place depending on what existed previously. However, the particular route to the establishment of a national system of education, must not obscure the general principle that it is the axiomatic imperative of the nation to provide schooling for its nationals that has spread schooling dramatically and globally over the last two centuries.

Phenomena, which have been labelled as the universaliation, bureaucratisation and formalisation of schooling, were part of the process by which nations transformed schooling to make it consistent with their need to mobilise the polity, to create solidarity and common bonds across ethnic and religious groups, and establish an overarching national identity above all other identities. In this new setting schooling became not only a means of bonding nationals by overt displays of loyalty to national symbols, and a mechanism of securing and developing loyalties which supersede all others, but also a right of all nationals.

The process that transformed schooling to serve the prerogatives of nations, nationhood and nationalism also transformed the teaching occupation. In the nation-state teaching became a full-time secular occupation. This is not to say that teaching as a religious career was discontinued, or that teaching was no longer combined with other occupations, but rather to say that full-time teaching of a secular nature became the modal form of the teaching occupation. This was principally because the scope and scale of schooling provided in nation states far exceeded the scope and scale of schooling that was provided in the Religious Age where schooling served the doctrinal, liturgical and personnel needs of denominations or churches.

As would be expected the transformation of schooling did not represent a clean break with the past. In moving forward in the creation of the national system of education, steps were taken to preserve several elements that characterised the religious schooling system. Indeed, what was created initially was not a secular system of schooling but a non-sectarian system that was broadly Protestant and decidedly Christian. It is subsequent reforms that have produced a secular system of schooling. In other words, operating in the intersection between the historical religious system of schooling and the emerging national system of education, the nineteenth century public school founders created new forms as well as conserved historical patterns.

It must be noted that the Catholic Church succeeded in retaining teaching as an occupation within the clergy by the establishment of religious orders with teaching either as their sole responsibility or one of their main endeavours. Monks and nuns, who previously taught in the monastery, or convent, were reorganised to teach schools that served the public. Cloisters were abolished but celibacy was retained as religious brothers, sisters and priests embarked upon teaching as their life's work.

The fundamentally new aspect of the national society was its assumption of political and social equality. The principal axiom of the nation-state is the equality of nationals irrespective of ethnicity, religious persuasion, their location in city or countryside, of class or gender. While constitutions and laws of nations may not immediately concede all aspects and elements of equality, the axiom takes on the quality of natural justice and becomes an overwhelming argument and rationale, which can be prosecuted by the groups that are disenfranchised. In other words, the axiom of equality of nationals is an assumption or hypothesis that invites empirical test in the actual situation. It is not an automatic concession. The parameters of the inequality must be established, exposed and enunciated before it will be eliminated, at least in law and on paper.

Because of its roots in religion, teaching had been mainly a masculine occupation. The transformation of teaching as a secular occupation in the nation did not and could not by itself demand a continuation of the masculine tradition seeing that nationality is not premised on gender. At the same time, the nation itself was emerging from the Religious Age marked with patriarchal forms that defined society and personhood in different terms and did not immediately accord women their national rights. The feminisation of teaching occurred in the transition of society from its religious to its national form. It is against this background of the transformation of teaching itself as a secular occupation that the feminisation of teaching must be interpreted.

WOMEN'S TRUE PROFESSION AND DOMESTICITY REVISITED

'True womanhood' and 'women's true profession' were stock phrases that were used in the arguments advocating the employment of women teachers in public schools in the nineteenth century. The position taken here is that that argument, and the advocacy related to it, was justification and not the cause of the feminisation of teaching in nineteenth century America. It legitimised the departure from the tradition of men teachers and therefore had to establish, in the particular situation, the rationale for the new pattern. As such it represents a contextual and not a universal aspect of the phenomenon of the feminisation of teaching.

American scholars, at the close of the twentieth century, have viewed the feminisation of teaching negatively, for different reasons. Grumet viewed it as a combination of denial and cruel oppression, which through its convolutions permitted male dominance to continue unchanged. Also that it was a divisive mechanism by which women were set against each other. Douglas wrote disparagingly of sentimental womanhood and American culture bent on establishing a perpetual Mother's Day. Sugg extended this line of argument to education generally and public school teaching in particular. Scholars of all persuasions seem to agree that school teaching, redefined as women's work, kept women in an extended domestic sphere, little different from their subservient roles in the home. It is hard to find any interpretation of feminisation by American researchers and scholars, of either critical or consensus theory leanings, that view the movement of women into teaching as authentic and unrelated either to nostalgia or some form of social pathology. It would appear that advocacy related to women's position in society, in the latter part of the twentieth century, has unduly jaundiced the interpretation of feminisation of teaching in nineteenth century America.

In interpreting and explaining the feminisation of teaching in the United States in the nineteenth century the position taken here is that there was nothing saccharine or sentimental, cruel or divisive, demeaning or domestic about the opportunity given to young White native-born middle class Protestant women to become teachers. Further, that the feminisation of teaching among native-born, White, middle class, Protestant Americans involved consenting men and women purposely acting in a collaborative manner. Stressing women's morality, gentleness and submissiveness was addressed to the middle classes who held firmly to the Victorian values of the day. Pointing to their cheapness compared to male teachers targeted the concerns of the cost conscious taxpayers who could sabotage the enterprise, since schooling is financed through property taxes in the United States. Highlighting women's capacity to teach was designed to convince single women, and their anxious parents, of their capability and the feasibility of the task. These along with all of the other arguments were addressed to particular constituencies either to allay fears or secure co-operation. These must not be confused with the more fundamental imperatives driving the process of feminisation of teaching among this group.

Faced with declining natural increase in their own ranks, immigrants flooding the ports and congesting the cities of the Northeast, rejected at the polls and their denominations disestablished by the constitution, these descendants of the founding colonists decided to act decisively and creatively against these seemingly overwhelming odds. The invitation to young White native-born middle class Protestant women to become teachers was an invitation to junior partnership, with their men as the senior partners, in the mission to preserve and promote the English/Protestant heritage in the new American nation. Nationalism and cultural heritage were at the core of this mission and its motivation.

If a charge of cruel oppression, exploitation and divisiveness is to be made then it is more appropriately made against the men and women of the native-born, White, middle class, English, Protestant group concerning their joint action against the other groups that composed the American society at that time. If the men are charged as the main perpetrators then the women cannot escape prosecution as co-conspirators and accessories before the fact. What is being highlighted here is that the primary social significance of the partnership route to feminisation is its impact on and consequences for subordinate and disadvantaged groups in society and not the internal conflicts among the partners.

This group that claimed primacy in the establishment of American society and culture was closing ranks, against all other groups, in seeking to preserve and promote their culture as dominant in the new nation. The women understood this, accepted it as noble and honourable and embarked upon teaching with that understanding. Naturally they combined group interest with their own personal ambitions. Pay differentials and limited promotional prospects denoted rank in the partnership. This mission has survived the initial feminisation of the school system and remains the unspoken imperative, in a revised format, consistent with changes in the circumstances over the last 150 years.

Where White native-born Protestant middle class men could not find sufficient numbers of teachers from among themselves, they recruited teachers from among women of their group since to do otherwise would be to allow men of groups, that they perceived as threats, to teach their children. However, this was not simply a defensive move to ensure that their children were taught by members of their own group, but it was combined with an offensive goal: to teach the children of all other groups in the society. Put another way, the school reformers in constructing the new national system of education in America, not being able to find all the male teachers from among their own group, recruited from among their women because the latter could be trusted and relied upon to be faithful to the agreed national project.

In this regard White native-born middle class American Protestants were acting no differently from royal men and women in Sumerian kingdoms in the third millennium BCE, or naditu and their families in Old Babylonia, or Jewish men and women in the Diaspora, or kings, princes, their wives, daughters and nieces in Anglo-Saxon England.

Grumet and Douglas are absolutely right that feminisation did not change the fundamental nature of patriarchy and that women complied with its preservation in the new circumstances. The point is that the abolition of patriarchy was not part of the national project. What was at stake was the preservation of the cultural heritage of White native-born English Protestants against immigrants, Catholics and Blacks and, to a lesser degree, lower class native-born Americans. It was this context that prompted the relaxation of patriarchal closure within the group, allowing women of the group to enter occupations that were previously inaccessible to them. Further, it is on those grounds that women co-operated with their men, against the interests of women of the other groups. Just as their men were not displaying gender solidarity with the men of the groups that were perceived as threat, so were the women not displaying similar gender solidarity with women of the other groups.

Disputes over pay differential between men and women and the glass ceiling in their promotional prospects constituted internal squabbles that did not in any way alter the hegemonic mission relative to the threatening groups, against whom they had closed ranks. In the process patriarchy in the private sphere of White, native-born English Protestant was enlarged in the public sphere as this group now exercised hegemony over all other groups.

Most of the scholars commenting on the justification of women as teachers on moral and religious grounds have stressed its relationship to the Victorian reconstruction of womanhood as having special powers different from men, and to Scottish common sense philosophers who differentiated between masculinity and femininity on the basis of powers of intellect and sensitivity. While these connections were no doubt made by the reformers, it would appear that the attempt made by the Protestant school reformers, laymen and ministers, to define themselves and female teachers went beyond the accepted wisdom and conventions of their times.

In moving forward to fashion teachers for the nation's schools, these reformers appeared also to be reaching backward to some of the masculine and feminine roots of teaching in Christianity and Judaism. They returned to the ethic of love and kindness and rejected punishment and fear. They also drew heavily on the broad paradigms that had developed within the Religious Age and adjusted them to the new context. In Judeo-Christian civilisation the masculine roots of teaching were in the prophetic tradition and in the clergy. In the transformation into the common school movement, the essential elements of the prophetic tradition were transferred from a religious to a nationalist setting. The prophetic rationale for schooling was to create the new nation and the new national society, within the context of America's unique and peculiar destiny and mission in human history as a democratic Republic. These nationalist prophets projected the essence of the nation and the national to be created, through the instrumentality of schooling, and worked to translate vision into reality.

The early school reformers were either Protestant ministers or laymen, or scholars of the main denominations. It is almost impossible not to make some linkages between the members of the American Institute of Education and the tradition of the prophets. The theology was a mixture of Protestantism, education and nationalism, combining and blending religion, nation building and learning. This imagery seems appropriate since it is not possible to explain their action solely in political terms as Whigs, or in terms of status seekers as Katz suggests, or as capitalists seeking to promote class interest and hegemony. Capitalists are not known to send their children to common schools with ordinary people or to promote such egalitarian values where it applies to themselves and their children.

Chastened by disestablishment of the churches, rejected at the polls, fearful of being overwhelmed in the future as their own numbers declined, they could think of only one answer: acculturate and assimilate everybody through education until they became like them. However quaint this may appear they were convinced of it and devised a programme to do just that. Their sincerity of purpose is beyond doubt even if there is disagreement with the intention.

The feminine roots of teaching in Christianity rested in the cult of the pure woman, the virgin. This was the foundation principle of female monasticism, the location of the inauguration of women's careers as teachers. The monasteries had been closed, but the post-Reformation Catholic Church had preserved that tradition in teaching orders of nuns. Catholic religious women teachers now challenged the Protestant churches in the mission of redemption through education. It does not seem far-fetched to suggest that in recruiting unmarried female teachers for schools the Protestant reformers were creating their version of the pure woman as teacher. This possibility becomes more probable when it is considered that the reformers did not design the system to accommodate the school dames who had long experience in teaching children. School dames as wives belonged to the penitential tradition. They were dispossessed in the new arrangements.

A defining feature of the Early Church and Catholic tradition of the pure woman as teacher was that it was completely separated from that of wife and mother and suitably sanctified by vow and demarcated by clothing. The Protestant reconstruction of the pure woman as teacher arranged the occupation of teaching sequentially with marriage and motherhood. The young women were first teachers and then moved unto the roles of wives and mothers. At the point of marriage she was either required, or expected, to resign from teaching. The Protestant reconstruction of the pure woman as teacher did not require her to make a life long commitment to teaching, as was the case with the Catholics. This is consistent with much of Protestant theology, which does not celebrate celibacy as a form of holiness. The virgin teacher having performed her angelic mission in redeeming the school was expected to proceed to her ordained earthly mission of founding and maintaining a family as faithful wife and loving mother. That was the rationale.

The common school movement, and later the public school system that evolved from it, recruited women as teachers, based on the concept of the pure woman and not mothers performing a nurturant role. Clifford (1991) showed that up to 1930 married women constituted only 17.9 per cent of women teachers. It is only in the postwar period that this pattern changed. Salvation and redemption of the school was the mission not the domestic task of caring for and nurturing the young.

Douglas, Grumet and Sugg were misguided in stressing nostalgia, sentimentality and mothering as the genesis of feminisation of teaching in the United States. The feminisation of teaching was predicated on the symbol of the virgin, the pure woman and not on wives and mothers. The women in partnership with men were not mothers but unmarried women who, on the assumption of their virginity, could act as men. Motherhood came after these unmarried women had performed their teaching role based on purity.

Nowhere is the significance of this sequence better highlighted than with respect to single women who made teaching a lifelong career. They found themselves in the invidious position of having performed the mission of purity in the school, but not having moved on to the domestic mission, which was in the home. In time, such women came to be perceived as flawed, unable to secure a husband in the marriage market and to experience motherhood (Oram, 1989). It is against this background that the spinster teacher became a comic character, stereotyped as a miserable and frustrated woman despite her faithful and meritorious service as a teacher. Woman's true profession had betrayed the spinster teacher by denying her due recognition for her teaching service in the public sphere because she had not moved to the domestic roles of wife and mother in the private sphere.

It is this combination of prophet as senior partner and pure woman as the junior partner that sets out on the joint mission to promote and preserve the new nation in their image. Many studies of the feminisation of teaching in the United States in the nineteenth century have recorded the work of this partnership as school systems were created in cities in the Northeast. However, cities were just one site of the operation of the partnership. The partnership in the city targeted the immigrants pouring in from Europe. Other sites at which this partnership can be observed at work are the expansion of schooling in the West and the creation of schooling for Blacks in the South following emancipation. Each example of the partnership requires some elaboration.

The Partnership at Work in the West

Kaufman (1984) gave a full description of women teachers in the West. Unless otherwise stated Kaufman's account will be summarised and interpreted here to illustrate the example of partnership of secular national prophet and pure woman creating the national system of schooling in the United States. As early as the 1820s Emma Williald and later Zilpah Grant began answering calls for female teachers in the West (Scott 1979). A primary impetus for this effort was competition with schools already set up by the Catholic Church. In 1831, the Rev Lyman Beecher, who was a member of the American Institute for Education, had relocated in Cincinnati and he along with Catharine began campaigning for teachers for the West (Hoffman 1981). One of Lyman Beecher's chief concerns was the head start that the Catholics had in establishing schools in the West.

By 1852, the recruitment of teachers had been formalised in the National Board that sent approximately 25 female teachers twice per year to fill teaching posts in the West. These Protestant women were of different denominations united in purpose not only to redeem the rugged frontier people but also to prevent them from being won over by this new rival, the Catholic Church.

Prior to being posted all applicants were trained at the Teachers' Institute at Hartford. Applicants had to be single, Protestant and evangelical. Each woman had to write about her conversion experience and provide supporting evidence of Christian witness from her ministers. Those unable to meet this religious test were deferred. In the six-week stay at the Institute candidates were not only tested to ensure their academic and pedagogic competence but also specifically instructed in methods of discipline that depended on moral suasion and example, as prescribed by the Golden Rule. In addition to callisthenics to improve their physical condition and health, they were given inspirational lectures, taken on visits to various kinds of institutions and oriented to life in the West.

Kaufman's analysis of the social background and correspondence of more than 600 of these female teachers sent to the West by the Board revealed the following:

- They were daughters of native-born Northeastern craftsmen or farmer families.
- Most were daughters of first generation literate women.
- Most were either already self-supporting while the remainder had a strong desire to live by 'their own exertions'.
- They were all fired with Republican zeal to prepare an educated citizenry in the new nation. They felt empowered by their Christian faith and had a strong sense of acting according to the will of God.
- Some wanted a change from New England and had a sense of adventure.
- A half had lost one or both parents or suffered adversely from the death of a family member.
- Most already had teaching experience, two-thirds having taught for more than three years before moving West.

In looking at their impact on the West, Kaufman's main findings were:

a) Two-thirds of them became settlers. The third who returned had less teaching experience and strong family ties in the East including both parents being alive.

b) Eighty per cent got married, a higher proportion than their peers in the East. Most of them married men of higher social position and were usually second wives of established men. Three-quarters of those who married were more than 25 when they got married.

c) Many of those who remained single continued teaching for the rest of their lives and some became legends in their communities.

d) Almost all were described as 'fixed centres of intellectual and religious influence'.

e) Several either became foreign missionary teachers for a time or joined the freedmen teaching corps in the 1860s.

Kaufman noted that several teachers reported having been discouraged by friends and families from taking the bold step of going West. Their courage is attested by the fact that it was not easy to get recruits to go West who matched all the criteria. Many who applied and were accepted changed their minds, some at the last minute before going. She made the point that their actions cannot be explained solely in terms of economic, social and religious factors since this would imply that all female teachers of evangelical persuasion who met the criteria and had the social characteristics would have gone West. Certainly individual choice and character played an important part.

The impact they had on the West is attested to by the fact that the female teacher from the East became part of the legend, literature and folklore. The schoolmistress of the East is portrayed in Western lore as the ideal woman: moral, self-sacrificing, discreet, dedicated to children and capable of bringing the best out of men. This does not appear to be just the propaganda of the Eastern schoolmen or their supporters in the press. It appeared to have had some lived reality, which approximated to this portrayal.

It is impossible to explain the actions of these women, and the men who organised and supervised the operations, simply in terms of market forces. At the same time, there is no gainsaying the fact that many of these pioneering teachers did well for themselves particularly in finding husbands, a traditional concern of women. Through marriage several enjoyed upward social mobility that probably would not have been theirs had they stayed in the East. However, there is a sense of mission and cause that is manifest in their actions that defies reduction to pedestrian purposes resident in domesticity, docility or sentimentalism. Belief, in the form of nationalism, cultural heritage and piety, albeit of a Protestant and evangelistic complexion, provide answers where supply and demand, gender roles, exploitation, bureaucratisation and school formalisation come to dead ends.

The Partnership at Work in Freedmen Education in the South

The Civil War, and the abolition of slavery associated with it, provided yet another challenge to which the Northeastern Protestant partnership of national prophets and pure women responded. The main groups providing assistance to this effort included evangelicals, liberals and Quakers. The evangelicals offered their assistance through the American Missionary Association, AMA, which generally combined teaching and missionary work in a non-sectarian alliance. The liberals offered their assistance through the American Freedmen Union Commission. They stressed secular reforms. The Friends Association for Aid and Elevation of the Freedmen took a position in-between the evangelicals and the liberals in that they stressed secular reforms but were also mindful of missionary activity.

The AMA entered the field of freedmen's education in 1862. They established schools staffed mainly with teachers from the Northeast. The criteria used to recruit teachers for the freedmen's schools included personal conversion experience, sound character as evidenced by testimonials, good health, energy and educational experience. The AMA discouraged both elderly and very young applicants. It did not appoint any applicant under the age of 22 years. Preferred candidates were those between the ages of 25 and 40 years (Morris 1981). In 1864 the AMA published an ideal letter from an applicant, in its monthly publication, which portrayed that applicant as a young woman possessed of a missionary spirit and devoid of mercenary or romantic motives. She was in good health, energetic, earnest, grave, experienced as a teacher and from an evangelical religious background (Jones 1979).

Several of these teachers had either previously served in the West, or were foreign missionaries. The Committee for West Indian Missions was a predecessor to the AMA and had supported the emancipation effort in Jamaica through the deployment of missionaries there. Participation in the Jamaica mission was part of the advocacy for abolition by showing from that example the feasibility of emancipation. As such the establishment of schools in Jamaica after 1834, and the support of those schools by American missionaries, provided training for the effort to educate freemen in the 1860s (Morris 1981).

In their selection of teachers the Unitarians, Rationalists and Universalists, who made up the bulk of the liberal Protestant faction, stressed personal virtue, social enlightenment, respect for man as a rational being, and recognition and respect for moral law. Stressing ethical considerations, intellectual culture, attainments in this life, female virtue, kindness and the priceless worth of simple human relations the liberals came to the same conclusion as the evangelicals, that assisting the freedmen was of the uttermost importance in facilitating their transition from slavery to full citizenship.

Irrespective of the criteria employed in the selection of the teachers, or the stated rationale of the particular societies for their involvement in freedmen's education, most of the teachers from the Northeast were female. They were native-born, single, White females, of Protestant conviction, below the age of forty years (Morris 1981). Their supervisors, superintendents and managers of the enterprises were more mature White males, usually married, of Protestant conviction, and in several instances ministers of various denominations. As Tyack and Hansot (1982) had noted for the public school system as a whole, men managed and women taught in the schools established in support of freedmen's education.

Jones (1979) observed, in her study of the archives of the AMA, that the Yankee women teachers reflected a wide range of opinions. Among them were views ranging from what could be regarded as modern feminist sentiments, to subtle forms of resistance, to outright acquiescence to the dictates of the Association. Of the 300 women included in her sample only three, one per cent, challenged the AMA on its policy of paying women less than men although they were openly critical of other decisions of the Association. Further, while the women insisted on consent as the guiding principle of governance, there was never any doubt that able men of earnest Christian conviction would always lead. Disagreements centred on incompetence or practices regarded as deviations from Christian teaching. In other words, the available evidence suggests that Yankee women were consenting partners in the AMA operations, differing from the males mainly with respect to questions related to the soundness of educational practices and the faithful observance of Christian principles.

Over 7000 Yankee women teachers went to the South to teach freed Blacks. They lived in Black communities, acted as teachers, preachers, doctors, domestic and political advisors and were generally involved in the life of the communities in which they lived. While this degree of engagement was not without tension on both sides, the Yankee teachers were much better received in the Black communities than by Southern Whites who were openly hostile to them, labelling them 'nigger lovers'. (Hoffman 1981).

In the North these young White middle class women teachers were perceived as embodying all the female virtues: grace, elegance, piety, patience, purity of purpose and self-sacrifice. Venturing into the war torn territory, their virtue fulfilled the sacrifice of blood made by the Yankee soldiers. The actions of these Yankee women teachers bore strong resemblance to the royal Anglo-Saxon women of the seventh and eighth centuries in England who, as abbesses and nuns, attempted to pacify the kingdoms won by the blood by their male kin. Female piety and purity following in the wake of male fury in warfare brought completeness, as it sought to bring to fruition the noble purpose which justified the conflict.

In the South, Yankee women teachers were not only hated by White Southerners, but also stereotyped in very unfavourable terms. They were portrayed as horse-faced, bespectacled, spare of frame, wanting in intellect, meddlers, bigoted, narrow-minded and fanatical (Hyatt-Brown 1994). Cash (1954) regarded them as comic figures at best, and at worse as dangerous fools playing with explosive forces they did not understand. To say that young single White Northern female teachers were operating in hostile territory is an understatement. To claim that all remained unaffected by that hostility would be an overstatement. As Morris (1981) pointed out some White Northern women teachers, in making conscious efforts to conform to White Southern mores on race mingling, discriminated against the Blacks whom they had come to serve. In this, they were by no means immune to the circumstances in which they sought to execute their nobly conceived mission.

Among the Blacks there were several points of tension. Blacks preferred teachers of their own race (Butchart 1994). They were suspicious of White philanthropy including the missionary effort. Northern White teachers and missionaries manifested a wide range of attitudes, views and personal opinions. Some were almost as prejudiced as the Southern Whites, while others were fiercely opposed to encroachments on the rights of the freedmen and vociferous in their defence of those rights (Brown 1994). Notwithstanding the tensions, misgivings, misperceptions, suspicions and prejudice the Northern missionaries and women teachers succeeded in establishing a bridge between Blacks and Whites. From this beginning in freedmen's education the partnership established links that endured the initial paternalism of missionary benevolence, doubts about the intellectual capacity of Blacks and suspicions on the part of Blacks of the genuineness of the motivation of the assistance offered (Anderson 1988). Indeed, the partnership won praise and acceptance from even a critical advocate such as W.E.B. Dubois (Morris 1981). Dubois regarded the Yankee women teachers as heroines.

Morris (1981) noted that neither the AMA nor the Commission took any precautions to conceal their prejudice against employing Catholics as teachers in the schools that they operated. Also, few Catholics were employed in the schools supported by the Freedmen's Bureau, which was a Federal agency in the War Department. Even then, these few Catholic teachers were reported on in an unfavourable manner. The prejudice was even deeper if they were Irish. The oft-expressed view was that the Pope desired to control Blacks in a manner similar to his control of the Irish. Indeed, Protestant groups competed in terms of which was better equipped and more effective in meeting the Catholic threat. In an article, *Rome in the Field* that was published in newspapers of both the evangelical and liberal groups, the Pope and Catholics were charged with being part of a plot to gain control of the US Government. The central element of the conspiracy was the formation of a political coalition between the European immigrants coming into the country and the Southern Blacks recently emancipated. A key strategy in defeating this conspiracy was the education of the freedmen and their conversion to the Protestant faith.

Just as White Protestant men and women of English ancestry were co-operating as managers and teachers in the growing school systems in rapidly expanding cities of the Northeast to ensure that the immigrants were assimilated and acculturated into American culture, and just as this partnership was operating in the Westward expansion of the frontier, so too it was at work in the aftermath of emancipation and in reconstruction in the South. The unique aspect of the Southern situation was the confrontation of the Northeast with its rival claimant to the White Protestant English heritage, the Southern planter elite and their allies.

The criteria used by these Northern agencies to select and hire teachers posed severe problems for teacher recruitment. What was interesting was that the Northern Protestant leadership found it much easier to compromise with their Southern rivals than with Catholics. Morris (1981) pointed out that the Freedmen's Bureau showed remarkable tolerance towards Southern Whites who offered themselves to teach Black students particularly persons who had been sufficiently humbled by circumstances namely 'women of reduced circumstances' and 'broken down schoolmasters'. Hence in Charleston in May 1865 of the 100 teachers in the city, 30 were Yankee teachers, 25 were Southern Blacks and 45 were Southern Whites. The clash between the South and the North was not with respect to the core values of the English Protestant heritage but rather with respect to who should dominate the Union. The war having settled the latter, it was possible to begin to find scope for co-operation with respect to the former despite the fact that White Southern teachers could not be expected to be zealous about the education of the freedmen.

The feminisation of teaching in nineteenth century America cannot be interpreted principally within the framework of industrialisation, urbanisation and class conflict. Its occurrence in rural areas, among Blacks and immigrants must be viewed against the wider background of nationalism, the imposition of a national culture and the competition between groups in the society for dominance in the new nation. White, Protestant Americans, largely of English ancestry, managed to preserve in the period of independence the dominance they had enjoyed within the colonial society. Feminisation of teaching was one of the processes and mechanisms by which this dominance was perpetuated and preserved.

Seven

THE TRANSFORMATION OF SCHOOLING AND TEACHING IN THE COMMONWEALTH CARIBBEAN

Commonwealth Caribbean populations are unique within the Americas by virtue of three demographic features. First, people of European ancestry constitute the minority in every country. Second, people of African or Asian ancestry comprise the majority in all the countries. Indeed, the Caribbean is the only region outside of Africa in which people of African ancestry constitute the majority in any country. Third, except in a few of the smaller islands and in Belize, Dominica, St Vincent, Suriname, and Guyana, the first Americans are virtually non-existent, having died out or retreated following European entry into the region. However, given the colonial history of the region Europeans have dominanted Commonwealth Caribbean society albeit as a dominant minority that had to contend with marginal majorities of people of other racial groups. To varying degrees all the peoples of the civilisations of the Old World confronted each other on Commonwealth Caribbean soil but with different positions relative to power, wealth and status.

A mix of geographical, cultural, political and demographic features combine to produce the unique Caribbean ethos which partially explains why Belize in Central America and Guyana and Suriname in South America have always identified themselves as Caribbean. Notwithstanding these unique features, the Caribbean shares several features with the rest of the New World. These can be listed as follows:

1. There were no aboriginal Caribbean people tracing their origins to antiquity. All the peoples of the Caribbean came from the Old World at different times, by diverse means and for divergent reasons.
2. The first people of the Caribbean were Asians who having migrated through continental America then settled the Caribbean. These first American were joined by small bands of explorers from Africa (van Sertima 1995) Their entry into the Caribbean predated European 'discovery' by more than a thousand years.
3. Since Columbus the first Americans have either been eliminated, or driven to the periphery of the societies to the extent that their influence on culture and the nature of society has been exceedingly marginal.

4. Since Columbus the region has been part of Western European civilisation. The particular version that dominates in different territories varies with territorial possession by specific Western European countries that exercised imperial control.

Caribbean diversity makes the region the closest approximation to a social laboratory that can be found in nature. In many instances geographical, political, cultural and linguistic borders coincide in these countries. However, the idiosyncratic tendencies that these coincidences promote occur against a background of shared history and social milieu, similar demographic and economic parameters and common imperatives in their interrelationships with the rest of the hemisphere and the world. The result is that any common economic, social or political stimulus can be expected to generate an array of responses in both time and space. The result is naturally occurring control and experimental groups. Systematic comparative analysis of Caribbean reality, therefore, has the potential to yield insights of wide generalisations about any particular phenomenon that is investigated.

After their 'discovery' by Colombus, Hispaniola and Cuba became the base from which Central America, the northern coast of South America and the Gulf of Mexico were explored and conquered. All trade from these mainland colonies of Spain, including the enormous exports of silver from Peru (carried across the Isthmus of Panama by mule train) had to pass through the Caribbean Sea. The silver fleet from Mexico joined the Peruvian silver at Havana. Peruvian and Mexican silver financed Spain's wars against the Dutch, the French and the English in the sixteenth century. These nations retaliated in two ways – by illicit trading with the Spanish colonies and by raids on the silver fleets and on ports in and around the Caribbean. They did not try to seize and settle territory till the seventeenth century. Spain defended the Greater Antilles and left all of the Bahamas and the Lesser Antilles, except Trinidad, to their competitors. In challenging Spain's hold on the Greater Antilles the English were successful in capturing Jamaica, while the French seized the more mountainous parts of Hispaniola thus sharing that island with Spain. The English settled Barbados, the Bahamas and some of the Lesser Antilles, while the French and the Dutch shared the rest of the Lesser Antilles between them.

Barbados was English from first colonisation and remained so, but several of the islands of the Lesser Antilles changed hands between European powers at some time in their history. Some did so several times. Grenada was French and became English. So too were St Lucia and Dominica. In these islands, while the official language became English, the vernacular of the people remained a French based Creole indicating their previous relationship and some degree of resistance to the change.

Commonwealth Caribbean nationalism has antecedents stretching back into the early decades of the eighteenth century through the successful wars fought against the British by the Maroons in Jamaica which culminated in the Treaties of 1739–40. As Campbell (1990) pointed out, the treaties established quasi-states within the colonial slave society in which the Maroons won for themselves freedom and a measure of autonomy.

Lewis (1983) pointed to elements of both cultural and political nationalism in the Commonwealth Caribbean from the latter part of the eighteenth century, of which the Fedon Rebellion in Grenada in the last decade of the eighteenth century is an important marker. Lewis also made the point that nationalism in the Commonwealth Caribbean has antecedents not only in rebellions and in cultural traditions of people of African ancestry but also to the constitutional traditions of Creole whites. From very early in the colonial period, English settlers had some control over taxation and legislation – which they regarded as the rights and freedoms of Englishmen – through the election of Assemblies modelled on the House of Commons. The only Commonwealth Caribbean islands which never had an elected assembly were St Lucia and Trindad, captured late in the eighteenth century from France and Spain, whose inhabitants were therefore not regarded as having English traditions. Opposition to the British government, as expressed by eighteenth century Creole Whites like Edward Long of Jamaica, was not 'nationalism' in the modern sense, but it was a very definite sense of interests different from those of Britain. There were often fierce quarrels between assemblies and governors attempting to carry out unpopular imperial policies. Benn (1987) maintained that Caribbean nationalism is clearly discernable, in an articulated form, from the middle of the nineteenth century and has continued in unbroken expression to the present time.

In the nineteenth century, Commonwealth Caribbean countries were still colonies. However, the abolition of slavery in 1838 set in train a series of developments designed to create free society based on the rights of citizens. Athough political sovereignity did not come until the latter half of the twentieth century the national society began to be constructed from the first half of the nineteenth century. It is not their external political status that is critical to this study but rather their internal institutional structures premised on freedom, citizenship and the rule of law. Of crucial importance to this study is the fact that schooling and teaching were vital elements in the construction of this free society following the abolition of slavery in 1838. This chapter will attempt to examine the beginning of the transformation of schooling and the masculine and feminine roots of teaching in the Commonwealth Caribbean in circumstances in which Europeans were the dominant minority who had to allow schooling to be provided to the marginal African and Indian majority.

A SYNOPSIS OF THE HISTORY OF COMMONWEALTH CARIBBEAN PEOPLES AND SOCIETY

Initially the English colonists who came to the Caribbean differed from those who settled on mainland America only in terms of the location they chose. Their time of arrival was about the same, beginning with St Christopher in 1624, Barbados in 1627, Nevis in 1628 and Antigua and Montserrat in the 1630s. Dunn (1972) pointed out that the English colonists in North America and those in the Caribbean islands established the same institutional arrangements. A governor, council and representative assembly administered each colony. Each colony was divided into parishes and vestries and had justices of the peace at the local level.

However, in North America, the colonists could be divided into two main groups: those who had come to settle largely for religious reasons and those whose main mission was the pursuit of material gain. The former desired to perfect their faith in permanent settlements in the New World. They prized and guarded jealously their right to make their own decisions. They cherished and worked toward a new vision of humanity and society, often practising a stern and austere lifestyle. The latter sought a fortune and kept alive the prospect of return to the Old World where they hoped to live in the style befitting the fortune made in the New World. They were not averse to external direction if this promoted material gain. In their sojourn in the Caribbean, these colonists practised a lifestyle that rejoiced in its release from the constraints and restrictions of European society as interludes of celebration punctuated work routines.

This is not to say that there was no attempt in the Caribbean to establish colonies where piety dominated the decision-making process. Indeed, this was the case with the Providence Company modelled on the Puritans of the Massachusetts Bay Company. The king chartered this company in 1630. Its mission was to establish in the Caribbean a godly commonwealth of similar ilk to the New England colonies. Three islands were settled with this stated mission: Providence (Santa Catalina), Henrietta (San Andreas), and Tortuga (Dunn 1972). However, the lure and opportunity of quick profit from pirating and buccaneer assaults on Spanish territory overwhelmed religious piety to such an extent that the Puritan missions in the Caribbean were shortlived. The temptation of quick and large profits undermined piety and corrupted its adherents.

The English first came to the New World during the Elizabethan era not to colonise but to trade with or raid Spanish settlements in the Caribbean and seize their ships. Starting with John Hawkins in the 1560s and followed by Francis Drake in 1573 and 1585 and Walter Raleigh in search of El Dorado between 1584 and 1604, English traders and privateers engaged in both illicit trade with and piracy against Spanish possessions in the Caribbean. Dunn (1972) estimated that between 1560 and 1630 London merchants invested more money in commerce and piracy in the Caribbean than in any other mode of overseas business including the East India Company.

The English colonists in the Caribbean had much in common with those in the Southern colonies. The plantation was the institutional framework of material gain. Servile labour was the main means of extracting wealth. The established Anglican Church provided ideological support and spiritual comfort.

At the same time, it would be misleading to conceive of the Caribbean colonies as Southern colonies replicated on the islands. The Caribbean colonies differed from those in the Southern United States in four important and interrelated respects.

1. The English colonists fast became a minority in circumstances in which people of African ancestry became the vast majority, later to be joined by large numbers of people from South Asia in some colonies like Trinidad and Guyana.

2. Active competition between the European powers within the region meant that colonies were not only vulnerable to attack but that the particular power in control of any colony had to take into account the policies of their rivals and developments in the neighbouring colonies.

3. Men without families constituted the majority of the colonists in most places. Hoping to return to England having made a fortune, they were reluctant to invest in permanent institutions essential to settled community.

4. The lifestyle within the Caribbean manifested tendencies towards licentiousness. The local hero was the 'Grandee': the man who rode hard, drank much, gambled recklessly and had a lot of 'brown skinned' progeny.

Each of these has left deep marks upon society and culture in the Caribbean as they evolved from these beginnings. For example, while Europeans dominated the society politically and economically, they had to contend with an African majority that consistently resisted domination by a variety of means including violence. As such, the European minority lived in fear of its safety, which occasioned oscillation between the imposition of brutal measures and substantial amelioration of conditions.

Ironically, although Hakluyt gathered much of his data about the New World from the privateers of the Elizabethan period, and while his book, *Principal Navigations of the English Nation* contained detailed descriptions of sailing between the islands, Hakluyt did not envision planting colonies in the Caribbean. His paradigm for English colonial expansion in the New World centred on continental America. Equally ironical was the fact that it was in the Caribbean that Hakyluyt's paradigm for colonisation achieved its immediate success. Starting with Barbados which switched from tobacco to sugar plantations in the 1640s, the English became efficient producers of sugar and captured the lion's share of the growing European sugar market as the taste for sweetness spread across that continent (Mintz 1985). The wealth generated by the Caribbean colonies in the late seventeenth and eighteenth centuries far outstripped that of the North American colonies. As such, the Caribbean colonies became more valuable and important to England than her North American possessions (Mintz 1974). In the inter-relationships between English colonies in the New World in these two centuries, the flow of assistance and expertise was from the islands to the mainland. While this position reversed itself in the nineteenth and twentieth centuries the recognition of the early importance of the English possessions in the Caribbean is critical to understanding several differences between this region and English North America.

There are four important observations to that which must be made regarding the early success of the Caribbean colonies.

1. Wealth generated in the Caribbean was a substantial contributor to English capital formation, which made the industrial revolution possible.

2. Because the wealth generated in the Caribbean colonies was exported, the Caribbean colonies experienced short-term prosperity but long term under-development since the benefits derived from their early comparative advantage in sugar production did not form the basis for diversification into other economic enterprises. As Best (1968) observed the Caribbean possessions were colonies of exploitation, to be contrasted with the colonies of settlement, which retained much more of the wealth they generated.

3. Contact between the mainland and island colonies was established early with respect to trade and fund-raising in which advantage rested with the Caribbean and not the American colonies. Wealth generated in the Caribbean helped to build several institutions in North America (Hill and Parboosingh 1951).

4. The colonists in the Caribbean were the first among the English to deploy large numbers of African slaves in plantation production. Many Caribbean planters were instrumental in passing on their knowledge to Southern planters.

THE CLASH OF CIVILISATIONS AND COSMOLOGIES IN THE CARIBBEAN

In a very profound way, practically all of the major civilisations and cosmologies that had emerged and evolved in human history converged and confronted each other on Caribbean soil. Western Europeans came in pursuit of profit or piety. Jews came disguised as Christians as they sought to escape the Inquisition in Spain. West Africans were brought by coercive means and by a cruel mode of transhipment. Later peoples of South Asia and China, offering themselves as indentured labourers, came in search of better economic prospects. Later still, Syrians and Lebanese from Western Asia came as petty traders, for much the same reasons as Indians and Chinese.

These Old World peoples did not come to the Caribbean at the same time or in the same numbers. They did not enter Caribbean society in the same positions of power, wealth and status. Inequality marked and marred the course of their interaction. Neither did all groups settle in similar numbers in the different Caribbean locations. Given these variations, therefore, their influence in shaping Caribbean society and culture were by no means uniform. Yet, what is indisputable is that in their entirety, these Old World peoples brought to the Caribbean the generic forms of all the civilisations and cosmologies that had evolved in human history and in so doing contributed to the shaping of the mosaic, which now constitutes Caribbean society and culture.

The Western Europeans, in the case of the Commonwealth Caribbean, were the English. They were by virtue of their position as conquerors the dominant civilisation and culture despite the fact that they were numerically in the minority. Enough has been written about the content of the English version of Western European civilisation in chapters 5 and 6 to require no further elaboration here, except to note the fact that the English cosmology that had official sanction in the Caribbean was not only Christian but Anglican Protestant. It is necessary, however, to give brief sketches of the cosmology of the non-European peoples who composed Caribbean society.

The Africans brought to the Caribbean as slaves constituted the majority in mid-millennium Caribbean societies. While they occupied a subordinate position in the society, their numerical position as the majority group imposed its own importance from the perspective of culture and civilisation. Further, all but the ignorant should immediately perceive that they brought with them the generic form of ancient civilisation with the West African variants that had evolved over six thousand years of recorded history.

Chevannes (1995) and Lawson (1996) gave a full description of the cosmology of the West Africans when they entered the Caribbean which can be summarised as follows:

- They believed in a polytheistic cosmology comprised of a High God and a pantheon of lesser gods.
- The High God was the supreme creator but was removed and remote from humans and the daily routines of life that were under the control of a large number of lesser gods who mediated between humans and the High God.
- The lesser gods were related to natural phenomena. One set were heavenly deities related to thunder, lightening, rain, and sky while others were earthly deities related to such phenomena as fertility, diseases, sea, river, crops etc.
- The Africans paid great and careful attention to the lesser gods because they controlled the forces of the world and daily life and acted decisively in human affairs for good or ill.
- Each lesser god had a cultic tradition comprised of rituals, festivals, priests and devotees. The priests presided at worship and devotees in special ritual moments could become mediums of the god who could be recognised by the demeanour or the dance of the devotee.
- Related to the pantheon of lesser gods were the spirits of the ancestors who were the guardians and guarantors of the village, lineage or kinship collective. Veneration of ancestors was a matter of life and death, well

being or ill heath. Misfortune was usually attributed to an angry ancestor punishing the living for neglecting to offer proper sacrifices or failing to perform some customary rite.

- Funeral ceremonies and burial rites were matters of great importance and complexity because they could interfere with the repose of the departed or affect their entrance into the spirit world. Customs that had to be observed included the preparation of the body for burial, the wake, the ceremonious interment, mourning after burial and the celebration of the ninth night after the death of the person.

While these elements defined the general contours of the cosmology of the West Africans, there was no uniformity among the various tribes. On the contrary, there were numerous variations. These were reflected in the names and attributes ascribed to the High God and to the lesser gods as well as the relative emphasis and importance given to deities and the spirits of departed ancestors. For example, while the Yoruba and the Ibo paid careful attention to the pantheon of lesser gods, the people of the Congo were far more respectful to the spirit-world and spirits embodied in trees, particularly cotton trees, and sacred medicines.

When analysed in terms of both its generic features and detailed content it is abundantly clear that the cosmology of the West African peoples who came to the Caribbean was that of the first civilisations in Mesopotamia and Egypt, outlined in chapter 2. This was the cosmology from which Judaism, Christianity and Islam had diverged to inaugurate the monotheistic civilisations of the Religious Age. What is ironic was that at the same time that Western Europe was reconnecting with ancient civilisation and its learning, Western Europeans met African purveyors of that civilisation on Caribbean soil and labelled them primitive.

History had come full circle. The people of the ancient civilisations that had their genesis in Central Africa, and that came to maturity in North Africa, Western Asia and the Indus Valley and then spread westward to Greece and eventually to Rome, had regarded the rest of the world as barbarians. This included Europeans who were latecomers to civilisation. As pointed out in chapter 6 up to the end of the fifteenth century, Western Christian civilisation was seen and regarded as the least among civilisations when compared to Eastern Christian, Islamic and ancient civilisations. However, when Western Christian civilisation met the ancient civilisation of the Africans, and all other civilisations, in the New World and the Caribbean, Western Christianity claimed superiority and became dominant on the basis of military might.

Not all the Western Africans slaves were devotees of a polytheistic cosmology. A minority were converts of Islam. For example, Africans of the Hausa tribe of Northern Nigeria and the Cameroons were Muslims. However, the numbers of Muslims were sufficiently small and their dispersion across the colonies and plantations sufficiently diverse as to severely subvert and undermine adherence to Islam among the offspring of these Africans. Hence while Islamic civilisation entered the Caribbean with the Africans in the seventeenth and eighteenth centuries, the establishment of Islamic communities came later with the entrance of peoples from South Asia in the nineteenth century.

The point to note is that Islam entered the Caribbean via Africa and South Asia and not directly from Western Asia. Moreover, when at a later date Arabs migrated to the Caribbean mainly from Lebanon and Syria they were for the most part Christians and not Muslims. Islamic communities in the Commonwealth followed the distribution of Indian indentured labourers across the region and were established mainly in Guyana and Trinidad and to a lesser extent in Jamaica. Even then, Muslims were a minority among the peoples of South Asia.

Judaism entered the Caribbean colonies from the time of Christopher Columbus, as Jews disguised as Christians fled the Inquisition in the Iberian Peninsula. Just as Jews were expelled from England in 1290, they were being evicted from Spain and Portugal at the time of the entrance of the Iberians into the New World. Jews were therefore part of the Spanish settlement of Jamaica but remained after the Spanish departed after the English capture in 1655. Small communities of Jews also existed in Trinidad, Barbados and Guyana.

All the institutional forms that characterised Jewish communities in the Diaspora, which maintained the Judaic cosmology, were evident in the Commonwealth Caribbean. Jews lived in closely knit urban communities led by rabbis. Synagogues were the centres of Jewish life. Most Jews pursued careers related to trade, finance and the professions. Separate Jewish cemeteries were maintained for the burial of the dead.

The ancient civilisation of the Indus Valley entered the Caribbean through the Hindus of South Asia. Indeed, the vast majority of the peoples of South Asia who came to the Caribbean were Hindus. By the latter half of the nineteenth century, there was not a single type of Hinduism being practised. Some of the classical tenets of Hinduism can be summarised as follows:

- A polytheistic pantheon of gods hierarchically organised and headed by the Sanskritic deities, by virtue of being conceived as the purest manifestation of the Absolute. At the lower end of the pantheon would be deities of villages traditionally associated with epidemics.
- Humans lived in different states of being from the Brahman, considered to be the purest state of being, to the Charmar, untouchables, the most impure.
- The correspondence between the hierarchy of deities and states of being, and the ritual definition of castes and parallel priestly orders related to the several castes such that only Brahman priests could approach the Sanskritic deities.
- Cultic traditions related to the various deities with temples, shrines, regional centres and priests.

- A wide array of ceremonies, rituals, sacrifices and ascetic penance related to initiation, preparation for worship, purification to reinstate appropriate pure states of being after contact with substances and persons deemed to be impure.
- The concepts of duty, dhara, the accumulated consequences of action, karma and cycles of rebirths into different states of being, samsara.
- Scriptures, providing the faithful with sacred textual sources for their guidance.

Vertovec (1992) pointed out that by the time Indians arrived in the Caribbean in the second half of the nineteenth century, bhakti tradition in Hinduism, which had been developing for centuries, had gained increasing popularity over classical village and regional centred Hinduism. Further, the circumstances of indentured service outside of India were not conducive to the practice of classical Hinduism. However, bhakti-centred Hinduism was much better suited to the Caribbean context. Accordingly, it was not surprising that Hindus in the Caribbean, particularly Trinidad and Guyana, embraced the bhakti traditions. In this regard, Hindus in the Commonwealth Caribbean in relation to Hinduism were in no different position from that of reformed and orthodox Jews to Judaism.

The defining features of the bhakti tradition in Hinduism can be listed as follows:

- Personal devotion to God, usually in the form of Krisha or Rama.
- Anti-caste and egalitarian ethics.
- Ecumenism, able to span geographical and caste differences and promote inter-caste fraternisation.
- Congregational worship involving the reading of scriptures, expositions by pundits and the singing of bhajans, hymns of praise.
- Justifying bhakti ideals through reference to Tulsidas' Ramayana, Bhagavata Purana and Bhagavad Gita scriptures.

CULTURAL DOMINANCE AND CREOLISATION

English culture and Western European cosmology and civilisation, undergirded by imperial power, became the dominant cultural framework in the Commonwealth Caribbean. The English version of Western European cosmology and civilisation was deemed superior and all other cosmologies and civilisations – African, Muslim, Hindu and Judaism – were consigned to inferiority. Further, the machinery of the state, the pronouncements of the church, the biases infused into social status and the pre-conditions of material advancement in the society were all deployed to persuade and coerce all non-English peoples to adopt the English version of Western European culture.

African religion and culture were singled out for special treatment. African civilisation was denied while African culture was classified not only inferior but as designated primitive and barbarian. West African cosmology was deemed mere superstition and the practise of their festivals and rituals damned as demonic and often made illegal. Accordingly, in the clash of civilisations that took place on Caribbean soil, African civilisation was not only denied but relegated to the lowest place in the hierarchy of cultural forms that Old World peoples brought to the region.

However, English cultural dominance had to contend with imperatives of creolisation that undermined and subverted its hegemony. The imperatives of creolisation were rooted in two sets of processes.

The first set of processes driving creolisation related to the fact that all civilisations and cultures in the Caribbean had been displaced and disconnected from their moorings in the Old World, including that of the English. The vast majority of peoples who constituted Caribbean society cherished hopes of returning to their 'motherland'. Nascent Caribbean societies, therefore, were not undergirded with sentiments of settlement and presumptions of permanence.

The vast majority of the English hoped to make a fortune and return to Britain. The Africans dreamed to be freed from slavery and repatriated to Africa. East Indians and Chinese expected their indenture to provide sufficient material returns to allow their return to India and China in better positions than the ones they had left. Continued presence in the Caribbean represented frustration of hopes of return, the shattering of dreams of freedom and repatriation, and the deferral of expectations of material advancement. Probably the only group that were not anticipating any return to a motherland was the Jews. Actually, the initial experience of all the Old World peoples that constituted Caribbean society was that of becoming part of a Diaspora of their particular people.

A brief contrast must be made between the English in North America, particularly New England, and the English in the Caribbean. The commitment of the former to the New World was long term. Their adjustments and adaptations in North America were marked with assumptions of permanence. They named the resulting cultural transformation, American. The English who remained in the Caribbean lived with a sense of being trapped by circumstances, which they perpetually hoped would change. Their adjustments to the imperatives of the Caribbean were largely a series of short-term expediencies. At the same time, the circumstances of Caribbean societies did not allow the wholesale continuation of all aspects of Western European culture in this region. For example, only a pale imitation of European class structure could be replicated in the Caribbean where the monarchy was remote and the titled aristocracy and landed gentry virtually absent. The product of the necessary but unintended cultural transformation was labelled Creole. While the designation American portended something new and different, the designation Creole connoted pollution and inferiority. While similar cultural adaptations and adjustments to the New World were taking place in both North America and the Caribbean, the former assumed positive connotations and the latter attracted negative insinuations.

Put another way, while the English in the Caribbean were not deliberately attempting to transform their parent culture, the imperatives of the Caribbean dictated change and required adjustments to the specific context. Without the socio-political and socio-cultural infrastructure of England, over time English culture in the Caribbean diverged from the classical forms that had evolved in the mother country. Without any over arching design or grand vision, Caribbean divergence from the parent English culture carried audible undertones of deviation from the ideal and constant insinuations of impurity, contamination and inferiority.

Both the process and product of creolisation were all embracing. It referred to persons, their language and their lifestyle. The English most recent from England were real English, but the English who were born in the Caribbean, or had lived most of their life here, Creole. The latter were assumed to have been contaminated and polluted in the Caribbean. The Creole designation therefore subverted and undermined the imposition of English cultural dominance because of its perceived lack of authenticity.

The second set of processes related to the interaction between the several cosmologies and cultures, particularly with that of the Africans. The English in the Caribbean were a small minority group notwithstanding their position of imperial power and cultural dominance. The Africans were the vast majority, later joined by East Indians in some colonies like Trinidad, Guyana, St Lucia and Jamaica. English culture and Western European civilisation, therefore, did not only have to contend with disconnection and displacement from the socio-political and socio-cultural infrastructure of Europe, but more profoundly it had to interact on a daily basis with African, and later Indian, majorities as a small minority segment. While the English could deny African civilisation and pronounce African culture to be inferior, and impose English ways by means of imperial power, English culture and Western Christianity had to confront African culture and cosmology on a daily basis from the position of numerical minority. This confrontation left none of the parent cultures unchanged.

The point is that creolisation affected all the civilisations, cultures and cosmologies that clashed on Caribbean soil, including that of the imperial power (Nettleford 1978). A full treatment of this subject is beyond the scope of this book but it is important to note the broad parameters and the major trends of these cultural interactions. Caribbean culture and civilisation can be said to have commenced its construction with Creolisation. The latter embodied processes related to essential adaptations of parent English culture to Caribbean imperatives and syncretic interactions between the civilisations of the other Old World peoples who comprised Caribbean society.

English imposition of their culture, met with a range of responses that included outright acceptance, partial acceptance, covert resistance and open rejection. Likewise, creolisation always had to contend with varying degrees of retention of numerous aspects of the parent cultures. The intersection and merging of these two tributaries of cultural change resulted in Caribbean culture.

Formal schooling and education were among the principal means by which the English imposed their cultural hegemony. All social and economic advancement was routed through formal schooling and required mastery of the English language, conversion to Christianity and, even if in only nominal terms, being loyal British subjects pledging allegiance to the Crown.

While all the formal institutions of society were configured and manipulated to support the dominance of English culture, the culture of the folk and the informal institutions of society became the loci of resistance to cultural domination and the retention of non-English cultures. For example, creolisation, in terms of interaction between languages, resulted in Africans retaining the morphology and syntax of their Western African languages while infusing a largely English vocabulary, with the resultant creation of dialects which became the lingua franca of each colony. As they were in the minority, even the English had to learn this Creole dialect in order to communicate. Similarly, many Europeans resorted to African herbal cures for numerous illnesses and some even consulted obeah men where diseases did not respond to the standard Western treatment.

The implication for schooling was that non-European parents did not send their children to school to learn their ancestral culture but rather to master English culture, which was the pre-condition for socioeconomic advancement. Likewise, schools did not include in their curricula content that addressed the cultures of Africa and Asia, or the history and civilisation of non-Europeans. The latter were acquired through the home, and through informal institutions within the community. Creolisation was largely excluded from formal schooling, which was firmly premised on models from England and English culture.

RACE, CLASS AND GENDER

Mills (1993) referred to race, class and gender in the Caribbean as the unholy trinity of oppression. Their importance in shaping Caribbean society cannot be overestimated. A very brief attempt will be made here to mention some of the ways in which these three criteria have shaped society in the Caribbean.

Race and Colour

The position taken in this study is that race is a social phenomenon and not a biological fact. This position rests heavily on findings in genetic research, referred to in Chapter 2, which in large measure repudiate the skin-colour division of humanity into white, black, yellow and red racial groupings. The human gene pool reflects no such differentiation of DNA. Indeed, natives of Africa living in Africa have been shown to have much wider differences in their genetic composition among themselves than other populations across the world, which are all sub-sets of the diversity of genetic sequences found in Africa.

Race in its modern social meaning derived much of its content and construction from the interaction of Old World peoples in the New World. Europeans came to the New World calling themselves races of Spanish, Portuguese, English, Irish, Scots, Welsh, French, Dutch, Danes, Swedes, etc. They met peoples whom they called races of Apache, Comanche, Arawaks, Ciboney, Caribs, etc. From Africa, through the slave trade, came people referred to as races of Ibo, Mandingo, Coromantin, Fanti, Ashanti, Yoruba, Hausa, etc. From Asia came Cantonese, Dravidians, and Aryans. From the Mediterranean came Lebanese, Syrians and Jews. Out of this cauldron of difference came the reconstructed definition of race that reduced the multiplicity of races to four colour coded groups labelled White, Black, Yellow and Red. Race in the Old World was defined implicitly in terms of common ancestry, generic language, shared culture and people originating from a specific geographical area. This notion of race was transformed into the notion of skin-colour groups with presumed blood relationships based upon continental origin.

These racial distinctions had immediate social meaning in the dichotomy between free and slave, minority or majority, dominant or subordinate. For example, in Trinidad, English, Irish, Spanish and French who in Europe had historically maintained differences in defining themselves, were thrown together toward the end of the eighteenth century, as minority groups of free people belonging to different segments of the dominant group in the society. While the old differences did not disappear, for reasons of safety, security and material advancement these traditional adversaries developed common bonds, forged shared identity and maintained solidarity as White people.

Likewise, people from Africa, most of whose paths had never crossed on that continent, faced with a common exploiter, and needing to resist oppression, developed common bonds, found shared identity and sought to maintain solidarity as Black people. Hence, although the assumptions of colour-coded races were fictional, their social relevance, within the Caribbean and New World settings, gave race social meaning that became embedded in the lives of all who lived there and institutionalised in the mechanisms of social intercourse.

However, Caribbean lifestyle and demographics immediately compromised and complicated the definition of race based upon colour and other phenotypic characteristics. White men and Black women developed liaisons that produced mulatto or coloured children. Many Black slave women negotiated manumission for their coloured children with the White slave masters who had fathered them. Some White men, faced with the contradictions of the child/slave status of their children responded in their lifetime by manumitting their children, some others did so posthumously. A new stratum therefore emerged in Caribbean society – the Free Coloureds. Initially, they were free people with restricted rights and privileges. Jews were categorised by law in this same tier, with the same restrictions in rights and privileges.

There can be no question that, given the asymmetry in power, European men raped and sexually exploited many African women in the Caribbean (Beckles 1989). The horrors and pain experienced by these African women cannot be overstated. However, it must be acknowledged that there were African women who were not only or merely victims of European male exploitation. Some African women entered into consenting sexual relations with White men motivated by their own intentions of seeking freedom for their children from slavery. As Mintz (1974) pointed out both the asymmetry of power between White slave master and Black slave woman and the scarcity of European women combined to make slave women a virtual sexual reservoir from which White planters and their employees recruited sex partners. Three patterns became evident. Many masters temporarily acquired sexual partners from among slave women while aspiring to return to Europe and marry. Some masters maintained mistresses from among slave women even though married to European wives who had accompanied them to the Caribbean. A few masters married slave women, where this was permitted, and legitimised their children.

In this way, sex became a means of social mobility in the Caribbean and also the major means of compromising any rigid distinctions between these racial groups that were being defined by other more circumscribed relations. These sexual liaisons evolved into what Lewis (1987) referred to as Caribbean pigmentocracy. A Black woman and a White man produced a Mulatto. A Mulatto woman and a White man produced a Quadroon. A Quadroon woman and a White man produced a Mustee and a Mustee woman and White man produced a Mestee who was regarded as White. A Mulatto woman and a Black man produced a Sambo, and a Sambo woman and a Black man produced a Black child. In other words, race as it was reconstructed in the Caribbean became a hierarchy of shades of skin colour between Black and White. Jamaica passed a law in 1733 that declared as White individuals three degrees removed from African ancestry provided that they had been baptised into Christianity (Cox 1984).

It must be noted that in circumstances in which there were limited numbers of available White women, the sexual liaisons which developed across the so-called racial divide went beyond rape, promiscuity and bastard children and included common-law familial relations that sometimes persisted even where some White men married women of their own race. In many instances the men involved assumed parental responsibilities for their children, accorded them a social status outside of slavery and in some instances left them inheritances.

Three of the social implications that arose from sexual liaisons and familial relations between Black women and White men in the Caribbean can be listed as follows:

1. Neither Black nor White was an immutable social category but rather ends of a colour continuum, which accommodated recognised shaded intermediaries connecting both ends.
2. Inter-racial unions were means of social mobility in a society structured and organised on the basis of race. Through these unions, the colour of offspring was lightened or darkened with the consequential social implications. The dynamic aspect of the colour continuum was that by a series of back-crosses through sex with White men it was possible to become White after about five or six generations.
3. A White bias in the selection of sexual partners developed since rights and privileges resided with this group. Initially this bias manifested itself in circumstances of Black and Coloured women having liaisons with White men. Later it was reflected in successful Black and Coloured men marrying White women.

The White, Coloured, Jew and Black hierarchy formed the quintessential racial/colour matrix of Caribbean societies. Fashioned during the period of slavery this social construction of race/colour acquired legal, political, economic, ideological and cultural meaning and significance. All other groups that came into the societies after emancipation were integrated within this matrix. These included East Indians, Chinese, Lebanese, Syrians, Portuguese, Germans and Africans. The present composition of Caribbean societies evolved from the varying sizes and mix of this primordial hierarchy in the particular territories and the variations in the numbers of the newcomers who settled in the different colonies. Actually, no two territories are exactly alike, which is the essence of Caribbean diversity.

The Class Dimension

It would be misleading to think that any racial group identified in Caribbean colonial slave societies was either uniform or homogenous. In each group there were wide variations in occupation, prestige, income and power. For example, Whites varied from planters owning large plantations to bond servants pledged to service. Some Coloureds were numbered among the planters even if they were owners of smaller plantations. At the same time, many Coloureds were slaves, (Beckles 1989). Some free Blacks were owners of commercial enterprises in the towns, although the majority were slaves on the plantation. Among the slaves, there were distinctions between house and field slaves, headmen, artisans and labourers.

Class, understood as status group, probably best described the socioeconomic and cultural differentiation that existed within each group. These distinctions were important in how people perceived themselves and related to each other. While the notion of race may have evoked tendencies to solidarity and shared identity, class differentiated and divided the particular groups in their internal relations. The colour/class groupings that this created opened possibilities of alliances both within and outside the group. For example, White and Coloured planters formed alliances in their mutual interest even if solidarity of colour was breached in the particular situation. Jews formed alliances with free Blacks although the colour line was crossed. Again, White planters sometimes employed Black slaves in ways that cut across both colour and class lines. Beckles (1990) pointed out that in Barbados during the latter part of the seventeenth century White planters replaced White artisans with Black slaves when the cost of servants rose higher than that of slaves, leaving those Whites even more impoverished than before.

The point to note is that while race segregated the society into well-defined groups, class divided the racial groups into different segments. However, race was the primary criterion and division. Hence, class positions within a particular racial group could not compensate for or mitigate the position of that racial group in the overall society. Low status Whites regarded themselves, and were regarded, as superior to high status free Blacks.

Gender and Patriarchy

All Old World peoples brought their patriarchal traditions with them to the New World. It was the older men of all groups who exercised final authority in family and lineage matters. Jews and Akans were matrilineal in tracing their line of descent while almost all other groups were patrilineal. However, this did not alter masculine control but rather mitigated the extent of women's marginalisation in the two genealogical traditions. In the matrilineal groups, women played a more prominent role in lineage matters because of their role in tracing genealogical descent. However, this did not give mothers final authority in family and lineage matters. Among the Akan it was uncles who had the final authority in lineage matters. In other words, older males exercised final authority with respect to lineage matters related to the sisters, nephews and nieces and not over their wives, sons and daughters, but this did not fundamentally alter the patriarchal framework.

Slavery subverted patriarchy among people of African ancestry because African men, either as fathers or uncles, could not exercise control over their households and could not protect their women or children or nieces or nephews. The slave owners and their overseers had final authority. In a real sense, therefore, slavery in the Caribbean undermined the patriarchal traditions of African peoples as it undermined the traditional role of fathers, husbands, uncles and men in general in relation to their households and lineage.

A similar pattern emerged among Indians. Jayawardena (1963) noted that under indentured service the plantation organisation did much to subvert the power of fathers in Indian families in that they were no longer the sole trustee of the domestic resources of the kinship collective. Adult sons and wives had access to economic resources and accommodation that were beyond the fathers' control. Further, European managers arbitrated in all inter-personal disputes among the indentured Indians including the complaints of wives, daughters-in-law and sons against husbands, fathers-in-law and fathers. If in the opinion of the European manager the Indian father or husband was behaving unreasonably then the former would reprimand the latter in the presence of the complainants, thus undermining the traditional authority of the latter in domestic matters related to his household.

African and Indian were engaged in many situations in performing the same tasks as their men, except for being trained as artisans. While women earned less than men for the same tasks, some measure of economic independence was implied in their wage earning capacity.

Women of European ancestry, because they were often the wives or relatives of officials or planters, usually managed their households and were not engaged in paid occupation. These households usually had large numbers of servants. The slave society therefore reinforced and heightened the patriarchal traditions of Europe and promoted its continuation in the Caribbean setting.

One indirect and not too subtle way in which slavery promoted European patriarchal traditions was through the access European men had to the sexuality of not only White women, but Coloured and Black women as well. Holding the pinnacle of power and wealth in the society not only facilitated sexual abuse and rape of women of the subordinate groups but also made attractive dependent relationships by women bearing in mind the protection and privileges that could possibly emanate from such illicit relationships. Like feudal lords exercising customary rights, slave masters, their managing attorneys and bookkeepers demonstrated their patriarchal power through sex.

SCHOOLING IN THE COMMONWEALTH CARIBBEAN

Education and schooling was established and evolved within the social and cultural milieu outlined in the foregoing description of Caribbean society and culture. When the English began colonising the Caribbean in the early seventeenth century, they brought with them the concepts of education that represented the most up to date ideas of schooling in England and Western Europe at the time of the Reformation. By virtue of such wholesale borrowing from England the Caribbean colonies, like the North American colonies, advanced to the frontier of the evolution of schooling without going through the stages that had guided its development in the ancient world and later in Western Europe. From this starting point, it is possible to identify three major eras in the evolution of Commonwealth Caribbean education, which parallel, for different reasons, similar developments in the British empire and English-speaking world.

1.   Education through family and philanthropy.
2.   The denominational school system with state support.

3. The state school system with denominational management.

Each of these will be discussed briefly.

EDUCATION THROUGH FAMILY AND PHILANTHROPY

Chapter 5 gave a full description of the evolution of schooling in England up to the Reformation, while chapter 6 showed how various types of schools that evolved in England were imported into the North American colonies. Three aspects of that history are relevant here. First, the gradual extension of education to the laity, which had occurred mainly during the latter part of the Middle Ages, had resulted in the creation of several different types of schools. Second, the Protestant doctrine that insisted that individuals were responsible before God for their own salvation, and that they could interpret the Bible for themselves, had consequently made literacy an essential prerequisite of faith and personal piety. Third, endowments had evolved as a mechanism for providing free schooling for parents who were unable to teach their children themselves or afford to pay tutors to provide the necessary instruction.

In Anglican England these tendencies translated into an approach to education that was premised on the following principles:

- The laity should be educated for reasons of piety. That is, everybody should learn to read and understand the Bible and thereby be able to follow its precepts for themselves. The educational implication of this tenet of Protestantism was universal adult literacy.
- Education was the responsibility of the family, particularly that of the head of the household. If families were unable to so educate their members, then they should employ persons capable of providing the required teaching.
- In the case of uneducated parents who were poor or indigent children who had become wards of the community, the provision of education should be through philanthropy offered by the church or community or individual patrons. Elementary schools, therefore, were provided only for the poor and were provided by the church or community or individual philanthropy. These charity schools, were the institutional means of compensating for the educational and financial deficit of some families and for discharging communal responsibility for the indigent.

English colonists in the Caribbean, like their brethren in the Southern colonies, adopted the Anglican approach to the provision of universal basic education for adult literacy. As such, they were at odds with the New England colonies that had followed the Calvinist philosophy of communal responsibility, which had also been adopted in Scotland (Anderson 1995). One major difference between the American and Caribbean colonies was the social composition of their societies. It was mainly families that colonised America, bringing with them much of the infrastructure of community. In the Caribbean colonies it was mainly men who came without their families, and they were located mainly on plantations. The family tradition of these Caribbean colonies therefore, was never strong. The demand for schooling as part of the infrastructure of the community was weak. The philanthropic orientation of the Anglican tradition therefore was greatly re-enforced by the nature of Caribbean society.

Those few colonists, who came with families and could afford it, provided privately for the education of their children or sent them back to Britain for their education. Those who could not afford to do these, benefited either from the charity of the church, through vestry schools, or from the philanthropy of individuals who, at death, bequeathed endowments for the establishment of schools. These schools were for poor White boys. The posthumous conscience for education was restricted to Whites and seldom extended to girls. The Vestry schools, and the endowed Free schools offered elementary education designed to serve the purpose of piety as prescribed by Protestant theology. They were fashioned on similar institutional arrangements to those that were pioneered prior to the English Reformation and became prevalent thereafter.

No formal education was provided for the slave population. The Caribbean planter took the same view as the Southern planter that education was subversive to slavery. Only in the last decade before emancipation was some instruction aimed at literacy provided through Sunday Schools. As Beckles (1987) pointed out, slaves who taught themselves to read had to keep their accomplishments a secret. While some may have justified the lack of provision for the slaves by denying their human status, the fear was that education would be subversive to both slavery and the plantation system. Indeed, the educational landscape during this era in the West Indian colonies was a mirror image of that in the Southern American colonies where slavery and the plantation dominated social, economic and cultural relations.

Most Caribbean historians have had great difficulty interpreting the educational developments of this period. The establishment of schools during the period of slavery is either completely ignored or treated as an aberration. Consequently, most histories of schooling in the Caribbean begin with the institutions established after emancipation. Yet the schools established in the seventeenth and eighteenth centuries are important and constitute an organic part of the evolution of schooling in the region.

The point being made here is that Commonwealth Caribbean education had its genesis in the educational ideas that prevailed in post-reformation England. In other words, schooling in the Caribbean was inaugurated in the region at the same time that it became a popular institution in Western Europe and was transplanted to North America. The early colonists borrowed the educational institutional framework that was emerging at that time, and with some pride, implanted them in their new setting. While schools were relatively few in number, and their proportion in relation to the size of Caribbean colonies was less than in Europe and North America, the institutional framework of education in the Caribbean shares origin and form with contemporary developments in seventeenth and eighteenth century Western Europe and North America.

As Caribbean society has been dominated by the plantation, no account of the history of education can be complete without reference to planter views on education which were consistent throughout the history of the region. They maintained that schooling for the mass of the population was unnecessary in the plantation economy. The planter elite was equally opposed to education for poor Whites, Blacks and Indians. This opposition to schooling was maintained from the beginning of the eighteenth century to well into the twentieth century.

There was only one twist to this consistent and impartial opposition to public schooling. A few, who conformed to this position during their lifetime, had a posthumous conscience about the non-provision of education for poor white boys and provided legacies for the establishment of schools for poor white boys. However, to underscore the fact that the grave cannot triumph over living resistance, many of the bequests were defrauded, mismanaged or left dormant. The schools that were established were few and modest in their provisions.

THE DENOMINATIONAL SCHOOL SYSTEM WITH STATE SUPPORT

In England it took more than 150 years before the Calvinist tradition, of collective responsibility of the community, supplanted the Anglican tradition of family responsibility and philanthropy. No doubt, the success of the Presbyterians in Scotland in establishing mass education could not be ignored by the Anglicans in England. Also, the enlargement and extension of the communal tradition by the absolutist monarchs of Central Europe in the eighteenth century to mean state responsibility had not escaped the English. Elementary education had been made free and compulsory in Prussia 1763, and in Austria and Bohemia in 1774 (Anderson 1995).

England embarked on its own mission to spread schooling across the land with the Education Act of 1833 which provided state support for church schools. In other words, England did not simply follow the pattern set in Central Europe. The state did not immediately take over the school system. Rather, state support was engrafted onto the system of church schools thus creating a state supported denominational system of education.

A companion measure to the Education Act of 1833 was the Act to establish schooling for the soon to be emancipated slaves and to create the Negro Education Grant which would provide financial support for that system of mass schooling in the British Caribbean. Both pieces of legislation were tabled in the House of Commons in 1833. Moreover, the same amount of money,

20,000 pounds, was provided for mass schooling in England, and for mass schooling in the British colonies. As in the case of England, the churches in the Caribbean would be partners with the imperial government in establishing schooling for the children of the ex-slaves. A denominational school system with state support was simultaneously created in England and the Caribbean.

The point to note here is that a mass system of elementary schooling, spearheaded by the churches and the imperial government, was inaugurated in England and the West Indian colonies at the same time, but for very different reasons. The same educational institutions, were created in two completely different settings. In England, the socioeconomic imperative was to address some of the social implications of the industrial revolution. In the Caribbean, it was for meeting the challenges of creating free societies following the abolition of slavery as the newly emancipated were to be incorporated as citizens with rights in free societies. What is highlighted is the robust nature of schools as institutional agents of social and political purpose.

From a comparative perspective, it needs to be noted that the 1833 reform of education in England marked the entry of the state into the domain of education in that country. The nature of the intervention was to provide both a financial and a regulatory framework for spreading elementary schooling to the mass of the population. At the same time the Massachusetts school reformers were advocating and commencing to implement similar intervention of the state into schooling in the United States. Likewise, in the Caribbean, churchmen with assistance from the imperial government were embarking on the same educational pathway. In each case, the contextual justification was different but the essence of the intervention was the same. Elementary schooling was to be extended to the mass of the population through financial assistance provided by the state. The goal of universal basic schooling and literacy advocated by the Protestant ethic had proven to be outside of the resources of the church. That goal, now based on notions of citizenship and access to education by the masses would now be supported by the state.

Once again, for its own peculiar imperatives, Caribbean education was pushed to the frontiers of the evolution of schooling. In a nutshell, the imperatives shaping the use of schooling as an ameliorating measure following emancipation could be listed as follows:

1. After nearly two hundred years of brutal exploitation in slavery, emancipation would not bring financial compensation for the slaves but rather for the planters, who were seen to be losing property. Schooling was presented as a form of 'restitution in kind' to the ex-slaves in lieu of the cash payments to planters. It was feared that the ex-slaves might be tempted to seek reprisal for the injustices of slavery. Education was presented as a peace offering. Schooling was offered as an incentive to the peaceful transition from slave to free society. British imperial policy was mindful of the reprisal against Whites in Haiti in the opening decades of the nineteenth century, which it hoped to

forestall by offering full membership in a free society along with the educational means of appropriating the implied opportunities of citizenship. Maintaining the peace was a paramount concern of the imperial government.

2. The imperial government was desirous of ensuring that the ex-slaves became loyal British subjects appropriately Anglicised. In this regard, the English language became an indicator and schooling a key instrument in ensuring this cultural goal.

3. The planters muted their long-standing opposition to mass schooling out of concern for their safety as well as with the hope that the system established would seek to persuade and socialise the ex-slaves and their descendants to be willing workers on the plantations on which they had been enslaved.

4. The Black and Brown population that had been enslaved accepted education as the mechanism by which they would enter the mainstream of the free society being created. Their motivation was the prospect of upward social mobility implied in access to educational opportunity.

5. The main mission of the churches was to Christianise the ex-slaves. This was not far removed from the Anglicising mission. Imperial assistance assumed the promotion of this cultural goal. The fact that the Anglican Church received most of the imperial aid for establishing schools underscored this association.

6. Some clergy, mainly among the Baptist, Moravian and Methodist churches embraced mass education not only for purposes of proselytising among the newly freed, but also to prove the personhood and potential of people of African ancestry as a means of refuting the assertion of racial inferiority that had undergirded slavery in the New World (Phillippo 1843)

For all of these overlapping reasons on the part of the providers, stakeholders and participants, mass schooling was inaugurated in the Caribbean at the same time that similar developments were taking place in Western Europe and North America. One historical result is that there are villages, districts and towns in the Caribbean that have had schools for as long as similar communities in the industrialised world. Likewise, there are teachers' colleges that have comparable histories in training teachers since they came into being at the same time that these institutions were established in England.

The educational innovations of the 1830s added a new component to the educational landscape that had not existed to that point. In addition to endowed and free schools, financed mainly by philanthropy, were added elementary schools and teachers' colleges financed initially by imperial subsidy, voluntary contributions of churches, and student fees. These two systems served two different segments of the society. The first schooled the children of Whites of modest means, Coloureds, Free Blacks and Jews. The second offered schooling to the children of the ex-slaves.

There was one striking difference between the education provisions in the Caribbean as compared to North America. That difference was with respect to university education. Theological and teacher education, for the training of local ministers and teachers, were the only forms of tertiary education established in the Caribbean. The evolution of theological colleges into universities and teachers' colleges into liberal arts colleges did not take place in this region. While much research remains to be done on this question, a worthwhile hypothesis appears to be that the imperial administrators did not provide this aspect of educational development as a means of justifying the continued importation of British personnel into the colonies (Miller 1990).

The decade 1836 to 1846 represented red-letter years in the history of Commonwealth Caribbean education. It saw the inauguration of elementary schooling for the former slaves including the building of schools and the creation of teacher training colleges. The imperial government through the Negro Education Grant contributed £25,000 in 1836. This was increased to £30,000 in 1837 and continued at this level to 1841. Between 1842 and 1846 the Grant was reduced by £6,000 per annum until it was fully withdrawn in 1846.

This grant permitted the building of schoolhouses, the training of teachers, recruitment of teachers from Britain, the provision of equipment as well as some support for operational costs, particularly teachers' salaries. The churches augmented the imperial grant with their own contributions of cash and kind. Their most significant contribution, however, was the management of the system. The imperial grant was not made to colonial assemblies but to the churches. The elementary system thus established was a denominational system in which the churches exercised control. The ex-slaves made their own contribution to the establishment of the school system. This was not only through paying school fees for their children from their meagre income, but also through contributions of cash and labour in the construction of school buildings. At the same time, through membership in the various denominations they had some voice in the policies and practices guiding the new school system.

The combined efforts of the imperial government, the churches and the Blacks created the public elementary system in less than a decade. This was a remarkable achievement. Because these groups established the system, their intentions prevailed. The elementary system was established as an agent of Anglicisation. Peace prevailed in the transition from slavery to freedom. The imperial government satisfied with the accomplishment of its intentions terminated the imperial grant in 1846. Thousands of Blacks were converted to Christianity. Blacks demonstrated that they were the equals of Whites in their capacity to learn. Missionaries basked in the glory of their success and thanked the Almighty and their own perspicacity. Blacks affirmed their personhood through education. However, upward social mobility was slow in coming. Since these were still early days they patiently continued to entertain their aspiration to be integrated into the mainstream of the society.

The period 1847 to 1865 could correctly be described in terms of the evaporation of hope and disillusionment with the promises of full citizenship. The imperial government, by discontinuing its financial support for the denominational system of elementary schooling had left its partners, the Blacks and the churches, to their own devices. While the Colonial Office implored the assemblies to give financial support to education, thereby taking up some of the slack left by the phasing out of the imperial grant, such support was in several colonies merely token amounts, which did not go very far. The contradiction and weakness of the imperial exhortation was that it was encouraging assemblies to contribute to education at the same time it was withdrawing its own support, a fact that was not lost on the local representatives.

The Anglicans had benefited most from the imperial grant. Not surprisingly, they suffered most from its withdrawal. The dissenting denominations that had benefited least were least affected. As would be expected the denominational system as a whole declined, although the dissenting denominations made substantial gains. The hopes of Blacks for upward mobility through education were deferred if not dashed. Many of the expectations of emancipation remained unfulfilled. Consistent with the history of the Caribbean, Blacks resorted to violence. They did so in Morant Bay, Jamaica, in October 1865. The rebels slew the Custos of the Parish of St. Thomas-in-the-East, a few English officials, a few members of the planting elite and Charles Price, one of the first Blacks to be elected to the Assembly (Hutton 1992). The peace of the entire Caribbean was disturbed.

The Morant Bay Rebellion was not an ordinary riot although judging from the scope of the violence involved it could justifiably be classified as such. St. Thomas-in- the-East was one of the three top sugar growing parishes of Jamaica. It was the parish in which the planters implemented some of the most unjust measures designed to coerce the newly freed Blacks to continue to work on the plantations. It was also the parish in which the Blacks led by the freeholders or small settlers, as they were called, confronted and met the challenge head-on. The so-called small settlers were the Blacks who had made the most marked educational and occupational progress following emancipation. Not content with their own success, and outraged by the restrictions and restraints imposed on Blacks in pursuing the goal of full citizenship in the society, they shared solidarity with the vast mass of their peers who had not progressed much from the conditions that existed during slavery.

The events of October 1865 were therefore not a spontaneous violent expression of frustration. It was the culmination of the ongoing post-emancipation confrontation between White planters and the Established Anglican Church on the one hand and Black freeholders, estate workers and the Native Baptists on the other hand, that played itself out in that eastern parish in Jamaica.

At the time of emancipation influential sections of the British government were convinced that the planter elite, who controlled the assemblies, was incapable of effectively governing a free society. They had invited those colonies that had Assemblies to voluntarily opt for Crown Colony Government. This offer was bluntly refused. The greatest fear of the English officials was that the planter government would so alienate the majority Black population that the latter would effectively mobilise to take over the government. Black rule was not an option that was viewed favourably in the British empire ascending to its zenith. At the same time that the British government was instrumental in the emancipation of the slaves and acted as their allies in the creation of pubic education, it was exploring ways to deny them the fullest expression of citizenship.

The developments and events in St Thomas-in-the-East played out the worst case scenario of White/Black relationships in the free society and confirmed the suspicions of the imperial government concerning the planters' inability to govern. Hutton (1992) showed that planters in St Thomas were leaders in the following practices after emancipation:

a)   Restricting land ownership to Whites in order to prevent the newly freed Blacks and Coloured from moving away from the plantation. Among the devices employed to this end was maintaining high sale prices, leasing and renting at exorbitant sums and charging high fees for the conveyance of land.

b)   Excessive use of the law of trespass to prosecute Blacks, who for whatever reasons strayed, squatted or grazed animals on unused land.

c)   Paying low wages and retaining one week's wage to ensure that the employees returned to work in the next week.

d)   Biasing and abusing the legal system by appointing planters or their agents as the vast majority of the magistrates hearing cases in the local courts. In a few instances planters, their managers or attorneys were complainants or defendants in cases in which they adjudicated.

e)   Creating artificial unemployment by blocking other sources of employment that were open to Blacks.

f)   Suppressing economic or social organisations established by Blacks for their advancement.

While many of these practices were Caribbean-wide, the planters of St Thomas-in-the-East in Jamaica were numbered among their chief exponents. Under this pressure from the planters, suitably justified in racist rhetoric, Blacks in the parish mobilised and organised in their defence. In fact, they became the leaders among the Blacks demanding radical reforms in the free society that had emerged following emancipation. As was pointed out previously, the leaders of this movement were not the Blacks who had remained on the plantation; the latter were the foot soldiers. The leadership came from those who had successfully moved away from the clutches of the plantation but had maintained solidarity with their less successful peers.

Hutton (1992) listed the following measures were adopted by Blacks in pursuit of their intentions and demands:

1. Writing petitions and passing resolutions, which were sent to the Governor or the Colonial Office.
2. Writing letters to the press.
3. Forming and sending deputations to wait on officials with respect to various grievances.
4. Taking strike action.
5. Organising mass meetings to denounce planter actions and to air their grievances.
6. Purchasing land in accordance with the voter requirements especially at the local government level of the Vestry.
7. Canvassing and campaigning to win the elected seats in the Vestry, this was achieved by the beginning of the 1860s.
8. Voting as a block in matters brought to the Vestry that materially affected the lives of Blacks.
9. Setting up an alternative judicial and court system with its own judges, attorneys, procedures including the issuing of summons and punishment.
10. Organising to disrupt the official courts where Blacks were being unjustly charged, according to popular opinion.
11. Resisting the White supremacy ideology of the planter elite by fashioning their own ideology of Black consciousness popularised on the slogan of 'Skin for Skin, Colour for Colour'.

Indeed, the trigger of the Morant Bay rebellion was a case in the Resident Magistrate Court of the Parish in which the Black man accused was found guilty by the judge and ordered to pay a fine plus legal costs. A large number of Blacks, following the proceedings, advised the man to pay the fine but not the legal costs. This incident on October 11 followed closely on the return of a deputation, led by Paul Bogle, that had journeyed on foot to Spanish Town, the capital, to wait on the Governor with petitions related to grievances concerning the state of affairs in the parish. The Governor had refused to receive the deputation. One of the grievances concerned the abuse of the courts by the planter magistrates. The disruption of the Court that followed was partially the response of the disgruntled Blacks to the Governor who was not prepared to listen to their concerns.

The implications of the Morant Bay rebellion that followed the court incident went much further than the otherwise sleepy and quiet environs of that east coast Jamaican town. Evidence of this comes from the fact that British troops were not only drawn from Barbados and Canada to put it down, but American military advisors fresh from the Civil War, Spanish warships from Cuba and French steamships from Martinique were invited to help to put down the insurrection and to maintain the peace thereafter. The Americans were concerned that Black rebellion could incite similar reaction in the South. The Spanish were alarmed that a successful Black rebellion of ex-slaves in Jamaica could have great impact in Cuba, where slavery still existed. The French displayed solidarity with their perennial opponents no doubt with memories of the Haitian uprising as the end of the eighteenth century. The full weight of Western imperial power was amassed against this small-town riot by Jamaican Blacks. The rebellion was crushed with great brutality. The atrocities committed by the official forces far outstripped those committed by the rebels.

The leaders of the Morant Bay Rebellion were mainly Black, with a few Browns, small farmers, freeholders, shopkeepers, contractors, elementary school teachers and tradesmen. In fact, two elementary school teachers were among those who were executed by the authorities for their participation as leaders in the rebellion. These small settlers were all literate and made extensive use of written instruments in promoting their cause. They led the estate workers who formed the bulk of the rebels. They were successful products of the newly created denominational education system. The list of grievances promulgated in their petitions and resolutions included the abuse of the legal system and courts, the neglect of education, repressive taxation, the artificially high price of land, high unemployment, low standard of living and racial discrimination. However, the most fundamental issue that was at stake was that of representative democracy in which Blacks desired to take over the internal government of the colony.

In the aftermath of the rebellion, the imperial government in London listened to grievances but rejected the claims of majority rule. The imperial government took over the grievances of the rebels and made them the agenda for reform in the Caribbean colonies. With respect to the fundamental issue of internal self-government by the majority Black population, the Crown took control of the government. After 1866, with the exception of Barbados, Crown colony rule was instituted in those colonies in which it had not existed prior to the Jamaican rebellion. Blacks were not given the political franchise. White planters were removed from the government. White officials representing the Crown assumed control.

The British government returned to its original intentions in education. It used schooling as a social incentive in order to help restore and maintain the social peace. The government therefore returned to its partnership in the denominational system. Acting upon instructions from the Colonial Office the governors in all the colonies enacted educational reforms of a standard nature. The Colonial Office may have entertained grave doubts about the ability of Blacks to take over the government, but they were entirely convinced that their proven capacity for rebellion demanded amelioration of the social conditions. Education was chief among instruments of amelioration.

The elements of the standard reforms implemented were:

1. Opening the local treasury to provide support for elementary schooling. This subsidy for the denominational system served to build

new schools, subsidise teachers' salaries and manage the schools. The most famous aspect of this subsidy was the introduction of payment by results.

2. Expansion of the denominational system to include larger numbers of children.

3. Quality control of denominational schools through government inspection.

4. Support for teacher training through the expansion of existing colleges and construction of new ones.

5. Bureaucratisation of educational administration by the appointment of full-time inspectors and the establishment of a Department of Education.

6. The passage of education laws, which included compulsory clauses. Such laws were passed in Guyana in 1876, Bahamas 1877, Barbados 1878, St Lucia 1879, Leeward Islands and Trinidad and Tobago 1890, Jamaica 1892, and Grenada 1896. This is not to say that the laws were enforced only to acknowledge that they were enacted.

It should be noted that these reforms did not all come at one time. State subsidy for elementary education, expansion of schooling, government inspection, and support for teacher training and the nucleus of an educational bureaucracy were policies that were immediately implemented by governors in the late 1860s and 1870s. Compulsory education laws and a state system were outgrowths of these earlier reforms and were inspired by the English reform of 1870. The important point to note was that there was no imperial financial support for these reforms. They were all paid for by local revenue. The Colonial office took over the colonial treasury from planter control and open the public purse to the denominational elementary system. The colonial office was now doing directly what it had pleaded with the Assembly to do from the mid-1840s.

The impact of the improvements in the denominational education system with state support could be judged by the response of the Black population to these developments. They flocked to the expanded and improved school system in droves. Demand outstripped supply. Peace prevailed. The British government and the churches again appeared as allies and champions of the disadvantaged Black majority. The planters again appeared as the only villains. They had frustrated developments, which could have occurred twenty-five years earlier. They had withheld support for education which was now so freely given.

Another measure of the impact of the reform measures was the general perception at that time that there was no difference in level or quality between the endowed and the elementary schools. Moreover, the integration of the teachers' college with the public elementary schools gave elementary schooling an advantage. In response the Browns, Jews and middle class whites charged the colonial administrators with compromising their position in the society. They maintained that an educational distinction should exist between themselves and the Blacks, and that with the reforms this was no longer the case.

The official response to their agitation and advocacy was the reorganisation of the trusts of the endowed schools to allow for the creation of a secondary school system. This trend started in Barbados in the early 1870s, followed by Jamaica in 1879 and was adopted by the rest of the region before the end of the century. The system of secondary schooling that was established virtually excluded Blacks. For the latter, the teachers' colleges served as both secondary school and teacher training institution.

This renewal of the partnership between the imperial government the churches and Blacks accomplished many aspects of the promise of post-emancipation education. There was no external assistance for education from the imperial government. The cost of this new intervention was borne by the colonies and continued contributions from the missionary societies. Funds were voted from local revenue to both expand the educational enterprise as well as to improve its quality. It was the injection of local financial resources, directed by the Colonial Office through the colonial governors, which inspired participation in elementary schooling to levels which paralleled Western Europe, the United States of America, Canada, Australia and New Zealand by 1900. The period 1870 to 1900 was the one in which the parallel system of endowed schools was reorganised into private elementary schools leading to public high schools, which had little or no relationship to the public elementary system and teachers' colleges.

THE STATE SYSTEM WITH DENOMINATIONAL MANAGEMENT

The decade of the 1890s was one of fundamental change in the structure, content and financing of public schooling in the Caribbean. The state assumed policy and financial responsibility for the public school system while leaving the denominations with the day-to-day management of the schools and teachers' colleges. Several factors contributed to this change.

The denominational school system had a glaring weakness: rivalry between churches for membership. This led to the establishment of many small schools in the same districts. Duplication of small schools in the same localities imposed an economic constraint on all the denominations engaged in providing public elementary schooling. The rapid expansion of the school systems between 1870 and 1890 exacerbated this economic weakness. Ironically, at the time that the churches had mobilised greater participation in the school system, they became increasingly unable to finance and sustain the system that they had created. The result was that the denominations invited greater state support.

It was in this very period that Western Europe, including Britain, had come firmly to the view that public education was the responsibility of the state. All over Europe, the state had assumed responsibility for the education system. This new posture combined with the financial difficulties of the churches in maintaining their schools made it easy for churches and imperial government to agree on greater state involvement in elementary education. However, the colonial state left denominations to continue the day-to-day management of the system but took control of policy in exchange for greater financial support.

The implications of these reforms were profound. Ostensibly, the Crown Colony government had removed the planter elite from the reins of colonial government. However, the existence of legislative councils to which governors appointed leading colonial citizens gave them some access to the corridors of power, if even through the side door. Changes in the constitution, beginning in 1884 in Jamaica, which allowed a number of elected members, expanded the access to power by the planting interest. Hence, the planting interest was in a position to influence policy although the state held control. State take-over of educational policy and free elementary education meant that finally the planting interest could influence educational policy. Their intentions had not changed since emancipation. In the planters views Blacks should serve the manual labour demands of the sugar plantations.

Not only did the change in locus of authority in the school system from church to state open the way to direct planter influence on public education but at the same time it also meant the loss by Blacks of any control over the education of their children. Membership in the churches and payment of school fees had been levers of Black influence in the denominational school system. Financial support of schools by parents was no longer a lever of influence. While relieved of school fees, Blacks no longer had any meaningful control or influence over the education system. Blacks were not represented in the Executive or Legislative Councils or the Department of Education, the new arena of education policy formulation and approval.

The first two interventions of the imperial power in education, following emancipation and after the Morant Bay Rebellion had allied the Black segments of Caribbean societies to the Crown. This third intervention alienated them. The Negro Education Grant and the Crown Colony reforms were in the interest of Blacks. This third intervention was decidedly against their interests. Nowhere is this better illustrated than with respect to the vocationalisation of the public education system. At the end of the nineteenth century the imperial power set out to do what the planters had repeatedly failed to do, use elementary education to channel Blacks into agricultural labour and domestic service.

By the 1890s, the imperial power had changed its attitudes to race and to Blacks. Jacobs (1973) attributed this shift to the British colonial experience in India. Perraton (1967) cited the colonisation of Africa as the source of the change. The point to note is that similar shifts in attitudes occurred in the United States about the same time. Hence, it is unlikely that any explanation limited to the British empire can adequately account for this shift. Brereton (1979) emphasised the pervasive acceptance and persuasive tenets of Social Darwinism. The truism emerging from this new science was that Whites dominated the world because they were the fittest in the human survival game. Also it would appear that the rise of Western European countries to dominance in the world brought to the fore their assertions of superiority as a people. This found full expression in the emerging scientific paradigms of that period.

James Anthony Froude gave full expression to this racist thinking in his book *The English in the West Indies*. However, notions of White supremacy did not go unchallenged by Blacks in the Caribbean. The responses included reasoned arguments in the same medium and with equal erudition to the proponents of White supremacy. From the perspective of a West Indian of African descent, John Jacob Thomas of Trinidad rebutted Froude's White supremacy/Black inferiority assertions in his book entitled *Froudacity*.

However, Whitehall and the Colonial Office were unconcerned with reasoned rebuttal of the premises of racism. Joseph Chamberlain, Colonial Secretary between 1896 and 1902, was a friend and admirer of Froude. He shared Froude's view and was a champion of the sugar interest. In 1897, he sent out the West India Royal Commission to investigate the sugar industry. The recommendations of this Commission included the establishment of an Imperial Department of Agriculture and the introduction of the teaching of agriculture in elementary schools and teachers colleges. While the imperial government's implementation of the overall recommendations of the Commission was modest, the recommendations concerning the Imperial Department of Agriculture and agricultural education in schools and teachers colleges were immediately implemented and backed by financial support.

This was only the second time in the history of Caribbean education that the British government actually granted financial support for education in the Caribbean colonies. The Imperial Department of Agriculture, with headquarters in Barbados, gave the required technical assistance for its implementation. By 1900, all Commonwealth Caribbean countries had made plans to introduce agricultural education and elementary school teachers were being trained to teach it.

The imperial government's support for the teaching of domestic economy to girls came from a different set of concerns. The concern was for the working class family in Britain, in the context of an industrial situation, where mothers and daughters, fathers and sons worked. The essence of this concern was manifested in the Commission established by the British government at the turn of the century to carry out a number of comparative studies on 'School training for the Home Duties of Women'. This concern is articulated in a passage in the Preface of the second volume of these Reports, which quoted a circular issued by the Minister of Agriculture, Industry and Public Works of Belgium in 1898. The quotation is lengthy but is key to understanding the attitude to the working class at that time.

Up to the present, leaving out of account the needlework which she learns at the primary school, a girl is supposed to serve her apprenticeship as future mother of a family at home. Assuredly this system would be the best, but is only possible if the girl can carry on, in her own home, a trade that enables her to earn her daily bread. Now the exigencies of the organisation of modern labour have rendered this method inapplicable in the industrial parts of the country. The girl can go out early in the morning to the local mines, to the works, to the factory; she often stays there all day and only returns home in the evening. She has, therefore, no opportunity of adapting herself to household duties, nor of acquiring the domestic virtues which will be necessary to her when, in her turn, she found a new home. And not only is the opportunity wanting, but there is no inclination. When her daily work is accomplished she considers herself indisposed to every other occupation. Having worked as industriously and as long as her father and her brothers, she believes herself justified in resting when they do.

It is, doubtless, but rarely that the thought of a preparation for future duties enters her mind. She thus arrives at the marriage almost a stranger to all the necessities, as to all responsibilities, of her new social condition. The girl's ignorance is still greater if, as is the case in certain industries, the mother of the family herself works in the factory and lives, for a great part of the day, separated from her children whom she confides to strangers or to charitable institutions.

It is not surprising that the new home, established under these unfavourable conditions, soon presents a spectacle of greatest moral and economic disorder. The income is squandered; the dwelling and the furniture is spoiled; the children are deprived of the necessary moral and physical care; the meals are badly and hastily prepared. Soon the head of the family, instinctively revolted by the appearance of the permanent mess which his home presents, yields to the temptations of the public house, and to the invitations of his comrades. Then the home, morally speaking, is dissolved. Continued discussions destroy the affection, and, as they grow up, the children left to themselves and their education neglected, tend to absent themselves more and more from a home where there is nothing to cheer their eyes and delight their hearts.

The evil inevitably increases from generation to generation, and we end by becoming accustomed to the idea that it is normal and that we cannot change any of it.

The answer to this 'inevitable evil' was teaching domestic economy in schools. The English adopted the Belgian proposals in English schools. If it was good enough for Belgium and England, surely it was good for the colonies.

Domestic economy for girls became the equivalent of agricultural education for boys in the imperial policy for Caribbean education. The Caribbean Creole elite knew better and embraced domestic economy for girls in elementary schools for a different reason. They knew from the Caribbean experience that the breakdown of Black family life was not simply working conditions and that it could not be remedied by mere curriculum innovation. But here was an excellent opportunity to solve one of their perennial complaints, the difficulty of getting good domestic help.

Brereton (1979) demonstrated that complaints against the quality of domestic help were an ongoing feature of the social history of the Creole elite. Eisner (1974) showed that during the late nineteenth, and early twentieth centuries, female domestic service was a 'growth industry'. Here was an inexpensive means by which domestic servants could be trained. Jamaica sent the principal of one government teacher training college, Shortwood, to the Southern United States to observe such training in the vocational institutes related to the Hampton-Tuskegee system. On her return to Jamaica she established a programme at the college which trained elementary school teachers side by side with domestics and interchangeably.

In summary it can be concluded that toward the end of the nineteenth century, Britain and France, major powers of that era, fully embraced for their own populations the educational outlook that had been pioneered by Germany, Austria, the United States, Australia and Canada. That view was that mass education was the responsibility of the state. However, England did not move to a full state system. The reforms of 1870 transformed the denominational system with state assistance into the state system with church management. The church/state partnership remained but the state assumed the role of the senior partner. The essence of the shift was in the relative position of the two partners. In the denominational system with state assistance, the churches were the major partner, and the state the minor player. In the state system with church involvement, the positions were reversed. The other major difference was that the state now mandated free and compulsory elementary education. Similar reforms were enacted in the Caribbean colonies in a decade.

However, in extending these reforms to the Caribbean colonies the imperial government switched sides.

a) It decreed that education should serve the interest of the sugar industry, and therefore the planters.

b) It capped education expenditure at no more than 10 per cent of public expenditure. The Barbados Assembly was the first to take such action in 1897. The Colonial Office directed the governors of Jamaica, Trinidad and Grenada to impose similar expenditure limits.

c) It closed schools as part of a programme of rationalisation of the denominational system. While there was justification for some closures, given the previous duplications of the denominational system, the overall effect was to deny easy access to schooling in several localities given the distances some children had to travel to the location of the new school.

d) It restructured the curriculum of elementary schools and teachers' colleges severely restricting the amount of liberal and general education offered and significantly expanding vocational education, a direction that the Black population had stoutly resisted for over sixty years.

The changes halted the expansion of the schools system in its trajectory to fully implement compulsory primary education. By closing schools, some children were denied access to education. Further, capping resources to the education system limited further expansion of the system. The impact of the reform was to undermine the motivation to participate in schooling. Blacks did not see schooling as the route to agricultural labour but as the means of liberation from its legacy. The combined effect of capped resources, the closure of some schools and diminished motivation was initial fall off in school attendance in the first decade of the twentieth century and stagnation in educational development until the 1930s.

By the end of the nineteenth century British imperialism had come to definite conclusions concerning the treatment of the 'darker races' of the empire and their place in the scheme of things. Vocational and not liberal education was the appropriate education for these members of the empire. For different reasons the same racist education policies that were adopted in the education of Blacks in the South in the 1890s were also implemented in the Caribbean. Part of the justification resided in the economic mission of the colonies in relation to the empire. The Caribbean colonies were to produce primary raw material for the manufacturers in the metropolis. The mission of the educational system was to serve this economic end. Although wealth was being created by industrialisation, the Caribbean colonies were to remain agricultural outposts of the empire.

At the end of the century, the government was not alone in retreating from the alliance with the Black segment of Caribbean society. So too were the churches. By the end of the nineteenth century Black male teachers and Black clergymen, were becoming thorns in the sides of the denominations, which were all run by missionaries. As Miller (1994) showed, Black clergymen began challenging the policies and practices of the missionary Societies. However, the missionaries controlled the purse strings. Teachers trained by the various denominations for their denominational schools began to resist the performance of church duties as part of their responsibilities in a state system of education. In addition, the denominations began to restructure their educational involvement in the state system, as well as their programmes of training local clergy.

The essence of the denominational system of education with state support was that the churches provided, financed and managed the education system, with some financial supplements and quality control offered by the state. The shift to the state system with church management was that the former would set policy, provide, finance and maintain quality while the latter would manage the day-to-day operation of schools. The continued involvement of the church was necessary because they owned most of the schools. The great boon offered to the consumers of education was that state provided elementary education would be free. By the 1890s, elementary education was free in the Caribbean. However, free elementary education disguised the loss of influence and control of policy, including curriculum content, by Blacks, the major clients of public primary education.

This change of governance and financing of the school system fundamentally altered the relationship of the state and churches to the mass of the people. In the denominational system, the churches and the imperial state were agents of liberation of the disadvantaged. In the State system both had become part of the mechanism of oppression. The churches and the imperial state had changed sides and had finally become agents of planter interests. What was to follow was decades of retrogression and stagnation in Caribbean education, which was not reversed until the violent social upheavals in the 1930s.

Data on the spread of elementary schooling in the world, compiled by Benavot and Riddle (1998) showed that up to 1900 Commonwealth Caribbean colonies achieved levels of participation in elementary schooling that were only surpassed by Australia, Canada, the United States, New Zealand and nine Western European countries. It is important to note that these are not simply post-hoc findings by researchers and historians. Contemporary officials both in the colonies and in the Colonial Office were aware of the progress made in education in the Caribbean. Indeed, in comprehensive reports that were written at the end of the nineteenth century, colonial administrators in the colonies proudly referred to these achievements by comparisons with the state of education in England and the Caribbean colonies (Miller 1994)

Recognition of Caribbean educational achievement in the nineteenth century went beyond officials in the colonies and Colonial Office in England. King (1998) showed that in 1884 General Eaton, the United States Commissioner of Education, invited Jamaican schools to participate in the International Congress on Education and its exhibition. About 30 to 40 Jamaican schools exhibited in New Orleans. The Jamaican exhibit was not only awarded a Diploma of Honour but aroused a great deal of interest with respect to its quality. Following this success Jamaica was one of the 'civilised countries' invited to participate in the International Congress of the World's Columbian Exhibition held in Chicago in 1893. At that Congress, several Jamaican educators and officials were recognised by appointments to honorary positions. Thomas Capper, Superintending Inspector, was Honorary Vice President of the Department Congress of School Supervision while George Hicks and J.R. Williams were Honorary Vice Presidents of the Department of Congress of Elementary Education (King 1998).

But at the beginning of the twentieth century while educational opportunities were continuing to expand in Western, Northern and Central Europe, North America, Australia and New Zealand, brakes were applied to continued educational development in the Caribbean colonies. The reward earned for substantial expansion of educational opportunity and international recognition for high quality was curtailment of these efforts. It is almost impossible not to conclude that the levels of education achieved in the Caribbean by the end of the nineteenth century was deemed by the imperial overlords as inappropriate for subject people who were mostly Black.

COMPARISONS AND CONTRASTS WITH ENGLAND AND THE USA

Schooling in the Caribbean had its genesis in the same generic ideas and ideals as that of England and the United States. However, the peculiar context of the Caribbean and its history provided it own imperatives and unique variations on the specifics of the evolution of schooling. Unlike England and the United States, which have attained imperial stature in the world, these Caribbean states have continued to be marginal entities in the geopolitical configuration of global power. However, with respect to education it seems accurate to say that Caribbean countries are Western nations of modest means.

Caribbean countries share with the West the same long history of the same types of schools. They also share similar conceptions of schooling. They hold to the same standards of cognitive achievement and enjoy comparable levels of participation in schooling at the primary and secondary levels. However, there are vast differences in the resources mobilised for educational purposes. Mintz (1974) put the matter bluntly by stating that the Caribbean region was westernised, modernised and developed before most of the colonial world had been colonised. Accordingly, the people of the Caribbean are urbanised but nearly without cities and industrialised but without factories. For these reasons, he observed, the similarities of the Caribbean with other Third World countries are deceptive and untrustworthy.

What this means in effect is that with respect to many schooling phenomena, the Caribbean offers the counterpoint to standard and conventional explanations. As Miller (1992) showed, for those who explain the spread of schooling in the world as a consequence of urbanisation and industrialisation, Caribbean data reveal comparable levels of schooling in countries that remained agricultural well into the twentieth century, with the vast majority of their population living in rural areas. Likewise, for those who explain the spread of schooling in relation to sovereignty and political independence, the Caribbean offers comparable participation in schooling in colonial territories. Similarly, for those explaining the spread of schooling in terms of the ruling elite seizing mass elementary schooling as a means of maintaining its hegemony over the proletariat, Caribbean data offer circumstances in which the ruling elite opposed elementary schooling as the mass of the people embraced it for their liberation. Additionally, for those holding ideas founded in racism, Caribbean data provide comparable levels of schooling in populations that were overwhelmingly Black. Finally, for those holding to the superiority of British colonialism compared to other European varieties, the Caribbean colonies attained levels of educational participation and attainment that were not repeated in colonies in other parts of the British empire.

When the history of Caribbean education is viewed in relation to that of the United States not only does it become patently clear that both systems of education had their genesis in the same sources, but that points of contact and comparison have been ongoing. During the period 1850 to 1890, it was the common school reforms of New England, and particularly the work of Horace Mann and the Massachusetts school reformers, that captured the interest and imagination of educators in the Caribbean. As King (1998) pointed out the *Boston Journal of Education* was read and frequently quoted in the region. In other words, although the Caribbean were still colonies of Britain the denominational educators, and government supervisors, drew inspiration from developments in the United States as well as in England. The models they drew upon were those related to the latest, most progressive and most liberal ideas about education and schooling that were embraced in the West. In addition, there was some exchange of personnel between the United States and the Caribbean particularly through missionary societies. Moreover, Caribbean educators while inspired by the developments in New England were proud of the fact that education in the Caribbean colonies was far in advance of that in the Southern States. They made constant comparisons to this effect (King 1998).

An important contrast between the Caribbean and the United States is that the denominations in the Caribbean were never internally divided into White and Black segments. The demography of the Caribbean did not accommodate this division. Initially denominations divided with respect to the segments of the populations they served. Roughly speaking the Anglicans served the big planters and the colonial administrators; the Presbyterians served the smaller planters and middle managers who were mainly Scottish and Irish; the Methodists had strong connections with the Free Coloureds; while the Moravians and the Baptists had strong connections with the Blacks. In Trinidad and Guyana, the Presbyterians later played a significant role in providing education to the Indian segment of the population. In large measure the Catholics were the most cosmopolitan in composition but generally represented congregations that had their roots in Spanish or French colonial experience before being captured or ceded to the British in the perennial competition for possessions in the region.

Following emancipation, and the disestablishment of the Anglican Church in the 1860s, all denominations competed for membership from among sections of the Black population. The result was that all denominations in the Caribbean have had mixed race memberships, although in particular localities in some colonies like Barbados, which had a relatively large White settler population, a few all White congregations were not unknown. It is against this background that the denominational system of education, serving mainly Blacks, took their inspiration from the most liberal and progressive educational models of schooling in the nineteenth century.

A fact, that should not go unnoticed, is that when the colonial administrators took control of the education system from the churches, not only did they put brakes on Caribbean education, but also they began to draw their examples, ideas and inspiration from the Hampton-Tuskegee model designed for Blacks in the Southern States. Also, the colonial administrators at the end of the nineteenth century fully supported an adaptation of British social philosophy in the Caribbean which when translated from its European source equated in the Caribbean to a White upper class, a Brown middle class and a Black working class. Race was added to European and British concepts of class to produce colour-class social stratification. As such, in reforming the education system to enable it to support and to reproduce British social philosophy, colonial officials adopted measures similar to those being applied to the education of Blacks in the Southern United States.

For very different reasons, the West Indian colonies followed very similar patterns to the North American colonies in the establishment of schools at the elementary and secondary levels. At the tertiary level, however, the patterns in North America and the Caribbean diverge sharply.

In the North American colonies colleges were founded very soon after schools were established. While nine colleges had been founded in the North American colonies before the declaration of American independence in 1776, up to the end of the eighteenth century not a single college had been established in the West Indian Colonies. It was not until 1830, nearly two hundred years after the founding of Harvard, when the Codrington Grammar School was transformed into a theological college, that the first tertiary institution was established in the Commonwealth Caribbean. In other words, elementary and secondary schools were founded in the Commonwealth Caribbean and operated for more than a hundred and fifty years before a single college was established in the region.

Over the seventeenth and eighteenth centuries, the pattern that had developed in the West Indian colonies was for those who could afford it to send their sons to England to university. Brathwaite (1971) in his study of colonial Creole society in Jamaica showed that between 1770 and 1820, 229 Jamaicans went to Oxford and Cambridge. The Jamaican practice mirrored a common pattern throughout the West Indian colonies.

It should also be noted that universities were established very early in the settlement of Spanish colonies. Sherlock and Nettleford (1990) pointed out that in the first half of the seventeenth century, the Spanish established the universities of Santo Domingo, Mexico and Lima. In the second half of the seventeenth century, Spain established five more universities in its New World colonies and followed this with the founding of another ten universities over the course of the eighteenth century. Put another way, the pattern of founding colleges in North America resembled the pattern that had previously been established by the Spanish in Latin America. The pattern in the Commonwealth Caribbean, however, differed from both Latin and North America.

THE TEACHING OCCUPATION IN THE COMMONWEALTH CARIBBEAN

It is necessary to trace briefly various trends in the transformation of the teaching occupation that were related to the evolution of schooling in the Commonwealth Caribbean. From the time of the inauguration of schooling in the Caribbean through the introduction of charity schools, to the present time, teaching in the Caribbean has been largely a full-time secular occupation. The pre-reformation tradition in England where the teachers of all types of schools, except writing schools, were priests was not transferred to the Caribbean. Rather, the evolving tendency where teaching was being separated from the clergy was the pattern that was established in the region. It would appear that the scarcity of priests in the Caribbean colonies dictated this pattern. The instances where priests were full-time teachers occurred mainly in theological colleges and to a lesser extent in teachers' colleges and secondary schools.

The fact that the majority of teachers in the Caribbean were not priests did not mean that teaching was divorced from the church and religious service. Invariably teachers were catechists or minor lay functionaries in the church. Gordon (1963) cited records that showed that in the licentious oriented slave society, teachers and priests were not particularly welcome among the planting elite on grounds of assumed piety. In the denominational school system, established following emancipation, teachers were expected to perform church duties in addition to their teaching responsibilities. This was particularly so in the Nonconformist denominations where a single clergyman serviced a circuit of churches. The teacher was expected to deputise for the clergyman in the church related to the school in which they taught. Up to the end of the nineteenth century, the vast majority of elementary schools in the Commonwealth Caribbean were single teacher institutions. The defining relationship of the denominational school system as it operated in communities was that of the minister/manager and the teacher/catechist. Schooling and Christianity were tied not only conceptually but also operationally.

Following the demise of the denominational system of schooling, and with the establishment of the state system with church management in the 1890s, the ties between teaching and church work changed from being obligations of the job to becoming voluntary engagement. This could be seen as yet another aspect of the separation of the teaching occupation from its roots in religion.

A defining difference between the United States and the Commonwealth Caribbean in the latter half of the nineteenth century is that although mass schooling was being inaugurated in both places, this was taking place in different institutional frameworks. In the United States, the common school paradigm prevailed. In the Commonwealth Caribbean, schooling was institutionalised consistent with the colour/class system. Wealthy Whites and Browns sent their children to England for schooling. Middle class Whites, Browns and Jews of more modest means sent their children to private schools and endowed secondary schools. The vast majority of Blacks, some Browns, and some poor Whites attended public elementary schools and teachers' colleges. The imperative was to provide access to schooling in the free colonial society, not to educate children of all races and classes in common schools. The private elementary/endowed secondary schools formed a system of education that not only catered to a different social clientele but was administered separately from the public elementary schools and teachers' colleges.

The imperatives of colonial administration and the social division in the institutional framework had important implications for who the teachers were in the two systems. The imperatives of colonial administration worked in such a manner that the kith and kin of the imperial power not only managed the system but also provided most of the teachers at the higher levels of both systems. Whites, mainly British, were the Superintendents and Directors of Education in the several colonies. They also constituted the vast majority of principals and lecturers in the theological and teachers' colleges and the head-teachers and qualified teachers of the secondary schools. Scattered among the college lecturers and the secondary school teachers were a sprinkling of Creole Whites, some Browns and one or two Blacks who had performed exceptionally well.

The general principle that obtained at the elementary level was that the teachers were locals and mirrored the social origins of the students in some fashion. This had different implications for social mobility in the different segments and strata. The teachers of the private schools were drawn from the middle strata of the colour/class system. They were not only teaching children of their social strata but also retaining their own social status.

In the case of the ex-slaves and indentured workers, elementary school teaching was one of the few non-manual occupations to which they had access. Accordingly, elementary education was a strategic occupation in the creation of the Black and Indian middle classes that began to emerge in the nineteenth century. Elementary school teaching was an occupation for upward social mobility for these social segments.

A critically important point to note is that the cultural paradigm for the training of elementary school teachers, in colleges within the Commonwealth Caribbean, was that of Black or Indo-Englishman. As one of the formal institutions offering upward social mobility, teachers' colleges conformed to the canons of cultural hegemony and emphasised mastery of English language and lifestyle, Christian commitment, loyalty to the Crown and superiority of the English version of Western European civilisation. It was of strategic importance that those who would teach children were purveyors and practitioners of the English culture. Hence, acquisition of academic knowledge and pedagogic skill were only part of the range and repertoire of learning that colleges offered. Assimilation of English culture was of equal importance and constituted the ethos of teacher training.

GENDER OF ELEMENTARY SCHOOL TEACHERS

Virtually no research has been done on the gender of teachers in the Commonwealth Caribbean during the period of the slave society. Since schooling was started in the seventeenth century with charity schools for poor White boys in can be assumed that the teachers were male. However, this is an assumption. By the eighteenth century, schools were also provided for girls. Again, an assumption could be made. However, it was not unusual at that time to find males teaching infants. It is therefore unwise to speculate about the gender of teachers for the entire period of the slave society.

Hard data on the gender of elementary school teachers, private and public, come from the comprehensive survey done by Latrobe during the years 1837 and 1838. He visited every colony in the Caribbean and every school in each colony and recorded details about these schools including facts about the teachers.

Latrobe found private schools in all the British West Indian colonies except Anguilla, Montserrat, St Lucia and Tobago. Table 1 shows the gender of private school teachers as reported by Latrobe.

Table 1: The Gender of Private School Teachers: 1837–38

Country	No. Male	No. Female	% Female
Antigua and Barbuda	1	7	87.5
Barbados	-	2	100.0
Dominica	-	5	100.0
Grenada	3	8	72.7
Guyana	7	9	56.3
Jamaica	42	81	65.9
St. Kitts and Nevis	4	3	42.9
St. Vincent and the Grenadines	3	7	70.0
Trinidad	6	8	57.1
Total	121	189	61.0

Source: (Miller 1998)

Table 1 shows that by the late 1830s private elementary school teaching was already a predominantly female occupation in the Commonwealth Caribbean: 61 per cent of teachers in private elementary schools were female. This pattern was most marked in the British Virgin Islands, Dominica and Antigua and Barbuda. The only colony in which private elementary school teachers were not predominantly female was St Kitts and Nevis. Given the relatively small numbers of private schools and teachers it is probably unwise to make much of the variation in proportion between the different colonies. The most pertinent observation is the fact that the private elementary school occupation was already a predominantly female occupation in the 1830s.

The private elementary school system of the Commonwealth Caribbean must therefore qualify among the earliest cases of the feminisation of teaching anywhere in the world. This feminisation has deepened since the 1830s, but it has never been reversed. For example, in Barbados female teachers were 51.8 per cent of private school teachers in 1838 and 87.2 per cent by 1911. The Latrobe Report recorded that the private schools teachers were White, Coloured and Jewish.

Public elementary school teaching manifested a somewhat different pattern. Table 2 shows in the 1830s.

Table 2: The Gender of Public Elementary School Teachers: 1837–38

Country	No. Male	No. Female	% Female
Anguilla	1	1	50.0
Antigua and Barbuda	19	46	70.8
Barbados	43	28	39.4
British Virgin Islands	5	3	37.5
Dominica	4	13	76.5
Grenada	9	8	47.1
Guyana	63	24	27.6
Jamaica	257	104	28.8
Montserrat	7	8	53.3
St. Kitts and Nevis	21	44	67.7
St. Lucia	5	0	0.0
St. Vincent and the Grenadines	15	8	34.8
Tobago	10	6	37.5
Trinidad	27	16	37.2
Total	486	309	38.9

Source: Latrobe Reports

Public elementary schooling was inaugurated at emancipation in 1834. Table 2 shows that public elementary teaching was inaugurated as a largely male occupation. The exception to this was in the Leeward Islands. In Antigua and Barbuda, St Kitts and Nevis and Montserrat public elementary school teachers were predominately female. The exception in the Leeward Islands was the British Virgin Islands, which followed the pattern in the rest of the region where the majority of public elementary school teachers were male. In the region as a whole 61.1 per cent of the public elementary school teachers were male and 38.9 per cent were female.

The Latrobe Reports showed that the vast majority of the teachers who inaugurated public elementary education were White males and females recruited from Britain. However, a significant minority of these teachers in the late 1830s were Brown and Jewish. Very few teachers were either Creole Whites or Black.

Gender and Public Elementary School Teachers in Jamaica

After the termination of the Negro Education Grant in 1846, local resources would not support teachers recruited from Britain. Therefore, teachers for the public elementary schools were recruited locally by the various denominations, which established Normal Schools for the training of these teachers. In these circumstances, public elementary school teaching became a predominantly Black male occupation by the 1850s (Miller 1998). For example, by 1872 in Jamaica, 90.5 per cent of public elementary school teachers were male and the vast majority were Black (Miller 1994b)

By the 1890s, when the denominational system with state support gave way to the state system with denominational management deliberate policies were adopted in the various countries that resulted in recruiting female teachers, mainly Blacks, to become the mainstay of the public elementary school system. There was a full debate in the Jamaican Legislative Council in 1891 in which the argument for recruiting female teachers can be summarised as follows:

- Fifty to 60 per cent of teachers in the United States were female and that system should be adopted in Jamaica.
- Women were found to be better teachers than men in elementary schools.
- It was cheaper to employ women. In the United States, women were half the cost of men.
- The tone and morale of schools run by women would be higher that those run by men.
- Schools run by women would be more efficient.
- Men were leaving teaching and seeking employment in other spheres.

The Superintendent of Schools explained that the Department of Education had great difficulty in finding women with the appropriate level of education to be trained as teachers. One member of the Council responded that women having not had any opportunity in getting employment in the past had not prepared themselves but given such opportunity would do so. This observation proved prophetic.

Miller (1994) reviewed the factors that contributed to the policies adopted by the colonial authorities in Jamaica to change the gender composition of public elementary in favour of females. He concluded that the policies were designed to:

1. Neutralise the potential development of a militant group of educated Black men.
2. Lessen the influence of the Church in the state controlled system of education by breaking the alliance between the minister/manager and the teacher/catechist.
3. Keep Black men as a source of cheap labour in the productive sector, mainly agriculture.
4. Reduce the cost of the teaching service by the lower salaries given to women.
5. Afford Black women the status of social equal and not Black men.

Like all other aspects of the Commonwealth Caribbean while countries may be responding to the same imperatives and may arrive at the same outcomes, the route taken varies in keeping with local contextual considerations. It is therefore instructive to look at the routes taken by Barbados, Trinidad and St Lucia in addition to the circumstances outlined for Jamaica.

Gender and Public Elementary School Teachers in Barbados

When the change in the gender composition of public elementary school teachers in Barbados in the closing decade of the nineteenth century is examined in the context of educational developments between 1838 and 1911, and alongside the societal factors which shaped these developments, the following observations and inferences appear warranted.

1. Public elementary schooling was established in the post-emancipation period as a segregated institution in a society segregated according to race. In the first decade, the teachers were predominantly Coloured, White and male.
2. In the denominational system operated between 1846 and 1878 with minimal government assistance and control, the system remained segregated and employed an increasing proportion of Black males as teachers. Females were employed mainly as infant school teachers.

3. Reforms in 1878 brought about the racial integration of public schools as poor whites were coerced into participating in the public elementary system. Poor Whites responded by sending their boys to the public schools but keeping their girls in privately supported schools. These reforms also brought about greater state assistance and control. Increasing numbers of female teachers were employed largely because of the growth of the number of infant schools after 1878.

4. The employment of women teachers continued to increase in the 1890s and the first decades of the twentieth century as the state promoted the employment of White and Coloured women as teachers and encouraged the enrolment of poor White girls in the public system. The employment of women as teachers was promoted by restricting infant school teaching to women only and by creating single-sex schools and mandating that students and teachers had to be of the same gender. These measures legally excluded men from teaching infants and girls, which they had done to that point. The men excluded were mainly Black and Brown. At the same time the pay policy introduced mandated that women be paid 75 per cent of the salary of male teachers.

5. By 1911, women constituted just over 50 per cent of elementary public school teachers in Barbados.

Gender and Public Elementary School Teachers in Trinidad

Between 1838 and 1869, public elementary school teaching in Trinidad was mainly if not exclusively a male occupation. Most of these male teachers were Black or Coloured. The reforms associated with the Keenan recommendations, including the employment of women as teachers, resulted in a shift to more female than male teachers, by 1891. This shift was related to several factors.

·   The creation of the dual structure in the public school system, by the inclusion of church schools. Church schools, as private schools, had employed a larger proportion of female teachers than the government schools.

·   The rapid expansion of the number of both government and church schools in the public system after 1875. In the twenty year period 1878 to 1898 the public school system had increased by 151 schools: 29 government and 122 church schools.

·   More female than male teachers were employed to meet the expanded demand for teachers in the enlarged public elementary school system.

The wider socioeconomic factors associated with the shift in the gender composition of public elementary school teachers can be summarised as follows:

- In the context of costly recruitment of immigrant labour from outside there was great pressure for native Black males to be retained as agricultural labourers. The ownership structure of the sugar industry had recently changed as well as its technology. Corporate ownership had largely replaced individual ownership and central factories using the vacuum-pan technology had replaced the windmill-run factories. The new investors had to be reassured that steps were being taken to ensure that there would be an adequate supply of labour.
- The French Creoles, in the 1870s were openly opposed to the limited upward social mobility offered to Coloureds and Blacks through the educational system. Such opposition brought the French Creoles into open conflict with those Coloureds and Blacks who used education as their major channel of upward social mobility. The French Creoles were insistent that upward social mobility for Coloureds and Blacks should be restricted.
- The Catholic Church and the government were arriving at some form of rapprochement after several decades of conflict over education.

The educational reforms, which successfully incorporated the churches into the state system of education, took place in circumstances of conflict between the French Creoles and Blacks; significant economic restructuring; and technological change which required state action to reassure the new corporate owners concerned about a steady supply of labour. Further, new alliances were being formed between the English and French Creole elites as the dominant groups in the society. Shifting the opportunities offered through teaching to females instead of males resonated with each group for different reasons. To the French Creoles it would further limit the prospects of upward mobility among the Coloured and Black males. To corporate capital it would help to ensure an adequate supply of labour. To the colonial officials it would reduce the number of literate Black men whom they regarded as social misfits and potentially dangerous politically as the Morant Bay Rebellion had proven. To the Catholic Church this shift was not problematic in that it was standard practice for elementary schools to be taught by females, albeit nuns.

The net result of the impact of the reforms of the first half the 1870s was to change the gender composition of elementary teaching from predominantly male to majority female by 1891.

Gender and Public Elementary School Teachers in St Lucia

To explain the establishment of elementary school teaching in St Lucia as a predominantly male occupation and its subsequent change to being a majority female occupation, by the end of the nineteenth century, it is essential to explain the role of the state in determining the education of the subordinate Black majority in St Lucian society. Three questions become relevant. Why did the state, after emancipation, invite and sponsor Mico schools? Why did the state sponsor a dual system of Protestant and Catholic education between 1859 and 1889? Why did the state take direct control of education after 1889 and then place it largely under Catholic management?

The answers to these questions relate to two broad axes of conflict in St Lucian society in the nineteenth century. These were conflicts between English and French cultural orientation and between the planter and the peasant modes of economic production. Each needs to be discussed in turn.

Mico schools were invited and sponsored after emancipation as the means by which the objective to Anglicise the Black segment of the society would be realised. The late start and limited involvement of Catholics in education up to 1859 is accounted for by the same factors. French priests who operated schools that employed French as the language of instruction confronted the colonial government directly. The government met the challenge head on by insisting that state assistance would only be given to schools that employed English as the language of instruction and had managers who could read and write English. However, even where nuns conducted Catholic schools in English, they were not immediately included in the public system. Up to 1859, colonial government did not trust Catholic commitment to Anglicisation.

The employment of male teachers from the local population was standard practice for the Mico Charity regionally. This was consistent with the patriarchal traditions of the church and the ex-slaves. It also served the purposes of Anglicisation since these male teachers, who were given college training, were leaders in the local community and lay preachers in the Protestant churches. A male oriented elementary school teaching cadre was not at odds with the Anglicising intentions of the state.

Mico elementary schools did not continue to operate in the rest of the Caribbean after the Negro Education Grant was terminated in 1846. The Mico Charity confined their efforts to teacher training in Jamaica and Antigua and only continued to operate model schools in conjunction with those colleges. The sole exception was in St Lucia. The continuation of the Mico schools in St. Lucia was quite definitely the result of the invitation of the government to continue to operate in circumstances in which the Protestant presence was not sufficiently large to prevent the Catholics from dominating the school system. Further, the failure of the state system that was attempted in the decade 1848 to 1858 perpetuated reliance on the Mico schools as a countervailing force to the Catholic influence. In 1859, the state abandoned its own schools and turned them over to Mico, an unusual occurrence indeed.

The inclusion of the Catholic schools in the public system after 1859 seems to be related to the Catholics' acceptance of Anglicisation as cultural policy, and the state's intention to co-opt the Catholic church in this mission. The terms of their incorporation were unequivocal: English would be the language of instruction; English language would be taught as a subject; and the managers of the schools should be able to read and write English. By their acceptance of these terms, the Catholic Church had become an agent of the policy of making St Lucia English. The colonial government had prevailed in the confrontation with the Catholic Church on the issue of cultural orientation.

By 1889, the Anglicisation policy and programme were settled as far as public elementary education was concerned. The conflict between the peasant and plantation modes of production was not. St Lucia was one of the few Caribbean countries that did not carry out the educational reforms of the 1870s that were mandated by the Colonial Office. Des Veoux, the Lt. Governor, in his long despatch to the Colonial Office in 1877 explained his reasons for deviating from the stated policy. He cited among others:

(i)   The dislocation of labour being caused by elementary education since there were no jobs available for those who were successful, and who in turn would not take the available jobs as agricultural labourers;

(ii) The social misfits being produced by the elementary system who conceived of themselves as being above their 'station' in society;

(iii) The social and political aspirations of educated Black males and the implications for destabilisation of the society.

By the 1880s the Colonial Office, the plantation managers in St Lucia and the foreign owners were united about the critical importance of the supply of labour to the sugar industry. St Lucian officials were among the first to request a regional commission to enquire into this question. The commission did not come until 1897 but the point is that the officials in St Lucia were early proponents of both the need for this commission and of its principal recommendations. Indeed, the findings and recommendations of the Commission were a foregone conclusion before its creation.

Emigration was seen as a critical factor crippling the availability of local labour. Elementary education was seen to be inspiring emigration because it was creating the desire for a better life. Emigration was contributing to the growth of the peasantry by providing them with capital to buy and develop account farms. Educational change was needed to persuade the Blacks to accept agricultural labour by making them satisfied with their lot in society.

By 1901, elementary education was vocationalised. Compulsory education laws were passed and were enforced. The Catholic Church, which enjoyed the confidence of the Blacks, had to be co-opted as an agent of the plantation interest. Mico departed St Lucia in 1891 after it was clear that they no longer had a purpose to serve. The schools, students and teachers in some instances, plus buildings in other cases, were turned over mainly to the Catholic Church.

St Lucia must be the only country in history that not once but twice turned over state schools to non-state agencies. It must be noted that by 1897 it was generally conceded in the Western world, and in the Caribbean, that elementary education was the responsibility of the state and not the church. The trend in the rest of the region was for the state to assume greater responsibility for elementary schooling. St Lucia was going in the opposite direction to the region and to the rest of the Western world. Measures to subordinate Blacks to the interests of the plantation had triumphed over notions of educational progress.

By turning over the schools to the Catholics the government was making it possible, by virtue of the size of the system, for the Catholic church to organise the elementary system along the lines of the economic interests of the sugar plantations. The Catholic Church was gaining control of the school system in exchange for using the weight of its influence to channel its Black adherents into agricultural labour and domestic service.

It is important to note the absence of outright confrontation between the state and the Catholic Church in St Lucia. Clearly there were suspicions on both sides. Priests attempted to undermine the state sponsored Mico schools by forbidding parents to send their children to those schools. However, there was never open confrontation. Romalis (1969) explained that the priests, at that time, came mainly from La Vendee a very conservative region of France that had resisted the French Revolution. In his opinion, the priests were unlikely to have been strong supporters of the principle of social equality. However, it has to be noted that the colonial government often acted in a conciliatory manner toward the Catholic Church. For example, in 1875, when the Anglican Church was being disestablished in the rest of the region the government in St Lucia started a system of annual grants to the Catholic church. By the last quarter of the nineteenth century, the state and the Catholics of St Lucia seemed to have reached an accommodation. The essence of this accommodation appeared to have been that if the Catholic Church served the interests of the state, then it would be allowed almost total freedom to minister to the soul, with state support. This was in direct contrast to the conflict that existed in the United States between the Catholic Church and the state.

There are those who may argue that while the state may have handed over the Mico and government schools to the Catholic church with the intention of co-opting the church as an agent in socialising Blacks to accept agricultural labour as their destiny, the state at no point prescribed single-sex schools, nor decreed the employment of female teachers. Also that the rule that pupil-teachers should be of the same gender as the principal was to protect teenage Black girls from lecherous Black male teachers who were sometimes cited for sexual exploitation of pupil/teachers and students. Accordingly, the shift of the gender composition of the teaching force from male to female was the consequence of moral considerations.

The weight of the evidence, however, suggests that concerns about the supply of labour for the sugar plantation and the political threat of educated Black males were the major factors related to the partial exclusion of Black males from elementary school teaching after 1900. Maintaining order was always an uppermost concern of colonial administrators. Village lawyers and petition writers, as literate Black men were labelled, were regarded as agent provocateurs and potential threats to social peace. The leadership of the Morant Bay rebellion had come from this group. That lesson was not forgotten at the end of the century.

It should be noted that financial consideration in terms of differential pay for male and female teachers did not occur until nearly forty years after elementary teaching became predominantly female. Even then, the differential was not great. At the lower and middle levels, women and men were paid the same salaries. However, at the top end of the pay scale women received between 80 and 87 ½ per cent of the salary of men. Parsimony was certainly not a consideration in the feminisation of teaching in St Lucia. Rather it was a belated bonus, and even then of modest size.

Common Features of the Commonwealth Caribbean Cases

The common features related to the gender of teachers could be summarised as follows:

1. In the Commonwealth Caribbean context, of marginal majorities and dominant minorities, the implicit assumption and the consistent and general practice has been for the teachers of the children of a particular segment of the society to be recruited mainly from persons from within that segment of the society.

2. Private elementary schools, catering mainly to the children of the dominant groups, have employed teachers from those groups. Private elementary school teaching has been a feminine occupation in the Caribbean from before 1838 and has remained unchanged since that time.

3. Where the mechanism for the employment of public elementary school teachers rested effectively with the subordinate majority groups, their agents and their allies, the patriarchal traditions of the subordinate groups prevailed. Both the opportunities to be employed and to be trained as teachers went mainly to the males of the subordinate groups. Teaching in these circumstances became and remained a masculine occupation for as long as the subordinate groups and their allies maintained effective control of the policies governing the hiring of teachers.

4. Where the dominant minority groups, through the state machinery, assumed effective control of the public elementary school system, including the training and employment of teachers, they implemented policies that resulted in the feminisation of public elementary school teaching. The exact measures used varied from country to country but their effect was the same.

5. The change in the gender composition of elementary school teaching took place within the context of expanding demand for teachers. More women than men were employed to meet the expanded demand for elementary school teachers. In the period that states took control of the public system, they expanded access to students but shifted the

gender composition of teachers in favour of females in circumstances of an absolute increase in the number of both male and female teachers.

The wider societal factors present in all British Caribbean colonies that were related to change in the gender of public elementary school teaching, in favour of females, at the end of the nineteenth century can be summarised as follows:

1. Conflict between the dominant and subordinate groups with respect to political, economic and social advantage in society and shifts in alliances between the groups in relation to that contest in different time periods.
2. State intervention in the conflict on the side of the dominant group in the closing decades of the nineteenth century.
3. Control of upward mobility opportunities by the dominant groups through the machinery of the state.
4. Tacit acceptance of the principle that social mobility opportunities arising from the public elementary teaching occupation should remain within the subordinate groups.

SCHOOLING, TEACHING AND THE CONSTRUCTION OF THE FREE SOCIETY

Schooling and teaching were handmaidens in the process of transforming the colonial slave society in the British West Indies into the colonial free society. Public elementary schools were the means by which ex-slaves were to become citizens with rights. Initially, the main partners in this process were the imperial government and the Protestant denominations. In first decade after emancipation, with funding from the Negro Education Grant the imperial administrators, the Protestant clergy and the majority of the teachers were British. They worked to create this future free society.

Following the termination of the Negro Education Grant, economic necessity dictated that the teachers for public elementary schools had to be recruited locally. The denominational structure of the system made it almost mandatory to recruit teachers from the ranks of their members who were the main clients of public education. As members of the church and fee paying clients of the system, Blacks could influence policies for the recruitment of teachers.

If the imperial administrators and the heads of the Protestant denominations could be classed as the architects of the system, then the missionaries were the main contractors and the teachers the foremen in the construction of education for Black citizens of the free colonial society. While the imperial administrators, heads of Protestant denominations and missionaries were British and White, the teachers were of African ancestry and Black. Herein lay the problem in the partnership. These Black male teachers belonged to the marginal majority of Commonwealth Caribbean society and were therefore the main rivals of the dominant minority in the free colonial society that was being constructed. The Black males qualified to be co-opted to the partnership by virtue of their conversion to Christianity, aptitude in mastering the English language and 'Englishness'. Their incentive to join the partnership was the upward social mobility offered by elementary school teaching and elevation to middle class status. The question was, could conversion and upward social mobility alone make and keep them loyal.

The point is that economic necessity, the structure of the denominational school system and the demographic fact that Blacks were the majority in the population and the principal clients of the school system, made it almost inescapable for the architects of the free colonial society to employ Black males as the mainstay of the teaching force in public schools. The architects of the common school movement in the United States had studiously avoided this risk.

By the end of the nineteenth century, a number of factors converged concerning Black male teachers. For example, they had organised in Jamaica to create the Jamaica Union of Teachers in 1894, at a time when trade unions were illegal. The main stimulus for this militant step was that in the newly created state system with denominational management, the Education Code allowed a teacher to be fired for not doing church work. Jamaican teachers were incensed by this clause. In addition, Black male teachers and Black clergy were no longer trophies of missionary grace but thorns in the flesh of the missionaries of the different denominations as they challenged the latter with respect to numerous aspects of the work of the denominations and the education system.

As Miller (1994) pointed out, in addition to challenges to constituted authority, the new corporate owners of plantations were concerned about the supply of labour for the sugar plantations. Creole Whites and Browns of the middle classes were concerned and complained about the growth of the Black middle class. Colonial bureaucrats were in a quandary with respect to the extent to which they could implement state policy in a system in which missionaries and Black male teachers had formed close bonds. The outcome of these political, economic, social and bureaucratic concerns was policies that began to exclude Black males from teaching through the shift in recruitment and employment policies in favour of female teachers.

These outcomes obtained in Protestant Barbados and Jamaica, and Catholic St Lucia and Trinidad. The Protestant/Catholic rivalry in education that remained unresolved in the United States was settled in the Commonwealth Caribbean by the end of the nineteenth century. Whatever the imperial government and colonial state was doing, the Protestant and Catholic Churches were complicit, for better or for worse.

TEACHING AND VIRGINITY IN THE CARIBBEAN

There is no evidence that female participation in the teaching profession in the Caribbean has ever been predicated on virginity. Unlike the United States and England, there were never any laws that required female teachers to resign or that legalised their dismissal, once they got married. Public or private elementary or secondary school teaching was never at any time restricted only to single women although many female teachers were single women.

The available records consistently showed that married women were employed in schools in the Commonwealth Caribbean throughout the nineteenth century. Latrobe in his 1837 and 1838 reports recorded married women as teachers in both public and private elementary schools. For example, of the 83 private primary school teachers found in Kingston, Jamaica in 1837, 63 were female and 30 of that number were married. Of the 298 teachers in public primary schools in Jamaica in 1868, there were 33 female teachers, eight of whom were married. By 1878, there were 638 teachers employed in public primary schools in Jamaica, 553 men and 86 women. Eighteen of the female teachers were married. In 1889, there were 100 female teachers in public primary schools in Jamaica fifteen of whom were married.

The major difficulty experienced by married women employed as teachers was the fact that there was no provision for maternity leave with pay. While they were able to return to their jobs after being away for maternity reasons, they received no pay for that period. In some instances pregnant married teachers had to resign, but they could be re-employed after the maternity period was over.

The Commonwealth Caribbean commenced practising the twentieth century pattern of employment of female teachers, without regard to marital status, nearly a century before this became standard practice in either the United States or England. While the Commonwealth Caribbean countries were colonies and not nations, the school systems that were established after 1834 were predicated on creating a free society in which all citizens had equal rights. While the principle of equal rights was violated with respect to race and class, it was observed with respect to gender in the context of employment in public and private elementary schools.

In Jamaica at the end of the nineteenth century women teachers in public elementary schools were paid the same salary as men despite agitation from several quarters to pay them less. In this regard, pay policy for public elementary school teachers in Jamaica was decades ahead of similar policies in the United States and England. It was also decades ahead of the pay policy in public secondary schools, which maintained pay differentials between male and female teachers until the middle of the twentieth century. Put another way in public schools catering to the dominant minority and staffed by recruits from that segment, differentials were maintained between the pay of male and female teachers, as was the case in Britain and the United States. However, in public schools serving the subordinate majorities women teachers were paid the same as male teachers.

Miller (1994) was of the view that the ethical justification for employing female teachers was premised on the narrower issue of sexual morality rather than on the wider concept of the 'pure woman'. It was repeatedly argued that it was not desirable for men to teach girls, particularly girls over ten years of age. To support this contention charges were made that many male teachers had commited acts of sexual immorality with female students. Female teachers were needed to either replace men in the teaching of girls or to act as chaperones where male teachers were employed. While the defenders of male teachers successfully challenged the evidence that would support widespread sexual misconduct among male teachers, nevertheless the charges were persistently made whenever the issue of the employment of female teachers was debated.

To underscore the conclusion that in the Caribbean ethical justification for employing female teachers centred on the issue of sexual morality and not virginity, the observation must be made that both the official regulations and the hiring and firing practices of school authorities precluded teachers, male or female, from retaining their teaching jobs, or from being trained as teachers, if they had children out of wedlock. It was not parenthood that was the focus of ethical considerations, but rather parenthood out of wedlock, that is, sexual morality as defined by the Victorian standards of those days.

Where teachers did have children out of wedlock, and the authorities knew this, they were dismissed. In several instances, however, unmarried teachers managed to conceal parenthood. Concealment was much easier for male than female teachers, but the latter was by no means impossible. In these cases, teachers officially denied parenthood but covertly carried out their parental responsibility in the capacity of uncles or aunts. It was not until the 1970s that clauses that required the dismissal of unmarried teachers who had children were removed from codes of regulations. By then, the rule and the practice were centred almost entirely on unmarried female teachers having children. Even then, it was maternity leave laws, granting maternity leave to all mothers irrespective of marital status that effected changes in the regulations governing the dismissal of unmarried teachers who became pregnant and decided to have the child. An unmarried mother as teacher was the ethical sticking point in Commonwealth Caribbean school systems. Married mothers, or married women, were never barred from public school teaching in the region. Virginity was never the issue in relation to the employment of female teachers in schools in the Commonwealth Caribbean.

This is not to say that the tradition of the pure woman as a teacher found no place in the school systems of the Commonwealth Caribbean. Indeed, several teaching orders of nuns taught in Roman Catholic schools that were part of the public school system in all Commonwealth Caribbean countries. The point is that the rationale undergirding the employment of female teachers in Commonwealth Caribbean schools was not predicated on notions of virginity and purity. The rationale for employment of both male and female teachers was the construction of a free society premised on equal rights and justice. It was the rights-based notion of society and not the religious rationale that underpinned the school systems of the Caribbean and the employment of teachers in the nineteenth century.

Up to the 1890s, that is, during the period of the denominational school system with state support, female teachers were employed mainly in two niches, as teachers of infants and as teachers of sewing. Both niches related to areas that could be called 'women's work': childcare and domestic economy. The exception to this pattern were the Catholic nuns who taught children of all ages and all subjects in the curriculum. In other words, Catholic nuns, rooted in the religious tradition of virginity and purity, taught and managed schools on the same basis as men. On the other hand, women identified with the emerging rights-based tradition were slotted into niches within the school system that related to areas conventionally related to women's work.

Campbell (1996) observed that in Trinidad and Tobago in the nineteenth century although males were employed to teach juveniles, children aged 7 to 15 years, females gradually began to be employed to teach infants since the consensus was that infants needed surrogate mothers. Campbell's observations about Trinidad and Tobago certainly hold true for the rest of the Commonwealth Caribbean. For example, in Barbados up to the 1880s almost all female teachers in public schools were employed in infant schools. Again, the first college for training female public school teachers in Jamaica was founded in 1861 to train infant school teachers.

The notion of female teachers being surrogate mothers is a relatively recent notion that begins to have institutional expression in school systems in the late nineteenth century. The teaching of infants begins to be one of the bases of justifying the employment of female teachers. It is at the level of the infant school that the notion of the female teacher as surrogate mother was most widely accepted and practised in the Commonwealth Caribbean. Even then, males continued to be employed as infant school teachers almost to the close of the nineteenth century. It is through laws passed toward the end of the nineteenth century that infant schools become the almost exclusive domain of female teachers.

The niche for women as sewing teachers followed the educational reforms that were implemented in the 1870s in the aftermath of the Morant Bay rebellion in Jamaica. Larger schools would have a single sewing teacher, while smaller schools in a particular locality would share an itinerant sewing teacher. Sewing teachers taught only girls. In a sense, their involvement in the school system was more limited than in the case of infant school teachers in that their duties were gender specific. Sewing was seen as a task that could not reasonably be assigned to male teachers who had general responsibility for instruction. Hence, the employment of specialists in sewing translated into opportunities for female teachers, given the gender definition of sewing as a specialist task of women.

In tracing the evolution of the feminine roots of teaching from its genesis in virginity and purity to its rights-based nation-building prerogatives in the context of the Commonwealth Caribbean, several intriguing paradoxes cannot be overlooked.

- It is within the denominational school system run by churches that the nation-building patterns began to emerge. It is schools run by churches that began the move away from the religious tradition of purity and virginity as the basis of employment of women as teachers to the modern presumption of teaching being women's work. This is true not only of Protestant denominations but also of the Catholic Church, where it employs females who were not nuns.
- It is the churches that began the practice of slotting women into gender niches within the school system, notwithstanding the long tradition of nuns teaching schools on the same basis as men. At the same time that the churches began to shift to the nation building ideology of a free society based on equal rights and justice, they also began to employ women to perform highly gendered roles in the school systems.
- British school superintendents and directors of education presided over employment policies that accepted the employment of married women, even though such policies ran contrary to the practices in Britain where women had to resign or were fired from their teaching jobs once they got married.

These paradoxes highlight the societal imperatives of the Caribbean, and the New World generally, which virtually mandated fundamental changes in rapidly expanding school systems. The imperatives for fundamental changes arose from the intense conflict between the groups that comprised these societies. It is in these marginal colonial societies that fundamental shifts occurred in the gender composition of the teaching profession at an earlier time than in the more powerful countries. The early advance of the Commonwealth Caribbean countries to the twentieth century pattern and justification of the employment of female teachers has to be understood in this context. Fundamental change begins in the margin.

Eight

VISION, VALUES AND VIRTUE: THE ESSENCE OF TEACHING

Why did teaching become a masculine occupation in the first place? Why did teaching remain a masculine occupation for over 4300 years? On what bases did women first make their entrance into the teaching occupation? Do the masculine and feminine roots of teaching cast any light on the social nature of the teaching occupation and its role in society? These were the main questions that this study set out to answer. In this concluding chapter, an attempt will be made to synthesise the findings and observations previously reported and discussed.

THE MASCULINE ROOTS OF TEACHING IN THE ANCIENT WORLD AND THE RELIGIOUS AGE

Why did teaching become a masculine occupation in the first place? In a nutshell, the findings of this study can be synthesised and summarised as follows:

1. Following the revolution in agricultural production in the ancient world, around 4000 BCE, kinship communes amalgamated into clans. Some clans formed associations that evolved into cities and kingdoms predicated on the covenant of kinship. The public sphere created by cities and kingdoms was largely limited to matters of religion and government. Patriarchy determined internal rank within lineages and clans. Accordingly, where non-manual occupational opportunities arose within the small public sphere created in religion and government, patriarchal rank determined that first choice of such opportunities should go to the males of the extended families and clans benefiting from the creation of these non-manual occupations. Consequently, fathers and then sons predominated as chiefs and kings and as priests and holy men.

2. The school was created as an institution to support the exercise of administrative power by palaces and temples in ancient city-states. As such, schooling was created as a single-tier institution. The same schools admitted children and graduated adults as scribes. At its creation,

schooling was exclusive and not inclusive. Formal schooling was restricted to supplying the very limited demand for scribes for temples and palaces.

3. Particular clans came to supply the scribes and consequently their teachers. Scribes were usually descendants of governors, city fathers, ambassadors, temple administrators, military officers, sea captains, tax officials, priests, accountants, supervisors, foremen, scribes and archivists. Scribes, therefore, were the offspring of persons who were pursuing non-manual occupations created in the rise of city-states. Teachers were drawn from the clans that populated non-manual occupations requiring scribal training.

4. The capacity of these clans to produce sons far exceeded the personnel demands of non-manual occupations. Patriarchal rank within the clans, that virtually owned these non-manual occupations by the practice and tradition of children inheriting the occupation of their fathers, determined that the sons of those clans should receive scribal training. Teachers were selected from this male pool with scribal training and therefore were males.

Concisely, teaching became a masculine occupation because in the early stages of the creation of city-state civilisation lineages and clans owned occupations which were passed on from one generation to the next. This tradition was carried over to the non-manual occupations created in government and religion. The public sphere that was created in government and religion was small in comparison to the numbers of children of the lineages and clans that owned the non-manual occupations within this small public sphere. Patriarchal rank within the lineages and clans gave sons preference over daughters with respect to access to opportunities that would preserve their interests and status in society. These circumstances gave rise to teaching as a male occupation.

JUDAISM, JEWISH COMMUNITIES AND THE MASCULINE ROOTS OF TEACHING

Judaism and the Jewish community represent a most interesting and important case in the study of the masculine roots of teaching for five principal reasons. First, Jews are one of but a few peoples of recorded history that have continuously retained a separate identity from their origins as Hebrews in the ancient world. Second, formal schooling has been a central activity in Jewish communities for over 2,500 hundred years. Third, Israel and Judah were marginal states in the ancient world and Jews have formed marginal communities in the Diaspora. They have no history as an imperial people. Fourth, after the dispersion of the ten tribes of the North Kingdom, Jews, with but a few notable exceptions, consistently observed the ancient code of accommodation with dominant powers. They accepted the hegemony of dominant powers in exchange for a level of autonomy in conducting the internal affairs of their communities. As a result, patriarchal structures were retained within Jewish communities notwithstanding their marginal positions in the political economy of the societies in which they resided. Fifth, for nearly two thousand years male teachers, rabbis, led Jewish communities within the Diaspora.

Teaching was inaugurated as a masculine occupation in Judah in circumstances in which prophets in this small marginal state envisioned that, faced with overwhelming military and cultural might of ruling empires, the only real chance of survival as a people resided in spiritual resistance as God's chosen people. The prophetic call to faithfulness to God was not only issued through preaching but through formal schooling. The school of the prophets had modest beginnings during the period of the monarchy. The purpose of this school was not teaching the scribal arts. Rather it was that of proclamation of a vision of Israel as God's chosen people and their survival against overwhelming odds.

The prophets became the teachers of the people during the Theocracy when priests became the rulers. Women were excluded from all levels of schooling, as students and teachers, during the period of classical Judaism. This was not entirely a unilateral decision of men. Rather, Jewish men and the majority of women co-operated in this sexual division of power, which left men responsible for spiritual resistance, the major strategy employed for their collective survival. This single gender structure of schooling, and the teaching occupation, was not imposed from outside. It was a decision of the Jewish community as a whole, from the inside. It was related to the fact that Judah accepted the hegemony and protection of the prevailing superpower, and in return was accorded a great measure of autonomy in its internal affairs including the operation of their own schools and colleges. Nested precariously in cities and kingdoms ruled by men of great political, economic and military might, and whose hegemony was accepted, Jewish communities chose to be led by male teachers schooled in spiritual resistance. In a fierce world ruled by men, in which their survival was always at risk, Jewish communities chose to be defended by their men, albeit through spiritual resistance and not military might.

Teachers became the leaders of the Jewish communities in the Diaspora, after the Temple was destroyed and the Romans dispersed Jews. Teaching continued as a masculine occupation as Jews lived precariously as marginal groups in the Islamic and Christian empires that superseded the ancient world of the city-states and imperial cities. Factors related to the masculine composition of teaching in the Diaspora during the Age of Religious empires were essentially the same as those which obtained during the period of the existence of Judah. These were as follows:

- Jewish communities in the Diaspora sought accommodation with the powerful in the states in which they found refuge.
- In return for accepting the hegemony of the powerful and for performing useful services, Jewish communities invariably negotiated autonomy in conducting their religious and educational affairs. The synagogue provided both worship and schooling and was the institutional means of maintaining religious and educational autonomy.
- While Jews were perennially made scapegoats by their powerful protectors, who then became their persecutors, and were repeatedly expelled from states providing temporary refuge, these circumstances became the mechanism through which the cycle repeated itself in new locations.
- What was preserved, however, was Jewish identity, solidarity, community and spirit.

THE FEMININE ROOTS OF TEACHING

On what bases did women first make their entrance as teachers? The short answer to this question resides in factors related to:

- The high ethic vision of Islam and Christianity;
- Celibacy;
- Hiatus in the male succession in passing on advantages within lineages and clans;
- The employment of women of the clan to preserve advantage;
- Partnership between males and females of royal and aristocratic lineages and clans to consolidate and preserve their position in society.

Each of these factors deserves some elaboration.

Islam and Christianity offered women limited opportunities at the highest levels of their ethical visions. The ascetic movement, in both religions, which rejected the world and retreated to the cloister of the monastery to serve God alone, accepted men and women based on equality. While their numbers were always much smaller than those of men, the seclusion of women in the private cloister of the monastery gave them access to the public sphere on the same basis as men.

In both religions, celibacy levelled the ground of social differences between men and women, and as such established a measure of equality that did not exist in the secular world in which the preservation of the clan through procreation was a pre-eminent and predominant consideration.

However, not even the cloister or virginity could completely isolate the mission of clans and families to perpetuate themselves and to retain advantage. Consequently in addition to opportunities provided to women through religion combined with virginity, families, lineages and clans holding some advantage in society often deployed their women in strategies intended to retain that advantage or to consolidate power. For example, in Islam women were recruited as teachers in circumstances where there was a hiatus in the supply of able males in families and clans that virtually owned particular hadiths. This process retained the hadiths within these families and clans. As such, women teachers were acting to defend and promote the interests of their kinship collectives. Hence, it was the wives, sisters and daughters of scholar/teachers who were most likely to be female teachers of hadiths in Islam as they substituted in instances of breaks in male succession in their particular family or lineage. Likewise, in Christian England it was members of the aristocracy whose sisters and daughters, and sometimes widows, were most likely to be the nun/teachers in the convents.

It should be noted that these two feminine roots of teaching in Islam and Christianity were exceedingly small compared to the masculine roots. While Christianity offered somewhat greater opportunities to women than Islam, the number of women teachers in the Religious Age was small.

The overwhelmingly important point to note is that women did not make their entrance into the teaching occupation based on nurturing children. Women teachers were not extending the role of mothers from the private sphere of the home into the public sphere of the school via the monastery or convent. Rather women first made their entrance into teaching because of virginity, that is, on the basis of turning their backs on the traditional roles of wives and mothers. Virginity opened the door for women to enter the teaching profession as 'men'. Teaching therefore was not an extension of motherhood but rather sharing in manhood.

Women teachers therefore shared in the proclamation of the prophetic vision as manifested in the high ethical visions of Islam and Christian. In this regard, they were the partners of their men folk, albeit junior partners. Likewise, they also shared in the preservation, conservation and consolidation of advantage or power in the families, lineages and clans to which they belonged. Again, they were partners of their men folk in promoting and ensuring the collective advantages of the group in which they shared identity, solidarity and the primordial sense of belonging. Women were sharing in men's work in building and maintaining religions, kingdoms and empires.

Teaching as women's work predicated on the nurturing roles of mothers is a nineteenth century conception and has become popular, and even standard, in the twentieth century. It is therefore a very recent rationale for women as teachers. With respect to the feminine roots of teaching, virginity not marriage and motherhood provide the rationale and justification for women to break through the masculine mystique that had permeated teaching.

WHY DID TEACHING REMAIN AS A MASCULINE OCCUPATON?

Why did teaching remain a predominantly male occupation, at all levels of schooling, for over 4300 years?

From the empirical perspective, it is possible to answer this question with reference to the following factors.

1. As some city-states conquered others and established empires, the pattern of conquest was to leave in place the authorities and structures of those cities that accepted the hegemony of their conquerors. Indeed this became the ancient code of imperial accommodation with vanquished cities and kingdoms. Where the vanquished refused to abide by this code, their cities were destroyed and their political, administrative and technical cadres were dispersed or eliminated. However, those cities and peoples that accepted the hegemony of their conquerors were rewarded with autonomy in conducting their internal affairs, including operating their own schools. This paradigm of governance fostered accommodation between dominant and subordinate groups and preserved patriarchal structures within both groups.

2. In the era of the Religious Empires schooling primarily served the personnel needs of religion. Monarchs and emperors drew administrative personnel for their courts almost exclusively from among the religious community. Teaching, like the priesthood, was one of the occupations within the religious community.

3. While the ethics and vision of Christianity and Islam declared the ideal of equality before God, and made no distinction between males and females in their obligations to God, the lived application of these religions, to societies organised on the basis of patriarchal criteria, compromised their ethical visions. Patriarchy infiltrated and altered the ethical visions of Christianity and Islam to a more profound extent than patriarchy was changed by these religions. In the process, both Christianity and Islam became bastions of patriarchy as they developed doctrines which justified and legitimised the latter and as they entrenched patriarchal structures within the institutions of the religions.

4. Schooling was limited and concentrated mainly at the upper levels of education as it was geared mainly to the personnel and learning needs of religion and the palace. In the context of the patriarchal organisation of society and limited demand for schooling, and therefore modest demand for teachers, the supply of men from those families or clans from which teachers were recruited was almost always adequate in relation to the demand for teachers.

5. Schooling started as a single tier institution and was subsequently differentiated into two levels, elementary and higher. The higher-level schools maintained the function to supply the administrative and technical expertise required by both the monarchy and religion. In the religious age, higher-level schools, academies, acquired the function of either affirming or opposing power as it was exercised by monarchs and emperors. Later when schooling was further differentiated into a three tier structure, the university continued to perform the functions of supplying administrative and technical expertise, and providing the ideological justification for either affirming the exercise of state power or for opposing it.

6. Teachers of the highest level of schooling, in two-tier or three-tier institutional structures, have continued to be predominantly male even in the Era of the Nation-State. This is mainly because the role and function of this level of schooling has not changed since the inauguration of schools in ancient Mesopotamia, neither has the predominance of male teachers.

The explanation from the theoretical perspective comes from applying the Theory of Place (Miller 1990). The Theory of Place asserts that the most critical consideration in unravelling complexity related to any social phenomena is that of identifying and analysing the criteria, the operational absolutes, on which the society is organised and their implications for understanding the particular phenomenon. It is instructive therefore to identify the operational absolutes on which the societies in the ancient city-states and Religious Empires were organised as well as the nation-state as represented by the United States in the early nineteenth century.

Table 1: The Rank Order of the Operational Absolutes in the Ancient City States and Societies organised on the Basis of Religion

Sumer	Judaism	Islam	Christian England	United States
City/Region	Religion	Religion	Religion	Religion
Ethnicity	Region	Ethnicity	Ethnicity	Ethnicity
Natality	Natality	Natality	Natality	Natality
Genealogy	Genealogy	Genealogy	Genealogy	Race
Gender	Gender	Gender	Gender	Gender
Generation	Generation	Generation	Generation	Generation

The point to note about the rank order of the operational absolutes of those societies is that the three primary criteria that were contested were religion, ethnicity and natality. In Sumer, cities fought each other for imperial dominance as Semites supplanted Sumerians. In Judah, it was Sadducees and

Pharisees that fought each other, and Jerusalem that declared the other regions as ritually impure. In Islam, it was Arabs, Persians and Turks that competed for imperial power and slaves that established the Mamluk kingdoms. In England, it was Angles, Saxons, Jutes, Danes, Vikings and Celts that contested power and slavery that was eliminated by the time of the Norman Conquest. Genealogy, generation and gender were virtually never challenged and therefore patriarchy remained unchanged as the social foundation of these societies.

In the era of the nation-state, as exemplified by the United States all the criteria employed in the construction of American society have been contested at some time including race, gender and generation. Established as Christian, mainly Protestant, colonies, religion has been officially excluded from the public sphere in the American constitution as Catholics and Jews consistently and persistently challenged the hegemonic position of Protestants. Indeed, the public school was an important arena in which these challenges were made. Likewise, Anglo-Saxon ethnicity and culture has been challenged in the solvent of the American melting pot. Similarly natality was challenged ending in civil war in the 1860s. More recently race, gender and generation have all been challenged as bases upon which the American society should be organised and structured.

The point is that in the era of the nation-state patriarchy has been fundamentally challenged, and declared unconstitutional and illegal for the first time in the history of human civilisation. This is in marked contrast to the conservation and preservation of patriarchy in the civilisation of the city-state and religious empires. It is in the context of the rights-based nation-state, therefore, that gender shifts in teaching have taken place. Men continued to predominate as teachers, at all levels of schooling, for as long as patriarchy continued to be preserved and conserved among the criteria upon which societies were organised.

THE TEACHING OCCUPATION AND ITS SOCIETAL RELATIONSHIPS

Do the masculine and feminine roots of teaching cast any light on the social nature of the teaching occupation and its role in society? In attempting to answer this question it is necessary to make some brief observations on some of the insights gained from this study in relation to teaching and the five dimensions of place: namely power, belief, resources, culture and status. Each will be discussed in turn.

Teachers and Power

Historically schooling, and the teaching occupation within it, was created as ancient cities were established and as some clans, through their activities in warfare, seized the government and founded monarchies. Monarchies in cities were established by military means but governance required more than arms and physical coercion. Newly established palaces, the centre of monarchical administration, could not rely on the temple for their administrators. Hence schooling was created to ensure a supply of scribes, administrators, for kings and their palaces.

The core of the relationship between teaching and power resided in their nexus with technology and knowledge. The emerging monarchs needed the new technology of writing, not only for its capacity to trace liability and establish accountability but also as justification of their right to rule. Likewise, scholars – soothsayers and prophets – claiming knowledge that enabled them to forecast or foresee the future became invaluable to the holders of power, even if their claim to such capability was highly suspect. Notwithstanding suspicions about the quality of the knowledge, decision-making by monarchs who claimed guidance from specialised knowledge and exclusive expertise was more acceptable and defensible in the body politic than those that appeared to be based solely on intuition.

Schooling and the occupation of teaching were created to perform affirmative functions with respect to exercise of newly acquired power by monarchs. The monarch and his scribes became wedded in the interstices of administrative power and their inseparability was immortalised in the art of the period, which routinely showed kings accompanied by their scribes. This imagery symbolised the affirmative nexus that had been forged between power and the educated, the products of schools and teaching. The common purpose of schooling, and the occupation of teaching, was to facilitate the consolidation and extension of the power of ancient monarchies in their mission to govern the cities that had been created around them and the empires some had acquired through conquest.

It was not long in history before schooling and the occupation of teaching became associated with power in the opposition or resistance mode. What emerged were two forms of resistance. The first was a resisting form of affirmation that constrained the powerful to act in accordance with some prescribed set of ethical principles. This association between schooling and teaching is also exemplified in Islam during its classical period in the relationship between emperors, governors and their courts and the ulama and in Israel with the rise of the prophets and their schools.

It is important to note the distinction between unqualified affirmation of power and resisting power affirmatively in any particular social context. While both are affirming power in the particular context, they are competitors in terms of how power should be structured and used and who should hold it. For example, while capitalism and communism affirmed the position of the industrialised countries in geopolitics, they were competitors with respect to how the industrialised countries should be organised and who should be the holders and users of power in those countries. Hence, conservative and socialist parties in any particular nation are but affirmative or opposing modes of the exercise of power in that nation, depending on which is the government at any particular time. However power is structured in any society, schooling and teaching can be deployed to affirm the organisation of power, and to oppose it affirmatively.

The second is an affirmative form of resistance, which overtly or covertly rejects and resists the structure and organisation of power in a particular societal context, while at the same time affirming an alternative vision and framework. While there is a range of relationships between the contestants from outright violent confrontation to benign accommodation, this type of resistance of power is both dangerous and explosive. Jews in the Diaspora exemplified benign accommodation with the powerful that invariably turned violent and explosive. The point is that schooling and teaching are critical elements to the resistance of power in this mode.

The occupation of teaching in contemporary times retains its relationship with all three modes of power. This is one of the reasons why teaching remains a strategic occupation in relation to the exercise of power in any society. The control of schooling and access to the occupation of teaching is strategic to all competing groups in society: from those seeking to impose their hegemony over other groups, to those resisting such imposition or to those accepting some aspects of the imposition on specific terms. Teaching therefore is never neutral in its relationship to power, neither is the relationship unidirectional. Schooling and teaching can serve the cause of those holding power in an affirmative manner. It can also serve the cause of those over whom power is exercised by being an instrument of resistance. The exact nature of the relationship between power and teaching in any setting depends upon how it is directed by those practising the profession, the alliances they make and the interests they serve.

Where access to schooling was restricted and limited only to certain cadres in society its power relations were far more easily identified and traced than in the circumstances in nation-states in which access to different levels is universalised or broad-based. In these latter circumstances schools become arenas in which the intentions and the agendas of the powerful and the weak, the dominant and the subordinate groups, contend. Teachers are not neutral actors in these arenas but agents of the contending groups. In this regard, teachers seldom constitute a monolithic group except in some small schools.

Teachers and Belief

The relation of the occupation of teaching to power is instrumental. However, teaching's relationship to belief is substantive. Scholar/teachers are responsible not only for disseminating knowledge but also for transmitting the high ethical vision of the society of which they are a part. For this reason, there is an inseparable connection between schooling and teaching on the one hand and religion, philosophy and ideology on the other hand. No holy man, philosopher or ideologue can stand aloof from teaching in some form, neither can any teacher perform tasks of instruction without reference to beliefs and the knowledge emanating from those beliefs. Teaching and belief are indispensable to each other. Schooling is the institutionalised form of that indispensable relationship in society, where beliefs are shared across families, clans, tribes and other forms of kinship and non-kinship solidarity.

It is in the dimension of belief that society seeks to address the inherent contradictions in its establishment. The ageless paradox in the society is between a social reality that is relative, temporary and unjust and an ethical imperative that is absolute, permanent but unreal. Realism versus idealism, pragmatism versus utopianism and reason versus revelation are but well-known representations of attempts to come to terms with this paradox. The poles of the paradox are that of reality that is time bound, relative and unjust and therefore condemned as immoral and that of the just, transcendental, eternal and absolute that can only be apprehended by faith but which is ultimately compromised by reality. Given the inseparable relationship between teaching and belief, taking account of the substance of the challenge confronted by belief, teaching finds itself forever caught between the poles of reason and revelation. In every era and society, teachers and schools divide in varying proportions and degrees between those relying on reason and those holding to revelation as the supreme value.

It is this relationship between teaching and belief that accounts for the difficulty of separating priests, scholars, teachers, ideologues and philosophers from each other and accounts for their potential to occupy central places in society. In addition, this relationship defines the legitimating role of belief concerning place in society and its affirmative or oppositional relationship to power, resources and status. Again, this relationship confers upon priests, scholars, teachers and philosophers the potential to exercise power or to become kingmakers. It also explains their potential threat to those holding or aspiring to powerful positions or commanding great resources.

It is important to note that it is almost impossible for teachers to be neutral in confronting competing belief systems. Invariably and inevitably, teachers are believers of a particular set of values, even if they dispassionately attempt to expose their students to opposing beliefs. Difficulties invariably arise where teachers hold to beliefs different from those that parents and communities or school authorities embrace. The point is that it is almost impossible for schooling and teaching to avoid indoctrinating its students in some belief system. The disputes about indoctrination invariably are more about fundamental disagreements with respect to particular beliefs or belief systems, than about indoctrination itself. Whether the beliefs are religious or secular, schooling and teaching are never neutral but are value laden.

It is necessary to note some aspects of the major trajectories in the evolution of belief systems since the commencement of civilisation. The polytheism, religious tolerance, hedonism and materialism of the ancient world of the city-states were challenged by the monotheistic religions that superseded it in the Religious Age. For these reasons the Religious Age disconnected from the beliefs and knowledge of the ancient world. Monotheistic religions brought with them religious intolerance, focus on the spiritual, moral and ethical and other-worldly rewards.

In similar fashion, monotheism itself was challenged, in the era of the nation-state, by a combination of atheism, agnosticism and secular belief exemplified in scientific dogma and nationalism. A distinction is made here between the practice of science and scientific dogma that attempts to explain all of life in terms of speculations claiming science as their basis. Over the last two hundred years scientific dogma in many instances supplanted religion as the primary belief system in explaining and interpreting human existence. Religion was relegated to superstition, while 'scientific explanations' were sought for everything.

At the end of the twentieth century atheism, agnosticism and secularism are being challenged by the reversion to some form of theism, even among scientists. The 'fundamentalist reaction' is yet another example of attempts to revert to more than logic and sense experience as the sources of explanation. The miracle of an intelligently ordered universe, morality, values and the human spirit have again become major concerns both in society and in education.

Teachers and Culture

It has almost become a truism that one of the main aims of education is the transmission of culture. By extension, this would also encompass schooling and teaching. However, the relationship between schooling and teaching on the one hand and the transmission of culture on the other hand, is somewhat more complex because the culture of any society is not uniform across all the clusters of places that compose the society. In addition, schooling and teaching always occur in the arena of contest between central and marginal groups in the society, and therefore between cultures.

Schooling and teaching conducted in the culture of the dominant groups invariably comes to be defined as education in the high culture of the society. The assumption is that it is the mastery of this culture that provides greatest access to central places in the society. Indeed, central groups usually make such a requirement mandatory for all candidates of upward social mobility. On the other hand, schooling offered in the culture of the subordinate groups is usually perceived as being designed to keep its clientele in their places. Invariably subordinate groups assume that their culture will be transmitted through informal channels and that the school's responsibility is to transmit the high culture. It is this relationship between schooling, teaching and culture that often results in teaching being offered in languages that are not the mother-tongue of the students, and parents prizing such teaching despite its very questionable pedagogy.

The most fundamental changes in the relationship between schooling, teaching and culture take place when subordinate groups replace dominant groups. With the rise of those previously marginalised to central places, the high culture is invariably redefined to include substantial elements of the culture of the subordinate groups leading the charge and replacing the former dominant group. In this transformation, sight must be kept of the fact that all aspects of the culture of those previously dominant are never replaced. The requirements of legitimacy of the new holders of central places include both change and conservation. It is this conservative aspect of cultural transformation that explains the fact that Sumerian continued to be used as the language of instruction, diplomacy and commerce for centuries after the Sumerians had disappeared as a distinct society in Mesopotamia. Similarly, Latin continued to be used, in much the same way as Sumerian, for centuries after the Romans had exited from the historic stage. Likewise, English has continued as the national language in many newly independent nations in which the mother tongues are other than English, long after the demise of the British empire.

What is highlighted here is the profound relationship that exists between teaching and conservation and change in culture in society. This relationship is conditioned by the structure of dominance and subordination between groups, mediated by the cyclical movements of places in society and reinforced by the external relationships of the particular society to the world of which it is an integral part. As in the case of power, teaching is a strategic occupation in the transmission of culture in society, particularly the high culture. In this regard, teachers are usually required to be exemplars of the culture they transmit, in both its conservative and changing aspects.

Teachers and Resources

Either by utility or by substance, teachers by the nature of their occupation can occupy a central position with respect to belief and culture. Their position with respect to resources is somewhat different. The teaching occupation has never been one through which its practitioners have garnered great material resources. It would appear that this is implicitly related to the nature of the occupation itself and not to a deficiency on the part of teachers. This is not a feature that is in any way related to gender but rather to the nature of teaching and the resource dimension.

While the belief dimension tends and is biased toward the transcendental aspects of society, the resource dimension is rooted in society's material reality. The two are not always compatible, since the latter could compromise the former. Teaching and teachers are often caught in the web of this incompatibility. In transmitting the high ethical vision of society, however this is conceived, material gain often casts a long shadow of doubt on both purity of purpose and sincerity of conviction. To enhance persuasion and to ensure purity and sincerity, some teachers eschew the aggressive pursuit of material resources in order to be convincing with respect to their integrity and credibility concerning the ethical vision they expound or seek to exemplify.

For these reasons there has been a long tradition of low pay, little better than a subsistence level of material resources, among teachers, which predates the feminisation process. While the latter has undoubtedly added to the degree of pecuniary pay among teachers in some circumstances, it certainly is not the source. Indeed, genteel poverty is a feature that the most revered teachers have shared with the most pious priests, prophets and holy men who by their disregard for material resources testify to their strict adherence to the pure, the just and the holy. This lifestyle of modest material possessions, of the holy man and teacher, was very much in vogue during the age of the Religious Empires.

In contemporary society where so much is measured in terms of material resources, shunning material resources appears not only quaint but also foolish. Far from adding credibility, it is a source of derision and disdain in many quarters. Teachers are currently faced with one of two choices. First, to adopt an aggressive stance to the acquisition of material resources to validate themselves within the prevailing materialistic value system, while risking unfavourable comparisons with their predecessors on the grounds of departing from the highest traditions of the profession. Or, second, to hold fast to the tradition of genteel poverty, and risk being ridiculed, disrespected and disregarded within the contemporary society while being exemplars of a high ethical vision of past eras.

Teachers and Status

The survey of teachers across the ages has shown that teaching included more than one occupation, which are regarded differently in terms of status. College and university teachers have always enjoyed the highest status. The higher status of the college/university teaching occupation is directly related to the level of mastery of matters related to the belief system and knowledge, as well as the relationship of these teachers with power either in the affirmative or resistance modes. University teachers have been the apologists of power both in the affirmative and resistance modes. Also, the power of knowledge and the knowledge of power are the defining features of the status of teachers. Consequently those perceived to possess the highest levels of these are accorded the highest status among teachers. In addition to knowledge however, the university teaching occupation has been populated mainly from the ranks of social contenders for power in society. This also contributes to its status.

By virtue of operating at the entry level of schooling, teachers at the elementary level are not perceived to have more than a rudimentary level of mastery, hence cannot command the deference and honour that their peers at the higher level can evoke. The relatively low status of elementary school teachers predates the feminisation of the occupation at this level. While this relatively low status is a factor why men of the dominant group, with access to occupations which offer greater power and status, do not take up teaching at this level, this is certainly not the cause of the feminisation.

Secondary school teaching occupies the middle position in terms of its location in the education hierarchy and its status. This level of schooling has long been associated with access to the university level of education. Indeed, the latter not only recruits its students from this level but sometimes its teachers. Further, given the elitist traditions that have surrounded schooling for most of its existence, probably to the latter half of the twentieth century, secondary school teachers have been invariably recruited mainly from the higher social strata in societies and particularly from their ruling elites. This has been the case in Judaism, Islam and Christianity during the Religious Age and within nation-states within modern times.

TEACHING AS AN OCCUPATION OF CIVILISATION

This study has sought to explore the masculine and feminine roots of teaching in the ancient civilisation of the city-states and in the age of the monotheistic religions. Those roots were traced to the prophets in Judaism, Christianity and Islam and the tradition of the virgin or pure woman in Christianity and to a lesser extent Islam. It is probably fitting that some attempt be made to point to the social legacy of these two roots to the teaching occupations as a whole.

In sociological terms, prophets can be defined as those who:

- Are fundamentally concerned with changing the social and political circumstances of their times not by changing leadership, but rather by changing the society itself from the bottom up. The accepted challenge is that of getting ordinary people to become constructively engaged with the extraordinary issues constantly confronting human society.
- Stubbornly disregard depressing conditions, debilitating circumstances, overwhelming odds and seeming hopelessness embedded in the social facts and political realities of their societies.
- Resolutely and uncompromisingly hold to a vision of an ennobling future construction of society based on egalitarian values, utopian and even transcendental ideals.
- Persistently and persuasively proclaim this ennobling vision while passionately condemning any departure from these egalitarian values or transcendental and utopian ideals.
- Zealously seek to inspire all to transform society by constructing the future in terms of the egalitarian, utopian and transcendental vision.

In sociological terms the 'virgin religious woman' could be defined as one who had:

- Voluntarily denied her natural desire for sex and children and therefore turned her back on the traditional roles of wife and mother.
- Committed herself, through religious vows, to help to spread the ethical vision, realise the transcendental and utopian ideals and promote egalitarian values of the prophets.
- Devoted her life to the upliftment of the less fortunate in society.

From a historical perspective the prophets and the virgins, who were teachers, lived and had their beings authenticated by the ethos and the high ethical visions of religions that created the empires of the Religious Age. In an age that drew its inspiration from the spiritual, the partnership in schooling and teaching between prophecy and purity was compelling. Their message was universal in terms of geography, time and the very nature of human existence and society. Schooling and teaching in these times were anchored to the eternal, the absolute and the high ethical vision of the particular religion. However, the effectiveness of schools and teachers in these times was constrained and limited by scarcity of the earthly means to encompass all within their embrace in addition to the resistance of significant segments to the vision of society predicated almost totally in spiritual terms.

The masculine and feminine roots of teaching as they evolved in the religious age invested teaching and teachers with a formidable mission in society with respect to its vision, values and virtues. This mission could be summarised as follows:

- Envisioning the future of a people in noble and ethical terms and inspiring especially the young to seek to realise that future despite social facts and overwhelming odds that would normally deter such actions.
- Proclaiming the high ethical vision of a people in terms that inspire especially the young to transcend their circumstances and themselves in ways that advance human civilisation.
- Denying natural desires and creature comforts in the process of becoming exemplars of the ethical vision, values and virtues being proclaimed.

The transformation of teaching in the era of the nation-state has been profound, even if the period of transition has lasted for just about a century and a half. In the era of the nation-state, the prophetic visions of the Religious Age have been secularised and territorialized within national borders. Actually, the ideological premises of the nation-state could be seen as a secular and agnostic reconstruction of the vision of the prophet. Prophets have become nationalists and nation-builders. These secular prophets now herald ennobling futures in the national construction of human society. However, compared to the prophets of the Religious Age, the nationalists and nation-builders are far more circumscribed in the scope of their vision and message. Far from being universal in time, geography and context, nationalism is restricted in place, time and content. Nationalism only seeks to advance the rights and well being of nationals. The exclusiveness of the nation undermines and subverts the majesty of a universal and utopian formulation of society and humankind. Further, the agnostic underpinning of nationalism robs its egalitarian and utopian values of transcendence and therefore makes it more vulnerable to materialism on the one hand and scepticism on the other. Notwithstanding these limitations, the nation-state and nationalism has retained several aspects of the masculine roots of teaching and the sociological definition of the prophet.

Nations have no need for virgins. Constitutional rights, not purity and self-denial, are the foundation of nation-states. While sacrificial purity is at the heart of religion, it occupies no such place in nation-states or nationalism. The foundation of nations is constitutional law enshrining the rights of nationals. Human and individual rights are among the central values of nations. Purity holds no special place and could be said to be redundant. Further, constitutional law has made gender of no legal significance. Hence, any distinction between women in terms of virgins and mothers, single or married, is superfluous. Men and women are equal with respect to national rights and responsibilities. Further, it is the state that has the responsibility for welfare related to those who have fallen between the cracks. There is therefore no unique role for pure women in the symbolic underpinnings of the nation-state.

With respect to the roots of teaching therefore, the masculine root has greatest relevance to the teaching occupation in the nation-state. Women teachers are nationalists and nation-builders on the same basis as men. Men and women can be the secular prophets of the national vision that is embraced. Nationalists and nation-builders are recruited to teaching on a unisexual basis. From the perspective of the values on which nation-states are constructed the fact that more women or men have been recruited to teach at any level of the school system should only constitute a problem with respect to the canons of equality. As such, imbalance at any level, and in favour of any gender, constitutes no ideological basis of concern.

The tasks of men and women teachers in nation-states are the same. They are to:

a) Build national identity and solidarity.
b) Mobilise the nation to compete successfully with other nations for power and resources. Accordingly, teachers must transmit the knowledge, skills and attitudes that are required for comparative advantage in these spheres.
c) Inform and educate their nationals about their rights within the nation and their obligations to the nation.

d) Preserve and promote the national culture.

Indeed, it must be acknowledged that the secular prophets of the nation-state have been far more successful in mobilising the earthly means, inspiring participation and in garnering voluntary support for schooling than the prophets of religion. Schooling therefore has expanded in the era of the nation-state to include far greater numbers than the religious vision ever inspired.

It must not be overlooked, however, that the masculine and feminine roots of teaching in prophesy and purity have left a great legacy to teachers with respect to persona, character and personality. Teachers continue to be perceived as:

- Shapers of the future society based on utopian and transcendental values and ideals;
- Paragons of virtue and moral stature in their communities.
- Individuals whose work is characterised by self-sacrifice in the service of others.

Concisely, teachers are expected to be at the frontiers of the construction of the future. They are expected to imbue their students with ideals. They themselves are expected to be virtuous persons and exemplars of the best in human nature. These attributes can all be traced back to the masculine and feminine roots of teaching in the ancient world and the religious age.

Some of the most contentious contemporary debates concerning teaching and teachers revolve around the national reconstruction of teaching and its legacy from its masculine and feminine roots. In the national reconstruction of teaching the private lives of teachers are separate from their public roles and responsibilities. Once teachers observe the laws of the land and respect the rights of their students and colleagues, their lifestyles and other involvement are not the concern of their employers. This was certainly not the case in past eras, where the private and public behaviour of teachers could not be separated. They are many who still hold to the view that teachers should be vignettes of virtue even in matters far removed from schools and their teaching responsibilities.

When the social history of the teaching occupation is taken as a whole, conclusion that seems almost impossible to avoid is that teaching is an occupation of civilisation. This has been the case whether the civilisation is that of the ancient city-states, of Western civilisation with its Judaeo/Christian foundations or Islamic civilisation or the civilisation of the nation-state. The mission of teaching has been to make its students civil, however civilisation is conceived. Teaching is rooted in the high ethical vision of civilisation however it is formulated.

Another conclusion is that teaching and schooling are much more about the construction of the future than about preserving the past. Teaching has a forward focus and not a backward gaze. Teaching is about a dynamic engagement with destiny, whatever this is conceived to be by a particular people. The awesome reality is that schools and teaching foretell the future and are a foretaste of what is to come. Recognition of this aspect of teaching can either terrify or console depending on the experience and perspective of the observer.

Another conclusion is that teaching is a prophetic occupation. It is fundamentally concerned with the social and political circumstances of a people. Teaching is about defining and developing purpose and meaning about human life and human society that is to be achieved by a particular people at some point in time. It is about social mobilisation from the bottom-up and from the top down. Teaching is about an ennobling upotian, and sometimes transcendental, vision of humanity and society and the values with which these should be endowed. Teaching is intentional and deliberate activity designed to proclaim vision and values. The core of that intention is development of the will to construct society and humanity with a particular purpose and to achieve a desired destiny.

Because of its high content in vision and values, teaching almost by default requires virtue in order to be most effective. The vision and the values require personal and symbolic expression in the process of persuading students. Who the teacher is, is as important as what the teacher does. Teachers are expected to exemplify some of the best qualities of human nature, however these are conceived in particular circumstances and in different ages. The essence of teaching as it has evolved from its ancient roots is vision, values and virtue. Devoid of these, teaching merely becomes instruction lacking in focus, purpose and meaning with respect to the larger issues with which each generation of humans must contend.

AN AFTERWORD

At the beginning of the twenty-first century nationalism has waned. The concept of the nation-state is in decline. Nationalism as a secular and territorial version of the prophetic vision has lost its lustre and panache. Its territorial limitations have robbed it of universality and its secular character has denied it transcendence. In the process, the inspriring ethical vision has descended into a materialistic dream limited only to nationals. The result is that the nationalist philosophy has been tarnished by xenophobia even where it has delivered partially on the materialistic dream as aliens are excluded from participating legally in benefits.

Clan and land no longer constitute the foundations upon which societies are organised. National borders have been compromised by information and communications technologies. The boundaries between virtual and real are becoming increasingly blurred. The doctrine of national sovereignty is challenged by the affirmation of universal human rights. Global and local are connected on television in nightly news on daily events. It is the here and the now that matters in material terms. Although the content of the new is not crystal clear, the contours are already clearly discernable. The individual is the unit of social organisation. The consumer is the centre of economic activity. The willing worker and the entrepreneur are the expected products of education. Material advancement and creature comforts constitute meaning and purpose in and of life. For the first time in the history of civilisation, it is the merchant's ethos that is pre-eminent.

The implication of these developments for teachers and teaching is profound. Over the last two hundred years, the teaching occupation has been pried and loosened from its roots in religion. It is now being untangled from its moorings in nationalism and nation building. Further, as materialism has gained pre-eminence through the wide acceptance of market forces, notions of comparative advantage and the global economy, the teaching occupation is plunged into crisis given its historical ambivalent and ambiguous relationship with the acquisition of the resources at the fountainhead of schooling. While single issues like the environment provide some relief with respect to universal concerns, most of the issues related to schooling give the impression of local and parochial considerations.

Teaching and teachers at the beginning of the twenty-first century, therefore, face some of the most profound challenges in coming to terms with their mission in society and the essence of their profession in contemporary times. There are many advocates of a return to the 'good old days'. Their concept of the future is a return to the past. Yet, if there are any lessons to be learned from this study of the evolution of schooling and teaching it is that schools and teachers are not about recapturing a past but must contend with destiny in constructing future society in bold new ways.

Bearing in mind that fundamental change begins in the margin, it is likely that the most creative and dynamic developments related to schooling and teaching and their relationships in society may indeed arise from among subordinate groups and marginal societies in the world. In these circumstances the leadership, if not the muscle, is likely to come mainly from the daughters and not the sons of these marginal groups and nations. The challenges to these daughters will be those traditionally faced by sons. In what manner and for what purpose will the collective power of people be mobilised to fashion and construct humanity, society and civilisation in the future? Probably it is this question that schooling and teaching should now address in the context of the contemporary construction of the prophetic vision of society and the sacrificial purity associated with virgins.

Bibliography

Ahlstrom, G. W. *Who Were The Israelites?* Winona Lake, Ind: Eisenbrauns, 1986.

Ahmed, L. *Women and Gender in Islam: Historical Roots of a Modern Debate.* New Haven: Yale University Press, 1992.

Ahmed, M.D. *Muslim Education and the Scholar's Social Status up to the Fifth Century Muslim Era.* Zurich: Verlag Der Islam, 1968.

Albright, W.F. *The Biblical Period.* Philadelphia: The Jewish Publication Society of America, 1966.

Alexander, M. V. C. *The Growth of English Education, 1348–1648.* University Park: Pennsylvania State University Press, 1990.

Ali, A. A. K. M. *History of Traditional Islamic Education in Bangladesh.* Draha: Islamic Foundation of Bangladesh, 1983.

Anderson, J. D. *The Education of Blacks in the South, 1860–1935.* Chapel Hill: University of North Carolina Press, 1988.

Anderson, R. D. *Education and the Scottish People 1750–1918.* Oxford: Clarendon Press, 1995.

Beckles, H. *Natural Rebels: Black Women as Slaves in Barbados.* London: Zed Books, 1989.

Beckles, H. *A History of Barbados: From Amerindian Settlement to Nation-State.* Cambridge: Cambridge University Press, 1990.

Benavot, Phyllis A. R. 'The Expansion of Primary Education, 1870–1940: Trends and Issues'. *Sociology of Education* 61(July 1998): 191–210.

Ben-Horin, M. 'From the Turn of the Century to the Late 1930s'. In *A History of Jewish Education in America*, edited by J. Pilch, 51–116. New York: American Association of Jewish Education, 1969.

Benn, D. *Ideology and Political Development: The Growth and Development of Political Ideas in the Caribbean 1774–1983.* Kingston: Institute of Social and Economic Research, University of the West Indies, Mona, 1987.

Berkey, J. *The Transmission of Knowledge in Medieval Cairo: A Social History of Islamic Education.* Princeton: Princeton University Press, 1992.

Biale, R. *Women and Jewish Law: An Exploration of Women's Issues in Halakhic Sources.* New York: Schocken Books, 1984.

Bickerman, E. J. 'The Historical Foundations of Post-Biblical Judaism'. In *The Jews: Their History, Culture and Religion*, edited by L. Finkelstein,(1) 70–114. Philadelphia: The Jewish Publication Society, 1966.

Bird, P.' Women's Religion in Ancient Israel'. In *Women's Earliest Records: From Ancient Egypt and Western Asia. Proceedings of the Conference on Women in the Ancient Near*

East Brown *University Providence, Rhode Island Nov. 5–7 1987*, edited by B. S. Lesko, 283–298. Atlanta: Georgia, Scholars Press, 1989.

Bonner, G. S. 'Religion in Anglo-Saxon England'. In *A History of Religion in Britain*, edited by S. Gilley and W. J. Sheils, 24–44. Oxford: Blackwell, 1994.

Borg, M. J. *Conflict, Holiness, and Politics in the Teaching of Jesus*. New York: Edwin Mellen Press, 1984.

Borg, M. J. *Jesus: A New Vision*. San Francisco: Harper & Row, 1988.

Brathwaite, E. *The Development of Creole Society in Jamaica: 1770–1820*. Oxford: Clarendon Press, 1971.

Brereton, B. *Race Relations in Colonial Trinidad*. London: Cambridge University Press, 1979.

Briggs, A. *A Social History of Britain: From the Ice Age to the Channel Tunnel*. London: Weidenfeld and Nicolson, 1994.

Broek, R.D. *Studies in Gnosticism and Alexandrian Christianity*. New York: E.J. Brill, 1996.

Bronowski, J. *The Ascent of Man*. Boston: Little, Brown, 1973.

Brown, G. H. *Bede the Venerable*. Boston: Twayne Publishers, 1987.

Brundage, J. A. 'The Merry Widow's Serious Sister: Remarriage in Classical Canon Law'. In *Matron and Marginal Women in Medieval Society*, edited by R. R. Edwards and V. Zeigler. Woodbridge: The Boydell Press, 1995.

Butchart, R. E. 'We Can Best Instruct Our Own People: New York African Americans in the Freedmen's Schools, 1861–1875'. In *African American Education in the South, 1861–1900*, edited by D. G. Nieman, 31–53. New York: Garland, 1994.

Campbell, M. C. *The Maroons of Jamaica: 1655–1796*. New Jersey: Africa World Press, 1990.

Cann, R. L., M. Stoneking, et al. 'Mitochondrial DNA and Human Evolution'. *Nature* 325 (1987): 31–36.

Cantor, A. *Jewish Women/Jewish Men: The Legacy of Patriarchy in Jewish Life*. San Francisco: Harper San Francisco, 1995.

Cash, W. J. *The Mind of the South*. Garden City: Doubleday, 1954.

Castle, E. B. *Ancient Education and Today*. Baltimore, Maryland: Penguin Books, 1961.

Chaudhri, A. G. *Some Aspects of Islamic Education*. Lahore: Universal Books, 1982.

Childe, G. V. *New Light on the Most Ancient East*. London: Routledge, 1952.

Clifford, G. J. 'Man/ Woman/Teacher: Gender, Family and Career in American Educational History'. In *American Teachers: Histories of a Profession at Work*, edited by D. Warren, 293–343. New York: MacMillan, 1989.

Clifford, J. 'Daughters into Teachers: Educational and Demographic Influences on the Transformation of Teaching into Women's Work in America'. In *Women Who Taught: Perspectives on the History of Women and Teaching*, edited by A. Prentice and M.R. Theobald, 115–135. Toronto: Toronto University Press, 1991.

Cook, M. 'Activism and Quietism in Islam: The Case of the Early Murji'a'. In *Islam and Power*, edited by A. S. Cudsi and A. E. H. Dessouki. Baltimore: Johns Hopkins University Press, 1981.

Cooper, J. S. 'Third Millennium Mesopotamia: An Introduction'. In *Women's Earliest Records from Ancient Egypt and Western Asia*, edited by B. S. Lesko, 115–135. Georgia: Scholars Press, 1989.

Cox, E. L. *Free Coloreds in the Slave Societies of St. Kitts and Grenada, 1763–1833*. Knoxville: University of Tennessee Press, 1984.

Cragg, K. *The Arab Christian: A History in the Middle East*. Louisville: Westminister/John Knox Press, 1991.

Crawford, H. *Sumer and Sumerians*. Cambridge: Cambridge University Press, 1991.

Cremin, L. A. *The American Common School: An Historical Conception*. New York: Columbia University, 1970.

Cremin, L. A. *American Education: The Colonial Experience, 1607–1783*. New York: Harper Torchbooks, 1970.

Cremin, L. A. *American Education: The National Experience, 1783–1876*. Cambridge: Harper and Row Publishers, 1980.

Crossan, J. D. *The Historical Jesus: The Life of a Mediterranean Jewish Peasant*. San Francisco: Harper & Row, 1991.

Cubberly, E. P. *Public Education in the United States: A Study and Interpretation of American Educational History*. Massachusetts: Houghton Mifflin, 1947.

Davidson, T. *Education and the Greek People*. New York: D. Appleton, 1903.

Diakonoff, I. M. 'The Structure of Near Eastern Society'. *Oikumene* 3 (1982): 7–100.

Douglas, A. *The Feminization of American Culture*. New York: Knopf, 1977.

Downing, F. G. *Christ and the Cynics: Jesus and Other Radical Preachers in First Century Tradition*. Sheffield: Sheffield Academic Press, 1988.

Drazin, N. *The History of Jewish Education: From 515 BCE to 220 CE*. Baltimore: Johns Hopkins Press, 1940.

Dunn, R. S. *Sugar and Slaves: The Rise of the Planter Class in the English West Indies, 1624–1713*. New York: Norton, 1972.

Ebner, E. *Elementary Education in Ancient Israel: During the Tannaitic Period (10–220 C.E.)*. New York: Bloch, 1956.

Eby, F. and Arrowood C. F. *History and Philosophy of Education: Ancient and Medieval*. New York: Prentice–Hall, 1940.

Eisner, G. *Jamaica 1830–1930: A Study in Economic Growth*. Westport, Connecticut: Greenwood Press, 1974.

Elkins, S. K. *Holy Women of Twelfth-Century England*. Chapel Hill: University of North Carolina Press, 1988.

Ellegard, A. *Jesus: One Hundred Years Before Christ*. London: Century, 1999.

Ellis, C. ' "A Remedy for Barbarism": Indian Schools, the Civilizing Program and the Kiowa-Comanche-Apache Reservation, 1871–1915'. *American Indian Culture and Research Journal* 18, no. 3 (1994): 85–120.

Engineer, A. A. *The Rights of Women in Islam*. London: C. Hurst, 1992.

Falkenstein, A. *The Sumerian Temple City*. Los Angeles: Undena Publications, 1974.

Finkelstein, L. *The Pharisees: The Sociological Background of their Faith*. Philadelphia: Jewish Publication Society of America, 1938.

Frerichs, E. S. 'Introduction to Ancient Israel'. In *Women's Earliest Records: From Ancient Egypt and Western Asia. Proceedings of the Conference on Women in the Ancient Near East Brown University Providence, Rhode Island Nov. 5–7 1987*, edited by B. S. Lesko, 261–264. Atlanta: Scholars Press, 1989.

Froner, S. 'In the Colonial Period'. *A History of Jewish Education in America*, edited by J. Pilch, 1–24. New York: American Association of Jewish Education, 1969.

Gabriel, R. A. *The Culture of War: Invention and Early Development*. New York: Greenwood Press, 1990.

Gadd, C. J. *Ideas of Divine Rule in the Ancient East*. London: Oxford University Press, 1948.

Gadd, C. J. *Teachers and Students in the Oldest Schools*. London: University of London, 1956.

Gartner, L. P. *Jewish Education in the United States*. New York: Columbia University, 1969.

Gelb, I. J. 'Household and Family in Early Mesopotamia'. In *State and Temple Economy in the Ancient Near East 1*, edited by E. Lipsinski. Leuven: Universiteite te Leuven, 1979.

Gellner, E. *Muslim Society*. Cambridge: Cambridge University Press, 1981

Gil'adi, A. *Children of Islam: Concepts of Childhood and Medieval Muslim Society*. Hampshire: MacMillan, 1992.

Gilchrist, R. *Gender and Material Culture*. London: Routledge, 1994.

Gilman, A. 'From Widowhood to Wickedness: The Politics of Class and Gender in New York City Private Charity, 1799–1860'. *History of Education Quarterly* 24, no. 1 (1984): 59–74.

Glassner, J.J. 'Women, Hospitality and the Honor of the Family'. In *Women's Earliest Records: From Ancient Egypt and Western Asia. Proceedings of the Conference on Women in the Ancient Near East. Providence, Rhode Island Nov. 5–7 1987*, edited by. B. S. Lesko, 71–90. Atlanta: Scholar's Press, 1989.

Goldin, E. J. 'The Period of the Talmud (135 C.E.–1035 C.E.)'. In *The Jews: Their History Culture and Religion 1*, edited by. L. Finkelstein, 115–215. Philadelphia: Jewish Publication Society of America, 1966.

Good, H. G. *A History of American Education*. New York: Macmillan, 1956.

Goody, J. *The Login of Writing and the Organization of Society*. Cambridge: Cambridge University Press, 1986.

Gordon, M. M. 'Patriots and Christians: A Reassessment of Nineteenth Century School Reforms'. *Journal of Social History* 11, no. 4(1978): 554–573.

Gordon, S. C. *A Century of West Indian Education: A Source Book*. London: Longmans, 1963.

Grant, R. M. *Early Christianity and Society*. San Francisco: Harper and Row, 1977.

Green, M. W. 'The Construction and Implementation of the Cuneiform Writing System'. *Visible Language* XV, no. 4(1981): 345–372.

Greenberg, S. 'Jewish Education Institutions'. *The Jews: Their History, Culture and Religion II*, edited by L. Finkelstein, 1254–1287 . Philadelphia: The Jewish Publication Society of America, 1966.

Grinstein, H. B. 'In the Course of the Nineteenth Century'. In *A History of Jewish Education in America*, edited by J. Pilch, 25–50. New York: American Association of Jewish Education, 1969.

Hall, H. R. *The Ancient History of the Near East*. London: Methuen and Company, 1916.

Hallo, W. W. 'A History of Sumerian Literature'. *Sumerological Studies in Honor of Thorkild Jacobsen on his Seventh Birthday*, edited by S. J. Lieberman, 181–203. Chicago: University of Chicago Press, 1975.

Harris, R. 'Independent Women in Ancient Mesopotamia'. In *Women's Earliest Records: From Ancient Egypt and Western Asia. Proceedings of the Conference on Women in the Ancient Near East. Providence, Rhode Island Nov. 5–7 1987*, edited by B. S. Lesko, 145–156. Atlanta: Scholar's Press, 1989.

Hawting, G. R. *The First Dynasty of Islam: The Umayyad Caliphate.* London: Croom Helm, 1986

Herrin, J. *The Formation of Christendom.* Princeton: Princeton University Press, 1987.

Hertzberg, J. *Judaism.* New York:, George Braziller, 1962.

Hill, K. R. and I. S. Parboosingh. 'The First Medical School of the British West Indies and the First Medical School of America'. *West Indian Medical Journal* 1, no. 21(1951).

Hill, R. 'From the Conquest to the Black Death'. *A History of Religion in Britain.* S. Gilley and W. J. Sheils, Oxford: Blackwell, 1994.

Hillgarth, J. N. *Christianity and Paganism: The Conversion of Western Europe 350–750.* Philadelphia: University of Pennsylvania Press, 1986.

Hoffman, N. *Woman's 'True' Profession: Voices from the History of Teaching.* New York: Feminist Press, 1981.

Horsley, R. A. *Sociology and the Jesus Movement.* New York: Crossroads, 1989.

Horsley, R. A. and J. S. Hanson. *Bandits, Prophets, and Messiahs: Popular Movements at the Time of Jesus.* Minneapolis: Winston Press, 1985.

Humble, R. *Warfare in the Ancient World.* London: Cassell, 1980.

Hutton, C. A. ' "Colour for Colour; Skin for Skin": The Ideological Foundations of Post-Slavery Society, 1838–1865 The Jamaican Case'. Department of Government, Kingston: University of the West Indies: 431, 1992.

Hyatt-Brown, B. 'Black Schooling During Reconstruction'. In *African American Education in the South, 1861–1900,* edited by D. G. Nieman, 426–445. New York: Garland Publishers Inc., 1994.

Jackson, J., G. *Introduction to the African Civilizations.* New York: Citadel Press Book, 1995.

Jacobs, H. P. *Sixty Years of Change, 1806–1866: Progress and Reaction in Kingston and the Countryside.* Kingston: Institute of Jamaica, 1973.

Jacobsen, T: 'Primitive Democracy in Ancient Mesopotamia'. *Journal of Near Eastern Studies* II, no. 3 (1943):159–172.

Jayawardena, C. *Conflict and Solidarity in a Guianese Plantation.* London: University of London, 1963.

Jones, J. 'Women Who Were More Than Men: Sex and Status in Freedmen's Teaching'. *History of Education Quarterly* 19, no. 3 (1979): 47–59.

Jones, T. B. 'Sumerian Administrative Documents: An Essay'. *Sumerological Studies in Honor of Thorkild Jacobsen on his Seventh Birthday,* edited by S. J. Lieberman, 41–63. Chicago: University of Chicago Press, 1975.

Kaestle, C. F. *The Evolution of an Urban School System: New York City,1750–1850.* Massachusetts: Harvard University Press, 1973.

Katz, B. *Dahl's History of the Book, Third English Edition.* London: The Scarecrow Press, 1995.

Katz, M. *The Irony of Early School Reform: Educational Innovation in Mid-nineteenth Century Massachusetts*. Massachusetts: Harvard University Press, 1968.

Kaufman, P. W. *Women Teachers on the Frontier*. New Haven: Yale University Press, 1984.

Kettle, A. J. 'Ruined Maids: Prostitutes and Servant Girls in Late Medieval England'. In *Matron and Marginal Women in Medieval Society*, edited by R. R. Edwards and V. Zeigler. Woodbridge: Boydell Press, 1995.

Khan, H. 'History of Muslim Education'. Paper presented at the Pakistan Education Conference, 1967.

King, R. 'Education in the Late 19th Century Jamaica: American Connections'. In *Before and After 1865*, edited by B. Moore and S. Wilmot, 13–22. Kingston: Ian Randle Publishers, 1998.

Kraemer, R. S. 'Jewish Women in the Diaspora World of Late Antiquity'. In *Jewish Women in Historical Perspective*, edited by J. Baskin, 43–67. Detroit: Wayne State University Press, 1991.

Kramer, S. N. *The Sumerians: Their History, Culture and Character*. Chicago: Chicago University Press, 1963.

Kramer, S. N. *History Begins at Sumer: Thirty Nine Firsts in Man's Recorded History*. Philadelphia: University of Pennsylvania Press, 1981.

Kretzmann, P. E. *Education among the Jews: From the Earliest Times to the End of the Talmudic Period 500 AD*. Boston: Badger, 1916.

Lamberg-Karlovsky, C. C. 'Comment on Zagarell: Trade, Women, Class and Society in Ancient Western Asia'. *Current Anthropology* 27, no. 5 (1986): 422–423.

Landsberger, B. *Three Essays on the Sumerians*. Los Angeles: Undena Publications, 1974.

Lawson, W. A. *Religion and Race*. New York: Peter Lang, 1996.

Leach, A. F. *The Schools of Medieval England*. London: Methuen, 1915.

Leahy, W. P. *Adopting to America: Catholics, Jesuits and Higher Education in the Twentieth Century*. Washington D. C.: Georgetown University Press, 1991.

Lewis, G. K. *Main Currents in Caribbean Thought*. Kingston: Heinemann Educational Books (Caribbean), 1983.

Lewis, G. K. *Grenada: The Jewel Despoiled*. Baltimore: Johns Hopkins University Press, 1987.

Leyser, H. *Medieval Women: A Social History of Women in England, 450–1500*. London: Weidenfeld and Nicolson, 1995.

Lyon, H. R. *Anglo-Saxon England and the Norman Conquest*. London: Longman, 1991.

Makdisi, G. *The Rise of Colleges: Institutions of Learning in Islam and the West*. Edinburgh: Edinburgh University Press, 1981.

Makdisi, G. 'Baghdad, Bologna and Scholasticism'. In *Centres of Learning: Learning and Location in Pre-Modern Europe and the East*, edited by J. W. Drijvers and A. A. MacDonald, 141–160. Leiden: E. J. Brill, 1995.

Maller, J. B. 'The Role of Education in the History of the Jews'. In *The Jews: Their History, Culture and Religion II*, edited by L. Finkelstein, 1234–1253. Philadelphia: The Jewish Publication Society of America, 1966.

Mayr-Harting, H. *The Coming of Christianity to Anglo-Saxon England*. University Park: Pennsylvania State University Press, 1991.

McClusky, N. G. *Catholic Education in America: A Documentary History*. New York: Columbia University, 1964.

McClusky, N. G. *Catholic Education Faces its Future*. New York: Doubleday, 1968.

Meyers, C. 'Women and the Domestic Economy of Early Israel'. In *Women's Earliest Records: From Ancient Egypt and Western Asia. Proceedings of the Conference on Women in the Ancient Near East Brown University Providence, Rhode Island Nov. 5–7 1987*, edited by B. S. Lesko, 265–278. Atlanta: Georgia, Scholars Press, 1989.

Miller, E. *Jamaican Society and High Schooling*. Kingston: University of the West Indies, 1990.

Miller, E. *Men At Risk*. Kingston: Jamaica Publishing House, 1991.

Miller, E. *Education For All: Caribbean Perspectives and Imperatives*. Washington, D. C.: The Johns Hopkins University Press, 1992.

Miller, E. *Marginalisation of the Black Male*. Kingston: Canoe Press, 1994.

Miller, E. 'Feminisation of Elementary School Teaching in the Commonwealth Caribbean'. In *Institute Annual*, edited by R. King. Kingston: University of the West Indies, 1998.

Miller, E. and J. Hatcher. *Medieval England: Rural Society and Economic Change, 1086–1348*. London: Longman, 1978.

Miller, E. and J. Hatcher. *Medieval England: Towns, Commerce and Crafts, 1086–1348*. London: Longman, 1995.

Mills, C. W. *A Comment on the Class, Race and Gender: The Unholy Trinity. Race, Class and Gender in the Future of the Caribbean*, edited by J. E. Greene, 111–114. Kingston: University of the West Indies, Mona, 1993.

Mintz, S. W. *Caribbean Transformation*. Baltimore: The Johns Hopkins University Press, 1974.

Mintz, S. W. *Sweetness and Power*. New York: Viking, 1985.

Monaghan, J. 'Literacy Instruction and Gender in Colonial New England'. *American Quarterly* 40, no. 1(1988): 17–41.

Moran, J. A. H. *The Growth of English Schooling 1340–1548: Learning, Literacy and Laicization in Pre-Reformation York Diocese*. Princeton: Princeton University Press, 1985.

Morison, S. E. and H. S. Commager. *The Growth of the American Republic*. New York: Oxford University Press, 1942.

Morley, S. G. *The Ancient Maya*. Stanford: Stanford University Press, 1956.

Morris, N. *The Jewish School: An Introduction to the History of Jewish Education*. New York: Jewish Education Committee Press, 1937.

Morris, R. *Reading 'Riting and Reconstruction: Education of Freedmen in the South, 1861–1870*. Chicago: Chicago University Press, 1981.

Mortley, R. *Womanhood. The Feminine in Ancient Hellenism, Gnosticism, Christianity and Islam*. Sydney: Delacroix Press, 1981.

Naff, T. 'Towards a Muslim Theory of History'. In *Islam and Power*, edited by A. S. Cudsi and A. E. H. Dessouki. Baltimore, Johns Hopkins University Press, 1981.

Nakosteen, M. K. *History of Islamic Origins of Western Education*. Boulder: University of Colorado Press, 1964.

Neusner, J. 'Religion and Society in the Formation of the Judaism of the Pentateuch'. In *Social Foundations of Judaism*, edited by C. Goldscheider and J. Neusner. New Jersey: Prentice Hall, 1990.

Niditch, S. 'Portrayals of Women in the Hebrew Bible'. In *Jewish Women in Historical Perspective*, edited by J. Baskin, 25–42. Detroit: Wayne State University Press, 1991.

Niebuhr, R. *An Interpretation of Christian Ethics*. New York: Harper Row, 1935.

Nieman, D. G. 'Introduction'. In *African American Education in the South, 1861–1900*. New York: Garland, 1994.

Noble, W. and Davidson, I. 'The Evolutionary Emergence of Modern Human Behavior: Language and its Archaeology'. *Man* 26 (1991):223–254.

Oberg, M. 'Indians and Englishmen at the First Roanke Colony: A Note on the Pemisapan's Conspiracy, 1585–86'. *American Indian Culture and Research Journal* 18, no. 2 (1994): 75–89.

Orme, N. *English Schools in the Middle Ages*. London:, Methuen, 1973.

_____. *Education in the West of England, 1066–1548*. Exeter: University of Exeter, 1976.

Parry, A. W. *Education in England in the Middle Ages*. London: University Tutorial Press Ltd., 1920.

Parsons, G. *The Stream of History*. New York: Scribner, 1932.

Penny, D., M. Steel, et al. 'Improved Analysis of Human mtDNA Sequences Support a Recent African Origin for Homo Sapiens'. *Molecular Biological Evolution* 12, no. 5 (1995): 863–882.

Perraton, H. D. 'British Attitudes Towards East and West Africa, 1880–1914'. *Race* 8, no. 3 (1967).

Perry, W. J. *The Growth of Civilization*. Harmondsworth: Penguin Books, 1937.

Phillippo, J. M. *Jamaica: Its Past and Present State*. London: John Snow, 1843.

Pilch, J. 'From the Early Forties to the Mid Sixties'. In *A History of Jewish Education in America*. New York, American Association of Jewish Education: 119–176, 1969

Powell, M., A. 'Three Problems in the History of Cuneiform Writing: Origin, Direction of Script and Literacy'. *Visible Language* XV, no. 4(1981): 419–440.

Powell, M. A. *The Jesus Debate: Modern Historians Investigate the Life of Christ*. Oxford: Lion, 1998.

Ramirez, F. and Boli, J. 'The Political Construction of Mass Schooling: European Origins and Worldwide Institutionalisation'. *Sociology of Education* 60 (1987): 2–17.

Rawlinson, G. *The Origins of Nations*. New York: Scribner, Welford and Armstrong, 1878.

Rigby, S. H. *English Society in the Later Middle Ages: Class, Status and Gender*. London: MacMillan, 1995.

Robinson, A. *The Story of Writing*. London: Thames and Hudson, 1995.

Romalis, C. *Barbados and St Lucia: A Comparative Analysis of Social and Economic Development in Two British West Indian Islands*. Washington: Washington University, 1969.

Sachar, A. L. *A History of the Jews*. New York: Knopf, 1948.

Sanders, E. P. *Jesus and Judaism*. Philadelphia: Fortress Press, 1985.

Sanders, E. P. *The Historical Figure of Jesus*. London: Penguin Press, 1993.

Schmandt-Besserat, D. 'An Archaic Recording System and the Origin of Writing'. *Syro-Mesopotamian Studies* 1, no. 2 (1977): 1–32.

Schmandt-Besserat, D. 'From Tokens to Tablets: A Re-Evaluation of the So-Called "Numerical Tablets"'. *Visible Language* XV, no. 4(1981): 321–344.

Schmandt-Besserat, D. and Alexander, S. M. *The First Civilization: The Legacy of Sumer*. Austin: University of Texas, 1975.

Schwantes, S. J. *A Short History of the Ancient Near East*. Michigan: Baker Book House, 1965.

Schweitzer, A. *The Quest for the Historical Jesus: A Critical Study of the Progress from Reimarus to Wrede*. New York: MacMillan, 1968.

Scott, A. F. 'The Ever Widening Circle: The Diffusion of Feminist Values from the Troy Female Seminary, 1822–1872'. *History of Education Quarterly* 19, no.1 (1979): 3–25.

Sedlak, M. W. 'Let Us Go Buy a School Master: Historical Perspectives on the Hiring of Teachers in the United States'. In *American Teachers: Histories of a Profession at Work*, edited by D. Warren, 257–290. New York: MacMillan, 1989.

Shalaby, A. *History of Muslim Education*. Karachi: Indus Publications, 1979.

Sheils, W. J. 'Reformed Religion in England, 1520–1640'. In *A History of Religion in Britain*. S. Gilley and W. J. Sheils, 77–89. Oxford: Blackwell,1994.

Sherlock, P. and Nettleford, R. *The University of the West Indies: A Caribbean Response to the Challenge of Change*. London: MacMillan Caribbean, 1990.

Sjoberg, A. W. 'The Old Babylonian Eduba'. In *Sumerological Studies in Honor of Thorkild Jacobsen on his Seventh Birthday*, edited by S. J. Lieberman, 159–179. Chicago: University of Chicago Press, 1975.

Smith, M. *Jesus the Magician*. New York: Harper & Row, 1978.

Smith, R. T., ed. 'Social Stratification, Cultural Pluralism and Integration in West Indian Societies'. *Caribbean Integration: Papers on Social, Political and Economic Integration*. Rio Piedras: Institute of Caribbean Studies, 1967.

Smith, W. A. *Ancient Education*. New York: Philosophical Library, 1955.

Smits, D. '"Squaw Men", "Half Breeds" and Amalgators: Late Nineteenth Century Anglo-American Attitudes Toward Indian White Race-Mixing'. *American Indian Culture and Research Journal* 15 no. 3 (1991): 29–61.

Sperber, D. 'Manuals of Rabbinic Conduct during the Talmudic and Rabbinic Periods'. In *Scholars and Scholarship: The Interaction between Judaism and other Cultures*, edited by L. Landman. New York: The Yeshiva University Press, 1990.

Stanton, C. M. *Higher Learning in Islam: The Classical Period AD 700–1300*. Maryland: Rowman and Littlefield Publishers Inc., 1990.

Stark, R. *The Rise of Christianity*. Princeton: Princeton University Press, 1996.

Steinsaltz, A. *Biblical Images: Men and Women of the Bible*. New York: Basic Books Inc Publishers, 1984.

Stoddart, W. *Sufism*. St Paul: Paragon House, 1985.

Stone, E. 'The Social Role of the Naditu: Women in Old Babylonian Nippur'. *Journal of the Economic and Social History of the Orient* XXV no.1(1982): 50–70.

Sullivan, S. M. X. *History of Catholic Education in the Archdiocese of Boston*. Washington: Catholic University of America, 1946.

Swift, F. H. *Education in Ancient Israel: From the Earliest Times to 70 AD*. Chicago: Open House, 1919.

Tanner, N. 'Piety in the Middle Ages'. In *A History of Religion in Britain*, edited by S. Gilley and W. J. Sheils, 61–76. Oxford: Blackwell, 1994.

Tewksbury, D. G. *The Founding of American Colleges and Universities Before the Civil War, With Particular Reference to the Religious Influences Bearing upon the College Movement*. Hamden: Archon Books, 1965.

Thompson, S. *Religious Women: The Founding of English Nunneries after the Norman Conquest*. Oxford: Clarendon Press, 1991.

Tibawi, A. L. *Islamic Education: Its Traditions and Modernization into Arab National Systems*. London: Luzac, 1972.

Totah, K. A. *Contributions of Arabs to Education.* New York: Columbia University, 1926.

Tritton, A. S. *Materials on Muslim Education in the Middle Ages.* London: Lazuc, 1957.

Tyack, D. B. and Hansot E. *Managers of Virtue: Public School Leadership in America, 1820–1980.* New York: Basic Books, 1982.

Ullman, B. L. *Ancient Writing and Its Influences.* New York: Longman, Green, 1980.

Van de Mieroop, M. 'Women in the Economy of Sumer'. In *Women's Earliest Records: From Ancient Egypt and Western Asia. Proceedings of the Conference on Women in the Ancient Near East. Providence, Rhode Island Nov. 5–7, 1987,* edited by B. S. Lesko, 53–66. Atlanta: Scholar's Press,1989.

van Sertima, I. 'African Presence in Early America'. In *Race, Discourse, And The Origin Of The Americas.* V. L. Hyatt and R. Nettleford. Washington: Smithsonian Institute Press, 1995.

Vanstiphout, H. J. J. 'On the Old Babylonian Curriculum'. In *Centres of Learning: Learning and Location in Pre-Modern Europe and the East,* edited by. J. W. Drijvers and A. A. MacDonald, 3–16. Leiden: E. J. Brill, 1995.

Vanstiphout, H. L. J. 'Lipit-Istar's Praise in the Edubba'. *Journal of Cuneiform Studies* 30, no. 1(1978): 33–64.

Vanstiphout, H. L. J. 'How Did They Learn Sumerian?' *Journal of Cuneiform Studies* 31, no. 2 (1979): 118–128.

Vertovec, S.:*Hindu Trinidad: Religion, Ethnicity and Socio-Economic Change.* London: MacMillan Education Caribbean, 1992.

Vinovskis, M. A. *Origins of Public High Schools: A Re-examination of the Beverly High School Controversy.* Madison: University of Wisconsin Press, 1985.

Vogelzang, M. E. 'Learning and Power During the Sargonic Period'. In *Centres of Learning: Learning and Location in Pre-Modern Europe and the East,* edited by J. W. Drijvers and A. A. MacDonald, 17–28. Leiden: E. J. Brill, 1995.

Wakeman, M. 'Ancient Sumer and the Women's Movement'. *Journal of Feminist Studies in Religion* 1, no. 2(1985): 7–28.

Warniche, R. M. *Women of the English Renaissance and Reformation.* Westport: Greenwood Press, 1983.

Wegner, J. R. 'Images and the Status of Women in Classical Rabbinic Judaism'. *Jewish Women in Historical Perspective,*edited by J. Baskin, 68–93. Detroit: Wayne State University Press, 1991.

Wilson, A. C. and Stoneking, M. et al. 'Ancestral Geographic States and the Peril of Parsimony'. *Systematic Zoology* 40 (1991): 363–365.

Witherington III, B. *Jesus the Sage: The Pilgrimage of Wisdom.* Minneapolis: Fortress Press, 1994.

Wogan-Browne, J. 'Rerouting the Dower: The Anglo-Norman Life of St Audrey by Marie (of Chatteris?)'. In *Power of the Weak: Studies on Medieval Women,* edited by J. Carpenter and S.B. MacLean, (27–56). Chicago: University of Illinois Press, 1995.

Wolpoff, M. H., W. X. Zhi, et al. 'Modern Homo Sapiens Origins: A general theory of hominid evolution involving fossil evidence from East Asia'. In *The Origins of Modern Humans: A World Survey of the Fossil Evidence,* edited by F. H. Smith and F. Spencer, 411–483. New York: Liss, 1984.

Wright, B. '"For the Children of the Infidels": American Indian Education in the Colonial Period'. *American Indian Culture and Research Journal* 12, no. 3(1988): 1–14.

Wright, N. T. *Jesus and the Victory of God. Christian Origins and the Question of God 2.* Minneapolis: Fortress Press, 1996.

Wright, Q. *A Study of War.* Chicago: 1965.

Yellen, J. E., Brooks A. S, et al. 'A Middle Stone Age Worked Bone Industry from Katanda, Upper Semliki Valley, Zaire'. *Science* 268 (1995): 553–556.

Zagarell, A. 'Trade, Women, Class and Society in Ancient Western Asia with CA Comment'. *Current Anthropology* 27, no. 5(1986): 415–430.

Zolty, S. P. *And All Your Children Shall Be Learned: Women and the Study of Torah in Jewish Law and History.* Northdale: Jason Aronson, 1993.

Index

DATE DUE

Demco, Inc. 38-293